McGRAW-HILL SERIES IN GEOGRAPHY

Edward J. Taaffe and John W. Webb, *Consulting Editors*

POPULATION GEOGRAPHY: A READER

GEORGE J. DEMKO
Department of Geography
Ohio State University

HAROLD M. ROSE
Department of Geography
University of Wisconsin
Milwaukee

GEORGE A. SCHNELL
Department of Geography
State University College
New Paltz, New York

McGRAW-HILL BOOK COMPANY

NEW YORK, ST. LOUIS, SAN FRANCISCO
DÜSSELDORF, LONDON, MEXICO
PANAMA, SYDNEY, TORONTO

POPULATION GEOGRAPHY:

A READER

Library of Congress Catalog Card Number 78-91964

1 2 3 4 5 6 7 8 9 0 H D B P 7 9 8 7 6 5 4 3 2 1 0

PREFACE

The absence of a suitable text and the inconvenience of preparing lengthy reading lists for population geography courses provided the stimuli for assembling this reader. This collection might serve as a text or as a supplement for use with an existing text. Above all, it is our intention to bring together some of the more important articles by geographers and others in order to aid the student in defining, identifying, and analyzing population problems of geographic significance. Most of the articles reflect clearly one of the primary intellectual concerns of geographers, questions of spatial variation and the spatial processes which give rise to such variation.

The problem of selecting suitable articles for inclusion in any reader is an exasperating one, usually resolved by compromise. Further, many excellent studies could not be included because of limitations on the number of articles which could be used or inability to secure permission for reprinting. A number of omissions should thus be apparent. There is no section devoted to urban populations, although a number of articles are addressed to urban problems. Similarly, no attempt has been made to provide balanced regional coverage; although emphasis is placed on the work of Western scholars, there are examples taken from Soviet and other materials. Because of such limitations, the student is urged to examine the selected supplementary bibliographies at the end of each section and the general list at the end of the book. Moreover, there exists an abundant literature on population, for in recent years the attention paid to this subject by a variety of scholars has produced a rich source of ideas, techniques, and approaches.

Thus, it is our hope that this reader serves as a useful pedagogical tool and plays at least some role in stimulating greater interest in population research by geographers.

With the exception of the cross references in the Introductions and in Selections One and Eighteen, the cross references in all the selections refer to citations in the original sources.

We gratefully acknowledge the help given by the many authors and publishers without whose cooperation this book could not have been produced. We are also grateful to Mr. Theodore Shabad of the American Geographical Society for permission to use his translations of the two Soviet articles included in the collection. The editors, however, accept sole responsibility for the selection and organization of materials and, therefore, are fully responsible for any shortcomings of such a collection.

GEORGE J. DEMKO
HAROLD M. ROSE
GEORGE A. SCHNELL

LIST OF CONTRIBUTORS

EDWARD A. ACKERMAN
Executive Officer
Carnegie Institution of Washington
Washington, D.C.

DONALD S. AKERS
Population Division
U.S. Department of Commerce
Bureau of the Census
Washington, D.C.

THEODORE ANDERSON
Director
Urban Community Studies Program
Department of Sociology
University of Iowa
Iowa City, Iowa

BRIAN J. L. BERRY
Professor of Geography
Department of Geography
and Director of Training Programs
The Center for Urban Studies
University of Chicago
Chicago, Illinois

GEORGE BLYN
Chairman
Department of Economics
Rutgers University
College of South Jersey
Camden, New Jersey

DONALD J. BOGUE
Professor of Sociology
and Director of Community and Family Study
   Center
University of Chicago
Chicago, Illinois

REID A. BRYSON
Professor of Meteorology
Department of Meteorology
University of Wisconsin
Madison, Wisconsin

GÖSTA CARLSSON
Professor of Sociology
Department of Sociology
University of Lund
Lund, Sweden

ROY CHUNG
Assistant Professor of Geography
Department of Social Science
University of Northern Iowa
Cedar Falls, Iowa

MICHAEL R. C. COULSON
Assistant Professor of Geography
Department of Geography
University of Calgary
Calgary, Alberta, Canada

KINGSLEY DAVIS
Professor of Sociology
and Director of International Population and Urban
   Research Institute
University of California
Berkeley, California

JOHN D. DURAND
Professor of Economics
Department of Economics
University of Pennsylvania
Philadelphia, Pennsylvania

JACK P. GIBBS
Professor of Sociology
Department of Sociology
Washington State University
Pullman, Washington

YEKATERINA NIKOLAYEVNA GLADYSHEVA
Head
Population and Manpower Section
Institute of Economics
Alma-Ata
Kazakhstan, U.S.S.R.

ALFONSO GONZALEZ
Chairman
Department of Geography
University of South Florida
Tampa, Florida

JOHN FRASER HART
Professor of Geography
Department of Geography
University of Minnesota
Minneapolis, Minnesota

DUDLEY KIRK
Professor of Demography
Food Research Institute
Stanford University
Palo Alto, California

EVERETT S. LEE
Head
Department of Sociology
University of Massachusetts
Amherst, Massachusetts

YURIY VLADIMIROVICH MEDVEDKOV
Head
Department of Geography
Institute of Science and Technical Information
Moscow, U.S.S.R.

RICHARD L. MORRILL
Professor of Geography
Department of Geography
University of Washington
Seattle, Washington

MALCOLM A. MURRAY
Head
Department of Geography
Georgia State College
Atlanta, Georgia

WARWICK NEVILLE
Professor of Geography
Department of Geography
University of Singapore
Singapore

LEO A. ORLEANS
China Research Specialist
(China Research Analyst)
The Library of Congress
Washington, D.C.

VIKTOR IVANOVICH PEREVEDENTSEV
Institute of the International Workers Movement
Moscow, U.S.S.R.

VADIM VYACHESLAVOVICH POKSHISHEVSKIY
Professor and Vice-President
Geographical Society of the U.S.S.R.

ARTHUR H. ROBINSON
Professor of Geography
Department of Geography
University of Wisconsin
Madison, Wisconsin

ANDREI ROGERS
Associate Professor of City and Regional Planning
Department of City and Regional Planning
University of California
Berkeley, California
and Counselor with the Regional Science Association

PETER SCOTT
Professor of Geography
Department of Geography
University of Tasmania
Hobart, Australia

JAMES W. SIMMONS
Associate Professor of Geography
Department of Geography
University of Western Ontario
London, Ontario, Canada

MORTIMER SPIEGELMAN
Chairman
Committee on Vital and Health Statistics Monographs
Statistics Section
American Public Health Association, Inc.
New York, New York

JOHN Q. STEWART
Professor of the Metaphysics of Science
Prescott College
Prescott, Arizona

GEORGE J. STOLNITZ
Professor of Economics
Department of Economics
Indiana University
Bloomington, Indiana

ROBERT J. TENNANT
Assistant Professor
Department of Geography
York University
Toronto, Canada

GLENN T. TREWARTHA
Professor of Geography
Department of Geography
University of Wisconsin
Madison, Wisconsin

VLADIMIR VASILYEVICH VOROBYEV
Head
Population and Historical Section of the Institute of Geography
Irkutsk, Siberia, U.S.S.R.

WILLIAM WARNTZ
Professor of Theoretical Geography and Regional Planning
and Director
Laboratory for Computer Graphics and Spatial Analysis
Department of City and Regional Planning
Graduate School of Design
Harvard University
Cambridge, Massachusetts

JULIAN WOLPERT
Associate Professor of Regional Science
Department of Regional Science
University of Pennsylvania
Philadelphia, Pennsylvania

WILBUR ZELINSKY
Professor of Geography
Department of Geography
The Pennsylvania State University
University Park, Pennsylvania

CONTENTS

PART ONE

GEOGRAPHY AND THE STUDY OF POPULATION

Selection One

THE GEOGRAPHIC STUDY OF POPULATION
G. J. Demko, H. M. Rose, and G. A. Schnell

The recent increase in the number of articles written by geographers on population and associated problems is related to the growing awareness by members of the profession of the importance of population geography and to an increasing agreement with, or acceptance of, the notion that geography is one of the social sciences. Perhaps most important in elevating population geography to a more prominent position among the many branches of the discipline has been the influence of Trewartha; his presidential address, delivered before the Association of American Geographers in 1953,[1] is one of the most explicit statements on the subject yet to appear. Since that time, the quantity and quality of work which could be described as population geography has increased markedly and the number of population courses taught in geography departments has grown commensurately, or nearly so. The more important question, however, centers on the path that population geography has traversed and the methodologies adopted by its practitioners in their progress toward gaining a better understanding of the spatial dimension of population and its attributes. The objectives of this paper are as follows: (1) to review and examine the conceptual notions of population geography as espoused by the major contributors to the field, and (2) to differentiate between population geography and other disciplines which include population study within their scope, as well as provide a workable definition of population geography.

A Review

The importance of Trewartha's case for population geography can hardly be minimized, especially his reminder to the members of the Association of their negligence with respect to the geographic study of population. In addition, Trewartha argued eloquently for a focus on man, a focus which would affirm the systematic nature of the field. In defining population geography, Trewartha indicated that its essence lay in "the understanding of regional differences in the earth's covering of peoples."[2] The major difficulty with such a definition is its implication of emphasis on the unique. Despite statements pleading the need for a study of dynamics, the dynamics are stressed with the goal of understanding areal differences.

Another prominent American population geographer, Zelinsky, defines the field as "the science that deals with the ways in which the geographic *character of places* is formed by, and in turn reacts upon, a set of population phenomena that vary within it through both space and time as they follow their own behavioral laws, interacting one with another and with numerous nondemographic phenomena."[3] Zelinsky identifies three types of concern in ascending order of importance: ". . . the simple description of the location of population numbers and characteristics [the where?], the explanation of the spatial configurations of these numbers and characteristics [the why where?], and the geographic analysis of population phenomena (the interrelations among areal differences in population with those in all or certain other elements within the geographic study area)."[4] The intent of such statements is not debatable, but the emphasis on the *character of places* and *areal differences*

minimizes, at the very least, the import of *spatial processes* and stresses difference at the expense of regularity.

Madame Beaujeu-Garnier, representing a Gallic point of view, presents the problem of the population geographer as one of describing "the demographic facts in their present environmental context, studying also causes, their original characteristics and possible consequences."[5] She, too, lists three levels of problems. Her hierarchy includes "the distribution of people over the globe, the evolution of human societies, and the degree of success that they have achieved."[6] Again, this denotes the spatial distribution theme as a primary level of problem identification, whereas recognition of process stemming from the notion of spatial interaction is conspicuous by virtue of its absence from the definition.

The statements of Clarke, a British population geographer, are similar to the preceding in that he indicates population geography's concern ". . . with demonstrating how spatial variations in the distribution, composition, migrations, and growth of populations are related to spatial variations in the *nature of places*."[7] Thus Clarke distinguishes population geography from demography by emphasizing the former's concern with understanding spatial variation of demographic variables by seeking measures of areal coincidence with other, related variables. A second distinction is made when he indicates that "While the demographer is devoted to numbers and depends heavily upon statistical methods, the population geographer relates numbers to area and relies upon maps."[8] Again, the primary emphasis is placed on geographic questions at the first level, questions of spatial distribution, in which only variations over area and place are stressed. Further, although the map is clearly a tool identified most closely with geography, it would be unfortunate to accept the implication that statistical methods are not, or should not be, closely associated with analysis in population geography. Indeed, the map has become even more useful by virtue of its value in portraying residuals from regression, statistical surfaces in trend surface analysis, and many other quantitative measures which are readily adaptable to graphic presentation.

Edward Ackerman, a prominent American geographer, has very clearly designated the distinctive role of geography in population research and delimited the problems of population geography at various levels.[9] In summarized form, Ackerman indicates that the first set of problems (assuming data collection completed or data availability) involves the identification of generic relations, which includes the categorization, classification, and differentiation procedures. This first step is consistent with the format followed in most, if not all, research undertakings, since it accomplishes two goals: it allows the researcher to establish the desired level of generalization, and it requires some selection process to determine which variables should be included by virtue of their pertinence to the categories or classes to be used. The next level of inquiry involves the establishment of genetic relationships, or the dynamic aspects (processes) of spatial distributions, in which the temporal variable is highly significant. Moreover, the why-where step, mentioned earlier, is initiated here as an attempt to identify and relate process to phenomena. Last, and most significant, is the determination of covariant relations; that is, the search for understanding of space relations or spatial processes, often expressed in terms of areal association and interaction between and among phenomena.

In sum, the main theme expressed by population geographers has been areal differentiation, beginning with observation and identification of patterns of spatial distributions leading to attempts at solution of problems of static relationships between variables. More important are the questions of spatial interaction, those questions concerning the spatial processes which give rise to, and explain, significant distributions. These are analogous to the genetic and covariant relations of Ackerman, who earlier identified the problem of emphasis on areal differentiation: "The concept of areal differentiation . . . did not often lead us to common ground with the other sciences. We see it also as ending in a somewhat static goal."[10] Population study by geographers should, therefore, lead to a better understanding of the processes creating areal distributions as expressed in the concepts inherent in, and by the study of, spatial interaction. This last step demands that population study by geographers treat those spatial systems which arise from, or lead to, the geographic character of populations.

Comment and Definition

As one of the many disciplines which include the formal study of human population as a component, geography occupies an important place. Although areal distributions concern each of these fields as an inherent trait (e.g., the dimension of area expressed by the existence of man in space, similar to his existence through time as an expression of the temporal dimension), it is the emphasis upon spatial distribution and the subsequent questions of spatial interaction, the *why where?* phase described above, that appropriately differentiates and thus delimits the place of population geography among the social sciences. Specifically, the collection, analysis, and presentation of data relating to spatial distributions and attendant regional patterns become meaningful in population geography only when carried forward a step to include inquiry into the processes which influence, indeed create, particular spatial distributions.

The extension of the work of human geographers of the late nineteenth and early twentieth centuries, beyond their inclusion of population as an intrusion upon the physical scene along with other evidences of man's occupancy and activities, thus demands more than the examination and presentation of population enumeration (or more than an indirect enumeration based upon the more nearly static evidence at hand — man's dwellings, for example). The counting of heads serves as the initial phase; the identification of population qualities — characteristics — as spatial distributions is the logical extension of such basic counts. Specifically, the spatial aspects of economic and social characteristics of a given population outweigh by far such simple enumerations in terms of their importance in better understanding the impact of the dynamic processes — migration, fertility, and mortality. Population study is, and should continue to be, an element of human geography and of regional geography, but, more importantly, population geography, as a formal and systematic subfield of the discipline, places far greater emphasis upon man. As a result, man becomes the focus of study in a more precise sense than as simply one of many phenomena which happen to occupy an area and are therefore included along with a wide variety of physical, economic, and cultural features for consideration. Thus, it is not our intention to modify the notion expressed by many geographers that the general measure of significance in geography is man. Rather, in addition to the inclusion of man's culture, his economic activities, and his general distribution at present or in the past (which signifies generally the place of population in human geography, economic geography, and regional geography, respectively), we believe there exists a need for better understanding of spatial aspects of population per se and that geographers must apply their special tools and techniques to such problems.

Population geography is, therefore, that branch of the discipline which treats the spatial variations in demographic and nondemographic qualities of human populations,[11] and the economic and social consequences stemming from the interaction associated with a particular set of conditions existing in a given areal unit. Moreover, population geography, unlike some other branches of the discipline, is highly sensitive to the time dimension. The weighty influence of time leads to an increasing emphasis on processes which account for the spatial expression of population composition at any specific time or through a time period. A situation of this type leads logically to the development of analytic techniques, or models, which better aid in providing an understanding of the processes which operate to produce any given set of population attributes within a spatial context.

Population geography as a relatively recent and largely underdeveloped branch of geography has not had its boundaries rigorously circumscribed, a condition which might work to its advantage. Yet, some attempts have been made to specify the limits of the field. Zelinsky has stated that the scope of the field should include a treatment of all of the variables present in the census schedules of advanced nations.[12] While this appears to simplify the problem of circumscribing the field, it does not totally resolve the problem at hand. Among the various advanced countries that have highly developed censuses there is no uniform listing of variables. The lack of uniformity among censuses is essentially related to the composition of the population itself, as well as to the relevance and sensitivity of social issues which result in the inclusion or exclusion of certain kinds of information, even among the more highly developed countries. This leads to the conclusion that no uniform set of population attributes which might happen to appear in the census schedules of even the most advanced countries can be employed to circumscribe the field. The increasing complexity of population problems will largely influence the nondemographic population data collected by individual countries. Therefore, the limits imposed on population geography are likely to be determined by the cultural and economic context in which individual population geographers conduct their work. Since it is in the area which Hauser and Duncan choose to call population study, as opposed to demography,[13] that most work by geographers has been conducted, it is not at all surprising that the cultural context has proven especially relevant in its influence upon the scope of population geography.

In conclusion, it is our hope that the

study of population geography will continue to expand and that, the comments made here notwithstanding, its future development will be shepherded by a significant proportion of geographers. Only then will the field of study gain a prominent role, both within and beyond the discipline, for it will have been subjected to the most rigorous of tests — time and scrutiny.

Notes

[1] G. T. Trewartha, "A Case for Population Geography," Annals of the Association of American Geographers, Vol. 43, #2 (June, 1953), pp. 71–97.

[2] *Ibid.*, p. 87.

[3] W. Zelinsky, *A Prologue to Population Geography* (Englewood Cliffs, N. J.: Prentice-Hall, 1966), p. 5. (editor's italics).

[4] *Ibid.*, pp. 5–6.

[5] J. Beaujeu-Garnier, *Geography of Population* (New York: St. Martin's Press, 1966), p. 3.

[6] *Ibid.*, p. 4.

[7] J. I. Clarke, *Population Geography* (Oxford, London, New York: Pergamon Press, 1965), p. 2.

[8] *Ibid.*, p. 2.

[9] E. A. Ackerman, "Geography and Demography" in Hauser and Duncan (eds.), *The Study of Population* (Chicago: The University of Chicago Press, 1959), pp. 717–727.

[10] E. A. Ackerman, "Where Is a Research Frontier?" Annals of the Association of American Geographers, Vol. 53, #4 (December, 1963), p. 434.

[11] Demographic characteristics are those employed to describe changes in the movement or state of the population, i. e., fertility, mortality, migration. The nondemographic characteristics usually relate to biological, social, and economic qualities. See R. Thomlinson, *Population Dynamics* (New York: Random House, 1965), pp. 5–6.

[12] Zelinsky, *op. cit.*, p. 7.

[13] P. M. Hauser and O. D. Duncan (eds.), *The Study of Population* (Chicago: The University of Chicago Press, 1959), pp. 2–3.

Selection Two

A CASE FOR POPULATION GEOGRAPHY*

Glenn T. Trewartha

Introduction

My thesis for your consideration may be very simply stated: the geography of population has been, and continues to be neglected, to the injury of geography in general, and a serious and sustained effort should be made to develop a working concept of population geography which may be applied broadly in teaching and research.

As I enter upon an elaboration of the above proposition I am very conscious of a pungent German proverb: "Weiss man nichts, so schreibt man über Methode," a proverb which I have adopted as something of a personal warning and guide. I am a conscientious objector as far as much methodological discussion and writing are concerned, and have long insisted that doing substantive work is far more important than talking or writing about how it should be done. Moreover my conviction is strong that methodological writing which is the outgrowth of ample experience in doing substantive research rests upon a more secure foundation than that which is developed by deductive philosophical reasoning. It follows, therefore, that those best qualified to engage in fruitful methodological discussion are the workers whose ideas have been tested in the fires of performance.

If the above reasoning is correct I would be the first to admit that my professional experiences and accomplishments do not qualify me to write as an expert concerning the position of population geography and

* Presidential address delivered before the Association on the occasion of its 49th annual meeting held in Cleveland, Ohio, Mar. 30–Apr. 2, 1953.

Reproduced by permission from the *Annals of the Association of American Geographers*, Vol. 43, #2, 1953, pp. 71–97.

of its organization, content, and subdivisions. But at the risk of being considered hoist on my own petard I venture to explore this field. I am somewhat emboldened by what appears to be the urgency of the case, and also by the paucity of professed specialists in population geography who might bring to the discussion a superior wisdom derived from experience. The conviction that the neglect of population geography constitutes a fundamental weakness in the general approach to modern geography urges me to delay no longer a preliminary statement of the case for the population element.

Fitzgerald in a recent paper has stated that "The chief difficulty in attaining a regional classification acceptable to the strictest canons of geographical methods, results from some remaining uncertainty as to the place of man within the frontiers of geography."[1] Here is a challenge and one that requires immediate acceptance. It is possible that the uncertainty referred to has been a discouraging factor and that clarification relative to the structure and facets of population geography, and to just where population fits and has a place within the geographical system, may have the effect of activating this field in research and teaching.

Population a Slighted Aspect of Geography

Judged by any one of several criteria I am obliged to conclude that geographers, and especially American geographers, have not made population one of their major concerns. In the way that climate, landforms, agricultural land use, and manufacturing, for example, have been made the subjects of special systematic treatment in geographic research and teaching, or that these same topics have been important and integral parts of holistic regional studies, population by comparison has been neglected.

SLIGHT RECOGNITION IN TREATISES ON CONTENT AND METHODOLOGY OF GEOGRAPHY

A scrutiny of a number of the standard works on the nature, content, and methods of geography reveals a complete omission of any reference to population geography by most writers. Of those analyzed, in only one is there an elaboration of the topic to the point where the reader is impressed by the author's recognition of its importance and of his awareness of where it fits into the geographical structure.

In the three-volume work of Siegfried Passarge, *Grundlagen der Landshaftskunde*, one of the most detailed analyses of geographical structure and content, there is a section entitled, "Der Mensch und seine Werke." The title is inappropriate, however, for the entire content is an analysis of the works of man, including house types, settlement forms, communications, and the different economies, but man himself, as population, is completely ignored. That this was not just an oversight in this earlier publication, dated 1920, is suggested by the continued omission of any reference to population in *Vergleichende Landschaftskunde* (1921–1930), *Beschreibende Landschaftskunde* (1929), and *Einführung in die Landschaftskunde* (1933), all published at later dates.

In *The Nature of Geography* by Hartshorne[2] various branches of the field such as physical geography, historical geography, political geography, and economic geography are singled out for special treatment, but no reference is made to population geography as a systematic subdivision. In the index to this volume it is indicated that the topic of population is referred to three times in the text, but the references are completely incidental and no comment on content or method is intended.

Dickinson and Howarth in their volume, *The Making of Geography*,[3] discuss the evolution of human geography, but make no mention of the place of population within this field. Economic, political, social, and historical geography are all analyzed, but population is omitted. Their index does not so much as contain the word population. Wooldridge and East's *The Spirit and Purpose of Geography*,[4] a more recent British contribution in the field of geographic content, is equally neglectful of any recognition of the population element.

Hettner in *Die Geographie; ihre Geschichte, ihr Wesen und ihre Methoden*,[5] by contrast with the others mentioned, does clearly single out population as a prime element for geographical study. Unfortunately this volume contains no index so that it is difficult to trace all references to the topic. In his treatment of the eight branches of geography, however, "Die Geographie des Menschen" is recognized as a major field and population geography, or *Bevölkerungsgeographie*, is cataloged as a principal subdivision of the larger field of human geography. Hettner proceeds to elevate population geography to an important position because, as he says, population has a great influence on all of the other geographic elements. He argues that *Bevölkerungsgeographie* and *Bevölkerungsstatistik* are essentially different, for geography limits itself to those aspects of population which are closely related to the nature of the land, and includes features in addition to density and movements. It goes beyond *Bevölkerungsstatistik* in that it analyzes population characteristics of areas for which there are few or no population statistics. But although Hettner specifically recognizes the field of population geography, he makes no serious attempt to analyze its content or methods.

A sampling of some of the better-known shorter pronouncements on geographic content and method reveals a considerable range of emphasis relative to the population element, but with outright neglect or casual reference being the most common forms of treatment. Camille Vallaux in his essay on Human Geography contained in the *Encyclopedia of the Social Sciences* avoids any mention of population. Carl Sauer in his chapter on Cultural Geography in the same source emphasizes material culture as the geographer's focus of attention and adds the positive statement that man himself is ". . . not directly the object of geographic investigation. . . ." In two other of his essays, however, "The Morphology of Landscape"[6] and "Recent Developments in Cultural Geography"[7] population density and mobility are included in diagrammatic representations of the forms of the cultural landscape. Significantly though, in Sauer's treatment of the content of the several branches of geography, no mention is made of a special field of population geography. Barrows in his essay, "Geography as Human Ecology,"[8] makes no specific reference to population. One of the most positive statements concerning population geography, its subdivisions and its position within the general field, is included in Sten de Geer's paper entitled, "On the Definition, Method and Classification of Geography."[9] In his essay he refers to the geography of population as a distinctive branch of the general field and presents an outline of its contents and subdivisions.

GENERAL TREATMENT OF POPULATION IN TREATISES ON HUMAN GEOGRAPHY

Further evidence concerning the evaluation of the population element is furnished by a glance at some of the substantive treatises on human geography.

Vidal de la Blache in his *Principles of Human Geography* clearly recognizes population as forming a primary element of the extensive field on which he is writing, for he devotes all of Part I, or about one-third of his volume, to the topic, distribution of population. The entire emphasis is on distribution of numbers and associated density patterns. There is no recognition of other geographical aspects of population; no attempt is made to arrange and classify its content, and I can detect no disposition to recognize population geography as a distinct and primary subdivision of the broader field of human geography.

Jean Bruhnes in his volume, *Human Geography*, restricts the content of that field to the visible evidences of man's occupation and use of the physical environment. The essential facts of human geography are the marks left by man upon the earth's surface. Bruhnes does, however, introduce order and classification into the treatment of the facts or elements of human geography, and of first rank among these facts he places the unequal covering of the earth's surface with people. Their numbers, not their qualities, are emphasized. The primary maps, according to Bruhnes, are those of water and men. But, he asks, "How does population reveal itself?" He answers that men are approached and measured through the habitation, for there they are caught and counted. The earth's covering of human dwellings accordingly is a phenomenon more geographical than the earth's covering of human beings. The one is the first visible sign of the second. "Truly geographical demography is above all the demography of the habitation," says Bruhnes. To that statement I feel obliged to dissent. One can readily agree that it is in connection with the size and spacing of settlement units that the ultimate details of population distribution are to be observed and mapped. But Bruhnes' subsequent discussion is not concerned with the size and spacing of population units as revealed by settlements, but rather with the morphology of houses and settlements. Unless one is to assume that degree of visual conspicuousness is the best measure of geographical importance there is no reason to substitute houses for people. One does not substitute barns for cattle, nor the factory structure for the goods produced. What is more, there are effective ways of studying some phenomena other than by first-hand personal observation. So, although Bruhnes specifically recognizes the geographical importance of the population element, he proposes to study it obliquely through the channel of habitation and settlement morphology and as a consequence makes little contribution to population geography as such. One searches in vain for an outline of content.

An analysis of Alfred Hettner's *Allgemeine Geographie des Menschen* leaves no doubt that this author viewed the study of population as an integral and important part of the general field of human geography. In his analysis of the separate branches of human geography he singles out *Bevölkerung* (popu-lation) and gives it equal prominence with such topics as settlements and dwellings, trade and transportation, the economies, and the State. Although his treatment of each of these separate branches of human geography is consistently brief, he gives unmistakable evidence of the high relative position which he accords to population, pointing out that men operate in the dual capacity of both producers and consumers, or as Hettner puts it, population may be thought of in one way as hands and in another way as mouths. Momentary numbers and densities, while important, are not sufficient; population must be treated dynamically according to Hettner, and hence involve the concepts of regional birth rates, death rates, immigration, and out-migration. Nor should the geographer's analysis be confined to biological phenomena only, for social qualities, dependent upon prevailing economic, political, and social-psychological conditions, are equally, if not more, important. Geography is obliged to consider, on the one hand, the comparative dependence of population on natural, economic, and social conditions, and, on the other hand, to describe and explain the contrasts in population numbers and densities in different parts of the earth. Thereby is laid the groundwork for answering the all-important question relative to the capacity of the earth and its individual regions to support population. Brief though Hettner's remarks on population geography are, still they are among the most direct and illuminating ones to be found on the topic. One could wish that this master had seen fit further to elaborate his ideas on the subject.

In *Handbuch der Geographischen Wissenschaft*,[10] Hassinger's comprehensive treatment of Die Geographie des Menschen does not appear to recognize population geography as a distinct branch of the subject as does Hettner. To be sure he proclaims that the dynamic element, man, is not of less importance in the cultural landscape than man's works, but his analysis of man, or population, is disappointingly anthropological.

Huntington and Shaw in their *Principles of Human Geography*[11] omit entirely any direct reference to, or organized treatment of, population. The book's index contains only two textual references to population and these are quite incidental.

THE GEOGRAPHY OF POPULATION AS SUCH

The single comprehensive treatment by a geographer of the facts of population geography, of which I am aware, is contained in a recent book by Pierre George of France which bears the title. . . . *Introduction a l'étude géographique de la population du monde.*[12] Here for the first time I believe has there been an attempt to present in book form and size a geographic study of the earth's population. Whether one agrees with the content, organization, and Marxian slant as developed by George seems to me less important than recognizing that here is a pioneer study and hence one of signal importance. The way is now open for others to improve upon this first attempt.

OTHER SOURCES OF EVIDENCE SUGGESTING THE INFERIOR POSITION OF POPULATION GEOGRAPHY

Additional evidence concerning the position accorded to population in geographical science may be obtained from noting such items as: 1) the number and quality of publications on population by geographers; 2) the attention given to the population element in holistic regional studies; 3) the number of doctoral dissertations in geography focusing on population themes; and 4) the amount and quality of professional training in population as indicated by the courses offered in the geography curricula of universities.

In a survey made of the publications of American geographers on the substantive aspects of population since 1925, a total of 45 titles were counted for a period which was approximately a quarter century.[13] As far as mere number of contributions is concerned this may not appear to suggest an unusual neglect of the field. However, a closer examination of these contributions indicates that by far the greater share of them were undertaken by investigators who were essentially amateurs. Most of the authors were one-paper contributors who did not continue to publish in the field of population. In a large number of cases they appear to have been young professionals who were primarily interested in other fields and who lacked the competence which previous experience or adequate training might provide. Their interest evidently waned after the production of a single paper. There were notably few repeaters. A number of the papers appear to have been inspired by the fact that a new decennial census had recently been published, suggesting a certain opportunistic attitude rather than one of developed and sustained interest. With due recognition of those in our profession who have authored meritorious studies on population, it still may fairly be said, I think, that the American literature on population geography is a diluted and watered one, with more shortcomings in quality than in mere quantity.

To supplement the survey made of American geographical literature, a hasty and entirely quantitative sampling was made of the contributions on population in certain European sources. Three standard geographical magazines were surveyed, viz., *Petermann's Geographische Mitteilungen, Annales de Géographie,* and *The Geographical Journal.* No attempt was made to judge the qualities of the contributions or the competence of the authors. The only result of the survey, therefore, relates purely to the number of titles which give evidence of dealing explicitly with population themes. All three of the foreign geographical periodicals reveal a scanty treatment of population topics. For example, a survey of *Petermann's Geographische Mitteilungen* over a recent four-decade period brought to light only three papers whose content was clearly in the field of population geography. In *The Geographical Journal* for the period 1910–1950 a total of 16 such papers were published and in the *Annales de Géographie,* 22.

A recent bibliography by Hans Dorries bearing the title "Siedlungs und Bevölkerungsgeographie (1908–38),[14] the only one of its kind of which I am aware, offers still another means for judging the relative position of population geography. Although the title suggests that the author considers settlement geography and population geography to be separate and coequal branches, an analysis of the bibliography's outline proves otherwise. In the introductory section, which covers the systematic aspects of the two fields, population is considered only under the sub-head, "Struktur der Siedlungslandschaft." This plan of organization indicates the subsidiary position in which the author places population geography in that it is made a branch of settlement geography. Moreover, out of the total 51 pages devoted to the listing of systematic titles, only 15 pages are devoted exclusively to population. The main body of the bibliography follows a regional organization and here again population is only one topical subdivision of each of the regional settlement landscapes. For example, under "British Settlement Landscapes" there are five subdivisions of which population is one. Two hundred ten titles are listed for various aspects of British settlement geography as compared with only 37 for population. A scanning of the titles listed under the heading of population indicates that a large proportion were authored by nongeographers and appeared in non-geographical publications.*

A much more difficult task than evaluating the place of population geography as such in the writings of geographers is to discover the prominence given to population as one element in holistic regional studies. The writer makes no pretense of having engaged in a comprehensive and careful inventory of large numbers of such studies, but only a rough sampling. For what such a sampling is worth, the conclusion reached from this type of analysis indicates that the population

element is commonly slighted in the holistic regional studies of American geographers. In not a few regional analyses population is never mentioned directly and one is obliged to infer the existence of people within the region being studied entirely by indirect evidence. Emphasis usually is upon men's creations—houses, settlements, fields, communications—but the originator and creator of the whole cultural scene, the dynamic element, is either omitted or slighted. The evidence shows that this neglect of the population element is less characteristic of the published regional studies of European geographers.

Further testimony bearing upon the deemphasis of population is furnished by a survey of doctoral theses in geography. Out of a total of 343 such dissertations completed at American universities to June 1946 only 11, or slightly over three per cent, were on population subjects. More significant, perhaps, is the fact that few of the authors of these eleven dissertations continued to publish on population, so that the research associated with the thesis topic appears not to have awakened a continuing enthusiasm for investigations along this line. Significant also is the fact that these eleven dissertations were undertaken at schools where little or no professional training in the field of population geography was offered and where no person on the geography staffs had a serious professional interest in population.

Neglect of the field is most clearly revealed perhaps by the training programs of the Departments of Geography in American universities as exhibited by their course offerings. An inventory of the programs in over 20 of the largest or most distinguished departments revealed that in not one of them is there a separate content course dealing exclusively with population. One department does list a course labeled "Settlement Patterns" in which, from the brief catalog description, one would judge some attention is given to the general topic of population. Two other departments listed graduate seminars on population. This indeed reveals a serious lack of training opportunities in the

* Some of the most noteworthy contributions to the field of population geography have come from sociologists and demographers and have appeared in the professional publications of those disciplines.

field of population geography. In view of the above fact, one cannot help but wonder why there should have been even as many as 11 doctoral dissertations in geography focusing on population topics, and whether the 45 substantive papers in the field of population geography over the past quarter century may not have been too many.

Written and oral inquiries made of foreign geographers, especially British, French, and German, reveal a similar neglect of population geography as a systematic field in European universities. Hassinger and Bobek of Austria; Waibel, Bartz, Müller-Wille, and Otremba of Germany; Sorre of France; and East and Darby of Britain were all interviewed personally on this topic or they have replied to letters of inquiry. Without exception their testimony witnesses to the fact that population geography is not a specialized branch of university geography in their countries and that lecture courses in this field are not offered in their geography institutions. Opinion is more divided relative to whether there is a similar neglect of the population element in holistic regional studies.

From the various kinds of evidence presented I am obliged to conclude that both at home and abroad population geography as a systematic branch is not given the attention and emphasis which its importance warrants. It is omitted or slighted in treatises on geographic content and method. Geography curricula almost without exception ignore it. Research in the field is relatively meager, and in general regional studies the population element, more often than not, is treated indifferently and without professional expertness.

Why Has Population Geography Been Neglected?

If it may be assumed that the evidence presented has revealed a neglect of population geography, it may be in order to inquire why this is the case. To be sure it has not been a consistent neglect, for the systematic treatment of population geography as a distinct and recognized branch of the parent field has received far less attention than might be assumed from merely counting the number of references to population in textbooks of geography or even enumerating the titles to papers focusing on population which have been published in geographical periodicals. Population numbers and distribution are items which appear rather frequently, but often incidentally, in geographical writings, and noteworthy papers have been produced. But isolated good papers and incidental treatment are not what I am discussing, however.† The question may fairly be asked relative to why there has been such a casual treatment of population as an element of geography and particularly why this element has not been singled out for a specialized topical development following the patterns set by agricultural geography, political geography, and industrial geography. I have no definitive answer to the question posed, but I propose to present a number of suggestions which have developed in my mind, some of which stem from conversations with professional colleagues.

In part the neglect may derive from the nature of one of the primary organizational divisions of our science which has long been recognized and almost universally accepted. I refer not to that division into regional (special) and topical (general), for I can see no valid reason why such an organizational plan should lead to a neglect of population. Certainly no adequate holistic study of an inhabited area may logically omit giving prime consideration to the population element. And since, as I hope to show later, population geography is the pivotal topical study within our field, either as applied to the earth as a whole or to most of its parts, there appears to be no good reason why it should have been neglected to an even greater extent in topical or systematic geography.

---

†As a recent sample of a geographic population study of monographic size see Pierre Gourou, *La Densité de la Population au Ruanda-Urundi*, Institut Royal Colonial Belge, Memoires—Collection in –8°. Tome XXI, fasc. 6, 1953.

It is that other organizational division of geography, the one which splits the field into physical and cultural, giving rise to the familiar breakdown into physical landscape and cultural landscape, which should share more of the blame. I have no quarrel with such a grouping of the geographic elements as a pedagogical device, but I do assert that the effect of the physical-cultural division in creating in the minds of many the rigid concept of two separate kinds of geography is fundamentally bad. Geography is a unitary science. Its single focus is its concern with the areas which comprise the earth's surface and no convenient organizational sub-division should be permitted to destroy this basic unity. I do believe, however, that a rigidity of thinking on the part of geographers which has caused them to classify all earth phenomena as either physical or cultural, results in the human animal, which fits logically into neither category, being considered something of an outsider and a misfit.

The ancestors of man at the precultural level may be considered a part of the natural earth. It was only when these ancestors became men and developed culture that the differentiation into a physical landscape and a cultural landscape became possible. Since culture originates with human beings, civilized man can scarcely be grouped with other living things within that branch of physical geography designated as biogeography. Yet the originator and creator of the cultural earth has appeared logically to be excluded from cultural geography as well. The creator can scarcely be classified as an element of his own creation. He stands outside and beyond culture. Sauer makes this position clear when in an essay on cultural geography previously referred to he writes, ". . . but because man, *himself not directly the object of geographic investigation,*[15] has given physical expression to the area by habitations, workshops, markets, fields, lines of communications. Cultural geography is therefore concerned with those works of man that are inscribed into the earth's surface and give to it characteristic expression."[16]

Following a similar line of reasoning, Jean Bruhnes, in the process of classifying the facts of human geography, devises an ingenious way of bringing population under the umbrella of geography. As noted earlier, he concludes that the earth's covering of human dwellings is a phenomenon more geographical than the people who created them and that geographical demography is essentially the demography of the habitation. "The human fact as a force applied to the transformation of the surface of the earth will manifest itself as an explanatory and cooperating factor in each of the visible and tangible results of transforming work: apropos of the cultivated field or the mine men will have to be studied insofar as they determine these facts and insofar as they remain connected with them."[17] "It is in connection with the house, the village, and the city that the question of the distribution of population must be examined—under its real and logical aspect— . . ."[18] And Bruhnes proceeds to classify and analyze the facts of human geography through a study of the works of man and not of man himself, or population.

It appears, therefore, that the common two-fold subdivision of geographical science into physical and cultural has failed to provide a special niche for population. Thus the utilizer of the natural resources, and at the same time the creator of the cultural earth, tends to be neglected. It is for this reason that I propose a basic modification in the structural outline of content for geography in order to give population a more explicit position and one which its importance rightfully warrants. In place of the customary bifurcation into natural and cultural elements I propose a three-fold organization of the elements in which man, the physical earth, and the works of man are the triad of elemental groupings. 1) Man, the creator and originator of the cultural landscape, as well as the beneficiary of his own production; 2) the natural earth, which provides the environment and the raw materials for the use of man the creator; and 3) the cultural earth, which is the product of man's creation from the natural stuff—these are essential groupings within a unitary geography. Thus, while the common binomial subdivision of elements into physical and cultural leaves population in a somewhat penumbral position, which may in part account for its neglect, the here-suggested trinomial organization results in giving man his deservedly explicit and important position within the unitary geographical structure. The only *final* value is human life or human living, and this being the case it is difficult to understand why geographers should judge the creations of man, and the environment out of which he creates them, relatively more important than man himself. Neither does it do justice to the importance of population to include it as a third-order subdivision within the geographical hierarchy—a branch of settlement geography, which in turn is a branch of human geography, which itself is one of the two main subdivisions of the parent stem. I am making a plea for a trinitarian approach to our science in order that population can no longer be neglected because it does not appear to fit satisfactorily into a structural classification which recognizes only physical and cultural elements.

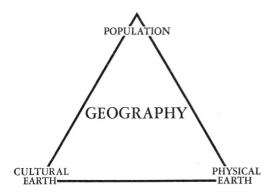

Lest my suggestion be misunderstood, I repeat that I abhor having this interpreted as meaning I would willfully aggravate the divisibility of our science by recommending three instead of two kinds of geographies. I reiterate my belief in a unitary geography. But I do contend it should be recognized that this sturdy plant has three main subdivisions

of its elements instead of the customary two.

A second reason which may be offered for the minimizing of the importance of population by geographers is associated with the inclination to define geography as the study of landscape and to make the two terms, geography and landscape, synonymous. Granted that the definitions of landscape are numerous, there is, nevertheless, a widespread tendency, both at home and abroad, to limit landscape to the visual aspect of an area or the external forms of the earth's surface. The expression, "the face of the earth," fairly well indicates what a large number of geographers apparently have in mind when they employ the term landscape, and make it synonymous with geography. It may be granted that, either individually or collectively, man usually is not a visibly conspicuous element of the total earth's surface, or of most of its individual areas, and one cannot escape the conclusion that this lack of conspicuousness may be a reason why morphologically-minded geographers give to population *per se* an unimportant position. One suspects it was this line of thinking that led Bruhnes to consider houses and settlements as more fundamentally geographic than the people who created them.

But man does not derive his geographical importance from the percentage of an area covered by the bodies of human beings or even from their total bulk. It is not so much the visibly conspicuous element of men, viz., their physical bodies, which change the face of the earth and are geographically significant, but rather men's minds or their knowledge, and these are not a visible landscape element. Geography is more than visual landscape although the visual landscape is often, and quite correctly, the starting point in a regional study. Nevertheless, it is this common preoccupation with the form or visual picture of an area which in part may account for population having been relegated to an inferior position in the geographic system.

Somewhat corollary to the second reason, as stated above, for the relative neglect of population geography may have been the increasing emphasis during the past several decades upon geography as a direct observational science utilizing skill in field observation. A high degree of preoccupation with the readily observable landscape features quite naturally led to emphasis upon first-hand observation. But the inconspicuous nature of human beings, as well as their fluidity of movement, makes it difficult to study many of the facts of population at first hand. As a result relatively more reliance must be placed upon the statistical and cartographic analysis of census materials. This inability to make as abundant use of direct observation methods in the study of population as compared with many other phenomena may, I believe, have tended to turn geographers away from the demographic aspects of their subject.

It has been suggested, also, that the relative recency of a demographic methodology and technique may have had a discouraging effect upon geographers interested in population studies. I am inclined to doubt the validity of this argument and for the reason that geographers did not make effective use of those methods that were currently employed by demographers. But even if one were to admit the argument as having been operative in the past, it needs to be emphasized that as of the present the situation is reversed, for the tools now employed by demographers are so numerous and so specialized as to require a high degree of technical training in order to be able to use them effectively. The total effect of the formidable modern demographic techniques may be more discouraging to geographers than was the alleged dearth of techniques in an earlier period.

The Position of Man in Geography

In our science, the central theme of which is area differentiation, the dynamic and pivotal element is human life, or population. This is not to claim that people should be directly the object of study to a greater extent than

climate, systems of land use, transportation patterns, etc., but rather to suggest that fundamentally geography is anthropocentric and, if such is the case, that numbers, densities, and qualities of the population provide the essential background for all geography. *Population is the point of reference from which all the other elements are observed and from which they all, singly and collectively, derive significance and meaning. It is population which furnishes the focus.*

PHYSICAL GEOGRAPHY

Reverting to my previous remarks concerning a division of the unitary field into physical and cultural elements, it may seem most difficult to apply the concept suggested in the preceding paragraph, in what is usually thought of as physical geography. There is no such thing as a non-cultural man, and for this reason men cannot be considered as elements of a non-cultural division of reality. Therefore my contention that geography, including physical geography, is anthropocentric, cannot rest upon a fallacious premise such as that which would classify primitive peoples as an element of nature. Rather it has its defense in historical precedents and in modern trends.

Of genuine importance to the argument is the fact that during that period of the late 18th century when the theoretical concepts of the new science of geography were being developed, and its foundations were being sought in the physical features of the earth, contemporary geography had a highly anthropocentric slant. Throughout this pre-Humboldt-Ritter period most geographers followed Kant in viewing physical features in terms of their resource potentialities for supporting human life.[19] To be sure, the central theme was the physical earth, but it was the physical earth as the home of man. And while there are many who subsequently have deviated from this point of view, it has never been abandoned. In fact, recent years have seen a reemphasis of the resource aspect of physical geography so that geographical climatology, geographical geomorphology, and geographical pedology are more to the forefront at present than ever before. Clearly the classifications of climate now in vogue among geographers have a point of view which emphasizes human use, as do those of soils and native vegetation. R. J. Russell's 1948 presidential address[20] before this Association made a plea for a more geographical treatment of surface configuration and in 1950 John E. Kesseli[21] spoke to the Association of Pacific Coast Geographers in the same vein. If not explicitly stated, it is certainly implicit in the published versions of these significant addresses that human-use quality is a major criterion to be used in the selection of those aspects of landforms to be geographically studied.

Consciously or unconsciously, therefore, a group of modern physical geographers is reemphasizing the resource aspects of the non-human earth in their writings. But the resource concept is functional; it always implies human needs. An earth without population lacks resources, for the very word resource implies human wants.[22] There is a distinction, therefore, between *physical earth* and *resource equipment*, for the latter is an expression of appraisal in terms of human usefulness, including both positive and negative elements. The concept of natural resources as so many bundles of raw materials piled up in a storehouse is false. Coal is black rock; it becomes a resource only to those populations who want it and know how to use it. Actually the term, resource, refers less to the corporeal aspects of a thing or substance than to the function which that thing or substance may perform. In a very real sense raw materials do not exist; they are human creations. Of necessity the resource concept is dynamic, not static, for it varies with the cultural stage of a people and with their economic development, so that the resource base changes as men's civilizations, and therefore their abilities and needs, change.

What I am attempting to say is that much of even physical geography is anthropocentric in character and its materials for study are selected having in mind their importance for the populations of the earth. (Admittedly it is those populations with European backgrounds that have provided the bases for selection.) The relative usefulness of the various physical elements is determined not by nature, but by man. It follows, therefore, that our systems of classification in physical geography must have a human basis, and that any physical geography oriented with respect to the resource concept is obliged to be cognizant of the population element. In view of the fact that it has been those with European backgrounds who have written most of the treatises on physical geography, it would be enlightening to see what might come from the hands of natives of the Congo, the Sahara, or the arctic tundra.

CULTURAL GEOGRAPHY

But if much of modern physical geography is anthropocentric in character because of the connection between the physical earth and population by means of the resource concept, how much closer and more direct is the connection between the cultural earth and population. At the risk of stating the commonplace, it may be noted that the cultural features which embellish the earth's surface in almost limitless combinations as developed through time are the evidence of successive periods of human occupance. From culture may be read the chronicle of population, its ebb and flow, its accomplishments and defeats, for culture accurately reflects the numbers, and even more precisely, the qualities of its creators. Man, the creature unlike all others, who has emancipated himself from passive adaptation and natural selection, is the one animal that is able to change the environment to fit his needs. His uniqueness and preeminence are to be discovered not so much in the excellent qualities of his body as in his superior wisdom and intelligence. To be sure, the resource base is still the foundation of human enterprise even in the most advanced civilizations, but to an ever increasing extent the resources of civilized man are not natural resources, but human inventiveness, experience, and knowledge. Thus the total culture within an area develops its unique and distinctive characteristics partly as a result of population numbers, which suggests intensity of use, but even more it reflects the socio-economic qualities of the occupying group. Quality of population counts for more than mere numbers, and culture is more the product of men's minds than of their bodies. The greatest transformation of the natural area results when population is not only numerous, but likewise advanced in technology.

Man's connection with the cultural earth is at the same time active and passive. He is ". . . both the most dynamic agent of production and the beneficiary of the entire process of resource development and utilization."[23] In his role as an agent of production he transforms the surface of the earth for his own use. But he is also the end object of the entire process of production for he reaps the harvest of material goods and enjoys the advantages of developing civilization. It is in this dual role, both as producer and as beneficiary of the civilization created, that population becomes the most potent and dynamic regional element. The cultural earth as an object of geographic study is thus a product of the totality of population attributes and is not to be understood apart from the human resource which produced it.

The Approach to Population Geography

I have indicated earlier my belief that geography is a unitary discipline. Physical and cultural, systematic and regional, general and special, are dualisms which appear at times to fog this oneness. As geographers I believe we are committed to the study of earth regions. But the concept of region cannot be divorced from the fact that an area has reality only in terms of the specific groups of interrelated elements which comprise it, and can be studied only in terms of these elements which are the topical or systematic specializations of geography. Moreover, the study of the elements of

areas, individually or in groups, where the regional concept is always implied, is no less "regional" in quality than is the holistic type of area analysis. Constant emphasis of the mosaic method of treatment as regional geography *per se* has obscured recognition of the fact that the topical approach can be equally regional. Consequently, in subscribing to the chorographic point of view, I am not thereby committing myself to a defense of the mosaic or holistic approach to studying areas, or of agreeing that such studies necessarily are the purest form of regional geography.

Among the various groups of elements which cause earth regions to differ, population is one. It is not just one among many, however, for as stated earlier, population is the pivotal element around which all the others are oriented. Indeed, it is only from man or population that these other elements derive geographical significance. Consequently, the study of population is logically the single most important topical approach to geography and one in which the regional concept has its broadest application. To be sure, geography does not claim to be the science of man, but it does include within its circumference man in his reciprocal relationship to the earth area.

For some time it has been my conviction, growing out of experience, that while an understanding of places may be the desirable goal in geographic research and instruction, the goal normally is best attained by the topical approach.[24] Experience seems to show that the groups of phenomena represented within most regions are too numerous and too complex to be handled expertly in their complicated interrelations by one person at one time. This may account for the fact that many of our holistic regional studies appear to be relatively superficial and lacking in fresh approach. It is as though the plowshare consistently reached to about the same depth and so did not involve new materials. As a consequence the mosaic method of geographic analysis has many times appeared monotonous.

Regional analysis of a superior quality requires the highest type of mature scholarship and is not to be undertaken by amateurs. In general, it must be based upon the work of systematic specialists, or it may be the combined product of several systematic specialists. For this reason I am led to conclude that the training of our advanced graduate students, even those who are professed regionalists in interest, should include work in a number of systematic fields and a greater degree of experience in at least one. This is only a recognition that the effective tools and techniques of regional analysis are provided by the several systematic branches of our science. It stems from a conviction, also, that regional geography is in danger of becoming sterile without constant insemination from the topical branches.

If the view is accepted that the most expert way of approaching an understanding of a region is by the route of topical analysis rather than that of mosaic description, and if in addition it is agreed that population is the pivotal element in geography, then it follows that an adequate treatment of the population element in regional studies requires that population geography be developed as a systematic specialty. Evidence already has been presented to indicate that such a systematic specialty does not exist either in this country or abroad. Here is a situation that requires correction. I entertain serious doubts whether the population element can possibly receive adequate treatment in comprehensive regional studies and in regional courses of instruction until the field of population geography is developed as a specialized systematic branch of our science. Concrete evidence pointing to a recognition of this fact is required in the form of 1) population specialists on our geography staffs; 2) courses of instruction in population geography in our professional training programs; and 3) a greater abundance of scholarly publications in this field.

A System for Population Geography

It is not my purpose here to establish a rigid plan or outline for population geography. I desire only to make suggestions relative to its core content, with this content arranged into a tentative and flexible system which will allow ample latitude for needed modifications growing out of different needs, variable data, and contrasting regions. Since this is in the nature of a first attempt to create such a system it is to be expected that it will be changed and modified as it is put to the test of continued use by workers in the field. There is bound to be lack of agreement on the full content of the field of population geography and admittedly there is no one way or best way of ordering and arranging the topics to be included. Still, in most disciplines and branches of disciplines, there is a core of content on which there is reasonable agreement, even though the full content and its arrangement may bear the stamp of individual authorship. This, it is believed, should be the case with population geography.

It is my hope that this preliminary attempt at the development of a system of content for population geography may have the effect of inducing others to share their experiences and to express their ideas on the topic. Such contributions should make it easier for geographers to plan courses on population and to visualize the research aspects and opportunities in the field. It will be of great value if the geographers working on population are enabled to work cumulatively, to the end that their research may build more rapidly toward a complete and unified structure. At the same time it is believed that the development of a system of content for population geography should have a beneficial effect upon regional geography in general, expressed either through courses of instruction or through research studies.

The geographer's goal in any or all analyses of population is an understanding of the regional differences in the earth's covering of people. Just as area differentiation is the theme of geography in general, so it is of population geography in particular. But I emphasize that the concept of differentiation applies to a wider range of population attributes than most geographers have ordinarily included within the scope of their studies. Simple distribution patterns and arithmetic densities are scarcely sufficient to establish a field of population geography.

The outline of content developed below is intended to be generally applicable to the area analysis of population. It is intended to fit areas of all sizes ranging from the earth as a whole down to localities. It is meant to be suggestive of the kinds of population features to be observed and compared in different areas.

POPULATION GEOGRAPHY

A tentative system of content and organization

I   Geography of population in the past—how the earth was populated.
1   Prehistoric
2   The ancient world
3   The medieval world
4   The modern world
    a   Pre-census periods
        a^1 Comparative population growth in the great world regions
        a^2 The European migration and the spread of western technology.
    b   The period of the great national censuses
        b^1 The differential quantity and quality of population data.

II   Population numbers
1   Gross pattern of world population numbers
2   Dynamics of numbers
    a   Differential rates of population growth
        a^1 Area natality and mortality patterns and differentials
        a^2 Age pyramids as indicators of future growth
        a^3 Area patterns involving crude rates of natural increase and net reproduction rates.
        a^4 Area change and variability of population
        a^5 Significance of area dif-

ferential rates of population growth.
3   Area aspects of overpopulation and underpopulation
4   Distribution of population
    a   Gross patterns of distribution
        a^1 The ecumene and the non-ecumene
        1   The frontiers of the ecumene
            a   The polar frontier
            b   The dry frontier
            c   The wet tropical frontier
        2   The expanding ecumene and population growth.
        a^2 Continental and subcontinental population distribution patterns.
    b   Population distribution by settlement types
        b^1 Size and spacing of settlement units as population clusters
    c   Distribution of population density patterns
        c^1 Arithmetic density
        c^2 Physiological density
        c^3 Agricultural density
        c^4 General economic density (the man-land ratio)
5   Migrations and movements of population
    a   International migrations
        a^1 Regions of out-migration and its effects
        a^2 Regions of in-migration and its effects
    b   Intranational and local migrations
        b^1 Rural urban migrations
        b^2 Seasonal migrations
        b^3 Diurnal movements

III   Qualities of population and their regional patterns of distribution
1   The physical qualities of population
    a   Body size, form and color
    b   Race and nativity
    c   Sex balance

d   Age composition
e   Health and disease
   e[1] Diet and nutrition
2   The social-economic qualities of population
  a   Religious beliefs
  b   Educational status
    b[1] Schooling
    b[2] Illiteracy
  c   Occupational status
  d   Marital status
  e   Residence; rural or urban, including size of settlement
  f   Stage of economic development
    f[1] Use of inanimate power of mechanical robots
  g   Customs, habits, prejudices, loyalties, etc.

Historical Population Geography

Little of a specific nature is known concerning the population of the earth and its individual parts for more than a few centuries back. Even at the present time no census data for any kind exist for perhaps as much as 8 per cent of the earth's people and for 25 to 35 per cent it is fragmentary and inadequate. A century ago at least 80 per cent of the earth's inhabitants had not been counted. Consequently any treatment of population growth in past centuries is based upon estimates derived from very fragmentary circumstantial evidence. Population figures prior to about 1750 are only the means of a number of inferences.

But if direct statistical evidence is lacking, there are still indirect methods available to the geographer for arriving at conclusions regarding the number, density, and quality aspects of population in the pre-modern world. The anthropologist, for example, has developed methods for relating population density to the stage of culture in which a people is found. It has been determined that it is very unusual for a race that has no knowledge of agriculture to reach a population density greater than one per square mile.[25] By means of stage of culture and other types of evidence Kroeber has attempted to reconstruct the pre-white Indian population of North America.[26] Attempts have been made, likewise, to relate present-day population distribution over the world to stage of economic development.[27] It appears to have been established by archaeologists that the first important upsurge in world population was contemporaneous with the Neolithic Revolution in which the food gathering of Paleolithic man was supplemented by the cultivation of crops and the domestication of animals. Still another acceleration of population growth is associated with the second revolution which witnessed the development of urban culture based upon trade and the processing of goods, the prelude to which was a series of epoch-making inventions.[28]

As a phase of historical geography this analyzing and mapping of population in past periods, both prehistoric and historic, appears to be a fertile field of research. It is of a type that suggests the need for interdisciplinary teamwork in which geographers with great profit might combine their efforts with those of anthropologists, demographers, and economic historians. My experience with a graduate seminar on population in which anthropology students were collaborators convinces me of the possibility for doing fruitful work in this frontier field of the historical geography of population.

The Dynamics of Population Numbers

Although there can be no doubt that among the data on regions used by geographers none is more important than numbers of people, in practice such data are treated usually in an abridged form, and less commonly in their dynamic aspects. For while present numbers are highly important, such data take on greatly added significance if they are viewed as a changing and developing fact that has both a past and a future. How the population of a locality, a region, a State, or even a continent, came to be what it is today in comparison with those of other areas, and how its population may compare at some future date, is associated with such items as birth rates, death rates, fertility ratios, net reproduction rates, in-migration, and out-migration; kinds of facts to which geographers ordinarily give little attention. The differential rates of population growth in the past, in localities as well as in States, have been of the utmost importance and will continue to be in the future. Any comprehensive geographical analysis of a region should, therefore, take into consideration this fact of differential growth both as it applies to areas beyond and outside the region in question, and likewise to the several localities which comprise the region. Both interregional and intraregional contrasts in differential rates of growth carry in their train economic, political, and social consequences which the student of social and cultural phenomena may not ignore.

The rapidity with which a population is reproducing itself is the most basic and significant of all social and economic phenomena. This being so, methods for accurately measuring human fertility and mortality are of paramount concern. Three principal indicators of fertility in human population have been developed. These are the birth rate, the fertility ratio, and the net reproduction rate. Most used of these, because it is simplest, is the birth rate, and the crude birth rate at that. But crude birth rate, or the ratio of births to total population, is a most unreliable gauge of human fertility. Variations in the age and sex composition of populations are great and unless allowance is made for these irregularities, it is impossible to compare the reproductive tendencies of the populations of different regions. Much the same criticism can be made for crude death rate figures. At least the specific death rates for particular age and sex groups should be used in making regional comparisons. Still more significant in the study of regional mortality differentials are data showing the average duration of life or the expectation of life.

Two relatively recent improvements have made the characteristically inadequate treatment by geographers of the population element in regional analyses somewhat indefensible. The first of these is the greater abundance of more accurate data on the population of more of the world's areas than were ever before available. This is only a relative improvement, to be sure, for the deficiencies are still discouraging. But as Hettner has pointed out, the geographer in his study of population, unlike the demographer, is not limited to areas for which a series of reliable censuses have provided good statistical data. Through the employment of such *indirect* methods as, 1) a study of large-scale maps showing settlements or physical characteristics, 2) the application of information on the nature and intensity of land use, and 3) an analysis of aerial photographs, as well as the *direct* method of personal observation in the field, the geographer is able to draw valuable conclusions regarding population in areas for which the census data are few and unreliable. The second improvement is the unusual progress made in recent decades in the techniques of statistical demography which provide greatly widened opportunities for geographical research, especially as it is related to comparative studies of regions and localities. No longer can the conscientious geographer be satisfied with a static treatment of numbers, or contented with a reliance on crude birth rates and death rates as tools for measuring probable population change.[29]

Population Distribution

It is in the distributional aspects of numbers of people that geographers appear to have made their chief contribution to population study. This may stem from the fact that number distribution lends itself particularly well to representation on maps.

All distributional aspects of numbers of people are nearly inseparable from the concept of population density. It is impossible to discuss distribution without indicating that there are more in some places, leading to relatively higher densities, and fewer in others, leading to lower densities. But much of our mapping of distributions, and our discussions likewise, are concerned with the patterns of *relative* density distributions and not with absolute densities. In this discussion the term density will be understood to refer to absolute density. For the moment, however, the concern is with the distribution of relative densities.

ECUMENE AND NON-ECUMENE

Distribution of people in its broadest aspect, or global scale, involves dividing the land portions of the earth into permanently inhabited as compared with uninhabited, or temporarily inhabited, parts. The terms ecumene and non-ecumene have been employed to represent these two major subdivisions. The non-ecumene is composed of extensive contiguous areas as well as of smaller non-contiguous islands imbedded within the ecumene. Principally the non-ecumene is composed of the cold lands (chiefly high latitudes, but also high altitudes), the dry lands, and the wet tropical lands. The foremost active settlement frontiers exist where population is endeavoring to establish itself in the face of increased duration of low temperatures, increased drought, and increased heat and humidity. The degree and rapidity to which population can force the advance of these frontiers is a topic which can scarcely help but attract investigation by geographers. During the past two centuries unprecedented overseas migrations of Europeans and their culture have expanded the ecumene on a scale never equalled previously so that it appears to some that the physical earth is at present well explored economically and population has become increasingly stabilized. In other words, present population differences more closely reflect the comparative economic potentialities of areas than at any time in world history.[30] While this may appear true, especially to peoples of European culture, there is less certainty as to whether Orientals and natives of the tropics would completely agree. It may be that our particular culture makes us myopic concerning the opportunities which portions of the non-ecumene offer.

The most active advance of settlement along the cold frontier within the last quarter century has certainly occurred in the European sector under the stimulus provided by the Russian Communist government. The methods and techniques employed, while deservedly under suspicion, are worthy of careful study. As of 1931 the population of the Soviet Far North had a population of about 1,000,000 people. In 1939 the same region contained about 2,500,000 people.

New interest in the dry frontier of settlement has very recently developed as a consequence of successful experimentation with methods of artificial rain-making. It is a certainty that supercooled clouds have been caused to precipitate as a result of seeding them with dry ice and silver iodide crystals. Among experts there are strong differences of opinion, however, relative to whether artificial rain-making can have sufficiently large-scale effects so as to be of genuine economic significance. Some who are doubtful about its value in humid climates appear to be willing to admit greater potentialities for cloud seeding in dry regions, especially where mountains are present.

Unlike the other two types of non-ecumene, the wet tropics, instead of having serious climatic deficiencies, actually are characterized by a superabundance of climatic energy. It is neither deficiency of heat nor deficiency of rainfall which has discouraged settlement in parts of these low latitude areas. Moreover, there are at present numerous examples of unusually dense native population in some areas within the wet tropics, although other sections, chiefly located in the New World, remain largely unpeopled. Here then is a frontier whose density differentials suggest problems of an importunate nature demanding attention. If the agricultural techniques of the Asiatic tropics could be transplanted to Africa and the Americas the effects upon population growth in the latter regions might be startling. Perhaps there is good reason for shifting our interest from the settlement potentialities of the wet tropics for white peoples, to one which focuses on the low latitudes as a pioneer area for the expansion of native tropical peoples and for Orientals.

POPULATION DISTRIBUTION BY TYPES OF SETTLEMENT

While geographers have tended to concentrate their attention upon the distributional aspects of population numbers, they have, on the other hand, limited their efforts chiefly to that phase of the topic dealing with what I shall call *gross* distribution. By comparison they have seriously slighted that other important aspect of distribution which seeks to understand the characteristic size groupings of population as exhibited by settlement units. It is this aspect of distribution which is most conspicuous when population is observed in the field rather than by means of the census.

Some of the finest and most detailed maps of population distribution known for any region of the earth are available for Japan, yet these do not exhibit that element of distribution arising from the degree of nucleation. A similar situation exists with respect to most other regions of the world. Almost all of the world's population shows some degree of clustering or nucleation. Man is a gregarious animal and, as a consequence, rarely lives singly and alone. In some parts of the world population is predominantly clustered in tiny units comprising single families. In others the population clusters are somewhat larger and form hamlets and villages, and in still others larger urban units predominate. Composites of these forms are common. One of the best examples of an attempt to combine the concepts of gross distribution and settlement distribution of population is Sten de Geer's study of Sweden.[31] Through the use of unarranged or scattered dots for dispersed population, clusters of arranged dots for small nucleated settlements, and graduated spheres for larger clustered settlements, this Swedish geographer has been able to produce a map which exhibits not only gross patterns of relative densities, but in addition certain elementary concepts of the degree of population clustering.

It is my belief that an analysis of population distribution in terms of settlement size and spacing is a neglected aspect of population geography worthy of serious attention. Much of this work may take the form of representative locality studies which will serve the purpose of supplementing other maps showing the gross patterns of distribution. Quite a different form of this type of study, and one representing the other extreme from the suggested locality study, was undertaken in one of my graduate seminars in which the goal set was a generalization of the patterns of rural population nucleation for the entire earth. The end product was a world map which by the use of four color tints showed the distribution of four degrees of nucleation. I consider the project to have been a success as far as it went, but the fact that the resulting map has never been submitted for publication indicates its tentative and incomplete character.

POPULATION DENSITY

Men and land are the ultimate elements in the life of human society so that the number of people in proportion to the amount of land is a fundamental consideration in population study. The concept of density, or the relationship between people and land, is usually expressed as a simple arithmetic ratio which divides total population by total area. This common expression of density, while it is not without some value geographically, in reality provides only the most superficial representation of the real pressure of population upon the resource base.[32] Such a simple ratio is unsatisfactory because it expresses a quantitative relationship between two elements which in themselves are highly inconstant. The numerator, or total population, represents men of greatly contrasting cultures and stages of economic development whose demands upon the physical earth stand in great contrast. The denominator of the ratio expressing units of area fails to take into consideration the variable capacities of different environments for supporting human life and satisfying human wants.

Because the data required by the ratio $\frac{\text{population}}{\text{area}}$ are the most readily obtainable, arithmetic density no doubt will continue to be used by geographers. However, their recognition of its unsatisfactory character will cause them to employ more accurate indices of population pressure on the resource base when the data and techniques are available. *Physiological* density, expressed by the ratio $\frac{\text{population}}{\text{arable area}}$ is a somewhat more refined concept of density since it eliminates from the denominator barren areas and others not suitable for agricultural production. On the other hand, it errs in eliminating all productive non-arable land such as forest, natural pasture, scenic land, mining land, etc. It likewise errs in continuing to evaluate all arable land as having the same productivity, and rating populations as having the same capacities no matter what their cultural background or stage of economic development. Some attempts have been made by geographers to express the physical productivity of agricultural land by means of numerical indices.[33] Thus far their success does not seem to be marked, but if a method could be found for evaluating quantitatively the agricultural productivity of different environments it would be possible to weigh the denominator in the physiological-density ratio so as to get a more realistic comparison of population density in different physical environments.

Agricultural density is expressed by the ratio $\frac{\text{agricultural population}}{\text{cultivated area}}$. Obviously it can serve as an index of general population density only in those regions where agricultural population forms a very large proportion of the total. It represents no advance over the other types of density in differentiating between different qualities of environment or of men.

But even these more specialized ratios still fall short of being able to express the man-land ratio in its fullest meaning, or what is called the *general economic density* of population. The numerator of such a ratio should involve not alone numbers of men but also their socio-economic qualities, including stage of technological advancement. The denominator should denote not just total area, or even cultivated area, but rather the sum total of the natural resource equipment, so that it essays to express the capacity of a region's natural environment to support human life at a particular stage of development. In primitive closed societies the carrying capacity of land may not be impossible to arrive at. But in highly complex dynamic societies a satisfactory means for measuring population pressure on the total resource base has never been accomplished. In advanced societies the means for supporting population often depends as much, or even more, upon items brought in from outside as upon those produced at home. A spatial gap is thereby created between the place of production and the place of consumption. Thus the internal carrying capacity of domestic resources becomes relatively less important as societies advance in technology and regional specialization.

Deficiencies both in data and in methodological tools, for expressing quantitatively the real man-land ratio, or economic density, may compel geographers for the time being to continue to use arithmetic density and other simple ratios in their population studies. Even work in arithmetic density is made difficult for large areas of the world for which fairly detailed population data are available, because of a lack of base maps showing the boundaries of minor civil divisions, and of information concerning the areas of these subdivisions. These serious lacks call for a unified assault by such an organization as the International Geographical Union. But dissatisfaction with arithmetic density as an index for expressing the true man-land ratio likewise presents a challenge to geographers to produce something better. It is a challenge that should not be shunned for it is difficult to see who is so well equipped professionally to make a contribution to this phase of population research as is the geographer.

POPULATION QUALITY

And finally I propose to direct my remarks to the topic of qualities of people, a facet of population study that has been much more seriously neglected by geographers than have the several aspects of number distribution. But numbers alone are deceiving and at best can provide only an incomplete, and often erroneous, impression of the relative importance of any phenomenon. Acres of wheat and numbers of livestock are important data to be sure, but their usefulness and significance are greatly increased if supplemented by other data indicative of quality, such as quantity and value of wheat per acre and quantity and value of output per animal. Each unit area under cotton in Egypt yields five times as much cotton fiber as a comparable area in India and the ratio is still more exaggerated if value is substituted for weight. What is being sought here is not mere number of acres or of animals, but, in addition, the *quality* of the crop or livestock as indicated by density of stand, value of output or some other measure of excellence or intensity.

But while most of the world's things are measured, and their distributions indicated, not alone in terms of numbers but also in terms of quality or value, geographers continue to treat human beings in terms of numbers almost exclusively. The identical number of points or dots is made to represent 1000 illiterate natives of Amazonia and 1000 highly civilized citizens of Sweden, even though they represent quite different potentialities both as producers and consumers. Certain it is that how man uses the earth and what he does to its surface, how much he produces and consumes, as well as his physical well being, in fact the sum total of his cultural accomplishments as expressed in

the inclusive term civilization, is related not alone to mere numbers of people, but even more to their qualities. The seven per cent of the world's population living in Anglo-America, trained to use inanimate power and mechanical robots, is said to accomplish one-half of the world's work.

Just what the qualities of population are which significantly modify and supplement the concept of numbers is not always so clear. However, two main classes or subdivisions of quality may readily be recognized: 1) those which are physical in character and are chiefly attributes of the bodies of men, and 2) those which are cultural characteristics, socio-economic in nature, and hence indices of civilization.

Many bodily features such as skull form and size, body weight and height, color of hair and skin, etc., appear to have little significance relative to man's potentialities either as a producer or a consumer. Of all of these, skin color alone may have some functional significance in this instance as it is related to climatic adaptation, but even such a connection is uncertain. Modern censuses usually tabulate three physical characteristics of population which are of considerable value in a comparative regional analysis of population quality. They are: race and nativity, balance between the sexes, and age composition. While race or nationality is not indicative of inherent potentialities, it is, nevertheless, often suggestive of cultural backgrounds, economic status, and differentials in terms of birth rates, death rates, intelligence quotients, and other important social indexes. The sex ratio of a population and its age composition likewise have far-reaching significance.

Most important, without doubt, of all the physical characteristics of a population, affecting both its production of wealth and its ability to enjoy the wealth produced, is the state of physical well-being of the people. The idea may be summed up in the word, health. That health is not identical with the absence of disease is obvious; still there is a relationship. Unfortunately medical science has paid little attention to people who are healthy, so that whatever information and statistics are available are those concerned with one negative aspect of health, viz., disease, and with individual diseases at that. Whole populations in part of the wet tropics are so infested with malaria, hookworm, dysentery, and other debilitating diseases as to make the people unfit for vigorous physical or mental effort and thereby adversely affecting the labor supply. Large parts of the world's population live at sub-standard levels of well being because their diets do not provide the necessary ingredients for good health. This problem of the differential health and well being of populations in various regions is a research frontier in population geography which has received altogether too little attention.

In addition to physical attributes which in a qualitative sense differentiate the earth's populations, there are those other qualities of individuals and groups which are cultural or socio-economic in character. These include, among others, religious beliefs, educational status, marital status, occupational status, place of residence (rural or urban), and stage of economic development, including use of inanimate power and machines. Less tangible qualities of a population, but perhaps no less significant, are such features as customs, habits, prejudices, degree of enterprise, and different kinds of loyalties and allegiances. Many of these qualities of population are not represented in census data, but are to be caught and examined only through first hand observation or by archival investigation. Some of these qualities greatly affect man as an agent of production; others are of more consequence in affecting man as a consumer and enjoyer of the fruits of his labors. Few of these socio-economic qualities as they affect the world's population have been worked out in even their general patterns, let alone their regional and locality details. They remain, therefore, a fructuous field for geographic research.

Conclusion

My conclusion is brief and can be expressed in the form of a syllogism.

Population geography as a topical subdivision of the general field has been, and continues to be, neglected, by students of social and cultural phenomena, including geographers who should have known better.

As the pivotal element in geography, and the one around which all the others are oriented, and the one from which they all derive their meaning, population cannot be neglected without doing serious injury to geographic science in general.

Therefore, it behooves professional geographers to correct the unfortunate situation that now exists just as promptly as possible. I shall refrain from making specific recommendations concerning the steps to be taken and instead urge that the Association of American Geographers undertake a study of the situation looking toward the proposal of a remedial program.

Notes

[1] W. Fitzgerald, "Progress in Geographical Method," *Nature*, CLIII (April 1944): 481.

[2] Richard Hartshorne, *The Nature of Geography*.

[3] Robert E. Dickinson and O. J. R. Howarth, *The Making of Geography*.

[4] S. W. Wooldridge and W. G. East, *The Spirit and Purpose of Geography*.

[5] Alfred Hettner, *Die Geographie; ihre Geschichte, ihr Wesen und ihre Methoden*.

[6] Carl O. Sauer, "The Morphology of Landscape," *University of California Publications in Geography*, 2, 1925.

[7] Carl O. Sauer, "Recent Developments in Cultural Geography," Chapter 4 in *Recent Developments in the Social Sciences*, Edward Cary Hayes, ed.

[8] Harlan H. Barrows, "Geography as Human Ecology," *Annals of the Association of American Geographers*, XIII (1924): 17–33.

[9] *Geografiska Annaler* (1923): 1–37.

[10] *Allgemeine Geographie, Zweiter Teil, Das Leben auf Der Erde*.

[11] Ellsworth Huntington and Earl B. Shaw, *Principles of Human Geography*, 6th edition.

[12] Along this line see also: Louis Chevalier, "Demographie et géographie," *Annales de géographie*, LVI (July–Sept., 1947). Chapter 28, "Population," in *Elements of Geography* by Vernor C. Finch and Glenn T. Trewartha represents a brief outline of the content of population geography.

[13] *Preliminary Report of the Committee on Rural and Urban Settle-*

ment Geography, National Research Council, July 1, 1951.

[14]*Geographisches Jahrbuch*, Band 55, 1, pp. 1–380.

[15]Italics mine.

[16]*The Encyclopedia of the Social Sciences*, Vol. 6, p. 622.

[17]*Human Geography*, pp. 65–66.

[18]*Ibid.*, p. 67.

[19]Richard Hartshorne, *The Nature of Geography*, pp. 47–48.

[20]Richard Joel Russell, "Geographical Geomorphology," *Annals of the Association of American Geographers*, XXXIX (March 1949): 1–11.

[21]John E. Kesseli, "Geomorphic Landscapes," *Yearbook of the Association of Pacific Coast Geographers*, XII (1950).

[22]For a more comprehensive treatment of this dynamic concept of resources see: Erich W. Zimmermann, *World Resources and Industries*, 2nd Ed., Part I; Isaiah Bowman, *Geography in Relation to the Social Sciences*, pp. 34–37; Isaiah Bowman, "The New Geography," a radio talk subsequently published by the United States Rubber Company; and Eugene Holman, "Our Inexhaustible Resources," *The Atlantic Monthly*, CLXXXIX (June 1952): 29–32.

[23]Zimmermann, *op. cit.*, p. 91.

[24]This point of view has been admirably expressed in an essay by Edward A. Ackerman in which he gathered together experiences resulting from his wartime services in Washington, D.C. See Edward A. Ackerman, "Geographic Training, Wartime Research, and Immediate Professional Objectives," *Annals of the Association of American Geographers*, XXXV (Dec. 1945): 121–143.

[25]A. M. Carr-Saunders, *Population*, p. 10. On this topic see also: A. B. Wolfe, "The Fecundity and Fertility of Early Man," *Human Biology*, V: 37–38, and Abraham Clarke, *Archaeology and Society*, pp. 174–182.

[26]Alfred Louis Kroeber, *Cultural and Natural Areas of North America*, pp. 131–181.

[27]Mark Jefferson, "The Anthro-pography of North America," *Bulletin of the American Geographical Society*, XLV (1913): 161–180.

[28]V. Gordon Childe, *Man Makes Himself*.

[29]Louis Chevalier, "Demographie et géographie," Annals de Géographie, LVI (July–September, 1947): 201–202.

[30]Carl O. Sauer in *Limits of Land Settlement*, Isaiah Bowman ed., p. 9.

[31]Sten de Geer, "A Map of the Distribution of Population in Sweden: Method of Preparation and General Results," *Geographical Review*, XII (1922): 72–83.

[32]For a discussion of different kinds of population-density indices, see Dr. Imre Ferenczi, *The Synthetic Optimum of Population*, International Institute of Intellectual Cooperation, League of Nations, 1938.

[33]See especially a group of papers in *Comptes rendus du Congres International de Géographie*, Amsterdam, 1938, Volume 2, Sec. 111b. *Economic Geography*, pp. 174–228.

Selection Three

GEOGRAPHY AND DEMOGRAPHY[1]

Edward A. Ackerman

Professional geographers have long interested themselves in the study of population, and those scholars concerned with human geography inevitably have studied attributes of human populations and their settlement characteristics. In this they have touched common ground with demographers. This chapter discusses the areas of common interest through the distinctive approach of the geographer in his research, the aspects of population study covered by geographers in the past, and the outlook for research in geography which bears upon the study of population.

Reprinted from *The Study of Population* by Philip M. Hauser and Otis Dudley Duncan (eds.), by permission of The University of Chicago Press. © 1959 by the University of Chicago. Published 1959. Fourth Impression 1964. Composed and printed by The University of Chicago Press, Chicago, Illinois, U.S.A.

The Character of Geographic Research

Geography is one of the oldest of the sciences. Like astronomy, geography is concerned with the content of space, and it treats the distributive relations of objects in space. The "universe" of geography[2] is mainly two dimensional, limited to the zone of contact between land surface, water surface, and atmosphere. It is particularly a science of spatial distribution, and the matrix for its distributional analysis is the earth's surface. (This presentation follows the methodological discussion of Ackerman, 1958.) Geography undoubtedly began with isolated students' attempts to establish the space relation of particular localities to other localities within the range of the individual's experience. We can only guess when this first took place, but embryonic geography certainly began in remote prehistory. It was present at the time when the written record of human cultures began.

Men in early Egypt and Babylon began to measure the relation of localities or points on earth to the movements of the sun and stars; with this they began a science which has continued through each passing generation. Throughout much of its long history, geography has been concerned with identifying the pattern of simple space relations among the physical and biotic features of the earth's surface—the pattern compounded from distance and extent, direction and orientation. Inevitably there has been included in this work the identification of the space relations of cultural features. Thus even the earliest maps included the location of the most readily recognized cultural features—routes, towns, or settlements—along with the location of physical features.

Modern geographical research has been carried on in several specific steps. It starts with the description of the earth as a site,[3] that is, with accurate determination of the shape and extent of the physical matrix. Explorers, geographers, and others took centuries to produce an accurate determination, but it was finally accomplished by navigational reckoning, surveying, geodesy, and cartography. The objective was to determine the exact position which points on the earth's surface have in relation to each other. While the major works in this step have been completed, refinement of detail and new geodetic data on poorly known regions like the Antarctic are still necessary.

A second step in modern research is identification of the specific phenomenal content of earth space: quantity, qualities, degree. This has been carried on for centuries, but generally in an unsystematic manner. The tools were field observation and the written word. As cartographic techniques have been developed, this work has become more precise. Aerial photography in particular has improved the geographer's capacity to observe and record

accurately, but other devices, like the use of fractional symbols in mapping, also have contributed.

The third step is the identification of generic relations: categorization, classification, differentiation. The objective of this is to reduce to comprehensible limits the myriad possible observations which may be made about the distribution of earth phenomena. This step may be illustrated by the classification of weather phenomena into climatic types, and further into climatic regions. Climatic regions and other special-purpose regions show space relations generically considered.

A fourth step is the identification of genetic relations; this seeks determination of the dynamic aspects of space content. For example, a land-forms region is not static but changing. The processes[4] at work, their speed of action, and the conditions under which they arrive at stable equilibrium are all significant to genetic relations. This is a phase of study which geography shares with other disciplines and in which it often carries a secondary role, but geography's view and its objectives are uniquely centered on distributional problems.

The fifth step is the determination of covariant relations among earth features. Settlement types may covary with transportation routes, transportation routes with land forms, land forms with climatic types, and so on. Study of covariant features is important in ascertaining space relations.

The integration of data on site, phenomenon, and process so as to reveal the full pattern of space relations is the final step. Geography is an "integrative" discipline, with some resemblance to history in this respect (Hartshorne, 1939, pp. 243–45). In this sense it culminates in an understanding of, and capacity to describe, those aspects of a region which are significant in areal differentiation. In this step the science is concerned with the analysis and synthesis of earth-space content in such a way that reality may be comprehended.

In its first modern flowering in the nineteenth century, geography concentrated on the physical and biotic world. This strong physical interest was continued until a relatively few years ago, but geography now has changed to a different form. Within the twentieth century, geographers have turned to a dominant interest in those phases of the discipline which collectively are known as human geography: study of the space relations of cultural attributes in the setting of the natural environment. While the cultural phases of geography were known as far back as the time of Strabo (63 B.C.?–A.D. 24?), methodical study appeared only on the eve of the twentieth century. Recording of population numbers within settlements and political groupings seems to have been among the most continued efforts toward cultural study in premodern geography.

Recent geographers have studied the features of culture in the same general manner as their immediate predecessors analyzed the physical environment. They have taken the cultural features of the earth, analyzed them generically and genetically in their space relations, and established co-variant relations of cultural features with each other and with those of the physical and biotic environment. Much of this study has concerned economic features, but distributional features of concern to demography also have been studied.

Geographic Studies of Population

During the period in which professional geographic activity has centered on human geography, there has been consistent attention to the description and analysis of the distributional aspects of population. Like population studies in other disciplines, such study has included a number of separate subjects. The following are considered significant from the point of view of demography: (1) design of the collection of demographic data; (2) an analysis and comprehensible synthesis of data on areal differentiation of population as shown by census enumeration; (3) study of the several population attributes in their distributional

aspects; (4) study of settlement patterns and settlement interrelation; and (5) study of the geographic pattern of population sustenance. Of these, the first four will be discussed in this chapter. The fifth is treated in chapter xxvi of this volume, under the title "Population and Natural Resources." The present chapter refers primarily to American studies and to the subjects considered distinctively suited to geographical research methods. (The European geographical literature in the fields is extensive, as illustrated in the bibliography by Dörries, 1940.) References, furthermore, will be illustrative rather than exhaustive.

Design of the Collection of Demographic Data

Every census enumeration must be conducted within a geographic framework, and few other research works or data collections are so closely tied to units of area on the earth's surface. It follows that perceptive understanding of the areal characteristics of the enumeration unit can facilitate a census considerably and make its results more meaningful. It is not surprising, therefore, that some of the earliest and most consistent geographic work related to demography has been applied to census design. Henry Gannett, as Geographer of the Census, in 1881 drafted a plan of territorial division to facilitate enumeration in the following census (James, 1954; Von Struve, 1940). Geographers have assisted in the design of each decennial United States census since Gannett's time. The Division of Geography of the United States Bureau of the Census in 1958 was staffed with fifteen professional geographers assisting in preparation for the 1960 enumeration.[5] Other countries—Japan, the Soviet Union, Great Britain, and some Latin-American countries—have used geographical assistance in census design.

Census design improvements have been at least partly dependent upon and related to other aspects of geographic population research, notably the study of settlement patterns. Problems attending census design have become increasingly complex as single urban areas have spread within the last thirty years over many adjacent units of political jurisdiction, but census design is an important research function because understanding of the regional economic structures which affect population dynamics depends in large part on the manner in which census data are organized.

Areal Differentiation of Population: Analysis and Comprehensible Synthesis

Once an enumeration has been made, problems of meaningful interpretation of the returns arise. Geographers have made analyses of the static areal differentiation shown in a single enumeration; they have compared a succession of returns so as to reveal the trends in areal distribution patterns; they have evaluated the returns according to how they reflect the actual situation; they have interpolated data to show actual geographical patterns; and they have studied the relation of the different units in population distribution (e.g., the rural-urban relations and the hierarchy of central places).

The earliest such studies of note are still relatively recent, dating mainly from the years following the First World War. In this period the work of the Inquiry, a research group directed by Isaiah Bowman, studied areal differentiation of Central European populations in unprecedented detail. While an important objective of the Inquiry was the study of cultural differentiation, other results rested on a thorough description of the details of numerical distribution (partly reported in Bowman, 1921). In the same period Sten de Geer (1922) undertook a classic study of the distribution of population in Sweden, in which a very helpful technique for urban-rural cartographic comparison was used for the first time. Aurousseau (1921, 1923) in France and Jefferson in the United States were other geographical scholars examining the problems of describing population distributions during the same years. Among other things, Aurousseau devoted attention to developing a usable method of distinguishing rural and urban population. Jefferson (1909, 1911) was among the first to study the shortcomings of enumerations within arbitrary census areas, and he noted the important difference between geographical concentrations and political cities (see James, 1954).

Since the time of Jefferson and Aurousseau, there has been a succession of geographical studies which try to analyze census and other statistical data and to present these data so as to show areal differentiation. Some have sought refinements of method, giving more realistic presentation of distributional patterns (Wright, 1936, 1937). Others have worked with the problem of meaningful distributional descriptions in the presence of fragmentary or unreliable data (Louis, 1952), and still others with the extension of distributional knowledge into areas of underdeveloped economies, poorly developed governmental structure, or other characteristics conducive to retarded or previously fragmentary information (e.g., Trewartha and Zelinsky, 1954a, b). Perhaps most numerous have been the straightforward interpretations of national or regional enumerations, which attempt to provide a description of the most recently known static pattern (e.g., Fawcett, 1932; James, 1938; Melón, 1952; Ahmad, 1953; Cumberland, 1953; Stevens, 1946).

Some of the most careful and interesting studies have concerned the dynamics of population distribution as they could be interpreted from a series of census returns. Even before 1900, one study based on the returns of 1870, 1880, and 1890 had appeared in the United States (Whitney, 1894). Stanley Dodge's work (1946) on the relation of population dynamics to the frontier in the United States is a good example of geographical methods applied to an illumination of trends. Dodge's study covers two and one-half centuries, and the entire country. More typically, geographical studies of this kind treat limited periods (Neuvy, 1956; Willatts and Newson, 1953; Friis, 1940) or limited areas (Kollmorgen and Jenks, 1951–52; Schwind, 1954).

Some prominent geographers consider these and other geographic studies of population of basic importance to the entire field of human geography (James, 1954). Trewartha (1953) especially has presented the case for geographic population study as "pivotal" to the entire field of human geography, and he urges greater attention to it. This would suggest that population distribution studies are likely to be undertaken by geographers as a necessity in their own field, whatever the relation of geographic study to demography. It would also suggest that the refinement and extension of demographic data are of great importance to the human geographer and will be a stimulus to his further application in this field.

Study of the Several Population Attributes in Their Distributional Aspects

Geographers generally have devoted less of their effort to distributional studies of specific demographic attributes beyond straight enumeration. Nonetheless, they have paid some attention to these subjects. Specific studies of natality and mortality are not common in geographical literature, but examples can be found—Dodge's (1946) study of population trends, for example, describes trends in United States' fertility rates specifically. For this reason, only a few original studies of population projection problems have been undertaken. (One example is Steigenga, 1954. Studies on natural resources or other economic phenomena—of indirect significance to projections—have been numerous.) Where needed, the projections used by the geographer generally have been drawn from the work of the demographer (for example, the projections used in the post-World War II sustenance study of Japan; see Ackerman, 1953, p. 7).

Distributional studies of other specific demographic attributes also have been undertaken. Migrations and their distributional consequences have been attractive subjects for geographers, as might be expected. Proudfoot's (1956) study of European refugee movements during and after the Second World War is the most detailed research undertaken by a geographer on this subject. While its content goes beyond the distinctively geographic, it illustrates well the geographer's affinity to problems of areal change in population. Geographers also have treated migration in terms of its mechanism (Porter, 1956) and its correlation with environmental features (Ullman, 1954) or settlement (Gottmann, 1957). A number of specific regional or national studies also might be cited, for example, Nelson (1953), Mather (1956), Dyer (1952), and Hart (1957).

Geographic studies describing ethnic distributions (Calef and Nelson, 1956; Price, 1953; Schroeder, 1956), health conditions, and age and sex ratios (Franklin, 1958) also have been undertaken. The extensive studies of disease distribution supported by the American Geographical Society have been noteworthy among these special distributional studies (e.g., May, 1952). They illustrate the results to be obtained from competent collaborative effort between geographers and workers in other disciplines in studying specialized aspects of demographic geography.

Settlement Patterns and Settlement Interrelation

The relation between population dynamics and economic and other societal phenomena has long been appreciated; in fact, investigation of this relation can be traced to the beginnings of demography. Prominent among the phenomena investigated have been settlement forms and the several determinants of economic productivity. In part because of the world's demographic history since 1940, we now know that the interrelations of these elements and population growth are extremely complex and intricate, subject to no simple interpretation (see United Nations, 1953). We perhaps are still closer to the beginning than to the completion of conclusive analysis of these elements and their interrelation.

One obvious entry into this complex field is through the study of settlement forms, their distribution, and the evolution of their distribution. This is one important point of contact between people and the earth to which they are bound. Geographers perhaps have pursued these studies more assiduously than any others related to demography. The field of urban geography has been particularly well cultivated, but studies of the general nature of settlement and of rural farm and non-farm settlement also have been pursued. German geographers have devoted much attention to analyzing settlement types and distinctions among them (e.g., Christaller, 1938; Gradmann, 1937).[6] This was a natural consequence of German geographic methodology's emphasis on *Länderkunde* and *Landschaftskunde*. (See Hartshorne, 1939, pp. 207–10, 224–27, for explanation of these terms.) While the German view has notably influenced the practice of American geography, United States studies have turned much more in the direction of urban geography. The pioneering studies of Jefferson (1921, 1931) indicated a choice of direction which since has become popular among American geographers, and a copious American, British, and European professional literature has accumulated on urban geography. (See Mayer, 1954a, pp. 162–66, for a recent illustrative bibliography of urban geographic studies, especially of the United States.) Many studies have treated the morphology and functions of towns or sections of cities, and there is a notable series undertaken under the direction of Charles C. Colby and others of the University of Chicago faculty (e.g., Klove, 1942; Harris, 1940). Treatment of mapping techniques (e.g., Jones, 1931; Applebaum, 1952) and a variety of specialized studies of the internal structure of cities also were undertaken (e.g., Proudfoot, 1937).

From a study of cities' morphology and functions a natural step is to investigate the over-all structural pattern of urban settlement and the relation of cities, towns, and villages to each other. While geographers recently have shared this subject increasingly with economists, sociologists, and planning analysts, provocative analysis was undertaken early by geographers (Christaller, 1933; Jefferson, 1939; Ullman, 1941). Their attention to it has been continued (e.g., Dickinson, 1947; Smailes, 1946; Mayer, 1954b). Further study has been devoted to articulating parts of the settlement pattern, especially the function of transportation (e.g., Brush, 1953). Although not specifically directed toward the problem of articulation, the very extensive set of regional studies which twentieth-century geography has produced could serve as background material for research in this field. (For a descriptive summary of the methods of regional geography, see Whittlesey, 1954.)

While less cultivated in recent years than urban geography, study of rural settlement also has been conducted by geographers in a number of countries. Much investigation has centered on forms related to agricultural pursuits (e.g., Demangeon, 1920; Barrows, 1910; Hall, 1931; Stevens, 1946; Thorpe, 1952),[7] but the treatment of rural nonfarm settlement also has appeared recently (e.g., Kant, 1957).

Studies of settlement often, and sometimes inevitably, have included attention to functions represented in the settlement forms. This interest has been extended into study of functional relations of different types of population distribution (e.g., McCarty, 1942) and of the relation of population dynamics to functions of settlements (e.g., Roterus, 1946). Geographers have undertaken studies which localize functional relations of interest to demographers and which investigate the meaning of local demographic events of concern to students of areal phenomena. At one stage in the field's progress, geographers' attraction to studies of the relation (or co-variation) of population distribution, settlement forms, and functions prompted one leading geographer (Barrows, 1923) to propose human geography as human ecology. However, geography has not followed the trend proposed by Professor Barrows, although it has continued to have a preoccupation with covariants in the composite pattern of physical and cultural features on the earth.

Common Interests of Other Disciplines in Fields Treated by Geography

Within recent years students from other disciplines also have become concerned with the manifold problems of distribution and distributional relations. This is illustrated in the discussion of human ecology and population distribution presented elsewhere in this volume (chap. xxviii). Although the Barrows proposal did not anticipate a trend in geography, it did anticipate the growth of another field of study. The common ground of human ecology and human geography is suggested by Duncan's reference to the works of ten different geographers in the presentation of his chapter. Distributional studies are of obvious concern to the human ecologist.

Sociologists, economists, physicists, and others have profitably turned their attention to distributional problems associated with depicting the reticulated structure of settlement, population agglomeration, and social function. The works of Bogue (1955) in sociology, Isard (1956) in economics, and of the physicist Stewart (1947) have been considered helpful contributions to the subjects which have preoccupied geographers for decades. These and similar works have been well received among geographers because they afforded fresh insights, although not necessarily conclusive approaches, to the increasingly complex problems of understanding the distributional structure of man's relation to the earth.

Logical Future Research Interest in Geography

At least two prominent American geographers in recent years have stressed the importance of population studies to their field. James (1954, p. 107) has summarized the situation: "The irregularity of the distribution of mankind over the earth and the differences from place to place in the racial and societal character of the population are facts which underlie all studies in social science, including those of human geography." Trewartha (1953, p. 83), in the most thoughtful American analysis of the meaning of geographic population studies, states that "numbers, densities, and qualities of the population provide the essential background for all geography. *Population is the point of reference from which all other elements are observed, and from which they all, singly and collectively, derive significance and meaning.*" While partisans of the landscape school of geography might dispute Trewartha's emphasis, the significance of population study was indorsed by one of the most influential methodologists in the field, Alfred Hettner (Trewartha, 1953, p. 75). Furthermore, even geographers of the landscape school have contributed studies of indirect importance to demography through studies of settlement. While relatively few geographers have undertaken comprehensive studies of geography of population per se (one exception is Pierre George, 1951), it is safe to say that a majority of them today would recognize a significant relation between geographic and demographic research. This seems especially true since the end of the Second World War, when the demographer began to broaden his vision in seeking an answer to population dynamics.

A further point of interest in this relation is the connection between geographic research, resource-use planning, and settlement planning. It is patent that the technology of the future will contain an increasing element of these techniques and that they must eventually be taken into account in any evaluation of population dynamics. The techniques of geographic research and its results are basic to efficient planning (see Mayer, 1954*a*, p. 162). Accordingly, any evaluation of the technological element in settlement influences and sustenance patterns as they affect population characteristics may be illuminated by appropriate geographic study.

If the above assumptions are accepted, a further view of the possible character of forthcoming geographical research may form a helpful conclusion. One view of this prospect has been presented as follows (see Ackerman, 1958, for an elaboration of the statement given here): Geography treats areal differentiations, and all significant areal differentiation has a time dimension. A near universal characteristic of space-relation patterns on the earth is constant change. Study of the *evolution* of space content on the earth's surface is geography's research frontier. Geographers can seek understanding of the evolution of earth distributions in the operation of at least eight different physical, biotic, and cultural processes: movement of the soil mantle; movement of water over land; climate; biotic processes, particularly the vegetative; demographic movement; organizational evolution; development of the resource-converting techniques; and development of the space-adjusting techniques.[8] Demographic movement is at the heart of these forces which influence the change in space content.

Within this framework the following general research problems are recognized: study of distributions in the abstract and development of the general theory of area distribution, perfection of techniques of observation, study of the action of the processes on a given class of phenomena, study of the covariance of the processes as reflected in space relations, and integration of data on the several processes with those of site. Quantification is considered a major problem in describing the space-relations effect of the significant processes causing change (see, for example, Robinson and Bryson, 1957), and observational techniques need much further development if they are to match the need for quantification. Finally, study of the covariance of the significant processes is only at its beginning.

In the future, geographic research is likely to proceed on the assumption that the cultural, physical, and biotic worlds are something of a continuum for the understanding of space relations. However, disaggregative research, stressing quantification may be most influential in determining the future direction taken by the discipline. In this the data and interpretations of demography will be very important to geography. Geography, on the other hand, will aspire to illuminate the scene on which population growth and decline runs its course.

Notes

[1]The author was assisted by Donald Patton of the University of Maryland. Dr. Patton's bibliographic research and recommendations are represented in many of the references cited.

[2]"Universe" here is used in the sense of the total field for investigation within which a science actually or potentially may be a valid instrument of inquiry and synthesis.

[3]The term "site" here denotes that attribute which gives a specific position in space to any phenomenon.

[4]"Process" here and hereafter denotes a succession of physical,

biotic, or cultural events dependent on characteristic energizing agents.

[5]Information supplied by the Division of Geography, United States Bureau of the Census, January, 1958.

[6]Christaller generally has been considered an economist; however, works like the *Siedlungsgeographie* have become part of geography's professional literature. While Christaller was an economist first, he was a geographer too.

[7]These are taken only to illustrate the time span and type of hundreds of studies in this subfield.

[8]Resource-converting techniques are

those which turn the materials of the physical world and the life products of the biotic world to satisfaction of the needs of men (i.e., land-use techniques, techniques of mineral exploitation, etc.).

Space-adjusting techniques are those which shorten the effective distance of travel and transportation or those which permit intensification of space employment beyond that possible on the natural land surface (e.g., civil engineering, architecture, city and regional planning).

Selected Bibliography

Ackerman, E. A. 1953. *Japan's Natural Resources.* Chicago: University of Chicago Press.
———. 1958. *Geography as a Fundamental. Research Discipline.* ("Department of Geography Research Series") Chicago: University of Chicago.

Ahmad, Q. S. 1953. "Distribution of Population in Pakistan," *Pakistan Geographical Review*, VIII, 94–112, maps.

Applebaum, W. 1952. "A Technique for Constructing a Population and Urban Land Use Map," *Economic Geography*, XXVIII, 240–43.

Aurousseau, M. 1921. "The Distribution of Population: A Constructive Problem," *Geographical Review*, XI, 563–92.
———. 1923. "The Geographic Study of Population Groups," *ibid.*, XIII, 266–82.

Barrows, H. H. 1910. *Geography of the Middle Illinois Valley.* (Illinois State Geological Survey Bulletin No. 15) Urbana, Ill.
———. 1923. "Geography as Human Ecology," *Annals of the Association of American Geographers*, XIII, 1–14.

Bogue, D. J. 1955. "Nodal versus Homogeneous Regions, and Statistical Techniques for Measuring the Influence of Each," preprint, *Proceedings of the Conference of the International Statistical Institute.* Rio de Janerio.

Bowman, I. 1921. *The New World: Problems in Political Geography.* New York and Chicago, 4th ed.; 1928.

Brush, J. E. 1953. "The Hierarchy of Central Places in Southwestern Wisconsin," *Geographical Review*, XLIII, 380–402, map.

Calef, W. C., and Nelson, H. J. 1956. "Distribution of Negro Population in the United States," *Geographical Review*, XLVI, 82–97.

Christaller, W. 1933, *Die zentralen Orte in Süddeutschland.* Jena: Fischer.
———. 1938. "Siedlungsgeographie und Kommunalwissenschaft," *Petermanns geographische Mitteilungen*, LXXXIV, 49–53.

Cumberland, Kenneth. 1953. "Population Growth in New Zealand: A Review of Recent Census Returns," *The Scottish Geographical Magazine*, LXIX, 97–105, map.

Demangeon, A. 1920. "L'habitation rurale en France: Essai de classification des principaux types," *Annales de géographie*, XXIV, 352–75.

Dickinson, R. E. 1947. *City, Region and Regionalism.* London: Kegan Paul, Trench, Trubner & Co.

Dodge, S. D. 1946. "Periods in the Population History of the United States," *Papers of the Michigan Academy of Science, Arts, and Letters*, XXXII, 253–60.

Dorries, H. 1940. "Siedlungs und Bevölkerungsgeographie (1908–38)," *Geographisches Jahrbuch*, LV, 3–380.

Dyer, D. 1952. "The Place of Origin of Florida's Population," *Annals of the Association of American Geographers*, XLII, 283–94, maps.

Fawcett, C. B. 1932. "Distribution of the Urban Population in Britain in 1931," *Geographical Journal*, LXXIX, 100–116.

Franklin, S. H. 1958. "The Age Structure of New Zealand's North Island Communities," *Economic Geography*, XXXIV, 64–79.

Friis, H. R. 1940. "A Series of Population Maps of the Colonies and the United States, 1625–1790." *Geographical Review*, XXX, 463–70

Geer, S. de. 1922. "A Map of the Distribution of Population in Sweden: Method of Preparation and General Results," *Geographical Review*, XII, 72–83.

George, Pierre. 1951. *Introduction à l'étude géographique de la population du monde.* Paris: Institut National d'Études Démographiques.

Gottman, J. 1957. "Expansion urbaine et mouvements de population," *Research Group for European Migration Problems Bulletin*, No. 5, pp. 53–61.

Gradmann, R. 1937. "Zur siedlungsgeographischen Methodik," *Geographische Zeitschrift*, XLIII, 353–61.

Hall, R. B. 1931. "Some Rural Settlement Forms in Japan," *Geographical Review*, XXI, 93–123.

Harris, C. D. 1940. *Salt Lake City: A Regional Capital.* Chicago: University of Chicago.

Hart, J. F. 1957. "Migration and Population Change in Indiana," *Indiana Academy of Science*, LXVI, 195–203.

Hartshorne, Richard. 1939. *The Nature of Geography: A Critical Survey of Current Thought in the Light of the Past.* Lancester, Pa.: Association of American Geographers.

Isard, Walter. 1956. *Location and Space Economy.* New York: Wiley.

James, P. E. 1938. "The Distribution of People in South America," in *Geographic Aspects of International Relations.* Chicago: University of Chicago Press.
———. 1954. "The Geographic Study of Population," in *American Geography: Inventory and Prospect*, ed. P. E. James and C. F. Jones. Syracuse N. Y.: Association of American Geographers.

Jefferson, Mark. 1909. "The Anthropogeography of Some Great Cities," *Bulletin of the American Geographical Society*, XLI, 537–66.
———. 1911. "The Real New York," *ibid.*, XLIII, 737–40.
———. 1921. "Great Cities of the United States, 1920," *Geographical Review*, XI, 437–41.
———. 1931. "Distribution of the World's City Folks," *ibid.*, XXI, 446–65.
———. 1939. "The Law of the Primate City," *ibid.*, XXIX, 226–32.

Jones, W. D. 1931. "Field Mapping of Residential Areas in Metropolitan Chicago," *Annals of the Association of American Geographers*, XXI, 207–14.

Kant, E. 1957. "Suburbanization, Urban Sprawl, and Commutation: Examples from Sweden," in *Migration in Sweden: A Symposium*, ed. D. Hannerberg *et al.* ("Lund Studies in Geography," Ser. B. "Human Geography," No. 13.) Lund: C. W. K. Gleerup.

Klove, R. C. 1942. *The Park Ridge-Barrington Area.* Chicago: University of Chicago Press.

Kollmorgen, W. M., and Jenks, G. F. 1951–52. "A Geographic Study of Population and Settlement Changes in Sherman County, Kansas," *Transactions, Kansas Academy of Sciences*, LIV, 449–94; LV, 1–37, map.

Louis, H. 1952. "Über Aufgabe und Möghchkeiten einer Bevölkerungsdichtekarte der Erde: Begleitworte zur beigegebenen Karte 1:80 Mill.," *Petermanns geographische Mitteilungen*, XCVI, 284–88.

McCarty, H. H. 1942. "A Functional Analysis of Population Distribution," *Geographical Review*, XXXII, 282–93.

Mather, D. B. 1956. "Migration in the Sudan," in *Geographical Essays on British Tropical Lands*, ed. R. W. Steel and C. A. Fisher. London: G. Phillip & Son.

May, J. M. 1952. "Map of the World Distribution of Dengue and Yellow Fever," *Geographical Review*, XLII, 283–86.

Mayer, H. M. 1954a. "Urban Geography," in *American*

Geography: Inventory and Prospect, ed. P. E. James and C. F. Jones, Syracuse, N. Y.: Association of American Geographers.

———. 1954*b*. "Urban Nodality and the Economic Base," *Journal of the American Institute of Planners*, XX, 117–21.

Melon, Amando. 1952. "La población de España en 1950 (datos y comentarios)," *Estudios geográficos*, XIII, 441–54.

Nelson, H. J. 1953. "Die Binnenwanderung in den USA, am beispiel Kaliforniens," *Die Erde*, II, 109–21.

Neuvy, Pierre. 1956. "L'évolution de la population japonaise," *Annales de géographie*, LXV, 40–53.

Porter, R. 1956. "Approach to Migration through Its Mechanism," *Geografiska Annaler*, XXXVIII, 317–43.

Price, E. T. 1953. "A Geographic Analysis of White-Negro-Indian Racial Mixtures in Eastern United States," *Annals of the Association of American Geographers*, XLIII, 138–55, maps.

Proudfoot, M. J. 1937. "City Retail Structure," *Economic Geography*, XIII, 425–28.

———. 1956. *European Refugees, 1939–52: A Study in Forced Population Movement*. Evanston, Ill.: Northwestern University Press.

Robinson, A. H., and Bryson, R. A. 1957. "A Method for Describing Quantitatively the Correspondences of Geographical Distributions," *Annals of the Association of American Geographers*, XLVII, 379–91.

Roterus, V. 1946. "Effects of Population Growth and Non-Growth on the Well-being of Cities," *American Sociological Review*, XI, 90–97.

Schroeder, K. 1956. "Bevölkerungsgeographische Probleme in Grenzraum der USA gegenüber Mexico," *Die Erde*, VIII, 229–63, map.

Schwind, M. 1954. "Bevölkerungsdichte und Bevölkerungsverteilung in Schleswig, 1800–1950," *Berichte zur deutschen Landeskunde*, XIII, 32–43, maps.

Smailes, A. 1946. "The Urban Mesh of England and Wales," *Transactions of the Institute of British Geographers*, No. 11 pp. 87–101, maps.

Steigenga, W. 1954. "Het Vraagstuk der regionale Bevolkingsprognose," *Tijdschrift voor economische en sociale Geographie*, XLV, 80–88.

Stevens, A. 1946. "The Distribution of Rural Population in Great Britain," *Transactions of the Institute of British Geographers*, No. 11, pp. 23–53.

Stewart, J. Q. 1947. "Empircal Mathematical Rules Concerning the Distribution and Equilibrium of Population," *Geographical Review*, XXXVII, 461–85.

Struve, A. W. von. 1940. "Geography in the Census Bureau," *Economic Geography*, XVI, 275–80.

Thorpe, H. 1952. "The Influence of Inclosure on the Form and Pattern of Rural Settlement in Denmark," *Transactions of the Institute of British Geographers*, No. 17, 111–29, maps.

Trewartha, G. T. 1953. "The Case for Population Geography," *Annals of the Association of American Geographers*, XLIII, 71–97.

———, and Zelinsky, W. 1954*a*. "Population Patterns in Tropical Africa," *Annals of the Association of American Geographers*, XLIV, 135–62, map.

———. 1954*b* "The Population Geography of Belgian Africa," *ibid.*, pp. 163–98, map.

Ullman, E. L. 1941. "A Theory of Location for Cities," *American Journal of Sociology*, XLVI, 853–64.

———. 1954. "Amenities as a Factor in Regional Growth," *Geographical Review*, XLIV, 119–32.

United Nations, Population Division. 1953. *The Determinants and Consequences of Population Trends*. New York: United Nations.

Whitney, J. D. 1894. *The United States: Facts and Figures Illustrating the Physical Geography of the Country and Its Material Resources. Supplement 1, Population: Immigration: Irrigation*. Boston: Little, Brown & Co.

Whittlesey, D. 1954. "The Regional Concept and the Regional Method," in *American Geography: Inventory and Prospect*, ed. P. E. James and C. F. Jones, Syracuse, N. Y.: Association of American Geographers.

Willatts, E. C., and Newson, Marion C. C. 1953. "The Geographical Pattern of Population Changes in England and Wales, 1921–1951," *Geographical Journal*, CXIX, 431–54, maps.

Wright, J. K. 1936. "A Method of Mapping Densities of Population: With Cape Cod as an Example," *Geographical Review*, XXVI, 103–10.

———. 1937. "Some Measures of Distributions," *Annals of the Association of American Geographers*, XXVII, 177–211.

A SELECTED SUPPLEMENTARY BIBLIOGRAPHY FOR PART 1

George, P., *Questions de géographie de la population*. Institut National d'Etudes Démographiques, Cahiers de "Travaux et Documents," No. 34. Paris: Press Universitaires de France, 1959.

Hooson, D. J. M., "The Distribution of Population as the Essential Geographical Expression," *Canadian Geographer*, Vol. 17, 1960, pp. 10–20.

James, P. E., "The Geographic Study of Population," *American Geography: Inventory and Prospect*, P. E. James and C. F. Jones (eds.). Syracuse: Syracuse University Press, 1954, pp. 106–122.

Melezin, A., "Trends and Issues in the Soviet Geography of Population," *Annals of the Asociation of American Geographers*, Vol. 53, 1963, pp. 144–160.

Pokshishevskiy, V. V., "Geography of Population and Its Tasks," *Soviet Geography: Review and Translation*, Vol. 3, 1962, pp. 3–13.

Stamp, L. D. "The Geographical Study of Population," *Applied Geography*. London: Penguin Books 1960, pp. 26–36.

PART TWO

POPULATION GROWTH: HISTORY, THEORY, AND POLICY

INTRODUCTION

The history, theory, and policy of population growth are closely related. The history details the events of significance that have taken place, as well as their causes and consequences. The theory represents an attempt to better understand reality by treating selected components in their ideal relations to one another for purposes of detailed analyses and the establishment of principles. The policy, in this context, is understood to mean the practical application of current knowledge through legislative or other channels to problems of excessive population growth. Although usually expressed in programs of fertility reduction and control, such programs include, if only by implication, the study of resources in terms of quantity, quality, distribution, and allocation.

Briefly, Durand treats the history of world population growth, comments on the factors which have controlled, or failed to control, past population increases, and speculates about the *carrying capacity* of the earth. "World Population: Trend and Prospects" is thus an apt companion piece to the second selection, "A Summary View of the Principle of Population," by Malthus, whose work on the relationships between growth in number of inhabitants and the means of subsistence is universally accorded a prominent place in the study of population.

Stolnitz adequately, if briefly, describes and analyzes the trends from high to low vital rates—*demographic transition*—which have characterized population history in those world regions which have evolved from an agrarian economy to a modern, urban-industrial status. Moreover, in applying his *perspectives* of past demographic transitions to the presently underdeveloped regions in Latin America, Asia, and Africa, he concludes that the speed with which these regions move through the period of declining mortality and high fertility (the preindustrial phase) to a stage of low rates of birth and death (the industrial characterization) is central to their future well-being.

In the concluding article in this section, Kingsley Davis introduces serious doubts concerning the prospects of current family planning programs as adequate solutions to problems of overpopulation. He arrives at this position after reviewing the nature of current programs, describing the dangers associated with acceptance of family planning and population control as adequate goals in various national policies, and introducing additional approaches which might further the chances of existing policy (such as it is) to succeed.

Returning to the original theme of this introduction, it might prove worthwhile for the reader if certain of the common themes which the selected papers exhibit were treated in greater detail, particularly the notion of demographic transition as it relates to today's underdeveloped regions and their inhabitants. Demographic transitions are historical events which, despite the lack of reliable data concerning specific trends in vital rates for those national populations whose fertility and mortality were so transformed during the eighteenth and nineteenth centuries, are well documented. As such, these evolutions in demographic behavior, usually observed as accompaniments to urban-industrial development, portray a rather optimistic picture. That is, given economic development, population growth trends are such that the problem of immoderate growth eventually corrects itself.

It must be recognized that, in gaining a modern demographic balance of low birth and death rates, Northwestern Europe, including England and Wales, experienced a rather lengthy period during which fertility remained at or near its preindustrial level while mortality declined. (Chung's "Space-Time Diffusion of the Transition Model: The Twentieth Century Patterns," in Part 5 includes several graphs depicting demographic transitions.) Therefore, as a theoretical model on which programs to combat excessive population growth (in currently underdeveloped regions) might be based, demographic transition is questionable. Indeed, if presently underdeveloped nations were to follow demographic trends similar to those of Europe, the positive checks detailed by Malthus and so antithetical to the European experience might produce results hardly consistent with the view that demographic transition leads to a slowly increasing, relatively affluent status for those who reside in such places.

With the imposition of extensive programs and projects aimed at reducing mortality and increasing longevity often enjoying a far greater degree of success than companion attempts at fertility reduction and control, the people of many underdeveloped nations have begun to feel the ill effects of demographic transition without experiencing any of its benefits. Mortality seems simple to reduce (a mechanical process of installing better medical facilities, improving sanitation techniques, and so forth) as compared to the cultural tangle one encounters in the battle to win acceptance of birth control and family planning. The reduction and control of fertility requires, it seems, a revolution in values (a population acting independently as families should,) but one in which the collective desire for a better quality of life is reflected in responsible demographic behavior.

All four selections included thus relate well to the widely publicized, popularized, often misunderstood, *population explosion*. Each, in its own way, directs attention to the relationships between population numbers and the resource base. This association is explicit in the work of Durand and that of Malthus (the earth's carrying capacity and the linkages between population growth and food are treated by these articles); Stolnitz, in his treatment of changing vital rates, relates trends in demographic behavior to industrial development; and, finally, Davis suggests ways of limiting reproduction and postponing marriage which would ". . . reduce the numbers, not the quality, of the next generation."

Selection Four

WORLD POPULATION: TREND AND PROSPECTS*

John D. Durand

The time in which we live could be described without exaggeration as the age of the peopling of the earth. Of course, the earth has been peopled to some extent for a long time—according to a conservative estimate, the origin of the human race dates back at least 100,000 years—but the majority of its growth since the beginning has been contributed by the last three or four generations. The world population in 1850 has been estimated at about 1,200,000,000; the present estimate is about 2,500,000,000. In other words, the growth during one century has been more than during all the previous ages. Moreover, the rate of growth has been rising for several hundred years; it is still rising and there are reasons for believing that it may rise higher in the future.

The exact rate of world population growth at present is not known because there are no censuses or vital statistics for many countries; and estimates for the past are still more uncertain than those for the present. Still, the order of magnitude of the figures and the direction of the trend are unmistakable. In round numbers, 30 or 35 million people are being added to the population each year. In percentage terms, the increase is now more than 1 per cent and perhaps nearly 1½ per cent per annum. During the last half-century, the rate averaged about one per cent.

An increase of 1 per cent does not seem very large, but its power of multiplication over a period of years is impressive. If the population continues to grow at the present rate, another two and one-half billion people will be added by the next two generations. Compared with what must have been normal in past ages, this rate is something like the speed of an express train compared to the pace of a tortoise. An Argentine demographer has calculated that if Adam and Eve and their descendants had multiplied constantly at 1 per cent per annum, they would now be so many that, standing shoulder to shoulder and breast to back, they would occupy the surface of a sphere with radius fourteen times that of Neptune's orbit. This is an understatement; the calculation was based on the scriptural dating of the Creation, only 7,000 years ago.

Actually, the population has not grown at any constant rate in the past. If the trend could be reconstructed it would look something like a staircase, with periods of more or

*Although the author is a member of the United Nations Secretariat, the contents of this lecture represent his personal views and not necessarily those of the United Nations.

Reprinted with permission of The Macmillan Company from *Population and World Politics* by Philip M. Hauser (ed.). © by The Free Press, a Corporation, 1958.

less rapid increase corresponding to times when the progress of civilization was unusually rapid, and intervening periods of slower growth or decline. During the whole paleolithic era the population must have remained exceedingly small, strictly limited by the quantities of game, edible plants, berries, etc., which nature offered in each area.

Professor Walter F. Willcox has made a painstaking estimate of the trend of world population back to 1650, using whatever statistics and other information could be obtained. There are only two earlier dates for which any estimates are possible in the present state of knowledge. One is just before the beginning of the neolithic revolution—when agriculture was first introduced—the other is about the time when Christ was born. The emperors of ancient Rome and China took some "censuses" of their dominions at about that time; these enumerations covered a large enough part of the world to permit rough estimates of the total population.

Consider first the time when the neolithic revolution began in the Near East. Of course, this transition is not something which occurred all at once, but a process which stretched out over a long period in each region. The timing also is uncertain, but if we choose the year 6000 B.C. we can be sure that what agriculture was being practiced in the world at that time was not of very great economic importance.

No one knows just how large the world population was in 6000 B.C. but something can be said about the upper and lower limits. It has been estimated on the basis of archaeological and anthropological studies that the maximum density of paleolithic hunting and food-gathering populations could hardly have exceeded one or two persons per square mile even in the most favored areas, and in most regions it must have been considerably less. The Indian population of North America before Columbus, for example, is believed to have had an average density of only about one person per ten square miles

in the areas where agriculture was not practiced. Taking into account the geography of the regions which are known to have been inhabited by paleolithic men, it appears that the world population could hardly have been more than five million, and it is difficult to understand how it could have been less than one million. If this is the correct range, the average rate of increase during the paleolithic period, assuming that it lasted only 100,000 years, works out to less than 1½ per cent per *century*.

The development of agriculture, even in a simple form, enormously increased the population-carrying capacity of the earth and at the same time made possible a great improvement in the conditions of life. L. R. Nougier's article on the prehistoric population of France, which appeared in the French journal *Population*, gives some idea of the population increase which took place in some regions during the neolithic era. Basing his calculations on a detailed survey of the archaeological findings in different parts of the country, he concluded that the population of the area which is now France prior to the "neolithic revolution" probably never amounted to more than about 20,000. During the fourth millenium B.C., when the first agricultural settlements appeared, he estimated that the population grew to about half a million, and in the next thousand years—4000 to 3000 B.C.—it jumped to five million.

A still greater impetus to population growth in some regions may have been given by the next great step in social and economic evolution, namely, the creation of the market economy and of city-centered societies of exchange. Trade over wide market areas permitted the division of labor to a degree that would not have been possible under the neolithic regime, with its small, self-sufficient villages. At this stage, the advance of civilization not only opened the way for population growth, but was itself encouraged by the increase of numbers. In fact, the society of exchange requires a certain minimum population size and density within the trading area to permit extensive specialization of functions. Furthermore, the growth of population under this regime made it possible to mobilize large forces of labor for works such as drainage, irrigation, and terracing, which greatly extended the useable land in some regions. In ancient Egypt, for example, the areas of farmland along the Nile were originally very small; in spite of their remarkable fertility they could not support much population until the swamps had been drained and irrigation works constructed on a large scale.

By the time of Christ, agriculture was being practiced in most of Europe and Asia, in large parts of Africa, and in much of Central America and northern South America. Societies of exchange with dense agricultural population and sizeable cities had been organized over a great area in the eastern hemisphere, extending from Spain to China and from India to the Baltic Sea. The trend reached culmination in the military and trading empires of ancient Rome, Persia, India, and China. Similar developments were beginning in Middle America and the Andes. These accomplishments were reflected by a large increase of world population. At this time the total is believed to have been between 200 and 300 million. If so, the average increase during the preceding six thousand years was at least 6 per cent and perhaps as much as 10 per cent per century.

The growth during the next sixteen centuries was slower. Willcox's estimate for 1650 A.D. is 470 million. Professor Carr-Saunders has estimated 545 million. If we accept a range from 450 to 550 million, it appears that the rate of increase between the time of Christ and 1650 was from 2½ to 5 per cent per century. This was a period when the pace of social and economic development was comparatively slow. There were no innovations that could be compared in importance with the invention of agriculture or the development of the exchange economy, nor with the subsequent development of the industrial economy. Progress took the form chiefly of extending earlier advances to

regions which had been retarded in their development. The growth of population likewise was confined mainly to the outlying regions. Within the historic centers of high culture, available estimates show little net increase during the first centuries of the Christian era or the Middle Ages.

Modern Growth

Since 1650, the rate of increase has risen far above what was estimated for any previous period. It has averaged at least 65 per cent per century during the last 300 years. This enormous spurt, like the smaller one in pre-Christian times, has been linked with important new developments in the social and economic spheres. Industrialization, with a whole host of connected improvements in techniques of production and social organization, has again added to the carrying capacity of the earth. Again, the course of economic development has demanded a growing population to supply markets and labor force for production on a larger scale with ever finer specialization of employments.

How has the link between population increase and economic and social development been made? Is it a rising birth rate or a falling death rate which has permitted population to expand when expansion was feasible and useful? How has expansion been checked when development slowed down?

For the pre-modern period, the answer is unknown. According to one hypothesis, the mores of almost all peoples have been oriented since very ancient times to the maintenance of a high birth rate, in order to guarantee survival in the face of high mortality risks. These mores are slow to change, according to the hypothesis, and therefore adjustments in the population trend have been effected chiefly by changes in the death rates. But it is now well known that various means of regulating the birth rate, including abortion, infanticide, coitus interruptus, limitation of marriage, and taboos affecting sex relations, have long been known and practiced by many peoples, both primitive and "civilized," in different parts of the world. It seems possible, therefore, that changing birth rates have had as much to do with population trends as changing death rates.

The same uncertainty applies to the acceleration of population growth in the early part of the modern period, that is, before records of vital statistics were established. However, so far as the recent past is concerned, the statistics have already demonstrated that it is rapidly falling death rates, and not rising birth rates, which have been primarily responsible for a faster increase of numbers.

Not everyone realizes how much death rates have been reduced in recent times. Two hundred years ago a new-born child could look forward on the average to only thirty-five or forty years of life, even in the countries where conditions of health were most favorable. Estimates for former times, including calculations of the life expectancy in medieval Europe, ancient Greece and Egypt, and in prehistoric times, show a still more dismal picture of early death. At present the expectation of life in many countries exceeds sixty-five years and all over the world it is being lengthened, thanks mainly to a great reduction in the number of children who die in infancy. This progress of death control is one of the most important achievements of the modern age. It is without any precedent in the past, and it has a powerful effect on the population trend.

Major reductions of death rates were first recorded in the vital statistics of various countries in northwestern Europe early in the nineteenth century. There were probably substantial reductions during the eighteenth century also, before the national systems of birth and death registration were established in most of the countries concerned. The trend was quickly communicated to the more prosperous areas of European settlement overseas, and, subsequently, to the countries of southern and eastern Europe. With minor interruptions, it has continued ever since; the average death rate today for European countries—around ten deaths annually per 1,000 population—is less than one-third of what it was in the early nineteenth century.

The initial effect on the population of Europe was a veritable mushrooming. The birth rates at first remained almost unchanged while the death rates fell. It has been estimated that between 1750 and 1900 the population of Europe and its emigrant offshoots overseas multiplied nearly fourfold.

The phase of rapid growth in the European population was finally brought to an end by falling birth rates. By 1900 the small-family idea was well established in the leading industrial countries of western, northern, and central Europe, and also in the United States, Canada, Australia, and New Zealand. Thirty years later the number of births in many of these countries was no longer sufficient to replace the population permanently, and their governments were beginning to consider the need for vigorous measures to avoid the threat of de-population. That threat has now disappeared, at least for the time being, thanks to a revival of birth rates. But Europe still appears on the world map as a region of low human fertility, and its rate of population growth is now only about one-half the world rate. The United States, Canada, Australia, New Zealand, and the Soviet Union have somewhat higher birth rates; their rate of increase is about the same as the world average, or slightly higher.

Any slackening of world population growth which might have been caused by lower birth rates in Europe was more than offset by falling death rates in other parts of the world, where birth rates were still high. The progress of death control in Latin America, Asia, and Africa has been most remarkable during the last few decades. Latin America as a whole now has a death rate not much higher than the average for Europe. The effect of this combined with the higher birth rate of the Latin American peoples is to make Latin America the fastest growing region of the world today. Most countries in that region have recently been adding to their population rates between 2 and 3 per cent per annum, that is, about twice the world average. The same is true of many countries in Asia and Africa: Egypt, Turkey, Ceylon, and the Philippines, for example.

In other Asian and African countries, the population is growing more slowly at present, not because they have lower birth rates than the countries above, but because they have higher death rates. Consider India as an example. The death rate in that country at present is two or three times as high as in the United States. Even with a birth rate far above the world average, the population of India grows at a comparatively modest rate —somewhere between 1 per cent and 1½ per cent per year.

For a long time the consensus of expert opinion has been that China's population was growing rather slowly. The death rate was presumed to be high even in good years, and it was thought to rise from time to time when there were large floods, famine, or other catastrophes. In this way the effect of a high birth rate was presumed to be counterbalanced. But the presumption could not be verified for lack of any reliable statistics. In 1953, a census was taken on the mainland and data on births and deaths as well as population were obtained. It was reported in the newspapers that the birth rate was found to be thirty-seven per 1,000 and the death rate seventeen per 1,000. If these are the correct figures, they mean that the Chinese population is now growing at 2 per cent per annum. But the figures should be taken with some reserve; experience has shown that birth and death statistics collected in censuses are subject to substantial errors.

China's population is about one-fourth the world total; with the rest of Asia it accounts for more than half of all mankind. If this huge population begins to multiply at the rate demonstrated in Latin America, the result will be a large boost to the rate of world population increase. If the Chinese census figures are correct, this has nearly

come to pass already in China; and if not, all that is needed to bring it about there, and in all Asia, is a repetition of what has happened in countries like Ceylon. With modern techniques and materials for public health work, it is entirely possible, and within a few years. Increasing at 2 per cent a year, Asia's people would add a billion to the world population in less than thirty years.

In Latin America, too, there is room for progress in cutting down death rates. In many cases they are still noticeably higher than the rates for the most advanced countries in Europe, for example. The fact that death rates can be reduced in practically every part of the world; and it is virtually certain that this will happen in the years to come—always barring the possibility of calamities such as another World War.

What can be said about the possibility that birth rates, too, will be reduced so that the rate of population growth will be kept at the present level or diminished? An effort in this direction will be made in some countries where too rapid an increase is found to be hindering progress toward a satisfactory level of living. India has announced a policy of taking steps to moderate the growth of population in accordance with the needs and capacity of the economy. Egypt is considering a similar policy; Japan already has a national system of birth control clinics, and other countries may follow suit. But it is not easy to make such a policy effective in an underdeveloped country with a low level of income and popular education, and poor facilities for the distribution of either ideas or materials. In view of the difficulties, it seems unlikely in the near future that any reduction of birth rates in underdeveloped countries will be great enough to counterbalance their falling death rates.

In the parts of the world where birth rates are lower—generally speaking, Europe, North America, and Australia—fertility may rise or fall; it is difficult to predict. But fewer births in those regions, representing only about one-third of world population, would hardly be sufficient to balance the acceleration of growth which seems almost inevitable in Asia, Africa, and Latin America.

Future Growth

The United Nations Population Division has made some tentative forecasts of future population up to 1980 for various parts of the world, taking into account the possibilities which have been briefly mentioned here. For the world total, the results indicate an increase from the present 2,500,000,000 to at least 3,300,000,000 and perhaps nearly 4,000,000,000 by 1980. They also imply that the underdeveloped continents of Asia, Africa, and Latin America can look forward to a larger share of world population than they already have.

It is not appropriate to enter here a discussion of the economic difficulties which this growth of numbers may create, particularly in the underdeveloped regions. But it is appropriate to point out the anomalous relationship between population trends and economic development which the recent changes in death rates have created. In Europe and the United States during the nineteenth century the increase in life expectancy and consequent growth of population could be regarded as symptoms of economic health. They were largely the direct results of higher real income for the masses, better nutrition and housing; in short, a rising standard of living. What was accomplished by the progress of medical science could also be considered an indirect effect of economic development, which increased the resources that could be devoted to the furtherance of science. In the underdeveloped countries today the situation is different. Spectacular reductions of death rates are achieved by such means as mass immunization, mosquito-control campaigns, and simple improvements in hygiene and protection of water supplies, without any great change in economic conditions. The people of the underdeveloped countries are certainly living longer than their fathers did,

but it is not because they are living better. And if they have managed to ease their conditions of life somewhat, they have done it in spite of the increase of their numbers and not because of it.

Perhaps we are only witnessing a passing phase in the changing relationship between population growth and economic progress. It is said that if the people of the less developed regions can reach a certain level of real income, with a certain degree of industrialization and a certain educational standard, they will moderate their increase with lower birth rates. It may be so, but the hypothesis is only based on an interpretation of past trends in the industrial countries of the West—and lately in Japan, the one industrial nation of the East. Its application to other cultural settings in other times is open to question.

It is also said that a balance of births and deaths must be achieved within a few more generations in any event; otherwise it will be imposed by mass starvation and strife due to exhaustion of the earth's resources. But the weight of evidence implies rather clearly that the resources are sufficient to support a growing population for some time to come, even with present technical knowledge, and it is impossible to foresee what technical and organizational improvements might be made in the more distant future.

He who wishes to enter this field of speculation should not ignore the relationship, in the broad sweep of history, between the growth of population and man's ability to turn the resources of nature to his advantage. We have seen the capacity of the earth expand, and seen population growth help to expand it, at each stage of economic evolution, from the hunting and food-gathering to the subsistence-agriculture regime, and thence to the regime of commercial agriculture and the industrial regime. There may be at least one more step in this evolution, and when that step has been taken, it may appear that the massive growth of population in our times was necessary for it.

Selection Five

A SUMMARY VIEW OF THE PRINCIPLE OF POPULATION
Thomas R. Malthus

The following essay, entitled "A Summary View of the Principle of Population," was published in 1830, after having appeared in slightly longer form in the 1824 supplement to the Encyclopaedia Britannica.

In taking a view of animated nature, we cannot fail to be struck with a prodigious power of increase in plants and animals. Their capacity in this respect is indeed almost infinitely various, according with the endless variety of the works of nature and the different purposes which they seem appointed to fulfil. But whether they increase slowly or rapidly, if they increase by seed or generation, their natural tendency must be to increase in a geometrical ratio, that is, by multiplication; and at whatever rate they are increasing during any one period, if no further obstacles be opposed to them, they must proceed in a geometrical progression.

In the growth of wheat, a vast quantity of seed is unavoidably lost. When it is dibbled instead of being sown in the common way, two pecks of seed wheat will yield as large a crop as two bushels, and thus quadruple the proportion of the return to the quantity of seed put into the ground. In *Philosophical Transactions* (1768) an account is given of an experiment in which, by separating the roots obtained from a single grain of wheat and transplanting them in a favourable soil, a return was obtained of above 500,000 grains. But without referring to peculiar instances or peculiar modes of cultivation, it is known that calculations have often been made, founded on positive experience of the produce of wheat in different soils and countries, cultivated in an ordinary way, and making allowance for all ordinary destruction of seed.

Humboldt has collected some estimates of

this kind, from which it appears that France, the north of Germany, Poland, and Sweden, taken generally, produce from five to six grains for one; some fertile lands in France produce fifteen for one; and the good lands in Picardy and the Isle of France, from eight to ten grains for one. Hungary, Croatia, and Slavonia yield from eight to ten grains for one. In the Regno de la Plata, twelve grains for one are produced; near the city of Buenos Aires, sixteen for one: in the northern part of Mexico, seventeen; and in the equinoctial regions of Mexico, twenty-four for one.[1]

Now, supposing that in any one country during a certain period and under the ordinary cultivation, the return of wheat was six grains for one, it would be strictly correct to say that wheat had the capacity of increasing in a geometrical ratio of such a nature as to sextuple itself every year. And it might safely be calculated hypothetically that if, setting out from the produce of one acre, land of the same quality could be prepared with sufficient rapidity and no wheat were consumed, the rate of increase would be such as completely to cover the whole earthy surface of our globe in fourteen years.

In the same manner, if it be found by experience that on land of a certain quality, and making allowance for the ordinary mortality and accidents, sheep will increase on an average so as to double their numbers every two years, it would be strictly correct to say that sheep have a natural capacity of increasing in a geometrical progression, of which the common multiple is two and the term two years; and it might safely be said that if land of the same quality could be provided with sufficient rapidity, and no

Reprinted from *On Population: Three Essays*, New York: The New American Library of World Literature, 1960, pp. 12–59, by permission of The Population Council. © 1958 by the Population Council.

sheep were consumed, the rate of increase would be such that if we were to begin with the full number which could be supported on an acre of land, the whole earthy part of the globe might be completely covered with sheep in less than seventy-six years.

If, out of this prodigious increase of food, the full support of mankind were deducted, supposing them to increase as fast as they have ever yet increased in any country, the deduction would be comparatively inconsiderable; and the rate of increase would still be enormous, till it was checked either by the natural want of will on the part of mankind to make efforts for the increase of food beyond what they could possibly consume, or, after a certain period, by their absolute want of power to prepare land of the same quality so as to allow of the same rate of progress.

Owing to these two causes combined, we see that notwithstanding this prodigious *power* of increase in vegetables and animals, their actual increase is extremely slow; and it is obvious that, owing to the latter cause alone, and long before a final stop was put to all further progress, their actual rate of increase must of necessity be very greatly retarded: it would be impossible for the most enlightened human efforts to make all the soil of the earth equal in fertility to the average quality of land now in use; furthermore the practicable approaches towards it would require so much time as to occasion at a very early period a constant and great check upon what their increase would be, if they could exert their natural powers.

Elevated as man is above all other animals by his intellectual faculties, it is not to be supposed that the physical laws to which he is subjected should be essentially different from those which are observed to prevail in other parts of animated nature. He may increase slower than most other animals, but food is equally necessary to his support; and if his natural capacity of increase be greater than can be permanently supplied with food from a limited territory, his increase must be constantly retarded by the difficulty of procuring the means of subsistence.

The main peculiarity which distinguishes man from other animals in the means of his support is the power which he possesses of very greatly increasing these means. But this power is obviously limited by the scarcity of land—by the great natural barrenness of a very large part of the surface of the earth—and by the decreasing proportion of produce which must necessarily be obtained from the continual additions of capital applied to land already in cultivation.

It is, however, specifically with this diminishing and limited power of increasing the produce of the soil that we must compare the natural power of mankind to increase in order to ascertain whether, in the progress to the full cultivation and peopling of the globe, the natural power of mankind to increase must not, of absolute necessity, be constantly retarded by the difficulty of procuring the means of subsistence; and if so, what are likely to be the effects of such a state of things.

In an endeavour to determine the natural power of mankind to increase as well as their power of increasing the produce of the soil, we can have no other guide than past experience.

The great check to the increase of plants and animals, we know from experience, is the want of room and nourishment; and this experience would direct us to look for the greatest actual increase of them in those situations where room and nourishment were the most abundant.

On the same principle, we should expect to find the greatest actual increase of population in those situations where, from the abundance of good land and the manner in which its produce is distributed, the largest quantity of the necessaries of life is actually awarded to the mass of the society.

Of the countries with which we are acquainted, the United States of America, formerly the North American Colonies of Great Britain, answer most nearly to this description. In the United States not only is there an abundance of good land, but from the manner in which it has been distributed and the market which has been opened for its produce, there has been a greater and more constant demand for labour, and a larger portion of necessaries has been awarded to the labourer than in any of those other countries which possess an equal or greater abundance of land and fertility of soil.

Here, then, we should expect to find that the natural power of mankind to increase, whatever it may be, would be most distinctly marked; and here, in consequence, it appears that the actual rate of the increase of population has been more rapid than in any known country, although, independently of the abundance of good land and the great demand for labour, it is distinguished by no other circumstances which appear to be peculiarly favourable to the increase of numbers.

It has been stated that all animals, according to the known laws by which they are produced, must have a capacity of increasing in a geometrical progression. And the question with regard to man is, what is the rate of this geometrical progression?

Fortunately in the country to which we should naturally turn our eyes for an exemplification of the most rapid rate of increase, there have been four enumerations of the people, each at the distance of ten years; and though the estimates of the increase of population in the North American Colonies at earlier periods were of sufficient authority, in the absence of more certain documents, to warrant most important inferences, yet as we now possess such documents, and as the period they involve is of sufficient length to establish the point in question, it is no longer necessary to refer to earlier times.

According to a regular census made by order of Congress in 1790, which there is every reason to think is essentially correct, the white population of the United States was found to be 3,164,148. By a similar census in 1800, it was found to have increased to 4,312,841. It had increased then during the ten years from 1790 to 1800 at a rate equal to 36.3 per cent, a rate which, if continued, would double the population in twenty-two years and about four months and a half.

According to a third census in 1810, the white population was found to be 5,862,092,[2] which, compared with the population of 1800, gives an increase in the second ten years at the rate of nearly 36 per cent, which, if continued, would double the population in about twenty-two years and a half.

According to the fourth census in 1820, the white population was found to be 7,861,710,[3] which, compared with the population of 1810, gives an increase in the third ten years, at a rate per cent of 34.1, which, if continued, would double the population in twenty-three years and seven months.

If we compare the period of doubling according to the rate of increase in the most unfavourable ten years of this series with twenty-five years, we shall find the difference such as fully to cover all the increase of population which would have taken place from immigration, or the influx of strangers.

It appears from a reference to the most authentic documents which can be collected on both sides of the Atlantic that the emigration to the United States during the last thirty years, from 1790 to 1820, falls decidedly short of an average of 10,000 a year. Dr. Seybert, the best authority on the other side of the water, states that from 1790 to 1810 it could not have been so much as 6,000 a year. Our official accounts of the number of emigrants to the United States from England, Ireland, and Scotland during the ten years from 1812 to 1821, inclusive, give an average of less than 7,000, although the period includes the extraordinary years 1817 and 1818, in which the emigrations to the United States were much greater than they were ever known to be before or after, up to 1820. The official American accounts, as far as they go, which is only for two years from the 30th September, 1819, tend to confirm this average,[4] and allowing fully for the emigrants from other European countries, the general average will still be under 10,000.

A new mode has, however, lately been

suggested[5] of estimating the amount of increase in any country derived from emigration. It has been justly stated that when a census is taken every ten years, and the population is distinguished into those above and those below ten years of age, all above ten years of age, exclusive of immigrants, must have existed in the census immediately preceding, and consequently, after having made a proper allowance for the mortality during these ten years, the excess above the remaining number must be attributed to immigration. If we had the means of estimating with accuracy the loss which would be sustained in America in ten years by a population not increased by additional births, this mode of estimating the amount of immigration would be unobjectionable, and often very useful.

But, unfortunately, the means are deficient. Even the annual mortality in the United States is not known. It was supposed by Dr. Price to be 1 in 50; by Mr. Barton, 1 in 45; and it is stated by Mr. Bristed in *America and Her Resources* that the annual deaths average throughout the United States 1 in 40, in the healthiest districts 1 in 56, and in the most unhealthy 1 in 35.

If, however, we could ascertain accurately the average annual mortality, we should still be unable to ascertain the amount of the loss in question, as, under any given law of mortality, it would depend so very much upon the rate at which the population was increasing. The truth of this observation

will be placed in a striking light by the following short table, with which we have been favoured by a very able calculator, Mr. Milne, author of a well-known *Treatise on Annuities and Assurances*. It is constructed on the supposition that the population, in each case, is always subject to the same law of mortality as that which prevailed in all Sweden and Finland during the five years ended with 1805, and that the number of births in the present year in each case is 10,000.

We see from this table that, under the same law of mortality, the difference of loss sustained in ten years by a people not increased by fresh births would, in the three cases supposed of a stationary population, a population doubling in fifty years, and a population doubling in twenty-five years, be as 1 in 5.3692, 1 in 6.6786, and 1 in 7.9396; and that when the population is doubling itself in twenty-five years, the loss would be very little more than one-eighth.

But the censuses must be allowed to form a prima-facie evidence that the population of the United States has for some time been going on doubling itself in twenty-five years; and assuming this evidence to be true, which we are warranted in doing till better evidence is produced on the other side, it will appear that the amount of immigration, deduced from the rule here referred to, is less than 10,000 a year.

Thus the white population of the United States in 1800 was 4,312,841.[6] This popula-

	THE POPULATION CONSTANTLY THE SAME.	THE POPULATION INCREASING, AND HAVING INCREASED IN GEOMETRIC PROGRESSION FOR MORE THAN 100 YEARS, SO AS TO DOUBLE ITSELF EVERY	
		50 YEARS.	25 YEARS.
Total population 10 years since	393,848	230,005	144,358
Total above 10 years of age now	320,495	195,566	126,176
Died during the term of 10 years out of those living at its commencement	73,353	34,439	18,182
Being one of	5.3692	6.6786	7.9396

tion, without further accession of births, would in 1810 be diminished one-eighth, or reduced to 3,773,736. In 1810, the population above ten years of age was 3,845,389; and subtracting the former number from the latter, the difference, or amount of immigration, will be 71,653, or 7,165 a year.

Again, the white population 1810 was 5,862,092, which, diminished by one-eighth in ten years, would be 5,129,331. The population above ten years of age in 1820, was 5,235,940.[7] Subtracting the former from the latter, the difference, or amount of immigration, is 106,608 or 10,660 a year—showing, as we should expect, a greater amount of immigration from 1810 to 1820 than from 1800 to 1810, but even in the latter ten years, and including emigrations from Canada as well as all other countries, little exceeding 10,000.

Altogether, then, we can hardly err in defect if we allow 10,000 a year for the average increase from immigration during the twenty-five years from 1795 to 1820; and applying this number to the slowest period of increase, when the rate was such as to double the population in twenty-three years and seven months, it may be easily calculated that in the additional year and five months, a population of 5,862,000 would have increased to an amount much more than sufficient to cover an annual influx of 10,000 persons, with the increase from them at the same rate.

Such an increase from them, however, would not take place. It appears from an account in the National Calendar of the United States for the year 1821, that of the 7,001 persons who had arrived in America from the 30th of September, 1819, to the 30th of September, 1820, 1,959 only were females, and the rest, 5,042, were males,[8] a proportion, which, if it approaches towards representing the average, must very greatly reduce the number from which any increase ought to be calculated.

If, however, we omit these considerations, if we suppose a yearly emigration from Europe to America of 10,000 persons for the twenty-five years from 1795 to 1820, the greatest part of which time Europe was

involved in a most extensive scene of warfare requiring all its population, and further, if we allow for an increase of all the emigrants during the *whole period* at the fullest rate, the remaining numbers will still be sufficient to show a doubling of the population in less than twenty-five years.

The white population of 1790 was 3,164,148. This population, according to the rate at which it was increasing, would have amounted to about 3,694,100 in 1795; and supposing it to have just doubled itself in the twenty-five years from 1795 to 1820, the population in 1820 would have been 7,388,200. But the actual white population of 1820 appears, by the late census, to be 7,861,710, showing an excess of 473,510, whereas an emigration of 10,000 persons annually, with the increase from them at 3 per cent, a rate which would double a population in less than twenty-four years, would only amount to 364,592.

But the most striking confirmation of the censuses of the United States, and the most remarkable proof of the rate of increase being occasioned almost exclusively by procreation, have been furnished to us by Mr. Milne. In his work on *Annuities and Assurances*, which contains much valuable and interesting information on the subject of population, he had noticed the effects of the frequent pressure of want on the labouring classes of Sweden, which, by increasing the proportion of deaths, rendered the law of mortality so accurately observed in that country by Professors Wargentin and Nicander inapplicable to other countries more favourably circumstanced. But the law of mortality was observed to be gradually improving from the time that Dr. Price constructed his Swedish table; and the period from 1800 to the end of 1805 was so free from scarcities and epidemics, and the healthiness of the country had been further so much improved by the introduction of vaccination, that he justly thought the law of mortality, as observed during these five years, might suit countries where the condition of the people was known to be much better than it had generally been in Sweden. On these grounds he applied the Swedish law of mortality during the term mentioned to the hypothesis of a population which had been increasing by procreation in geometrical progression for more than a hundred years so as to double every twenty-five years. Assuming this population to be one million, he distributed it, according to such supposed law of mortality, into the different ages referred to in the American censuses, and then compared them with the same number of persons distributed according to the actual returns of the ages in the American censuses for the three periods of 1800, 1810, and 1820.

The results are as follows:

Distribution of a population of 1,000,000 persons in the under-mentioned intervals of age.

BETWEEN THE AGES OF	THE HYPOTHESIS.	ACCORDING TO UNITED STATES CENSUS OF 1800.	CENSUS OF 1810.	CENSUS OF 1820.
0 & 10	337,592	334,556	344,024	333,995
10 & 16	145,583	154,898	156,345	154,913
16 & 26	186,222	185,046	189,227	198,114
26 & 45	213,013	205,289	190,461	191,139
45 & 100	117,590	120,211	119,943	121,839
0 & 100	1,000,000	1,000,000	1,000,000	1,000,000
Under 16	483,175	489,454	500,369	488,908
Above 16	516,825	510,546	499,631	511,092

The general resemblance in the distribution of the ages in the three different censuses to each other and to the hypothesis clearly proves—

First, that the distribution of the ages, in the different enumerations, must be made with some care, and may, therefore, be relied on as in the main correct.

Secondly, that the law of mortality assumed in the hypothesis cannot deviate essentially from the law of mortality which prevails in the United States.

Thirdly, that the actual structure of the American population differs very little from what it would be if it were increasing regularly from procreation only, in geometrical progression, so as to double itself every twenty-five years; and that we may therefore safely infer that it has been very little disturbed by immigration.

If to these proofs of the rapid increase of population which has actually taken place we add the consideration that this rate of increase is an average applying to a most extensive territory, some parts of which are known to be unhealthy; that some of the towns of the United States are now large; that many of the inhabitants must be engaged in unwholesome occupations and exposed to many of those checks to increase which prevail in other countries; and further, that in the western territories, where these checks do not occur, the rate of increase is more rapid than the general average, after making the fullest allowance for immigration—it must appear certain that the rate at which the population of the whole of the United States has actually increased for the last thirty years must fall very decidedly short of the actual capacity of mankind to increase under the most favourable circumstances.

The best proof that can be obtained of the capacity of mankind to increase at a certain rate is their having really increased at that rate. At the same time, if any peculiarly rapid increase which had appeared to take place in a particular country were quite unsupported by other evidence, we might be disposed to attribute it to error or accident, and might scarcely be justified in founding important conclusions upon it. But this is far from being the case in the present instance. The rate of increase which has at times taken place in other countries, under the operation of great and obvious checks to the progress of population, sufficiently shows what might be expected if these checks were removed.

The countries most resembling the United States of America are those territories of the New World which lately belonged to Spain. In abundance and fertility of soil they are indeed superior; but almost all the vices in the government of the mother country were introduced into her colonial possessions, and particularly that very unequal distribution of landed property which takes place under the feudal system. These evils, and the circumstance of a very large part of the population being Indians in a depressed state and inferior in industry and energy to Europeans, necessarily prevent that rapid increase of numbers which the abundance and fertility of the land would admit of. But it appears from the instructive and interesting account of New Spain, which M. Humboldt has not long since given to the public, that for the last half of the eighteenth century, the excess of the births above the deaths and the progress of the population have been very great. The following are the proportions of burials to baptisms in the registers of eleven villages, the details of which were communicated to M. Humboldt by the curates:

	BURIALS.	BAPTISMS.
Dolores	100	253
Singuilucan	100	234
Calymaya	100	202
Guanaxuato	100	201
St. Anne	100	195
Marsil	100	194
Queretaro	100	188
Axapuzco	100	157
Yguala	100	140
Malacatepec	100	130
Panuco	100	123

The mean proportion is 100 to 183.

But the proportion which M. Humboldt considers as best suited to the whole of the population is 100 to 170.

In some of the villages above mentioned, the proportion of the births to the population is extraordinarily great and the proportion of deaths very considerable, showing in a striking point of view the early marriages and early deaths of a tropical climate and the more rapid passing away of each generation.[9]

At Queretaro, it appears that the baptisms were to the population as 1 to 14, and the burials as 1 to 26.

At Guanaxuato, including the neighbouring mines of St. Anne and of Marsil, the baptisms were to the population as 1 to 15, and the burials as 1 to 29.

The general result from all the information which could be collected was that the proportion of births to the population for the whole of the kingdom of New Spain was as 1 to 17, and of the deaths as 1 to 30. These proportions of births to deaths, if they were continued, would double the population in twenty-seven and a half years.

M. Humboldt further observes that the information which he had collected respecting the proportions of the births to the deaths, and of these to the whole population, proves that if the order of nature were not interrupted by some extraordinary and disturbing causes, the population of New Spain ought to double itself every nineteen years.[10]

It is known, however, that these causes do occur in the actual state of things: consequently we cannot consider the actual rate of the increase of population in New Spain as greater than according to the former calculation. But a rate of increase such as to double the population in twenty-seven and a half years, in spite of all the obstacles enumerated by M. Humboldt, is very extraordinary. It is next to the increase of the United States, and greatly superior to any that can be found in Europe.

Yet in Europe, the tendency to increase is always very strongly marked, and the actual increase for periods of some length is sometimes much greater than could be expected beforehand, considering the obstacles to be overcome.

It appears from Sussmilch[11] that the population of Prussia and Lithuania, after the great plague in 1709 and 1710, doubled itself in about forty-four years, from the excess of the births above the deaths enumerated in the registers.

In Russia, the whole population in 1763 was estimated by enumeration and calculation at twenty millions, and in 1796 at thirty-six millions.[12] This is a rate of increase which would occasion a doubling in less than forty-two years.

In 1695, the population of Ireland was estimated at 1,034,000. According to the late returns in 1821, it had increased to the prodigious amount of 6,801,827. This is an example of an actual increase for 125 years together at a rate which would double the population in about forty-five years; and this has taken place under the frequent pressure of great distress among the labouring classes of society and the practice of frequent and considerable emigration.

But for the proof of the power of population to increase under great obstacles of the preventive as well as of the positive kind, we need not go out of Great Britain. The rate of increase since our enumerations have commenced has been very remarkable for a country which was considered as well peopled before, and some of the details accompanying the returns tend strikingly to illustrate the principle of population.

The population of Great Britain according to the late enumerations was, in 1801, 10,942,646, and in 1811, 12,596,803.[13] This is a rate of increase during the ten years of rather above 15 per cent, a rate which, if continued, would double the population in between forty-nine and fifty years.

By the last enumeration of 1821, it appears that the population was 14,391,631[14] which, compared with the population of 1811, gives a rate of increase during the ten years of 14.25 per cent, a rate which would double the population in about fifty-two years.

According to these numbers, the rate of increase during the last ten years was slower than that of the first; but it appears from the excess of the number of males above females in the enumeration of 1811—so opposite to the state of the population in 1801 and 1821 when the females exceeded the males, particularly at the latter period—that of the large number added to the population for the army, navy, and registered merchant ships in 1811, a considerable proportion must have been foreigners. On this account, and on account of the further difficulty of knowing what part of this number might properly belong to Ireland, it has been proposed to estimate the percentage rate at which the population has increased in each of the ten years by the females only; and according to this mode of computation the population increased during the first period at the rate of 14.02 per cent, and during the second at the rate of 15.82. This last rate of increase would double the population in less than forty-eight years.

The only objection to this mode of computation is that it does not take into consideration the greater destruction of the males during the war. In 1801, the females exceeded the half of the population by 21,031, and in 1821 by 63,890, while, at the intermediate period, owing to the causes above mentioned, the females fell short of the half of the males by 35,685.

When, however, a proper distribution has been made of the army and navy among the resident population, and taking England and Wales alone, it appears that from 1801 to 1811 the population increased at the rate of 14.5 per cent, and from 1811 to 1821, at the rate of 16.3 per cent.[15] At the former of these rates, the period of doubling would be rather above fifty years, at the latter, under forty-six years, and taking the whole period, the time of doubling would be about forty-eight years. Yet in Great Britain there is a much larger proportion of the population living in towns and engaged in occupations considered as unhealthy than in any other known country of the same extent. There are also the best reasons for believing that in no other country of the same extent is there to be found so great a proportion of late marriages, or so great a proportion of persons remaining unmarried, as in Great Britain, And if, under these circumstances, a demand for labour and an increase of the funds for its maintenance could for twenty years together occasion such a rate of increase as, if continued, would double the population in forty-eight years and quadruple it in ninety-six years, it is in the highest degree probable that if the encouragements to marriage and the means of supporting a family were as great as in America, the period of doubling in Great Britain would not be more than twenty-five years, even in spite of her great towns and manufactories, and would be decidedly less if these obstacles were removed.

Taking, therefore, into consideration the actual rate of increase, which appears from the best documents to have taken place over a very large extent of country in the United States of America, very variously circumstanced as to healthiness and rapidity of progress; considering further the rate of increase which has taken place in New Spain, and also in many countries of Europe, where the means of supporting a family and other circumstances favourable to increase bear no comparison with those of the United States; and adverting particularly to the great increase of population which has taken place in this country during the last twenty years under the formidable obstacles to its progress which must press themselves upon the attention of the most careless observer, it must appear that the assumption of a rate of increase such as would double the population in twenty-five years as representing the natural progress of population, when not checked by the difficulty of procuring the means of subsistence or other peculiar causes of premature mortality, must be very decidedly within the truth.

It may be safely asserted, therefore, that population, when unchecked, increases in a geometrical progression of such a nature as to double itself every twenty-five years.[16]

It would be unquestionably desirable to have the means of comparing the natural rate of the increase of population when unchecked with the possible rate of the increase of food in a limited territory, such as that in which man is actually placed; but the latter estimate is much more difficult and uncertain than the former. If the rate of the increase of population at a particular period of some little extent can be ascertained with tolerable exactness, we have only to suppose the continuance of the same encouragements to marriage, the same facility of supporting a family, the same moral habits, with the same rate of mortality, and the increase of the population at the same rate after it had reached a thousand millions would be just as probable as at any intermediate and earlier period; but it is quite obvious that the increase of food in a limited space must proceed upon a principle totally different. It has been already stated that while land of good quality is in great abundance, the rate at which food might be made to increase would far exceed what is necessary to keep pace with the most rapid increase of population which the laws of nature in relation to human kind permit. But if society were so constituted as to give the fullest scope possible to the progress of cultivation and population, all such lands, and all lands of moderate quality, would soon be occupied; and when the future increase of the supply of food came to depend upon the taking of very poor land into cultivation, and the gradual and laborious improvement of the land already cultivated, the rate of the increase of food would certainly have a greater resemblance to a decreasing geometrical ratio than an increasing one. The yearly increment of food would, at any rate, have a constant tendency to diminish, and the amount of the increase of each successive ten years would probably be less than that of the preceding.

Practically, however, great uncertainty must take place. An unfavourable distribution of produce, by prematurely diminishing the demand for labour, might retard the increase of food at an early period in the same manner as if cultivation and population had been further advanced; while improvements in agriculture, accompanied by a greater demand for labour and produce, might for some time occasion a rapid increase of food and population at a later period in the same manner as if cultivation and population had been in an earlier stage of their progress. These variations, however, obviously arise from causes which do not impeach the general tendency of a continued increase of produce in a limited territory to diminish the power of its increase in future.

Under this certainty with regard to the general tendency, and uncertainty in reference to particular periods, it must be allowable, if it throws light on the subject, to make a supposition respecting the increase of food in a limited territory which, without pretending to accuracy, is clearly more favourable to the power of the soil to produce the means of subsistence for an increasing population than any experience which we have of its qualities will warrant.

If, setting out from a tolerably well-peopled country such as England, France, Italy, or Germany, we were to suppose that by great attention to agriculture, its produce could be permanently increased every twenty-five years by a quantity equal to that which it at present produces, it would be allowing a rate of increase decidedly beyond any probability of realization. The most sanguine cultivators could hardly expect that in the course of the next two hundred years each farm in this country on an average would produce eight times as much food as it produces at present, and still less that this rate of increase could continue so that each farm would produce twenty times as much as at present in five hundred years, and forty times as much in one thousand years. Yet this would be an arithmetical progression and would fall short, beyond all comparison, of the natural increase of population in a geometrical progression, according to which the inhabitants of any country in five hundred years, instead of increasing to twenty times, would increase to above a million times their present numbers.

It will be said, perhaps, that many parts of the earth are as yet very thinly peopled and, under proper management, would allow of a much more rapid increase of food than would be possible in the more fully inhabited states of Europe. This is unquestionably true. Some parts of the earth would no doubt be capable of producing food at such a rate as to keep pace for a few periods with an unrestricted increase of population. But to put this capacity fully into action is of all things the most difficult. If it is to be accomplished by the improvement of the actual inhabitants of the different parts of the earth in knowledge, in government, in industry, in arts, and in morals, it is scarcely possible to say how it ought to be commenced with the best prospect of success, or to form a conjecture as to the time in which it could be effected.

If it is to be accomplished by emigration from the more improved parts of the world, it is obvious that it must involve much war and extermination besides all the difficulties usually attendant upon new settlements in uncivilized countries; and these alone are so formidable, and for a long time so destructive that, combined with the unwillingness which people must always naturally feel to quit their own country, much distress would be suffered at home before relief would be sought for in emigration.

But supposing for a moment that the object could be fully accomplished—that is, supposing that the capacity of the earth to produce the necessaries of life could be put fully into action, and that they were distributed in the proportions most favourable for the growth of capital and the effective demand for labour—the increase of population, whether arising from the increase of the inhabitants of each country or from emigrants issuing from all those countries which were more advanced in cultivation, would be so rapid that in a period comparatively quite short, all the good lands would be occupied and the rate of the possible increase of food would be reduced much below the arithmetical ratio above supposed.

If merely during the short period which has elapsed since our Revolution of 1688 the population of the earth had increased at its natural rate when unchecked, supposing the number of people at that time to have been only 800 millions, all the land of the globe, without making allowance for deserts, forests, rocks, and lakes, would on an average be equally populous with England and Wales at present. This would be accomplished in five doublings, or 125 years; and one or two doublings more, or a period less than that which has elapsed since the beginning of the reign of James the First, would produce the same effect from the overflowings of the inhabitants of those countries where, owing to the further progress of cultivation, the soil had not the capacity of producing food so as to keep pace with the increase of an unrestricted population.

Whatever temporary and partial relief, therefore, may be derived from emigration by particular countries in the actual state of things, it is quite obvious that, considering the subject generally and largely, emigration may be fairly said not in any degree to touch the difficulty. And whether we exclude or include emigration—whether we refer to particular countries, or to the whole earth—the supposition of a future capacity in the soil to increase the necessaries of life every twenty-five years by a quantity equal to that which is at present produced must be decidedly beyond the truth.

But if the natural increase of population, when unchecked by the difficulty of procuring the means of subsistence or other peculiar causes, be such as to continue doubling its numbers in twenty-five years, and if the greatest increase of food which, for a continuance, could possibly take place on a limited territory like our earth in its present state, be at the most only such as would add every twenty-five years an amount equal to its present produce then it is quite clear that a powerful check on the increase of population must be almost constantly in action.

By the laws of nature man cannot live without food. Whatever may be the rate at which population would increase if unchecked, it never can actually increase in any country beyond the food necessary to support it. But by the laws of nature in respect to the powers of a limited territory, the additions which can be made in equal periods to the food which it produces must, after a short time, either be constantly decreasing, which is what would really take place or, at the very most, must remain stationary so as to increase the means of subsistence only in an arithmetical progression. Consequently, it follows necessarily that the average rate of the *actual* increase of population over the greatest part of the globe, obeying the same laws as the increase of food, must be totally of a different character from the rate at which it would increase if *unchecked*.

The great question, then, which remains to be considered, is the manner in which this constant and necessary check upon population practically operates.

If the soil of any extensive well-peopled country were equally divided amongst its inhabitants, the check would assume its most obvious and simple form. Perhaps each farm in the well-peopled countries of Europe might allow of one, or even two doublings, without much distress, but the absolute impossibility of going on at the same rate is too glaring to escape the most careless thinker. When, by extraordinary efforts, provision had been made for four times the number of persons which the land can support at present, what possible hope could there be of doubling the provision in the next twenty-five years?

Yet there is no reason whatever to suppose that anything besides the difficulty of procuring in adequate plenty the necessaries of life should either indispose this greater number of persons to marry early, or disable them from rearing in health the largest families. But this difficulty would of necessity occur, and its effect would be either to discourage early marriages, which would check the rate of increase by preventing the same proportion of births, or to render the children unhealthy from bad and insufficient nourishment, which would check the rate of increase by occasioning a greater proportion of deaths—or, what is most likely to happen, the rate of increase would be checked partly by the diminution of births and partly by the increase of mortality.

The first of these checks may, with propriety, be called the *preventive check* to population; the second, the *positive check;* and the absolute necessity of their operation in the case supposed is as certain and obvious as that man cannot live without food.

Taking a single farm only into consideration, no man would have the hardihood to assert that its produce could be made permanently to keep pace with a population increasing at such a rate as it is observed to do for twenty or thirty years together at particular times and in particular countries. He would, indeed, be compelled to acknowledge that if, with a view to allow for the most sanguine speculations, it has been supposed that the additions made to the necessaries produced by the soil in given times might remain constant, yet this rate of the increase of produce could not possibly be realized; and that if the capacity of the soil were at all times put properly into action, the additions to the produce would, after a short time and independently of new inventions, be constantly decreasing till, in no very long period, the exertions of an additional labourer would not produce his own subsistence.

But what is true in this respect in reference to a single farm must necessarily be true of the whole earth, from which the necessaries of life for the actual population are derived. And what would be true in respect to the checks to population if the soil of the earth were equally divided among the different families which inhabit it, must be true under the present unequal division of property and variety of occupations. Nothing but the confusion and indistinctness arising from the largeness of the subject could make persons deny in the case of an extensive territory, or the whole earth, what they could not fail to acknowledge in the case of a single farm which may be said fairly to represent it.

It may be expected, indeed, that in civilized and improved countries, the accumulation of capital, the division of labour, and the invention of machinery will extend the bounds of production; but we know from experience that the effects of these causes, which are quite astonishing in reference to some of the conveniencies and luxuries of life, are very much less efficient in producing an increase of food; and although the saving of labour and an improved system of husbandry may be the means of pushing cultivation upon much poorer lands than could otherwise be worked, yet the increased quantity of the necessaries of life so obtained can never be such as to supersede, for any length of time, the operation of the preventive and positive checks to population. And not only are these checks as absolutely necessary in civilized and improved countries as they would be if each family had a certain portion of land allotted to it, but they operate almost exactly in the same way. The distress which would obviously arise in the most simple state of society from the natural tendency of population to increase faster than the means of subsistence in a limited territory is brought home to the higher classes of an improved and populous country in the difficulty which they find in supporting their families in the same rank of life with themselves, and to the labouring classes, which form the great mass of society, in the insufficiency of the real wages of common labour to bring up a large family.

If in any country the yearly earnings of the commonest labourers determined, as they always will be, by the state of the demand and the supply of necessaries compared with labour, be not sufficient to bring up in health the largest families, one of the three things before stated must happen; either the prospect of this difficulty will prevent some and delay other marriages; or the diseases arising from bad nourishment will be introduced and the mortality be increased; or the progress of population will be retarded, partly by one cause, and partly by the other.

According to all past experience and the best observations which can be made on the motives which operate upon the human mind, there can be no well-founded hope of obtaining a large produce from the soil but under a system of private property. It seems perfectly visionary to suppose that any stimulus short of that which is excited in man by the desire of providing for himself and family and of bettering his condition in life, should operate on the mass of society with sufficient force and constancy to overcome the natural indolence of mankind. All the attempts which have been made since the commencement of authentic history to proceed upon a principle of common property have either been so insignificant that no inference can be drawn from them, or have been marked by the most signal failures; and the changes which have been effected in modern times by education do not seem to advance a single step towards making such a state of things more probable in future. We may, therefore, safely conclude that while man retains the same physical and moral constitution which he is observed to possess at present, no other than a system of private property stands the least chance of providing for such a large and increasing population as that which is to be found in many countries at present.

But though there is scarcely any conclusion which seems more completely established by experience than this, yet it is unquestionably true that the laws of private property, which are the grand stimulants to production, do themselves so limit it as always to make the actual produce of the earth fall very considerably short of the *power* of production. On a system of private property no adequate motive to the extension of cultivation can exist unless the returns are sufficient not only to pay the wages necessary to keep up the population, which at the least must include the support of a wife and two or three children, but also afford a profit on the capital which has been employed. This necessarily excludes from cultivation a considerable portion of land which might be made to bear corn. If it were possible to suppose that man might be adequately stimulated to labour under a system of common property, such land might be cultivated, and the production of food and the increase of population might go on till the soil absolutely refused to grow a single additional quarter, and the whole of the

society was exclusively engaged in procuring the necessaries of life. But it is quite obvious that such a state of things would inevitably lead to the greatest degree of distress and degradation. And if a system of private property secures mankind from such evils, which it certainly does in a great degree by securing to a portion of the society the leisure necessary for the progess of the arts and sciences, it must be allowed that such a check to the increase of cultivation confers on society a most signal benefit.

But it must perhaps also be allowed that under a system of private property, cultivation is sometimes checked in a degree and at a period not required by the interest of society. And this is particularly likely to happen when the original divisions of land have been extremely unequal and the laws have not given sufficient facility to a better distribution of them. Under a system of private property, the only effectual demand for produce must come from the owners of property; and though it be true that the effectual demand of the society, whatever it may be, is best supplied under the most perfect system of liberty, yet it is not true that the tastes and wants of the effective demanders are always, and necessarily, the most favourable to the progress of national wealth. A taste for hunting and the preservation of game among the owners of the soil will, without fail, be supplied if things be allowed to take their natural course; but such a supply, from the manner in which it must be effected, would inevitably be most unfavourable to the increase of produce and population. In the same manner, the want of an adequate taste for the consumption of manufactured commodities among the possessors of surplus produce, if not fully compensated by a great desire for personal attendance, which it never is, would infallibly occasion a premature slackness in the demand for labour and produce, a premature fall of profits, and a premature check to cultivation.

It makes little difference in the actual rate of the increase of population, or the necessary existence of checks to it, whether that state of demand and supply which occasions an insufficiency of wages to the whole of the labouring classes be produced prematurely by a bad structure of society and an unfavourable distribution of wealth, or necessarily by the comparative exhaustion of the soil. The labourer feels the difficulty nearly in the same degree, and it must have nearly the same results, from whatever cause it arises; consequently, in every country with which we are acquainted where the yearly earnings of the labouring classes are not sufficient to bring up in health the largest families, it may be safely said that population is actually checked by the difficulty of procuring the means of subsistence. And, as we well know that ample wages, combined with full employment for all who choose to work, are extremely rare—and scarcely ever occur, except for a certain time, when the knowledge and industry of an old country is applied, under favourable circumstances, to a new one—it follows that the pressure arising from the difficulty of procuring subsistence is not to be considered as a remote one which will be felt only when the earth refuses to produce any more, but as one which not only actually exists at present over the greatest part of the globe, but, with few exceptions, has been almost constantly acting upon all the countries of which we have any account.

It is unquestionably true that in no country of the globe have the government, the distribution of property, and the habits of the people been such as to call forth in the most effective manner the resources of the soil. Consequently, if the most advantageous possible change in all these respects could be supposed at once to take place, it is certain that the demand for labour and the encouragement to production might be such as, for a short time in some countries and for rather a longer time in others, to lessen the operation of the checks to population which have been described. It is specifically this truth constantly obtruding itself upon our attention which is the great source of delusion on this subject and creates the belief that man could always produce from the soil much more than sufficient to support himself and family. In the actual state of things, this power has perhaps always been possessed. But for it we are indebted wholly to the ignorance and bad government of our ancestors. If they had properly called forth the resources of the soil, it is quite certain that we should now have but scanty means left of further increasing our food. If merely since the time of William the Conqueror all the nations of the earth had been well governed, and if the distribution of property and the habits both of the rich and the poor had been the most favourable to the demand for produce and labour, though the amount of food and population would have been prodigiously greater than at present, the means of diminishing the checks to population would unquestionably be less. That difficulty in procuring the necessaries of life which is now felt in the comparatively low wages of labour almost all over the world, and is occasioned partly by the necessary state of the soil and partly by a premature check to the demand for produce and labour, would then be felt in a greater degree and would less admit of any relaxation in the checks to population because it would be occasioned wholly and necessarily by the state of the soil.

It appears, then, that what may be called the proportionate amount of the necessary checks to population depends very little upon the efforts of man in the cultivation of the soil. If these efforts had been directed from the first in the most enlightened and efficient manner, the checks necessary to keep the population on a level with the means of subsistence, so far from being lightened, would, in all probability, be operating with greater force; and the condition of the labouring classes, so far as it depends on the facility of procuring the means of subsistence, instead of being improved, would, in all probability, be deteriorated.

It is to the laws of nature, therefore, and not to the conduct and institutions of man, that we are to attribute the necessity of a strong check on the natural increase of population.

But, though the laws of nature which determine the rate at which population would increase if unchecked and the very different rate at which the food required to support population could continue to increase in a limited territory, are undoubtedly the causes which render necessary the existence of some great and constant check to population, yet a vast mass of responsibility remains behind on man and the institutions of society.

In the first place, they are certainly responsible for the present scanty population of the earth. There are few large countries, however advanced in improvement, the population of which might not have been doubled or tripled, and there are many which might be ten, or even a hundred times as populous, and yet all the inhabitants be as well provided for as they are now, if the institutions of society and the moral habits of the people had been for some hundred years the most favourable to the increase of capital, and the demand for produce and labour.

Secondly, though man has but a trifling and temporary influence in altering the proportionate amount of the checks to population or the degree in which they press upon the actual numbers, yet he has a great and most extensive influence on their character and mode of operation.

It is not in superseding the necessity of checks to population in the progress of mankind to the full peopling of the earth (which may with truth be said to be a physical impossibility), but in directing these checks in such a way as to be the least prejudicial to the virtue and happiness of society, that government and human institutions produce their great effect. Here we know from constant experience that they have great power. Yet, even here it must be allowed that the power of government is rather indirect than direct, as the object to be attained depends mainly upon such a conduct on the part of individuals as can seldom be directly enforced by laws, though it may be powerfully influenced by them. This will appear if we consider more

particularly the nature of those checks which have been classed under the general heads of preventive and positive.

It will be found that they are all resolvable into *moral restraint, vice* and *misery*. And if, from the laws of nature, some check to the increase of population be absolutely inevitable, and human institutions have any influence upon the extent to which each of these checks operates, a heavy responsibility will be incurred if all that influence, whether direct or indirect, be not exerted to diminish the amount of vice and misery.

Moral restraint, in application to the present subject, may be defined to be abstinence from marriage, either for a time or permanently, from prudential considerations, with a strictly moral conduct towards the sex in the interval. And this is the only mode of keeping population on a level with the means of subsistence which is perfectly consistent with virtue and happiness. All other checks, whether of the preventive or the positive kind, though they may greatly vary in degree, resolve themselves into some form of vice or misery.

The remaining checks of the preventive kind are the sort of intercourse which renders some of the women of large towns unprolific; a general corruption of morals with regard to the sex, which has a similar effect; unnatural passions and improper arts to prevent the consequences of irregular connections. These evidently come under the head of vice.

The positive checks to population include all the causes which tend in any way prematurely to shorten the duration of human life, such as unwholesome occupations, severe labour and exposure to the seasons, bad and insufficient food and clothing arising from poverty, bad nursing of children, excesses of all kinds, great towns and manufactories, the whole train of common diseases and epidemics, wars, infanticide, plague, and famine. Of these positive checks, those which appear to arise from the laws of nature may be called exclusively misery; and those which we bring upon ourselves, such as wars, excesses of all kinds, and many others which it would be in our power to avoid, are of a mixed nature. They are brought upon us by vice, and their consequences are misery.

Some of these checks, in various combinations and operating with various force, are constantly in action in all the countries with which we are acquainted and form the immediate causes which keep the population on a level with the means of subsistence.

A view of these checks, in most of the countries of which we have the best accounts, was taken in the *Essay on Population*. The object was to trace in each country those checks which appeared to be most effective in repressing population; and to endeavour to answer the question generally, which had been applied particularly to New Holland by Captain Cook, namely, By what means is the population of this country kept down to the number which it can subsist?

It was hardly to be expected, however, that the general accounts of countries which are to be met with should contain a sufficient number of details of the kind required to enable us to ascertain what portion of the natural increase of population each individual check which could be traced had the power to overcome. In particular, it was not to be expected that any accounts could inform us of the degree in which moral restraint prevails, when taken in its strictest sense. It is necessary, therefore, to attend chiefly to the greater or smaller number of persons who remain unmarried or marry late; and the delay of marriage owing to the difficulty of providing for a family, when the degree of irregularity to which it may lead cannot be ascertained, may be usefully called the prudential restraint on marriage and population. And this will be found to be the chief mode in which the preventive check practically operates.

But if the preventive check to population—that check which can alone supersede great misery and mortality—operates chiefly by a prudential restraint on marriage, it will be obvious, as was before stated, that direct legislation cannot do much. Prudence cannot be enforced by laws without a great

violation of natural liberty and a great risk of producing more evil than good. But still, the very great influence of a just and enlightened government and the perfect security of property in creating habits of prudence cannot for a moment be questioned. The principal causes and effects of these habits are thus stated in the *Principles of Political Economy*, iv, p. 250.

From real high wages, or the power of commanding a large portion of the necessaries of life, two very different results may follow; one, that of a rapid increase of population, in which case, the high wages are chiefly spent in the maintenance of large and frequent families; and the other, that of a decided improvement in the modes of subsistence, and the conveniencies and comforts enjoyed, without a proportionate acceleration in the rate of increase.

In looking to these different results, the causes of them will evidently appear to be the different habits existing among the people of different countries and at different times. In an inquiry into the causes of these different habits, we shall generally be able to trace those which produce the first result to all the circumstances which contribute to depress the lower classes of the people, which make them unable or unwilling to reason from the past to the future and ready to acquiesce for the sake of present gratification in a very low standard of comfort and respectability; and those which produce the second result, to all the circumstances which tend to elevate the character of the lower classes of society, which make them approach the nearest to beings who "look before and after," and who, consequently, cannot acquiesce patiently in the thought of depriving themselves and their children of the means of being respectable, virtuous, and happy.

Among the circumstances which contribute to the character first described, the most efficient will be found to be despotism, oppression, and ignorance; among those which contribute to the latter character, civil and political liberty, and education.

Of all the causes which tend to encourage prudential habits among the lower classes of society, the most essential is unquestionably civil liberty. No people can be much accustomed to form plans for the future who do not feel assured that their industrious exertions, while fair and honourable, will be allowed to have free scope; and that the property which they either possess or may acquire, will be secured to them by a known code of just laws impartially administered. But it has been found by experience that civil liberty cannot be permanently secured without political liberty. Consequently, political liberty becomes almost equally essential; and in addition to its being necessary in this point of view, its obvious tendency to teach the lower classes of society to respect themselves by obliging the higher classes to respect them, must contribute greatly to all good effects of civil liberty.

With regard to education, it might certainly be made general under a bad form of government, and might be very deficient under one in other respects good; but it must be allowed that the chances, both with regard to its quality and its prevalence, are greatly in favour of the latter. Education alone could do little against insecurity of property; but it would powerfully assist all the favourable consequences to be expected from civil and political liberty, which could not indeed be considered as complete without it.

The varying prevalence of these habits owing to the causes above referred to, combined with the smaller or greater mortality occasioned by other customs and the varying effects of soil and climate, must necessarily produce great differences in different countries, and at different periods, in the character of the predominant checks to population and the force of each. And this

inference, which inevitably follows from theory, is fully confirmed by experience.

It appears, for instance, from the accounts we have received of ancient nations and of the less civilized parts of the world, that war and violent diseases were the predominant checks to their population. The frequency of wars and the dreadful devastations of mankind occasioned by them, united with the plagues, famines, and mortal epidemics of which there are records, must have caused such a consumption of the human species that the exertion of the utmost power of increase must, in many cases, have been insufficient to supply it; and we see at once the source of those encouragements to marriage and efforts to increase population which, with inconsiderable exceptions, distinguished the legislation and general policy of ancient times. Yet there were some few men of more extended views who, when they were looking to the settlement of a society in a more improved state, were fully aware that under the most beautiful form of government which their imagination could conceive, the greatest poverty and distress might be felt from a too rapid increase of population. And the remedies which they proposed were strong and violent in proportion to the greatness of the evil which they apprehended. Even the practical legislators who encouraged marriage seemed to think that the supplies of children might sometimes follow too rapidly for the means of supporting them; and it appears to have been with a view to provide against this difficulty, and of preventing it from discouraging marriage, that they frequently sanctioned the inhuman practice of infanticide.

Under these circumstances, it is not to be supposed that the prudential restraint on marriage should have operated to any considerable extent. Except in a few cases where a general corruption of morals prevailed which might act as a preventive check of the most vicious kind, a large portion of the procreative power was called into action, the occasional redundancy from which was checked by violent causes. These causes will be found resolvable almost wholly into vice and misery, the first of which, and a large portion of the second, it is always in the power of man to avoid.

In a review of the checks to population in the different states of modern Europe, it appears that the positive checks to population have prevailed less, and the preventive checks more, than in ancient times, and in the more uncultivated parts of the world. The destruction occasioned by war has unquestionably abated, both on account of its occurring on the whole less frequently, and its ravages not being so fatal either to man or the means of his support as they were formerly. And although in the earlier periods of the history of modern Europe, plagues, famines, and mortal epidemics were not unfrequent, yet as civilization and improvement have advanced, both their frequency and their mortality have been greatly reduced, and in some countries they are now almost unknown. This diminution of the positive checks to population, as it has been certainly much greater in proportion than the actual increase of food and population, must necessarily have been accompanied by an increasing operation of the preventive checks; and probably it may be said with truth, that in almost all the more improved countries of modern Europe, the principal check which at present keeps the population down to the level of the actual means of subsistence is the prudential restraint on marriage.

Yet in comparing together the accounts and registers of the different countries of modern times, we shall still find a vast difference in the character and force of the checks which are mainly in action; and it is precisely in this point of view that these accounts afford the most important instruction. Some parts of Europe are yet in an unimproved state and are still subject to frequent plagues and mortal epidemics. In these countries, as might be expected, few traces are to be found of the prudential restraint on marriage. But even in improved

countries the circumstances may be such as to occasion a great mortality. Large towns are known to be unfavourable to health, particularly to the health of young children; and the unwholesomeness of marshy situations may be such as in some cases to balance the principle of increase, even when nearly the whole of the procreative power is called into action (which is very seldom the case) in large towns.

Thus in the registers of twenty-two Dutch villages given by Sussmilch,[17] the mortality (occasioned, as may be supposed, chiefly by the natural unhealthiness of the country) was as high as 1 in 22 or 23, instead of the more common proportion of 1 in 35 or 40; and the marriages, instead of being in the more usual proportion to the population of 1 in about 108 or 112, were in the extraordinary high proportion of 1 in 64,[18] showing a most unusual frequency of marriage, while, on account of the great mortality, the number of inhabitants was nearly stationary and the births and deaths about equal.

On the other hand, in Norway, where the climate and modes of living seem to be extremely favourable to health and the mortality was only 1 in 48, the prudential restraint on marriage was called more than usually into action, and the marriages were only 1 in 130 of the population.[19]

These may be considered as extreme cases, but the same results in different degrees are observable in the registers of all countries; and it is particularly to be remarked that in those countries where registers of births, deaths, and marriages have been kept for a considerable time, the progressive diminution of mortality occasioned by the introduction of habits more favourable to health, and the consequent diminution of plagues and mortal epidemics, have been accompanied by a smaller proportion of marriages and births. Sussmilch has given some striking instances of the gradual diminution in the proportion of the number of marriages during a part of the last century.[20]

In the town of Leipzig, in the year 1620, the annual marriages were to the population as 1 to 82; from the year 1741 to 1756, they were as 1 to 123.

In Augsburg, in 1510, the proportion of marriages to the population was 1 in 86; in 1750 as 1 to 120.

In Danzig, in the year 1705, the proportion was as 1 to 89; in 1745, as 1 to 118.

In the Dukedom of Magdeburg, in 1700, the proportion was as 1 to 87; from 1752 to 1755, as 1 to 125.

In the principality of Halberstadt, in 1690, the proportion was as 1 to 88; in 1756, as 1 to 112.

In the Dukedom of Cleves, in 1705, the proportion was 1 to 83; in 1755, 1 to 100.

In the Churmark of Brandenburg, in 1700, the proportion was 1 to 76;[21] in 1755, 1 to 108.

Instances of this kind are numerous, and they tend to show the dependence of the marriages on the deaths in all old countries. A greater mortality almost invariably produces a greater number of early marriages; and it must be equally certain that except where the means of subsistence can be adequately increased, a greater proportion of early marriages must occasion a greater mortality.

The proportion of yearly births to the whole population must evidently depend principally on the proportion of marriages and the age at which they are contracted; and it appears consequently from registers that in countries which will not admit of any considerable increase of population, the births and marriages are mainly influenced by the deaths. When an actual decrease of population is not taking place, the births will always supply the vacancies made by death, and exactly so much more as the increasing wealth of the country and the demand for labour will admit. Everywhere in the intervals of plagues, epidemics, and destructive wars, the births considerably exceed the deaths; but while from these and other causes the mortality in different countries is extremely various, it appears from registers that, with the allowance above stated, the births vary in the same proportion.[22]

Thus, in 39 villages of Holland, where the deaths at the time to which the registers refer were about 1 in 23, the births were also 1 in 23. In 15 villages around Paris, the births bore the same or even a greater proportion to the whole population on account of a still greater mortality, the births being 1 in 22.7 and the deaths the same. In the small towns of Brandenburg, which were in an increasing state, the mortality was 1 in 29, and the births 1 in 24.7. In Sweden, where the mortality was about 1 in 34.5, the births were 1 in 28. In 1,056 villages of Brandenburg, in which the mortality was about 1 in 39 or 40, the births were about 1 in 30. In Norway, where the mortality was 1 in 48, the births were 1 in 34.

Of all the countries reviewed in *The Essay on Population*, there is none which so strikingly illustrates the most important fact of the dependence of the proportions of marriages and births on the deaths, and the general principles of population, as Switzerland. It appears that between 1760 and 1770, an alarm prevailed respecting the continued depopulation of the country; and to ascertain the point, M. Muret, minister of Vevay, made a very laborious and careful search into the registers of different parishes, from the time of their first establishment. He compared the number of births which had taken place during three different periods of seventy years each, the first ending in 1620, the second in 1690, and the third in 1760. And finding by this comparison that the number of births was less in the second period than in the first, and less in the third period than in the second, he considered the evidence of a continued depopulation of the country from the year 1550 as incontrovertible.[23] But the accounts which he himself produces, clearly show that in the earlier periods to which he refers, the mortality was very much greater than in the latter; and, that the greater *number* of births found in the registers formerly was not owing to a greater population but to the greater *proportion* of births which almost always accompanies a greater mortality.

It appears from accounts which are

entirely to be depended on that during the last period, the mortality was extraordinarily small and the proportion of children reared from infancy to puberty extraordinarily great. At the time when M. Muret wrote his paper, in 1766, the proportion of deaths to the population in the Pays de Vaud was 1 in 45, of births 1 in 36, and of marriages 1 in 140. These are all very small proportions of births, deaths, and marriages compared with other countries; but the state of things must have been totally different in the sixteenth and seventeenth centuries. M. Muret gives a list of all the plagues which had prevailed in Switzerland from 1520, from which it appears that this dreadful scourge desolated the country at short intervals during the whole of the first period, and extended its occasional ravages to within twenty-two years of the termination of the second. We may safely conclude that in these times the average mortality was very much greater than at present. But what puts the question beyond a doubt is the great mortality which prevailed in the neighbouring town of Geneva in the sixteenth century, and its gradual diminution in the seventeenth and eighteenth. It appears from calculations published in the *Bibliothéque Britannique* (IV, 328), that in the sixteenth century, the probability of life, or the age to which half of the born lived, was only 4.883, or under four years and eleven months; and the mean life, or the average number of years due to each person 18.511, or about eighteen years and a half. In the seventeenth century, the probability of life in Geneva was 11.607, about eleven years and seven months; the mean life 23.358, or twenty-three years and four months. In the eighteenth century, the probability of life had increased to 27.183, twenty-seven years and two months; and the mean life to thirty-two years and two months.

There can be no doubt, from the prevalence of the plague and its gradual extinction as noticed by M. Muret, that a diminution of mortality of the same kind, though not perhaps to the same extent, must have taken place in Switzerland; but if with a mortality which could not have been less than 1 in 30 or 32, the proportion of births had been what it was when M. Muret wrote, it is quite evident that the country would have been rapidly depopulated. But as it is known from the actual amount of births found in the registers that this was not the case, it follows as a necessary consequence that the greater mortality of former times was accompanied by a greater proportion of births. And this at once shows the error of attempting to determine the actual population, either of different countries or of different periods in the same country, by the amount of the births, and the strong tendency of population to fill up all vacancies, and very rarely to be limited by any other cause than the difficulty of supporting a family.

Switzerland and the Pays de Vaud afford other most striking instances of the dependence of the births on the deaths; and the accounts of them are perhaps more to be depended upon as they appear to contradict the preconceived opinions of the person who collected them.

Speaking of the want of fruitfulness in the Swiss women, M. Muret says that Prussia, Brandenburg, Sweden, France, and indeed every country the registers of which he had seen, give a greater proportion of baptisms to the number of inhabitants than the Pays de Vaud, where this proportion is only as 1 to 36. He adds that from calculations lately made in the Lyonnois, it appeared that in Lyons itself the proportion of baptisms was 1 in 28, in the small towns 1 in 25, and in the villages 1 in 23 or 24. What a prodigious difference, he exclaims, between the Lyonnois and the Pays de Vaud, where the most favourable proportion, and that only in two small parishes of extraordinary fecundity, is not above 1 in 26, and in many parishes it is considerably less than 1 in 40. The same difference, he remarks, takes place in the mean life. In the Lyonnois it is little above twenty-five years; while in the Pays de Vaud, the lowest mean life, and that only in a single marshy and unhealthy parish, is twenty-nine and one half years, and in many places it is above forty-five years.

"But whence comes it," he says, "that the country where children escape the best from the dangers of infancy, and where the mean life, in whatever way the calculation is made, is higher than in any other, should be precisely that in which the fecundity is the smallest? How comes it again, that of all our parishes, the one which gives the mean life the highest, should also be the one where the tendency to increase is the smallest?"[24]

To resolve this question, M. Muret says, "I will hazard a conjecture, which, however, I give only as such. It is not that, in order to maintain in all places a proper equilibrium of population, God has wisely ordered things in such a manner as that the force of life in each country should be in the inverse ratio of its fecundity? In fact, experience verifies my conjecture. Leyzin, a village in the Alps, with a population of 400 persons, produces but a little above 8 children a year. The Pays de Vaud, in general, in proportion to the same number of inhabitants, produces 11, and the Lyonnois 16. But if it happen that at the age of twenty years, the 8, the 11, and the 16 are reduced to the same number, it will appear that the force of life gives in one place what fecundity does in another. And thus the most healthy countries, having less fecundity, will not over-people themselves, and the unhealthy countries, by their extraordinary fecundity, will be able to sustain their population."

These facts and observations are full of the most important instruction and strikingly illustrate the principle of population. The three gradations in the proportion of births which are here so distinctly presented to our view, may be considered as representing that variety in the proportion of births which is known to take place in different countries and at different periods; and the practical question is whether, when this variety prevails without a proportionate difference in the rate of increase, which is almost universally the case, we are to suppose, with M. Muret, that a special providence is called into action to render women less prolific in

healthy countries and where improved habits of cleanliness have banished plagues and mortal epidemics; or to suppose, as experience warrants, that the smaller mortality of healthy and improved countries is balanced by the greater prevalence of the prudential restraint on marriage and population.

The subject is seen with particular clearness in Switzerland on account of the population of some of the districts being stationary. The number of inhabitants on the Alps was supposed to have diminished. This was probably an error; but it is not improbable that they should have remained stationary, or nearly so. There is no land so little capable of providing for an increasing population as mountainous pastures. When they have been once fully stocked with cattle, little more can be done; and if there be neither emigration to take off the superabundant numbers, nor manufactures wherewith to purchase an additional quantity of food, the deaths must equal the births.

This was the case with the Alpine parish of Leyzin before referred to, where for a period of thirty years the mortality and the proportion of births almost accurately kept pace with each other; and where, in consequence, if the positive checks to population had been unusually small, the preventive checks must have been unusually great. In the parish of Leyzin, according to M. Muret, the probability of life was as high as sixty-one years;[25] but it is obvious that this extraordinary degree of healthiness could not *possibly* have taken place under the actual circumstances of the parish with respect to the means of subsistence if it had not been accompanied by a proportionate action of the prudential restraint on marriage; and accordingly, the births were only 1 in 49, and the number of persons below 16 was only one quarter of the population.

There can be little doubt that in this case the extreme healthiness of the people, arising from their situation and employments, had more effect in producing the prudential check to population than the prudential check in producing the extreme healthiness; yet it is quite certain that they must constantly act and react upon each other, and that if, when the circumstances are such as to furnish no adequate means for the support of an increased population and no relief in emigration, the prudential check does not prevail, no degree of natural healthiness could prevent an excessive mortality. Yet to occasion such a mortality, a much greater degree of poverty and misery must have taken place than in districts less favourably circumstanced with regard to health; and we see at once the reason why, in countries of mountainous pasture, if there be no vent in emigration, the necessity of the prudential check should be more strongly forced on the attention of the inhabitants, and should, in consequence, prevail to a greater degree.

Taking countries in general, there will necessarily be differences as to natural healthiness in all the gradations, from the most marshy habitable situations to the most pure and salubrious air. These differences will be further increased by the nature of the employments of the people, their habits of cleanliness, and their care in preventing the spread of epidemics. If in no country was there any difficulty in obtaining the means of subsistence, these different degrees of healthiness would make a great difference in the progress of population; and as there are many countries naturally more healthy than the United States of America, we should have instances of a more rapid increase than that which has there taken place. But as the actual progress of population is, with very few exceptions, determined by the relative difficulty of procuring the means of subsistence and not by the relative natural powers of increase, it is found by experience that except in extreme cases, the actual progress of population is little affected by unhealthiness or healthiness; but that these circumstances show themselves most powerfully in the character of the checks which keep the population down to the level of the means of subsistence, and occasion that sort of variety in the registers of different countries which was noticed in the instances mentioned by M. Muret.

The immediate cause of the increase of population is the excess of the births above the deaths; and the rate of increase, or the period of doubling, depends upon the proportion which the excess of the births above the deaths bears to the population.

The excess of births is occasioned by, and proportioned to, three causes: first, the prolificness of the marriages; secondly, the proportion of the born which lives to marry; and, thirdly, the earliness of these marriages compared with the expectation of life, or the shortness of a generation by marriage and birth compared with the passing away of a generation by death.

In order that the full power of increase should be called into action, all these circumstances must be favourable. The marriages must be prolific, owing to their being contracted early;[26] the proportion of the born living to marry must be great, owing both to the tendency to marriage, and the great proportion of births rising to the age of puberty; and the interval between the average age of marriage and the average age of death must be considerable, owing to the great healthiness of the country and the expectation of life being high. Probably these three causes, each operating with the greatest known force, have never yet been found combined. Even in the United States, though the two first causes operate very powerfully, the expectation of life and, consequently, the distance between the age of marriage and the average age of death is not so favourable as it might be. In general, however, the excess of births which each country can admit being very far short of the full power of increase, the causes above mentioned contribute to the required supply in very various proportions, according to the different circumstances and habits of each state.

One of the most interesting and useful points of view in which registers can be considered is in the proofs which they afford of the varying prevalence of the prudential check to marriage and population in different countries and places. It has been not an uncommon opinion, and has even been strongly expressed of late years although the subject has been much better understood than formerly, that the labouring classes of people, under the circumstances in which they are placed, cannot reasonably be expected to attend to prudential considerations in entering upon the marriage state. But that this opinion does them great injustice is not only obvious to common observation, by which we can scarcely fail to see that numbers delay marriage beyond the period when the passions most strongly prompt to it, but is proved by the registers of different countries, which clearly show either that a considerable number of persons of a marriageable age never marry, or that they marry comparatively late and that their marriages are consequently less prolific than if they had married earlier. As the prudential restraint on marriage may take place in either of these ways, it may prevail nearly in the same degree with a different proportion of marriages to the whole population; and further, with the same proportion of marriages there may be a very different proportion of births and rate of increase. But on the supposition of the same natural prolificness in the women of most countries, the smallness of the proportion of births will generally indicate with tolerable correctness the degree in which the prudential check to population prevails, whether arising principally from late and consequently unprolific marriages, or from a large proportion of the population dying unmarried.[27]

We must refer, then, to the different proportions of births in different countries as the best criterion of the different degrees in which the prudential restraint on marriage operates. These proportions vary from about 1 in 36 to about 1 in 19, or even 17, in different countries, and in a much greater degree in different parishes or districts.

A particular parish in the Alps has already been mentioned where the births were only a forty-ninth part of the population; and it appears by the late returns of the parish registers of England and Wales, that the births in the county of Monmouth are only 1 in 47, and in Brecon, 1 in 53; which, after making ample allowance for omissions, would show the prevalence of the prudential restraint on marriage in a high degree.

If in any country all were to marry at twenty or twenty-one, the proportion of the births would probably be more than 1 in 19; and this result would be still more certain if the resources of the country could not support an accelerated rate of increase than if the means of subsistence were in the greatest abundance and the demand for labour as effectual as it has ever been in the United States. On the latter supposition, taking the births at one-nineteenth and the expectation of life the same as it is in England, the effect would be to occasion a most rapid increase of population; and the period of doubling, instead of being about forty-six or forty-eight years, would be less than in America. On the other hand, if the resources of the country could not support a more rapid increase than that which has taken place in England and Wales during the ten years previous to the census of 1821, the effect would be a great diminution in the expectation of life. If the births were 1 in 19 instead of 1 in 30, the same rate of increase would take place as at present, if the annual mortality were increased to about 1 in 26.5; and in that case, the expectation of life would be reduced in the proportion of from 41; or, as is more probable, from above 45[28] to less than 26. This is the kind of effect which must inevitably follow the absence of the prudential check to marriage and population; and it cannot be doubted that a considerable part of the premature mortality which is found to take place in all parts of the world is occasioned by it. The laws of nature, in application to man as a reasonable being, show no tendency to destroy half of the human race under the age of puberty. This is only done in very particular situations, or when the constant admonitions which these laws give to mankind are obstinately neglected.

It has been said that a tendency in mankind to increase at such a rate as would double the population in twenty-five years, and, if it had full scope, would fill the habitable globe with people in a comparatively short period, cannot be the law of nature, as the very different rate of increase which is actually found to take place must imply such an excessive degree of mortality and destruction of life as to be quite irreconcilable with actual facts and appearances. But the peculiar advantage of a law of increase in a geometrical progression is that though its power be absolutely immense if it be left unchecked, yet when this becomes impossible, it may be restrained by a comparatively moderate force. It can never, of course, happen that any considerable part of that prodigious increase which might be produced by an uninterrupted geometrical progression should exist and then be destroyed. The laws of nature which make food necessary to the life of man, as well as of plants and animals, prevent the continued existence of an excess which cannot be supported, and thus either discourage the production of such an excess, or destroy it in the bud in such a way as to make it scarcely perceptible to a careless observer. It has been seen that in some countries of Europe where the actual progress of the population is slower than in many others, as in Switzerland and Norway, for instance, the mortality is considerably less. Here, then, the necessity of a greater check to the natural progress of population produces no increase of mortality. And it appears, farther, that even the degree of mortality which in each year would be sufficient to destroy that excess of births which would naturally be produced if all married young and all could be supported, might take place, and often does take place in particular situations, and yet is very little noticed. About the middle of last century, the mortality of Stockholm and London was about 1 in 19 or 20. This is a degree of mortality which would probably keep the births on a level with the deaths even though all married at twenty. And yet numbers resorted both to Stockholm and London from choice, the greater part probably not aware that by so doing, they would shorten their own lives and those of their children, and the rest thinking that the difference was not worth attending to, or was at least

balanced by the advantages of society and employment which the town presented. There is nothing, therefore, in the actual state of the mortality observed to take place in different countries and situations which, in the slightest degree, contradicts the supposition of a natural tendency to increase quite as great as that which has been stated.

It has been further remarked that as, in point of fact, it very rarely happens that mankind continue to increase in a geometrical progression of any kind, and only in a single instance in such a one as to double the population in twenty-five years, it is useless and absurd to lay any stress upon tendencies which never, for any length of time together, produce their natural effects. But it might really as well be said that we are not to estimate the natural rate of increase in wheat or sheep, as it is quite certain that their natural tendency to increase has never practically continued to develop itself for so long a time together as that of mankind. Both as a physical, and even economical question, it is curious and desirable to know the natural law of increase which prevails among the most important plants and animals. In the same view, it must be still more interesting to know the natural law of increase with respect to man. It may be said, indeed with truth, that the actual appearances all around us—the varying rate of increase in different countries, its very slow progress, or stationary state in some, and its very rapid progress in others—must be a mass of anomalies, and quite contrary to the analogies of all the rest of animated nature, if the natural tendency of mankind to increase be not, at the least, as great as that which is developed under the most favourable circumstances, while in all others it is kept down by the varying difficulties which the state of the soil and other obstacles oppose to it. But the question as it applies to man assumes at once a tenfold importance in reference to the moral and political effects which must result from those checks to increase, the existence and operation of which, in some form or other, no human exertions can by possibility prevent. A field is here opened for the most interesting inquiries which can engage the friends of human happiness.

But as a preliminary to these inquiries, it is obvious that we must know the degree of force to be overcome, and the varying character of the checks which, in the different countries of the world, are practically found to overcome it; and, for this purpose, the first step must be an endeavour to ascertain the natural law of population, or the rate at which mankind would increase under the fewest known obstacles. Nor can this tendency to increase ever safely be lost sight in the subsequent inquiries, which have for their object the improvement of the moral condition of man in society.

The existence of a tendency in mankind to increase, if unchecked, beyond the possibility of an adequate supply of food in a limited territory, must at once determine the question as to the natural right of the poor to full support in a state of society where the law of property is recognised. The question, therefore, resolves itself chiefly into a question relating to the necessity of those laws which establish and protect private property. It has been usual to consider the right of the strongest as the law of nature among mankind as well as among brutes; yet, in so doing, we at once give up the peculiar and distinctive superiority of man as a reasonable being and class him with the beasts of the field. In the same language, it may be said that the cultivation of the earth is not natural to man. It certainly is not to man, considered merely as an animal without reason. But to a reasonable being, able to look forward to consequences, the laws of nature dictate the cultivation of the earth, both as the means of affording better support to the individual and of increasing the supplies required for increasing numbers, the dictates of those laws of nature being thus evidently calculated to promote the general good and increase the mass of human happiness. It is precisely in the same way, and in order to attain the same object, that the laws of nature dictate to man the

establishment of property and the absolute necessity of some power in the society capable of protecting it. So strongly have the laws of nature spoken this language to mankind and so fully has the force of it been felt, that nothing seems to be thought so absolutely intolerable to reasonable beings as the prevalence in the same society of the right of the strongest; and the history of all ages shows that if men see no other way of putting an end to it than by establishing arbitrary power in an individual, there is scarcely any degree of tyranny, oppression, and cruelty which they will not submit to from some single person and his satellites rather than be at the mercy of the first stronger man who may wish to possess himself of the fruit of their labour. The consequence of this universal and deeply seated feeling inevitably produced by the laws of nature, as applied to reasonable beings, is that the almost certain consequence of anarchy is despotism.

Allowing, then, distinctly, that the right of property is the creature of positive law, yet this law is so early and so imperiously forced on the attention of mankind that if it cannot be called a natural law, it must be considered as the most natural as well as the most necessary of all positive laws; and the foundation of this pre-eminence is its obvious tendency to promote the general good, and the obvious tendency of the absence of it to degrade mankind to the rank of brutes.

As property is the result of positive law, and the ground on which the law which establishes it rests is the promotion of the public good and the increase of human happiness, it follows that it may be modified by the same authority by which it was enacted, with a view to the more complete attainment of the objects which it has in view. It may be said, indeed, that every tax for the use of the government, and every county or parish rate, is a modification of this kind. But there is no modification of the law of property, having still for its object the increase of human happiness, which must not be defeated by the concession of a right of full support to all that might be born. It may be safely said, therefore, that the concession of such a right, and a right of property, are absolutely incompatible and cannot exist together.

To what extent assistance may be given, even by law, to the poorer classes of society when in distress without defeating the great object of the law of property, is essentially a different question. It depends mainly upon the feelings and habits of the labouring classes of society, and can only be determined by experience. If it be generally considered as so discreditable to receive parochial relief, that great exertions are made to avoid it, and few or none marry with a certain prospect of being obliged to have recourse to it, there is no doubt that those who were really in distress might be adequately assisted with little danger of a constantly increasing proportion of paupers; and, in that case, a great good would be attained without any proportionate evil to counterbalance it. But if, from the numbers of the dependent poor, the discredit of receiving relief is so diminished as to be practically disregarded, so that many marry with the almost certain prospect of becoming paupers, and the proportion of their numbers to the whole population is, in consequence, continually increasing, it is certain that the partial good attained must be much more than counterbalanced by the general deterioration in the condition of the great mass of the society and the prospect of its daily growing worse: so that, though from the inadequate relief which is in many cases granted, the manner in which it is conceded, and other counteracting causes, the operation of poor-laws such as they exist in England might be very different from the effects of a full concession of the right,[29] and a complete fulfilment of the duties resulting from it, yet such a state of things ought to give the most serious alarm to every friend to the happiness of society, and every effort consistent with justice and humanity ought to be made to remedy it. But whatever steps may be taken on this subject, it will be allowed that with any prospect of legislating for the poor with

success, it is necessary to be fully aware of the natural tendency of the labouring classes of society to increase beyond the demand for their labour or the means of their adequate support, and the effect of this tendency to throw the greatest difficulties in the way of permanently improving their condition.

It would lead far beyond the limits which must be prescribed to this summary to notice the various objections which have been made by different writers to the principles which have been here explained. Those which contain in them the slightest degree of plausibility have been answered in the late editions of the *Essay on Population*, particularly in the appendix to the fifth and sixth, to which we refer the reader.[30] We will only, therefore, further notice the objection which has been made by some persons on religious grounds; for, as it is certainly of great importance that the answer which has been given given to it should be kept in mind, we cannot refuse a place to a condensed statement of it at the end of this summary.

It has been thought that a tendency in mankind to increase beyond the greatest possible increase of food which could be produced in a limited space impeaches the goodness of the Deity, and is inconsistent with the letter and spirit of the Scriptures. If this objection were well founded, it would certainly be the most serious one which has been brought forwards; but the answer to it appears to be quite satisfactory, and it may be compressed into a very small compass.

First, it appears that the evils arising from the principle of population are exactly of the same kind as the evils arising from the excessive or irregular gratification of the human passions in general, and may equally be avoided by moral restraint. Consequently, there can be no more reason to conclude, from the existence of these evils, that the principle of increase is too strong than to conclude, from the existence of the vices arising from the human passions, that these passions are all too strong and require diminution or extinction instead of regulation and direction.

Secondly, it is almost universally acknowledged that both the letter and spirit of Revelation represent this world as a state of moral discipline and probation. But a state of moral discipline and probation cannot be a state of unmixed happiness, as it necessarily implies difficulties to be overcome and temptations to be resisted. Now, in the whole range of the laws of nature, not one can be pointed out which so especially accords with this scriptural view of the state of man on earth, as it gives rise to a greater variety of situations and exertions than any other, and marks, in a more general and stronger manner, and nationally as well as individually, the different effects of virtue and vice—of the proper government of the passions, and the culpable indulgence of them. It follows, then, that the principle of population, instead of being inconsistent with Revelation, must be considered as affording strong additional proofs of its truth.

Lastly, it will be acknowledged that in a state of probation, those laws seem best to accord with the views of a benevolent Creator, which, while they furnish the difficulties and temptations which form the essence of such a state, are of such a nature as to reward those who overcome them with happiness in this life as well as in the next. But the law of population answers particularly to this description. Each individual has, to a great degree, the power of avoiding the evil consequences to himself and society resulting from it, by the practice of a virtue dictated to him by the light of nature and sanctioned by revealed religion. And, as there can be no question that this virtue tends greatly to improve the condition and increase the comforts both of the individuals who practice it, and through them, of the whole society, the ways of God to man with regard to this great law are completely vindicated.

Notes

[1] *Essai Politique sur le Royaume de la Nouvelle Espagne*, IV, ix, 98.

[2] These numbers are taken from Dr. Seybert's *Statistical Annals*, p. 23.

[3] This number is taken from the American National Calendar for 1822, and has since been compared with the original census as published for the use of the members of Congress.

[4] American National Calendar for 1821, p. 237, and *North American Review*, October, 1822, p. 304.

[5] This mode was suggested by Mr. Booth in Mr. Godwin's *Inquiry Concerning Population*.

[6] Seybert's *Statistical Annals*, p. 23.

[7] American National Calendar for 1822, p. 246.

[8] The details for the next year were not then printed, but it is known that the whole number of passengers arriving in the United States was 10,722, of which 2,415 were from the United States, leaving 8,307 foreigners.—*American Review*, October, 1822, p. 304.

[9] The details which M. Humboldt has given of the population of New Spain are highly interesting, as they are the first of any consequence which the public has yet received of a tropical climate. The peculiarities which mark them are exactly of the kind which might have been expected, though the proportion of births is still greater than we could have ventured to suppose.

[10] *Essai Politique sur le Royaume de la Nouvelle Espagne*, II, iv, 330, et seq. Vol. I.

[11] *Gottliche Ordnung*, Vol. I, Table XXI.

[12] Tooke's *View of the Russian Empire*, II, 126.

[13] *Population Abstract* (1821), "Preliminary Observations," p. 8.

[14] *Population Abstract* (1821), "Preliminary Observations," p. 8.

[15] *Population Abstract* (1821), "Preliminary Observations," p. 32.

[16] This statement, of course, refers to the general result, and not to each intermediate step of the progress. Practically, it would sometimes be slower and sometimes faster.

[17] *Gottliche Ordnung*, I, 128.

[18] This very large proportion of marriages could not all have been supplied from the births in the country, but must have been occasioned in part by the influx of strangers.

[19] *Essay on Population* (6th ed.), I, 260.

[20] *Gottliche Ordnung*, I, 134, et seq.

[21] Some of these high proportions of marriages could not have taken place except under a shorter duration of human life, and a great proportion of second and third marriages, which have always a most powerful effect. In all considerable towns, also, the inhabitants of the neighbouring country increase the lists of marriages.

[22] Sussmilch, *Gottliche Ordnung*, I, 225; *Essay on Population* (6th ed.), I, 331.

[23] *Mémoires, &c., par la Société Economique de Berne* (1776). pp. 15, et seq.; *Essay on Population* (6th ed.), I, 338, et seq.

[24] *Mémoires, &c, par la Société Economique de Berne* (1776), pp. 48 et seq.

[25] *Mémoires, &c., par la Société Economique de Berne* (1776), Table V, p. 65 of the Tables.

[26] By *early* is not meant a premature

age; but if women marry at 19 or 20, there cannot be a doubt that, on an average, they will have a greater number of births than if they had married at 28 or 30.

[27]It is impossible to form any judgment of the natural prolific-ness of women in different countries from the proportions of births to marriages in their registers, because those proportions are always pro-digiously affected by the rate of increase, the number of second and third marriages, and the proportion of *late* marriages. The registers of a country might mark four births to a marriage, and yet the women who in country situations marry at twenty might have on an average seven or eight births.

[28]This may be presumed from the small annual mortality in this country during the ten years from 1810 to 1920.

[29]The grand objection to the lan-guage used respecting the *right of the poor to support* is that, as a matter of fact, we do not perform what we promise, and the poor may justly accuse us of deceiving them.

[30]In the answer to Mr. Arthur Young, the question of giving land to cottagers is discussed; and it is a curious fact, that after proposing a plan of this kind, Mr. A. Young is obliged to own, "that it might be prudent to consider the misery to which the progressive population

might be subject as an evil which it is absolutely and physically im-possible to prevent." The whole of the difficulty, in fact, lies here. The grand distinction between colonies in England and Ireland and colonies in Canada is that in the one case there will be no demand for the progressive population from the colonists, and the redundancy of labour after a short time will be aggravated: in the other, the de-mand will be great and certain for a long time, and the redundancy in the emigrating countries essentially relieved.

The answer to Mr. Weyland, in the Appendix, contains much that is applicable to present objections.

Selection Six

THE DEMOGRAPHIC TRANSITION: FROM HIGH TO LOW BIRTH RATES AND DEATH RATES

George J. Stolnitz

Demographic transitions rank among the most sweeping and best-documented his-torical trends of modern times. The following discussion of transition patterns summarizes past declines of vital rates and the prospects for future ones in comparatively global fashion. Its focus is on modern population movements in broad terms, on major regions of the world rather than individual countries, and on some major implications only. Details will be kept in the background. It is important to keep in mind, therefore, that the general picture to be described is based upon hundreds of investigations, covering a host of specific places, periods and events. Indeed, it is the very multiplicity of these building blocks which accounts for the impressiveness of the over-all structure.

The main outlines of the structure can be summarized briefly. All nations in the

Modern Era which have moved from a traditional, agrarian-based economic system to a largely industrial, urbanized base have also moved from a condition of high mor-tality and fertility to low mortality and fertility. In so doing they have almost all experienced enormous increases in popula-tion along with massive shifts in their relative numbers of children, adults and aged. Partly as cause and partly as result have been associated sweeping changes in the relation between population and natural resources, in the relation between numbers of con-sumers and size of labor force, in investment patterns and in the distribution of people between rural and urban areas.

To give these generalizations even skeletal form requires some perspectives. A first perspective is that the periods needed for maturation of the vital trends just outlined have not been short. Although they vary greatly from country to country and case to case, they have always been long-run, more like quarters of a century or generations than decades, and surely more like decades than single years. We need to remember this when considering the relevance of the experience in the industrialized nations for the underdeveloped economies of today.

A second perspective is that the pace of the trends to modern, lower vital rates marked a vast break with the past, without precedent in human history. The mortality declines which have occurred in many areas over the past century almost certainly exceed by far the cumulative movement in any part of the globe over the preceding twenty centuries. In their own proportions, the declines in fertility have been similarly precipitous by previous standards.

A third perspective is that the trends appear without exception to have become irreversible wherever they have occurred. This too marks a significant break with the past. Premodern decreases in mortality must have been succeeded by more or less equal increases, subject to the vagaries of the harvest and the whims of a threatening natural environment. It is true that one can only surmise this interpretation, but indirect evidence makes it seem most probable. Even apart from wars, the time path of human survival before about 1800 was one of fluctuations rather than sustained movement. In contrast, the modern path has been to ever higher, more secure ground. Given peace, the current levels of medical technology and economic well-being in the industrialized nations are more than ample to initiate rising longevity. They seem super-abundantly capable of preventing declines.

Similarly, the prospect for significant reversal of past fertility declines in industrialized societies seems remote. The closest to an exception has been the rise in the birth rate of many of these areas after the war. Some partial reversal of the long-term trend in fertility may well have occurred in at least some areas. But at most, the return was to the years before the unusually depressed conditions of the 1930s, not to traditional high fertility. Although childless and small-size families in a number of countries have recently become less frequent than a generation ago, large-size families have also continued to become less frequent. The postwar experience is better described as a "trendlet" rather than a trend, compared to long-run fertility movements, even where the recent increases have been greatest. Moreover the crest of the rise has already been reached and become dated in numerous cases and gives evidence of being left behind in others. But perhaps above all, the context of the postwar fertility increases in industrialized areas has been one of ever spreading family planning and control over its size. It may well be that the nations in the vanguard of fertility transitions have reached something like a bottom plateau, involving the two-child family. Future fertility in these areas may fluctuate sometimes above this level, sometimes below, depending upon economic conditions and social fashion. Or it may resume a further downtrend. In any event a sustained long-run uptrend seems inconceivable. By all available indications, the break with the historical past appears to be complete.

A fourth general perspective to keep in mind is a close variant of an ancient bit of folk wisdom: it's not what you do but the way you do it that makes the final difference. The low birth and death rates encountered today in the modernized economies could have been reached by many paths through time. In fact, however, the death rate has either come down first or has moved more rapidly than has the birth rate. The result almost everywhere among such economies was a rapid acceleration in their population growth rates and numbers, which lasted for decades. Eventually the gap between their birth and death rates closed and decelerated growth ensued, but only after lengthy periods of transition. Experience of a full transition process was needed before the low growth rates of their pre-transition history reappeared.

A fuller account of these effects would have to take heed of the great transatlantic migrations before World War I, which lessened the acceleration in Europe and enhanced it in the newer nations of North America and Oceania. Also France, Ireland and perhaps the United States provide exceptions to the general prototype, each for its individual reasons.

Nevertheless the proposition stands, with very high probability, that demographic transition implies a substantial speeding up in the growth of population both as compared to the pre-transition period and to its later phases. The probability approaches certainty in the case of the newly developing, low-income countries of today. The initial widening observed between birth and death rates in past transitions has not been accidental, and an analogous widening seems even more likely in future transitions. Among the reasons for this anticipation are several that merit special attention.

Thus, on the one hand, lower mortality is a universally desired and accepted social goal, at least in peace and off the highway. Nineteenth-century declines in death rates among the then developing economies were an outcome of effective new methods of disease control and rising levels of living; they did not result in a significant way from changes in the social order or from altered social values. Today methods exist for reducing high mortality that are more effective in a technical sense than ever before, that require relatively low expenditures and small numbers of skilled personnel, and that can be divorced sharply from the general socioeconomic environment. Applied in the form of public health, sanitation and mass medical programs, such methods can be superimposed by governments upon populations that are technologically backward in most or all other respects.

On the other hand, lower fertility and the means for achieving it have long been subjects of religious controversy and deep-rooted ethical, social and individual debate, both within the household and in the community at large. Previous transition experience suggests that sustained down-trends in fertility often begin as a result of forces whose momentum develops slowly. Such downtrends require a shift in attitudes from the traditional fatalism typical of peasant societies to a belief that one's destiny can be affected by one's deeds, in

childbearing as in other spheres of behavior. Another major factor in the past has been the growing importance of secular education, which refashioned old attitudes and proposed new values, along with fresh opportunities for putting these to work. Increasing urbanization was typically a third major factor, with its emphasis on a skilled and better-educated labor force and with its tendency to reduce the importance of the family as a center of employment opportunities, economic security, education and recreation. Children on the farm could be, and usually were, put to work early. In the city equal numbers of children became a much greater drain on family resources, a lesser source of income, a more potent competitor with basic family needs such as housing, and a threat to earning capacity on the part of women. As a rule, therefore, the spread of small-family ideals has tended to be more rapid in an urban context than in rural cultures. The specific knowledge and motivations needed to convert such ideals into effective behavior, in particular knowledge of contraceptive methods and willingness to apply them, also tend to be more rapidly acquired in urban environments. In contrast to medical innovations, whose effectiveness is largely a technological matter, adoption of contraceptive methods may require a wholesale reorientation of social values and attitudes.

All of these classes of causal factors—changing value structures, shifting occupational and residential composition of population, and rising educational levels—are relatively long-run in nature. It is true that the weight and timing of these factors are not easily traced; their causal influence in quantitative terms remains obscure even in the cases where their importance stands out most clearly. It is also true that other factors have sometimes appeared capable of initiating marked fertility downtrends, as in France, Ireland and the United States. As of now, however, the weight of evidence from past transition patterns leans heavily toward the expectation that future departures from traditional fertility patterns will come slowly. And even if this is not the case, mortality in many areas with high birth rates has already come down, or promises to do so, more rapidly than has ever been the case before.

There is another dimension to the point that the process of transition is important, in addition to its end result. The nations with low vital rates today could have had the same increases in numbers if their fertility and mortality trends had been smaller than the ones they actually experienced. In other words, ignoring migration, the rate of population growth depends upon the difference between birth and death rates, not upon their level. A birth rate of 25 per 1000 and a death rate of 15 per 1000 yields the same growth as does a birth rate of 20 per 1000 and a death rate of 10 per 1000. In both cases the growth is 10 per 1000.

Yet there is an important difference between the two, involving the age composition of the population. Declines in mortality tend to have only limited effect on the fractions of a population belonging to the young ages, or roughly under fifteen, the main adult ages, or fifteen to sixty-five, and the old ages, sixty-five and over. If only mortality had declined in the industrially advanced nations while fertility had remained unchanged, their age composition today would be much as it was in 1850. A demonstration of this rather startling conclusion is given in the essay following, by Ansley Coale. For present purposes we can simply accept it as true, though it seems to fly in the face of common sense and in fact eluded the attention of professional demographers until quite recently. Age composition, in short, tends to remain quite unaffected by movements from high to low mortality. In contrast, declines in fertility have a sharp effect on age structure, leading directly to a decline in the fraction under fifteen. The larger the decline in the one, the sharper is the decline in the other. The second side of the coin, of course, is that the fraction of adults increases.

We have here in a nutshell an explanation of one of the great historical shifts of the Modern Era. As fertility in the industrially advanced nations came down rapidly during the late nineteenth and early twentieth centuries, their age profiles shifted commensurately. Young populations became young adult populations and consumers became, increasingly, producers as well. Moreover this was at a time when productive capacity, rather than aggregate demand, was the key to economic progress. Output which would otherwise have gone to support the young could be applied to private and collective investment, without sacrifice of consumption levels. Not only was labor efficiency rising, because of new technology and new forms of economic organization, but the average laborer had fewer persons to support.

A substantial component of the rise in the per capita income of the industrializing nations between about 1870 and 1920 can be traced to these facts. And conversely a substantial segment of the economic difficulties confronting the newly developing countries of today stems from a continuing unfavorable balance among their age groups.

A fifth and final perspective is that only a minority of the world's population has already made a substantial demographic transition or is clearly in process of doing so. As already indicated, all industrially advanced nations have reached a stage of both low fertility and low mortality. A number of other nations, at an intermediate stage economically because development came later or was retarded, are also as a rule in an intermediate stage demographically. But even if both of these groups of areas are combined, they are far outnumbered by the rest of the world, where economic development has not begun or is barely incipient.

The demographic situation in the underdeveloped areas is mixed only with respect to mortality. Substantial numbers of such areas have already experienced large declines in the death rate, especially during the last two decades. The basic reason has been that modern public health methods and medical technology are both cheap and effective enough to keep people living much longer—

even in the face of chronic hunger, general economic misery and ever present risks of mass disease. The instances where this pattern has recently occured in low-income areas are so numerous and so widely distributed that it seems safe to predict its recurrence in many other such areas, where mortality has yet to make a major move pending the introduction of modern disease-control systems.

A central question, especially in the densely settled low-income nations, is how long these achieved or prospective mortality declines can be preserved under unfavorable conditions of life in general. For fertility—the other side of the transition process and the component much more resistant to change—has yet to give any significant signs of decline in the underdeveloped world.

In short, current mortality trends in the world's low-income areas are in good part independent of the pace of development, while fertility remains unresponsive to its first stirrings. The result has been a growing number of burgeoning populations, whose rates of growth are without parallel anywhere in the past. For the present at least, the difficulties of accommodating the growth in numbers are far more clearly in sight than the signs of relief. It is true that past economic development in the industrially advanced nations has always brought with it lower fertility, as an apparently inevitable by-product. But so far as our current information goes, the inevitable in today's newly developing economies may well come slowly.

These summary comments should make it clear that past and current world population movements need to be sharply classified by regions or economic status. In order to take a closer look at international transition processes and their implications, it is useful and convenient to make a threefold classification of populations by area. One group includes the nations of Northern, Western and Central Europe and their offshoot populations overseas in the new lands of the nineteenth century, mainly the United States, Canada, Australia and New Zealand. For

simplicity and with no political undertones intended, this group may be termed "the West." A second group is Eastern and Southern Europe, the intermediate-stage region referred to earlier. It is true that the overlap of demographic characteristics in this region and the West has increased rapidly since the war. However, the typical differences between member nations in the two groups have been very substantial in earlier periods, both in terms of the levels of their vital rates and the timing of their transitions. Significant differences exist on the average even today, though with numerous individual exceptions. Thus a good deal more is gained for our purposes by distinguishing the two groups than by lumping them together.

The third group comprises the countries of Latin America, Asia and Africa (really the non-white populations of the last). No doubt a lumping of densely settled India with the sparsely settled Middle East, or the newly created nations of Middle Africa with Latin America, does violence to many facts. Nevertheless the procedure is justified for brevity and as a working approximation. Economic modernization is just beginning or has barely begun in all but a small part of any of these continents, while fertility is at traditional, premodern levels almost everywhere. The exceptions, Japan and a very few other nations such as Argentina, are better treated individually than as a basis for further subclassifications. Moreover, in all three continents the statistical record is scattered and fragmentary up to the end of the interwar period. Enormous data gaps remain the rule today and the generalizations we can safely make must therefore be rather unrefined. All in all, we can make the main points to be indicated for the underdeveloped world by treating it as a whole.

Turning to a closer look at the three groups, the heartland of the transition process has clearly been the West. The nations of the West began their economic modernization first, have progressed the furthest in productive capacity and income levels per capita, and have been exposed the longest to interactions between demographic evolution and rapid long-run economic change. Since economic and statistical development tend to go together, the West also provides the most extensive statistical record of such interactions.

Unfortunately the record is too short even here. We can surmise only indirectly and in retrospect that mortality in a number of Western areas eased downward during the century or two before the industrial revolution. As suggested earlier, the downdrift was marked by extensive fluctuations about an unemphatic trend. The course of fertility is still more speculative. The first available figures on national birth rates in the West are typically well below the ones encountered today in Latin America and Asia among populations not practicing birth control. Little is known about why this should be the case. Sweden, the only Western nation with records going back to 1750, showed little change in the birth rate for a century thereafter but had already reached the low initial level of 30 to 35 per 1000. France had also attained this level by roughly 1800 and moved slowly to lower levels after the Napoleonic period. The United States apparently started with a much higher birth rate in 1800 and witnessed a much sharper drop in the next half century, although it should be cautioned that the available estimates are extremely tentative. In any event by about 1850, when extensive data first became available, most Western nations may have experienced a kind of preliminary transition, though one whose time path is uncertain and whose causal mechanisms are most obscure.

The middle decades of the nineteenth century constituted a long lull in the demographic history of the West. The forces working for transition gathered strength, as it were, for a more decisive onslaught. The storm broke in the last quarter of the century. In country after country fertility and mortality began to decline at a pace without any previous precedent. Not the least remarkable aspect of the event was its almost simultaneous occurrence in so many areas, despite substantial differences in their po-

litical and social structures, in economic conditions and trends, and in historical contexts. A giant diffusion process, so to speak, until then undetected by contemporary observers, was suddenly released and has been alive in the West ever since.

Mortality has continued downward since the 1870s, almost undeterred in trend by the two world wars. It would be difficult, for example, to distinguish neutrals from belligerents by mortality as of 1925 after the First World War or as of 1955 after the Second. For many decades Western nations have experienced ever more similar as well as declining mortality. Expectation of life at birth a century ago in the West averaged about forty years. Today it is close to or above seventy years, the biblical threescore and ten long cited in history as a limit to man's stay on earth. The trend to still higher levels of longevity seems certain to continue, though it may well slow down substantially. In the past the main contribution to increasing length of life came from mortality declines in the young ages. Today mortality before age fifty is already so small that even its total elimination would lead to only moderate gains in average longevity. Of course should major breakthroughs be achieved against the diseases of old age, notably heart and cancer, the horizons would open again much as they did in the past following breakthroughs against the infectious diseases.

On the side of fertility, the trends launched about 1875 gathered momentum for many decades. By the end of the interwar period, birth rates ranged from 15 to 20 per 1000, roughly half the size of the rates about 1850. The fertility increases in many parts of the West since the war therefore represent the first break in trend in close to a century. They also mark an interruption of the convergence of reproductive patterns throughout the region. At the moment, fertility in the European parts of the West is well below the levels found in its non-European parts, i.e. North America and Oceania.

It may be, as previously suggested, that the West has embarked upon a new phase in its fertility history. Only time will permit secure judgment. But it does seem certain that Western fertility in the future will not undo the long-term changes of the past.

The specific time sequences of the vital trends just summarized were such as to produce enormous increases in numbers, together with large-scale shifts in age composition. Among the long-settled nations of the West, population between 1850 and 1950 rose by two to three times in Norway, Denmark, England and Wales, Sweden, and the Netherlands. We need to recall that these increases developed despite very large out-migration. The newer parts of the West increased much more rapidly, of course, partly because of immigration but also largely because of their own excess of births over deaths. The two exceptions to the typical Western experience of rapid growth are France, where population increased only slightly as a result of her long-declining birth rate, and Ireland, where population decreased sharply because of emigration and uniquely low rates of marriage after the potato famine of the 1840s. As to age, in 1850 the percentage of population under fifteen tended to be about 35 in Western nations. By 1950 the typical value was 25 per cent. Although there was also a rise in the per cent over sixty-five, most of the shift went to the intermediate ages, fifteen to sixty-five, the main years of labor-force activity.

Eastern and Southern Europe—the second group of populations singled out—has had a much briefer recorded history of modern demographic movements. These can therefore be summarized more rapidly.

Details apart, perhaps the main point to be noted is that a decided transition process took place outside the West, under vastly different cultural, social, and economic circumstances. Moreover the process was no pale imitation of Western experience but occurred in its own time and manner. In retrospect, to be sure, the movement to lower mortality was quite unsurprising, given the effectiveness of twentieth-century medical technology and the universal appeal of longer life. Much more surprising—even startling—is that the appeal of lower, con-

trolled fertility has also not been space-bound or time-bound. Eastern and Southern Europe shows clearly that this appeal has extended well beyond the centers of Western culture in the past.

As of about 1900, when a sizable collection of data first became available for Eastern and Southern Europe, both mortality and fertility were typically above the Western average in 1850. Unlike the West, therefore, the break with tradition in most parts of the region has been an event of the present century. And once it began, the transition was far more rapid. In little more than a decade during the interwar period—between the early 1920s and the late 1930s—birth rates in many parts of Eastern and Southern Europe dropped by amounts it took the West more than a generation—about thirty to sixty years—to achieve during its own early transition. Again unlike the West, the birth rate has often continued to fall in the postwar period, especially in countries with relatively high fertility, as the transition has continued its course. Today mortality and fertility in the region are still above the West on the average, but the gaps of a half century ago are a relic of the past. Birth rates in many countries are below 20 per 1000 or not much above this level. Thus fertility is often well below that in large parts of the West; Hungary today has the lowest birth rate of any nation in either region. Expectation of life at birth is typically well over sixty to sixty-five years, which most Western countries reached only one or two decades ago.

With respect to the underdeveloped areas, or nearly all of Latin America, Asia, and Africa, some of the most salient points have already been reviewed. Fertility remains at traditional levels almost everywhere in all of these continents. Indeed it may even be rising in some areas as a result of lower mortality, though the data are often not reliable enough to judge. Of course it may also be that some declines have taken place but been similarly obscured. In any event, there is certainly no evidence of any sharp or even early transition in fertility. Meanwhile mortality in a large and growing number of countries has been falling at a headlong pace since the war, without precedent in previous trends. It is a remarkable fact that, in every underdeveloped country of these continents for which fairly reliable information exists, the mortality declines in the last decade or two have matched or exceeded the maximum rates of decline in any part of the West during its known history. Recent declines in a number of underdeveloped areas with less reliable data have been less dramatic, though they have certainly been rapid. In still other areas, such as Middle Africa and the Middle East, sustained mortality declines can be expected with confidence in the near future, as governments mobilize the tools of known medical technology.

The result, increasingly encountered since 1950, has been population growth at an enormous pace. National rates exceeding 2.5 per cent annually are now common, and rates exceeding 3 per cent not infrequent. The near prospect is for many other areas to reach these levels. We need to remember that such rates imply a doubling of population in only about twenty-five years. It is also worth noting that the same rates are about double the maximum rates of population growth in the European parts of the West during their century-long transition. Since Latin America, Asia, and Africa comprise the bulk of the world's population, an acceleration of their numbers implies also an acceleration in the world total. More important than global aggregates, the greatest increases in the foreseeable future will occur in the very regions with least developed economic resources. Growth in the West or Eastern and Southern Europe will be much slower.

This is not the occasion to examine closely the economic implications of such a rising tide of numbers. The densely settled agrarian areas such as India and China will clearly suffer greatly in terms of human costs, as economic needs for investment come into conflict with human needs for consumption. The less densely settled areas such as Brazil can accommodate added numbers more readily in their agrarian sectors, but even here the density picture will change radically if the expected trends come to pass. And

in all underdeveloped areas, continued high fertility will imply an unfavorable age structure, with something like 40 per cent under age fifteen compared to the 25 or 30 per cent found elsewhere. The typical worker in the underdeveloped economies of Latin America, Asia and Africa will have fewer productive resources to work with and also more mouths to support. Similarly, at the government level, undeveloped fiscal systems will be confronted with especially severe demands for collective consumption by the young, as in education.

This does not mean, despite the many voices of alarm one hears, that the population problem in the underdeveloped areas threatens catastrophe. The newly developing economies have so far been successful enough in accommodating the problem. Economic growth has occurred in fact and per capita income has risen in many areas, even densely settled ones, despite the numerous political, social, and administrative obstacles attendant upon early development. Indeed, the increases in per capita income found in a fair number of underdeveloped areas over the past decade compare favorably with the trends in most Western nations during their own early periods of development. The race between people and product may not always be so successful in the long run, but at least the areas in question seem capable of winning a kind of breathing space for themselves, during which both rapidly increasing numbers and rising per capita product can be reconciled. Moreover, it may be that the forces making for reduced fertility are gathering strength and that the present is yet another temporary "lull," much as in the West a century ago and in Eastern and Southern Europe about a half century ago. There are indications of a widespread desire for lower fertility among important segments of the population in many underdeveloped areas. Such desires may become effective behavior in the fairly near future, as governments become increasingly committed to explicit birth-control programs, as new cheap and effective methods of contraception become available for the first time, or as economic modernization itself gains momentum. Taiwan, India, Pakistan, Malaya, and possibly Egypt and mainland China may be early cases in point in significant areas. On the side of mortality again, declining death rates and the reduction of debilitating disease may have significant favorable effects on worker productivity, while increasing numbers of survivors among the total number of children born may help undermine the values supporting uncontrolled childbearing.

It may also be that a fertility downtrend in the underdeveloped areas, when and if it occurs, would be more rapid than precedent would suggest. This has typically been the case for latecomers to the transition process, such as Germany in the West, Eastern and Southern Europe after the West, and again Japan during this century. The last is the outstanding example of a non-Western, non-European culture which has gone through

something like a full transition sequence. Unfortunately we know very little about Japanese vital trends during the formative years of development, between 1870 and 1920. But we do know that fertility was already declining by 1920, continued to fall within the interwar years, and has plummeted downward since the war. Today Japan's fertility ranks well below Western levels and her mortality not much above.

These comments, to be sure, represent hopes rather than confirmed expectations. At the most, one can be a qualified non-pessimist at the moment. One final conclusion, however, is sure. Whether the underdeveloped areas embark upon a transition to lower fertility—and if they do, the time and speed with which the process would occur—will have a dominant effect upon the future well-being and security of the great majority of the world's population.

Suggestions for Further Reading

C. P. Blacker. "Stages in Population Growth." *Eugenics Review*, Vol. 39, No. 3 (Oct. 1947), pp. 88–102. A five-stage classification of long-run population changes.

F. W. Notestein. "The Economics of Population and Food Supplies." *Proceedings of the Eighth International Conference of Agricultural Economists*. London: Oxford University Press, 1953, pp. 15–31. A stock-taking of transition doctrines and experience by one of the early students of the subject.

G. J. Stolnitz. "Interrelations between Economic Development, Levels of Living and Demographic Trends," in D. Bogue, editor, *Applications of Demography: The Population Situation in the United States*

in 1975. Oxford: Scripps Foundation and University of Chicago, 1957, pp. 5–13. A critical review of some major evidence on the timing of past transition movements.

I. B. Taeuber. "Japan's Demographic Transition Re-examined." *Population Studies*, Vol. 14, No. 1 (July 1960), pp. 28–39. Some aspects of the main non-Western transition experience on record.

L. van Nort and B. P. Karon. "Demographic Transition Re-examined." *American Sociological Review*, Vol. 20, No. 5 (Oct. 1955), pp. 523–27. An analytical review of the possibility of developing a theory of demographic transitions.

Selection Seven

POPULATION POLICY: WILL CURRENT PROGRAMS SUCCEED?

Kingsley Davis

Grounds for skepticism concerning the demographic effectiveness of family planning are considered.

Throughout history the growth of population has been identified with prosperity and

Reprinted from *Science*, **158** (10 November 1967), 730–739, by permission of the author and publisher. Copyright 1967 by the American Association for the Advancement of Science.

strength. If today an increasing number of nations are seeking to curb rapid population growth by reducing their birth rates, they must be driven to do so by an urgent crisis. My purpose here is not to discuss the crisis itself but rather to assess the present and prospective measures used to meet it. Most observers are surprised by the swiftness with which concern over the population problem has turned from intellectual analysis and debate to policy and action. Such action is a welcome relief from the long opposition, or timidity, which seemed to block forever any governmental attempt to restrain population growth, but relief that "at last something is being done" is no guarantee that what is being done is adequate. On the face of it, one could hardly expect such a fundamental reorientation to be quickly and successfully implemented. I therefore propose to review the nature and (as I see them) limitations of the present policies and to suggest lines of possible improvement.

The Nature of Current Policies

With more than 30 nations now trying or planning to reduce population growth and with numerous private and international organizations helping, the degree of unanimity as to the kind of measures needed is impressive. The consensus can be summed up in the phrase "family planning." President Johnson declared in 1965 that the United States will "assist family planning programs in nations which request such help." The Prime Minister of India said a year later, "We must press forward with family planning. This is a programme of the highest importance." The Republic of Singapore created in 1966 the Singapore Family Planning and Population Board "to initiate and undertake population control programmes" (*1*).

As is well known, "family planning" is a euphemism for contraception. The family-planning approach to population limitation, therefore, concentrates on providing new and efficient contraceptives on a national basis through mass programs under public health auspices. The nature of these programs is shown by the following enthusiastic report from the Population Council (*2*):

No single year has seen so many forward steps in population control as 1965. Effec-

tive national programs have at last emerged, international organizations have decided to become engaged, a new contraceptive has proved its value in mass application, . . . and surveys have confirmed a popular desire for family limitation . . .

An accounting of notable events must begin with Korea and Taiwan . . . Taiwan's program is not yet two years old, and already it has inserted one IUD [intrauterine device] for every 4–6 target women (those who are not pregnant, lactating, already sterile, already using contraceptives effectively, or desirous of more children). Korea has done almost as well . . . has put 2,200 full-time workers into the field, . . . has reached operational levels for a network of IUD quotas, supply lines, local manufacture of contraceptives, training of hundreds of M.D.'s and nurses, and mass propaganda . . .

Here one can see the implication that "population control" is being achieved through the dissemination of new contraceptives, and the fact that the "target women" exclude those who want more children. One can also note the technological emphasis and the medical orientation

What is wrong with such programs? The answer is, "Nothing at all, if they work." Whether or not they work depends on what they are expected to do as well as on how they try to do it. Let us discuss the goal first, then the means.

Goals

Curiously, it is hard to find in the population-policy movement any explicit discussion of long-range goals. By implication the policies seem to promise a great deal. This is shown by the use of expressions like *population control* and *population planning* (as in the passages quoted above). It is also shown by the characteristic style of reasoning. Expositions of current policy usually start off by lamenting the speed and the consequences of runaway population growth. This growth, it is then stated, must be curbed—by pursuing a vigorous family-planning program. That family planning can solve the problem of population growth seems to be taken as self-evident.

For instance, the much-heralded statement by 12 heads of state, issued by Secretary-General U Thant on 10 December 1966 (a statement initiated by John D. Rockefeller III, Chairman of the Board of the Population Council), devotes half its space to discussing the harmfulness of population growth and the other half to recommending family planning (3). A more succinct example of the typical reasoning is given in the Provisional Scheme for a Nationwide Family Planning Programme in Ceylon (4):

> The population of Ceylon is fast increasing. . . . [The] figures reveal that a serious situation will be created within a few years. In order to cope with it a Family Planning programme on a nationwide scale should be launched by the Government.

The promised goal—to limit population growth so as to solve population problems—is a large order. One would expect it to be carefully analyzed, but it is left imprecise and taken for granted, as is the way in which family planning will achieve it.

When the terms *population control* and *population planning* are used, as they frequently are, as synonyms for current family-planning programs, they are misleading. Technically, they would mean deliberate influence over all attributes of a population, including its age-sex structure, geographical distribution, racial composition, genetic quality, and total size. No government attempts such full control. By tacit understanding, current population policies are concerned with only the *growth* and *size* of populations. These attributes, however, result from the death rate and migration as well as from the birth rate; their control would require deliberate influence over the factors giving rise to all three determinants. Actually, current policies labeled population control do not deal with mortality and migration, but deal only with the birth input. This is why another term, *fertility control*, is frequently used to describe current policies. But, as I show below, family planning (and hence current policy) does not undertake to influence most of the determinants of human reproduction. Thus the programs should not be referred to as population control or planning, because they do not attempt to influence the factors responsible for the attributes of human populations, taken generally; nor should they be called fertility control, because they do not try to affect most of the determinants of reproductive performance.

The ambiguity does not stop here, however. When one speaks of controlling population size, any inquiring person naturally asks, What is "control"? Who is to control whom? Precisely what population size, or what rate of population growth, is to be achieved? Do the policies aim to produce a growth rate that is nil, one that is very slight, or one that is like that of the industrial nations? Unless such questions are dealt with and clarified, it is impossible to evaluate current population policies.

The actual programs seem to be aiming simply to achieve a reduction in the birth rate. Success is therefore interpreted as the accomplishment of such a reduction, on the assumption that the reduction will lessen population growth. In those rare cases where a specific demographic aim is stated, the goal is said to be a short-run decline within a given period. The Pakistan plan adopted in 1966 (5, p. 889) aims to reduce the birth rate from 50 to 40 per thousand by 1970; the Indian plan (6) aims to reduce the rate from 40 to 25 "as soon as possible"; and the Korean aim (7) is to cut population growth from 2.9 to 1.2 percent by 1980. A significant feature of such stated aims is the rapid population growth they would permit. Under conditions of modern mortality, a crude birth rate of 25 to 30 per thousand will represent such a multiplication of people as to make use of the term *population control* ironic. A rate of increase of 1.2 percent per year would allow South Korea's already dense population to double in less than 60 years.

One can of course defend the programs by saying that the present goals and measures are merely interim ones. A start must be made somewhere. But we do not find this answer in the population-policy literature. Such a defense, if convincing, would require a presentation of the *next* steps, and these are not considered. One suspects that the entire question of goals is instinctively left vague because thorough limitation of population growth would run counter to national and group aspirations. A consideration of hypothetical goals throws further light on the matter.

Industrialized nations as the model.

Since current policies are confined to family planning, their maximum demographic effect would be to give the underdeveloped countries the same level of reproductive performance that the industrial nations now have. The latter, long oriented toward family planning, provide a good yardstick for determining what the availability of contraceptives can do to population growth. Indeed, they provide more than a yardstick; they are actually the model which inspired the present population policies.

What does this goal mean in practice? Among the advanced nations there is considerable diversity in the level of fertility (*8*). At one extreme are countries such as New Zealand, with an average gross reproduction rate (GRR) of 1.91 during the period 1960–64; at the other extreme are countries such as Hungary, with a rate of 0.91 during the same period. To a considerable extent, however, such divergencies are matters of timing. The birth rates of most industrial nations have shown, since about 1940, a wavelike movement, with no secular trend. The average level of reproduction during this long period has been high enough to give these countries, with their low mortality, an extremely rapid population growth. If this level is maintained, their population will double in just over 50 years—

a rate higher than that of world population growth at any time prior to 1950, at which time the growth in numbers of human beings was already considered fantastic. The advanced nations are suffering acutely from the effects of rapid population growth in combination with the production of ever more goods per person (*9*). A rising share of their supposedly high per capita income, which itself draws increasingly upon the resources of the underdeveloped countries (who fall farther behind in relative economic position), is spent simply to meet the costs, and alleviate the nuisances, of the unrelenting production of more and more goods by more people. Such facts indicate that the industrial nations provide neither a suitable demographic model for the nonindustrial peoples to follow nor the leadership to plan and organize effective population-control policies for them.

Zero population growth as a goal.

Most discussions of the population crisis lead logically to zero population growth as the ultimate goal, because *any* growth rate, if continued, will eventually use up the earth. Yet hardly ever do arguments for population policy consider such a goal, and current policies do not dream of it. Why not? The answer is evidently that zero population growth is unacceptable to most nations and to most religious and ethnic communities. To argue for this goal would be to alienate possible support for action programs.

Goal peculiarities inherent in family planning.

Turning to the actual measures taken, we see that the very use of family planning as the means for implementing population policy poses serious but unacknowledged limits on the intended reduction in fertility. The family-planning movement, clearly devoted to the improvement and dissemination of contraceptive devices, states again and again that its purpose is that of enabling couples to have the number of children they want. "The opportunity to decide the number and spacing of children is a basic human right," say the 12 heads of state in the United Nations declaration. The 1965 Turkish Law Concerning Population Planning declares (*10*):

Article 1. Population Planning means that individuals can have as many children as they wish, whenever they want to. This can be ensured through preventive measures taken against pregnancy. . . .

Logically, it does not make sense to use *family* planning to provide *national* population control or planning. The "planning" in family planning is that of each separate couple. The only control they exercise is control over the size of *their* family. Obviously, couples do not plan the size of the nation's population, any more than they plan the growth of the national income or the form of the highway network. There is no reason to expect that the millions of decisions about family size made by couples in their own interest will automatically control population for the benefit of society. On the contrary, there are good reasons to think they will not do so. At most, family planning can reduce reproduction to the extent that unwanted births exceed wanted births. In industrial countries the balance is often negative—that is, people have fewer children as a rule than they would like to have. In underdeveloped countries the reverse is normally true, but the elimination of unwanted births would still leave an extremely high rate of multiplication.

Actually, the family-planning movement does not pursue even the limited goals it professes. It does not fully empower couples to have only the number of offspring they want because it either condemns or disregards certain tabooed but nevertheless effective means to this goal. One of its tenets is that "there shall be freedom of choice of method so that individuals can choose in accordance with the dictates of their consciences" (*11*), but in practice this amounts to limiting the individual's choice, because the "conscience" dictating the method is usually not his but that of religious and governmental officials. Moreover, not every individual may choose: even the so-called

recommended methods are ordinarily not offered to single women, or not all offered to women professing a given religious faith.

Thus, despite its emphasis on technology, current policy does not utilize all available means of contraception, much less all birth-control measures. The Indian government wasted valuable years in the early stages of its population-control program by experimenting exclusively with the "rhythm" method, long after this technique had been demonstrated to be one of the least effective. A greater limitation on means is the exclusive emphasis on contraception itself. Induced abortion, for example, is one of the surest means of controlling reproduction, and one that has been proved capable of reducing birth rates rapidly. It seems peculiarly suited to the threshold stage of a population-control program—the stage when new conditions of life first make large families disadvantageous. It was the principal factor in the halving of the Japanese birth rate, a major factor in the declines in birth rate of East-European satellite countries after legalization of abortions in the early 1950's, and an important factor in the reduction of fertility in industrializing nations from 1870 to the 1930's (*12*). Today, according to *Studies in Family Planning* (*13*), "abortion is probably the foremost method of birth control throughout Latin America." Yet this method is rejected in nearly all national and international population-control programs. American foreign aid is used to help *stop* abortion (*14*). The United Nations excludes abortion from family planning, and in fact justifies the latter by presenting it as a means of combating abortion (*15*). Studies of abortion are being made in Latin America under the presumed auspices of population-control groups, not with the intention of legalizing it and thus making it safe, cheap, available, and hence more effective for population control, but with the avowed purpose of reducing it (*16*).

Although few would prefer abortion to efficient contraception (other things being equal), the fact is that both permit a woman to control the size of her family. The main drawbacks to abortion arise from its illegality. When performed, as a legal procedure, by a skilled physician, it is safer than childbirth. It does not compete with contraception but serves as a backstop when the latter fails or when contraceptive devices or information are not available. As contraception becomes customary, the incidence of abortion recedes even without its being banned. If, therefore, abortions enable women to have only the number of children they want, and if family planners do not advocate—in fact decry—legalization of abortion, they are to that extent denying the central tenet of their own movement. The irony of anti-abortionism in family-planning circles is seen particularly in hair-splitting arguments over whether or not some contraceptive agent (for example, the IUD) is in reality an abortifacient. A Mexican leader in family planning writes (*17*):

> One of the chief objectives of our program in Mexico is to prevent abortions. If we could be sure that the mode of action [of the IUD] was not interference with nidation, we could easily use the method in Mexico.

The questions of sterilization and unnatural forms of sexual intercourse usually meet with similar silent treatment or disapproval, although nobody doubts the effectiveness of these measures in avoiding conception. Sterilization has proved popular in Puerto Rico and has had some vogue in India (where the new health minister hopes to make it compulsory for those with a certain number of children), but in both these areas it has been for the most part ignored or condemned by the family-planning movement.

On the side of goals, then, we see that a family-planning orientation limits the aims of current population policy. Despite reference to "population control" and "fertility control," which presumably mean determination of demographic results by and for the nation as a whole, the movement gives control only to couples, and does this only if they use "respectable" contraceptives.

The Neglect of Motivation

By sanctifying the doctrine that each woman should have the number of children she wants, and by assuming that if she has only that number this will automatically curb population growth to the necessary degree, the leaders of current policies escape the necessity of asking why women desire so many children and how this desire can be influenced (*18*, p. 41; *19*). Instead, they claim that satisfactory motivation is shown by the popular desire (shown by opinion surveys in all countries) to have the means of family limitation, and that therefore the problem is one of inventing and distributing the best possible contraceptive devices. Overlooked is the fact that a desire for availability of contraceptives is compatible with *high* fertility.

Given the best of means, there remain the questions of how many children couples want and of whether this is the requisite number from the standpoint of population size. That it is not is indicated by continued rapid population growth in industrial countries, and by the very surveys showing that people want contraception—for these show, too, that people also want numerous children.

The family planners do not ignore motivation. They are forever talking about "attitudes" and "needs." But they pose the issue in terms of the "acceptance" of birth control devices. At the most naive level, they assume that lack of acceptance is a function of the contraceptive device itself. This reduces the motive problem to a technological question. The task of population control then becomes simply the invention of a device that *will* be acceptable (*20*). The plastic IUD is acclaimed because, once in place, it does not depend on repeated *acceptance* by the woman, and thus it "solves" the problem of motivation (*21*).

But suppose a woman does not want to use *any* contraceptive until after she has had four children. This is the type of question that is seldom raised in the family-planning literature. In that literature, wanting a specific number of children is taken as complete motivation, for it implies a wish to control the size of one's family. The problem woman, from the standpoint of family planners, is the one who wants "as many as come," or "as many as God sends." Her attitude is construed as due to ignorance and "cultural values," and the policy deemed necessary to change it is "education." No compulsion can be used, because the movement is committed to free choice, but movie strips, posters, comic books, public lectures, interviews, and discussions are in order. These supply information and supposedly change values by discounting superstitions and showing that unrestrained procreation is harmful to both mother and children. The effort is considered successful when the woman decides she wants only a certain number of children and uses an effective contraceptive.

In viewing negative attitudes toward birth control as due to ignorance, apathy, and outworn tradition, and "mass-communication" as the solution to the motivation problem (*22*), family planners tend to ignore the power and complexity of social life. If it were admitted that the creation and care of new human beings is socially motivated, like other forms of behavior, by being a part of the system of rewards and punishments that is built into human relationships, and thus is bound up with the individual's economic and personal interests, it would be apparent that the social structure and economy must be changed before a deliberate reduction in the birth rate can be achieved. As it is, reliance on family planning allows people to feel that "something is being done about the population problem" without the need for painful social changes.

Designation of population control as a medical or public health task leads to a similar evasion. This categorization assures popular support because it puts population policy in the hands of respected medical personnel, but, by the same token, it gives responsibility for leadership to people who think in terms of clinics and patients, of pills and IUD's, and who bring to the handling

of economic and social phenomena a self-confident naiveté. The study of social organization is a technical field; an action program based on intuition is no more apt to succeed in the control of human beings than it is in the area of bacterial or viral control. Moreover, to alter a social system, by deliberate policy, so as to regulate births in accord with the demands of the collective welfare would require political power, and this is not likely to inhere in public health officials, nurses, midwives, and social workers. To entrust population policy to them is "to take action," but not dangerous "effective action."

Similarly, the Janus-faced position on birth-control technology represents an escape from the necessity, and onus, of grappling with the social and economic determinants of reproductive behavior. On the one side, the rejection or avoidance of religiously tabooed but otherwise effective means of birth prevention enables the family-planning movement to avoid official condemnation. On the other side, an intense preoccupation with contraceptive technology (apart from the tabooed means) also helps the family planners to avoid censure. By implying that the only need is the invention and distribution of effective contraceptive devices, they allay fears, on the part of religious and governmental officials, that fundamental changes in social organization are contemplated. Changes basic enough to affect motivation for having children would be changes in the structure of the family, in the position of women, and in the sexual mores. Far from proposing such radicalism, spokesmen for family planning frequently state their purpose as "protection" of the family—that is, closer observance of family norms. In addition, by concentrating on *new* and *scientific* contraceptives, the movement escapes taboos attached to old ones (the Pope will hardly authorize the condom, but may sanction the pill) and allows family planning to be regarded as a branch of medicine: overpopulation becomes a disease, to be treated by a pill or a coil.

We thus see that the inadequacy of current

population policies with respect to motivation is inherent in their overwhelmingly family-planning character. Since family planning is by definition private planning, it eschews any societal control over motivation. It merely furnishes the means, and, among possible means, only the most respectable. Its leaders, in avoiding social complexities and seeking official favor, are obviously activated not solely by expediency but also by their own sentiments as members of society and by their background as persons attracted to the family-planning movement. Unacquainted for the most part with technical economics, sociology, and demography, they tend honestly and instinctively to believe that something they vaguely call population control can be achieved by making better contraceptives available.

The Evidence of Ineffectiveness

If this characterization is accurate, we can conclude that current programs will not enable a government to control population size. In countries where couples have numerous offspring that they do not want, such programs may possibly accelerate a birth-rate decline that would occur anyway, but the conditions that cause births to be wanted or unwanted are beyond the control of family planning, hence beyond the control of any nation which relies on family planning alone as its population policy.

This conclusion is confirmed by demographic facts. As I have noted above, the widespread use of family planning in industrial countries has not given their governments control over the birth rate. In backward countries today, taken as a whole, birth rates are rising, not falling; in those with population policies, there is no indication that the government is controlling the rate of reproduction. The main "successes" cited in the well-publicized policy literature are cases where a large number of contraceptives have been distributed or where the program has been accompanied by some

decline in the birth rate. Popular enthusiasm for family planning is found mainly in the cities, or in advanced countries such as Japan and Taiwan, where the people would adopt contraception in any case, program or no program. It is difficult to prove that present population policies have even speeded up a lowering of the birth rate (the least that could have been expected), much less that they have provided national "fertility control."

Let us next briefly review the facts concerning the level and trend of population in underdeveloped nations generally, in order to understand the magnitude of the task of genuine control.

Rising Birth Rates in Underdeveloped Countries

In ten Latin-American countries, between 1940 and 1959 (*23*), the average birth rates (age-standardized), as estimated by our research office at the University of California, rose as follows: 1940–44, 43.4 annual births per 1000 population; 1945–49, 44.6; 1950–54, 46.4; 1955–59, 47.7.

In another study made in our office, in which estimating methods derived from the theory of quasi-stable populations were used, the recent trend was found to be upward in 27 underdeveloped countries, downward in six, and unchanged in one (*24*). Some of the rises have been substantial, and most have occurred where the birth rate was already extremely high. For instance, the gross reproduction rate rose in Jamaica from 1.8 per thousand in 1947 to 2.7 in 1960; among the natives of Fiji, from 2.0 in 1951 to 2.4 in 1964; and in Albania, from 3.0 in the period 1950–54 to 3.4 in 1960. The general rise in fertility in backward regions is evidently not due to failure of population-control efforts, because most of the countries either have no such effort or have programs too new to show much effect. Instead, the rise is due, ironically, to the very circumstance that brought on the population crisis in the first place—to improved health and lowered mortality. Better health increases the probability that a woman will conceive and retain the fetus to term; lowered mortality raises the proportion of babies who survive to the age of reproduction and reduces the probability of widowhood during that age (25). The significance of the general rise in fertility, in the context of this discussion, is that it is given would-be population planners a harder task than many of them realize. Some of the upward pressure on birth rates is independent of what couples do about family planning, for it arises from the fact that, with lowered mortality, there are simply more couples.

Underdeveloped Countries with Population Policies

In discussions of population policy there is often confusion as to which cases are relevant. Japan, for instance, has been widely praised for the effectiveness of its measures, but it is a very advanced industrial nation and, besides, its government policy had little or nothing to do with the decline in the birth rate, except unintentionally. It therefore offers no test of population policy under peasant-agrarian conditions. Another case of questionable relevance is that of Taiwan, because Taiwan is sufficiently developed to be placed in the urban-industrial class of nations. However, since Taiwan is offered as the main showpiece by the sponsors of current policies in underdeveloped areas, and since the data are excellent, it merits examination.

Taiwan is acclaimed as a showpiece because it has responded favorably to a highly organized program for distributing up-to-date contraceptives and has also had a rapidly dropping birth rate. Some observers have carelessly attributed the decline in the birth rate—from 50.0 in 1951 to 32.7 in 1965—to the family-planning campaign (26), but the campaign began only in 1963 and could have affected only the end of the trend. Rather, the decline represents a

TABLE 7.1   Decline in Taiwan's fertility rate, 1951 through 1966

YEAR	REGISTERED BIRTHS PER 1000 WOMEN AGED 15–49	CHANGE IN RATE (PERCENT)[1]
1951	211	
1952	198	−5.6
1953	194	−2.2
1954	193	−0.5
1955	197	+2.1
1956	196	−0.4
1957	182	−7.1
1958	185	+1.3
1959	184	−0.1
1960	180	−2.5
1961	177	−1.5
1962	174	−1.5
1963	170	−2.6
1964	162	−4.9
1965	152	−6.0
1966	149	−2.1

[1]The percentages were calculated on unrounded figures. Source of data through 1965, *Taiwan* Demographic Fact Book (1964, 1965); for 1966, *Monthly Bulletin of Population Registration Statistics of Taiwan* (1966, 1967).

response to modernization similar to that made by all countries that have become industrialized (27). By 1950 over half of Taiwan's population was urban, and by 1964 nearly two-thirds were urban, with 29 percent of the population living in cities of 100,000 or more. The pace of economic development has been extremely rapid. Between 1951 and 1963, per capita income increased by 4.05 percent per year. Yet the island is closely packed, having 870 persons per square mile (a population density higher than that of Belgium). The combination of fast economic growth and rapid population increase in limited space has put parents of large families at a relative disadvantage and has created a brisk demand for abortions and contraceptives. Thus the favorable response to the current campaign to encourage use of the IUD is not a good example of what birth-control technology can do for a genuinely backward country. In fact, when the program was started, one reason for expecting receptivity was that the island was already on its way to modernization and family planning (*28*).

At most, the recent family-planning campaign—which reached significant proportions only in 1964, when some 46,000 IUD's were inserted (in 1965 the number was 99,253, and in 1966, 111,242) (*29*; *30*, p. 45) could have caused the increase observable after 1963 in the rate of decline. Between 1951 and 1963 the average drop in the birth rate per 1000 women (see Table 1) was 1.73 percent per year; in the period 1964–66 it was 4.35 percent. But one hesitates to assign all of the acceleration in decline since 1963 to the family-planning campaign. The rapid economic development has been precisely of a type likely to accelerate a drop in reproduction. The rise in manufacturing has been much greater than the rise in either agriculture or construction. The agricultural labor force has thus been squeezed, and migration to the cities has skyrocketed (*31*). Since housing has not kept pace, urban families have had to restrict reproduction in order to take advantage of career opportunities and avoid domestic inconvenience. Such conditions have historically tended to accelerate a decline in birth rate. The most rapid decline came late in the United States (1921–33) and in Japan (1947–55). A plot of the Japanese and Taiwanese birth rates (Fig. 7.1) shows marked similarity of the two curves, despite a difference in level. All told, one should not attribute all of the post-1963 acceleration in the decline of Taiwan's birth rate to the family-planning campaign.

The main evidence that *some* of this acceleration is due to the campaign comes from the fact that Taichung, the city in which the family-planning effort was first concentrated, showed subsequently a much faster drop in fertility than other cities (*30*, p. 69; *32*). But the campaign has not reached throughout the island. By the end of 1966, only 260,745 women had been fitted with an IUD under auspices of the campaign, whereas the women of reproductive age on the island numbered 2.86 million. Most of the reduction in fertility has therefore been a matter of individual initiative. To some

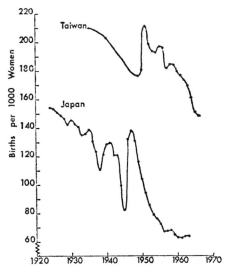

Figure 7.1 Births per 1,000 women aged 15 through 49 in Japan and Taiwan

extent the campaign may be simply substituting sponsored (and cheaper) services for those that would otherwise come through private and commercial channels. An island-wide survey in 1964 showed that over 150,000 women were already using the traditional Ota ring (a metallic intrauterine device popular in Japan); almost as many had been sterilized; about 40,000 were using foam tablets; some 50,000 admitted to having had at least one abortion; and many were using other methods of birth control (*30*, pp. 18, 31).

The important question, however, is not whether the present campaign is somewhat hastening the downward trend in the birth rate but whether, even if it is, it will provide population control for the nation. Actually, the campaign is not designed to provide such control and shows no sign of doing so. It takes for granted existing reproductive goals. Its aim is "to integrate, through education and information, the idea of family limitation *within the existing attitudes, values, and goals* of the people" [*30*, p. 8 (italics mine)]. Its target is *married* women who do not want any more children; it ignores girls not yet married, and women married and wanting more children.

With such an approach, what is the maximum impact possible? It is the difference between the number of children women have been having and the number they want to have. A study in 1957 found a median figure of 3.75 for the number of children wanted by women aged 15 to 29 in Taipei, Taiwan's largest city; the corresponding figure for women from a satellite town was 3.93; for women from a fishing village, 4.90; and for women from a farming village, 5.03. Over 60 percent of the women in Taipei and over 90 percent of those in the farming village wanted 4 or more children (33). In a sample of wives aged 25 to 29 in Taichung, a city of over 300,000, Freedman and his co-workers found the average number of children wanted was 4; only 9 percent wanted less than 3, 20 percent wanted 5 or more (34). If, therefore, Taiwanese women used contraceptives that were 100-percent effective and had the number of children they desire, they would have about 4.5 each. The goal of the family-planning effort would be achieved. In the past the Taiwanese woman who married and lived through the reproductive period had, on the average, approximately 6.5 children; thus a figure of 4.5 would represent a substantial decline in fertility. Since mortality would continue to decline, the population growth rate would decline somewhat less than individual reproduction would. With 4.5 births per woman and a life expectancy of 70 years, the rate of natural increase would be close to 3 percent per year (35).

In the future, Taiwanese views concerning reproduction will doubtless change, in response to social change and economic modernization. But how far will they change? A good indication is the number of children desired by couples in an already modernized country long oriented toward family planning. In the United States in 1966, an average of 3.4 children was considered ideal by white women aged 21 or over (36). This average number of births would give Taiwan, with only a slight decrease in mortality, a long-run rate of natural increase of 1.7 percent per year and a doubling of population in 41 years.

Detailed data confirm the interpretation that Taiwanese women are in the process of shifting from a "peasant-agrarian" to an "industrial" level of reproduction. They are, in typical fashion, cutting off higher-order births at age 30 and beyond (37). Among young wives, fertility has risen, not fallen. In sum, the widely acclaimed family-planning program in Taiwan may, at most, have somewhat speeded the later phase of fertility decline which would have occurred anyway because of modernization.

Moving down the scale of modernization, to countries most in need of population control, one finds the family-planning approach even more inadequate. In South Korea, second only to Taiwan in the frequency with which it is cited as a model of current policy, a recent birth-rate decline of unknown extent is assumed by leaders to be due overwhelmingly to the government's family-planning program. However, it is just as plausible to say that the net effect of government involvement in population control has been, so far, to delay rather than hasten a decline in reproduction made inevitable by social and economic changes. Although the government is advocating vasectomies and providing IUD's and pills, it refuses to legalize abortions, despite the rapid rise in the rate of illegal abortions and despite the fact that, in a recent survey, 72 percent of the people who stated an opinion favored legalization. Also, the program is presented in the context of maternal and child health; it thus emphasizes motherhood and the family rather than alternative roles for women. Much is made of the fact that opinion surveys show an overwhelming majority of Koreans (89 percent in 1965) favoring contraception (38, p. 27), but this means only that Koreans are like other people in wishing to have the means to get what they want. Unfortunately, they want sizable families: "The records indicate that the program appeals mainly to women in the 30–39 year age bracket who have four or more children, including at least two sons . . ." (38, p. 25).

In areas less developed than Korea the

degree of acceptance of contraception tends to be disappointing, especially among the rural majority. Faced with this discouragement, the leaders of current policy, instead of reexamining their assumptions, tend to redouble their effort to find a contraceptive that will appeal to the most illiterate peasant, forgetting that he wants a good-sized family. In the rural Punjab, for example, "a disturbing feature . . . is that the females start to seek advice and adopt family planning techniques at the fag end of their reproductive period" (*39*). Among 5196 women coming to rural Punjabi family-planning centers, 38 percent were over 35 years old, 67 percent over 30. These women had married early, nearly a third of them before the age of 15 (*40*); some 14 percent had eight or more *living* children when they reached the clinic, 51 percent six or more.

A survey in Tunisia showed that 68 percent of the married couples were willing to use birth-control measures, but the average number of children they considered ideal was 4.3 (*41*). The corresponding averages for a village in eastern Java, a village near New Delhi, and a village in Mysore were 4.3, 4.0, and 4.2, respectively (*42, 43*). In the cities of these regions women are more ready to accept birth control and they want fewer children than village women do, but the number they consider desirable is still wholly unsatisfactory from the standpoint of population control. In an urban family-planning center in Tunisia, more than 600 of 900 women accepting contraceptives had four living children already (*44*). In Bangalore, a city of nearly a million at the time (1952), the number of offspring desired by married women was 3.7 on the average; by married men, 4.1 (*43*). In the metropolitan area of San Salvador (350,000 inhabitants) a 1964 survey (*45*) showed the number desired by women of reproductive age to be 3.9, and in seven other capital cities of Latin America the number ranged from 2.7 to 4.2. If women in the cities of underdeveloped countries used birth-control measures with 100-percent efficiency, they still would have enough babies to expand city populations senselessly, quite apart from the added contribution of rural-urban migration. In many of the cities the difference between actual and ideal number of children is not great; for instance, in the seven Latin-American capitals mentioned above, the ideal was 3.4 whereas the actual births per women in the age range 35 to 39 was 3.7 (*46*). Bombay City has had birth-control clinics for many years, yet its birth rate (standardized for age, sex, and marital distribution) is still 34 per 1000 inhabitants and is tending to rise rather than fall. Although this rate is about 13 percent lower than that for India generally, it has been about that much lower since at least 1951 (*47*).

Is Family Planning the "First Step" in Population Control?

To acknowledge that family planning does not achieve population control is not to impugn its value for other purposes. Freeing women from the need to have more children than they want is of great benefit to them and their children and to society at large. My argument is therefore directed not against family-planning programs as such but against the assumption that they are an effective means of controlling population growth.

But what difference does it make? Why not go along for awhile with family planning as an initial approach to the problem of population control? The answer is that any policy on which millions of dollars are being spent should be designed to achieve the goal it purports to achieve. If it is only a first step, it should be so labeled, and its connection with the next step (and the nature of that next step) should be carefully examined. In the present case, since no "next step" seems ever to be mentioned, the question arises, Is reliance on family planning in fact a basis for dangerous postponement of effective steps? To continue to offer a remedy as a cure long after it has been shown merely to ameliorate the disease is either quackery or wishful thinking, and it thrives most where the need is greatest. Today the desire to solve the population problem is so intense that we are all ready to embrace any "action program" that promises relief. But postponement of effective measures allows the situation to worsen.

Unfortunately, the issue is confused by a matter of semantics. "Family *planning*" and "fertility *control*" suggest that reproduction is being regulated according to some rational plan. And so it is, but only from the standpoint of the individual couple, not from that of the community. What is rational in the light of a couple's situation may be totally irrational from the standpoint of society's welfare.

The need for societal regulation of individual behavior is readily recognized in other spheres—those of explosives, dangerous drugs, public property, natural resources. But in the sphere of reproduction, complete individual initiative is generally favored even by those liberal intellectuals who, in other spheres, most favor economic and social planning. Social reformers who would not hesitate to force all owners of rental property to rent to anyone who can pay, or to force all workers in an industry to join a union, balk at any suggestion that couples be permitted to have only a certain number of offspring. Invariably they interpret societal control of reproduction as meaning direct police supervision of individual behavior. Put the word *compulsory* in front of any term describing a means of limiting births— *compulsory sterilization, compulsory abortion, compulsory contraception*—and you guarantee violent opposition. Fortunately, such direct controls need not be invoked, but conservatives and radicals alike overlook this in their blind opposition to the idea of collective determination of a society's birth rate.

That the exclusive emphasis on family planning in current population policies is not a "first step" but an escape from the real issues is suggested by two facts. (i) No country has taken the "next step." The industrialized countries have had family planning for half a century without acquiring control over either the birth rate or population increase. (ii) Support and encouragement of research on population policy other than family planning is negligible. It is precisely this blocking of alternative thinking and experimentation that makes the emphasis on family planning a major obstacle to population control. The need is not to abandon family-planning programs but to put equal or greater resources into other approaches.

New Directions in Population Policy

In thinking about other approaches, one can start with known facts. In the past, all surviving societies had institutional incentives for marriage, procreation, and child care which were powerful enough to keep the birth rate equal to or in excess of a high death rate. Despite the drop in death rates during the last century and a half, the incentives tended to remain intact because the social structure (especially in regard to the family) changed little. At most, particularly in industrial societies, children became less productive and more expensive (*48*). In present-day agrarian societies, where the drop in death rate has been more recent, precipitate, and independent of social change (*49*), motivation for having children has changed little. Here, even more than in industrialized nations, the family has kept on producing abundant offspring, even though only a fraction of these children are now needed.

If excessive population growth is to be prevented, the obvious requirement is somehow to impose restraints on the family. However, because family roles are reinforced by society's system of rewards, punishments, sentiments, and norms, any proposal to demote the family is viewed as a threat by conservatives and liberals alike, and certainly by people with enough social responsibility to work for population control. One is charged with trying to "abolish" the family, but what is required is selective restructuring of the family in relation to the rest of society.

The lines of such restructuring are suggested by two existing limitations on fertility. (i) Nearly all societies succeed in drastically discouraging reproduction among unmarried women. (ii) Advanced societies unintentionally reduce reproduction among married women when conditions worsen in such a way as to penalize childbearing more severely than it was penalized before. In both cases the causes are motivational and economic rather than technological.

It follows that population-control policy can de-emphasize the family in two ways: (i) by keeping present controls over illegitimate childbirth yet making the most of factors that lead people to postpone or avoid marriage, and (ii) by instituting conditions that motivate those who do marry to keep their families small.

Postponement of Marriage

Since the female reproductive span is short and generally more fecund in its first than in its second half, postponement of marriage to ages beyond 20 tends biologically to reduce births. Sociologically, it gives women time to get a better education, acquire interests unrelated to the family, and develop a cautious attitude toward pregnancy (50). Individuals who have not married by the time they are in their late twenties often do not marry at all. For these reasons, for the world as a whole, the average age at marriage for women is negatively associated with the birth rate: a rising age at marriage is a frequent cause of declining fertility during the middle phase of the demographic transition; and, in the late phase, the "baby boom" is usually associated with a return to younger marriages.

Any suggestion that age at marriage be raised as a part of population policy is usually met with the argument that "even if a law were passed, it would not be obeyed." Interestingly, this objection implies that the only way to control the age at marriage is by direct legislation, but other factors govern actual age. Roman Catholic countries generally follow canon law in stipulating 12 years as the minimum *legal* age at which girls may marry, but the actual average age at marriage in this countries (at least in Europe) is characteristically more like 25 to 28 years. The actual age is determined, not by law, but by social and economic conditions. In agrarian societies, postponement of marriage (when postponement occurs) is apparently caused by difficulties in meeting the economic prerequisites for matrimony, as stipulated by custom and opinion. In industrial societies it is caused by housing shortages, unemployment, the requirement for overseas military service, high costs of education, and inadequacy of consumer services. Since almost no research has been devoted to the subject, it is difficult to assess the relative weight of the factors that govern the age at marriage.

Encouraging Limitation of Births within Marriage

As a means of encouraging the limitation of reproduction within marriage, as well as postponement of marriage, a greater rewarding of nonfamilial than of familial roles would probably help. A simple way of accomplishing this would be to allow economic advantages to accrue to the single as opposed to the married individual, and to the small as opposed to the large family. For instance, the government could pay people to permit themselves to be sterilized (51); all costs of abortion could be paid by the government; a substantial fee could be charged for a marriage license; a "child-tax" (52) could be levied; and there could be a requirement that illegitimate pregnancies be aborted. Less sensationally, governments could simply reverse some existing policies that encourage childbearing. They could, for example, cease taxing single persons more than married ones; stop giving parents special tax exemptions; abandon income-tax policy that discriminates against couples when the wife works; reduce paid maternity leaves; reduce family allowances (53); stop awarding public housing on the basis of family size; stop granting fellowships and other educational aids (including special allowances for wives and children) to married students; cease outlawing abortions and sterilizations; and relax rules that allow use of harmless contraceptives only with medical permission. Some of these policy reversals would be beneficial in other than demographic respects and some would be harmful unless special precautions were taken. The aim would be to reduce the number, not the quality, of the next generation.

A closely related method of de-emphasizing the family would be modification of the complementarity of the roles of men and women. Men are now able to participate in the wider world yet enjoy the satisfaction of having several children because the housework and childcare fall mainly on their wives. Women are impelled to seek this role by their idealized view of marriage and motherhood and by either the scarcity of alternative roles or the difficulty of combining them with family roles. To change this situation women could be required to work outside the home, or compelled by circumstances to do so. If, at the same time, women were paid as well as men and given equal educational and occupational opportunities, and if social life were organized around the place of work rather than around the home or neighborhood, many women would develop interests that would compete with family interests. Approximately this policy is now followed in several Communist countries, and even the less developed of these currently have extremely low birth rates (54).

That inclusion of women in the labor force has a negative effect on reproduction is indicated by regional comparisons (18, p. 1195; 55). But in most countries the wife's employment is subordinate, economically and emotionally, to her family role, and is readily sacrificed for the latter. No society has restructured both the occupational system and the domestic establishment to the point of permanently modifying the old division of labor by sex.

In any deliberate effort to control the birth rate along these lines, a government has two powerful instruments—its command over economic planning and its authority (real or potential) over education. The first determines (as far as policy can) the economic conditions and circumstances affecting the lives of all citizens; the second provides the knowledge and attitudes necessary to implement the plans. The economic system largely determines who shall work, what can be bought, what rearing children will cost, how much individuals can spend. The schools define family roles and develop vocational and recreational interests; they could, if it were desired, redefine the sex roles, develop interests that transcend the home, and transmit realistic (as opposed to moralistic) knowledge concerning marriage, sexual behavior, and population problems. When the problem is viewed in this light, it is clear that the ministries of economics and education, not the ministry of health, should be the source of population policy.

The Dilemma of Population Policy

It should now be apparent why, despite strong anxiety over runaway population growth, the actual programs purporting to control it are limited to family planning and are therefore ineffective. (i) The goal of zero, or even slight, population growth is one that nations and groups find difficult to accept. (ii) The measures that would be required to implement such a goal, though not so revolutionary as a Brave New World or a Communist Utopia, nevertheless tend to offend most people reared in existing societies. As a consequence, the goal of so-called population control is implicit and vague; the method is only family planning. This method, far from de-emphasizing the family, is familistic. One of its stated goals is that of helping sterile couples to *have* children. It stresses parental aspirations and responsibilities. It goes along with most aspects of conventional morality, such as condemnation of abortion, disapproval of premarital intercourse, respect for religious teachings and cultural taboos, and obeisance to medical and clerical authority. It deflects hostility by refusing to recommend any change other than the one it stands for: availability of contraceptives.

The things that make family planning acceptable are the very things that make it ineffective for population control. By stressing the right of parents to have the number of children they want, it evades the basic question of population policy, which is how to give societies the number of children they need. By offering only the means for *couples* to control fertility, it neglects the means for societies to do so.

Because of the predominantly pro-family character of existing societies, individual interest ordinarily leads to the production of enough offspring to constitute rapid population growth under conditions of low mortality. Childless or single-child homes are considered indicative of personal failure, whereas having three to five living children gives a family a sense of continuity and substantiality (56).

Given the existing desire to have moderate-sized rather then small families, the only countries in which fertility has been reduced to match reduction in mortality are advanced ones temporarily experiencing worsened economic conditions. In Sweden, for instance, the net reproduction rate (NRR) has been below replacement for 34 years (1930–63), if the period is taken as a whole, but this is because of the economic depression. The average replacement rate was below unity (NRR = 0.81) for the period 1930–42, but from 1942 through 1963 it was above unity (NRR = 1.08). Hardships that seem particularly conducive to deliberate lowering of the birth rate are (in managed economies) scarcity of housing and other consumer goods despite full employment, and required high participation of women in the labor force, or (in freer economies) a great deal of unemployment and economic insecurity. When conditions are good, any nation tends to have a growing population.

It follows that, in countries where contraception is used, a realistic proposal for a government policy of lowering the birth rate reads like a catalogue of horrors: squeeze consumers through taxation and inflation; make housing very scarce by limiting construction; force wives and mothers to work outside the home to offset the inadequacy of male wages, yet provide few childcare facilities; encourage migration to the city by paying low wages in the country and providing few rural jobs; increase congestion in cities by starving the transit system; increase personal insecurity by encouraging conditions that produce unemployment and by haphazard political arrests. No government will institute such hardships simply for the purpose of controlling population growth. Clearly, therefore, the task of contemporary population policy is to develop attractive substitutes for family interests, so as to avoid having to turn to hardship as a corrective. The specific measures required for developing such substitutes are not easy to determine in the absence of research on the question.

In short, the world's population problem cannot be solved by pretense and wishful thinking. The unthinking identification of family planning with population control is an ostrich-like approach in that it permits people to hide from themselves the enormity and unconventionality of the task. There is no reason to abandon family-planning programs; contraception is a valuable technological instrument. But such programs must be supplemented with equal or greater investments in research and experimentation to determine the required socioeconomic measures.

Notes

[1]*Studies in Family Planning, No. 16* (1967).

[2]*Ibid.*, No. 9 (1966), p. 1.

[3]The statement is given in *Studies in Family Planning* (1, p. 1), and in *Population Bull.* **23**, 6 (1967).

[4]The statement is quoted in *Studies in Family Planning* (1, p. 2).

[5]*Hearings on S. 1676, U. S. Senate, Subcommittee on Foreign Aid Expen-* *ditures, 89th Congress, Second Session, April 7, 8, 11* (1966), pt. 4.

[6]B. L. Raina, in *Family Planning and Population Programs*, B. Berelson, R. K. Anderson, O. Harkavy,

G. Maier, W. P. Mauldin, S. G. Segal, Eds. (Univ. of Chicago Press, Chicago, 1966).

[7]D. Kirk, *Ann. Amer. Acad. Polit. Soc. Sci.* 369, 53 (1967).

[8]As used by English-speaking demographers the word *fertility* designates actual reproductive performance, not a theoretical capacity.

[9]K. Davis, *Rotarian* **94**, 10 (1959); *Health Educ. Monographs* **9**, 2 (1960); L. Day and A. Day, *Too Many Americans* (Houghton Mifflin, Boston, 1964); R. A. Piddington *Limits of Mankind* (Wright, Bristol, England, 1956).

[10]*Offical Gazette* (15 Apr. 1965); quoted in *Studies in Family Planning* (*1*, p. 7).

[11]J. W. Gardner, Secretary of Health, Education, and Welfare, "Memorandum to Heads of Operating Agencies" (Jan. 1966), reproduced in *Hearings on S. 1676 (5)*, p. 783.

[12]C. Tietze, *Demography* 1, 119 (1964); *J. Chronic Diseases* 13, 1161 (1964); M. Muramatsu, *Milbank Mem. Fund Quart.* 38, 153 (1960); K. Davis, *Population Index* 29, 345 (1963); R. Armijo and T. Monreal, *J. Sex Res.* **1964**, 143 (1964); Proceedings World Population Conference, Belgrade, 1965; Proceedings International Planned Parenthood Federation.

[13]*Studies in Family Planning, No. 4* (1964), p. 3.

[14]D. Bell (then administrator for Agency for International Development), in *Hearings on S. 1676 (5)*, p. 862.

[15]*Asian Population Conference* (United Nations, New York, 1964), p. 30.

[16]R. Armijo and T. Monreal, in *Components of Population Change in Latin America* (Milbank Fund, New York, 1965), p. 272; E. Rice-Wray, *Amer. J. Public Health* **54**, 313 (1964).

[17]E. Rice-Wray, in "Intra-Uterine Contraceptive Devices," *Excerpta Med. Intern. Congr. Ser. No. 54* (1962), p. 135.

[18]J. Blake, in *Public Health and Population Change*, M. C. Sheps and J. C. Ridley, Eds. (Univ. of Pittsburgh Press, Pittsburgh, 1965).

[19]J. Blake and K. Davis, *Amer. Behavioral Scientist*, 5, 24 (1963).

[20]See "Panel discussion on comparative acceptability of different methods of contraception," in *Research in Family Planning*, C. V. Kiser, Ed. (Princeton Univ. Press, Princeton, 1962), pp. 373–86.

[21]"From the point of view of the women concerned, the whole problem of continuing motivation disappears, . . ." [D. Kirk, in *Population Dynamics*, M. Muramatsu and P. A. Harper, Eds. (Johns Hopkins Press, Baltimore, 1965)].

[22]"For influencing family size norms, certainly the examples and statements of public figures are of great significance . . . also . . . use of mass-communication methods which help to legitimize the small-family style, to provoke conversation, and to establish a vocabulary for discussion of family planning." [M. W. Freymann, in *Population Dynamics*, M. Muramatsu and P. A. Harper, Eds. (John Hopkins Press, Baltimore, 1965)].

[23]O. A. Collver, *Birth Rates in Latin America* (International Population and Urban Research, Berkeley, Calif., 1965), pp. 27–28; the ten countries were Colombia, Costa Rica, El Salvador, Ecuador, Guatemala, Honduras, Mexico, Panama, Peru, and Venezuela.

[24]J. R. Rele, *Fertility Analysis through Extension of Stable Population Concepts*. (International Population and Urban Research, Berkeley, Calif., 1967).

[25]J. C. Ridley, M. C. Sheps, J. W. Lingner, J. A. Menken, *Milbank Mem. Fund Quart.* **45**, 77 (1967); E. Arriaga, unpublished paper.

[26]"South Korea and Taiwan appear successfully to have checked population growth by the use of intra-uterine contraceptive devices" [U. Borell, *Hearings on S. 1676 (5)*, p. 556].

[27]K. Davis, *Population Index* **29**, 345 (1963).

[28]R. Freedman, *ibid.* **31**, 421 (1965).

[29]Before 1964 the Family Planning Association had given advice to fewer than 60,000 wives in 10 years and a Pre-Pregnancy Health Program had reached some 10,000, and, in the current campaign, 3650 IUD's were inserted in 1965, in a total population of 2½ million women of reproductive age. See *Studies in Family Planning, No. 19* (1967), p. 4, and R. Freedman *et al.*, *Population Studies* 16, 231 (1963).

[30]R. W. Gillespie, *Family Planning on Taiwan* (Population Council, Taichung, 1965).

[31]During the period 1950–60 the ratio of growth of the city to growth of the noncity population was 5:3; during the period 1960–64 the ratio was 5:2; these ratios are based on data of Shaohsing Chen, *J. Social Taiwan* 1, 74 (1963) and data in the United Nations *Demographic Yearbooks*.

[32]R. Freedman, *Population Index* 31, 434 (1965). Taichung's rate of decline in 1963–64 was roughly double the average in four other cities, whereas just prior to the campaign its rate of decline had been much less than theirs.

[33]S. H. Chen, *J. Soc. Sci. Taipei* 13, 72 (1963).

[34]R. Freedman *et al.*, *Population Studies* 16, 227 (1963); *ibid.*, p. 232.

[35]In 1964 the life expectancy at birth was already 66 years in Taiwan, as compared to 70 for the United States.

[36]J. Blake, *Eugenics Quart.* 14, 68 (1967).

[37]Women accepting IUD's in the family-planning program are typically 30 to 34 years old and have already had four children. [*Studies in Family Planning No. 19* (1967), p. 5].

[38]Y. K. Cha, in *Family Planning and Population Programs*, B. Berelson *et al.*, Eds. (Univ. of Chicago Press, Chicago. 1966).

[39]H. S. Ayalvi and S. S. Johl, *J. Family Welfare* 12, 60 (1965).

[40]Sixty percent of the women had borne their first child before age 19. Early marriage is strongly supported by public opinion. Of couples polled in the Punjab, 48 percent said that girls *should* marry before age 16, and 94 percent said they should marry before age 20 (H. S. Ayalvi and S. S. Johl, *ibid.*, p. 57). A study of 2380 couples in 60 villages of Uttar Pradesh found that the women had consummated their marriage at an average age of 14.6 years [J. R. Rele, *Population Studies* 15, 268 (1962)].

[41]J. Morsa, in *Family Planning and Population Programs*, B. Berelson *et al.*, Eds. (Univ. of Chicago Press, Chicago, 1966).

[42]H. Gille and R. J. Pardoko, *ibid.*, p. 515; S. N. Agarwala, *Med. Dig. Bombay* 4, 653 (1961).

[43]*Mysore Population Study* (United Nations, New York. 1961), p. 140.

[44]A. Daly, in *Family Planning and Population Programs*, B. Berelson *et al.*, Eds. (Univ. of Chicago Press, Chicago, 1966).

[45]C. J. Goméz, paper presented at the World Population Conference, Belgrade, 1965.

[46]C. Miro, in *Family Planning and Population Programs*, B. Berelson *et al.*, Eds. (Univ. of Chicago Press, Chicago, 1966).

[47]*Demographic Training and Re-*

search Centre (India) Newsletter
20, 4 (Aug. 1966).
[48]K. Davis, *Population Index* **29**,
345 (1963). For economic and
sociological theory of motivation
for having children, see J. Blake
[Univ. of California (Berkeley)],
in preparation.
[49]K. Davis, *Amer. Economic Rev.*
46, 305 (1956); *Sci. Amer.* **209**, 68
(1963).
[50]J. Blake, *World Population Conference [Belgrade, 1965]* (United
Nations, New York, 1967), vol.
2, pp. 132–36.
[51]S. Enke, *Rev. Economics Statistics*

42, 175 (1960); ——, *Econ.
Develop. Cult. Change* 8, 339 (1960);
——, *ibid.* **10**, 427 (1962); A. O.
Krueger and L. A. Sjaastad, *ibid.*,
p. 423.
[52]T. J. Samuel, *J. Family Welfare
India* **13**, 12 (1966).
[53]Sixty-two countries, including 27
in Europe, give cash payments to
people for having children [U.S.
Social Security Administration,
*Social Security Programs Through-
out the World, 1967* (Government
Printing Office, Washington, D.C.,
1967), pp. xxvii-xxviii].
[54]Average gross reproduction rates

in the early 1960's were as follows:
Hungary, 0.91; Bulgaria, 1.09;
Romania, 1.15; Yugoslavia, 1.32.
[55]O. A. Collver and E. Langlois,
Econ. Develop. Cult. Change **10**,
367 (1962); J. Weeks, [Univ. of
California (Berkeley)], unpublished
paper.
[56]Roman Catholic textbooks con-
demn the "small" family (one with
fewer than four children) as being
abnormal [J. Blake, *Population
Studies* **20**, 27 (1966)].
[57]Judith Blake's critical readings
and discussions have greatly helped
in the preparation of this article.

A SELECTED SUPPLEMENTARY BIBLIOGRAPHY FOR PART 2

Aird, J. S., "Population Policy in Mainland China,"
Population Studies, Vol. 16, 1962, pp. 38–57.

Bogue, D. J., "The End of the Population Explosion,"
The Public Interest, No. 7, 1967, pp. 11–20.

Boulding, K. E., "The Malthusian Model as a General System," *Social and Economic Studies*, Vol.
4, 1955, pp. 195–205.

Brown, H., *The Challenge of Man's Future.* New
York: The Viking Press, 1954.

Coontz, S. H., *Population Theories and the Economic
Interpretation.* London: Routledge and Paul, 1957.

Davis, K., "The World Demographic Transition,"
*Annals of the American Academy of Political and
Social Science*, Vol. 237, 1945, pp. 1–11.

Deane, P., and Cole, W. A., *British Economic Growth
1688–1959.* Cambridge: Cambridge University
Press, 1967.

Deevey, E. S., "The Human Population," *Scientific
American*, Vol. 203, 1960, pp. 195–204.

Eldridge, H. T., *Population Policies: A Survey of
Recent Developments.* Washington, D.C.: The

Committee on Investigation of Population Policies,
The International Union for the Scientific Study
of population, 1954.

Enke, S., "Government Bonuses for Smaller Families,"
Population Review (Madras), Vol. 4, 1960, pp.
47–54.

Jefferson, M., "Looking Back at Malthus," *Geographical Review*, Vol. 15, 1925, pp. 177–189.

Spengler, J. J., and Duncan, O. D. (eds.), *Population
Theory and Policy: Selected Readings.* New York:
The Free Press of Glencoe, 1956.

Stangeland, C. E., *Pre-Malthusian Doctrine of Population: A Study in the History of Economic Theory.*
New York: Columbia University Press, 1904.

Thompson, W. S., "The Spiral of Population," W. L.
Thomas, Jr. (ed.), *Man's Role in Changing the
Face of the Earth.* Chicago: The University of
Chicago Press, 1956, pp. 970–985.

Woytinsky, W. S., and Woytinsky, E. S., *World
Population and Production; Trends and Outlook.*
New York: Twentieth Century Fund, 1953.

PART THREE

POPULATION DATA ANALYSIS AND TRANSFORMATION

INTRODUCTION

This section is primarily concerned with techniques of data transformation and data analysis and is purposely placed among the early sections of the reader so that its importance will not be diminished. It should also be noted that there has been no selection included which covers cartographic representation or transformation of population data specifically, inasmuch as there are a number of excellent and readily accessible sources on cartographic techniques.* The major emphasis in these articles is on the use of mathematical concepts and application of quantitative techniques in population study. The value of such concepts and techniques no longer requires any defense in the light of their contribution to social science research in the recent past.

The first selection by Robinson and Bryson ("A Method of Describing Quantitatively the Correspondence of Geographical Distributions") addresses itself to the question of describing and mapping areal

---

*For example, see L. E. Tavener, "Population Maps: Problems and Methods of Demographic Cartography," *Genus* (Comitato Italians Per Lo Studio Del Problemi Della Populazione), 1956, pp. 88–101; F. J. Monkhouse and H. R. Wilkinson, "Population Maps and Diagrams" in *Maps and Diagrams* (London: Methuen, 1952), pp. 217–280.

associations with precision. The use of the correlation coefficient in correlation analysis is found to be of limited value when dealing with spatial problems inasmuch as it is the departures or residuals from correspondence that are significant. Density of rural farm population and the average annual precipitation of Nebraska are the two variables chosen to exemplify the problems of (1) relating variables which have a different range of values and (2) the seeming incomparability of concepts (precipitation and population). Population is regressed on precipitation and the resultant residuals or departures of each areal unit are mapped producing a pattern of *abnormalities* which may suggest other hypotheses for testing. Another procedure is suggested for examining correspondence between two distributions which involves the use of orthogonal polynomials in curvilinear regressions.

Anderson's study ("Potential Models and the Spatial Distribution of Population") has as its focus a statistical explanation of variation in population density. The analysis can be divided into three parts. The first is a theoretical discussion concerned with describing density variations via mathematical functions. Secondly, the analysis utilizes a resource potential model which attempts to describe relative density as a function of resource surplus in an area or areas. The approach used is similar to that of the familiar gravity model. In the subsequent step, a population potential model is designed where the independent variable becomes the population size of a given unit. The interpretation in this case stems from the fact that distance is significant in determining where people will live relative to others with whom they interact.

Stewart and Warntz ("Physics of Population Distribution"), in a highly quantitative study, employ some of the concepts of social physics in the study of population distribution and density. Such notions as *adhesion*, *cohesion*, and *demographic gravitation* are defined and used in analyses of urban and rural population patterns. Again, the value

of gravity models and the importance of distance in contemporary social systems are stressed.

Rogers ("Matrix Methods of Population Analysis"), in an elegantly succinct article, demonstrates the unique value of concepts from matrix algebra in population study. Matrix methods are applied to migration data and used to show the impact of mortality and fertility on population change. A distinct spatial application of matrix methods is illustrated by an interregional model of population growth which incorporates fertility, mortality, and migration and their effect on an age-disaggregated population changing through time.

The final article in this section ("Applications of Mathematics to Population Geography") by a young Soviet geographer, Yuriy Medvedkov, is a more general discussion of the value of quantitative techniques in population geography. Three levels of complexity in the applications of such techniques are discerned. The first level focuses on problems of quantity or the problem of precise expression of information, and questions of data reliability, variability of magnitudes, and data comparability are examined. The second level in the hierarchy is concerned with the search for empirical relationships and their expression as mathematical functions or formulas which allow greater precision and comparability than verbal or usual cartographic techniques. Medvedkov's third and most complex level relates to causal relationships in the search for explanation via deductive, theoretical means.

The selection of articles in this section is but a sample of the use of some exciting and innovative tools in the study of spatial problems of population. As a sample it is intended as a stimulant rather than as an expository collection of *how to do* statements. It is similarly important to note Medvedkov's caution that the use of mathematics to create new and particular methods is *not* the main objective; rather, it is a tool in formulating theory.

A METHOD FOR DESCRIBING QUANTITATIVELY THE CORRESPONDENCE OF GEOGRAPHICAL DISTRIBUTIONS[1]

Arthur H. Robinson and Reid A. Bryson

The Problem of Cartographic Correlation

The subject to be considered in this paper is the development of a logically sound and easily applied method by means of which one may quantitatively describe and map, for an area, the manner in which the continuous variations within one class of phenomena correspond to the variations within another class. Nothing is more fundamental in geographical research than the recognition and description of similarities and differences in cultural and physical behavior from place to place. Although this concept of spatial association is central to the science of geography, the techniques presently employed to recognize and describe such relationships are often somewhat less than rigorous. A recent monograph clearly states the problem and the need for methods to solve it:

It seems clear that geographic investigation is concerned with discovering and describing areal variations in the occurrence of phenomena on the earth's surface, and also with the search for other areally associated factors that may help to explain the observed distributions. In all such cases, questions are bound to arise as to the degree of association that exists between two (or more) phenomena. Areal association is indicated when a variation from place to place in the occurrence of one variable is accompanied by a similar place-to-place variation in the occurrence of another.

In geographic research, areal associations in the occurrence of related phenom-

ena (such as wheat yields and rainfall) have often been discovered by comparing maps of the distributions of those phenomena; and the resulting generalizations have usually taken a form such as, "In this region, there is a tendency for wheat yields to decrease as rainfall decreases." Vague generalizations such as these leave much to be desired, but they have been extremely useful in teaching and explaining areal variations in land-use patterns. Many associations, however, are not so clearly discernible as the wheat-rainfall association to which we have just referred. In those situations in which associations are less clearly defined, it has often been difficult to secure agreement even among competent professional geographers as to the degree, or even the existence, of such associations. Under these circumstances, it is impossible to escape the conclusion that these types of generalizations would have more value if they could be quantified. If some objective, quantified measure of association could be applied that would make such expressions as "slight tendency" or "strong tendency" more precise, it appears that the advancement of geographic analysis would be expedited materially.[2]

A number of geographical studies have employed ordinary statistical procedures to describe the association that exists between the attributes of a series of individuals. For example, the individuals may be years and the attributes rainfall and corn yield at a given place. By pairing the attributes one can calculate the ordinary correlation coefficient, which is a kind of index of the degree of average correspondence in the time change of the two variables for the

Reproduced by permission from the *Annals of the Association of American Geographers*, Vol. 47, 1957, pp. 379–391.

particular years in question. The relationship can also be described by a regression equation which expresses how the two series have covaried through *time;* that is, one can conclude, all other factors remaining constant, that, on the average, given so much rainfall one could expect so much corn. The areal distribution of correlation coefficients over area may also be instructive, as has been shown by several studies. Rose has suggested the use of the term "isocorrelates" for the isopleths employed to describe the pattern.[3] Foster correlated annual rainfall at Omaha with 27 other stations within about 500 miles.[4] Stidd plotted the correlation of Tennessee Valley rainfall with meteorological variables at a number of points in the United States.[5] The resulting charts show surprisingly smooth patterns of variation which suggests that even correlations which are too small to be statistically "significant" nevertheless may play an important role in determining a *pattern* of correlation.

The problem becomes somewhat different when the individuals become *place* instead of time. Here also there have been some previous studies. Fisher illustrates the use of regression equations in a problem having to do with rainfall, position, and altitude.[6] Brooks and Carruthers refer to some of the problems involved in the correlation of spatial factors.[7] Earlier, Mowrer calculated the coefficient of correlation of two distributions over area by measuring the areas of paired superimposed isopleths and used the resulting readings as frequencies.[8] It should be noted that his purpose was only to test whether the isopleth map was a reasonably faithful description of a distribution. He did this by comparing the coefficient arrived at with one derived from unmapped data, and he went on to suggest that such an isopleth map would be useful for "graphic correlation," i.e. visual comparison.

Naturally when one is comparing two distributions he would like a descriptive measure of the degree of similarity in the variations from place to place of the two distributions; for this the ordinary correlation

coefficient may be employed, as indicated above. In such an instance, however, the concern is with changes in two dimensions (space) instead of only one (time), and consequently the single summary index does not reveal anything about the *areal distribution* of the correspondence. In addition, therefore, one would like somehow to *map* the spatial covariation so that relative departures from correspondence may also be located. It is the relative amount and direction of this, at different points on the map, that one wishes to know. This may well be more significant in geographical research than merely a summary index of the degree of correlation. Insofar as is known, mention of attempts to solve this particular aspect of the geographer's fundamental problem of spatial correlation has not appeared in the geographical literature until recently.[9]

Some Basic Concepts and Assumptions

The proposed method will be illustrated by using two representative continuous distributions and the isoline maps prepared from them as examples to be compared. Before describing the method, however, it will be necessary to review briefly the general concept of the isoline, since the numerical and spatial assumptions on which such maps are based are of some importance in the method of comparison here suggested. It will also be helpful for the reader to think in terms of simple three-dimensional space. Any position in earthly space can be located with reference to three coordinates: the ordinary x and y coordinates of the horizontal "plane" and the z coordinate perpendicular to the horizontal. For example, any point on the irregular surface of the earth can be expressed in terms of its longitude (x), its latitude (y), and its elevation above some datum (z). Contours result from passing planes of given z values through the surface parallel to both x and y. A number of other familiar derivatives are computed from the three coordinate values. For example, land slope or gradient is the rate of change of z

with change in x and y; if z is made atmospheric temperature or pressure instead of elevation, temperature or pressure gradients may be computed, and so on.

Isopleths and isarithms, although well known, are not commonly thought of as the "contours" which describe the topography of an *assumed* three-dimensional surface. This surface is developed as follows: One first plots at selected x and y locations on a map some numbers, for example, population density. Then, in theory, there is erected at each location, i.e., control point, a vertical column proportional in height to the number, the z coordinate, according to some scale, e.g., persons per square mile. Next, still in theory, the spaces between the columns are filled and a continuous z surface is created, ordinarily by linear interpolation. The resulting "statistical surface" is theoretically the same as the surface of a topographic model.[10] It differs, however, in one fundamental respect, namely, that the z values (the vertical scale) have no relation whatever with the x and y values; they are numbers which represent population density and therefore have no natural dimensional reality. Herein lies one element of the problem: there is, at present, no way in terms of the x and y relationships of the earth surface to describe the magnitude of the ups and downs of the z surface, since both the "elevations" of points and the "slopes" between points are derived from an entirely arbitrary dimensional scale and bear no relation to horizontal distance. A series of horizontal planes passed through such a statistical surface provide isarithms or "contours."[11] It is important also to realize that the vertical, or z, scale of the statistical surface or model can be changed without changing the x and y positions of its isarithms; all that is necessary is that the chosen isarithmic values bear a constant relationship to whatever z scale is used.[12] It is this fact that makes it possible to compare two isarithmic maps (regardless of the kinds of numbers involved in their construction) when the vertical scale of one distribution is transformed in a way that makes it comparable with the vertical scale of the other.

If a second statistical surface formed from other data were prepared for the same area, e.g., average annual precipitation, it could vary from exact correspondence with the first surface (complete positive correlation) through various degrees of similarity or dissimilarity to an exact mirror image surface (complete negative correlation). High positive correlation would show many high spots on the one surface to be high on the other. High negative correlation would mean the reverse, i.e., many of the high spots on one would be low spots on the other.

If the two surfaces were formed of thin plastic and their vertical scales somehow brought into accord, then if they were perfectly correlated positively they would fit snugly on top of one another; if negatively, the mirror image of one would fit the other. Since the degree of coincidence between two such surfaces would rarely reach perfection, the problem is to locate, to express in quantitative terms, and to symbolize in some fashion the areas where the two surfaces do and do not "fit" one another. Such an analysis of the relation between the two surfaces would present the geographer with what might be called ready-made hypotheses to be tested—and with many questions: What accounts for the demonstrated coincidence? Is it a cause-and-effect relationship or are the two variables dependent upon still another to which they both react? What different factors are involved in different areas? The list of such questions is long and aims at the heart of the geographers' problem—the explanation of, and the recognition of the principles involved in, differences from place to place.

It is possible to measure and map the relationship between two such statistical surfaces. The procedure involves merely a combination of well-known and easily applied cartographic and statistical processes. The general method may be applied in several ways and with different scales of detail.

The General Method of Cartographic Correlation

For the purpose of illustrating the method and the procedures involved in applying it to a particular problem, the following two distributions for the state of Nebraska are employed:

1   Figure 8.1 (top). *Density of Rural Farm Population*. The values were computed from county data in the *1950 United States Census of Population*. Values were rounded off to the nearest whole number, control points were located near the centers of the counties, and the isopleths were interpolated linearly to an interval of two persons per square mile. In the subsequent discussion, values of persons per square mile derived from this map will be designated as D (density).
2   Figure 8.1 (bottom). *Average Annual Precipitation*, from *Climate and Man*, 1941 Yearbook of Agriculture. The isohyets are those on the map on p. 977. In the subsequent discussion, values of inches derived from this map will be designated as P (precipitation).

When the two maps are compared visually it will be seen that population density decreases westward as precipitation decreases. Also apparent are what seem to be departures from this general relationship, as for example in far western Nebraska in the Scotts Bluff area. To describe the general relationship in any quantitative terms, or to map the distribution of varying degrees of correspondence between the two maps would, however, be impossible from visual inspection alone. The major problems involved in a quantitative comparison of the maps derived from the two sets of data are the facts that (1) the two variables, P and D, are in different ranges of numbers, and (2) the numbers refer to seemingly incomparable concepts: persons per square mile on the one hand and inches of precipitation on the other.

In order to illustrate the first of these difficulties Figure 8.2 has been prepared. A regular grid has been placed over the map,

and at each intersection of the grid the z values of the continuous surfaces of D (density) and of P (precipitation) have been determined by interpolation. Since the x and y position of each D and P value at a point is identical, any concern with their comparability in those two dimensions is removed. Each north-south column of grid values for each distribution has been separately averaged, and these column averages have been plotted on the graph at the top and joined with straight lines. The ordinates extend far enough to include both ranges of z values, and the abscissas are simply evenly-spaced x positions (east-west). The sole purpose of these two crude "average east-west profiles" is to illustrate the problem which arises because two different scales of measurement are employed.

In order to measure the relationship between two variables expressed as numbers it is rather obviously necessary that the two scales be made comparable. This can be done in two ways: (1) by expressing both series in terms independent of the scales of measurement used for either one, or (2) by transforming one series to the scale used for the other. The first of these transformations is called normalizing the data. It is accomplished by expressing each number of one series as a departure from the mean of the series and then dividing each departure by the standard deviation of the series. In symbolic terms any given z value of density (D) is transformed to a normalized value (D_n) by $D_n = (D - \bar{D})/\sigma_d$, in which $\bar{D}$ is the mean of D and σ_d is the standard deviation of D. The same is then done for the other scale.[13] The numbers of the normalized scale will bear the same relationship to one another that they did before normalizing. Unfortunately, however, the numbers of a normalized series, being merely numbers expressing departures from the mean in units of the standard deviation, do not have any obvious meaning in terms of the original quantities. This inconvenience can be obviated, and essentially the same result can be accomplished by expressing one series in terms of the other. This will illustrate the

NEBRASKA

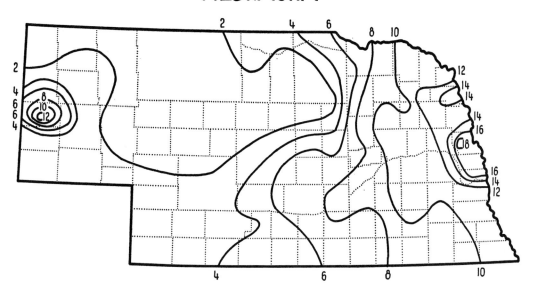

RURAL FARM POPULATION
PERSONS PER SQUARE MILE 1950

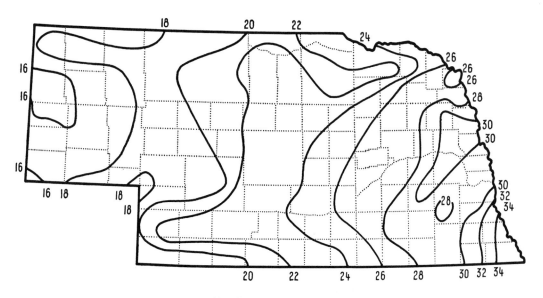

AVERAGE ANNUAL PRECIPITATION
INCHES

Figure 8.1 The two maps upon which the demonstration of the method is based. The precipitation map was copied from *Climate and Man;* the population map was prepared from county data in the 1950 U.S. census.

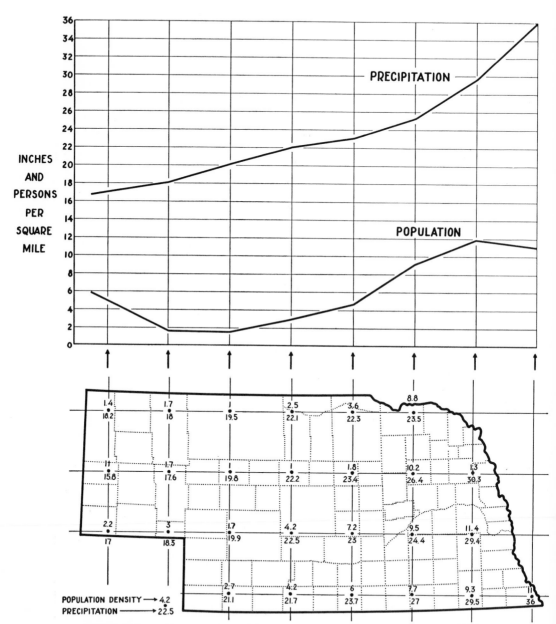

DIAGRAMMATIC E-W PROFILES OF NEBRASKA'S FARM POPULATION
DENSITY AND ANNUAL PRECIPITATION FROM AVERAGES OF N-S GRID VALUES

Figure 8.2 Each grid-point pair of values (average annual precipitation above, and rural farm population density below) on the bottom map is derived by interpolation from the two maps in Figure 8.1. Each north-south column of grid-point values on the map is averaged and these averages are plotted on the graph at the top; the lines which result when these averages are joined may be considered as generalized east-west "profiles."

process more clearly, and it has the further advantage of retaining the numbers in a meaningful form. How this may be done will be explained below.

Assuming, for the moment, that both the *D* and *P* scales have been made comparable by normalizing the numbers of which they are composed, the two series cannot yet be compared properly unless the relationship between them is known. One should not employ simple averages. For example, it is clear even from visual inspection that as the average annual precipitation decreases westward across Nebraska there is, in some degree, a corresponding decrease in population density. To map departures merely from the state mean for each series and then to compare the values at various points with these state averages would likely result in relatively meaningless numbers. The reason for this can be easily illustrated by turning our attention to eastern Nebraska where both annual precipitation and population density are above average; but by how much requires calculation. The average rural farm population density in Nebraska is approximately 5 persons per square mile and the average annual precipitation is about 22 inches. Saunders County in central eastern Nebraska has 11 rural persons per square mile and annually receives about 26 inches of precipitation. Therefore, it exceeds the state averages by 6 persons per square mile and 4 inches of annual precipitation, or, to state it another way, it exceeds the averages of population and precipitation by the seemingly rather large amounts of 120 percent and 18 percent, respectively. No matter how these numbers may be manipulated they do not tell us much of anything, for they do not take into account the obvious fact that as precipitation increases so does population. Instead, the significant fact against which we would like to compare Saunders County is the rate at which population changes with change in precipitation in Nebraska. It may turn out that Saunders County, in spite of its impressive population of 120 percent above the state average, is actually not far from what could be expected considering the change in precipitation amount. Instead, then, it is necessary to derive and describe in some reasonable fashion the *relationship* between the two distributions, and then express the comparisons of different places as departures from this relationship. In other words, how do the variations in population correspond to the variations in precipitation?

For this the regression of population on precipitation may be employed. Figure 8.3 shows a scatter diagram of the original values of the paired *P* and *D* values obtained from each of the intersections of the grid employed in Figure 8.2. These are plotted on a graph with a *Y* axis of population and an *X* axis of precipitation. The straight line of best fit shows the linear relationship between the two series of numbers. This is an ordinary regression line whose position and slope may be expressed by the general linear equation $Y = a + bX$. In a linear regression equation the coefficient *a* is the *Y* intercept of the line and *b* is the slope. The values of *a* and *b* are calculated from the paired *X* and *Y* values, obtained in this case from the 26 grid intersections in Figure 8.2, i.e., $X = P$ and $Y = D$.[14]

The function of the regression equation is illustrated in the graph above the scatter diagram of Figure 8.3. On this graph the two solid lines are the same as those in Figure 8.2, but there has been added a dashed line. This is the original precipitation profile, which appears at the top, expressed with a different vertical scale. It has been adjusted by means of the regression equation so that the series of 26 average annual precipitation values now has the same mean and standard deviation as the series of population density values. The regression equation has merely been entered with actual *P* values to give comparable population values (D_c), i.e., $D_c = -7.939 + 0.5826P$ (the subscript *c* in D_c stands for "computed"). Thus, for example, according to the relationship derived from this sample, we may "expect" a place in Nebraska that has 20 inches of average annual precipitation to have a rural farm population density of 3.7 persons per square mile ($-7.939 + 0.5826 \times 20 = 3.7$).

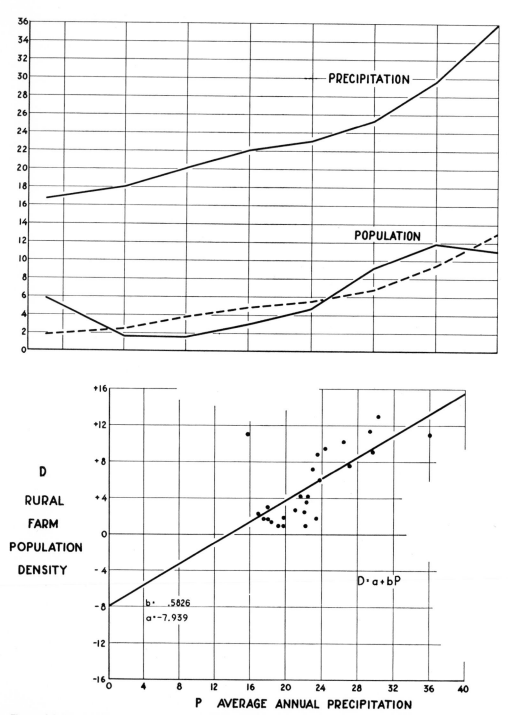

Figure 8.3 The scatter diagram at the bottom shows the covariation among the values of average annual precipitation and population density at the grid points shown on the map in Figure 8.2. Using the constants of the regression of population on rainfall, the east-west "profile" of actual precipitation on the graph at the top (same graph as in Figure 8.2) has been made comparable by converting the precipitation values to equivalent population values; the result is symbolized by the dashed line.

Actually what has been done is to combine the processes of (1) normalizing the scales and (2) deriving the relation between them. The original (actual) population "profile" and the adjusted (computed) precipitation "profile," stated in equivalent persons per square mile, can now be compared since they are expressed in the same numerical terms.

In similar fashion the isarithms of the original precipitation map can be given new z values by using the regression equation. The isarithms retain their original x and y positions on the map; only their numbering changes. In effect we now have *two* population density maps. One is the actual distribution of population in Nebraska, while the other shows what the population distribution would be if it were entirely dependent upon the distribution of average annual precipitation as defined by the average relation (the linear regression) between the two computed from the values estimated at the grid points.

The next step is to apply the relationship

that has been derived. This is done by comparing the two population maps, i.e., the renumbered precipitation map and the original population map. In other words, the "relief" of each of the two statistical surfaces is to be compared. If the correspondence of the population and precipitation distributions were perfect the two surfaces would coincide. The correlation is not perfect, but about 0.8; so in some places the two surfaces will depart from one another. The differences between them are measured on a vertical scale which is, in this instance, expressed as persons per square mile. When the plus or minus departures $(D - D_c)$ of the actual population density surface (D) from the "precipitation–population" surface (D_c) as indicated at the sample points are plotted, isopleths of departures from correspondence can be drawn.

Figure 8.4 is the map that results from the comparison; the white areas are the regions of greatest correspondence, i.e., the darker the shading the less is the correspondence

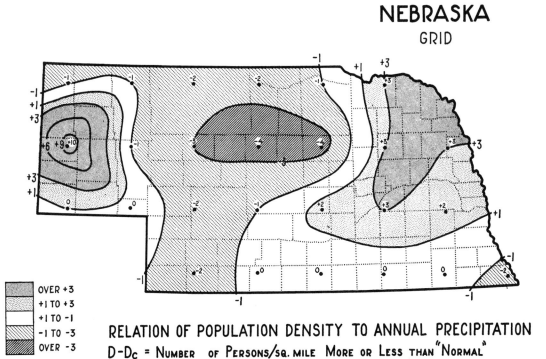

RELATION OF POPULATION DENSITY TO ANNUAL PRECIPITATION

$D - D_c$ = NUMBER OF PERSONS/SQ. MILE MORE OR LESS THAN "NORMAL"

"NORMAL IS $D = -7.939 + .5826P$

Figure 8.4 A map of the degree to which the two maps of Figure 8.1 (average annual precipitation and rural farm population density) correspond to one another, based only on the values at the sample grid points.

between the two original maps.[15] The Scotts Bluff area in western Nebraska shows a marked plus value, that is, the population surface rises well above the precipitation surface. The central area is a minus region, as is the extreme southeastern corner of the state. In the northeastern section the population surface again rises above the precipitation surface. Although this particular map is relatively crude it is nonetheless interesting. One immediately begins to speculate as to what other factors are associated with the more significant divergences. Such elements as distance from Sioux City and Omaha, soil or drainage characteristics of the Sand Hills, and the extent of irrigation pop up as possible factors, to be used as variables in a further analysis.

Sources of Error in the Method

The science of geography is plagued by the fact that its investigations are concerned with phenomena containing an enormous number of constantly changing variables, many of which are incapable of very precise observation. Furthermore, many of its basic techniques of cartographic notation require assumptions which turn its maps into what amount to generalized distributions of concepts. The two distributions here employed are representative examples. A map of average annual precipitation is subject to a large number of possible errors, including such things as bias, instrumental errors, variable length of record, etc.[16] The assumptions and kinds of errors inherent in the concept of population density and its computation are even more frightening, as is clear from the literature. All maps are subject to more or less error, especially isarithmic maps. Statistical techniques are also based upon various assumptions, e.g., normality, to name only one, which in given situations may possibly operate further to decrease the precision of results. To catalog all the *possibilities* of error inherent in this method would be out of order; most of them are already available in the cartographic and statistical literature. It is merely necessary to recognize that the usual sources of error are also present in this method.

A further observation is, however, in order here lest one infer more from the results of this method of comparison than is warranted, even assuming no error. The correlation coefficient (r) computed for the state as a whole from the paired sample values is about 0.8. From this it may be inferred that over 60 percent of the variations in population density can be accounted for (statistically) by the variations in average annual precipitation. Consequently, there may be a tendency to conclude that the plus or minus regions on the map are the only areas where other factors in addition to precipitation are involved. This is quite incorrect, since in such a complex thing as population density many other factors are no doubt involved in many ways in many places. A regression equation (and a correlation coefficient) are ways of describing the relation between two series of numbers; they *explain* nothing. Secondly, and of vital importance, it should be remembered that the regression of population density on precipitation is a relationship derived for the state *as a whole*, assuming the sample values to be representative.

The above cautionary comments should not be construed to mean that the map of the comparison between the maps of population density and average annual precipitation has no value. On the contrary, the map is a scientific generalization which in quantitative terms describes the manner in which the two original maps correspond to one another using the linear regression between them as a point of departure. The pattern and the direction (positive or negative) of discordance are facts every bit as good as the assumptions and the data on which they are based. It is simply necessary to keep in mind that all scientific generalizations are based upon assumptions and observations, and are subject to more or less error. When derived rigorously in proper scientific fashion the possible sources of error in the procedure can be recognized, and stated, if not well known.

Application of the Method without Mapping

The preceding example of the method started with two general maps and then employed a quick form of sampling to arrive at a small number of paired observations. This was done, not only to illustrate more easily the method through the use of "average east–west profiles" but also to test its applicability to studies wherein a *more* careful analysis was not desired. The procedures and the mathematics are quite elementary and the entire operation, starting with the two isarithmic maps, required only a few hours. Such a rough and quick approximation or test will be useful in many instances.

A more detailed and thorough comparison of two such distributions introduces a number of problems. Certainly, to prepare detailed maps and to change the nature of the sample so that the results will be subject to less error is not an efficient process when the values from which the maps are to be made are readily available. Stated in statistical terms, it would be foolish to go to the trouble of sampling a universe when it would be easier to work with the universe values themselves. Essentially the same procedure may be followed. One does, however, encounter the problem that the county values relate to areas of different size, and consequently computations to find the regression of population on precipitation must take into account these discrepancies. This problem was solved and the results, of general interest in several connections, were reported earlier in the *Annals*.[17]

The 93 counties of Nebraska were employed as individuals and the average rural farm population density of each was paired with the average annual precipitation of the county.[18] Taking into account the discrepancies in county sizes, the regression of population on precipitation was calculated. The relationship of $D - D_c$ was obtained for each county, and the plotted values together with isopleths of departures from correspondence are shown on Figure 8.5; the scatter diagram is shown at the bottom. A more detailed map results which must be considered better than the one which resulted from the small sample.

The Orthogonal Polynomial Method

Another method of arriving at the correlation between two areal distributions is to be found in the use of orthogonal polynomials.

In the preceding discussion the equation of a straight line of best fit (linear regression) was used to describe the statistical relation between average annual precipitation and rural farm population density. This idea may be applied to the example in Figure 8.2 to introduce the concept of the polynomial approach. The regression of *average precipitation* against *east–west position* in the state of Nebraska could readily be computed from the data used to construct the "average east–west profiles" in the graph at the top of Figure 8.2. The average values of P (computed from the columns of grid point estimates) at the various longitudes x would be paired, and the linear regression would be calculated by the method given in footnote 14. The regression equation would have the usual form of $P = a + bx$, in which P is the precipitation, a and b are the regression coefficients, and x is position east–west. It is apparent that such a straight line of best fit would not describe very precisely the relationship of the precipitation averages with the longitudes, being especially in error for eastern Nebraska. A better description of the relation between the two sets of numbers could be obtained by employing more coefficients and computing the nonlinear regression having the form $P = a + bx + cx^2$. The fit would be still better if the form $P = a + bx + cx^2 + dx^3$ were used, and, if a sufficient number of terms were employed, a perfect description of the relation could be written. To compute a regression equation with many coefficients is a major mathematical chore. To enable one to have the advantage of multiple terms, but to obviate the very great difficulties of solving many simultaneous equations, the orthogonal polynomials of Tschebycheff may be

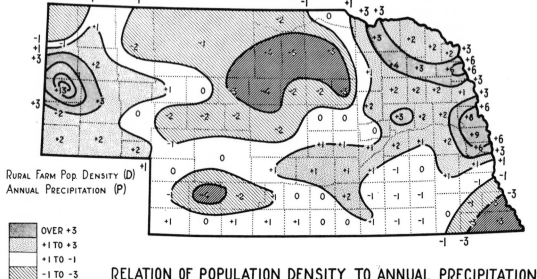

NEBRASKA
COUNTIES

RURAL FARM POP. DENSITY (D)
ANNUAL PRECIPITATION (P)

OVER +3
+1 TO +3
+1 TO -1
-1 TO -3
OVER -3

RELATION OF POPULATION DENSITY TO ANNUAL PRECIPITATION
$D - D_c$ = NUMBER OF PERSONS/SQ. MILE MORE OR LESS THAN "NORMAL"
"NORMAL" is $D_c = -12.150 + .7735P$

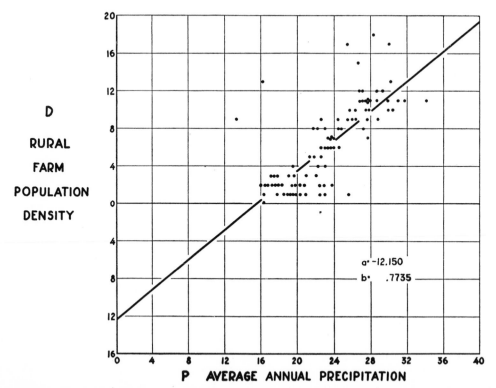

$a = -12.150$
$b = .7735$

D

RURAL

FARM

POPULATION

DENSITY

P   AVERAGE ANNUAL PRECIPITATION

Figure 8.5 The scatter diagram at the bottom shows the regression of population on precipitation based on county values. The map at the top results from employing these regression constants. It differs from Figure 8.4 in two ways: (1) the regression constants are somewhat different, and (2) a correspondence value was determined for each of the 93 counties, whereas only the 26 values at the grid points were employed for Figure 8.4.

employed. They have the special advantage that coefficients may be fitted one at a time until the reduction in the sums of the squares is no longer of importance, i.e., until the description of the relation is as precise as is desired.

A description of the manner by which orthogonal polynomials are utilized to obtain the desired coefficients is out of place in this paper. Their widespread use in studies involving curvilinear regression is relatively recent, and examples are found in the literature of many fields, such as agriculture, biology, and meteorology. In all instances the studies have been made by researchers with considerable mathematical and statistical backgrounds, and, as a result, the descriptions of the procedures are difficult for the non-statistician to follow. Nevertheless, since curvilinear regression analysis appears to offer much of value for future research in geography it is appropriate to mention the technique here.[19] The polynomial equations that result describe, as precisely as desired, the nature of the statistical surfaces. They may be normalized in the same general fashion as was done in the case of the preceding linear regression discussed. The

curvilinear regression of one surface on another may be employed to derive and map the relation between the two surfaces in the same fashion as previously illustrated. Unfortunately the computation and the manipulation of the normalized orthogonal polynomial coefficients is a rather laborious process; this difficulty can be readily surmounted by the use of high-speed electronic computers, such as the IBM 650 or its equivalent. The machine program for doing this is given in Bryson and Kuhn.[20]

As a sample case, the precipitation and population density values were interpolated from the maps of Figure 8.1 at intersections of an equally-spaced grid of 37 points east–west and 19 north–south. Data from adjoining states were used to fill in the corners of the grid. After punching the data on IBM cards, two minutes of machine computation produced the result that the two distributions were correlated 0.83, a not-surprising result in light of the previous discussion. Table 8.1 shows the coefficients of the polynomial terms for each of the maps.[21]

One useful property of the normalized equations is that the correlation between the two statistical surfaces described by them

TABLE 8.1   Illustration of the correlation between precipitation (p) and the population density (d) of Nebraska by the use of orthogonal polynomial coefficients[1]

POLYNOMIAL TERM	p COEFFICIENT	d COEFFICIENT	PARTIAL CORRELATION
East–west			
a^1	−.95	−.84	+.7980
b^1	+.06	+.35	+.0210
c^1	+.01	+.16	+.0016
d^1	−.02	−.07	+.0014
e^1	+.01	−.01	−.0001
f^1	−.01	+.05	−.0005
g^1	.00	−.03	−.0000
h^1	−.01	+.02	−.0002
North–south			
a^1	+.13	+.02	+.0026
b^1	−.04	−.06	+.0024
c^1	−.04	−.04	+.0016
d^1	+.01	+.05	+.0005
	Correlation		+.8283

[1]Computed by James F. Lahey.

may be computed very quickly. If the coefficients of the polynomial equation, after normalizing, are designated by a^1, b^1, c^1, etc. (since they correspond in a way to the a and b of a linear regression equation), and if the subscripts p and d refer to the precipitation and population density maps, respectively, then the correlation (r) between the two maps is given by $r = a_p^1 a_d^1 + b_p^1 b_d^1 + c_p^1 c_d^1 \ldots$ etc. There is also the additional advantage that the contribution of each term to the over-all correlation may be seen at a glance, as shown in Table 8.1. Thus the table shows that (1) most of the correlation is associated with the linear aspect of the distribution (the first term), and (2) that most of the correlation results from the fact that both precipitation and population density change in an east–west direction.

This method, while relatively elegant, would take considerably more time for the computation of a single study of two distributions as here illustrated; but for a much larger area or a more intensive study of an area, where *many* such correlations of distributions are to be made, it provides a powerful research aid.

Notes

[1]This study was supported by the Graduate School of the University of Wisconsin. While the senior author was working on the cartographic problem of correlating distribution maps by simple procedures with considerable assistance from Professor Bryson of the Meteorology Department, the latter was engaged in a study involving the use of orthogonal polynomials and machine computing methods to describe in numerical terms the distribution of meteorological data over area. Although the aims of the two studies were very different, the statistical concepts involved are fundamentally similar. Consequently they decided to issue a joint report. The authors express their appreciation to James F. Lahey, who carried out the machine computations necessary for the last example (Table 8.1).

[2]Harold H. McCarty, John C. Hook, and Duane S. Knos, *The Measurement of Association in Industrial Geography* (Iowa City: State University of Iowa, 1956), p. 20. Pages 20–53 contain an excellent summary of presently available techinques as well as suggestions for methods of measuring some other aspects of areal association.

[3]John K. Rose, "Corn Yields and Climate in the Corn Belt," *Geo-graphical Review*, Vol. 26 (1936), pp. 88–102.

[4]Edgar E. Foster, "A Climatic Discontinuity in the Areal Correlation of Annual Precipitation in the Middle West," *Bulletin of the American Meteorological Society*, Vol. 25, No. 7 (1944), pp. 299–306. The pattern of correlation in this case showed that stations within the "prairie peninsula" core correlated with each other better than with stations outside that region, even though they were farther apart. Qualitatively, the shape of the correlation isopleths fits the "prairie peninsula" surprisingly well.

[5]C. K. Stidd, "The Use of Correlation Fields in Relating Precipitation to Circulation," *Journal of Meteorology*, Vol. 11, No. 3 (1954), pp. 202–13.

[6]R. A. Fisher, *Statistical Methods for Research Workers* (12th ed.; New York: Hafner Publishing Co., 1954), p. 160 ff.

[7]C. E. P. Brooks and N. Carruthers, *Handbook of Statistical Methods in Meteorology* (London: Her Majesty's Stationery Office, 1953), pp. 226–28.

[8]E. R. Mowrer, "The Isometric Map as a Technique of Social Research," *American Journal of Sociology*, Vol. 44 (1938), pp. 86–96.

[9]Arthur H. Robinson, "A Method for Expressing Quantitatively the Correspondence of Mapped Distributions" (abstract), *Annals*, Association of American Geographers, Vol. 46 (1956), pp. 270–71, and McCarty, Hook, and Knos, *op. cit.*

[10]There are a great many sources of error inherent in the isarithmic map, such as the location of the control points, the validity of the average employed, the kinds of error involved in its derivation, and the manner in which the positions of the isarithms are determined through interpolation. A discussion of these is not appropriate here, and the maps and theoretical statistical surfaces subsequently employed are assumed to reflect truly the actual variations over area of the given quantities.

[11]Contours of a population density surface are more properly called isopleths since no point on such a surface can have an actual value, for the very definition of the z values involves area.

[12]For example, on a rainfall map one may change inches to millimeters or divide all values by any given number; the numbers of the z scale change and the range changes, but the isarithms remain in position. Of course, their numerical values will change.

[13]See Paul G. Hoel, *Introduction to Mathematical Statistics* (2d ed.; New York: John Wiley and Sons, Inc., 1954), pp. 117–19.

[14]The computation is a relatively simple operation involving only arithmetic; machine computation methods may of course be employed if the sizes of the sums are likely to get out of hand. If original values are employed, the general formulae are:

$$a = \frac{\Sigma X^2 \cdot \Sigma Y - \Sigma X \cdot \Sigma XY}{N \cdot \Sigma X^2 - (\Sigma X)^2}$$

$$b = \frac{N \cdot \Sigma XY - \Sigma X \cdot \Sigma Y}{N \cdot \Sigma X^2 - (\Sigma X)^2}$$

X = independent variable, Y = dependent variable, N = the number of pairs, and Σ is the summation sign. When actual values of P and D are substituted for X and Y in the above formulae, the computations are:

$$\Sigma X = 592.6 \qquad \Sigma Y = 138.8$$
$$\Sigma X^2 = 14{,}068.2 \qquad \Sigma XY = 3{,}490.7$$
$$(\Sigma X)^2 = 351{,}174.8 \qquad N = 26$$

$$a = \frac{14{,}068.2 \times 138.8 - 592.6 \times 3{,}490.7}{26 \times 14{,}068.2 - 351{,}174.8} = -7.939$$

$$b = \frac{26 \times 3{,}490.7 - 592.6 \times 138.8}{26 \times 14{,}068.2 - 351{,}174.8} = 0.5826$$

The values of a and b obtained from this small sample are probably relatively crude. The sample was deliberately made small for illustrative purposes, and the points chosen so as to have a convenient grid from which to construct the "average east-west profile" employed in Figure 8.2.

There are other ways of determining the values of a and b; the section on regression in any good statistics textbook will provide directions. These with no familiarity with statistical methods will find W. A. Neiswanger, *Elementary Statistical Methods* (New York, 1948) especially easy to follow.

[15]Saunders County turns out to be only slightly (2–3 persons per square mile) above what could be expected according to the defined relationship.

[16]See, for example, David I. Blumenstock, "The Reliability Factor in the Drawing of Isarithms," *Annals*, Association of American Geographers, Vol. 43 (1953), pp. 289–304.

[17]Arthur H. Robinson, "The Necessity of Weighting Values in Correlation Analysis of Areal Data," *Annals*, Association of American Geographers, Vol. 46 (1956), pp. 233–36.

[18]The county values for average annual precipitation employed were taken from *Climate and Man*, and were for a single station in each county. For the purpose at

hand the single station was assumed to be representative of the county.

[19]The work in English stems from the investigations of R. A. Fisher, "The Influence of Rainfall on the Yield of Wheat at Rothamstead," *Phil. Trans. Royal Soc. of London*, Series B, Vol. 213 (1925), pp. 89–142. A relatively clear account of the use and manipulation of orthogonal polynomials in an uncomplicated study is E. E. Housman, *Methods of Computing a Regression of Yield on Weather*, Research Bulletin 302, Iowa Agricultural Experiment Station (Ames: 1942), pp. 863–904. Their use in meteorological research is illustrated by: Don G. Friedman, "Specification of Temperature and Precipitation in Terms of Circulation Patterns," *Journal of Meteorol-*

ogy, Volume 12 (1955), pp. 428–35; William D. Sellers, ed., "Studies in Synoptic Climatology," *Final Report, ONR Contract N5048–07883*, Department of Meteorology, Massachusetts Institute of Technology (1956); and Reid A. Bryson and Peter M. Kuhn, "Half Hemispheric 500 mb Topography Description by Means of Orthogonal Polynomials, Part I, Computation," *Scientific Report No. 4 under Air Force Contract AF 19 (604)–992*, University of Wisconsin, Department of Meteorology (Madison: 1956).

[20]*Ibid.*

[21]It was clear that in this study so many coefficients would be unnecessary, but they were added for illustrative purposes.

Selection Nine

POTENTIAL MODELS AND THE SPATIAL DISTRIBUTION OF POPULATION

Theodore R. Anderson

The general problem with which this paper is concerned is the statistical explanation of the variation in population density between small areas (such as counties) within a large region, country, or land mass (such as the

Reprinted from *Papers and Proceedings of the Regional Science Association*, **2**, 1956, 175–182, by permission of the editor.

United States). Solving the problem involves, first, finding an equation which will describe the relative density (H) of any county as a function of certain variables (X) and certain parameters (a) holding time (t) constant. That is, an equation is desired of the form

(i) $\qquad H = f(X_1, X_2, \ldots a_1, a_2, \ldots t)$.

Once the static distribution of density is specified by such an equation the second aspect of the problem emerges: namely, describing the patterns of change in the density of a given area across time. Theoretically, the parameters in equation (i) describe the state of the system of densities at any given time. Hence, a series of equations representing these parameters as functions of time will describe changes in the system over time. Such equations will take the form

(ii) $$a_i = g_i(t).$$

Of course, these equations will not be functions of time in an abstract sense, but rather will be functions of variables which exist only across time and not in cross section. The problem, then, is the specification of the functions, f and g_i. Primary attention will be devoted to the function, f, since, until f is known, the parameters in terms of which the functions, g_i, have meaning cannot be known. Verbally this means that this paper is concerned primarily with the problem of describing density variations at one point of time.

The problem of finding a function, f, is, in turn, two-fold. First, there is the problem of locating the family of functions within which the particular function resides. Second, there is the problem of specifying the particular function within the family which best represents or describes the observed densities. The first problem is primarily theoretical, while the second is mainly methodological and empirical. Since the empirical research to be carried out on this problem is only now being initiated this paper will discuss only the theoretical problem of locating a sensible family of functions, whose members should adequately describe variations in density under a variety of conditions.

The Basic Model

Having introduced the problem, it is now appropriate to discuss the general kind of model which should solve the problem. Let the variable X_j be some characteristic of the jth area in the region being considered. Let D_{ij} be the distance between areas i and j. Consider the functions $F_{ij} = KX_j/D_{ij}$ and $H_i = \Sigma_j F_{ij}$, where the summation occurs over all j except i.

H_i will be called the potential of area i. A brief discussion of this general model is desirable. The variable X can, in general, be any characteristic of area j though in practice the characteristic should be theoretically and empirically meaningful or appropriate. F_{ij} is a function defining the contribution of area j to the potential of area i. It states that the contribution of area j varies directly with the value of X_j and inversely with the distance between areas i and j. The model in this form is familiar as the gravitational model as used by Dodd, Zipf, Stouffer, Stewart and many others when studying interaction and the movement of goods and persons. If the contribution of each area to the potential of area i is specified by the equation $F_{ij} [= KX_j/D_{ij}]$, then it follows that the total potential of area i is some combination of the contributions of each separate area. The equation, $H_i [= \Sigma_j F_{ij}]$ represents a reasonable means of combining the individual contributions, under the assumption that the individual contributions do not interact and, hence, add together to form the total potential.

This model, when X has been properly identified, should be very useful in describing the variations in density which occur between small areas such as the counties of the United States. Indeed, this paper will discuss two interpretations of X which render the model very plausible. In so far as the model actually is descriptive under each interpretation a final problem, of course, concerns combining the various models into a final, single, equation yielding density expectations. This final problem will not be considered fully in this paper.

Before proceeding to the possible interpretations of X it is useful to consider how the model would appear visually. In the limit as the size of each area is decreased the equation $C = \Sigma F_{ij}$, where C is a constant, would appear as a contour line on a map of the United States. This line would identify all points in the country possessing the same potential. A series of these lines (for different values of C) would present the variations in potential as a kind of contour map of the country. These lines will occasionally be referred to either as lines of potential or lines of force. It must be recognized at the outset, however, that the process of subdivision of the areas cannot proceed to the limit without destroying whatever claims the model may have to being an accurate description, for men are discrete entities, either occupying a given small area of space or not occupying it. It can only be hoped that 160 million odd (or 1 million odd) persons are enough to permit the model to have useful applications to important large-scale theoretical and practical problems.

A Note on Distance

Turning to the denominator of the model, $D_i{}^a{}_j$, it is reasonable to assert that distance is important in human life only when it must be traversed by something—human beings, various kinds of goods, or messages and signals of various kinds. Traversing distance always requires energy. But energy, being scarce, must be conserved, to some extent at least, through human organization: hence distance as an inverted or denominator factor. But the impact of distance will tend to vary with the types of energy converters which are available to man. Some ecologists would substitute for spatial distance what is called "time-cost" distance—that is, they would measure distance in terms of the time and cost involved in traversing it. While such a modification appears sound it is very hard to apply and, more importantly, creates a space in which nothing in the space itself is constant from one time period to another. While the issue is, at this stage of social science knowledge, to some extent a matter of personal opinion, it does seem preferable to let distance connote the amount of physical space intervening between two

points since this distance remains constant regardless of the society occupying the space and hence is literally a variable which is entirely independent of the society and not subject to variations induced by social change.

But some provision must be made in any model using distance for the impact of changing technologies. It seems reasonable to assume that the parameter a (that is, the power to which distance is raised) is flexible enough to contain these technological variations. That such a position is tenable seems clear in that any technological innovation will, in general, decrease the energy consumed in traversing a constant distance. This effect can be represented simply by decreasing the value of a.

First Interpretation of X: Resources

Turning now to possible interpretations of X attention may first be directed to considering X as a measure of productivity within area j. This interpretation can be illustrated by considering food production. Since any population requires food, the population which can be supported on a given area of land must bear a direct relationship to the amount of food energy which can be brought to the area. Let X_j measure the food energy surplus that can be produced in area j. This surplus is available to area i save for the energy loss involved in transportation. Assuming that the energy loss per unit distance is a decreasing function of distance: $F_{ij} = KX_j/D_{ij}{}^a$ becomes a reasonable model of the process.

When the parameter a is large transportation costs are high and area i must receive its food supply primarily from very nearby areas. When a is small transportation costs are low and the potential population at area i is large since it can draw its food supply from more distant areas.

It is important to note that under this model D_{ij} could never be less than 1 or area i could get more energy from area j than area j could produce. This limitation can be removed by introducing an additive constant 1 into the denominator, or in a variety of other ways, none of which change the basic structure of the model. It is also very important to note that the population potential defined in this manner will never equal the actual population since the food energy of any given area is simultaneously distributed over all other areas in the model. Hence, it is necessary to hypothesize that the actual density distribution will bear some direct, perhaps proportional, relationship to the potential population.

Under this hypothesis the general implications of the model are quite realistic in that it implies that when transportation is inefficient (i.e., a is large) population will be concentrated in fertile areas, but that when transportation is relatively efficient (i.e., a is small) population will be concentrated in the most accessible areas. These implications become more forceful if the model is modified so that the interpretation of a is changed somewhat. Instead of regarding a as an over-all system constant, it may be regarded as a variable whose value depends on the type of space intervening between the areas i and j and on the kind of transportation facilities available for traversing the distance. Thus variations in a might take into account whether the distance was over water or over land, whether upstream or downstream if on rivers, or, in recent times, whether by rail or otherwise if overland. Due to the limited number of types of terrain and the limited number of transportation facilities available to a society at any one time, it may be assumed quite safely that the number of different values which a will need to take on at any given time will be quite small, thus preserving the parameter efficiency of the model. If it is desirable to interpret transportation costs as a function of distance, the parameter a may be expressed as such a function rather than as a simple number.

Of course, this model by itself can hardly be expected to describe the actual population density distribution except in a very general way for it fails to take into account the social system which may modify considerably the distribution of the food supply and hence the distribution of population. In the long run, however, the factors included in this model should be efficacious. Thus, one would expect that the model would be more descriptive in India than in the United States since the population distribution in the United States is still strongly influenced by the points of entry of the population into the country.

Since human populations depend not alone upon food but also upon many other resources, the model might well be generalized to include these other resources as well. Retaining this form, a model could be constructed separately for each resource. The resulting models, which need not be considered in detail since they would be very similar to the food model, may, in general, be called resource potential models. These models, in combination, should prove fairly powerful as a description of population distribution under a variety of conditions. But they are limited in that they consider only the distribution of resources and the costs involved in converting and transporting these resources. They do not consider the fundamental social science fact that human beings find their adjustment to their environments through interaction with other human beings. That which holds the technological structure of society together is a complex maze of variegated patterns of interaction. These patterns place their stamp on the distribution of population as surely as does the distribution of resources. Societies exist through interaction as well as through consumption.

Second Interpretation of X: Population

The second major interpretation of X in the potential model to be discussed here generates the meaning of X_j from the interactional context in which man lives. If distance is a crucial factor in determining where men will live in relation to resources, which must but intermittently and sporadically be transported, distance must also be a crucial factor in determining where men will live in relation to other men with whom they interact, for interaction is a practically continuous phenomenon and also requires traversing distance with something which consumes energy.

Since a vast quantity of interactions are face-to-face, that which must be carried across the space is often man himself. Thus, men must be distributed in such a way that the energy consumed through crossing space so that interaction can occur is maintained at a more or less efficient level. But this means that men in interaction will tend to live close to each other. This tendency will strengthen as the rate of interaction per person increases and will tend to diminish as the transportation and communication systems become more efficient.

The simplest way to incorporate this principle into the potential model is to assume that each individual in the society possesses the same inherent interaction rate through his roles, or that the force exerted by each individual on the distribution of other individuals is constant. The force which is exerted on one area by another area will then be directly proportional to the number of individuals in the area. In other words, X_j in the potential model can now be interpreted as the population size of the jth area. The density potential of any area due to population is now specified by the model, which can thus be called the population potential model.

The model in this form is, of course, not predictive since one must, in effect, know the densities before one can reproduce them with the model. It must be remembered, though, that a predictive model is not being sought, but rather one which represents a useful means of describing the distribution of population at one point of time. If a population potential effect actually is operating, then it must be included in any theory of population distribution, whether it is predictive or not. It is actually quite easy to demonstrate that such an effect actually is operating, at least in the sense of F_{ij}. For instance, the largest population mass in this

country is situated along the northeastern coast of the United States, centering in New York City. According to this F_{ij} model, the density distribution in the rest of the country should be describable in part in terms of the force exerted by this one area. As a test, a random sample of 100 counties in the United States was drawn and the F_{ij} formula computed using distance from New York City. Since only one area was used, the population of New York City became part of the constant leaving only the distance from New York City as an independent variable. The linear correlation between the log of this distance and the log of the density of each county was $-.606$. In other words, about 36 per cent of the variance in density between counties in the United States (in 1950) can be statistically explained on the basis of the distance of the county from the largest population mass in the country. If distance from Chicago (the second largest population mass) is included, the explanation increases to about 46 per cent. It would be hard to find more convincing evidence that a population potential effect is operating. Bogue, in the Structure of the Metropolitan Community, has convincingly demonstrated that the model also operates in the region around each major population mass (or metropolis). whether the population be urban, rural nonfarm, or rural farm.

Thus, there appears to be little reason to doubt the existence of a population potential effect. But these demonstrations only indicate that a model of the form F_{ij}, where the area j is the densest in the region, is appropriate. They do not support the idea that a combination of F_{ij}s is desirable (except the New York and Chicago test). To determine whether summing the F_{ij}s of various areas improved the reproduction, all counties nearer Birmingham, Alabama than any other metropolis were studied. The density of these counties had a correlation of only .012 with distance from Birmingham. But when P/D was computed for each of the 12 nearest metropolises and summed, the correlation rose to .406, definitely indicating that large population masses other than the nearest have their effects and that a summation of contributions is appropriate. Of course this single example is only suggestive, but it is rather strongly suggestive. Bogue found essentially the same thing within the metropolitan region in that he found that large cities within the region had what he called a subdominant influence, thus presumably adding to the effect of the metropolis, though Bogue did not actually make the combination.

Once the importance of the population potential model is realized, the question arises as to how it can be made flexible enough to handle the variety of conditions arising in the world. First, of course, as in the resource potential model, the parameter *a* may be allowed to range over a small number of values rather than being restricted to only one value. That such variations are reasonable in a similar situation was demonstrated earlier by the author when it was found in a study of migration and Zipf's hypothesis that the power to which distance should be raised varied inversely with the population size of the source area. Such a relationship might easily persist in the general population potential model.

The model might also be modified by changing the assumption that each individual or role demanded the same rate of interaction or that the force of attraction per individual was constant. It is quite possible that the rate of interaction of the individual varies with his role in society. Thus, it is possible that farmers, for instance, are found to predominate in the more distant areas, or the areas where the population potential is relatively low not only because of the land requirements of their job, but also because their job requires less interaction with other men. Similar variations may well exist between functions or roles within the urban context. If so, then the force of attraction of an area will be related to the occupational composition of the occupants of the area. Thus, it could be hypothesized that areas whose occupants are primarily engaged in manufacture have less force per unit population than areas whose occupants are primarily engaged in commercial enterprises, or the government. The systematic testing of hypotheses of this type obviously requires a sensible classification of population re their functions, perhaps along the lines of the Harris-Kneedler classification.

Modifications and Conclusions

Before concluding this paper certain limitations of the potential model should be discussed. First, the model, in its population form at least, cannot predict or reproduce the location of the major population centers. It can only reproduce (if it works) the average density along each line of force or line of equal potential. Centers tend to arise as foci of interaction. It is quite possible that these centers are more likely to arise along certain lines of equal potential than along others (due, perhaps, to some operation of centrifugal and centripetal forces on interaction patterns). At least, in a very superficial sense, it is interesting to note that large cities tend to be located at about the same distance from the next larger city. For instance, Detroit, Cleveland, Cincinnati, St. Louis, and Minneapolis–St. Paul all are about 350 miles from Chicago (plus or minus 50 odd miles). Boston, Baltimore and Washington, D.C. are all about 200 miles from New York City. Many other such patterns exist in the United States, suggesting, to some extent at least, the hypothesis that centers do tend to exist along only certain lines of force. It is also quite possible that cities tend to arise at points of intersection of certain lines of force generated from different potential models. While these ideas are mere speculations at the present time, they do suggest a kind of research which might yield very interesting findings.

Second, the methodological problems associated with applying the potential models must be discussed. These problems result from the use of a model involving the summation of products where the factors in the products possess power parameters to be estimated. The use of summation almost precludes the use of logs as a means of getting simple equations from which, say, least squares estimates may be made. At the present time, only the arbitrary testing of a variety of parameter points or a very complicated iterative method (discussed by the author in a letter to the editor, American Sociological Review, Dec. 1955) appear feasible. Time does not permit more detailed discussion of the methodological issues here.

In conclusion, let it simply be said that the population potential model is capable of describing the structure of population distribution because it is a model of the way that the energy which binds men into societies operated in a spatial context. This model should describe the binding energy (or the results of the existence of the binding energy) in much the same sense that chemical models describe the structural relationships of the components of liquids and gases. But like liquids and gases, human populations are always found in a container of some sort.

The shape of the resulting empirical figure is modified to meet the conditions of the container. So is the shape of the human aggregate modified to meet the conditions of its container through the operation of the energy or resources potential model. In this conceptualization the analogy is intended merely to illustrate the idea, not to suggest any functional similarities. The crucial idea is that the population potential model does not actually identify or consider forces in the sense of externally operating phenomena as much as it attempts to describe the internal relationships of the aggregates of men in interaction which are called societies. In particular, no element within the system creates conditions or acts independently of the other elements in the system as long as the system remains closed. These particular models may or may not be adequate to the task set for them, but they are plausible enough to make extended research based on them well worth the effort involved.

Selection Ten

PHYSICS OF POPULATION DISTRIBUTION

John Q. Stewart and William Warntz

This report describes on-the-average regularities which have been proved to exist in the distribution of people within cities and in rural areas and across countries as a whole. A review is included of a good deal of previously published work, but new data are presented as well. In particular, none of the tables and figures has appeared in print before, although many of the tables are assembled from social physics notebooks of eight or ten years ago—when this sort of approach had not achieved its current degree of acceptability.

The "social mechanics" principles indicated in the present paper are necessarily

Reprinted from *Journal of Regional Science*, **1**, 1958, 99–123, by permission of the authors and publisher.

inadequate to deal with other wide areas of human behavior which also have significance for social science. But then mechanics is only one aspect of physics. Space here is not available to describe how, by developing ideas about "social energies," the approach becomes powerfully broadened.

Population Densities within a City

Every city tends to conform to a common pattern of internal population distribution, although a variety of local disturbing factors may in individual cities obscure or severely modify it. Not a single city exists which would be so free from these as to exhibit exactly the standard pattern. The standard

TABLE 10.1   Evidence for the relation of the area to the population of U. S. cities, 1940

RANK OF CITY	LOG C	RANK OF CITY	LOG C	RANK OF CITY	LOG C
1	2.67	31–35	2.44	151–165	2.61
2	2.59	36–40	2.48	166–180	2.60
3	2.62	41–45	2.41	181–195	2.55
4	2.47	46–50	2.45	196–210	2.65
5	1.98	51–55	2.54	211–225	2.54
6	2.60	56–60	2.41	226–240	2.56
7	2.55	61–65	2.58	241–255	2.56
8	2.64	66–70	2.54	256–270	2.61
9	2.76	71–75	2.59	271–285	2.48
10	2.65	76–80	2.51	286–300	2.57
11	2.58	81–85	2.63	301–315	2.52
12	2.70	86–90	2.64	316–330	2.53
13	2.70	91–95	2.48	331–345	2.63
14	2.73	96–100	2.62	346–360	2.48
15	1.98	101–105	2.69	361–375	2.52
16–20	2.49	106–120	2.58	376–390	2.51
21–25	2.37	121–135	2.55	391–405	2.46
26–30	2.52	136–150	2.68	406–412	2.55

Log C is the logarithm to base 10 of C, where $C = P^{3/4}/A$, P being the population of any city and A the land area in square miles within its political limits (Census of 1940). The rank in the first column is the order of their population size, New York being rank 1, Chicago 2, etc. Los Angeles, rank 5, is notorious for the excessive area within its city limits. The largest 15 cities are listed individually. After that only medians are listed—of groups of 5 cities each to rank 105, then of groups of 15 for the smaller cities (84323 to 25087). Where medians are tabulated, P is the median population of the group and A the median land area: as a rule these values do not then refer to the same city.

The same rule, the proportionality of area to the three-fourths power of population, held for the 140 metropolitan districts (listed in the 1940 census for all cities above 50,000); but for these the value of C in the formula is only 45 instead of 357.

In addition, five more values of log C were computed for medians of five groups of, respectively, 11, 11, 11, 41, 41 small cities each. These have median populations of 11087, 8186, 6253, 4134, 2577 and median land areas of 3.9, 2.3, 1.8, 1.3, 1.2 sq. mi. For these groups, log C was found to be, respectively, 2.44, 2.57, 2.59, 2.60, 2.48. This shows sais- factory agreement with the formula for cities as small as 2500. With the inclusion of these five, 59 values of log C are listed. Their average is 2.553, corresponding to $C = 357$, and $A = P^{3/4}/357$. (Data compiled by Catherine Kennelly.)

city is circular in shape. The density of population, D, within it is maximum at the center where it is D_0. The density drops radially from the peak in all directions, according to the exponential formula:

$$D = D_0 2^{-r/b},$$

where r is the distance from the center, and b is a short distance which is a constant for the given city.

We call b the "halving distance," because every increase in r by that amount carries to a ring where the density is cut in half. Thus contours of equal density are concentric circles. Their common center is the center of the "residential city." (In the next section we shall consider the "occupational city.")

In 1940 and earlier the standard city had a definite edge at some radius, a, where the edge density, D', was

$$D' = D_0 2^{-a/b},$$

D' being constant for all cities in the United States, and equal to about 2000 persons per square mile. The city's total population, P_c, is the integral of the density, D, taken over the whole area out to the boundary radius, a, successive ring by ring from center to edge. The area, A, of course is πa^2.

The first indication of this pattern of concentric rings decreasing exponentially in population density followed from the observation that on the average the area, A, of a city was proportional to the three-fourths

TABLE 10.2   Peak densities for tracted cities, 1940

NUMBER OF CITIES	MEDIAN POPULATION	MEDIAN PEAK DENSITY
1	7,455,000	264,000
3	1,931,000	71,000
5	859,000	90,000
7	587,000	48,000
11	368,000	32,000
13	282,000	28,000
13	152,000	35,000
7	86,000	29,000

From city maps published by the Census for the 60 cities for which population by census tracts was listed in 1940, the tract of highest population density in each city was determined from estimation of tract areas. These densities are presented in the form of medians for small groups of cities arranged by size of city. The 60 individual cities ranged in size from that of New York to that of Macon, Ga. (population 58,000). The median densities of the densest tracts are given in people per square mile of the tract area (areas of streets not deducted). Scales of miles published with the census maps of cities were in some instances suspect—indeed the computed density for the peak tract of Atlantic City, N.J., was at first so out of line with the general relation that the published scale was checked on the ground and found to be in error. The resultant correction eliminated the discrepancy.

Other scattered inspections on the ground in the 1940's indicated that the peak densities for typical smaller cities likewise tended to decrease regularly with population, to about 4000 per square mile for cities of 2500, the census lower limit. Thus U.S. cities in 1940 tended to conform to a common pattern of internal population distribution, with peak density (in units of persons per square mile) roughly equal to 75 times the square root of a city's total population. But see also Table 10.4.

power of the population, P_c.[1] Table 10.1 presents the original statistics. The only reasonable mathematical formula for internal density distribution which can yield such a relation between area and a power of the population is the exponential one for D as a function of r which is given above.

Then study of 1940 census data for all tracted United States cities, as well as inspection of several actual cities, indicated the value of D'. To fit the three-fourths power rule the halving distance, b, has to increase very slowly with the population P_c. In addition, examination of density variation within several tracted cities confirmed directly the tendency to the law of exponential decrease outward. That law independently

has been published by the economist, Colin Clark.[2] See also a note by Stewart.[3]

Table 10.2 gives further confirmation and clarification of the pattern, showing how the central density, D_0, depended on the population, P_c, in 1940. These data suggest that the halving distance, b, increases from about a third of a mile for the smallest cities, of 2500 population, to perhaps 4 miles for the largest ones. Note that D_0 is roughly proportional to the square root of P_c. As population increases the increased "attraction" (demographic gravitation) between people weighs down on and compresses the central population.

Evidence for the proportionality of the area, A, to the three-fourths power of P_c for cities in the United States and Europe was found to extend back at least to 1890, and there can be little doubt that cities were so structured a long time ago. Table 10.3 and Figure 10.1, compiled recently by Warntz, exhibit the same rule for British cities in 1951. Table 10.4 shows that cities in areas where general potential of population[4] is low tend to have larger areas than others of the same size-class located where the base potential (i.e., potential in the adjoining rural district produced by the remainder of the country) is high. This is confirmed also in the British study.

Full data as to the effect of base potential of population in changing D_0, D', and b have not been compiled. It must be emphasized that the center of population density is not the business center except in the smallest cities. Of interest is the slow increase in the number of stories in dwellings in the central region of peak density from the smallest to the largest cities. Their height rises from one or two stories in cities of a few thousand people to six or seven stories in walk-up tenements in New York's lower East Side.

To explain the sharp edge density of a city—a fall in a few hundred feet from 2000 people per square mile to rural densities of less than 200—one resorts to the concept of "cohesion" among city dwellers. The provision of the urban facilities which con-

TABLE 10.3   Areas and populations of cities in England and Wales, 1951

RANK	CITY	POPULATION (IN THOUSANDS)	AREA (IN THOUSANDS OF ACRES) ACTUAL	"EXPECTED"
1	London	3,348	74.8	105
2	Birmingham	1,112	51.1	46
3	Liverpool	790	27.3	35
4	Manchester	703	27.3	32
5	Sheffield	513	39.6	26
6	Leeds	505	38.3	25
7	Bristol	442	26.4	23
8	Nottingham	306	16.2	17
9	Kingston upon Hull	299	14.1	16
10	Bradford	292	25.5	16
11	Newcastle upon Tyne	292	11.1	16
12	Leicester	285	17.0	16
13	Stoke on Trent	275	21.2	15
14	Coventry	258	19.1	15
15	Croydon	250	12.7	14
16	Cardiff	244	15.1	14
17	Portsmouth	233	9.2	14
18	Harrow	219	12.6	13
19	Plymouth	209	13.1	13
20	Ealing	187	8.8	12
21–25	—	180	8.4	11
26–30	—	163	12.5	10
31–35	—	147	10.3	9.5
36–40	—	141	8.1	9
41–45	—	121	4.3	8
46–50	—	115	6.6	8
51–55	—	110	8.0	7.5
56–60	—	106	7.0	7.5
61–70	—	103	6.5	7
71–80	—	85	8.1	6.5
81–90	—	81	7.0	6
91–100	—	73	4.7	5.5
101–110	—	68	8.2	5
111–125	—	66	5.2	5
126–140	—	58	5.8	4.5
141–157	—	53	6.0	4.5

In Figure 10.1 land area in acres has been plotted against population on log-log paper for the 157 English and Welsh cities of over 50,000 persons in 1951. Land areas are in statute acres for the official political units (including inland water) as reported in the General Register Office's Census 1951, England and Wales, Preliminary Report, London, 1951. The leading twenty cities are shown individually. The next forty cities are indicated by means of medians of area and population for groups of five each. Groups of ten are employed for the next fifty cities. Following are two groups of fifteen each and finally one of seventeen. The above line indicates that the area of a city varies directly as the three-fourths power of the population. The equation relating area and population and used to compute "expected" values in Table 10.3 was found by a linear least squares solution of the logarithmic values of the variables for the first twenty cities. Stated in the power form this equation is: Area (in acres) equals 1.33 times population to the three-fourths power. If areas are to be stated in square miles, then the formula becomes: Area equals population to the three-fourths power divided by 481. (The coefficient of correlation, r, was found to be 0.87.) Compare this value of 481 to the ones similarly obtained in the United States of 357 in 1940 and 400 in 1890. In each of these cases the exponent of population was found to be three-fourths. Grouped data for the remaining 137 cities were also plotted in Figure 10.1 and indicate that the same relationship holds. The strong and well defined relationship of area to population is demonstrated.

Such scatter around the lines as exists can be further reduced by recourse to the macroscopic variable, base potential of population. Examination of the data clearly reveals that high potentials tend to constrict the area whereas at low

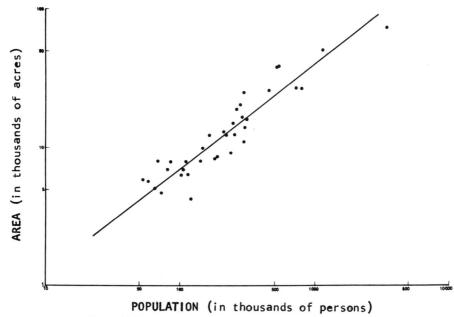

POPULATION (in thousands of persons)

Figure 10.1 Relation of area to population for English and Welsh cities, 1951

vert farm acreage into city lots requires joint cooperation supported by the inhabitants. Similarly the molecules within a water-drop stick together, and their mutual cohesional energy supports the "surface tension" of their boundary. Molecules cannot freely "evaporate" across the boundary—unless by addition of heat the temperature is raised to the boiling point, when cohesion is overcome and the surface tension and the boundary itself disappear. Molecules in a gas have independent careers, and do not so stick together.

Over and above the capital energy released in any region, rural or urban, by demographic gravitation, additional energy is released from cohesion in a city. This shows itself in increased activities of various sorts—more local motor traffic, more local telephone calls. In large cities demographic gravitation is relatively more important, and cohesion in small ones.

We can also speak of "adhesion," a clinging of people to desirable land (or, negatively, their repulsion from unfavorable sites). A main transportation route running out of a city is an example of desirable land, and despite the gravitational attraction of the city, residences "rise" along it as water rises in a capillary tube (because of adhesion to the glass). But glass repels mercury (relative to the force of cohesion of liquid mercury particles for one another), so a surface of mercury is depressed within an inserted capillary tube. Similarly, people tend to avoid areas naturally or artificially "unattractive."

Our lake-front cities are not circular but are drawn out as semiellipses as the result of adhesion to the shore. Population density in the Pine Barrens of New Jersey has been below that in neighboring fertile land in every census from 1790 on. A small city in a narrow valley is elongated—although the

potentials cities of a given population tend to occupy a larger area than indicated by the relationship of population alone. The effect of base potential is more pronounced for the less populous cities. (Potentials for the United Kindgom are mapped in Figure 10.2.) In the final analysis, each city is a unique case and a complete explanation would entail a complex of microscopic factors such as local topography, a multitude of personal decisions, and the like. The point to be stressed is that social scientists must learn the value of first approximations and develop the abilities to make them. Of course the local planner whose job is an engineering one must learn to appreciate both the general and the particular.

TABLE 10.4   Area of cities: variation with base potential and size

| POPULATION | POTENTIALS OF POPULATION | | | | |
	170,000	260,000	370,000	520,000	730,000
1,000,000+	—	—	172	127	299
500,000	—	—	61	46	—
200,000	45	53	38	18	19
100,000	50	38	20	19	10
50,000	13	14	10	10	5
33,000	11	12	9	7	6
25,000	7	9	6	6	4

All the 412 United States cities over 25,000 population in 1940 are represented. Their areas in square miles are presented in terms of median areas for groups of cities classified by population and by "base potential of population." The latter is the potential of population produced in the neighborhood of a city by all other people in the country, excluding those in the city itself. The rows refer to cities of the indicated population classes: namely, over 1,000,000, 500,000 to 1,000-000, ...25,000 to 33,000. The columns run according to base potentials, with median values 170,000, 260,000, 370,000, 520,000, 730,000—in 1940.

Evidently deviations in city areas from the one-variable relation of Table 10.1 are in part systematic, being well correlated with base potential as a second variable. Higher values of the latter are associated with a "compression" in city areas (related no doubt to greater land values of surrounding rural acreage). Warntz's examination of a number of British cities indicates the same effect (Table 10.3).

demographic gravitation usually is strong enough to crowd houses on steep slopes near the center.

While we have no adequate explanation as yet for the causes of the standard city pattern, cohesion must play a major role, along with demographic gravitation—and adhesion can account for some of the observed distortions.

The daily, even hourly, movings about of people increase with technological and economic advancement—just as the kinetic energy of molecules in the physical world increases with temperature. One's daily observations show how the automobile (much more effectively than the older forms of transport) operates to lower the boundary tension of cities. Widespread electric power networks, consolidated rural schools, state police protection of rural residents, and so on, have the same effect. Very important also is the fan of good highways extending out from every city, built and maintained at general expense rather than by direct assessment of those who choose to live along them. The combination of increased real incomes per capita with state and federal subsidies for local improvements and for rural amenities is breaking down the old constant high edge density. In "star" pat-

terns along the highways each city now in effect extends out well beyond the old bounding radius that was set by the high D'. The edge density now has perhaps fallen until it is almost indistinguishable from the rural density of the general countryside.

Plausibly, the standard city pattern is not otherwise changed. But many millions of people are listed now in the census as rural non-farm dwellers who might more properly be listed as urban. If this is so, the 1960 count of the urban fraction will, by former standards, be low by as much as 10 per cent.

Already in 1950, when the total population of the United States was 150,700,000, and there were 4284 cities, empirical regularities which had held from the first census[5] would have suggested an urban fraction of 64 per cent, instead of the tabulated 58.8. The reduction in the edge density of cities has changed the old balance of city and country. Further investigation is needed to arrive at a full theoretical explanation of the intra-urban equilibrium—the density pattern outlined above and the changing rural-urban equilibrium. "Microscopic" studies of cities one at a time emphasize local distortions and necessarily have failed to reveal the existence of the standard city pattern.[6] "Natural law" has been demonstrated to

TABLE 10.5 Municipal taxes per capita: by city size-class and base potential

| | POTENTIALS OF POPULATION | | | | |
POPULATION	170,000	260,000	370,000	520,000	730,000
1,000,000+	—	—	36	38	73
500,000	—	—	37	72	—
200,000	19	29	18	54	70
100,000	19	16	16	41	52
50,000	17	15	15	57	50
33,000	14	22	14	37	51
25,000	14	19	14	38	39

The form is identical with that of Table 10.4, but with medians of municipal taxes, in dollars per year per capita in 1940, presented for the same 412 United States cities. Whereas higher base potential compressed the areas, it increased the city taxes.

hold in social science as in physical science. City and regional planners who ignore tendencies of mass behavior do so at peril of serious failure in their designs.

Remarks on Other Characteristics of Cities

The residential city pattern has impressed itself also upon urban statistics other than those for population distribution. A correlation of urban rents with population and base potential existed in 1940 (before rent controls were effective as another influence).[7] Table 10.5, having the same sort of arrangement as Table 10.4, reveals the same two-variable dependence for municipal taxes per capita as for areas upon population and base potential—although where high values of the latter reduce the area they tend to increase the tax. Table 10.6 shows a like

dependence in the excess of urban births over deaths per 1000 people.

Thus it is clear that the customary grouping of city statistics by size-class alone, regardless of base potential, can obscure significant regularities. Base potential is a macroscopic variable, which no amount of microscopic study can reveal.

The density pattern discussed in the first section is for the residential city, as has been stated. Before the advent of modern rapid transit the "occupational city"—the spatial distribution of people at their jobs within cities—necessarily closely coincided with the residential city. Nowadays it seems that proper census statistics—which should be taken on a sampling basis—would define the occupational city, superimposed upon the residential one.

We may guess that the mathematical

TABLE 10.6 Excess of urban births over deaths: by city size-class and base potential

| | POTENTIALS OF POPULAITON | | | | |
POPULATION	170,000	260,000	370,000	500,000	730,000
1,000,000+	—	—	6.2	2.4	3.5
500,000	—	—	4.6	2.8	—
200,000	9.2	5.8	4.3	3.1	3.4
100,000	6.0	7.1	6.4	2.5	4.2
50,000	8.4	4.9	6.0	3.2	3.2
33,000	11.1	4.8	6.7	4.9	5.0
25,000	9.7	7.6	5.8	5.5	4.9

Some 412 cities as in Tables 10.4 and 10.5, 1940. Listed are medians of the excess of urban births over deaths (per 1000 total population annually). Here base potential was even more effective than city size in reducing the excess.

equations for the two would be the same, and that the two "cities" would differ only in the numerical values of the parameters, P_c, A, a, D_0, b, D'. (From discussion above it is clear that these six represent only two independent variables, P_c and D',—providing we ignore the effect of base potential, which is a third independent variable.)

Observations as one travels about the country indicate that the same factors which have reduced edge density, D', for the residential city have likewise reduced it for the occupational city. We shall return to this point below.

Hitherto unpublished data compiled from the 1940 United States census by Catherine Kennelly relate to the distribution among leading cities of a few sample occupations. Just as the city residential populations conform to the well-known "rank-size" or Pareto rule,[8] so also do the special subpopulations of residents listed city by city in specified occupations.

The rank-size rule states that, R being the rank of a given city in the list, the population for it equals MR^{-n}, M being the population of the largest city, of rank 1, and n an exponent constant for the sequence of all cities. When P_c is thus ranked, n for United States cities has long been unity, with New York at rank 1. If now "authors" are counted, New York again in 1940 had the largest contingent, 2765 of them, and the exponent n remained unity. Los Angeles ranked 2, whereas in the total population list it was 5. Denver was 7 instead of 24; Cambridge, Mass., 26 instead of 78; and Buffalo 42 instead of 14.

For real estate agents and brokers, n was again unity. New York led with 10884; Miami ranked 17 instead of 48, Pittsburgh 22 instead of 10. For operatives making automobiles and auto equipment, n was roughly 3/2; Detroit ranked 1 instead of 4; Flint was 2 instead of 56, New York was 12. This sort of statistic is a useful addition to the methodology of classifying cities with respect to their assumed special roles— a tricky business.[9]

What would one mean by the population P_c, of the occupational city? It would be the number of individuals whose places of employment lie within the boundary of a given city. Walter Isard emphasizes three factors which relate to the concentration or dispersal of places of employment.[10]

The first of these, economy of scale, is related in part to the technological factors in a given industry and to the limited divisibility of certain factors of production. For certain kinds of manufacturing, low per unit costs of output can be achieved when many units per time period are produced at one location by a single firm. Thus, mass production economies up to a certain level of output tend to concentrate a large output at a given geographical point.

In the second place, economies of localization may be experienced when several similar firms in an industry cluster around a given geographical point in close proximity to one another.

Thirdly, urban economies which depend upon city utilities and facilities, local labor supply, etc., have brought the plants into actual cities.

Today ample observable evidence makes it clear that the lowering of a city's edge density for industry is becoming even more pronounced than for residences. No large-scale "decentralization" is resulting. Our once tightly bound cities surround themselves with "evaporated" dwellings and plants— but the escape is only from local urban cohesion and not from the major national demographic gravitation. Only if the level of real national income increases tremendously will the high-density concentrations of residence and industry in the existing "manufacturing belt" thin out by removals to outlying situations of low population potential. To maintain the level of sociological intensity when people move farther apart demands that genuinely new and adequately profitable resources be tapped thereby.[11] Even then an associated increase in the birthrate probably would tend to maintain existing peaks of potential.

Figure 10.2 Potentials of population in thousands of persons per square mile in the United Kingdom, 1951

Rural Density; Interpenetrating Regions

Figure 10.2 is a hitherto unpublished map of population potentials for the United Kingdom, 1951. It permits testing there the relation of rural population density to the potential of population (produced by all the people). Results are given in Figure 10.3 and Table 10.7. Once again the rural density, D_R (in persons per square mile) is found to vary as the square of the potential, V, (in persons per mile). We have

$$D_R = kV^2,$$

where k (with the units stated) is determined for England and Wales as roughly 5.55×10^{-10}.

Table 10.8 compares with this other values of k found as multipliers in the same proportionality of D_R to V^2 in the United States at different dates, in Europe, and in Mexico. Respective total populations, P_T, are listed along with corresponding rural populations, P_R, and the ratio, w, of rural to total population. Tabulated also for each case is the computed value of a certain pure number, q, derived as follows:

TABLE 10-7   Potentials of population and rural population densities, England and Wales, 1951

COUNTY	POTENTIAL OF POPULATION IN THOUSANDS OF PERSONS PER MILE	RURAL DENSITIES IN PERSONS PER SQUARE MILE	
		ACTUAL	EXPECTED
Surrey	1,040	383	620
Derbyshire	786	386	350
Lancashire	780	298	345
Hertfordshire	775	364	340
Bedfordshire	745	235	315
Warwickshire	737	232	305
Nottinghamshire	723	234	295
Buckinghamshire	709	286	285
Staffordshire	703	234	280
Yorkshire (W. R.)	694	233	270
Essex	689	208	265
Leicestershire	665	257	250
Cheshire	661	251	245
Durham	636	378	225
Oxfordshire	628	183	220
Kent	626	262	215
Worcestershire	604	202	205
Northamptonshire	573	146	180
Gamorganshire	569	453	180
Denbighshire	563	149	175
Gloucestershire	561	246	175
Berkshire	558	285	170
Sussex	557	233	170
Shropshire	550	120	165
Rutlandshire	542	126	160
Monmouthshire	541	119	160
Hampshire	536	215	160
Flintshire	533	332	155
Cambridgeshire	526	163	150
Herefordshire	516	93	145
Huntingdonshire	506	122	140
Suffolk	501	142	137
Wiltshire	499	163	135
Somersetshire	483	162	130
Lincolnshire	482	122	128
Randnorshire	481	30	127
Norfolk	450	155	111
Yorkshire (N. and E. R.)	449	91	110
Breconshire	443	55	107
Northumberland	440	54	106
Dorsetshire	432	122	103
Caernarvonshire	422	102	97
Merionethshire	412	40	92
Westmorland	404	51	89
Montgomeryshire	402	38	88
Anglesey	397	121	86
Cardiganshire	395	53	85
Cumberland	394	89	85
Carmarthenshire	381	112	79
Pembrokeshire	335	79	60
Devonshire	333	104	60
Cornwall	301	131	49

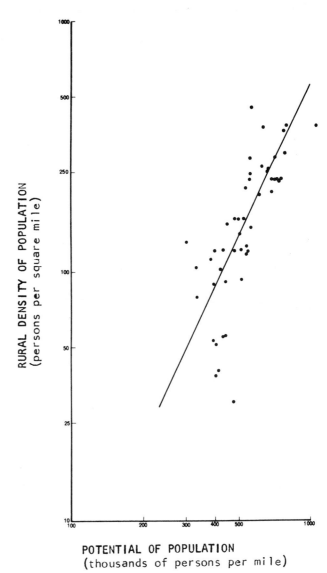

POTENTIAL OF POPULATION
(thousands of persons per mile)

Figure 10.3 Density of population in rural districts and potential of population, English and Welsh counties, 1951

Presented here in tabular form are the data of Figure 10.3. Fifty-two counties in England and Wales are shown. (London and Middlesex counties had no rural population in 1951.) The potential of population values (given above in thousands of persons per mile) are the ones computed as control point values for the drawing of the map in Figure 10.2. Actual density of population in rural districts (averaged by county) was obtained from the 1951 census data. The "expected" rural density was computed in the following way: Let D = rural density in persons per square mile and V = potential of population in persons per mile, then $D = 5.55 \times 10^{-10}V^2$.

Of course potential of population does not give final accuracy. It is, however, a single macroscopic integrative index which introduces a powerful unifying first approximation into the study of the geographical variation of sociological phenomena. Its effects must be supplemented by local factors in individual cases. The ruggedness of the terrain in such Welsh counties as Radnor, Montgomery, and Merion presumably offers a strong deterrent to rural settlement whereas the gentler slopes and more fertile soils in certain other places encourage it.

TABLE 10.8   Parameters for rural population density

REGION		P_T MILLIONS	P_R MILLIONS	$10^{12}k$	w	q
U. S.,	1900	76.0	45.8	880	0.603	0.111
	1930	122.8	53.8	425	0.438	0.119
	1940	131.7	57.2	351	0.435	0.106
Europe,	1930's	499.7	321.8	149	0.644	0.116
Mexico,	1930	16.4	11.0	3820	0.671	0.093
England & Wales, 1951		43.7	8.4	555	0.192	0.126

The columns list, respectively, for six different cases studied, total population, rural population, the value of k (multiplied by a million million), the numerical ratio, w, of rural population to total population, and, finally, another pure number, q, defined as equal to $P_T k/w$ (see text). In each case D_R, the rural density anywhere in the country, was approximately kV^2, V being the potential of population at the point, and k a parameter constant over the country at the time. The value of k as listed was determined by a median fit to the observed values of D_R, without any regard to the later computation of q. The greatest relative concentration of population near the center is indicated for Mexico, because q comes out smallest there.

Let A be the total area over which the populations P_T and P_R are dispersed. Therefore

$$P_R = \int D_R \, dA = k \int V^2 \, dA,$$

where k, being constant throughout the area, can be written outside the integral sign. The integration is over the entire area. Let there be a pure number q, where

$$q = \frac{P_T^2}{\int V^2 \, dA};$$

then

$$k = \frac{P_R}{P_T^2} \cdot q;$$

and, since

$$w = \frac{P_R}{P_T},$$

$$k = \frac{wq}{P_T} \quad \text{or} \quad q = \frac{P_T \cdot k}{w}.$$

Inasmuch as the potential V is that produced at any point by the whole population, P_T, divided by distance, while area always has the dimension of the square of distance, $\int V^2 \, dA$ has the dimension P_T^2, and q comes out dimensionless, a pure number, as is w.

Table 10.8 shows that q is remarkably stable from case to case. For a population uniformly distributed over a circular disk (Table 10.10 below), q is readily computed as about 0.11.

The listed values of k in Table 10.8 were obtained by fitting a median straight line of slope 2, on log-log graph paper, to plotted values of observed D_R at various points of known potential, V. Then q was computed from the said k in each case. Now q could have been determined directly by summing terms $V^2 \, dA$.

It can be shown that $\int V^2 \, dA$ computed over an assigned area for a fixed total population, P_T, is larger if the population is strongly concentrated near the center of the area— and smaller if instead most of the people are placed near the boundary rim of the area. Hence a small value of q indicates central concentration of the population; a medium value of q indicates roughly uniform distribution; and a larger q means boundary concentration.

So we have in q, thus computed, a new general index of distribution.

If, in computing V, people are assigned different weights it is required to take P_T not as the sum of the actual people, but as the sum of the product of people by their respective weights. None of the cases listed in Table 10.8 involved weights other than unity throughout. But weights suggested in different sections of the United States in 1940 would have increased the effective value of P_T by about 11,000,000 standard people.

The tendency of rural density to be proportional to the square of the potential, across a great country, is a well established fact. This indicates that such a country as the United States possesses demographic unity of a certain type. The applicability of the rank-size rule for cities also indicates a unity. Therefore we conclude that any subdivision into separated "regions" can have only special sorts of meaning—there are no unique regions.

The fact that there are no unique regions has already been recognized in the wide use by regional analysts of two classes of regions: the "homogeneous" and the "nodal." As an example of the homogeneous, there are regions where the rural density runs rather consistently high or low—the Pine Barrens of New Jersey being an example of low density of population in every census from 1790 on. This is a kind of homogeneous region which is identifiable by its systematic deviation from a general regularity. Besides the proportionality of rural density to the square of the potential, other demographic or economic terms are known to vary as the square or as some other power of potential. For each such relation across the country, systematic deviations of actual from expected values may define a different set of regions.

Examples of nodal regions are the campus of a seasoned, privately endowed, "national" university and the dispersed residences of its students, a metropolitan newspaper and its territory, a seaport and its hinterland. They are all very special: the hinterland of a given port may differ for different commodities. The competition of nodal regions of a given sort may be "interpenetrating" as for colleges, or "all-or-none" as for newspapers in different great cities. Thus sales of the old St. Louis "Star Times" by counties around the city were proportional to the respective potentials of population there of the counties, but only out to where that newspaper's territory was rather sharply bounded by competition of papers in Kansas City, Chicago, Memphis. In contrast, leading colleges each draw students from every part of the country.

Even where subdivision into regions is for administrative purposes, as into states,

counties, Federal Reserve districts, relations to population potential (or to income potential) make themselves evident, again confirming the general sociological unity of the country.[12]

Some Fundamentals of the Gravity Model

The recent rapid increase in the number of papers and articles employing the so-called "gravity models," while attesting (however belatedly) to the fact that distance is truly a dimension of social systems, has unfortunately brought with it much confusion concerning the exponent of distance to be employed. Whereas the "weights" assigned to people must be adjusted to fit observations, the function of distance is not such an arbitrarily adjustable parameter.

It appears that at present, potential of population, V, is the most widely known aspect of the gravity model. Knowledge of numbers of people, P, and their distances apart, r, are at once necessary and sufficient for the computation of potentials and the ultimate plotting of lines of equipotential on a map. Other demographic measures which can also be derived from these primitive quantities or "dimensions," and which are consistent with potential of population, include density, D, energy, E, and gradient, g. Time and velocity and acceleration are also consistent with the above but will not be considered here. Time is another primitive.

Potential of population is a "scalar" quantity (having no direction in space) and is equal to number of people divided by their distance away. The potential which a given population concentration creates at a distant point Q is:

$$V_Q = \frac{P}{r}.$$

But, the total potential at any point is produced by all groups of people. If the distribution may be regarded as continuous over a surface, the following formula applies:

$$V_Q = \int \frac{1}{r} D \, dA,$$

where dA signifies an infinitesimal element of the area over which the integration is extended.

Since density of population has the dimensions of persons per unit area, and area has the dimension of distance squared, the derived potential of population has the dimensions of number of people per unit distance.

If the values of potential have been computed for a sufficiently large number of appropriately spaced "control points" then a map such as Figure 10.2 can be drawn to exhibit lines of equipotential or "contours."

If a constant contour interval is maintained throughout the map, the gradient of potential is inversely as the spacing of the contours—gradient being the rate of change of potential with distance. Whereas potential is a scalar quantity, gradient is a vector directed at right angles to the equipotential contour at any place. Thus the unit of gradient has the dimensions of persons per mile squared. It should be noted that gradient and density thus have the same dimensions.

Although much analysis has centered upon the relation of the potential field to the geographical variation in certain sociological and economic phenomena, gradient has been shown to be important with regard to location theory.[13]

If only two separated groups of people are considered, their mutual "demographic energy" can be computed as:

$$E = \frac{P_1 P_2}{r}.$$

The unit of energy therefore is persons squared per mile. The energy alternatively can be interpreted as the product of the population of either group times the potential contributed there by the other group. If one wishes to compute the energy of any group of people, say a city population, in relation to the total population, this can be found by multiplying the population of the city by the total potential contributed there by all people. Again the unit of energy is persons squared per mile.

Thus a rigorous and consistent set of measures exists of a population as it is distributed spatially. It should in particular be noted that the above formulas include without disagreement the case of W. J. Reilly's "breakpoint" between competing market cities.[14] He published the rule of inverse square of distance because he investigated gradients, not potentials.

Both Reilly and Stewart found their respective exponents as empirical regularities without any a priori postulates.

Remarks and Formulas in Relation to Potential Theory

Mathematical statisticians have seldom blazed the difficult trail which leads from observations of the world to new branches of science. Their convention-bound methods come into play only after discovery of the leading concepts and relations of the new field. Statistics necessarily is microscopic. It deals with the data of special cases, and can work with broad data only if the cases already have been put together by connections discovered in studies in the field in question. The operation of a principle may be obscured by the simultaneous effects of other principles, and mere statistics cannot, in complete ignorance of conditions, sort out the principles.

Very wide ramifications are possessed by the formula for the influence of people at a distance—as directly proportional to the number of people (weighted in whatever numerical ratio may be necessary) and inversely to the first power of the distance. The present paper indicates many of the ramifications, and in addition suggests some of the other factors which can add their own peculiar effects.

Naturally a mathematics-statistics hopper, however recondite and busy, which lumps confusedly together all these factors will be incapable of closely verifying the law of inverse distance. This description, we suggest, applies to the recent study by Hammer and Ikle of long-distance telephone calls and airplane trips between certain cities.[15] When in their study people were weighted equally, the formula for "mutual energy" of the two city populations (their product divided by the distance apart) was roughly verified. But, when the machine was allowed (subject only to the hidden conventions of mathematical statistics) to select the weights assigned to the people of each city, the exponent of distance came out as something like the negative three-halves power.

No comparative test was made with the approximate weights previously published by others—namely, 2, 1, and 0.8 for different sections of the United States, nor, alternatively, per capita income. The actual observations of telephone calls and travel were not tabulated. One would not expect that airline trips among the given cities in the single month of March, 1950, would furnish a stable sample. Nor have experts of the A. T. and T. Co. compiled or released a broad table of phone calls among cities of all sizes. (Likewise the Federal Reserve System has made no adequate compilation of the interdistrict flow of bank checks.)

It can be mathematically fallacious to assume a scalar "potential," or index, equal to population divided by distance to the nth power where n is any exponent. For example, if n is greater than 2, the index would have infinite values for finite distributions of population density. This is because $\pi r^2 D/r^n$ equals $\pi D/r^{n-2}$, and, if n is greater than 2, approaches infinity as r approaches zero. The same objection applies with the gradient if n is greater than 1 in the potential. Consequently it is a misnomer to use the name "gravity model" unless potential and gradient are defined as in the present paper. In three dimensional space there are not gravity models, only the gravity model. People are distributed in three dimensional space, although for convenience demography often can neglect the third dimension.

The published observational evidence for the usefulness of a scalar index operating to the inverse first power of distance is direct, varied and remarkably strong as social science evidence goes. Mathematical statistics can be a good servant; but only a weak social science, intent on becoming weaker, will welcome it as a master.

Local Peaks of Potential.—Suppose a small city lies in a rural district where, apart from the city's own contribution, the contours of equipotential are, nearly enough, parallel straight lines, equally spaced. In section 4, gradient is defined as the rate of change of potential with the distance at right angles to the contours of equipotential. So here the general gradient, g, is uniform. The small city, if all alone, would be surrounded by contours more or less circular, sloped "downhill" radially outward. Superposition of these two sets of contours results in the single system illustrated schematically in Figure 10.4.

If instead of a city we had only a village, the hatched contour in the figure, and the circular ones included within its closed loop, would not come into existence. There would only be a short downhill ridge raised above the general level across the village. No local peak would then be formed, and no closed contours around the town. The condition that there be a local peak is roughly this: within the loop of the hatched contour the density of the local population must exceed the uniform gradient, g—the latter being measured at a distance away, outside the local influence. (As stated in section 4, gradient and population density have the same dimensions.)

The phenomenon of "urban sprawl" is well known near great cities. The gradient away from the central city is so large that even fairly sizable concentrations of local population do not match or exceed it. Local closed contours of potential are not achieved, and unless its internal cohesion is very great the would-be small city can have no independent demographic existence. As with the planet Saturn, the powerful gravitation of the central metropolis tears apart satellite towns. Is it possible for planners to provide the high cohesion which would preserve the character of such precariously perched neighborhoods?

A Theorem of Topology.—The contours

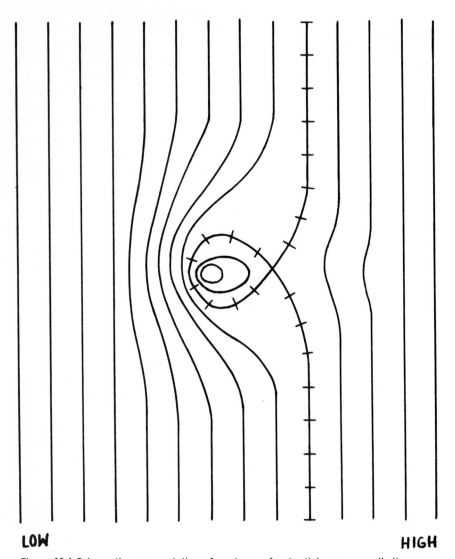

LOW   **HIGH**

Figure 10.4 Schematic representation of contours of potential near a small city

of potential are mathematically determined when the density of population is known throughout the whole country. Certain distributions of population produce "pits" as well as "peaks" of potential. Of course the bottom of a pit may itself be at a high potential; the requirement merely is that the slope be upward in all directions in the immediate neighborhood.

An interesting theorem of topology applies within any closed contour of equipotential on a surface, as first stated scores of years ago by the great physicist, Clerk Maxwell, and later by the well-known mathematician,

Marston Morse. The number of peaks plus the number of pits minus the number of passes equals one, always. Thus in the situation of Figure 10.4 a second and major peak is necessarily implied, far to the right (e.g., for the United States at New York City), and the portrayed parallel straight line contours really are parts of great sweeping arcs concave toward the major peak. In general, each separate city peak on the general massif is accompanied by its own neighboring pass on the New York side. Three otherwise isolated cities near together and forming a triangle would be separated by three passes on its three sides, and a pit would exist within the triangle.[16]

Potential Near the Center of a Small Populated Area.—If a circular disk of radius r has uniform population density, $\bar{D}$, throughout, then the total population, P, is $\pi r^2 D$. The increment of potential at the center produced by a ring of radius r and infinitesimal width dr is $2\pi\bar{D}dr$. Hence the total central potential is

$$V_c = 2\pi\bar{D}r = \frac{P}{(r/2)}.$$

For an irregular area, A, not too different in shape from a circle, the same formula approximately applies, if by r we understand the value determined by setting $\pi r^2 = A$, again, even though A be irregular. But if some actual area, A, is elongated, an ellipse will approximate it better. Mere inspection of the map will suggest a plausible approximation to α/β, the numerical ratio of the semi-major to the semi-minor axis. The area of the chosen ellipse would be $\pi\alpha/\beta$. However, Table 10.9 requires only estimation of the ratio α/β. One computes r as before, as though the assigned area A belonged to a circle. The potential near its center approximates

$$V_c = \frac{P}{fr/2},$$

where f is the number read from Table 10.9 as a function of α/β.

By these means it is easy to approximate the potential of a given population "on itself," inasmuch as if the area, A, is small the assumption of uniform density, $\bar{D}$, is nearly always moderately good.

Table 10.10 shows how the potential within the uniform circular disk falls off with increasing distance out from the center.

Additional Formulas for the "Standard City."—In section 1 we had

$$D = D_0\, 2^{-r/b},$$

which we now rewrite,

$$D = D_0\, e^{-r/b'},$$

where $b' = b/\log 2$, the logarithm being to base e.

The population of an infinitesimal ring of radius r and width dr is

$$dP_e = 2\pi D_0\, r\, e^{-r/b'}\, dr.$$

Hence the potential at the center is

$$V_0 = 2\pi b'(D_0 - D'),$$

TABLE 10.9 Table for computing the potential at the center of an elliptical disk

RATIO OF AXES α/β	ECCENTRICITY	VALUE OF f
1.0	0.000	1.00
1.5	0.745	1.01
2.0	0.866	1.02
2.5	0.917	1.06
3.0	0.943	1.09
4.0	0.968	1.12
5.0	0.980	1.15
6.0	0.986	1.20
8.0	0.992	1.27
10.0	0.995	1.33

For a uniformly distributed population over a circular disk (i.e., an ellipse with eccentricity zero), the potential at the center is equal to the population divided by half the radius, r. Values of f in the table (computed using elliptic integrals) permit ready computation of the potential at the center of an elliptical disk having a uniform distribution of population, as equal to the population divided by the quantity, half the equivalent radius times f. By equivalent radius we mean the radius of a circle which would have just the area of the chosen ellipse. The central potential of the elliptical disk is less than that of this circular disk (with the same population) in the ratio of 1 to f. This is because of the elongation of the ellipse, which puts the population farther away from the center. The first column gives the ratio of the semi-major axis, α, to the semi-minor one, β. The text describes the procedure when this table is used to approximate the potential "on itself" of a small populated area.

D_0 being as before the central density, and D' the edge density, with

$$D' = D_0\, e^{-a/b'}$$

Now

$$\int r\, e^{-r/b'}\, dr = -b'(r - b')e^{-r/b'},$$

so we see that the whole population out to the bounding radius a is

$$P_e = 2\pi\left[b'^2 D_0 - b'(a + b')D'\right].$$

TABLE 10.10 Potential within a uniform circular disc, as a function of the distance from the center

RATIO c/r	RELATIVE POTENTIAL
0.00	1.00
0.05	1.00
0.15	0.99
0.25	0.98
0.35	0.97
0.45	0.95
0.55	0.92
0.65	0.88
0.75	0.84
0.85	0.78
0.95	0.70
1.00	0.65

If a population, P, are distributed uniformly over a circular disk of radius r, the potential at the center is $2P/r$. This value is written in the table as, relatively, 1.00. The relative potential falls as shown with increasing distance c from the center, reaching only 0.65 at the edge (where c is equal to r). At a considerable distance beyond the edge, where the ratio c/r is large, the relative potential is approximately $r/2c$; thus at a distance of 5 radii from the center, where c/r is 5, it is 0.10, about. For at a distance the entire population P can be considered as though concentrated at the center, and the potential there is about P/c. Note that even at the very edge this approximate formula would give 0.50 for the relative potential, as compared with the accurate value of 0.65 tabulated.

Empirically it was shown that the radius a increases in proportion to the three-eighths power of the population, P_c; and that D_0 is proportional to the square root of P_c. The constants of the two proportions are invariant for all the cities at a given time (if we ignore the effect of base potential), but are expected to change from census to census, slowly. The edge density also was constant for the sequence of cities in 1940, ideally.

Hence the above equation determines b' as a function of P_c, at any rate for 1940 when we have all the empirical constants. Solutions can be tabulated; a/b' is a useful parameter.

World Map of Population Potential:— Inasmuch as the inverse distance formula for potential is good in three dimensions, potentials at representative points all over the earth can be computed once population densities everywhere are known. Distances must be measured not as arcs on the surface of the globe but as straight-line chords direct from point to point. (For one thing, the arc distance is ambiguous because it can be measured either way around the great circle through any two points.) Obviously populations of the various regions must be weighted. Per capita income weightings are perhaps available. "Social mass" per person would be better—perhaps 3000 tons in the United States, only a few hundred pounds for Australian aborigines on their native deserts.

Sociological Intensity

In a quasi-equilibrium, the contours of population potential are observed in the simplest situations to outline coinciding "isotherms" of human social activity of various sorts. For instance, in the United States in 1950 the number of cities per 100,000 square miles of populations 25,000 to 35,000 varied about as the cube of the income potential.

However, other factors, as indicated in section 2, may combine with the potential to raise or depress social activity in a region. It is suggested that the indicated isotherms depict levels of "sociological intensity," and that this, rather than potential of population, is the active operating agent in bringing about such correlations as the one just stated for small cities. It corresponds to the statistical concept of temperature in physics.

While potential is objectively defined, the problem of an equally objective definition of sociological intensity or "social temperature" is still being studied. The relation for small cities refers to one type of combination of man-with-lands or income-with-land. Dr. J. D. Hamilton, one of our associates in the social physics group, has suggested a close relationship between rules governing such combinations and the rules of physical chemistry governing molecular compounds.

Notes

[1]John Q. Stewart, "Suggested Principles of Social Physics," Science, 106, 1947, pp. 179–180.

[2]Colin Clark, "Urban Population Densities," Journal of the Royal Statistical Society Ser. A, Vol. 114, Part 4, 1951, pp. 490–496.

[3]John Q. Stewart, "Urban Population Densities," The Geographical Review, XLIII, 1953, p. 575.

[4]For a recent discussion of demographic gravitation and potentials of population see John Q. Stewart and William Warntz, "Macrogeography and Social Science," The Geographical Review, XLVIII, 1958, pp. 167–184. See also Section 4 of the present paper.

[5]John Q. Stewart, "Empirical Mathematical Rules Concerning the Distribution and Equilibrium of Population," The Geographical

Review, XXXVII, 1947, pp. 461–485.

[6]Homer Hoyt, The Structure and Growth of Residential Neighborhoods in American Cities, Federal Housing Administration, Washington, D.C., 1939.

[7]John Q. Stewart, Chapter 2, Theory in Marketing, edited by Reavis Cox and Wroe Alderson, Chicago, 1950.

[8]John Q. Stewart, The Geographical Review, loc. cit., p. 464.

[9]Cf. an excellent and broadly stimulating paper by Otis Dudley Duncan, "Population Distribution and Community Structure," Cold Spring Harbor Symposia on Quantitative Biology, XXII, 1957, pp. 357–371.

[10]Walter Isard, Location and Space-Economy, New York, 1956, p. 172.

[11]John Q. Stewart and William Warntz, The Geographical Review, loc. cit., p. 178.

[12]John Q. Stewart and William Warntz, The Geographical Review, loc. cit., p. 173.

[13]E.g., John Q. Stewart and William Warntz, The Geographical Review, loc. cit., p. 178.

[14]W. J. Reilly, "Method for the Study of Retail Relationships," University of Texas Bulletin, No. 2944, 1929.

[15]Carl Hammer and Fred Charles Ikle, "Intercity Telephone and Airborne Traffic Related to Distance and the 'Propensity to Interact,' " Sociometry, 20, pp. 306–316, 1957.

[16]For four cities at the corners of a square, with a pit inside, see John Q. Stewart, The Geographical Review, loc. cit., p. 475.

Selection Eleven

MATRIX METHODS OF POPULATION ANALYSIS

Andrei Rogers

Current population forecasting efforts generally adopt variants of the cohort-survival projection method. This technique summarizes the pattern of fertility and mortality to which a population is subject and explicitly introduces the effects of net migration. That is, an initial age distribution is carried forward through a time period, say five years, by the appropriate application of age-specific birth and death rates and the allowance for changes due to net migration. A degree of refinement may be added by further disaggregating the population into sex- and race-differentiated cohorts which then are separately survived through time.

Recently, several researchers have taken advantage of the conceptual elegance and computational simplicity of matrix representation of population change and move-

Reprinted by permission of the *Journal of the American Institute of Planners* (Vol. XXXII, No. 1, January, 1966).

ment. Together, their efforts point to a fertile area for significant research. More immediately, they provide a means for developing cohort-survival population projections in matrix terms. Such an approach allows the projection process to be treated independently of the population to which it is applied This separation enables us to study the consequences of applying the same projection process to another population and thereby permits a clearer focus on the projection process itself and its long-term implications.

For example, the long-run consequences of a particular survivorship structure may be traced,[1] the long-run distributional implications of different mobility patterns may be quickly assessed, and, in a limited sense, the effects of policy intervention may be explored.[2]

This paper develops an integrated interregional population projection model which easily may be programmed for any of the current generation of digital computers. The discussion proceeds in several parts. First, the effects of mortality and fertility are shown to be expressible by matrix multiplication. Migration is then described in terms of transition matrices. Finally, an integrated matrix model of population growth is presented in which the effects of fertility, mortality, and migration are applied to an age-disaggregated population as it is adjusted forward through successive time periods.

Mortality

Consider a population disaggregated into n age groups of equal time span at some point in time, t. Denote this age distribution by a column vector w_t. We are interested in defining a matrix, D, which when applied to w_t will "age" the population to the next time period, $t + 1$. More specifically, we are seeking a matrix operator which satisfies the following equation:

$$Dw_t = \overset{**}{w_{t+1}} \qquad [1]$$

The two asterisks over the derived age distribution, w_{t+1}, serve to remind us that the effects of births and net migration still need to be incorporated.

A matrix operator which will premultiply an initial population vector to age survivors into the next age groups is of the following form:

$$\underset{n \times n}{D} = \begin{bmatrix} 0 & 0 & 0 & . & . & . & . & . & 0 \\ d_1 & 0 & 0 & . & . & . & . & . & 0 \\ 0 & d_2 & 0 & . & . & . & . & . & 0 \\ 0 & 0 & d_3 & . & . & . & . & . & 0 \\ . & . & & . & & & & & . \\ . & . & & & . & & & & . \\ . & . & & & & . & & & . \\ 0 & 0 & 0 & . & . & . & d_{n-1} & 0 \end{bmatrix} \qquad [2]$$

The only non-zero terms are on the sub-diagonal and denote for each age group the proportion which will be survived forward during one time-period. Since these proportions always lie between zero and unity, they may be interpreted as probabilities, that is, d_r is the probability that an individual

selected at random from the rth age group will survive another unit interval of time. This unit interval equals the number of years spanned by an age group. Thus, for a population disaggregated into n age groups we can define $n - 1$ survival probabilities.

A simple example may clarify the above discussion. Consider a population disaggregated into four age groups: 0–14; 15–29; 30–44; 45 and over. Assume that at time t, a total population of 4,000 people is equally divided among these four age groups. Further, assume that all survival probabilities are equal and have the value $d_r = .9$. Then by equation [1] our survival calculation becomes:[3]

$$\begin{bmatrix} 0 & 0 & 0 & 0 \\ .9 & 0 & 0 & 0 \\ 0 & .9 & 0 & 0 \\ 0 & 0 & .9 & 0 \end{bmatrix} \begin{bmatrix} 1000 \\ 1000 \\ 1000 \\ 1000 \end{bmatrix} = \begin{bmatrix} 0 \\ 900 \\ 900 \\ 900 \end{bmatrix}.$$

Several interesting points should be observed. First, notice that after the 15-year interval, the first age group is empty. This, of course, is due to the absence of births. Note, too, that D^2 is the matrix operator which will carry the original age distribution forward two 15-year periods:

$$D^2 = \begin{bmatrix} 0 & 0 & 0 & 0 \\ 0 & 0 & 0 & 0 \\ .81 & 0 & 0 & 0 \\ 0 & .81 & 0 & 0 \end{bmatrix}.$$

This can be verified by premultiplying the above survived age distribution by D and observing that the same results occur if the original age distribution is premultiplied by D^2. The process can be extended to higher powers of D.

Fertility

The ordinary way of incorporating births into a cohort-survival model begins by applying age-specific birth rates to the total number of women in each child bearing age group during the given time period. This figure is then decomposed into male and female births and adjusted to allow for deaths of children under x years of age, where x is the time interval being used.

A cruder method must be adopted in the absence of a sex breakdown. The overall procedure is the same, however. A crude age-specific birth rate now is applied to the *total* number of people in each of the child bearing age groups and the results are then summed to arrive at the total number of births during the time period.

As in the case of mortality, the matrix representation of this fertility process consists of the premultiplication of an age distribution by a suitably constructed fertility matrix, B. Such a matrix has zeroes everywhere except in these first row elements which correspond to the child bearing age groups:

$$\underset{n \times n}{B} = \qquad\qquad\qquad\qquad\qquad\qquad [3]$$

$$\begin{bmatrix} 0 & 0 & \ldots & 0 & b_1 & b_2 & \ldots & b_v & 0 & \ldots & 0 \\ 0 & 0 & & & & & & & & & 0 \\ \cdot & \cdot & & & & & & & & & \cdot \\ \cdot & & & & & & & & & & \cdot \\ \cdot & & & & & & & & & & \cdot \\ \cdot & & & & & & & & & & \cdot \\ \cdot & & & & & & & & & & \cdot \\ 0 & 0 & \ldots & & & & & & & \ldots & 0 \end{bmatrix}$$

Returning to our example and assuming age-specific birth rates of .7 for the 15–29 age group and of .5 for the 30–44 age bracket, we have the fertility process:

$$\begin{bmatrix} 0 & .7 & .5 & 0 \\ 0 & 0 & 0 & 0 \\ 0 & 0 & 0 & 0 \\ 0 & 0 & 0 & 0 \end{bmatrix} \begin{bmatrix} 1000 \\ 1000 \\ 1000 \\ 1000 \end{bmatrix} = \begin{bmatrix} 1200 \\ 0 \\ 0 \\ 0 \end{bmatrix}.$$

This operation generates the number of births during the 15-year interval and enables us to go on to simultaneously take into account births, deaths, and the process of aging.

Mortality, Fertility, and the Interregional System

The effects of mortality and fertility may be combined, in order to find their joint contribution to the total projection process, simply by adding the matrices B and D to define a "survivorship" matrix operator, S, where:

$$\underset{n \times n}{S} = B + D = \qquad\qquad\qquad [4]$$

$$\begin{bmatrix} 0 & 0 & \ldots & b_1 & b_2 & \ldots & b_v & 0 & \ldots & 0 \\ d_1 & 0 & 0 & & & & & & & 0 \\ 0 & d_2 & 0 & & & & & & & 0 \\ 0 & 0 & d_3 & & & & & & & 0 \\ \cdot & & & \cdot & & & & & & \cdot \\ \cdot & & & & & & & & & \cdot \\ \cdot & & & & & & & & & \cdot \\ \cdot & & & & & & & & & \cdot \\ 0 & 0 & 0 & \ldots & & & \ldots & d_{n-1} & 0 \end{bmatrix}$$

Again returning to our example, we have:

$$S = \begin{bmatrix} 0 & .7 & .5 & 0 \\ .9 & 0 & 0 & 0 \\ 0 & .9 & 0 & 0 \\ 0 & 0 & .9 & 0 \end{bmatrix}$$

and

$$\overset{*}{w}_{t+1} = Sw_t =$$

$$\begin{bmatrix} 0 & .7 & .5 & 0 \\ .9 & 0 & 0 & 0 \\ 0 & .9 & 0 & 0 \\ 0 & 0 & .9 & 0 \end{bmatrix} \begin{bmatrix} 1000 \\ 1000 \\ 1000 \\ 1000 \end{bmatrix} = \begin{bmatrix} 1200 \\ 900 \\ 900 \\ 900 \end{bmatrix}.$$

Once again an asterisk reminds us that the migration component still needs to be considered. Also notice that the premultiplication is the sum of the separate premultiplications Dw_t and Bw_t.

So far, the development of matrix methods for tracing the effects of mortality and fertility on an age distribution has been limited to a consideration of a single region's population. Extension of the method to an interregional system of regions is straightforward. We simply replace vectors by matrices and each matrix by a set of matrices. That is, the vector w_t now becomes a matrix W_t, in which columns are geographic areas and rows are age groups. The survivorship matrix S now receives a subscript, i, identifying it with a particular region. Thus we transform the operation:

$$\overset{*}{w}_{t+1} = Sw_t,$$

into

$$\overset{*}{w}_{i,t+1} = S_i w_{i,t}.$$

If we are willing to assume that age-specific mortality and fertility rates are the same for all regions, the process simplifies to:

$$W^{*}_{t+1} = SW_t. \qquad [5]$$

Let us now consider migration as a component of change in an interregional system of m regions. Associated with every region, i, is a population w_i. During each unit of time, for example, five years, a certain proportion of the ith region's population, in any given age group, r, migrates to region j. Thus, for each age group one may construct an interregional flow matrix, K_r, which describes the number of people, in the rth age group, $_rk_{ij}$, who during the specified time period, move from region i to region j:

$$\underset{m \times m}{K_r} =
\begin{bmatrix}
_rk_{11} & _rk_{12} & . & . & . & _rk_{1m} \\
_rk_{21} & _rk_{22} & . & & & . \\
. & & . & & & . \\
. & & & . & & . \\
. & & & & . & . \\
_rk_{m1} & _rk_{m2} & . & . & . & _rk_{mm}
\end{bmatrix}, \qquad [6]$$

$$,(r = 1,2, \ldots, n).$$

Transform this $m \times m$ flow matrix into a transition matrix by dividing each element, $_rk_{ij}$, by its corresponding row sum, $_rw_i$. This defines a transition matrix, P_r, with elements

$$_rP_{ij} = \frac{_rk_{ij}}{_rw_i}. \qquad [7]$$

Each entry of P_r represents the fraction of people, in the rth age group, who start in the ith region at time t and who will be in the jth region at time $t + 1$. Further, it is easily shown that each entry of a power of P_r, that is, of $P_r{}^n$, denotes the proportion of people who, having started in the ith region, will be in the jth region after n time periods. As in the case of mortality, since $0 \leqq {}_rp_{ij} \leqq 1$, we may think of these elements of the transition matrix as probabilities.

Given a particular P_r and the distribution among regions of the population in the rth age group, w'_r (that is, the rth row vector in the population matrix W), one may retrieve the flow matrix K_r which corresponds to this age group. Thus, if one is willing to assume

that the transition structure (that is the $_rP_{ij}$) will remain constant over time, it becomes relatively a simple matter to project the K_r of the subsequent time period. One merely applies the transition matrix P_r to a diagonal matrix, A_r, whose non-zero elements denote each region's population in the rth age group.

Once again our example will clarify the procedure. First, we will expand our system by adding two more regions and name the three regions: A, B, and C. Assume, for convenience, that regions A and C have identical age distributions and that region B's distribution is double that of A's. Thus we have:

$$W_t =
\begin{array}{c}
\\
\\
0\text{–}14 \\
15\text{–}29 \\
30\text{–}44 \\
45 +
\end{array}
\begin{array}{ccc}
w_A & w_B & w_C \\
\begin{bmatrix}
1000 & 2000 & 1000 \\
1000 & 2000 & 1000 \\
1000 & 2000 & 1000 \\
1000 & 2000 & 1000
\end{bmatrix}
\begin{array}{c}
w_1' \\
w_2' \\
w_3' \\
w_4'
\end{array}
\end{array}$$

with *Region* on the vertical axis and *Age range* along it.

Assume, further, that 80 percent of the population of each region remain where they are during the 15-year time interval and that the remaining 20 percent are distributed equally among the other two regions. Let this transition structure be the same for each of the four age groups. That is assume:

$$P_r = \begin{array}{c} A \\ B \\ C \end{array}
\begin{array}{c}
\begin{array}{ccc} A & B & C \end{array} \\
\begin{bmatrix}
.8 & .1 & .1 \\
.1 & .8 & .1 \\
.1 & .1 & .8
\end{bmatrix}
\end{array}.$$

Now by writing the row vectors of W as separate diagonal matrices A_1, A_2, A_3, and A_4, we may proceed to derive K_1, K_2, K_3, and K_4.

$$K_1 = K_2 = K_3 = K_4 =$$

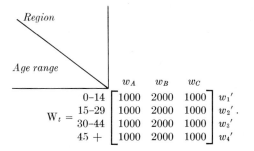

$$
\begin{array}{cc}
A_r & P_r \\
\begin{bmatrix}
1000 & 0 & 0 \\
0 & 2000 & 0 \\
0 & 0 & 1000
\end{bmatrix}
&
\begin{bmatrix}
.8 & .1 & .1 \\
.1 & .8 & .1 \\
.1 & .1 & .8
\end{bmatrix}
\end{array}
$$

$$= \begin{array}{c} K_r \\
\begin{bmatrix}
800 & 100 & 100 \\
200 & 1600 & 200 \\
100 & 100 & 800
\end{bmatrix}
\end{array}.$$

Since for simplicity we have assumed that $A_1 = A_2 = A_3 = A_4$ and $P_1 = P_2 = P_3 = P_4$, our K_r are all equal.

Having derived the total number of people in each age group who move from region i to region j during the interval of time $(t, t + 1)$, we can find the age-distributed net migration component for each of the m regions by subtracting the total number of out-migrants from the total number of in-migrants. In matrix notation:

$$n_{i,t} = 1'K_i - (K_i 1)'$$

where 1 *represents an* $n \times 1$ *unit vector,*

and

$$N_t = \begin{bmatrix} n'_{1,t} \\ n'_{2,t} \\ \cdot \\ \cdot \\ \cdot \\ n'_{n,t} \end{bmatrix} \qquad [8]$$

For our example, we have:

$n'_{1,t} = $ *total in-migrants* $-$ *total out-migrants*
$= 1'K_i - (K_i 1)'$

$= [1,1,1] \begin{bmatrix} 800 & 100 & 100 \\ 200 & 1600 & 200 \\ 100 & 100 & 800 \end{bmatrix}$

$- \left(\begin{bmatrix} 800 & 100 & 100 \\ 200 & 1600 & 200 \\ 100 & 100 & 800 \end{bmatrix} \begin{bmatrix} 1 \\ 1 \\ 1 \end{bmatrix} \right)'$

$= (1100, 1800, 1100) - (1000, 2000, 1000)$
$= (100, -200, 100).$

Since all flow matrices K_r are equal, clearly all net migration vectors will be equal and:

$$n'_{1,t} = n'_{2,t} = n'_{3,t} = n'_{4,t} = (100, -200, 100),$$

or collecting the four row vectors into a matrix N_t:

$$N_t = \begin{array}{c} \\ 0\text{--}14 \\ 15\text{--}29 \\ 30\text{--}44 \\ 45+ \end{array} \begin{array}{ccc} A & B & C \\ \begin{bmatrix} 100 & -200 & 100 \\ 100 & -200 & 100 \\ 100 & -200 & 100 \\ 100 & -200 & 100 \end{bmatrix} \end{array}.$$

A Growth Model

Having developed matrix methods for handling each of the major components of population change, we now can combine these into a population growth model:

$$W_{t+1} = SW_t + N_t \qquad [9]$$

where

$W_t = $ *a population matrix whose rows denote age groups and whose columns denote regions;*
$S = $ *a survivorship matrix which is constant over time and over the m regions of the system;*
$N_t = $ *a net migration matrix whose rows denote age groups and whose columns denote regions.*

Applying this model to our example of three regions:

$$W_{t+1} = \begin{bmatrix} 0 & .7 & .5 & 0 \\ .9 & 0 & 0 & 0 \\ 0 & .9 & 0 & 0 \\ 0 & 0 & .9 & 0 \end{bmatrix} \begin{bmatrix} 1000 & 2000 & 1000 \\ 1000 & 2000 & 1000 \\ 1000 & 2000 & 1000 \\ 1000 & 2000 & 1000 \end{bmatrix} +$$

$$\begin{bmatrix} 100 & -200 & 100 \\ 100 & -200 & 100 \\ 100 & -200 & 100 \\ 100 & -200 & 100 \end{bmatrix} = \begin{array}{ccc} A & B & C \\ \begin{bmatrix} 1300 & 2200 & 1300 \\ 1000 & 1600 & 1000 \\ 1000 & 1600 & 1000 \\ 1000 & 1600 & 1000 \end{bmatrix} \end{array}$$

Thus, in our hypothetical three-region system, the population has declined during the 15-year time interval $(t, t + 1)$ from 16,000 to 15,600. The regional distribution has shifted from a 4–8–4 division to a 4.3–7–4.3 allocation. The initial equi-distributed age composition has become skewed toward the 0–14 age group which now has 4,800 people, 800 more than before. The changes in the distribution and composition of the three regions may be studied simply by reiterating the whole process with W_{t+1} taking the place of W_t in the previous iteration.

A Growth Model for California Regions

The matrix population growth model, outlined above, has been used with considerable success to project California's interregional population, by five-year cohorts, to 1980.[4] Focusing on the State's 19 State Economic Areas as the fundamental areal unit, the model was calibrated using 1955–1960 data. A survivorship matrix was derived (Figure 11.1, on the following page), and 17 age-specific transition matrices were estimated. An initial 1960 age distribution was obtained for each of the 19 SEA's and the rest of the United States was carried along as a twentieth region to close out the system. For

FIGURE 11.1 Survivorship matrix for California*

0.	0.	0.	0.28840	0.77620	0.49690	0.27620	0.13800	0.03210	0.	0.	0.	0.	0.	0.	0.	0.	0.
0.96640	0.	0.	0.	0.	0.	0.	0.	0.	0.	0.	0.	0.	0.	0.	0.	0.	0.
0.	0.99770	0.	0.	0.	0.	0.	0.	0.	0.	0.	0.	0.	0.	0.	0.	0.	0.
0.	0.	0.99790	0.	0.	0.	0.	0.	0.	0.	0.	0.	0.	0.	0.	0.	0.	0.
0.	0.	0.	0.99490	0.	0.	0.	0.	0.	0.	0.	0.	0.	0.	0.	0.	0.	0.
0.	0.	0.	0.	0.99290	0.	0.	0.	0.	0.	0.	0.	0.	0.	0.	0.	0.	0.
0.	0.	0.	0.	0.	0.99320	0.	0.	0.	0.	0.	0.	0.	0.	0.	0.	0.	0.
0.	0.	0.	0.	0.	0.	0.99220	0.	0.	0.	0.	0.	0.	0.	0.	0.	0.	0.
0.	0.	0.	0.	0.	0.	0.	0.98760	0.	0.	0.	0.	0.	0.	0.	0.	0.	0.
0.	0.	0.	0.	0.	0.	0.	0.	0.98140	0.	0.	0.	0.	0.	0.	0.	0.	0.
0.	0.	0.	0.	0.	0.	0.	0.	0.	0.96860	0.	0.	0.	0.	0.	0.	0.	0.
0.	0.	0.	0.	0.	0.	0.	0.	0.	0.	0.95070	0.	0.	0.	0.	0.	0.	0.
0.	0.	0.	0.	0.	0.	0.	0.	0.	0.	0.	0.92880	0.	0.	0.	0.	0.	0.
0.	0.	0.	0.	0.	0.	0.	0.	0.	0.	0.	0.	0.89240	0.	0.	0.	0.	0.
0.	0.	0.	0.	0.	0.	0.	0.	0.	0.	0.	0.	0.	0.84270	0.	0.	0.	0.
0.	0.	0.	0.	0.	0.	0.	0.	0.	0.	0.	0.	0.	0.	0.75850	0.	0.	0.
0.	0.	0.	0.	0.	0.	0.	0.	0.	0.	0.	0.	0.	0.	0.	0.62740	0.	0.
0.	0.	0.	0.	0.	0.	0.	0.	0.	0.	0.	0.	0.	0.	0.	0.	0.39420	0.

*Used as S in the calculation of $w_{t+1}^{*} = Sw_{t}$.

further details, the reader is referred to the published report.[5]

Conclusion

The application of matrix methods to population analysis is of relatively recent origin. Concrete theoretical achievements, therefore, are only beginning to be made. Despite its infancy, however, a few interesting investigations should be noted. Work on survivorship matrices begun by Keyfitz in a previously cited article continues; his recent efforts have focused on the study of the stability of survivorship matrices, the interpretation of their latent roots, and the relation of the discrete matrix process to the continuous integral equation formulations of Lotka.[6] In the area of migration analysis, Rogers has attempted to investigate changes in migration stream structure and to study migration differentials by means of equilibrium distributions.[7] Policy intervention and its distributional effects, too, have been explored.[8] Others have sought to apply a "mover-stayer" hypothesis to migrants.[9] They hold that some persons are more mobile and tend to move more frequently, while others are less so. Finally, work in other subject areas, focusing on the study of change in the presence of response uncertainty, is very suggestive and worthy of examination for its potential applicability to migration problems.[10]

Notes

[1]Nathan Keyfitz, "Matrix Multiplication as a Technique of Population Analysis," *The Milbank Memorial Fund Quarterly* XLII (October 1964), 75–82.

[2]Andrei Rogers, "A Markovian Policy Model of Interregional Migration," *Papers and Proceedings of the Regional Science Association*, 15 (1965), forthcoming.

[3]The reader unacquainted with matrix algebra is referred to any of the myriad of texts on the subject that are currently available. For example: A. M. Tropper, *Matrix Theory for Electrical Engineers* (Reading, Mass.: Addison-Wesley, 1962).

[4]Andrei Rogers, *Projected Population Growth in California Regions: 1960–1980*, Preprint No. 12, Center for Planning and Development Research, University of California, Berkeley (forth-coming).

[5]*Ibid.*

[6]Nathan Keyfitz, "The Population Projection as a Matrix Operator," *Demography*, I (1964), 56–73.

[7]Andrei Rogers, *An Analysis of Interregional Migration in California*, Preprint No. 13, Center for Planning and Development Research, University of California, Berkeley (forthcoming).

[8]Andrei Rogers, "A Markovian Policy Model of Interregional Migration," *op. cit.*

[9]Isadore Blumen, Marvin Kogan, and Philip J. McCarthy, *The Industrial Mobility of Labor as a Probability Process*, VI, Cornell Studies of Industrial and Labor Relations (Ithaca, New York: The New York State School of Industrial and Labor Relations, Cornell University, 1955).

[10]James S. Coleman, *Models of Change and Response Uncertainty* (Englewood Cliffs, New Jersey: Prentice-Hall, Inc., 1964).

Author's Note:
The preparation of this paper was financed in part through an urban planning grant from the Housing and Home Finance Agency, under the provisions of Section 701 of the Housing Act of 1954, as amended. The development of matrix analysis of mortality and fertility borrows heavily from the seminal ideas of Nathan Keyfitz, particularly as expressed in his recent article: "Matrix Multiplication as a Technique of Population Analysis," The Milbank Memorial Fund Quarterly XLII (October 1964), 68–84. The author's principal contributions are the regionalization of Keyfitz's efforts and the introduction of the effects of migration.

Selection Twelve

APPLICATIONS OF MATHEMATICS TO POPULATION GEOGRAPHY

Yu. V. Medvedkov

Abstract: *Three levels of application of mathematics are considered in order of increasing complexity. The first level involves measurements of processes and phenomena, the second the derivation of empirical relationships, and the third the construction of deductive models reflecting the basic mechanism of processes and phenomena. Examples of the three levels are given: Boyce's city-shape index illustrates the first; and Clark's formula for population density within cities is given as an example of the second. The second level is also illustrated by Medvedkov's procedure for forecasting the interplay of natural and mechanical movement of population, involving the use of matrix algebra. On the third level, Medvedkov constructs models of flows of pedestrians doing their shopping on their way home from work to determine an optimal distribution of retail outlets.*

At least three levels must be distinguished in the application of mathematics to population geography. The "levels" refer to differences in the complexity of the problems to be solved; as a general rule, increasing complexity of problems requires an increasing complexity of the mathematical apparatus. In general terms, problems of the first level answer the question "how much"; the second "what are the relationships"; and the third "what are the causes."

The *first level* calls for the introduction of quantitative measurements of phenomena and processes. Actually this only sets the stage for the use of the actual mathematical tools. Our objective is to express information with numerical precision, and this requires, above all, clear definitions. Equally important is the choice of rational measurements and allowance for the variability of magnitudes and reliability of data. Special techniques are used for the numerical representation of inherently qualitative features,

Translated by Theodore Shabad from *Nauchnyye Problemy Geografii Naseleniya* (Research Problems in Population Geography), Moscow, Moscow University, 1967, 225–237.

for example, the binary system (presence of the feature—absence of the feature). Among the mathematical techniques most commonly used in such problems are the theory of measurements, group theory, descriptive statistics, and information theory.

A characteristic aspect of geographic research on population and settlement is the wide use of the data of statistical services. The use of population statistics has always been accompanied by a borrowing of analytical techniques. Many accounting categories or indicators have been adopted in ready form: employed population, age groups, coefficients of population growth, of natural increase, migration, and others. Population geography has long accumulated a reservoir for the application of mathematics, which made possible rapid progress in this area.

In quantitative evaluations the geographer must be constantly on guard against the pitfall of "false accuracy" in a situation where poorly defined concepts are so common. As a general rule, each numerical evaluation should be accompanied by a cross-check of the methods used in the collection of the relevant information. War should resolutely be declared against nebulous definitions and noncomparable figures.

In urban research, for example, it would be difficult to ignore the question of delimiting the real boundaries of a city. Official city limits do not define each city in equivalent fashion. Of great interest, therefore, are attempts to define the actual city boundaries on the basis of aerial photographs or data on population density, everyday contacts among the population, etc.

Conclusions concerning the density of settlement of a territory, which are so important for geography, should not be derived simply from data relating to a network of political-administrative divisions. Minor civil divisions vary greatly in size and may introduce distortions unless special operations are employed. Good results have been obtained through recalculation of density figures for a network of equal-area territories. A number of geographers in Poland, the United States, Finland, and Sweden use hexagonal territories for that purpose.

Many geographers are avoiding altogether the use of conventional density maps in order to represent more faithfully the discrete character of settlement. Instead they are introducing maps of the demographic potential, on which a measure of the nearness of population is computed for each point (j):

$$jV = \sum_{i=1}^{n} \frac{H_i}{R_{ji}} \tag{1}$$

(where H_i is the population, one by one, of all the places within the given territory; R_{ji} is the distance from each of these places to point j). The compilation of maps of the demographic potential involves a tremendous amount of computing, which can be facilitated by the use of electronic digital computers. Work on the compilation of demographic-potential maps is carried on widely in Poland, the United States, Sweden, and several other countries.

An example of an innovation typical of the first level of application of mathematics is the urban-shape index proposed by Ronald R. Boyce of the United States. A precise and objective characterization of shape is achieved by strictly qualified conditions of measurement. The index is computed on the basis of the length (R_i) of all the radial lines (1, 2, $3 \ldots i, \ldots n$) extending at equal angular intervals along n azimuths from the city's center to its boundaries. The formula of the index takes the form:

$$1 = \sum_{i=1}^{n} \left| \frac{R_i}{\sum\limits_{i=1}^{n} R_i} 100 - \frac{100}{n} \right| \tag{2}$$

The values of I range from 0 to 200. In a city of strictly circular form, $R_i = R_{i+1}$ and therefore $I = 0$. A city consisting of a single radial street would have a shape index $I = 200$. The values of the shape index for some cities are: Bucharest 16.1; Washington 16.2; Warsaw 24.9; Belgrade 31.1; Baku 39.2.

These figures are correct for a level of generalization corresponding to a map scale of 1:125,000, with measurements conducted along twelve radial lines. The figures are undoubtedly useful for city comparisons since they provide a precise and unambiguous statement of the shape of a city. But this is not the main point. The principal usefulness of this index lies in its ability to suggest whether the city shape affects certain urban functions. The nearness of population to places of employment in the center of the city would obviously vary, depending on whether the city is compact or extends in a long-narrow shape. Boyce noted in particular that the city shape affects the share of retail business in the central district. If we designate that share of the retail business by Y, then $Y = C \cdot 1^{-a}$, where C and a are constants.

A particularly complex case of measurements involves evaluation of the degree of the regularity of systems of settlement. Here we need a technique for filtering out interfering phenomena or noise. A solution proposed by the author involves the computation of the entropy of systems. As a basic definition, we consider a system to be regular if the entropy equals zero ($H = 0$). Once the distribution of the nearest-neighbor distances of places is expressed in frequencies (p_i), the entropy of the system can be found easily by Shannon's formula:

$$H = - \sum_i p_i \log_2 p_i \qquad [3]$$

For a completely regular system, the nearest-neighbor distances would be identical and therefore $H = 0$. A completely random system constitutes a Poissonian plane field of points. There the probability of encountering nearest-neighbor distances in the class ($r_{i+1} - r_i$) would be:

$$p(r_{i+1} - r_i) = \exp(-r_i^2 \alpha) - \exp(r_{i+1}^2 \alpha), \qquad [4]$$

where α is the mean number of points within a circle with a one-kilometer radius. A comparison of graphs and tables suggests the weight of the regular component and the Poisson component in any study system. The regularity features in systems of settlement turned out to be so strong that there were grounds for giving greater attention to the settlement theories of Christaller and Lösch.

The *second level* of application of mathematics is related to a search for empirical relationships in the vast body of numerical data available to population geography. The relationship between phenomena is to be expressed with a certain degree of approximation in the form of mathematical functions. This, in turn, opens the way to the cognition of causal relationships. Facts are generalized and become known at greater depth since their identification with functions helps to uncover the whole range of properties inherent in general in the given type of function. The theory of correlation, the theory of functions, methods of statistical testing of hypotheses—these are examples of branches of mathematics typical of the second level.

Some people regard empirical formulas as they would models of reality. Actually such formulas only approximate real relationships; out of the total mass of accompanying influences, a tendency emerges. The situation

under study is thus reproduced with a certain degree of schematism. Examples of empirical formulas that serve as models of real relationships in the sphere of settlement and population geography are: the Zipf equation for the population of cities combined into a system; the Clark equation for population density in cities; the Reilly equation for the boundary of the spheres of influence of two neighboring cities. These formulas are as follows:

$$H_j = k^{-1} H_1 j^{-a}; \; D_x = D_o e^{-bx}; \; R_{xB} = \frac{R_{AB}}{1 + \sqrt{\dfrac{H_A}{H_B}}} \;. [5\text{-}7]$$

In working with empirical formulas, we must distinguish between the structure of the formulas and the values of the parameters of the local characteristics. As the set of these characteristics increases, the formulas may correspond more precisely to the real situation. In principle we can even reflect completely all the nuances in the initial situation, but little is to be gained from it. There is no sense in introducing into the equations all the errors in measurements or secondary details. A wide diversity of parameters of local characteristics is essential in any large-scale study of a situation where local conditions are at the center of attention. Such an approach is essential in forecast computations, but it complicates formulas to such an extent that their structure is no longer clearly discernible. In generalizations, however, the principal aspect is the structure of the formulas and the set of parameters can be reduced to a minimum.

The three formulas above are given in a notion that corresponds to a highly generalized interpretation of settlement data. A formula looks entirely different if it is to be applied to large-scale studies. For example, Clark's formula would have to be replaced by the following expression, which has been proposed by the present author:

$$D\rho = D_o e^{(q-x)[\alpha_o + \Sigma k(\alpha h \, \cos \, h\rho + \beta_h \, \sin \, h\rho)]} \qquad [8]$$

This notation reflects the distribution of population within a city with virtually the same degree of detail as a dot map. The formula is more convenient than a map for computing the number of persons living within the limits of given radii and sectors; it is a faithful expression of the specific features of a radius-and-ring structure of urban settlement.

Empirical formulas, as a general rule, do not pretend to be able to delve in depth into causal relationships. They employ mathematics for descriptive purposes. Compared with textual or cartographic description, these formulas achieve greater compactness, precision, and comparability. An important advantage of formulas is the ease with which they can be transformed from one form into another, thus facilitating all sorts of logical computations. Value theoretical deductions can be derived in the course of mathematical generalizations of empirical formulas, for example, the results achieved by B. L. Gurevich and Yu. G. Saushkin in interpreting Clark's formula (see B. L. Gurevich and Yu. G. Saushkin, "The mathematical method in geography," *Vestn. MGU, geogr.*, 1966, No. 1; translated in *Soviet Geography*, April 1966).

Empirical formulas often find practical applications in forecast computations. It is extremely important to be able to mount experiments on the basis of formulas (models). Economic-geographic processes in themselves are not suitable for experimentation; any findings would be obtained at too high a cost. Quite another thing is the computation of alternatives in the course of a process involving simply changes in parameters in an empirical formula; this makes it possible to observe the consequences of such changes. Such computations are controlled by formal rules, which provide a guarantee against subjective judgments of the research; any findings, moreover, can be submitted to a cross check. The use of standard rules raises the productivity of labor and makes it possible to feed many operations into electronic computers.

To illustrate the advantages of a formalized forecasting procedure, let us now examine in greater detail the relationships between the natural and the mechanical movement of population. This subject is important in any geographic study of migration. Any hypothesis concerning population movement must encompass data on both age groups and regional distribution. A matrix form of notation is most suitable for this purpose. Matrix algebra makes it possible to reduce the whole forecasting procedure to simple equations.

We will use the following designations:

$\|H\|$—the matrix of the initial age composition of the population and the population distribution by regions;

$\|H_T\|$—same, after T years, i.e., at the end of the segment of time covered by the forecast;

$\|E_i\|$—the operator of natural movement of population;

$\|S\|$—the matrix of the migration balance;

$\|M_i\|$—the matrix of interregional population flows during T years.

In matrices $\|H\|$, $\|H_T\|$, and $\|S\|$ the vertical columns correspond to the regions of the country, and the horizontal rows to age groups. In practice the most suitable matrix form is a square. The matrices $\|M_i\|$ must be compiled for each age group separately; there the rows and columns must represent regions so that the sum along the rows would represent the situation at the initial time, and the sum along the columns the situation after T years. The matrices $\|E_i\|$ may be constructed for each region to reflect changes in birth and death coefficients. However, for the sake of simplicity we will assume that $\|E_i\|$ is the same for all regions, i.e., that there are no differences in birth and death coefficients between regions.

In order to predict the age composition and regional distribution of population by regions over a period of time T, all we need to know is the magnitudes of $\|H\|$, $\|E\|$, and $\|M_i\|$. The basic equation has the form

$$\|H_T\| = \|E\|\hat{\diamond}\|H\| + \|S\|, \qquad [9]$$

where $\|S\|$ consists of vector rows $\|s_i\|$ for which

$$\|s_i\| = \|1\|'\hat{\diamond}\|M_i\| - (\|M_i\|\cdot\|1\|)'. \qquad [10]$$

In expression 10 the symbol $\|1\|$ designates a unit vector-row.

The present author made the appropriate computations for the United States to forecast a situation as of 1981 (assuming no change in 1964 birth and death rates until 1981 and no changes in migration factors; the only assumption was a decline in the rate of migration as the population in the region of out-migration decreases). The total out-migration from a region during a period of T years is given by formula

$$m_{iT} = m_o \frac{e^{pT} - 1}{p}, \qquad [11]$$

where m_0 is the out-migration in the initial year at the beginning of the period covered by the forecast, and p is the rate of decline of population (H), so that $p = \dfrac{dH}{HdT}$. Expression 11 is obtained by integration of equation $H_T = H_0 e^{-pt}$ between the limits $t = 0$ and $t = T$.

The initial data relate to 1964 (see matrices below). In these matrices the columns (reading from left to right) correspond to three regions of the United States: the North, the South, and the West. The rows in $\|H\|$ and $\|E\|$ (reading from top to bottom) correspond to three age groups: 1–17 years; 18–34 years; 35 years and older. These three age groups are shown in the same sequence in matrices $\|M_1\|$, $\|M_2\|$, and $\|M_3\|$, where the rows represent the regions of out-migration.

The values of the elements shown in the matrices were computed from data published in statistical sources of the United States (*Statistical Abstract of the United States*, 1965; *Current Population Reports*, Series P-20, No. 141, Sept. 7, 1965. The latter source gives age-group data on interregional migration for the year ending March 31, 1964). All figures are given in thousands.

$$\|H\| = \begin{pmatrix} 34{,}407 & 20{,}286 & 10{,}815 \\ 20{,}682 & 12{,}195 & 6{,}501 \\ 42{,}242 & 24{,}906 & 13{,}278 \end{pmatrix}$$

$$\|E\| = \begin{pmatrix} 0.0983 & 1.434 & 0.3020 \\ 0.9895 & 0 & 0 \\ 0 & 0.976 & 0.666 \end{pmatrix}$$

$$\|M_1\| = \begin{pmatrix} 27{,}018 & 4{,}617 & 2{,}965 \\ 3{,}160 & 13{,}669 & 3{,}448 \\ 1{,}739 & 2{,}272 & 6{,}620 \end{pmatrix}$$

$$\|M_2\| = \begin{pmatrix} 12{,}099 & 4{,}871 & 3{,}805 \\ 5{,}220 & 4{,}073 & 3{,}012 \\ 2{,}375 & 2{,}601 & 1{,}322 \end{pmatrix}$$

$$\|M_3\| = \begin{pmatrix} 37{,}087 & 2{,}321 & 2{,}956 \\ 1{,}926 & 21{,}140 & 1{,}843 \\ 1{,}436 & 1{,}565 & 10{,}152 \end{pmatrix}$$

The figures for $\|H\|$ were taken directly from the statistical sources. In view of the incompleteness of 1964 data, the average national age structure of the United States had to be used for each region. In matrix $\|E\|$ the elements of the first row represent birth-rate coefficients by ages minus infant mortality. The figures were computed in the usual way for the three age groups and cover 17 years (assuming no change in the 1964 rates). The other elements in $\|E\|$, apart from zero, represent the complements that must be added to the death-rate coefficients by ages to yield 1, again assuming no change in the 1964 rates. [*Editor's note:* The complements in essence represent the probability of representatives of the three original age groups remaining alive at the end of the seventeen-year period.] The elements m_{iT} that make up $\|M_i\|$ are derived by formula 11. Here it must be explained that the formula should not be used to derive the diagonal elements in $\|M_i\|$. The elements of the main diagonal are derived from the equality of the sums $\Sigma\Sigma m_0 = \Sigma\Sigma m_{iT}$.

In the actual forecast computations, the first step consists of the operations shown in formula 10, which yield the difference between the sums along the rows and columns of the matrices $\|M_i\|$. We can illustrate this by means of the age group 1–17 years:

$$(1,1,1)\begin{pmatrix} 27{,}018 & 4{,}617 & 2{,}965 \\ 3{,}160 & 13{,}669 & 3{,}448 \\ 1{,}739 & 2{,}272 & 6{,}620 \end{pmatrix}$$

$$- \left[\begin{pmatrix} 27{,}018 & 4{,}617 & 2{,}965 \\ 3{,}160 & 13{,}669 & 3{,}448 \\ 1{,}739 & 2{,}272 & 6{,}620 \end{pmatrix}\begin{pmatrix} 1 \\ 1 \\ 1 \end{pmatrix} \right]' =$$

$$= (31{,}917, 20{,}558, 13{,}033)$$
$$- (34{,}600, 20{,}277, 10{,}631)$$
$$= (-2{,}683, 281\ 2{,}402) = \|s_1\|$$

In the same way we then obtain the migration balance for the other age groups. The vector-rows $\|s_i\|$ are then used to construct the migration-balance matrix $\|S\|$. For the United States over the period 1964–81, we obtain:

$$\|S\| = \begin{pmatrix} -2{,}683 & 281 & 2{,}402 \\ -1{,}081 & -760 & 1{,}841 \\ -1{,}915 & 117 & 1{,}798 \end{pmatrix}$$

In accordance with equation 9 we get the final answer:

$$\|H_T\| = \begin{pmatrix} 0.0983 & 1.434 & 0.3020 \\ 0.9895 & 0 & 0 \\ 0 & 0.976 & 0.666 \end{pmatrix}$$
$$\cdot \begin{pmatrix} 34{,}407 & 20{,}286 & 10{,}815 \\ 20{,}682 & 12{,}195 & 6{,}501 \\ 42{,}242 & 24{,}906 & 13{,}278 \end{pmatrix}$$
$$+ \begin{pmatrix} -2{,}683 & 281 & 2{,}402 \\ -1{,}081 & -760 & 1{,}841 \\ -1{,}915 & 117 & 1{,}798 \end{pmatrix}$$
$$= \begin{pmatrix} 43{,}114 & 27{,}285 & 16{,}797 \\ 32{,}965 & 19{,}313 & 12{,}542 \\ 46{,}404 & 28{,}606 & 16{,}986 \end{pmatrix}$$

When we compare matrices $\|H\|$ and $\|H_T\|$, we find that by 1981 the contrasts between the North and the West in total population will be reduced to the greatest extent in the 1–17 age group and to the smallest extent in the 34+ age group. This finding, one of the results of the forecast, is far from trivial. Without these computations one would have thought that representatives of the older age groups would become distributed more uniformly through the regions than younger people, who will have had far less time to take advantage of the opportunity of migrating westward. But such a supposition ignored the age differentiation in birth and death rates. The use of formula 9, on the other hand, took full account of the interplay of the processes of natural and mechanical movement of population.

In the case of these matrix formulas, mathematical generalization involves the determination of the probability character of the forecasting operations. Actually matrix $\|E\|$ may be regarded as the sum of the matrix operators of the birth rate (R) and the death rate (C): $\|E\| = \|R\| + \|C\|$. Matrix $\|C\|$ contains all the elements of $\|E\|$ except those in the first row (which are replaced by zeros); these figures then repre-

sent the probability that the members of a given age group will remain alive through the entire period T. Matrix $\|M_i\|$ can be easily converted into a matrix $\|P_i\|$, representing the probability operator of migrations, by dividing the elements of $\|M_i\|$ by the sums of their rows. The values of the elements in $\|P_i\|$ indicate the probability that persons living in a given region at the initial time will migrate during the period T. The diagonal elements of $\|P_i\|$ show the probability of anyone's not migrating to another region. The matrix $\|M_i\|$ can easily be derived from $\|P_i\|$ by means of the rule $\|M\| = \|B_i\| \cdot \|P_i\|$, where B_i is a diagonal matrix consisting of the elements of the row in $\|H\|$ that corresponds to the required age group (the subscript i designating that group).

Probability evaluations can also be found behind the figures in the upper vector-row of matrix $\|E\|$. Here we are dealing with the frequency of births occurring in various population groups.

After the conversion to probabilities has been completed, one further step is possible, namely to reflect the variability of the parameters by means of the concept of the density of distribution. A compilation of a series of forecasts for periods T, $2T$, $3T \ldots$, NT makes possible the use of the theorems of addition and multiplication of probabilities. All this facilitates complete evaluations with a minimum of computations and helps clarify the prospects of development of migrations and other demographic processes.

The *third level* of application of mathematics involves the most difficult aspect—the discovery of the mechanism of phenomena through deductive, theoretical thought processes. Here the derivation of laws is not postponed until that indefinite time when all details can be given size and shape in the form of empirical formulas or the most accurate maps; the goal can be reached far more rapidly through the use of intuition and imagination. Starting from a few well known facts, we are required to re-create in our mind all the deep-seated causes and effects. This time the problem is to construct models of laws, i.e., the most basic regularities, and not the external and obvious relationships that are sometimes reflected by means of empirical formulas. Suppositions represented in the form of formulas have the invaluable advantage of being susceptible to verification. The making of a guess is thus promptly followed by a comparison with the facts, and only those models that meet the test are then applied to research.

Creative thought processes that enable us to re-create a picture of the whole from just a few details find their application in all aspects of life. The descriptive sciences—and geography was long one of them—have underestimated the value of a scientific imagination. Anyone who saw his main purpose in the registration and accumulation of facts naturally shied away from bold guesses and hypotheses. But when we start to deal with problems of explanation prediction, and control, we can no longer get along without deductive reasoning. The application of mathematics enables us to insure the necessary discipline, rigorousness, and keenness of scientific guesswork.

We will start our acquaintance with the third level of application of mathematics with very simple examples. Such examples arise especially in the large-scale study of populated places. Let us take one such problem relating to the processes of movement of people in a city who are shopping for food during the peak evening hours when stores are expected to operate with maximum efficiency. Experience shows that not all the stores have the same number of customers, even if there is no difference in the range of goods offered for sale. What pattern of distribution of food stores would insure an equal customer load during the peak shopping period?

Anyone analyzing the behavior of members of pedestrian flows on the streets of a large city has to deal with such a mass of material that it would be difficult to expect him to register all the individual decision-making. The only way of solving this problem is to construct guesswork-based models and to test them.

For a precise formulation of the problem, let us take the simplest example. We will imagine a street with a single type of housing and, at one end of the street, a point of exit of pedestrians rushing home from work (say, a subway station). We will assume that all the stores along the street have the same assortment of goods for sale and each pedestrian makes one purchase only.

The first model is based on the assumption that the pedestrians tend to do their shopping closer to home. The linear density of housing is uniform, and therefore the flow of pedestrians will be according to the law

$$1_x = 1_o - ax, \qquad [12]$$

where x is the distance from the subway exit, and a is a certain constant. Along equal segments of the street, the same number of pedestrians will enter their homes. Let this number of people (ΔI) represent an optimal number of customers for a single store. It will be easily seen that a uniform distribution of customers per store will then require a uniform distribution of stores along the line of movement of the pedestrians.

The second model is based on the assumption that the pedestrians do their shopping in the busiest places on the ground that the actions of some serve as a reminder to others. In this case, the number of shopping contacts, or the rate of decrease of potential customers $(-d\mu)$, at any point along the street will be proportional to the number of pedestrians who have yet to do their shopping (μ). If ω is the coefficient of proportionality, then the situation can be expressed by the formula

$$\frac{d\mu}{\mu} = -\omega dx. \qquad [13]$$

We will now introduce the following symbols: M for the total number of pedestrians living on the street, and L for the length of the street. We will assume that μ is the number of pedestrians living along a street segment of length dx. Consequently

$$\mu = dM = \frac{M}{L} dx. \qquad [14]$$

Since $\dfrac{d\mu}{\mu} = d \ln\mu$, we can derive from (13) the expression dM_x, which is the total number of persons (the residents of dx) who have yet to do their shopping before reaching the point x:

$$\int_{\mu_0}^{\mu_x} d \ln\mu = - \int_0^x \omega dx. \quad [15]$$

The answer will be $\ln\mu_x - \ln\mu_0 = -\omega x$, whence $\mu_x = \mu_0 e^{-\omega x}$ or

$$dM_x = dM e^{-\omega x}. \quad [16]$$

Let us now take along that street a second point h, such that $h > x$. According to the conditions of the problem, the segment $dh = dx$ also accounts for μ residents from among the pedestrians. Of these, dM_x persons will not have done their shopping by the time they reach point x; among these, the number of persons who will do their shopping along segment dx is:

$$m_x = \omega dM_x dx = \omega dx dM e^{-\omega x}. \quad [17]$$

In view of (14), we should write 17 in another form:

$$m_x = \omega dx \frac{M}{L} dh \, e^{-\omega x}. \quad [18]$$

The persons who can do their shopping along segment dx are the residents of all the houses situated between x and L. We can find the number of these shoppers by integrating the right part of 18 with respect to the variable h between the limits L and x. We get:

$$m_{x\Sigma} = \frac{M}{L} \omega dx e^{-\omega x} \int_x^1 dh = \omega \mu e^{-\omega x}(L - x). \quad [19]$$

Taking into account 14, when $x = 0$ we have $m_{0\Sigma} = M\omega dx$, which reflects the large number of shopping contacts at the beginning of the street along a segment having the length dx. Using the last equation as a definition, we can write the finding 19 in the more compact form

$$m_{x\Sigma} = m_{0\Sigma} \frac{L - x}{L} e^{-\omega x}. \quad [20]$$

On the initial segments of the street $\dfrac{L - x}{L} \approx$ 1 so that formula 20 becomes even simpler:

$$m_{x\Sigma} = m_{0\Sigma} e^{-\omega x}. \quad [21]$$

Finally, let us designate by N_x the linear

density of shops along the street sufficient to serve $m_{x\Sigma}$ shoppers during peak hours. It is obvious that $N_x = N_0 m_{x\Sigma} \dfrac{1}{m_{0\Sigma}}$. By substituting the value of $m_{x\Sigma}$ from 21, we get

$$N_x = N_0 e^{-\omega x}. \quad [22]$$

Thus, according to the second model, a store distribution most convenient for a flow of pedestrians follows the exponential law.

Which of these two models is closer to reality? To seek an answer to that question we used known facts about the distribution of mobile retail outlets—pushcarts and open-air stands. Surveys made along Moscow streets have shown that the actual situation tends to correspond more often to the second model. In many situations, aspects of both models are combined.

Having thus explained the character of the three levels of application of mathematics, we must stress the close interrelationships between the various levels. The upper levels cannot develop without the lower ones, and the existence of both gives rise to a multitude of connecting ideas. A given set of mathematical tools can be used for a broad category of problems. The formal operations involving the algebraic symbols of population geography will be the same no matter whether the model is empirical or deductive in character.

At this mathematical stage of maturity, it should be noted that population geography has already been pervaded by a large range of problems borrowed from economics. These are problems involving the search for the extreme values of functions. Such problems play an important role in constructive applications of science. Computations of extreme values are found both in empirical and in deductive models.

An example is the problem of the location of an industry at a minimum distance from several populated places. We require that the sum of the squares of the commuting distances be a minimum. Using Cartesian coordinates, we will designate the unknown location by the abscissa x_c and the ordinate

y_c. For n places with coordinates x_i, y_i, the condition of minimization is expressed in the form

$$\sum_{}^{n} (x_i - x_c)^2 + \sum_{}^{n} (y_i - y_c)^2 = \text{min.} \quad [23]$$

Transformation by means of the binomial formula and subsequent differentiation with respect to x_i, and then y_i, shows that $x_c = \frac{1}{n}\Sigma x_i$, $y_c = \frac{1}{n}\Sigma y_i$. The coordinates of the unknown industrial site are thus the arithmetic means of the abscissas and the ordinates of all the places.

Functions are usually minimized or maximized by the method of linear programming. This method has proved itself in the construction of an optimal distribution of housing districts and places of employment in a city. In principle, the composition of available labor resources and the composition of industrial enterprises could also be coordinated.

There is a large literature on the subject of linear programming. Attempts have also been made to enlarge the range of programming by including nonlinear relationships and dynamic processes.

In geographic problems there is always a spatial aspect. Little benefit can be derived from findings relating to "population in general," as if it were located in a single point. The trouble is that matrix operations in programming do not always leave room for the spatial aspect. There is much room for improvement in achieving a geographic formulation of programming problems. An approach to this problem has been suggested by L. I. Vasilevskiy in his lectures on "The mathematical apparatus of the economic geographer" delivered in the Moscow branch of the Geographical Society USSR in 1965–66. He proposed the creation of algorithms for three-dimensional programming matrices or the maximization (minimization) of the complex index with a spatial component.

Although all three levels of mathematical application are important in population geography, the author basically favors deductive models. This is not just a matter of personal preference. There is a vast baggage of empirical research in population geography, but it has not been properly thought through. This has given rise to a dangerous gap—the absence of a solid and specific theory. Efforts to arrive at theoretical generalizations in verbal form have been fragmentary, and their results are therefore difficult to use. Unfortunately, the highly valuable content of traditional theory tends to be clothed in amorphous and ambiguous definitions that give rise to a great deal of unnecessary discussion (for example, the question of optimal city size).

It would be a mistake to see the main benefit of mathematical application in the creation of certain new and particular methods. Mathematics serves as the most precise and rational language for all modern science, especially when it comes to formulating theory. The conversion of all the valuable results of traditional theory into this new language is now needed and would be a fruitful undertaking. It would provide an overview of past achievements, and would open up new problems and previously unsuspected ways of solving them.

In a popular treatment of mathematics, Academician Ya. B. Zel'dovich had the following instructive comment: "The author knows from experience that the work he was unable to do (and was in the meantime done by others) remained undone because the author limited himself to general statements and was not bold enough to write down equations or to formulate the problem in mathematical terms; computational difficulties in a precisely formulated problem . . . can always be overcome—if not by exact calculation, then at least by approximating methods" [Ya. B. Zel'dovich. *Vysshaya matematika dlya nachnayushchikh* (Higher Mathematics for the Beginner). Moscow: Fizmatgiz, 1960, p. 69].

The application of mathematics is opening up new horizons in population geography. But until now we have been slow and not very successful in realizing the potentialities. For a number of reasons, geographers in the

USSR were late in beginning to master the new mathematical techniques. It is not unusual for problems at the second and third levels of complexity to be so poorly grasped that the talk revolves only around "quantitative methods." Members of adjacent disciplines have advanced far ahead of us in mathematical literacy. Few Soviet geographers thus far have been familiarizing themselves with foreign research and its rich mathematical baggage. There is a danger that we may be left behind world advances in the area of population geography.

A number of useful steps have been taken in the last few years to remedy this situation. A seminar on new methods is meeting regularly under the Moscow branch of the Geographical Society USSR [see *Soviet Geography*, April 1966, pp. 35–54]. In 1966 the society's branch and the Geography Faculty of Moscow University convened a conference on the mathematical method [see *Soviet Geography*, March 1967], followed by a summer school on "Mathematics in geography" [see the report in the present issue of *Soviet Geography*]. Judging from reviews, the first monographs containing mathematical analyses of settlement data (N. I. Blazhko and others) have been received with approval (V. M. Gokhman, "A valuable contribution to the use of mathematical research methods and models in economic geography, "*Izv. AN SSSR, ser. geogr.*, 1966, No. 2, 134–38).

Soviet geographers have a vast experience in research with traditional methods in population geography. The application of mathematics must of necessity flow out of past work and be based on it. That is why we are confident of early and decisive success in the development of this new and promising method of our discipline.

A SELECTED SUPPLEMENTARY BIBLIOGRAPHY FOR PART 3

Barclay, G. W., *Techniques of Population Analysis*. New York: John Wiley and Sons, Inc., 1958.

Clark, P. J., and Evans, F. C., "Distance to Nearest Neighbor as a Measure of Spatial Relationships in Population," *Ecology*, Vol. 33, 1960, pp. 445–453.

Hagerstrand, T., "A Monte Carlo Approach to Diffusion," *European Journal of Sociology*, Vol. 6, 1965, pp. 43–67.

Jaffe, A. J., *Handbook of Statistical Methods for Demographers*. Washington, D.C.: U.S. Government Printing Office, 1951.

Macarthur, N., *Introducing Population Statistics*, South Pacific Commission and the Australian National University. Canberra, Melbourne, New York: Oxford University Press, 1961.

Milbank Memorial Fund Conference, *Emerging Techniques in Population Research*. New York, 1963.

Monkhouse, F. J., and Wilkinson, H. R., "Population Maps and Diagrams," *Maps and Diagrams*. London; Methuen, 1952, pp. 217–280.

Robinson, A. H., *Elements of Cartography*, 2nd ed. New York: John Wiley and Sons, Inc., 1960, pp. 136–177.

Robinson, A. H., Lindberg, J. B., and Brinkman, L. W., "A Correlation and Regression Analysis Applied to Rural Farm Population Densities in the Great Plains," *Annals of the Association of American Geographers*, Vol. 51, 1961, pp. 211–221.

Rogers, A., *Matrix Analysis of Interregional Population Growth and Distribution*. Berkeley: University of California Press, 1968.

Spiegelman, M., *Introduction to Demography*. Chicago: Society of Actuaries, 1955.

Stewart, J. Q., "Empirical Mathematical Rules Concerning the Distribution and Equilibrium of Population," *Geographical Review*, Vol. 37, 1947, pp. 461–485.

Tavener, L. E., "Population Maps: Problems and Methods of Demographic Cartography," *Genus*, Comitato Italians per lo Studio dei Problemi della Popolazione, 1956, pp. 88–101.

U.S. Department of State, A.I.D., *Demographic Techniques for Manpower Planning in Developing Countries*. Washington, D.C.: U.S. Government Printing Office, 1963.

Wolfenden, H. H., *Population Statistics and Their Compilation*. Chicago: The University of Chicago Press, 1954.

Wolpert, J., "Stability in Inter-Regional Migration Streams," Paper read at Meetings of the Population Association of American, Cincinnati, Ohio, February 17, 1966.

Wright, J. K., "Some Measures of Distributions," *Annals of the Association of American Geographers*, Vol. 27, 1937, pp. 177–211.

PART FOUR

POPULATION DISTRIBUTION AND DENSITY: SPATIAL CHARACTERISTICS AND CHANGING PATTERNS

INTRODUCTION

The study of spatial distributions has long occupied geographers. The where? and the why where? constitute disarmingly simple, yet extremely complicated questions which can be asked about all manner of phenomena. The purpose here is to apply such questions to a single phenomenon—population. In so doing, a wide range of subjects are, by necessity, included; for the study of population distribution and density and the dynamic aspects of each of these topics embraces many demographic and nondemographic subjects. The first class, the demographic, involves the description and analysis of the array of mankind over area. In addition, mode of residence and trends in urban and rural populations, components of population change (including the study of mortality, fertility, and migration as they combine to effect changing distributions and densities), and the reciprocal relationships between and among population characteristics and distribution and density are included. Such relationships are perhaps best expressed as the manner in which population characteristics relate to the processes which combine to produce trends in distribution and density—natural increase and migration. Included in the nondemographic subjects germane to this section are physical, cultural, and economic factors which, singly and in combination, affect distribution and density. Topics treated by the various authors represented here range from physical environmental influences to differential economic opportunity, and include discussions of city form and function, and the impact of resources on distribution.

The lead article by Bogue describes traditional studies of population distribution as generally *aggregative* in approach, studying entire national populations ("the whole"), with no attempt at working with smaller political units ("the parts"). The *distributive* approach requires a shift in scale and, like the aggregative, may be used to examine most, if not all, of the topics of population study. Interestingly, it is this concern with areal variation and regularity through time, utilizing parts of the whole as statistical units, which seems to characterize the geographer's approach to population study—and Bogue, a sociologist, aptly describes the importance of such disaggregation.

Gibbs tests five hypothetical stages in "The Evolution of Population Concentration," using the forty-eight conterminous states of the United States as his study area. His discussion starts with the dawn of cities and ends in a description of a trend toward less territorial disparity in population density.

A basis in theory is provided for the empirically derived expression of negative exponential density patterns, which illustrate the influence of distance from city center on population density, in "Urban Population Densities: Structure and Change," by Berry, Simmons, and Tennant. Their paper treats the utility of urban activities and their effect upon population densities; such factors as city age, form, and density gradient as they influence central density; and changes in density through time and the disparities between Western and non-Western cities (industrial and preindustrial).

At the microlevel, Morrill investigates the patterns of population change occurring within major American cities today, the most obvious of which involves racial occupancy. Thus, the phenomenon of the evolution of the Negro ghetto is studied in some detail. A secondary contribution associated with this essay is the description of an operating spatial model. Hopefully, Morrill's "Alternatives to the Ghetto" section heralds increasingly widespread interest by geographers and others in such fundamental problems of urban America.

The last article deals with distributional trends of the population of Communist China. Orleans explains in detail the reasons for China's unbalanced pattern of population density. His statements concerning stability of such imbalance are well reasoned considering, as the author states, that ". . . quantitative data from China, . . . are, in most instances, either incomplete, of dubious reliability, or non-existent." It is noteworthy that most migrations in China have been the product of calamity of one sort or another. Orleans emphasizes the importance of the *push*, the pressure created within the place of origin, as opposed to the *pull*, the inviting circumstances often associated with the prevalence of better conditions in the place of destination, in his discussion of migration and distributional trends.

Selection Thirteen

POPULATION DISTRIBUTION[1]

Donald J. Bogue

The Field of Population Distribution Defined

The population of a whole country may be studied in two ways—as the residents of a single areal universe or as the residents of a congeries of sub-universes of which each sub-universe has a particular location in space. The first approach, the "aggregative," emphasizes the whole; the second approach, the "distributive," emphasizes the parts. These two approaches are complementary, since each answers a class of questions that the other cannot. Both may be used to study population composition, population trends, and the dynamics of population change. In fact, any population phenomenon that can be studied by one approach may be studied also by the other, and with profit in most instances.

The distinction between the two approaches may be clarified by an example. In the United States (as in many other nations) mortality rates declined throughout most of the nineteenth century and in the present century. The aggregative approach would trace this decline for the total population over the years. It would stratify the population by sex, age, marital status, occupation, and a variety of other characteristics; compute rates for each stratum or combination of strata; and note the trend over time within each. Age-sex-color specific rates (and other specific rates) of mortality for the entire United States for a series of time periods would be the statistical evidence to be examined and interpreted by this approach. A comparison of the rates for the various strata and an interpretation of the

Reprinted from *The Study of Population* by Philip M. Hauser and Otis Dudley Duncan (eds.), by permission of The University of Chicago Press. © 1959 by The University of Chicago. Published 1959. Fourth Impression 1964. Composed and printed by The University of Chicago Press, Chicago, Illinois, U.S.A.

difference found would constitute a major share of this analysis. Such research would be termed a study of differential mortality in the population at large.

At any one time the mortality rates for a nation may vary considerably from place to place. Rates in some regions may be higher than those in other regions; rates in the cities may be higher than those in rural areas; rates for certain neighborhoods within the cities may be higher than those for other neighborhoods. Thus there is internal diversity, or "place variance," in mortality. What appeared at first to be a single rate for the nation now appears to be simply the average of the rates for the subareas—the subarea rates being weighted in proportion to their relative shares of the whole. This place variance may be important for both theoretical and practical reasons. If mortality rates are persistently higher in some areas than in others, there must be particular reasons for the diversity. The distinguishing feature of population distribution research is its concern for place variance. In the example being considered here, the distribution approach to mortality would specify that rates should be established for each of various subdivisions of the country in addition to those established for the country as a whole. The major research task would be to interpret the interarea variance in rates and the trend in this variance.

To account for the diversity among areas, or place variance, one may postulate two types of explanations—differential composition and differential incidence or prevalence of the phenomenon being studied. If wide differences in mortality are noted among a sample of areas, these differences may be due to the fact that the populations of some areas are concentrated in the age groups at which mortality is high, while the populations of other areas contain disproportionately large shares of persons in the ages where mortality rates are low. Similarly, differential race, sex, and other composition can lead indirectly to differential mortality. Study of how differential population composition leads to differential population behavior is one of two major aspects of distributional analysis.

There is also a possibility that in some areas mortality operates with greater force upon particular age-sex-color (and other) groups than upon others. The extent of this variation, with the compositional aspect held constant, is the second important aspect of distributional study. By controlling differential composition, one is able to study the impact of a variety of social and economic conditions upon a population phenomenon. In mortality analysis, one could standardize the rates for subareas for sex, age, color, occupation, income (and possibly other factors) in order to determine whether the interarea differences that persist can be accounted for in terms of differences in climate, medical and health services, and the knowledge and health practices of the residents. A major practical contribution of this analysis is that it locates unique residence groups in the population that deviate from the average. These may be problem areas in need of special administrative action, or they may be areas of outstandingly good performance, perhaps indicating a type of administrative action that should be adopted in other areas.

A type of distributive population research performed frequently is the investigation of single local populations. For example, the trends in the size and composition of the population of a particular city or state are frequently the object of intensive research. These studies do not isolate a universe of variance but usually note only the difference between the single population studied and the universe from which it was drawn (such as nation, region, state). Another type of analysis, not strictly of the distributive type, is exploratory research. For studies of this type, a particular local population is taken as being roughly representative of the general population, and the interrelationships in this population are assumed to be similar to those in the general population or in some major segment of it. The emphasis is not upon variation but upon presumed lack of significant variation.

To summarize, the field of population distribution research may be defined as the study of a nation's or a community's population in terms of areal subdivisions, such as regions, states, socioeconomic areas, urban-rural residence, and census tracts. This includes the study of the composition of population residing in the smaller areal units as well as the study of the total number of inhabitants. It includes mobility research (studies of migration and movement within and between these units of area). It also includes studies over time of change in size and composition of the population of areal units.

The number and variety of studies in population distribution are very large and are increasing rapidly. Yet this is an area of study with which many professional demographers have only a slight familiarity, for their research has tended to be of the aggregative type. Much of the distributive population research has been done by persons who would not regard themselves as population specialists. As a result, the field is amorphous. It has few underlying methodological, conceptual, or theoretical principles by which continued research could lead to cumulative increase in predictability and control of population events in local areas.

The objective of this paper is to inventory this field of research, to describe each of its major subtypes, and to summarize briefly a theoretical viewpoint and methodology that could be of use in bringing greater coherence and validity to the findings of future population research.

An Inventory of Research in Population Distribution

In order to ascertain the present status of research in this particular field of population, a comprehensive bibliography was compiled.

The following sources were consulted: Joint Reference Library,[2] *Public Affairs Information Service, Population Index,* the annual census of research of the American Sociological Society, and the annual report of degrees granted, in the *American Journal of Sociology,* July issues, 1950–55. Articles dealing with some phase of the distributive aspect of population were included. (Because it was impossible to make a complete international list, the bibliography was confined to the work of analysts in the United States. It would have been highly desirable to include a listing of work being done in other countries, but the resources for performing this task were not available, and the compiler was not qualified.) In addition, letters were addressed to eighty-two persons in the United States who are known to be interested in this type of work or who are chairmen of sociology departments where such research could be performed. In spite of this determined effort to gain a complete coverage of recently completed and current research on population distribution, many items may have been inadvertently missed.

The items in this bibliography have been grouped into the following categories, by type of areal unit:[3] regions, states, and local—general; metropolitan and urban (including suburbs and fringes); rural (total) and rural nonfarm; and rural farm and agricultural. The subjects with which this research deals are listed in the stub of Table 13.1. The entries of Table 13.1 are a cross-classification of the nine categories of areal units against most of the possible research topics in the field of population distribution. By noting the combination of areal units and subjects, it is possible to state which are favored topics and which are neglected or bypassed. From the tabulation of Table 13.1, from familiarity with the titles, and from actually examining as many of the reports as could be obtained, the following conclusions have been reached:

1   There is a primary emphasis in distributional research on the number of inhabitants and growth in total size.

The total population, density of population, trends in total population growth, and forecasts of total population are items of extraordinary interest. By comparison, the specific demographic processes receive much less research attention.

2   In a high proportion of cases interest centers on single areas; consequently, much of the research consists of case studies in which the history of development and description of present conditions constitute the major part of the work. Workers who are employed by municipal governments or who teach in city universities tend to write about the city of their residence. Workers who are employed by state governments or who teach in state universities tend to write about the state of their residence. There appears to be a widespread sense of responsibility for maintaining a current analysis of the local population as a service to the local community or state.

3   There is also a heavy emphasis upon description and history rather than upon statistical inference. The recent trends and present composition of the population are recited, frequently with only a brief statement (or no statement at all) of the specific processes that could give rise to these results. Most of this descriptive work is coupled with exclusive interest in a single area—city or state. This means that the deviation of the local area from the national total is often described but not interpreted. The end product in many cases is a dot map or a shaded map showing where and how intensively the population is concentrated. Although the production of such maps is certainly a worthwhile activity, it is only the beginning of distributional analysis.

4   There is comparatively little intensive analysis of the distributional aspects of particular population events. Instead, the approach has tended to be of a "shotgun" variety, wherein all population events for a particular area are

TABLE 13.1   Population distribution research studies completed, 1950–55, and under way, May, 1955, by subject

SUBJECT OF RESEARCH	COMPLETED RESEARCH					RESEARCH UNDER WAY			
	TOTAL ALL AREAS	REGIONS, STATES, OR COMBINATIONS OF AREAS	URBAN AND METROPOLITAN	RURAL (TOTAL) AND RURAL NON-FARM	RURAL FARM AND AGRICULTURAL	TOTAL ALL AREAS	REGIONS, STATES, OR COMBINATIONS OF AREAS	URBAN AND METROPOLITAN	RURAL INCLUDING FARM AND NON-FARM
Total all topics	553	264	228	32	29	150	82	50	18
Total population size and growth	84	29	48	5	2	10	4	4	2
Population estimates and forecasts	71	52	16	0	3	8	6	1	1
General population composition and trends	131	51	64	10	6	45	26	14	5
Components of population change	5	4	1	0	0	3	1	1	1
Patterns of population distribution density, or land use	25	2	22	1	0	10	2	6	2
Migration and mobility	69	42	20	3	4	23	16	4	3
Race, color, nativity, ethnic orgin	21	9	10	1	1	8	4	4	0
Age	15	11	2	1	1	4	2	2	0
Sex	2	2	0	0	0	1	0	1	0
Mortality, longevity, life tables	18	14	1	3	0	3	3	0	0
Fertility	16	7	6	1	2	10	8	2	0
Family and household	12	4	5	0	3	3	0	2	1
Marriage, divorce, widowhood	6	4	2	0	0	3	2	1	0
Health, morbidity, medical services	17	10	3	3	1	1	1	0	0
Education	4	4	0	0	0	2	2	0	0
Labor force, employment status	26	11	10	3	2	4	0	2	2
Income	2	2	0	0	0	0	0	0	0
Occupation	3	1	2	0	0	4	3	1	0
Level of living economic conditions	9	4	1	1	4	0	0	1	0
Retail trade, manufacturing, goverment, service industries in relation to population	9	1	8	0	0	1	0	1	0
Commuting	7	0	7	0	0	1	0	1	0
Other	1	0	1	0	0	6	2	3	1

considered (frequently in a very cursory fashion). Where intensive studies of particular aspects of population have been undertaken, all too often the scope of the inquiry has continued to be largely historical and descriptive rather than analytical and explanatory. Studies of the population of states by counties and of cities by census tracts have frequently demonstrated and described intercounty and intertract variation for a given event and have shown how it has changed over time but have not undertaken to explain the variation. In some instances, analysts in neighboring areas have performed essentially the same analysis for their respective areas independently of each other. Because they used slightly different techniques, categories, and combinations of data, their results are not fully comparable. Because the analysis of particular events has proceeded on this area-by-area basis, there is a proliferation of studies on certain popular topics and a deficit of distributional studies on others. Several important topics have been left unstudied for some of the major states, metropolitan area, and cities. This must mean that much statistical information tabulated for these areas remains unanalyzed. In the inventory of current and recently completed research, the number of studies which are complete distributional analyses for a single topic is very small.

5 Many of the agencies who sponsored population distribution research are not research but administrative agencies. Many research persons in this field work in close alliance with local administrative agencies, and in many instances this orientation causes the research to be biased and selective in its interpretation. However, the frequency with which the studies are published by local administration bodies attests to the fact that local officials consider the studies important. One of the outstanding characteristics of population distribution research is that it has tried to be useful to local administrative groups. Population distribution research is one of the few types of social research for which local agencies have found use and for which they show enthusiasm.

6 There is scarcely a topic that has been studied at the national level that has not been studied at the local level at least once.

7 By and large, the distributional analysis for urban and metropolitan populations is much more developed than that for rural. The rural farm population has received much more attention than the rural non-farm. In fact, the rural village population is a badly neglected area of study; almost the only attention given it has been as a part of state and regional studies. Even here, attention has been turned almost entirely to total population and size of place rather than to socioeconomic characteristics and demographic processes in village population.

8 Also neglected are the small and medium-size cities. Metropolitan areas have received a large share of the distributional analysis for urban populations. The hinterland city is allowed to remain virtually unstudied; yet it is among such cities that some of the widest variations in population phenomena are to be found.

9 Several compositional aspects of population have received very little distributional analysis. Among them are race, nativity, educational attainment, school enrolment, income, occupation, marital status, family composition, and sex composition. Even the topics of major interest to demographers have been badly neglected on the distributional level. Distributional fertility and mortality studies are not numerous; they averaged less than one per seven states and less than one per twenty metropolitan areas.

10 An outstanding "popular" topic for distributional analysis is migration and spatial mobility. This topic ranks fourth in frequency, falling after studies of total population size, general composition, and population estimates and forecasts.

11 Within recent years there has been a movement to enlarge the scope of inquiry and to allow groups of persons to work together in order to encompass a larger territory and to integrate their

findings. As yet, this movement has been much more pronounced in the study of rural population than in the study of urban population. The current work of the Division of Farm Population, Agricultural Marketing Service, in organizing, systematizing, and integrating the distributional research of state colleges is outstanding in this respect.

12   A hasty check of the authors' names shows that a surprisingly high percentage of them are not members of the Population Association of America. Many of their studies show evidence of little rigorous training in demographic methods. This indicates that population analysis, as a profession and field of specialization, has not yet had its full impact upon the field of population distribution.

Table 13.1 also shows that the volume of research under way at the present time is very large and that the characteristics of this research are similar to those stated for published research. At the present time, more time and more funds are being spent for the study of internal population distribution and redistribution than for any other single phase of demography. Unfortunately this research is largely piecemeal, unintegrated, and descriptive. Much of it is pure fact-reporting and trend-tracing aimed at testing no particular hypothesis or arriving at no fundamental explanation. Yet this is one of the most widely supported types of population research. Administrative agencies of many types support this work, read it and attempt to use it in arriving at solutions to their problems. Studies that do attain scientific validity are widely read and appreciated, and scientific statements that validly apply to particular local areas are needed. In their concern with the cosmic problems, demographers may have failed to appreciate the fact that population problems become, in effect, problems of local areas. In their drive to be scientific and objective they have separated themselves from a group of professional city planners, welfare workers,

businessmen, and others who are anxious to make use of their services.

Given this situation, the problem becomes what to do about it. How can the population researcher perform work that would lead to a more scientific study of population distribution, a study that will still retain and even enhance its usefulness to local persons?

A Philosophy for the Study of Population Distribution

WHY STUDY LOCAL AREAS AT ALL?

The following questions can be asked: Is not the extent of interarea variation greatly overemphasized? Would not a detailed and comprehensive analysis for the entire United States, for each population topic listed in the stub of Table 13.1, provide sufficiently precise information to satisfy the needs of population experts and public administrators alike? The answers to these questions are negative. The extent of interarea variation, or deviation from the national average, is much greater than many demographers seem to realize. Only a very few local areas in a nation can use the national averages and national trends as a reliable guide and an interpretation of what to expect in a local area.

As a fundamental example, take the facts of rate of growth. The population of the United States grew by 14.5 per cent between 1940 and 1950, but the individual counties of the nation varied considerably (see Table 13.2). Only 364 of the 3,103 counties and independent cities fall in the growth-interval in which the average national rate falls. Instead of following the national trend, almost one-half of the units lost population. This situation is typical. For almost any population event, the statistics for the nation are only an average value; the individual areas of the nation deviate widely from this average. Usually the coefficient of variation (the standard deviation divided by the arithmetic mean) is at least 50 per cent. This is the point at which many statisticians would claim that an average begins to lose its meaning and usefulness as a measure of central tendency, for it is characteristic of only a small proportion of cases.

However, much of this variation is not of a random, unexplainable variety. It reflects the operation of unique combinations of local conditions. Variations in physical environment, social conditions, and type of economy may be expected to exert a marked influence upon population events. It is well known that these factors vary greatly among the parts of most nations.

TABLE 13.2 Distribution of counties by rate of population change, United States: 1940–50

RATE OF CHANGE	NUMBER OF COUNTIES	PER CENT OF COUNTIES
Total	3,103	100.0
Increase:		
20 per cent or more	520	16.8
10.0 to 19.9 per cent	364	11.7
5.0 to 9.9 per cent	307	9.9
0.0 to 4.9 per cent	394	12.7
Decrease:		
0.0 to 4.9 per cent	414	13.3
5.0 to 9.9 per cent	396	12.8
10.0 to 19.9 per cent	520	16.8
20.0 per cent or more	188	6.1

The population rates and proportions for a local area do not deviate aimlessly from year to year from corresponding measures of the national population; instead, they tend to show a persistent direction, degree, and rate of change. Their behavior is much more orderly than the wide range of variation about the national total might lead one to presume. But this orderliness results from differential population composition and differential environmental conditions—the force of unique conditions in the local area upon the relative status of these local areas. Only by studying population events in small-area units can these conditions and statuses be incorporated into the analysis as explanatory factors.

HOW CAN THE POPULATION ANALYST "BREAK THROUGH" THE DESCRIPTIVE PHASE?

Because his area deviates from the national average and because he suspects that this situation is not accidental but due to a unique combination of local conditions, the population analyst interested in a particular area tends to resort (as has been stated) to a complete description of a population event. He lets this substitute for an explanation of the event. It is readily apparent that this is not all that is needed. Any local area has numerous unique attributes. By description alone, it is difficult to determine which of these attributes is responsible for deviant population events. The factors that produce given population events can be ascertained only by a broad comparative analysis, such as observation of the variation of the events and attributes in a number of different areas and observation of which characteristics that vary among the areas covary with the population event. This requires that a hypothesis be formulated about what specific aspects of the environment are related to the population events. If a given factor varies independently of the population event (does not covary with it), it may be presupposed not to be an explanatory factor for the deviation of the local area from the national average.

An example will help clarify this. Figure 13.1 is the scattergram of infant mortality rates for the white population in the United States (infant deaths per 1,000 births) for 1950, by geographic division. The average (national) rate is drawn through these points as a horizontal dotted line. Median family income is the scale of the X-axis. The infant mortality rates of white infants are plotted as a scattergram against median family income in each of the nine geographic divisions. If the factor "family income" were independent of the population event "infant mortality," the data of Figure 13.1 would be scattered randomly around the horizontal line. However, this is not the case. Infant mortality rates tend to be scattered about a regression line that specifies a progressive decline in infant mortality

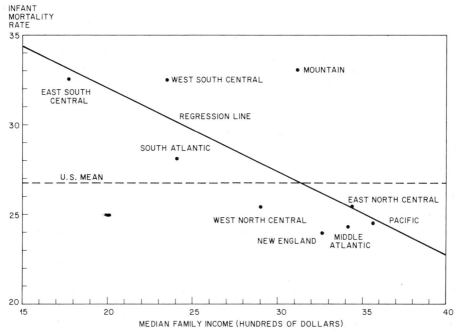

Figure 13.1 Scattergram of infant mortality rates for the white population of the U.S plotted against income of families, by geographic divisions, 1950

with the rise in median family income—the solid line of Figure 13.1. Thus, variations in infant mortality rates tend to be systematically related to variations in family income.

Data for observing this directly are not available, for births and deaths are not tabulated according to the income of the family into which they are born. This relationship can be observed only by subdividing the land area of the total universe in such a way that both infant mortality and family income may be observed to vary from one area to another. The fact that they tend to covary inversely leads to the hypothesis that they are related, either directly or through a common variable.

MULTIPLE AND ALTERNATIVE HYPOTHESES

Family income is not the only factor with which infant mortality may covary. There is great variation among local areas in such other factors as occupation, education of parents, color, age of mother, health of mother, medical care, and housing facilities.

A regression line between infant mortality and each of the above traits may show that all are significantly related to the rate of infant deaths. This does not necessarily mean that all are causally related. Certain of these factors may have common elements. Controlling these elements may remove the apparent effect of certain factors; thus, in order to arrive at a more comprehensive explanation, it is necessary to test all possible hypotheses. This testing requires the use of analytical methods capable of handling several factors simultaneously. These methods must be capable of measuring the effect attributable to each variable while holding constant the effect of the other variables. By such a procedure, it may be possible to explain a large share of the initial variance from the national average by the multiple covariance in a set of environmental factors. However, the "environmental factors" considered as variables are not conceived of as exerting a direct effect upon population. They are assumed to be indexes of forces and influences that are greater at a given time in a given type of socioeconomic system.

UNCONTROLLED ASSIGNMENT OF TREATMENTS
AND UNCONTROLLED REPLICATION

This view of population distribution is not one of regional causation; instead, it is a particular type of research design. It is no more than a reasoning by analogy from certain research designs employed by statistical analysis in the biological sciences, wherein varying quantities of various factors are assigned as treatments to individuals, with replication for sets of individuals to permit estimation of uncontrolled variables. The population researcher is powerless to determine the amount of each factor to be administered to each group, and he cannot specify how many times an experiment is to be repeated. If he employs these same statistical methods, he must do so under conditions of uncontrolled assignment of treatments and uncontrolled replication. His classification of the population according to traits, behaviors, or conditions is a substitute for assignment of treatment. His division of the entire area into subareas, each with its unique attributes, is a substitute for replication of the experiment. Both of these acts are accomplished after the events being studied have taken place and do not have the effect of randomizing errors—as in the case of controlled assignment of treatment and controlled replication. The population behavior of each subarea, together with the unique combination of traits observed for each subarea, becomes raw data for a multiple-variable analysis in which the data for each area are a single set of observations.[4]

This line of approach is indirect, and the factors which it finds to be non-randomly related to population events cannot be interpreted as being causal. Cause must be inferred from theoretical considerations and (if possible) from more direct measurement. In the example considered above, if infant births and deaths were both classified by income of parents, the relationship could have been established directly by cross-tabulation. Unfortunately, the array of

"causal factors" with respect to which population data are cross-tabulated is very small. There are only two approaches by which information about these factors may be brought to bear upon population phenomena: the "ecological" approach outlined here and direct field enumeration of the population. Neither of these can be a complete substitute for the other. Rapid progress in demography calls for a greatly accelerated development of both.

CROSS-CLASSIFICATION VERSUS AREAL DISTRIBUTION

From the foregoing, it is evident that if a given attribute, characteristic, or condition is regarded as being a factor in population behavior, it may be incorporated into the research study in two ways. It may be introduced distributively, as a varying attribute of the areas, or it may be introduced directly, as an attribute of the persons enumerated. In the latter case, it would be statistically manipulated by cross-classifying it with the population events. Hence, in some circumstances, there may be a choice of the way in which a variable is introduced. In this case, a distributive analysis would be made for each cell of the cross-classification or for certain summary measures derived from the cross-classification. Thus, if mortality data for subareas were tabulated by age, color, and sex, a mortality index standardized for these three factors might be computed for each area before launching into an analysis of other factors related to the areas.

Successive reduction of the size of the area for which observations are made would make it possible eventually to identify persons in terms of the space which they occupy. Similarly, progressive multiple cross-classification would make it possible to identify individuals in terms of combinations of characteristics which they alone possess. Thus, at the extreme, one approach excludes the other. Any research study must be a compromise between the degree of cross-classification and the size of the areal unit employed in a distributive analysis. In most instances a distributional approach without cross-classification is undesirable, and vice versa. The extent to which each approach should be emphasized will vary with the problem. Where there are no cross-classifications or where the population being studied is too small to support elaborate cross-classification, the distributional approach may receive emphasis. On the other hand, direct information available from cross-classification should be used as long as it is reliable. The distributional approach presupposes that the population for each local area will be cross-classified by a variety of factors, for there is interarea variation in relationships inferred from cross-classified data, as there is in single distributions. Under very few circumstances could an elaborate multiple-variable cross-classification of the population for an entire country be more informative than a less elaborate cross-classification with some area detail.

SUMMARY

When carried out as a "shotgun" approach to the description of a particular local area, population distribution studies are less effective than they might otherwise be, either as contributors of scientific knowledge or as the basis for administrative decisions concerning problems in the area. However, when undertaken as a multiple-variable analysis of particular population events for a sample of areas, population distribution studies are capable of contributing a great deal of indirect information about the environmental factors that underlie population events. This manner of approach, which may be called "ecological," is a gross analogy to the field experiments of agronomists and biologists. It should be employed where direct cross-tabulated information for the local areas is not available, and it should make the maximum possible use of cross-tabulated information that is available. Knowledge provided by this approach is especially useful because it keeps the analyst informed about the adequacy of his explanations and because it may be expressed in a form which permits its application to specific local areas.

Areas for Use in the Analysis of Population Distribution

To this point, the discussion has proceeded as if the choice of areas to be used in distributional analysis were self-evident or immaterial, but this is not the case. Given a particular territory whose surface is diverse, there is an infinite variety of ways in which it may be carved into subareas. If an average value is to be computed for each subarea, it is evident that the range of variability of the averages may be made arbitrarily small or arbitrarily large and that the "average of the averages" may be raised or lowered simply by gerrymandering the boundaries. There are two major schools of thought among geographers and other distributional analysts in their delimitation of areas.[5] One is the "homogeneous area" school, and the other is the "nodal area" school. The first group maintains that to be of maximum usefulness for scientific analysis areas should be of maximum internal homogeneity. Data collected for homogeneous areas show a greater range of variation for phenomena and for factors selected as explanatory variables. Each set of observations (data for a single area) tend to be confounded with fewer other variables. Thus, both population events and the variables that may be used to explain variations occur in their "purest" form when collected for units of area where internal homogeneity with respect to the factors being considered has been maximized.

The maximization of homogeneity should not be confused with the maximization of relationships. If one were interested in demonstrating a given relationship by appropriate gerrymandering, it would be possible to bias the analysis in the direction desired. This would be accomplished by maximizing the covariation of the variables involved. However, if there are points of disjuncture in the distribution of particular variables, and if the distribution for each of a number of variables is studied so that singly each distribution covers a minimum range of values, independent of the range of values covered by distributions for other variables, the variation of the means for the areas delimited will have been maximized without necessarily biasing the data collected for these units of area. This is especially true where homogeneous areas are delimited by a "unique set of characteristics" approach (in which the particular characteristics that are of outstanding economic and social significance in a given locale are given greater weight in arriving at the definition) rather than by the "fixed characteristics" approach.

The "nodal area" school maintains that modern economies are highly organized divisions of labor, in which particular territories orient their activities toward nodal centers—in most cases, large metropolitan centers. Thus this school is committed to emphasizing metropolitan regionalism. The obvious units of area to be employed in the statistical analysis are metropolitan regions, with each region perhaps divided into a few major subareas. Boundaries to such areas are determined not by homogeneity of characteristics but by functional interrelationships—lines of flow of goods and services and points at which competing nodes serve the hinterland areas. Internally, nodal regions are marked by diversity of characteristics rather than by homogeneity. One of the characteristics of metropolitan centers is their tendency to lie at or near the boundaries of major discontinuities in homogeneity. Seemingly, one function of such nodes is to articulate and integrate the special needs of adjoining areas that are unlike each other.

Unfortunately, students of distribution have adopted an "either-one-or-the-other" approach to these two ideas. Although they are not mutually exclusive, neither are they compatible. Each has been able to demonstrate, by the most trustworthy statistical tests, that it represents a valid point of view, holding constant variables representing the point of view of the other. In view of these facts, it is naïve to contend that one of these schools is wholly "correct" and that the other is "incorrect." A more tenable view is that a refined distributional analysis is one which takes account of both

ideas simultaneously. This view asserts that uniform (homogeneous) areas and nodal areas are two equally valid and equally important ways of viewing an inhabited territory.

Recent research (Bogue, 1949, 1954) has delimited both nodal areas and homogeneous areas for the United States, but no research has been published that employs both units simultaneously. The premises upon which such research would be conducted may be described, however. Since nodal regions are integrated in terms of exchange and flows, their internal structure consists of the routes of movement, the volume of movement, and the types of commodities moved from each part to every other part. Because the node is the organizing center, most of the routes will converge upon it, and the indexes of movement for most types of commodities will diminish with increased distance from the node to the outer boundary. The distance gradient, which is so often reported in studies of functional areas, is thus a major device for studying the internal structure of nodal areas. It would be an erroneous conclusion, however, to presume that distance gradients and other measures of internal structure of nodal areas are uninfluenced by the characteristics of the territory to which they pertain. Gradients for mountainous areas would differ from those for a semiarid prairie, and both could be unlike the gradient for a fertile and well-watered prairie. The boundaries of uniformity tend to be points of discontinuity or change in slope of gradients or points at which other changes in division-of-labor relationships occur.

It is here that the importance of recognizing uniform regions in the study of nodal areas becomes important. The territory that actually is integrated by a given node is not the "uniform fertile plain" postulated by Von Thünen and assumed by most subsequent students. Instead, the hinterland is characterized by a variety of conditions. Some parts may be mountainous regions devoted to mining and cattle-raising, as in the Denver metropolitan hinterland. Still other parts may be less fertile upland where small subsistence farms predominate, as in the Nashville metropolitan hinterland. Instead of working with "ideal types" or trying to visualize metropolitan relations from the data for rare territories where absolute uniformity is approached, nodal relationships should be observed in real-life situations. This can be done by explicitly introducing environmental differences as an additional set of factors. The homogeneous regions and subregions may be used as an economic and geographic base to show what activities the node integrates. They may, therefore, become an integral part of the internal structure of particular nodal regions. Without this all-important economic base, the hinterlands of all nodes appear to be identical. The unique functions which individual metropolitan centers perform are determined, in no small part, by the unique characteristics of their hinterlands; unless these unique features are known, it is difficult to comprehend how or why a particular metropolis performs the combination of functions it does. Thus, a realistic approach to the question, "Should population distribution analysis make use of homogeneous units of area or nodal units of area?" is "Use should be made of both—simultaneously in many cases."

The Region as a Set of Interrelated Variables

The preceding discussion has an important implication: if one simultaneously introduces several environmental characteristics as independent variables into a distributional analysis (where a population event is assumed to be the dependent variable) and if together these variables succeed in "explaining" or "accounting for" the phenomenon, does not this very finding destroy the significance of regions and regionalism? Why use the term "regionalism" or "regional effect" as a sort of mysterious force if the elements that compose this force are known? Do not the units of area used in the analysis suddenly cease to be important in their own right? Are they not merely a

not-too-important vehicle for arriving at the measurement of a statistical relationship? For example, a multiple-variable analysis may show that all differences among geographic units in mortality rates disappear when interregional differences in urban-rural occupational, racial, and income distribution are taken into account simultaneously. If this happens, should we not stop talking about "The South" and other "regions" as if they are distinctive socio-economic and geographic units and regard regional events as being fully explained by a series of explicit variables? The rules of parsimony require us to discard a concept when it is no longer necessary, and the "region" concept may be merely an intervening variable that we can abandon as soon as we know what variables it represents. Moreover, it is not true that as a nation undergoes industrialization, urbanization, and integration into a nodal (metropolitan) structured economy, the geographic and other differences that give local areas their unique characteristics tend to become ineffective as differentiators of the population? It may well be asked whether the concept of "regional effect" is not simply a worn-out idea left over from the heyday of environmental determinism in geography.

Although this argument may sound plausible, it is not valid. It mistakes basic assumptions employed in our measuring devices for reality. Most statistical systems for handling several variables simultaneously assume that variables can occur in almost every conceivable combination. Actually, the variables which may be used to measure the various aspects of environment cannot and do not occur in this way; they occur in space in more or less distinctive combinations and ranges of value, and the boundaries of the areas within which a particular combination is present are quite distinct. (In some cases such boundaries are sharp lines, while in others they are fairly narrow bands of transition.) Moreover, the particular combination of variables that occurs in a given place tends to be unmistakably related to geography, market position, or other traits rendered significant by the type of technology and economy present. The term "region" is merely a shorthand term for a unique cluster of interrelated conditions, traits, or forces present in an area at a given time. These clusters are so distinctive that not only geographers but economists, administrators, and even the general public take note of them.

Multiple-variable analysis helps to clarify the substantive content of a particular set of regions but does not become a synonym for regions. Instead of rendering the concept superfluous, it gives added and deeper meaning by helping to evaluate the relative weight of the forces at work in each of the distinctive socioeconomic clusters that we call regions.

Moreover, the notion that progressive urbanization and industrialization will cause these distinctive clusters to disappear cannot be supported either by theory or by observation. In fact, the contrary appears to be true. A market economy seems to cause places to seize upon whatever unique site, locational or physical characteristics they have that may provide the basis for profitable specialization. This is simply one form of adjustment to maximize their share of income in the total economy. For example, slight variations in soil quality, climate, and terrain can, under the influence of the modern market, differentiate "tobacco land" from other farmland or cause one section to specialize in "cash grain," another in livestock farming, and still a third in dairying. The economists of location have long argued that a similar situation holds for non-agricultural activities—there is a general region or regions within which a given industry can survive because the cost of assembling the necessary materials and marketing the product is less than it would be in other areas.

Thus, instead of minimizing geographic differences, the modern metropolitan economy may emphasize them. In this process, interregional differences that once were large may disappear, while new differences may appear. Instead of becoming a homogeneous mass, industrialized populations tend to become a patchwork of specialized populations tied together by a geographic as well as intracommunity and intercommunity division of labor. Modern research is helping to underscore the usefulness of regional variables as a readily observable set of major national divisions.

Limitations of the Distributive Approach

The mode of analysis that has been illustrated—relating the behavior of population groups to some factor that characterizes the group or its environment (or to changes in such factors)—has definite limitations. Since the units of observation are areas, the findings cannot be generalized to persons but must be applied to areas, although the relationships established for samples of areas (the so-called ecological correlations) do have significant implications for the expected results among random samples of persons drawn from each area. Procedures for evaluating and refining these implications have not been adequately explored, but it is plausible to expect that the implications would be greatly enhanced if the areas under observation had maximum homogeneity.

Another limitation arises from the fact that areas are not independent of each other but are contiguous to or have explicit location in relation to each other area. This may give rise to a covariation among the variables based solely on contiguity or proximity. The error may be expected to decline as the number of variables considered simultaneously is increased. This is especially true if the factors that express the covariance due to contiguity are explicitly introduced as separate variables.

Because of these limitations, the findings of a distributive analysis must be applied only to problems in which the unit of study is the area. Even here, the findings should be accepted as being tentative and approximate. Only after a given analysis has been replicated should the findings be considered verified generalizations. If this seems a heavy price to pay, it should be remembered that the same price must be paid in many other lines of social research before a comparable level of plausibility is reached.

Illustrative Hypotheses for Distributional Analysis

The preceding review of population distribution research has been critical of much current work in the field. The review has outlined principles for delimiting areal units and has proposed a philosophy for a revised mode of procedure. It is now appropriate to discuss concrete research programs of population distribution that may be undertaken. Two such programs are described. They are illustrations only; a similar approach could be made for virtually all topics of population study.

A DISTRIBUTIONAL ANALYSIS OF MORTALITY AND MORBIDITY

Although mortality rates have declined to a low level and although area-to-area differences have lessened in the last quarter-century, such differences still exist. It is generally agreed that differences in mortality are due largely to differences in social, economic, and health conditions among the areas; to the quality of medical services per capita; and to attitudes, knowledge, and concern with health among the residents. However, it is not known how much of these differences in mortality and morbidity are due to each of these factors, independent of the others. The following questions could be asked for total mortality, for total morbidity, for each cause of death, and for each type of illness: What factors are associated with varying incidence? What special factors are associated with unusually low and high incidence? How much change is associated with how much variation in each factor? What is the relative importance of each factor? Where are the areas of highest concentration of incidence, and what remediable factors appear to be responsible in each area? Where are the areas of greatest de-

cline in incidence, and what factors are responsible in each area? In all the above examples, comparisons should be controlled for population composition. In order to answer these questions, a multiple-variable analysis should be made for a sample of subareas, such as state economic areas. This would require tabulation by age, color, and sex for each subarea. It is impossible to perform such a study now because of the lack of data; state units are too large and heterogeneous for such an analysis, and county data are not cross-tabulated in sufficient detail. Life tables, with only a few exceptions, cannot now be prepared for any truly homogeneous area. Life expectancy, longevity, and mortality by cause of death need to be studied among local environments—both within metropolitan areas and within regions.

DISTRIBUTIONAL FERTILITY ANALYSIS

Variations in fertility among the population are greater than variations in mortality. It has been demonstrated that much interarea variation persists when age and color composition are controlled, and much work has been devoted to showing that fertility differentials exist among various occupational, income, religious, social, and other groups. But as yet there has been no measure of how much variation in fertility each factor explains when all others are controlled or of how much variation remains when all these factors are considered simultaneously. These questions need to be answered not only for a single instant of time but for several instants, so that changes and trends can be noted. This would call for a multiple-variable distribution analysis of fertility measures for the white and non-white population separately, controlled for age and marital status. It would involve a study design similar to that proposed for the study of mortality. Fertility data with the necessary cross-tabulations are not now available for such a study. At present, demographers are devoting a large amount of energy to the question of *how* fluctuations in fertility occur; yet of equal importance is the unanswered question of *why* they occur in a sociological and socioeconomic sense. An intensive distributional analysis of interarea variation in fertility and of interarea change in differences in fertility should throw considerable light on this subject, although a major handicap is the lack of generally accepted measures of fertility for use in an "open" population (a population that can be influenced by migration).

Population Distribution, Comparative International Demography, and Underdeveloped Countries

At the present time the international aspects of demographic events are being stressed, with greatest emphasis being placed upon underdeveloped countries. It is currently fashionable to compare the size, growth trends, and composition of the population of whole countries and to discuss the population problems of whole countries. These procedures assume, implicitly, either that each country is a homogeneous area or else that it is a single nodal unit. In almost all cases this is not true; most of the principal countries of the world are internally diverse. Hence, as the study of international demography progresses, there will be an increasing emphasis upon the comparison of countries in terms of their regions and subregions. The demographers of each country will appreciate that they do not have a single "population problem" but that their population problems are manifold, with each problem having spatial location within some one part of the country. Each problem can be expected to have special complications that are related to the geographic, economic, cultural, and historical traits that are unique to its locus. Administrators in each country will also come to see that their national population problems are the problems of particular areas and that the solutions must be devised in terms of the environmental circumstances.

In addition, the processes of industrialization and commercialization will lead to extensive mobility and migration among the population. Urbanization and metropolitanization may be expected to be a by-product of the industrialization process. Demographers in all nations will undoubtedly become much more concerned about internal migration than they are at present.

In short, although the attention of international demographers is now focused intently upon national aggregates, it may be predicted with a fair degree of assurance that this will be altered in the near future and that international demography will enter a phase of intensive distributional analysis. If this proves to be the case, one can hope that the transition from aggregative to distributional analysis will be made directly, without the discipline's having to go through the wasteful case-study descriptive phase that has characterized much of the work in the field to date.

Summary and Conclusion

The study of population distribution, in terms of volume of effort expended, is the largest single field of population study. Unfortunately, it has developed largely outside the main stream of population thought and has been carried forward by people who have been considered as "fringe" demographers by the professional population analysts. Most of the world's leading demographers have been concerned largely with national aggregates.

This chapter has tried to show that the distributional approach need not be one of descriptive case study. In fact, this approach can be a method which provides information about interrelationships between population events and environmental conditions obtainable in no other way. It is to be hoped that the study of population distribution will be accepted as one of the core areas of population study and that a scientific philosophy and methodology will be worked out in greater detail. Recent trends in research indicate that this will prove to be the case.

This chapter has purposely avoided some of the topics traditionally discussed under the term "population distribution." This includes a discussion of the relation of population to physical resources, the "carrying capacity" of land, optimum population, "population pressure," population trends toward increased agglomeration and urbanization with increasing technological complexity, and the intraregional and interregional interdependence that develops as a population distributes itself to exploit its environment. These are important aspects of the subject, but they all involve specific applications of the principles developed here. The object here has been to spell out some of the basic principles of study design in the field of population distribution so that work on these problems may produce a more rapid cumulation of scientific knowledge in the field of demography.

Notes

[1] This paper expresses a theoretical and research viewpoint that has guided eight years of research in the field of population distribution. The funds for this long-term study were granted by the Rockefeller Foundation. In addition, much of the presentation relies upon the responses of fellow demographers to an inquiry about their recent and current research activities. The author acknowledges with thanks the splendid response which permits him to speak with confidence about the present status of research in this particular area.

[2] The valuable help of Georgia Keck and Marianne Yates, librarian and assistant librarian of the Joint Reference Library, Chicago, is gratefully acknowledged.

[3] Donald J. Bogue (comp.), *Bibliography of Research in Population Distribution, Published and Under-way: 1950–55* (Oxford, Ohio: Scripps Foundation, Miami University). This document is too large to include in this chapter, but a copy may be obtained from the publisher at a nominal cost.

[4] This phase of the philosophy of population distribution has been stated in detail in Bogue and Harris (1954), chap. 1.

[5] These two approaches are discussed in greater detail in Bogue (1955).

Selected Bibliography

Bogue, Donald J. 1949. *The Structure of the Metropolitan Community*. Ann Arbor: University of Michigan Press.

———, 1954. "An Outline of the Complete System of Economic Areas," *American Journal of Sociology*, LX, 136–39.

———, 1955. "Nodal versus Homogeneous Regions, and Statistical Techniques for Measuring the Influence of Each." preprint. *Proceedings of the Conference of the International Statistical Institute*, Rio de Janeiro.

———, and Harris, Dorothy, L. 1954. *Comparative Population and Urban Research via Multiple Regression and Covariance Analysis*. ("Scripps Foundation Studies in Population Distribution," No. 8.) Oxford, Ohio: Scripps Foundation, Miami University.

Selection Fourteen

THE EVOLUTION OF POPULATION CONCENTRATION

Jack P. Gibbs

Studies of urbanization typically view population concentration in strictly quantitative terms, namely, as an increase in the proportion of the population who reside in cities. Urbanization is in fact the major factor in the process of population concentration,[1]

Reprinted from *Economic Geography*, **39**, 1963, 119–129, by permission of the editor.

but the process involves more than an increase in the proportion of city residents. Specifically, there is evidence of a particular order of stages in population concentration. This paper sets forth suggested major stages and reports a test of their applicability to the demographic history of the 48 coterminous states of the United States up to 1960.

Stages of Population Concentration

The following stages of population concentration are suggested:

1   Cities come into being, but the percentage increase of the rural population equals or exceeds the percentage increase of the urban population at the time cities first appear.
2   The percentage increase of the urban population comes to exceed the percentage increase of the rural population.
3   The rural population undergoes an absolute decline.
4   The population of small cities undergoes an absolute decline.
5   There is a decline in the differences among the territorial divisions with regard to population density, that is, a change toward a more even spatial distribution of population.

The stages are not mutually exclusive; consequently, it is logically possible for a society to be in two or more of the stages simultaneously. For example, during a given period both the rural population and the population of small cities may be declining. In such a case, the society may be said to be in both stages III and IV. However, the central question in such a case would be concerned with whether the rural population declined before the small cities began to lose population. This question could not be answered *a priori*, because it is logically possible for a society to reach stage IV before stage III; but the prediction is that stage III precedes stage IV. Thus, the theory states that population concentration occurs through the five stages set forth above and that each stage is reached in the order indicated.

STAGE I
Little is known about population growth in the first cities, but it appears likely that it was not of any great magnitude[2] and may have been less than in the rural areas. The growth of a nation's population is largely dependent, at least early in the history of the

nation, on an increase in the food supply. Accordingly, an increase in food production is likely to generate both rural and urban growth. This appears to be generally true, but it is more problematical for the urban population. An increase in food production is almost certain to benefit rural residents, because they have immediate access to the increase, whereas the influence of the same increase is less certain as far as the urban population is concerned. Whether or not the increase actually reaches the urban population depends largely on transportation technology; and, to the extent that efficiency of transportation is not improved relative to the increase in the food supply, the increase will not stimulate as much growth in the urban as in the rural population. For example, imagine a rural population which is producing 1,000,000 units of food per day, with each unit sufficient to support one person under the prevailing consumption standard. If the technology permits the transportation of only 10,000 food units from farms to cities, the urban population would number about 10,000 and the rural population would number about 990,000. Now suppose that some agricultural innovation (or the acquisition of new land) raises food production to 1,500,000 units. If the transportation technology remains unchanged, the urban population will not grow as a direct result of the increase in food production, whereas the rural population could conceivably increase more than 50 per cent. Some improvements in transportation would be likely to occur eventually; but initially they follow advances in food production. It is also in the period of an inefficient transportation technology that rural-urban migration is most likely to be at a minimum.

STAGE II
This stage of the concentration process begins when the rate of growth of the urban population exceeds that of the rural population. The immediate cause of a higher urban growth rate is rural-urban migration,[3] but advances in per capita food

production and improvements in transportation are the major underlying factors. Improvements in transportation make increases in food production available to urban residents and reduce the friction of space as an impediment to rural-urban migration.[4] Stage II also reflects the accumulation of several generations of slow urban growth in stage I and the eventual appearance of fairly large cities. This concentration of population makes possible a high degree of division of labor,[5] and through it the appearance of new functions which offer opportunities for employment and a higher standard of living to potential rural-urban migrants.[6]

STAGE III

As the volume of rural-urban migration reaches a high level, the number of migrants exceeds natural increase in the rural population which, therefore, undergoes an absolute decline.[7] This decline, which marks the beginning of stage III, is not altogether a product of an increase in the number of migrants from farms to cities; it also reflects a decline in rural natural increase, brought about by the fact that rural-urban migration is selective of individuals in their reproductive years.[8]

STAGE IV

As the volume of rural-urban migration increases in stage III, the number of potential migrants becomes less and less,[9] but the "pull" factor is still present. Just as the large centers offer opportunities not present in rural areas, so do they offer opportunities that far exceed those in the small towns. Accordingly, migration to large cities continues, but it is now primarily a movement from small centers to larger ones, with the ultimate outcome being a decline in the population of small places.[10] This decline marks the initiation of stage IV in the concentration process. It results from: (1) the same factors which produced the earlier decline in the rural population; and (2) a loss of functions in small centers that offer services to a now declining rural population.

STAGE V

It might appear that stage IV would continue to the point where virtually all of the national population is located in one huge urban center,[11] but such is not the case. Even if the transportation and agricultural technology could support such concentration, it would not take place. Continued improvements in transportation and communication make it possible for a population to obtain services and maintain existing socioeconomic relations without a high degree of concentration and, consequently, there is a movement from high density areas.[12] Persons who work in or otherwise depend on large cities come to live at a distance, in small towns or in settlements that have low population densities. The result is eventually stage V, which is characterized by a change toward a more even spatial distribution of population.[13] This is the final stage in the concentration process, and one that could conceivably continue to the point where the population is more evenly distributed than in the case of stage I. However, unlike the situation in stage I, the basis of population distribution in stage V is residential dispersion and not a decline in interdependence; this means that the deconcentration does not result in widely-scattered communities that have virtually no economic relationships with one another. Stated otherwise, stage V is not a product of the "force of diversification" postulated by George K. Zipf, even though it may eventually involve industrial decentralization at the regional level.[14]

Some Qualifications

Considered as a theory, the sequence of stages of population concentration bears some resemblance to nineteenth-century evolutionary ideas. In recent decades, the notion of an evolutionary course in sociocultural change has been sharply questioned. Evolutionary theories have suffered from at least two defects, namely, a vagueness in terminology and inadequate qualifications. The vagueness has precluded rigorous tests, while the absence of qualifications made it possible for isolated exceptions to invalidate the theory in question.

The present theory has been formulated with a view to avoiding the glaring errors in grand evolutionary schemes. For one thing, the theory is so stated that it can be subjected to systematic empirical tests. Of greater importance, however, are the qualifications attached to the theory. It is not suggested that all populations inevitably move through the specified stages. On the contrary, a population may remain indefinitely in stage I or a later stage. Furthermore, a population may regress to an earlier concentration stage, and the process may then start over again from that stage. Thus, there is no suggestion that change is inevitable or irreversible. The theory holds only that if concentration takes place it will follow the stages in the order specified.

A second major qualification relates to types of human populations. It is not suggested that the concentration process follows the specified sequence of stages in all populations. The hypothesized sequence will appear without exception only in indigenous and isolated populations, that is, populations that have always been ecologically closed systems.

The necessity for the qualifications is obvious. The migration of contemporary Europeans to unoccupied lands would in all probability never result in stage I; the population might well be in stage II at the outset. Moreover, contacts between the two populations may substantially alter the sequence of stages of concentration. For example, with a steady stream of immigrants there is no necessity for urban growth to result in rural depopulation. The immigrants may either move into cities or replace rural persons who have moved to cities. In general, then, to the extent that contact between populations takes the form of migration or an exchange of food or technology, there is no necessity for the specified stages of concentration to hold.

The qualifications immediately suggest a major criticism of the theory. At present there are no populations that meet the qualifications; and, therefore, it might be argued that the theory is neither testable nor useful. But this ignores the fact that the validity of any theory is contingent upon the qualifications imposed. Moreover, even if the qualifications of a theory create a null class, the validity of the theory can still be assessed indirectly. To the extent that conditions approximate those specified in the qualifications, predictions based on the theory should be correct. For example, the stages of population concentration should hold more consistently for nations than for small territorial divisions (such as counties in the U.S.A.). Small territorial divisions are least likely to approximate an ecologically-closed system, because there is usually a steady stream of migration, technological devices, and food from one division to the next. Finally, a theory does have utility even when applied to conditions that do not meet in all respects those specified in its qualifications. If predictions are to be made, if some kind of order in events is to be sought, then any generalization is better than none.

A Test of the Theory

Of all existing populations, those delimited by national boundaries most nearly satisfy the qualifications imposed on the theory. However, current international statistics are not suited for a test of the theory. In only a few countries do demographic statistics extend over long periods, and even in these cases the information necessary for determining stages is often not available, particularly with regard to the distant past. Furthermore, in some countries the census definition of urban and of rural has changed from time to time, thereby making historical comparisons difficult if not impossible.

Considering the present nature of demographic statistics, the most feasible approach is to test the theory on large territorial divisions of nations that have population data suitable for long-range historical comparisons. The United States provides such an opportunity, since the individual states are large and their demographic statistics extend back, in some cases, to the first census year, 1790. Moreover, the census classifications of urban, rural, and city size ranges can be made comparable through each of the past eighteen decennial censuses.

This does not mean that the states are ideal territorial units for a test of the theory. On the contrary, in no state is the population indigenous and isolated; and, since colonial times, there has been an appreciable interstate and international flow of migrants, technological devices, and food. Nevertheless, the states do provide a basis for assessing the utility of the theory. If its predictive power is reasonably high, this would indicate that populations may deviate considerably from the conditions stipulated in the qualifications and yet still conform approximately to the theory:

THE DETERMINATION OF STAGES IN THE DEMO-GRAPHIC HISTORY OF THE UNITED STATES Increases in the urban and rural population cannot be compared *for the time* the first city came into existence, because at least one urban place (defined by the census as a place of 2500 or more inhabitants) was already present in 18 states when their first census was taken.[15] However, some observations concerning stage I can be made. Of the 30 states with no urban place at the time of the first census, six states[16] had a percentage growth of rural population exceeding that of the urban population for the first census decade after an urban place had come into being; 24 of the 30 states had an urban growth rate higher than that for the rural population. These facts suggest that most of the states by-passed stage I, and that this stage is particularly dependent on the conditions specified in the qualifications of the theory. However, the experience of six states indicates that stage I is a possibility, and this is rather important since we are accustomed to the notion

that urban growth uniformly exceeds rural growth. It is also of some significance that, whereas in six states the rural growth rate exceeded that of the urban population in the first decade after urban centers came into existence, this was true for only two states in the second decade.[17] A comparison of the differences between rural and urban growth in the first and second decades after the appearance of urban centers is also instructive. For the 30 states without an urban center at the time of the first state census, the average percentage increase in the urban population during the initial decade was 253 as compared with 108 for the rural population in the same decade. Corresponding figures for the second decade are 142 and 43. The average percentage increase in the urban population was 2.35 times that of the average percentage increase in the rural population in the first decade, but 3.30 times in the second decade.

In the absence of adequate historical data pertaining to stage I of the concentration process, the test of the theory is concerned with the remaining four stages. The major question is, thus, the extent to which the 48 states have passed through stages II, III, IV, and V in the predicted order.

To answer this question it is necessary to determine for each state at each decennial census: (1) the rates of growth for the rural and urban population, (2) the population of small cities, and (3) a measure of population movement toward concentration or deconcentration at the state level.

The most feasible way to determine urban and rural growth is to accept the intercensal percentage increase for the two populations in each state as reported by the Bureau of the Census.[18] For the period 1790–1940, these figures are based on a definition of urban which, for all practical purposes, encompasses only incorporated places of 2500 or more inhabitants. For purposes of comparability, this definition was extended to the 1940–1950 and 1950–1960 decades, even though the Bureau of the Census applied a new urban definition in the

1950 and 1960 censuses.[19] These data make it possible to determine when the percentage of urban growth first came to exceed that of the rural (stage II), and when the rural population first declined (stage III).

To determine when a state has reached stage IV, it is necessary to compare the number of inhabitants of small cities, at each census year, with a decline in the number marking the onset of the stage. In the present test of the theory, the size range 2500–4999 was selected as representing small cities. This size range was selected because the minimum corresponds to the definition of urban as employed by the Bureau of the Census and because the population of smaller places (less than 2500 inhabitants) is not consistently reported in census publications.

The historical statistics in the 1950 census publications show the number of inhabitants of places 2500–4999 for only the census years 1900 through 1950,[20] and the latest census extends this series up to 1960.[21] Thus an inter-censal decline in the population of small cities has been determined over only the years 1900–1960. This ignores the possibility that the population of small cities declined in some states before 1900, but the over-all sixty-year trend indicates otherwise.

The identification of stage V presents the greatest difficulty of all. Deconcentration at the state level is a movement toward a more even distribution of population throughout the state. This movement can be expressed numerically by determining, for each census year, what percentage of the state's population would have to move from one component territorial division to another to bring about an even distribution of population. When this percentage figure begins to decline, deconcentration has commenced.[22]

For purposes of illustration, a direct measure of population concentration has been applied to Texas and Rhode Island for each census year from 1930 onward, using counties as territorial divisions. The results are shown in Table 14.1. The figures in Table 14.1 show that a continuous increase in con-

centration has occurred in Texas during the past 30 years, whereas exactly the opposite is true for Rhode Island.

Two comments on this method of assessing deconcentration should be made. First, the value of such a measure is always relative to the territorial divisions employed; in general, the smaller the divisions the better. In the case of Texas, for example, it is possible that deconcentration has been going on *within* certain counties, whereas *among* counties the process has been one of concentration. Second, although the measure of population concentration applied to Texas and Rhode Island could be applied to all states at each census year, it would require over 120,000 computations. The use of this direct measure of concentration is accordingly not feasible for an investigation with limited resources for research.

The percentage increase of the urban relative to the rural population provides one basis for gauging deconcentration indirectly. Just as an excess of the percentage urban growth over the rural indicates concentration, so the reverse is indicative of deconcentration. Some support for treating a higher rural rate of growth as indicative of deconcentration is found in a comparison of Texas and Rhode Island.

The percentage of the population that would have to move from one county to the next to bring about an even distribution of population is shown for both states in Table 14.1, along with the difference between the percentages of urban and rural growth during each census decade. Note that for each of the four census years the measure of population concentration is greater for Texas than Rhode Island, and the excess of the urban growth rate over the rural is also greater for Texas. Note also that in Rhode Island, between 1920 and 1950, the percentage growth of the rural population exceeded that of the urban, and that the values of the measure of concentration have declined since 1930. The exception in the case of Rhode Island is the decade 1950–1960; the measure of concentration declined, but the percentage growth was greater for the urban

TABLE 14.1 Comparison of two indicators by population concentration for Rhode Island and Texas, 1930–1960[1]

	RHODE ISLAND		TEXAS	
YEAR	INCREASE OF URBAN POPULATION OVER PRECEDING DECADE MINUS INCREASE OF RURAL POPULATION DURING SAME DECADE (%)	MEASURE OF POPULATION CONCENTRATION[2]	INCREASE OF URBAN POPULATION OVER PRECEDING DECADE MINUS INCREASE OF RURAL POPULATION DURING SAME DECADE (%)	MEASURE OF POPULATION CONCENTRATION[2]
1930	8.8	39.65	49.0	44.99
1940	−12.4	38.47	19.8	46.33
1950	−66.3	34.03	70.0	51.35
1960	27.7	28.25	66.6	57.73

[1]Source of data: Census reports for 1930, 1940, 1950, and 1960. Old definitions (1940) employed in determining rural and urban growth.
[2]Percentage of the state's population that would have to move from one county to another to bring about an equal population density for all counties.

than the rural population. In Texas, population concentration increased over the past decades; this is in line with the fact that since 1920 the percentage increase of the urban population has been higher than the percentage increase of the rural population. However, as is witnessed by the exception in the case of Rhode Island, this does not mean that the difference between the rural and urban growth rates is a perfectly adequate substitute for a direct measure of population concentration. The difference between the rural and urban growth rates was used to identify the appearance of stage V only because limitations in resources for research precluded direct measures of population concentration. To sum up, when the percentage growth of the rural population comes to exceed that of the urban population, the state is considered to be in stage V. But this criterion cannot be applied without qualification. Although the test of the theory cannot incorporate a consideration of stage I, there is evidence of a tendency toward this stage in some states. If such a tendency did exist, then the earliest period in which the percentage rural growth exceeded the percentage urban growth represents stage I and not stage V. But stage

I should occur very early in the history of the state, if it appears at all. Accordingly, the final criterion for the identification of stage V is a percentage increase of the rural population which exceeds that of the urban population *after* the first three census decades in which an urban population was present.

The application of the above criterion is based on the old (1940) urban definition for all census years, including 1950 and 1960. The extension of this definition to 1950 and 1960 can be questioned, despite the fact that it is the *only* way to achieve comparability over time. It could be argued that a higher percentage increase in rural population merely reflects the expansion of urban territory beyond municipal limits. This is doubtless true but the areas of expansion represent, on the whole, low residential densities. Thus, although the higher rate of rural growth may be a product of the failure of municipal boundaries to expand in accordance with population movement, the movement nonetheless suggests deconcentration.

SEQUENCE OF STAGES FOR INDIVIDUAL STATES
Table 14.2 shows the decade in which each

TABLE 14.2   Stages of population concentration in the forty-eight coterminus states of the United States up to 1960[1]

STATE	STAGE II EARLIEST CENSUS DECADE IN WHICH PERCENTAGE URBAN GROWTH EXCEEDED PERCENTAGE RURAL GROWTH	STAGE III EARLIEST CENSUS DECADE IN WHICH RURAL POPULATION UNDERWENT A DECLINE	STAGE IV EARLIEST CENSUS DECADE, 1900–1960, IN WHICH POPULATION OF URBAN PLACES OF 2500–4999 UNDERWENT A DECLINE	STAGE V EARLIEST CENSUS DECADE (30 YEARS AFTER APPEARANCE OF 1ST URBAN PLACE) IN WHICH PERCENTAGE RURAL GROWTH EXCEEDED PERCENTAGE URBAN GROWTH
Maine	1800–10	1860–70	1910–20	1950–60
New Hampshire	1800–10	1850–60	1900–10	1930–40
Vermont	1850–60	1860–70	1920–30	1960–70[3]
Massachusetts	1790–00[2]	1860–70	1910–20	1930–40
Rhode Island	1790–00[2]	1790–00[2]	1900–10	1930–40
Connecticut	1790–00[2]	1890–00	1910–20	1930–40
New York	1790–00[2]	1860–70	1930–40	1930–40
New Jersey	1810–20	1960–70[3]	1960–70[3]	*1930–40*
Pennsylvania	1790–00[2]	1960–70[3]	*1930–40*	1930–40
Ohio	1810–20	1880–90	1910–20	1930–40
Indiana	1840–50	1900–10	1900–10	1930–40
Illinois	1840–50	1880–90	1960–70[3]	*1930–40*
Michigan	1840–50	1910–20	1940–50	*1930–40*
Wisconsin	1850–60	1920–30	1920–30	1960–70[3]
Minnesota	1860–70	1920–30	1930–40	1960–70
Iowa	1850–60	1900–10	1900–10	1960–70[3]
Missouri	1830–40	1900–10	1910–20	1960–70[3]
North Dakota	1890–00	1930–40	*1920–30*	1960–70[3]
South Dakota	1880–90	1930–40	*1900–10*	1960–70[3]
Nebraska	1880–90	1930–40	*1920–30*	1960–70[3]
Kansas	1860–70[2]	1890–00	1920–30	1960–70[3]
Delaware	1840–50	*1830–40*	1940–50	*1920–30*
Maryland	1790–00[2]	1880–90	1940–50	*1920–30*
Virginia	1790–00[2]	1830–40	1940–50	1960–70[3]
West Virginia	1840–50	1940–50	*1920–30*	1930–40
North Carolina	1830–40	1960–70[3]	1960–70[3]	1960–70[3]
South Carolina	1800–10	1860–70	1900–10	*1830–40*
Georgia	1810–20	1920–30	1960–70[3]	1960–70[3]
Florida	1860–70	1960–70[3]	1960–70[3]	1960–70[3]
Kentucky	1810–20	1940–50	*1920–30*	1930–40
Tennessee	1830–40	1910–20	1920–30	1960–70[3]
Alabama	1830–40	1940–50	*1900–10*	*1870–80*
Mississippi	1840–50	1910–20	*1900–10*	*1870–80*
Arkansas	1860–70	1940–50	1940–50	1960–70[3]
Louisiana	1820–30	1940–50	*1930–40*	*1840–50*
Oklahoma	1890–00[2]	1930–40	*1920–30*	1960–70[3]
Texas	1850–60[2]	1940–50	1960–70[3]	1960–70[3]
Montana	1870–80[2]	1920–30	*1900–10*	1910–20
Idaho	1900–10	1960–70[3]	*1950–60*	1960–70[3]
Wyoming	1880–90	1940–50	1960–70[3]	*1910–20*
Colorado	1870–80	1960–70[3]	*1920–30*	*1910–20*
New Mexico	1860–70	1860–70	1930–40	1960–70[3]
Arizona	1890–00	1950–60[3]	*1920–30*	1920–30
Utah	1870–80	1960–70[3]	*1940–50*	1960–70[3]
Nevada	1870–80	1880–90	1900–10	1900–10
Washington	1880–90	1960–70[3]	1960–70[3]	*1930–40*
Oregon	1860–70	1960–70[3]	*1910–20*	1930–40
California	1850–60[2]	1960–70[3]	*1920–30*	1930–40

of the 48 states reached stages II, III, IV, and V of the concentration process. According to the theory, each decade within the rows of Table 14.2 should be later than the decade to the immediate left. Where two adjacent dates are the same, there is no way of determining which stage was reached first during the decade, and such cases constitute evidence neither for nor against the theory.

On the whole, the states conform to the theory. Disregarding cases of adjacent dates that are the same, it is found that stage II appeared before stage III in 45 or 98 per cent of 46 comparisons, that stage III preceded stage IV in 23 or 58 per cent of 40 comparisons, and that stage IV preceded stage V in 28 or 70 per cent of 40 comparisons. Altogether, 96 or 76 per cent of the 126 comparisons indicate that the stages succeeded one another in the order specified by the theory. Such a proportion, or a greater one, would occur on the basis of chance in less than one out of every 100 cases.

DEVIANT CASES

Inspection of Table 14.2 reveals that, in 16 states, the percentage rural growth came to exceed that of urban growth between 1930 and 1940. It might be argued that this is largely the consequence of the economic depression and not a stage in an evolutionary concentration process. This may be partially true, but in 11 of the 16 states the percentage rural increase was greater than the percentage urban increase during both the periods 1930–1940 and 1940–1950.[23] The fact that some of the states reached stage V between 1930 and 1940 (on the basis of the rural-urban differential growth) actually produces several cases of error in prediction. Had they entered stage V after 1940 or 1950, the order of stages would have been more consistent with the theory.

The majority of errors in prediction in-

volve stage IV. Whether this is true because this particular stage is more sensitive to the conditions specified in the qualifications of the theory or whether it is due to a failure to employ a lower size range for small cities (under 1000 or 1000–2499, rather than 2500 or more) is a question for further study. However, since the populations of places of less than 2500 inhabitants are not consistently reported in United States census publications, research on lower size ranges will have to be conducted for other countries.

Conclusions

The results of the test of the theory suggest a tendency for population concentration to occur through a certain order of stages. But the evidence suggests nothing more than a tendency, as several states in the United States have not moved through the stages in the sequence predicted by the theory. Whether this merely reflects the fact that the states do not meet the conditions specified in the qualifications of the theory or whether it means that the theory is inherently deficient can be determined only through further investigation. If it can be shown that the stages hold better for countries (or intranational territorial units) that have not experienced an appreciable amount of international trade, immigration, or emigration, then the argument for the theory would be strengthened considerably. Tests of the theory at the international level will be difficult, largely because of the problems involved in obtaining the necessary data; but the results of the present investigation, while by no means conclusive, would seem to justify further research.

Further research on the subject should go beyond observations on the order of stages and consider variables related to the rationale for each stage. For example, is it true

---

[1]Source of data: United States Bureau of the Census, *United States Census of Population: 1950*, Vol. I, and individual state reports for the 1960 census. Statistics based on old (1940) urban and rural definitions. Italics indicate errors in prediction — cases in which the decade is earlier and not later than the preceding one.

[2]No earlier census data.

[3]Earliest possible decade.

that a decline in rural fertility (as measured by the crude birth rate) typically occurs before the rural population declines in absolute numbers? Answers to this and to other questions pertaining to the dynamics of population concentration might well be more significant, particularly for underdeveloped countries, than the order of stages.

Notes

[1] See, for example, Hope Tisdale, "The Process of Urbanization," *Social Forces*, Vol. 20, 1942, pp. 311–316.

[2] See Kingsley Davis, "The Origin and Growth of Urbanization in the World," *Amer. Journ. of Soc.*, Vol. 60, 1955, pp. 430–432.

[3] Conrad Taeuber, "Rural-Urban Migration," *Agric. History*, Vol. 15, 1941, pp. 151–160; Robert I. Crane, "Urbanism in India," *Amer. Journ. of Soc.*, Vol. 60, 1955, p. 466; Ana Casis and Kingsley Davis, "Urbanization in Latin America," *Milbank Memorial Fund Quarterly*, Vol. 24, 1946, p. 299; Harold F. Dorn, "Migration and the Growth of Cities," *Social Forces*, Vol. 16, 1938, p. 329; Harley L. Browning, "Recent Trends in Latin American Urbanization," *Annals of the Amer. Acad. of Polit. and Soc. Science*, Vol. 316, 1958, p. 118; United Nations, *The Determinants and Consequences of Population Trends*, New York, 1953, pp. 109–111.

[4] Stated in the way of a generalization: a high urban growth rate through rural-urban migration is a product of economic development and related advances in transportation and communication. See Kingsley Davis, "Internal Migration and Urbanization in Relation to Economic Development," *Procs. of the World Population Conference*, 1954, Vol. 2, New York, 1955, pp. 783–799; and United Nations, *op. cit.*, p. 126.

[5] Amos H. Hawley, *Human Ecology*. New York, 1950, pp. 122–123.

[6] United Nations, *op. cit.*, pp. 124–126.

[7] See, for example, Conrad Taeuber, "Recent Trends of Rural-Urban Migration in the United States," *Milbank Memorial Fund Quarterly*, Vol. 25, 1947, pp. 203–213.

[8] United Nations, *op. cit.*, p. 149.

[9] Kingsley Davis and Hilda Hertz Golden, "Urbanization and the Development of Pre-Industrial Areas," *Econ. Development and Cultural Change*, Vol. 3, 1954, p. 11. England is a classic illustration of the process by which the pool of potential rural-urban migrants comes to diminish. See A. K. Cairncross, "Trends in Internal Migration, 1841–1911," *Trans. Manchester Stat. Soc.*, 1938–1939, pp. 21–29.

[10] A connection between small population size and loss of population is suggested by the findings of several studies. See, for example, Edmund de S. Brunner and T. Lynn Smith, "Village Growth and Decline, 1930–1940," *Rural Sociology*, Vol. 9, 1944, pp. 103–115; S. C. Ratcliffe, "Size as a Factor in Population Changes of Incorporated Hamlets and Villages, 1930–1940," *Rural Sociology*, Vol. 7, 1942, pp. 318–328; William Fielding Ogburn, "Size of Community as a Factor in Migration," *Sociology and Social Research*, Vol. 28, 1944, pp. 255–261; C. C. Zimmerman, *Farm Trade Centers in Minnesota, 1905–1929*. Univ. of Minnesota Agric. Experiment Station, Bull. 269, 1930. As the small places decline, the large urban centers grow; both trends contribute, of course, to population concentration. See, for example, Floyd and Lillian Dotson, "Urban Centralization and Decentralization in Mexico," *Rural Sociology*, Vol. 21, 1956, p. 44.

[11] Application of Stewart's formulas to trends in the United States yields a forecast of an eventual disappearance of the rural population and a population decline in small urban places which progresses up the size scale to a point where all of the national population reside in one urban center. See John Q. Stewart, "Empirical Mathematical Rules Concerning the Distribution and Equilibrium of Populations," *Geogr. Rev.*, Vol. 37, 1947, pp. 461–485.

[12] Edward Gross, "The Role of Density as a Factor in Metropolitan Growth in the United States of America," *Population Studies*, Vol. 8, 1954, pp. 113–120; Noel P. Gist, "Developing Patterns of Urban Decentralization," *Social Forces*, Vol. 30, 1952, pp. 257–267; J. Douglas Carroll, Jr., "The Relation of Homes to Work Places and the Spatial Pattern of Cities," *Social Forces*, Vol. 30, 1952, pp. 271–282; Henry S. Shryock, Jr., "Redistribution of Population: 1940 to 1950," *Journ. of the Amer. Stat. Assn.*, Vol. 146, 195, pp. 417–437; Leo F. Schnore, "The Growth of Metropolitan Suburbs," *Amer. Soc. Rev.*, Vol. 22, 1957, pp. 165–173; Leo F. Schnore, "Metropolitan Growth and Decentralization," *Amer. Journ. of Soc.*, Vol. 63, 1957, pp. 171–180; Donald J. Bogue, *Metropolitan Decentralization: A Study of Differential Growth*, Oxford, Ohio, 1950; Donald J. Bogue, "Changes in Population Distribution Since 1940," *Amer. Journ. of Soc.*, Vol. 56, 1950, pp. 43–57; and Homer Hoyt, "Forces of Urban Centralization and Decentralization," *Amer. Journ. of Soc.*, Vol. 46, 1941, pp. 843–852.

[13] Deconcentration involves, but should not be confused with, the expansion of urban boundaries, decline in urban population densities, or what is often referred to as "decentralization" within urban areas. (See Colin Clark, "Urban Population Densities," *Journ. Royal Stat. Soc.*, Vol. 114, 1951, pp. 490–496; and Henry S. Shryock, Jr., "Population Redistribution Within Metropolitan Areas: Evaluation of Research," *Social Forces*, Vol. 35, 1956, pp. 154–159.) Deconcentration *within* urban or metropolitan areas may take place at the same time that concentration is taking place at the regional level. (See Hans Blumenfeld, "On the Growth of Metropolitan Areas," *Social Forces*, Vol. 28, 1949, pp. 59–64.) The type of deconcentration which characterizes stage V occurs only through an increase in the relative population density of terri-

torial units which are far removed from the major centers of concentration. It involves, in addition to population redistribution within urban areas, the appearance of new centers and shifts in the size hierarchy and spacing of urban centers. See Charles T. Stewart, Jr., "The Size and Spacing of Cities," *Geogr. Rev.*, Vol. 48, 1958, pp. 222–245; and Otis Dudley Duncan, "Population Distribution and Community Structure," *Cold Spring Harbor Symposia on Quantitative Biology*, Vol. 22, 1957, pp. 357–371.

[14]See George Kingsley Zipf, *Human Behavior and the Principle of Least Effort*, Cambridge, Mass., 1949, Chap. 9; and George T. Renner, "Geography of Industrial Location," *Econ. Geog.*, Vol. 23, 1947, pp. 187–189.

[15]The 18 states are: New Hampshire, Massachusetts, Rhode Island, Connecticut, New York, Pennsyl-

vania, Kansas, Maryland, Virginia, South Carolina, Louisana, Oklahoma, Texas, Montana, Colorado, New Mexico, Arizona, and California.

[16]North Dakota, Nebraska, North Carolina, Georgia, Mississippi, and Utah.

[17]Maine and Wyoming.

[18]United States Bureau of the Census: *United States Census of Population: 1950*, Vol. I, Table 15.

[19]Urban and rural population for 1950 and 1960 are reported by the Bureau of the Census under both the old urban definition (1940) and the new (1950) definition. 1960 census figures were obtained from reports on individual states as they were released.

[20]United States Bureau of the Census, *op. cit.*, Table 3 in each state part.

[21]From reports on individual states.

[22]This is not true for countries or regions with an expanding frontier

of settlement. See Edgar M. Hoover, Jr., "Interstate Redistribution of Population, 1850–1940." *Journ. of Econ. History*, Vol. 1, 1941, pp. 199–205. Where population movement involves principally the settlement of unoccupied territory rather than redistribution, the measure must be adjusted so as to reflect only the relative decline of density in territorial units that were above average in the ratio of inhabitants to land at the start of the period.

[23]States in which the percentage rural increase exceeded the percentage urban increase in both 1930–1940 and 1940–1950: New Hampshire, Massachusetts, Rhode Island, Connecticut, New York, New Jersey, Pennsylvania, Ohio, Michigan, Oregon, and California. States in which the situation held for 1930–1940 but not for 1940–1950: Indiana, Illinois, West Virginia, Kentucky, and Washington.

Selection Fifteen

URBAN POPULATION DENSITIES: STRUCTURE AND CHANGE

Brian J. L. Berry, James W. Simmons, and Robert J. Tennant

More than a decade ago the economist Colin Clark introduced an article on urban population densities[1] with the remark that this branch of geography appeared to be relatively neglected. He then produced evidence in support of his argument that regardless of time or place the spatial distribution of population densities within cities appears to conform to a single empirically derived expression:

$$d_x = d_o e^{-bx}, \qquad [1]$$

where d_x is population density d at distance x from the city center, d_o is central density, as extrapolated, and b is the density gradient, indicating the rate of diminution of density with distance, a negative exponential decline.

Reprinted from *The Geographical Review*, **53**, 1963, 389–405, by permission of the editor.

However, despite much recent attention, both theoretical and empirical, and despite Clark's clear identification of his topic as lying within the province of urban geography (indeed, the germ of these ideas is to be found in the work of Mark Jefferson in 1909[2]), both the topic and Clark's stimulating and fundamental contribution remain neglected by geographers. For example, not a single reference to Clark's paper appears in "Readings in Urban Geography."[3] There is evidently a need for a careful review of Clark's work, especially in the light of the recent related contributions of Muth, Weiss, Stewart and Warntz, Alonso, Winsborough, Beckmann, and others.[4] This is the first objective of the present paper. A variety of interesting questions emerge from an inspection of the available evidence. For example: How widespread is the regularity? Does it have a theoretical rationale? What factors influence variations in b from place to place? Why should b diminish through time in Western cities yet remain relatively constant in "non-Western" ones?[5] These and similar questions are examined here.

The Negative Exponential Distribution

Clark argued that equation [1], which says that urban population densities decline in a negative exponential manner with increasing distance from the city center, "appears to be true for all times and all places studied, from 1801 to the present day, and from Los Angeles to Budapest." In fact, he provided thirty·six examples in which the equation

$$ln \ d_x = ln \ d_o - bx \qquad [2]$$

appeared to be a good fit to the sample data at his disposal.[6]

One thing he did not do, however, was to provide a theoretical rationale for his formula. And thirty-six cases hardly enable one to assert complete universality for equation [1] regardless of time or place, especially when a sound theoretical base is lacking. Other empirical support is necessary, and it is abundantly provided in the references cited here in footnote 4.

In Chicago, the classic laboratory for urban analysis in the United States, Winsborough[7] shows the pattern to hold for every census year from 1860 to 1950, with the *weakest* correlation between density and distance −0.97. Similarly, Kramer shows that the fit is better for *net* residential densities in Chicago than for gross densities, and that the rate of decline varies by radial sector.[8] Muth, and independently Weiss, found that the pattern holds for all large United States cities studied in 1950.[9] Sherratt fitted a similar model to data for Sydney, Australia; and Newling found that equation (2) provided a satisfactory fit for Kingston, Jamaica.[10] However, the only evidence provided for Asia relates to Calcutta, in which Kar shows that a negative exponential pattern existed in 1881, 1901, 1921, and 1951. Kar's graphs are presented

in Figure 15.9. We can now fill in this gap a little; for Robert J. Tennant[11] has recently found that Clark's model also applies in Colombo, Hyderabad, Manila, Rangoon, Singapore, Djakarta, and Tokyo (and, independently of Kar, in Calcutta). The relationship for Hyderabad is shown in Figure 15.1.

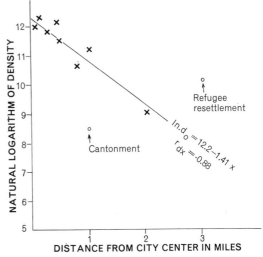

Figure 15.1 Density-distance relationship for Hyderabad

Almost a hundred cases are now available, with examples drawn from most parts of the world for the past 150 years, and no evidence has yet been advanced to counter Clark's assertion of the universal applicability of equation [1]. To be sure, the goodness of fit of the model varies from place to place, but in every place so far studied a statistically significant negative exponential relationship between density and distance appears to exist.

Theoretical Rationale

The basic theory of urban land use is by now well known. The argument runs as follows. Sites within cities offer two goods —land and location.[12] Each urban activity derives utility from a site in accordance with the site's location. Utility may be translated into ability to pay for that site. The most desirable locational property of urban sites is centrality (or maximum accessibility in the urban area, since transport routes converge at the center). For any use, ability to pay is directly related to centrality. The less central the location, the greater are the transport inputs incurred and the lower the net returns. Bid-rent functions thus decline with distance from the city center. However, the intercept (utility derivable from maximum centrality) and the slope (rent-distance trade-off) of this function differ for different activities, and in competitive locational equilibrium, with each site occupied by the use that pays most for the land, the resulting spatial structure of land use is one that is zoned according to relative accessibility. Land prices diminish outward; and as they do, regardless of other changes, land inputs will be substituted for other inputs, and intensity of land use will diminish. Thus declining residential densities should be expected.[13]

Most parts of a city are occupied by residential land uses of different kinds. Alonso[14] has shown that bid-rent functions are steeper for the poorer of any pair of households with identical tastes. Hence, in equilibrium, one expects the poor to live near the center on expensive land, consuming little of it, and the rich at the periphery, consuming more of it. Since land consumed by each household increases with distance from the city center, population densities must drop, with due allowance for variation in size of household.

Muth[15] goes further. Making assumptions about relative perfection of competition in the housing market, maximizing or minimizing behavior as appropriate, diminution of price of housing with distance from city center,[16] and a demand function for housing linear in the logarithm of price at the center and population, he develops a model in which price per unit of housing, rent per unit of land, and output of housing per unit of land all decline, and per capita consumption of housing increases, with distance from the city center. Net density (output of housing per unit of land divided by per

capita consumption of housing) must therefore also decline.[17] Moreover, if the price-distance function is assumed to be negative exponential and the production function for housing logarithmically linear with constant returns to scale, then net population density must decline negative exponentially with distance from the city center.

For the model to hold, a negative exponential price-distance relationship must exist. Also, since Muth's model considers only residential competition, we should expect the negative exponential to be a better fit for net than for gross residential densities, since the gross include all land regardless of use.[18]

Evidence can be provided to verify both these points. Figure 15.2 shows that front-foot values for residential land diminish negative exponentially in all parts of Chicago where undeveloped lots are available for sale. However, the more central parts of the city are largely filled, since the older the development, the less land is available, the less active the land market, and the lower the price. The earliest developments are the most central and are occupied by the lowest socioeconomic groups.[19] Indeed, within a six- or seven-mile radius of the center of Chicago the only market for residential lots is related to renewal activity or intended for conversion to new highways, at condemnation prices, except within the Loop or where private investment is committed to residential renewal. Hence it should be no surprise that the negative exponential price-distance relationship does not begin to take form until newer areas with an active land market for residential use are reached. Notice also in Figure 15.2 how the rate of decline varies by sector.[20]

Since a negative exponential price-distance relationship holds, we should now find a negative exponential decline of densities. Figure 15.3 shows this to be the case, and the fit for net densities is better than that for gross. Equation [1] is therefore a logical outcome of urban-land-use theory. The theory of urban land use, which originated with Hurd and Haig, and which owes its

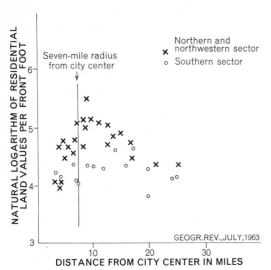

Figure 15.2 Residential land values, two sectors of the Chicago metropolitan area, 1961. Source: Olcott's *Blue Book of Land Values* for Chicago, 1961.

recent improvements to Ratcliff, Alonso, and Muth, provides the needed rationale for the appearance of Clark's empirical regularity.

Implications of the Model

From [1] it follows that the population residing within a distance r of the city center is

$$\int_o^r d_o e^{-bx}(2\pi x)dx = P_r,$$ [3]

which equals

$$2d_o\pi b^{-2}[1 - e^{-br}(1 + br)] = P_r,$$ [4]

assuming, of course, that a full 360° is concerned.[21] When $r = \infty$, this becomes

$$2d_o\pi b^{-2} = P_\infty.$$ [5]

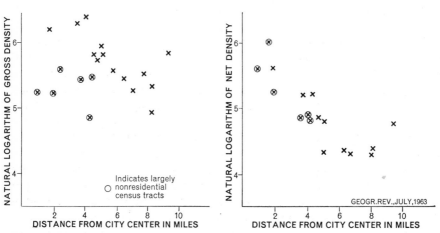

Figure 15.3 Gross and net density gradients, Chicago, 1960. Note how use of gross densities is complicated by presence of substantial nonresidential areas in certain census tracts

If population is held constant in [5], we thus expect

$$d_o = (2\pi)^{-1}b^2,$$ [6]

and this indeed appears to be true.

In Figure 15.4, d_o is graphed against b for United States cities in 1950.[22] Isolines of city size have been interpolated to hold P constant. Cities in any size class trend upward with the appropriate slope.

However, another expression exists for central density, d_o. Weiss[23] found that for the

United States in 1950 the density-distance gradient b could be calculated for any city by using the expression

$$b = (10^5/P_m)^{1/3} \text{ in } mi^{-1},$$ [7]

where P_m is the population of the metropolitan area. From this

$$P_m = 10^5 b^{-3}.$$ [8]

Muth's data, for central cities, P_c, indicate the exponent of b to be -2.65, which is of the right relative order of magnitude.[24]

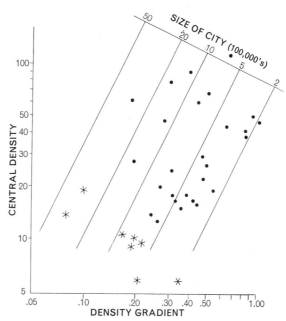

Figure 15.4 Central densities and density gradients related to city size, U.S. cities 1950

Substitution of [8] in [5] results in the expression

$$d_o = (10^5/2\pi)b^{-1}, \qquad [9]$$

which obviously differs from [6], in which population is held constant. Apparently [9] applies to different subsets of cities (for example, the subset starred in Figure 15.4 which has the correct slope of −1) defined in terms of factors influencing central density, d_o, regardless of city size.[25] Equation [6] applies to subsets of cities of the same size, and equation [9] to subsets of cities with similar histories of development.

Equation [8] is of further interest. It says that as the population of a city increases, the density gradient diminishes, or that small cities are more "compact" than larger cities by virtue of their steeper density gradients. Figure 15.5 shows how the relationship holds for thirty-six United States cities in 1950.[26] Asian cities are graphed in Figure 15.6.[27]

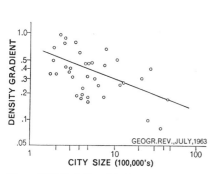

Figure 15.5 Relationship between city size and density gradient, U.S. cities, 1950

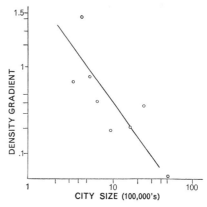

Figure 15.6 Relationship between city size and density gradient, selected Asian cities, postwar

It is obvious that Asian cities, with a greater intercept and a steeper slope, are far more compact than their United States counterparts of equivalent size, yet the generalization that compactness diminishes with size again holds.

Factors Influencing Central Density and Density Gradient

Enough has been said in connection with equations [6] through [9] to indicate that a more penetrating analysis is required of factors influencing central density and the density gradient in any cross section of cities. For purposes of analysis, Muth's data for United States cities will be used, since he has already provided the parameters d_o and b for each in 1950.

The most obvious influence on population densities near the city center is the age and mode of development and building. Older cities built with small lots and subdivisions will have higher densities than cities built at other times with other modes of subdivision. Winsborough[28] follows Boulding[29] in arguing for the controlling influence of timing of development on subsequent form. "At any moment the form of any object, organism, or organization is the result of its laws of growth up to that moment," and "Growth creates form, but form limits growth."[30]

But age of cities is useful only in defining similar subsets of cities for which equation [9] holds regardless of size. Holding size constant, central density is related to the density gradient, which in its turn may be influenced by a variety of additional factors. Thus central density is a function both of age and, as a composite surrogate for these other factors, of density gradient. A regression equation computed to quantify this functional relationship yielded the expression

$$d_o = 0.5302 + 0.6362 \text{ age} - 3.495\, b^{-1}. \quad [10]$$

Both age[31] and density gradient were significant at the 0.01 significance level, and 61 per cent of the variance of d_o was accounted

for.[32] This is pleasing, since Muth's estimates of d_o were subject to error, but it also indicates that additional factors should be investigated in connection with the definition of subsets of cities in equation [9]. A better measure of age should be found, probably one indicative of the nature of the growth process, accounting for differences in local transportation technology, in particular.[33]

Equations [3], [4], and [5] assume a circular city, with integration of equation [1] proceeding over the full 360° of the circle and the city center located at the center of the circle. Yet cities that conform to these assumptions are hard to find. Asymmetry and lopsidedness are common, elongations and crenulations many. Theoretically at least, one would expect the density gradient to diminish as shape distortions increase, because areas that would normally be occupied by certain densities are now no longer available, and uses that prefer these densities must move outward to the nearest available sites (though with some inevitable changes because of substitution effects). We must find out whether this is so, and if shape distortion, size of city, and so on interact to create the overall density gradient.[34]

Muth,[35] after a detailed multiple regression analysis, rejected no fewer than nine different variables hypothesized to have some influence in determining density gradient: density of local transit systems; quantity of local transit trackage; area of the standard metropolitan area (SMA) in 1950; proportion of SMA growth 1920–1950; median income; proportion of SMA sales in the central business district; proportion of central-city dwelling units substandard; proportion of urbanized-area male employment in manufacturing; and average density of central city. Only size of SMA and proportion of manufacturing outside the central city clearly appeared to bear significant relationships to b, though per capita car registrations showed a significant partial correlation, and the signs of other items, such as median income, indicated behavior in the right direction. Muth argued that

TABLE 15.1   Central densities and density gradients in Chicago,* 1860–1950

DECENNIAL CENSUS	CENTRAL DENSITY	DENSITY GRADIENT	DECENNIAL CENSUS	CENTRAL DENSITY	DENSITY GRADIENT
1860	30.0	0.91	1910	100.0	0.36
1870	70.8	0.87	1920	73.0	0.25
1880	96.6	0.79	1930	72.8	0.21
1890	86.3	0.50	1940	71.1	0.20
1900	100.0	0.40	1950	63.7	0.18

*Urbanized area.

size of city was significant only because other variables existed which were significant, and which could be approximated in sum by such a surrogate.

This leads us to postulate that density gradient is a function of size of city, shape distortion, and proportion of manufacturing outside the central city. A regression equation of the form

$$\log b = 3.08 - 0.311 \log P - 1.0 \log A + 0.407 \log M \quad [11]$$

resulted for the sample of forty-six United States cities.[36] Only size of city (P) was significant at the 0.05 level, and scarcely 40 per cent of the variance of b was explained. However, there is reason to believe that at such conventionally high significance levels the risk of making errors of the other kind (rejecting true hypotheses) is somewhat too large for comfort, and there is thus reasonable doubt whether shape distortion (A) and spatial pattern of employment in manufacturing (M) should be rejected, the more so since Muth did find M to be significant. A final decision cannot be made at this time, and further work is required. The only positive conclusion is to reiterate the relationship already found by Weiss and Muth, and remarked briefly in passing by Clark, that b diminishes as size of city increases, so that smaller cities are more compact than larger.

Changes through Time

The size-compactness relationship so far derived is cross-sectional. It applies to different cities in a region at the same period of time. One can argue from this cross-sectional pattern that as cities grow they should experience diminishing density gradients and degrees of compactness.

All the evidence indicates this to be true in cities of Europe, North America, and Australia. Clark[37] found diminishing gradients through time for London, Paris, New York, Chicago, Berlin, and Brisbane, for example. The curves for London are reproduced in Figure 15.7. Table 15.1 lists central densities for Chicago from 1860 to 1950 by decades.[38] A progressive decline in density gradient is evident, together with first an increase, and later a decrease, of central density. This phenomenon reappears in Clark's results, and Winsborough associated it with a shift in local transport technology. For example, in 1890, when mass transit was the most rapid and flexible transportation system available, there was a positive correlation between population concentration[39] and intensive use of mass transit in Chicago; but by 1950, when mass transit was competing with automobiles, the direction of the correlation was reversed.[40] Figure 15.8 shows the relation of Chicago's density-gradient time path to the 1950 cross-sectional picture for the United States.

Contrasting Changes in Western and Non-Western Cities

As Western cities grow through time they experience steady decreases in density gradient, and therefore in degree of compact-

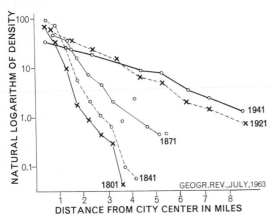

Figure 15.7 Density-distance gradients for London, 1801–1941 (after Clark).

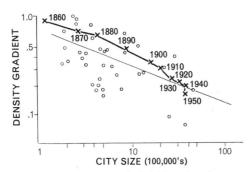

Figure 15.8 Chicago's diminishing density gradient, 1869–1950, compared with the 1950 United States cross section

ness, whereas central densities first increase and later decrease. But the same changes do *not* occur in non-Western cities. Figure 15.9 shows density gradients and central densities for Calcutta from 1881 to 1951.[41] Central density increased steadily, but although the urbanized area did expand, the density gradient remained constant. This tendency toward increased overcrowding with maintenance of a constant degree of compactness appears to be characteristic not only for the rest of the Indian urban scene[42] but also more generally in the non-Western world.

Figure 15.10 summarizes the cross-sectional and temporal patterns that may therefore be identified. At any point in time the empirical regularities to be observed are the same for both Western and non-Western cities. But through time the patterns differ.

In the West central densities rise, then fall; in non-Western cities they register a continual increase. In the West density gradients fall as cities grow; in non-Western cities they remain constant. Hence, whereas both degree of compactness and crowding diminish in Western cities through time, non-Western cities experience increasing overcrowding, constant compactness, and a lower degree of expansion at the periphery than in the West.[43]

Colin Clark[44] observed that there are "two possibilities for development, if the population is increasing. Either transport costs are reduced, enabling the city to spread out; or they cannot be reduced, in which case density has to increase at all points." In this, however, he identified the permissive factor for the accelerated *sprawl* of Western vis-à-vis non-Western cities (on the supply side) rather than the real reason for accompanying differentials in density gradient (which is on the demand side).

Alonso[45] showed that the rich, in Western cities, live at the periphery on cheap land and consume more land at lower densities than the poor do who live at the center. The Western world has also experienced a revolution in levels of living such that the richer, more mobile groups have increased not only numerically but also proportionally. Hence accelerated sprawl facilitated by improved transportation systems has been

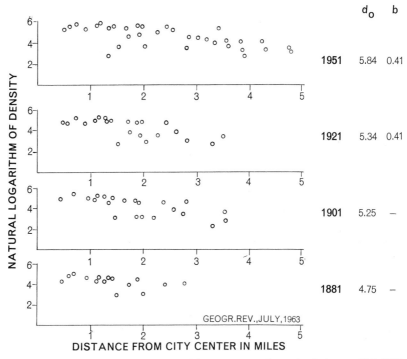

Figure 15.9 Density gradients for Calcutta, 1881–1951

stimulated by greater demands for peripheral lower-density land, with attendant reductions of the density gradient. The Western world has experienced significant changes in the nature of *demand* for residential land. Changed transport systems have merely ensured an adequate supply to meet the demands.

However, the socioeconomic pattern of non-Western cities is markedly different. Sjoberg[46] writes:

. . . the feudal city's land use configuration is in many ways the reverse of that in the highly industrialized communities. The latter's advanced technology fosters, and is in turn furthered by, a high degree of social and spatial mobility that is inimical to any rigid social structure assigning persons, socially and ecologically, to special niches.
[There are] three patterns of land use wherein the non-industrial city contrasts sharply with the industrial type: 1) the pre-eminence of the "central" area over the periphery, especially as portrayed in the distribution of social classes, 2) certain finer spatial differences according to ethnic, occupational, and family ties, and 3) the low incidence of functional differentiation in other land use patterns.[47]

Chatterjee[48] reiterates the regularity:

The influence of the caste system is reflected in the usual concentration of the higher castes in the central areas of good residential localities, while the lower caste groups usually occupy the fringe . . . The people still attach more importance to these centrally-situated residential areas . . . Thus, in spite of the modern development of road transport, the residential decentralization or movement towards the fringe outside the old residential areas is not very marked.[49]

If in Western cities the poor live at the center and the more mobile rich at the periphery, in non-Western cities the reverse is true. The least mobile groups occupy the

URBAN POPULATION DENSITIES

A. CROSS-SECTIONAL, WESTERN AND NONWESTERN

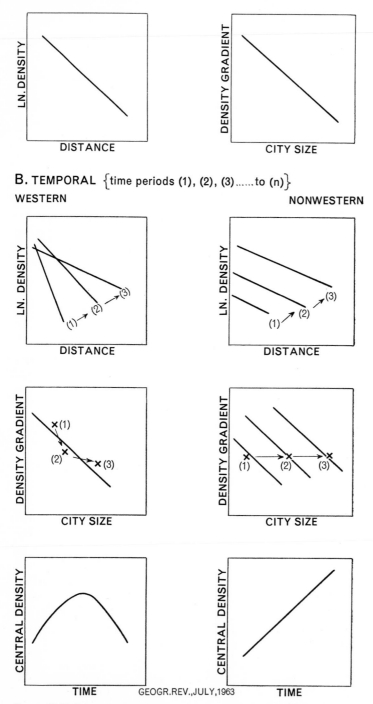

B. TEMPORAL {time periods (1), (2), (3)......to (n)}

Figure 15.10 Cross-sectional and temporal comparisons, Western and non-Western cities

periphery. Any income improvements lead to greater demands for central locations, and increased overcrowding. Sprawl reflects projection of the overall surface outward as densities increase throughout, in a periphery of degrading and depressing slums. Degree of compactness of the non-Western city remains, therefore, relatively unchanged, with the least mobile groups located at the periphery. In spite of reductions of transport costs in non-Western cities, the groups located where the possibilities of saving are greatest are the groups least able to take advantage of the possibilities. Changes on the supply side occasioned by transport improvements are of little utility. Differences in movements of central densities and density gradients through time are a function of the inverted locational patterns of socioeconomic groups within Western and non-Western cities, and attendant contrasts in demands for residential land.

Regardless of time or place, the expression

$$d_x = d_o e^{-bx} \qquad [1]$$

provides a statistically significant fit to the distribution of population densities within cities. Apparently, this negative exponential decline of density with distance represents a condition of competitive locational equilibrium in an active housing market, and it may be derived from traditional theories of urban land economics under a set of very simple assumptions.

The two parameters, d_o (central density, indicating concentration or crowding) and b (density gradient, indicating compactness), vary from city to city. In any temporal cross section, central density appears to be determined by the growth history of the city up to that time, and the density gradient is a function of city size.

Western and non-Western cities differ, however, in the ways in which d_o and b change through time. In Western cities d_o increases, then decreases, and b steadily drops. Later stages are characterized by deconcentration (falling d_o) and suburbanization (falling b, or "decompaction"). Non-Western cities, however, experience continued increases in d_o (overcrowding) and relative constancy of b (hence urban expansion without suburbanization in the Western sense). The contrast results from differing patterns of location displayed by higher- and lower-level socioeconomic groups in these cities.

Given the universal existence of the negative exponential density pattern, a large number of interesting applications become possible. Weiss,[50] for example, shows how equation [7] may be integrated with Zipf's rank-size rule for the United States to create a model that facilitates optimal location of market-oriented servicing units. The effectiveness of urban geography as an applied science is likely to increase in the world as more such findings are produced.

Notes

[1]Colin Clark: Urban Population Densities, *Journ. Royal Statist. Soc., Ser.* A, Vol. 114, 1951, pp. 490–496. See also his "Urban Population Densities," *Bull. Inst. Internatl. de Statistique*, Vol. 36, Part 4, 1958, pp. 60–68.
[2]Mark Jefferson: The Anthropography of Some Great Cities, *Bull. Amer. Geogr. Soc.*, Vol. 41, 1909, pp. 537–566. This article also contains interesting discussions of the reasons for the growth of very large cities (p. 539), of the definition of cities (pp. 543–544), and of the

dangers of "fictitious accuracy" of measurements, together with the need for recording both point estimates (means) and variances (size of errors) (pp. 555–556).
[3]Harold M. Mayer and Clyde F. Kohn, edits.: Readings in Urban Geography (Chicago, 1959).
[4]Richard F. Muth: The Spatial Structure of the Housing Market, *Papers and Proc. Regional Science Assn.*, Vol. 7 (7th Annual Meeting), 1961 (Philadelphia, 1962), pp. 207–220; Herbert K. Weiss: The Distribution of Urban Population

and an Application to a Servicing Problem, *Operations Research*, Vol. 9, 1961, pp. 860–874; John Q. Stewart and William Warntz: Physics of Population Distribution, *Journ. of Regional Science*, Vol. 1, 1958; pp. 99–123. William Alonso: A Theory of the Urban Land Market, *Papers and Proc. Regional Science Assn.*, Vol. 6 (6th Annual Meeting), 1960 (Philadelphia, 1961), pp. 149–158; Halliman H. Winsborough: A Comparative Study of Urban Population Densities (unpublished Ph.D. dissertation, Department of Sociology, The University of Chicago, 1961); Martin J. Beckmann: On the Distribution of Rent and Residential Density in Cities (paper presented to the Interdepartmental Seminar on Mathematical Applications in the Social Sciences, Yale University, 1957): G. G. Sherratt: A Model for General Urban Growth, *Management Science — Models and Techniques*, Vol. 2, 1960, pp. 147–159; Bruce E. Newling: Urban Population Densities — A Comment on Colin Clark's Paper with Special Reference to Kingston, Jamaica (unpublished manuscript, Northwestern University, 1960); Hans Blumenfeld: Are Land Use Patterns Predictable? *Journ. Amer. Inst. of Planners*, Vol. 25, 1959, pp. 61–66; Carol Kramer: Population Density Patterns, *C[hicago] A[rea] T[ransportation] S[tudy] Research News*, Vol. 2, 1958, pp. 3–10; "Chicago Area Transportation Study (Final Reports)," Vols. 1 and 2, 1959–1960; "Residential Density Model, Seattle Metropolitan Area, 1961" (King County Planning Department; mimeographed); Willard B. Hansen: An Approach to the Analysis of Metropolitan Residential Expansion, *Journ. of Regional Science*, Vol. 3, 1961, pp. 37–56; Beverly Duncan, Georges Sabagh, and Maurice D. Van Arsdol, Jr.: Patterns of City Growth, *Amer. Journ. of Sociology*, Vol. 67, 1961–1962, pp. 418–429; N. R. Kar: Growth, Distribution and Dynamics of the Population Load in Calcutta (1962; mimeographed); Lowdon Wingo, Jr.: An Economic Model of the Utilization of Urban Land for Residentail Purposes, *Papers and Proc. Regional Science Assn.*, Vol. 7 (7th Annual Meeting), 1961 (Philadelphia, 1962), pp. 191–205; *idem:* Transportation and Urban Land (Resources for the Future, Inc., Washington, D.C., 1961); Wilbur Smith and associates: Future Highways and Urban Growth (New Haven, 1961), especially pp. 14–18.

[5]The terms "Western" and "non-Western" are preferred to Sjoberg's "industrial" and "preindustial" (Gideon Sjoberg: The Preindustrial City — Past and Present [Glencoe, Ill., 1960]), though they have the same connotation.

[6]Clark, *Journ. Royal Statist. Soc.* [see footnote 1 above]. Most of Clark's historical materials were derived from Adna F. Weber's monumental source, "The Growth of Cities in the Nineteenth Century" (Columbia University Studies in History, Economics and Public Law, Vol. 11; New York, 1899).

[7]*Op. cit.* [see footnote 4 above], pp. 13–21.

[8]This information was used as a basis for projecting density distributions in the Chicago Area Transportation Study.

[9]Forty-six in Muth's case.

[10]Newling also shows the use of the model in defining the "real" limits of the city. See also Winsborough's comments on deconcentration, suburbanization, and so on.

[11]Robert J. Tennant: Population Density Patterns in Eight Asian Cities (paper read at West Lakes Division meeting of the Association of American Geographers, 1961).

[12]Alonso, *op. cit.* [see footnote 4 above].

[13]For a review of these ideas, see William L. Garrison and others: Studies of Highway Development and Geographic Change (Seattle, 1959), pp. 61–65. Rural analogies via a Von Thünen formulation are collected together in Michael Chisholm: Rural Settlement and Land Use (London, 1962). Beverly Duncan, in her paper "Variables in Urban Morphology" (Population Research and Training Center, The University of Chicago, 1962; mimeographed), shows extremely high correlations between a number of variables and measures of accessibility, distance from city center, and so on. Winsborough, *op. cit.* [see footnote 4 above], provides a systematic integration of views of land economists with those of human ecologists (especially Burgess, Hawley, Quinn, and Duncan).

[14]*Op. cit.* [see footnote 4 above].

[15]*Op. cit.* [see footnote 4 above].

[16]This decline is exemplified nicely for many different kinds of housing by W. C. Pendleton in "The Valuation of Accessibility" (The University of Chicago, 1962 [a prospective dissertation in urban land economics]; mimeographed).

[17]Since the model considers only the housing market, Muth is talking about *net* residential densities, though he always says *gross*.

[18]This was pointed out by Winsborough, *op. cit.* [see footnote 4 above], pp. 23–24.

[19]Alonso, *op. cit.* [see footnote 4 above], and Duncan, *op. cit.* [see footnote 13 above].

[20]One can go to Homer Hoyt's classic "One Hundred Years of Land Values in Chicago" (Chicago, 1933) and construct similar graphs for different times from 1836 on, supplementing for the last three decades with George C. Olcott's annual *Blue Book of Land Values for Chicago*, and find a repetition of the negative exponential pattern.

[21]Expressions (3), (4), and (5) are due to Clark, *Journ. Royal Statist. Soc.* [see footnote 1 above].

[22]The parameters are to be found in Muth, *op. cit.* [see footnote 4 above], Table 1.

[23]*Op. cit.* [see footnote 4 above].

[24]Computed from Muth's Table 1.

[25]Winsborough argues that the most significant of these factors is age of growth of the city.

[26]Muth's Table 1 is again the source.

[27]From Tennant, *op. cit.* [see footnote 11 above].

[28]*Op. cit.* [see footnote 4 above], pp. 9–10.

[29]K. E. Boulding: Toward a General Theory of Growth, *in* Population Theory and Policy (edited by Joseph J. Spengler and Otis Dudley Duncan; Glencoe, Ill., 1956), pp. 109–124.

[30]This is Boulding's "first principle of structural growth." Winsborough says that "the timing of growth affects the density patterns . . . different influences on the pattern of development at different times and the resultant structure of the city sets limits on its subsequent growth . . ."

[31]Years since the city reached a population of 50,000.

[32]See James W. Simmons: Relationships between the Population Density Pattern and Site of Cities (unpublished M.A. thesis, The University of Chicago, 1962) for an elaboration of these results.

[33]Winsborough, *op. cit.* [see footnote 4 above], shows that the implied central density of Chicago increased until 1900 or 1910 and decreased thereafter, apparently as a result of a shift in local transport that superimposed its effects on the established growth processes. Also, the total population density of a city, D, he found to be positively correlated with percentage of old dwellings, size of city, and percentage of population in manufacturing, and negatively correlated with percentage of dwelling units one-unit detached. For any city

he showed D to be a function of d_o, regardless of b; thus by implication d_o is a function of age, population, and employment. In turn, we shall see that b is a function of the last two variables. For an analysis of declining urban densities (D) in the decade 1950–1960 in the United States, see Ronald R. Boyce; Changing Patterns of Urban Land Consumption, *Professional Geographer*, Vol. 15, No. 2, 1963, pp. 19–24.

[34]Note that Weiss uses only population of metropolitan area in equation (7).

[35]*Op. cit.* [see footnote 4 above], Table 7.

[36]Simmons, *op. cit.* [see footnote 32 above]. The index of shape distortion, A, was constructed as the ratio of the sum of distances of points arranged in a regular network within the boundaries of the city's urbanized area from the city center to the sum of distances of points in the same regular network from the center of a circle of the same area as the city. A is 1.0 for a perfectly circular city and increases as distortion of shape does. The index is highly sensitive to elongation or lopsidedness, but not to crenulations, and only slightly to a starfish pattern created by radiating transportation routes. It appears to be fairly highly correlated with physically created distortions, especially the presence of water bodies; thus A is also an index of the influences of city sites on population density patterns. The correlation between

A and a site index S was 0.584. S was defined as WT where $W = 1 -$ (water area/total area) in a circle of the same area as the city centered on the CBD, and $T = 1 -$ tan (average slope). $S = WT = 1.0$ for a circular city on a level plain. Of the correlation between A and S, the greatest proportion of the covariance was accounted for by the W component, an indication that major shape distortions are largely a function of location alongside water bodies.

[37]*Journ. Royal Statist. Soc.* [see footnote 1 above].

[38]Computed from data in Winsborough, *op. cit.* [see footnote 4 above].

[39]Measured as b^{-1}.

[40]These review comments are drawn from "Comparative Urban Research: Progress Report to The Ford Foundation, May, 1962" (Population Research and Training Center, The University of Chicago), which summarizes Winsborough's findings and those of several related studies.

[41]This figure was provided by Professor N. R. Kar of Presidency College, University of Calcutta. The authors wish to express their gratitude to him.

[42]See Roy Turner, edit.: India's Urban Future (Berkeley, 1962).

[43]Winsborough, *op. cit.* [see footnote 4 above], points out the problems of differentiating between "deconcentration" and "suburbanization" in Chicago. Kar, *op. cit.* [see footnote 4 above], describes the absence of suburbs around Calcutta.

[44]*Journ. Royal Statist. Soc.* [see footnote 1 above], p. 495.

[45]*Op. cit.* [see footnote 4 above].

[46]*Op. cit.* [see footnote 5 above], especially pp. 95–103. Quotations on pp. 103 and 95–96 respectively.

[47]See also John E. Brush: The Morphology of Indian Cities, *in* India's Urban Future [see footnote 42 above], pp. 57–70. Contrast this picture with that provided throughout his book by James M. Beshers: Urban Social Structure (Glencoe, Ill., 1962). Paul Wheatley has pointed out (conversation) that the larger Southeast Asian cities do not have what we have termed the "non-Western" socioeconomic pattern, though the smaller and medium-sized towns do, and the result is that population redistribution follows the Western pattern in the larger cities.

[48]A. B. Chatterjee: Howrah: An Urban Study (unpublished Ph.D. dissertation, University of London, 1960), p. 233.

[49]It might be noted that the same social pattern is being repeated in new Indian towns. Le Corbusier's plan for the new Punjab (India) capital of Chandigarh has the best-quality residences at the center, grading outward to the poorest at the periphery.

[50]*Op. cit.* [see footnote 4 above]. Another interesting outcome of his model is the ability to calculate how many people reside in the most densely settled parts of the United States. For example, the 3000 most densely occupied square miles today contain the homes of 45,000,000 people.

Selection Sixteen

THE NEGRO GHETTO: PROBLEMS AND ALTERNATIVES

Richard L. Morrill

"Ghettos," as we must realistically term the segregated areas occupied by Negroes and other minority groups, are common features of American urban life. The vast majority of Negroes, Japanese, Puerto Ricans, and

Reprinted from *The Geographical Review*, **55**, 1965, 339–361, by permission of the editor.

Mexican-Americans are forced by a variety of pressures to reside in restricted areas, in which they themselves are dominant. So general is this phenomenon that not one of the hundred largest urban areas can be said to be without ghettos.[1]

Inferiority in almost every conceivable material respect is the mark of the ghetto.

TABLE 16.1 Major destinations of net 3,000,000 Negroes moving north, 1940–1960 (*Estimates only*)

New York	635,000	Washington, D. C.	201,000
Chicago	445,000	San Francisco	130,000
Los Angeles	260,000	Cleveland	120,000
Detroit	260,000	St. Louis	118,000
Philadelphia	255,000	Baltimore	115,000

But also, to the minority person, the ghetto implies a rejection, a stamp of inferiority, which stifles ambition and initiative. The very fact of residential segregation reinforces other forms of discrimination by preventing the normal contacts through which prejudice may be gradually overcome. Yet because the home and the neighborhood are so personal and intimate, housing will be the last and most difficult step in the struggle for equal rights.

The purpose here is to trace the origin of the ghetto and the forces that perpetuate it and to evaluate proposals for controlling it. The Negro community of Seattle, Washington, is used in illustration of a simple model of ghetto expansion as a diffusion process into the surrounding white area.

From the beginning of the nineteenth century the newest immigrants were accustomed to spend some time in slum ghettos of New York, Philadelphia, or Boston.[2] But as their incomes grew and their English improved they moved out into the American mainstream, making way for the next group. During the nineteenth century

TABLE 16.2 Minority populations of major urbanized areas, United States, 1960

	CITY	MINORITY POPULATION	TOTAL POPULATION	MINORITY %
1	New York City	2,271,000	14,115,000	16
	Negro	1,545,000		
	Puerto Rican	671,000		
2	Los Angeles	1,233,000	6,489,000	19
	Negro	465,000		
	Mexican	629,000		
	Asian	120,000		
3	Chicago	1,032,000	5,959,000	17
4	Philadelphia	655,000	3,635,000	18
5	Detroit	560,000	3,538,000	16
6	San Francisco	519,000	2,430,000	21
7	Washington, D. C.	468,000	1,808,000	26
8	Baltimore	346,000	1,419,000	24
9	Houston	314,000	1,140,000	28
10	San Antonio	303,000	642,000	47
11	St. Louis	287,000	1,668,000	17
12	Cleveland–Lorain	279,000	1,928,000	15
13	New Orleans	265,000	845,000	31
14	Dallas–Fort Worth	252,000	1,435,000	18
15	Atlanta	207,000	768,000	27
16	Birmingham	201,000	521,000	38
17	Memphis	200,000	545,000	37

Sources: Census of Population, 1960: Vol. 1, Chap. C, General Social and Economic Characteristics; Vol. 2, Subject Reports: Nonwhite Population by Race.

the American Negro population, in this country from the beginning but accustomed to servitude, remained predominantly southern and rural. Relatively few moved to the North, and those who did move lived in small clusters about the cities. The Negro ghetto did not exist.[3] Even in southern cities the Negroes, largely in the service of whites, lived side by side with the white majority. Rather suddenly, with the social upheaval and employment opportunities of World War I, Negro discontent grew, and large-scale migration began from the rural south to the urban north, to Philadelphia, New York, Chicago, and St. Louis, and beyond.

The influx was far larger than the cities could absorb without prejudice. The vision of a flood of Negroes, uneducated and unskilled, was frightening both to the whites and to the old-time Negro residents. As the poorest and newest migrants, the Negroes were forced to double up in the slums that had already been created on the periphery of business and industrial districts. The pattern has never been broken. Just as one group was becoming settled, another would follow, placing ever greater pressure on the limited area of settlement, and forcing expansion into neighboring areas, being emptied from fear of inundation. Only in a few cities, such as Minneapolis–St. Paul and Providence and other New England cities, has the migration been so small *and* so gradual that the Negro could be accepted into most sections as an individual.

America has experienced four gigantic streams of migration: the European immigration, which up to 1920 must have brought thirty million or more; the westward movement, in which from 1900 to the present close to ten million persons have participated; the movement from the farms to the cities, which since 1900 has attracted some thirty million; and the migration of Negroes to the North and West, which has amounted since World War I to about five million, including some three million between 1940 and 1960 (Table 16.1). The pace has not abated. Contributing also to the ghetto population have been 900,000 Puerto Ricans, who came between 1940 and 1960, largely to New York City; about 1,500,000 Mexicans, descendants of migrants to the farms and cities of the Southwest; and smaller numbers of Chinese, Japanese, and others.[4] Economic opportunity has been the prime motivation for all these migrant groups, but for the Negro there was the additional hope of less discrimination.

The rapidity and magnitude of the Negro stream not only have increased the intensity and size of ghettos in the North but no doubt have also accelerated the white "flight to the suburbs" and have strongly affected the economic, political, and social life of the central cities.[5] In the South, too, Negroes have participated in the new and rapid urbanization, which has been accompanied by increased ghettoization and more rigid segregation.

As a result of these migrations, the present urban minority population consists, in the North and West, of 7.5 million Negroes and 4 million others, together 12.5 percent of the total regional urban population; in the South, of 6.5 million Negroes, 20 percent; in total, of 18 million, 14 percent.[6] The proportion is increasing in the North, decreasing in the South. Minority populations in large American cities are presented in Table 16.2.

The Nature of the Ghetto

If we study the minority population in various cities, we can discern real differences in income, education, occupational structure, and quality of homes.[7] For example, median family income of Negroes ranges from $2600 in Jackson, Mississippi, to $5500 in Seattle; and as a proportion of median white family income, from 46 percent to 80 percent respectively. The United States median family income for Negroes in urban areas is only $3700, as compared with $6400 for whites, but it is more than double the figure for Negroes still living in rural areas, $1750. It is not hard, therefore, to understand the motivation for Negro migration to the northern cities, where striking progress has really been made.

But the stronger impression is of those general characteristics which are repeated over and over. The ghetto system is dual: not only are Negroes excluded from white areas, but whites are largely absent from Negro areas. Areas entirely or almost exclusively white or nonwhite are the rule, areas of mixture the exception. The ghettos, irrespective of regional differences, are always sharply inferior to white areas; home ownership is less and the houses are older, less valuable, more crowded, and more likely to be substandard.[8] More than 30 percent of Negro urban housing is dilapidated or without indoor plumbing, as compared with less than 15 percent for whites. The ghetto is almost always in a zone peripheral to the central business district, often containing formerly elegant houses intermingled with commerical and light industrial uses. As poor, unskilled labor, Negroes settled near the warehouses and the railroads, sometimes in shacktowns, and gradually took over the older central houses being abandoned by the most recently segregated groups—for example, the Italians and the Jews—as their rise in economic status enabled them to move farther out. More than one ghetto may appear on different sides of the business district, perhaps separated by ridges of wealthy, exclusive houses or apartments.

The Negro differs fundamentally from these earlier groups, and from the Mexicans and Puerto Ricans as well. As soon as economic and educational improvements permit, the lighter-skinned members of the other groups may escape the ghetto, but black skin constitutes a qualitative difference in the minds of whites, and even the wealthy Negro rarely finds it possible to leave the ghetto. Color takes precedence over the normal determinants of our associations.[9]

In the southern city Negroes have always constituted a large proportion of the population and have traditionally occupied sections or wedges, extending from the center of the city out into the open country. Indeed, around some cities, such as Charleston, South Carolina, the outer suburban zone is largely Negro. Figure 16.1 depicts the ghetto pattern for selected cities.

The impact of the ghetto on the life of its residents is partly well known, partly hidden. The white person driving through is struck by the poverty, the substandard housing, the mixture of uses, and the dirt; he is likely to feel that these conditions are due to the innate character of the Negro. The underlying fact is, of course, that Negroes on the average are much poorer, owing partly to far inferior educational opportunities in most areas, but more to systematic discrimination in employment, which is only now beginning to be broken. Besides pure poverty, pressure of the influx into most northern cities itself induces deterioration: formerly elegant houses, abandoned by whites, have had to be divided and redivided to accommodate the newcomers, maintenance is almost impossible, much ownership is by absentee whites. Public services, such as street maintenance and garbage collection, and amenities, such as parks and playgrounds, are often neglected. Residential segregation means de facto school segregation. Unemployment is high, at least double the white average, and delinquency and crime are the almost inevitable result. A feeling of inferiority and hopelessness comes to pervade the ghetto. Most important is the enormous waste of human resources in the failure to utilize Negroes to reasonable capacity. The real cost of maintaining the ghetto system is fantastic. In direct costs the city spends much more in crime prevention, welfare payments, and so forth than it can collect.[10] The ghetto is the key to the Negro problem.

What are the forces that operate to maintain the ghetto system? Four kinds of barriers hinder change: prejudice of whites against Negroes; characteristics of the Negroes; discrimination by the real-estate industry and associated financial institutions; and legal and governmental barriers. Naked prejudice is disclaimed by a majority of Americans today. Today's prejudice is not an outright dislike; it is, rather, a subtle fear, consisting of many elements. The typical

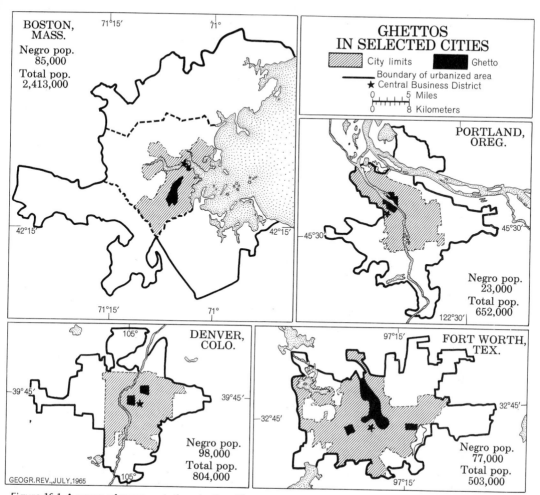

Figure 16.1 A group of representative ghettos. The dashed-line boundary on the Boston map indicates the inner urbanized area. Source: 1960 census data.

white American may now welcome the chance to meet a Negro, but he is afraid that if a Negro moves into his neighborhood it will break up and soon be all Negro. Of course, on a national average there are not as many Negroes as that—only one or two families to a block—but the fear exists because that is the way the ghetto has grown. A greater fear is of loss in social status if Negroes move in. This reflects the culture-bred notion that Negroes are inherently of lower standing. Some persons are terrified at the unlikely prospect of inter-marriage. Finally, people are basically afraid of, or uncertain about, people who are different, especially in any obvious physical

way. These fears combine into powerful controls to maintain segregation: refusal to sell to Negroes, so as not to offend the neighbors; and the tendency to move out as soon as a Negro enters, in order not to lose status by association.

The Negro himself contributes, however unwillingly, to ghettoization. It is difficult to be a minority as a group, but more difficult still to be a minority alone. Consequently the desire to escape the ghetto and move freely in the larger society is tempered by a realization of the problems in store for the "pioneer" and hesitancy to cut neighborhood ties with his own kind. Few people have such courage. In most cities, even if there were no housing discrimination, the ghetto would still persist, simply because a large proportion of Negroes could not afford, or would be afraid, to leave. Most Negroes achieve status and acceptance only within the Negro community. Usually Negroes who leave the ghetto prefer Negro neighbors; the risk is that this number, however small, is enough to initiate the conversion to full-scale ghetto.[11]

The Negro today suffers from his past. The lack of initiative and the family instability resulting from generations of enforced or inculcated subservience and denial of normal family formation are still present and are a barrier to white acceptance. The far lower levels of Negro income and education, no matter how much they are due to direct neglect and discrimination by the white majority, are nevertheless a strong force to maintain the ghetto. Studies show that whites will accept Negroes of equivalent income, education, and occupation.[12]

The strongest force, however, in maintaining the ghetto may well be real-estate institutions: the real-estate broker and sources of financing. It has always been, and continues to be, the clear-cut, official, and absolute policy of the associations of real-estate brokers that "a realtor should never be instrumental in introducing into a neighborhood a character of property or occupancy, members of any race or nationality, or any individuals whose presence will clearly be detrimental to property values in that neighborhood."[13] Many studies have attempted to resolve this problem. In the long run, property values and rents exhibit little if any change in the transition from white to Negro occupancy.[14] Sale prices may fall temporarily under panic selling, a phenomenon called the "self-fulfilling prophecy"—believing that values will fall, the owner panics and sells, and thus depresses market values.[15]

The real-estate industry opposes with all its resources not only all laws but any device, such as cooperative apartments or open-occupancy advertising, to further integration. Real-estate and home-building industries base this policy on the desirability of neighborhood homogeneity and compatibility. Perhaps underlying the collective action is the fear of the individual real-estate broker that if he introduces a Negro into a white area he will be penalized by withdrawal of business. There is, then, a real business risk to the individual broker in a policy of integration, if none to the industry as a whole. Segregation is maintained by refusal of real-estate brokers even to show, let alone sell, houses to Negroes in white areas. Countless devices are used: quoting excessive prices, saying the house is already sold, demanding unfair down payments, removing "For sale" signs, not keeping appointments, and so on. Even if the Negro finds someone willing to sell him a house in a white area, financing may remain a barrier. Although his income may be sufficient, the bank or savings institution often refuses to provide financing from a fear of Negro income instability, and of retaliatory withdrawal of deposits by whites. If financing is offered, the terms may be prohibitive. Similar circumstances may also result when a white attempts to buy a house—for *his* residence—in a heavily minority area.

Through the years many legal procedures have been used to maintain segregation. Early in the century races were zoned to certain areas, but these laws were abolished by the courts in 1917. The restrictive covenant, in which the transfer of property contained a promise not to sell to minorities, became the vehicle and stood as legal until 1948, since when more subtle and extralegal restrictions have been used.

Until 1949 the federal government was a strong supporter of residential segregation, since the Federal Housing Administration required racial homogeneity in housing it financed or insured. As late as 1963, when the President by Executive order forbade discrimination in FHA-financed housing, the old philosophy still prevailed in most areas. Finally, many states, and not just those in the South, still encourage separation. Even in the few states with laws against discrimination in housing, the combined forces for maintaining segregation have proved by far the stronger.

The Process of Ghetto Expansion

The Negro community in the North has grown so rapidly in the last forty years, almost doubling in every decade, that even the subdivision of houses cannot accommodate the newcomers. How does the ghetto expand? Along its edge the white area is also fairly old and perhaps deteriorating. Many whites would be considering a move to the suburbs even if the ghetto were not there, and fears of deterioration of schools and services, and the feeling that all other whites will move out, reinforce their inclination to move. Individual owners, especially in blocks adjoining the ghetto, may become anxious to sell. Pressure of Negro buyers and fleeing white residents, who see the solid ghetto a block or two away, combine to scare off potential white purchasers; the owner's resistance gradually weakens; and the transfer is made.

The role of proximity is crucial. On adjacent blocks the only buyers will be Negroes, but five or six blocks away white buyers will still be the rule. In a typical ghetto fringe in Philadelphia the proportion of white buyers climbed from less than 4 percent adjacent to the ghetto itself to 100 percent five to seven blocks away.[16] Figure 16.2 illustrates the great concentration of initial entry of new street fronts in a band of two or three blocks around a ghetto. The "break" zone contains 5 percent or fewer Negroes, but 60 percent of the purchases are by Negroes. Typically, a white on the edge does not mind one or two Negroes on the block or across the street, but if a Negro moves next door the white is likely to move out. He is replaced by a Negro, and the evacuation-replacement process continues until the block has been solidly transferred from white to Negro residence. Expansion of the ghetto is thus a block-by-block total transition.

In this process the real-estate agent is also operative. If the demand for Negro housing

can be met in the area adjacent to the ghetto, pressure to move elsewhere in the city will diminish. The real-estate industry thus strongly supports the gradual transition along the periphery. After the initial break the real-estate broker encourages whites to sell. The transition is often orderly, but the unscrupulous dealer sometimes encourages panic selling at deflated prices, purchasing the properties himself and reselling them to Negroes for windfall profits. The probability of finding a white seller is high in the blocks adjacent to the ghetto but falls off rapidly at greater distances, as whites try to maintain familiar neighborhood patterns and conceive this to be possible if the Negro proportion can be kept small. The process of transition is destructive to both groups, separately and together. Whites are in a sense "forced" to sell, move, and see their neighborhoods disband, and Negroes are forced to remain isolated; and total transition reinforces prejudice and hinders healthy contact.

Spread of the Negro ghetto can be described as a *spatial diffusion* process, in which Negro migrants gradually penetrate the surrounding white area. From some origin, a block-by-block substitution or diffusion of a new condition—that is, Negro for white occupancy—takes place. The Negro is the active agent; he can move easily within the ghetto and can, though with difficulty, "pioneer" outside it. The white is passive, an agent of resistance or inertia. Resistance against escape of Negroes from the ghetto takes two forms: rebuff of attempts to buy; and diminishing willingness to sell with increasing distance from areas or blocks that already have Negores. On the average the Negro will have to try more than once to consummate a sale, or, conversely, the owner will have to be approached by more than one buyer. Once the block is broken, however, resistance falls markedly, and transition begins. Although a complete model would take into account that a few whites continue to purchase in transition areas, the rate is insufficient, the net flow clear-cut, and the transition inevitable.

The proposed diffusion model is of the

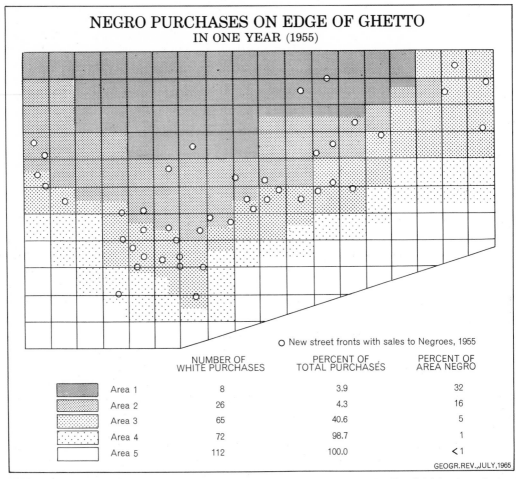

NEGRO PURCHASES ON EDGE OF GHETTO
IN ONE YEAR (1955)

O New street fronts with sales to Negroes, 1955

		NUMBER OF WHITE PURCHASES	PERCENT OF TOTAL PURCHASES	PERCENT OF AREA NEGRO
▓	Area 1	8	3.9	32
▒	Area 2	26	4.3	16
░	Area 3	65	40.6	5
∴	Area 4	72	98.7	1
□	Area 5	112	100.0	< 1

GEOGR. REV., JULY, 1965

Figure 16.2 Distribution of Negro purchases on the edge of the ghetto, showing initial entry of street fronts, 1955. Adapted from diagram in Rapkin and Grigsby, The Demand for Housing in Racially Mixed Areas (see text footnote 11 for reference), p. 76.

probabilistic simulation type.[17] It is probabilistic rather than deterministic for several reasons. We do not have sufficient definite information concerning the motivations for specific house-to-house moves of particular persons, but only general ideas concerning the likelihood of movement and how far. We are not dealing with a large aggregate of migrants, but with only a few individuals in a short period of time in a small area. If we had a thousand migrants, we could safely predict how many would move how far, but at the micro-level a probabilistic approach is required to evaluate individual decisions in the face of a complex of possible choices. Rather than determine that a specific migrant moves from one particular house to

another, we find the probability of a typical migrant's move from a block to any and all other blocks, and we use random numbers to decide which destination, among the many possible, he chooses. We thus obtain a spatial pattern of moves, which spreads settlement into new blocks and intensifies it in old blocks.

The model is simulated rather than "real" because it does not purport to predict individual behavior of actual people, but to simulate or pretend moves for typical households. Simulation is a valuable technique in science and technology, in which a model is constructed to depict artificially certain *major* features of some real process.

The simulation of diffusion model is

important in biology, in rural and general sociology, and in communications, and has been used in geography.[18] It is an ideal vehicle for the characteristics of ghetto expansion—a process of growth in time, concerning behavior of small groups in small areas in small units of time, in which a powerful element of uncertainty remains, even though the general parameters of the model tend to channel the results. This randomness is evident in the real situation, since we observe that the ghetto, like a rumor or an innovation, does not progress evenly and smoothly in all directions but exhibits an uneven edge and moves at different rates in different directions, here advancing from block to block, there jumping over an obstacle.

We do not expect the simulated patterns to match precisely the actual patterns. We do want the model to generate a pattern of expansion that corresponds in its characteristics to the real pattern, and we can satisfy ourselves of the correspondence by visual and statistical tests. The purpose and hope are to discover and illustrate the nature of the ghetto expansion process, in full knowledge that the detail of the ultimate step is omitted—how the actual individual decides between his specific alternatives. The omission is justified, because we know that the combined effect of many individual decisions can often be described by a random process. The real test here is whether the spread, over a period of time, has the right extent, intensity, solidity or lack of it, and so on.

The Model

A model of ghetto expansion must incorporate several elements: natural increase of the Negro population; Negro immigration into the ghetto; the nature of the resistance to Negro out-migration and its relation to distance; land values and housing characteristics; and the population size limits of destination blocks.

Beginning with the residential pattern at a particular time (in the Seattle example,

1940), migration and the spread of Negro settlement are simulated for ten two-year periods through 1960. The steps are as follows.

A   Taking into account natural increase for each period of the Negro population resident in the Seattle ghetto, at the observed rate of 5 percent every two years.

B   Assigning immigrants who enter the study area from outside at the observed mean rate of 10 percent every two years of the Negro population at the beginning of a period. These are assigned by random numbers, the probability that an area will be chosen being proportional to its present Negro population. Presumably, immigrants entering the area will find it easier to live, at least temporarily, and will find opportunities in houses or apartments or with friends, in approximate reflection of the number of Negro units available. After initial residence in the ghetto, the model allows these immigrants to participate in further migration.

C   Assigning internal migrants, at the rate of 20 percent of the Negro households (including natural increase and immigration) of each block every two years, in the following manner:

1   Each would-be migrant behaves according to a migration probability field (Fig. 16.3) superimposed over his block. This migration probability field can be shifted about so that each would-be migrant can in turn be regarded as located at the position indicated by X. The numbers in the blocks show where the migrant is to move, depending on which number is selected for him in the manner described below. Blocks adjoining position X have three numbers (for example, 48–50); more distant blocks have two numbers (for example, 54–55); and the most distant have one number (for example, 98). Since 100 numbers are used, the total number of these numbers used

in any one block may be regarded as the probability, expressed as a percentage, that any one migrant will move there. Thus a movable probability field, or information field, such as this states the probabilities of a migrant for moving any distance in any direction from his original block. Probability fields are often derived, as this one was, from empirical observations of migration distances. That is, if we look at a large number of moves, their lengths follow a simple frequency distribution, in which the probability of moving declines as distance from the home block increases. Such probabilities reflect the obvious fact of decreasing likelihood of knowing about opportunities at greater and greater distances from home. Thus the probability is higher that a prospective migrant will move to adjacent blocks than to more distant ones. The probability field provides a mechanism for incorporating this empirical knowledge in a model.

2 Randomly selected numbers, as many as there are migrants, are used to choose specific destinations, according to these probabilities, as will be illustrated below. The probability field as such makes it as likely for a Negro family to move into a white area as to move within the ghetto. A method is needed to take into account the differential resistance of Negro areas, and of different kinds or qualities of white areas, to Negro migration. Modification of the probability field is accomplished by the following procedures.

a If a random number indicates a block that already contains Negroes, the move is made immediately (no resistance).

b If a random number indicates a block with no Negroes, the fact of contact is registered, but no move is made.

c If, however, additional numbers indicate the same block contacted in b, in the same or the next two-year period, and from whatever location, then the move is made. This provides a means for the gradual penetration of new areas, after some persistence by Negroes and resistance by whites. Under such a rule, the majority of Negro contacts into white areas will not be followed by other contacts soon enough, and no migration takes place. In the actual study area chosen, it was found that resistance to Negro entry was great to the west, requiring that a move be allowed there only after three contacts, if the simulated rate of expansion was to match the observed rate. This is an area of apartments and high-value houses. To the north and east, during this period, resistance varied. At times initial contacts ended in successful moves and transition was rapid; at other times a second contact was required. These facts were incorporated into the operation of this phase of the model.

D There is a limit (based on zoning and lot size) to the number of families that may live on a block. Thus when the population, after natural increase and immigration, temporarily exceeds this limit, the surplus must be moved according to the procedures above. Obviously, in the internal-migration phase no moves are allowed to blocks that are already filled. The entire process is repeated for the next and subsequent time periods.

Hypothetical Example of the Model

Immigration (A and B) Let us assume at the start that the total Negro population— that is, the number of families—including natural increase is one hundred, distributed

1	2	3	4	5	6	7	8	9
10	11	12	13	14–15	16	17	18	19
20	21	22	23	24–25	26	27	28	29
30	31	32	33–34	35–37	38–39	40	41	42
43	44–45	46–47	48–50	X	51–53	54–55	56–57	58
59	60	61	62–63	64–66	67–68	69	70	71
72	73	74	75	76–77	78	79	80	81
82	83	84	85	86–87	88	89	90	91
92	93	94	95	96	97	98	99	00

GEOGR.REV.,JULY,1965

		2	2		
1	5	10	10	5	1
5	10	15	15	15	4

		1–2	3–4		
5	6–10 /	11–20 //	21–30	31–35	36
37–41	42–51 //	52–66 //	67–81 /	82–96 //	97–00

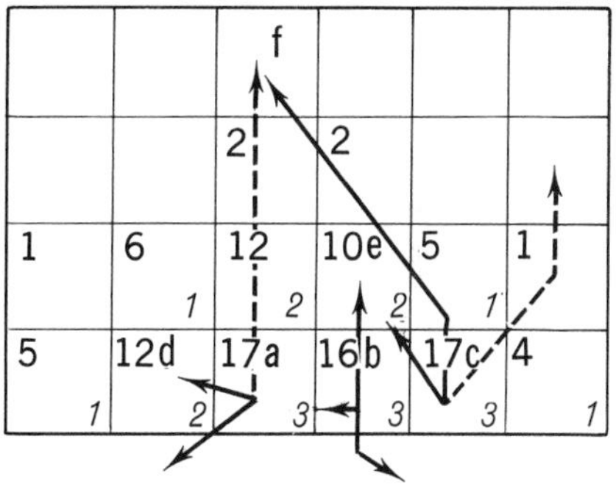

Figure 16.3 The migration probability field (left)
Figure 16.4 Negro residents at start of period (upper right)
Figure 16.5 (Center) Distribution of immigrants. Tally marks indicate entry into appropriate blocks.
Figure 16.6 (Lower right) Movement of migrants from three sample blocks. Large figures, resident Negroes; italic figures, number of migrants; broken lines, contact only; solid lines, actual moves.

spatially as in Figure 16.4. Here the numbers indicate the number of families in each block. Ten immigrant families (10 percent) enter from outside. The probability of their moving to any of the blocks is proportional to the block's population and here, then, is the same in percentage as the population is in number. In order that we may use random numbers to obtain a location for each immigrant family, the probabilities are first accumulated as whole integers, from 1 to 100, as illustrated in Figure 16.5. That is, each original family is assigned a number. Thus the third block from the left in the second row has two of the one hundred families, identified by the numbers 1 and 2, and therefore has a 2 percent chance of being chosen as a destination by an immigrant family. The range of integral numbers 1–2 corresponds to these chances. The bottom left-hand block has a 5 percent probability, as the five numbers 37–41 for the families now living there indicate. If, then, the random number 1 or 2, representing an immigrant family, comes up, that family will move to the third block in the second row. For the ten immigrant families we need ten random numbers. Assume that from a table of random numbers we obtain, for example, the numbers 91, 62, 17, 08, 82, 51, 47,

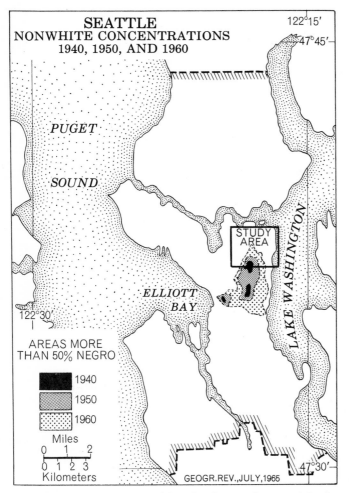

Figure 16.7 The ghetto area of Seattle. Source: Census data for the relevant years.

77, 11, and 56. The first number, 91, falls in the range of probabilities for the next to the last block in the bottom row. We place an immigrant family in that block. The second number, 62, places an immigrant family in the third block from the left in the bottom row. This process is continued until all ten random numbers are used. The final distribution of immigrant families is shown by the small tally marks in various blocks in Figure 16.5. The population of blocks after this immigration is shown in Figure 16.6. Here the large numerals indicate the number of families now in the blocks. It should be made clear that the migrants could not have been assigned exactly proportional to population,

because there are not enough whole migrants to go around. The first two blocks, for example, would each have required two-tenths of a migrant. In the probabilistic model, however, this difficulty does not exist.

Local migration (C) Twenty percent of the Negro families of each block, rounded off to the nearer whole number, are now taken as potential migrants. The rounding off yields a total of nineteen families who will try to migrate from the blocks, as indicated by the italic numerals in Figure 16.6. To illustrate, let us consider migration from the three blocks identified by *a*, *b*, and *c* in the bottom row. Random numbers are

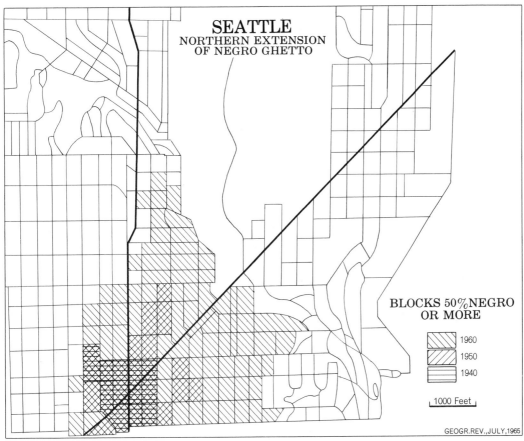

Figure 16.8 Blocks predominantly Negro in the northern part of Seattle's ghetto. Source: Census of Housing, 1960. (Block statistics for Seattle)

now needed to match against the migration probability field, Figure 16.3. Let the random numbers now obtained from the table of random numbers be 49, 75, 14, 50, 36, 68, 26, 12, and 33. The first migrant from *a* is represented by the random number 49. This provides a location one block to the left of the migrant's origin, *X*, to *d*. The second migrant's random number, 75, provides a location two blocks down and one to the left, which is beyond the study area. We interpret this as moot, as though he were replaced by another migrant from outside the area. The third migrant's number, 14, provides a location three blocks up, location *f*. Since this block has no Negroes, this is only a contact, and no move is made at the time. This is indicated by a dashed line. Now

let us proceed to migration from block *b*. The first migrant's number, 50, provides a location one block to the left, in block *a*, and the move is made. The second migrant's number, 36, provides a location one block up, in block *e*, and the move is made. The third migrant's number, 68, provides a location beyond the area. From block *c* the first migrant's number is 26, a location two blocks up and one to the right. This is an area with no Negroes, and only a contact path is shown. The second migrant's number, 12, provides a location three blocks up and two to the left. This location coincides with the contact made earlier by the third migrant from block *a*, and the move is made. The third migrant's number, 33, provides a location one block up and one to the left, or

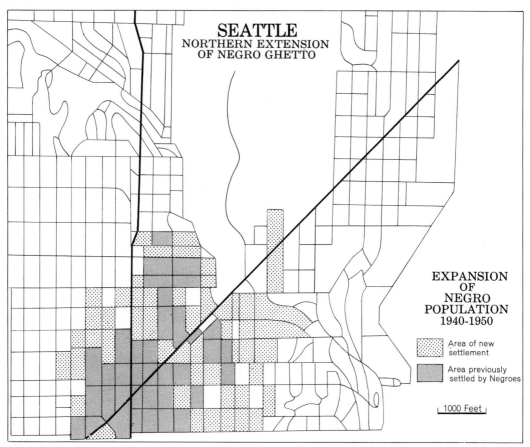

Figure 16.9 Source: Census of Housing, 1950 (Block statistics for Seattle)

block *e* again, and the move is made. The net result of all this migration is the opening of one new block to settlement, the reinforcement of three blocks, and two lost contacts.

Northward Expansion of the Ghetto in Seattle

The ghetto in Seattle, with only 25,000 residents, is of course smaller than those in the large metropolises, and it may seem less of a threat to the surrounding area.[19] Nevertheless, the nature of expansion does not differ from one ghetto to another, though the size of the ghetto and the rate of expansion may vary.

The expansion of the Seattle ghetto is shown on Figure 16.7, on which the study area is indicated. From 1940 to 1960 the Negro population in the study area more than quadrupled, from 347 families to 1520. Except for a few blocks just north and east of the 1940 Negro area, expansion was into middle-class single-family houses. To the west, where expansion was least, apartments offer increasing resistance, and to the northwest along the lake to the east houses reach rather expensive levels. Expansion was easiest along the major south-north and southwest-northeast arterial streets, and northward along a topographic trough where houses and land were the least valuable. The solidity of the ghetto core, the relatively shallow zone of initial penetration, and the consequent extension of the ghetto proper are shown on Figures 16.8 to 16.10. As the ghetto became larger and thus more threatening, transition became more nearly solid.

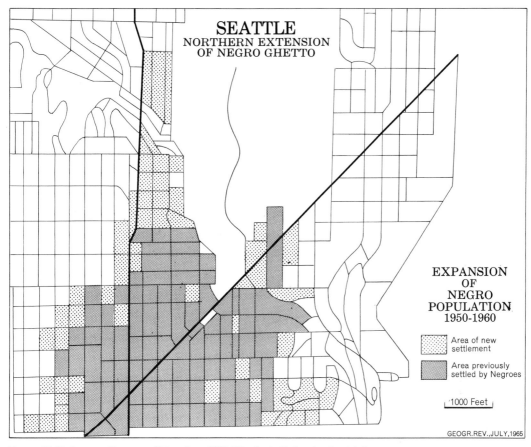

Figure 16.10 Source: Census of Housing, 1950 (Block statistics for Seattle)

The model was applied to the study area for ten two-year periods, beginning with the actual conditions of 1940 and simulating migration for twenty years. For each two-year period the natural increase of the Negro population was added to the resident population at the beginning of the period. Immigrants were assigned as in the model. Migrants were assigned according to the probability field (Fig. 16.3) and the rules of resistance. One example of the simulation of migration is shown on Figure 16.11, for 1948–1950. Typically, out of 147 potential migrants, 131 were successful and 16 made contacts, but only 8 of the movers pioneered successfully into new blocks. The results of the simulation are illustrated by Figures 16.12 and 16.13, which summarize the changes within two larger periods, 1940–1950 and 1950–1960.

Evaluation of the Results

A comparison of Figures 16.9 and 16.12, and 16.10 and 16.13, showing actual and simulated expansion of the Seattle ghetto for 1940–1950 and 1950–1960 respectively, indicates a generally close correspondence in the patterns. The actual pattern extended more to the north and the simulated pattern more to the northwest. A field check revealed that neither the quality nor the value of homes was sufficiently taken into account in the model. Topography, too, was apparently crucial. By 1960 the Negroes were rapidly filling in the lower-lying, nonview land. The ridge and view properties remained more highly resistant. The model did not recognize the rapid movement northward along the topographic trough.

According to the most stringent test of

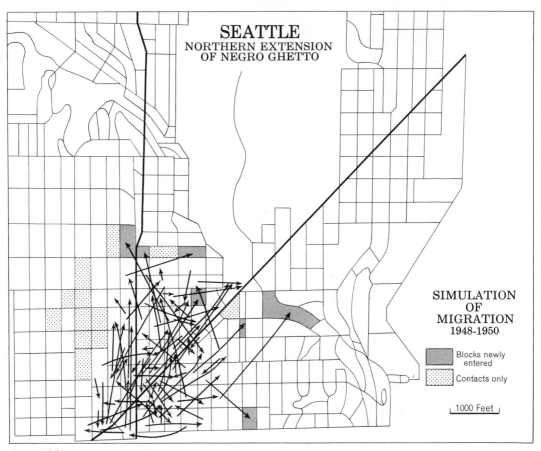

SEATTLE
NORTHERN EXTENSION
OF NEGRO GHETTO

SIMULATION
OF
MIGRATION
1948-1950

Blocks newly
entered

Contacts only

1000 Feet

Figure 16.11

absolute block-by-block conformity the model was not too successful. Less than two-thirds of the simulated new blocks coincided with actual new blocks. However, the model was not intended to account for the exact pattern. Sufficient information does not exist. The proper test was whether the simulated pattern of spread had the right extent (area), intensity (number of Negro families in blocks), and solidity (allowing for white and Negro enclaves), and in these respects the performance was better. The number of blocks entered was close, 140 for the simulation to 151 for the actual; the size distribution of Negro population was close; and similar numbers of whites remained within the ghetto (with the model tending toward too great exclusion of whites). This similarity, rather than conformance, indicated that both the actual and the simulated patterns *could have occurred* according to the operation of the model. This is the crucial test of theory.

A predictive simulation, as a pattern that could occur, using as the base the actual 1960 situation, was done for the periods 1960–1962 and 1962–1964 (Fig. 16.14). A limited field check showed that this pattern is approximately correct, except, again, with too much movement to the northwest and not enough to the north. No prediction from 1964 has been attempted, because of risk of misinterpretation by the residents of the area.

Alternatives to the Ghetto

The model attempted merely to identify the process of ghetto expansion and thus helps

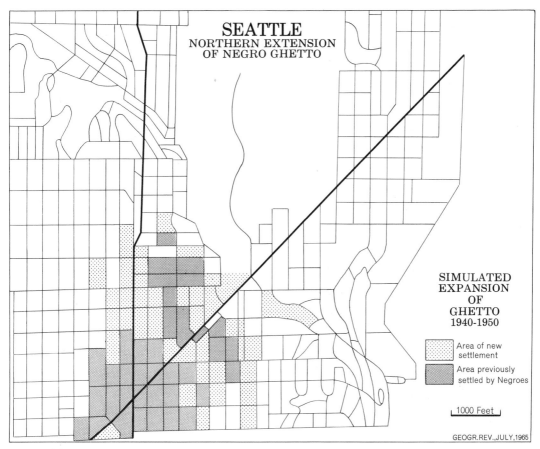

Figure 16.12

only indirectly in the evaluation of measures to control the ghetto. We know that such a diffusion process is common in nature—the growth from an origin or origins of something new or different within a parent body. Reduction of this phenomenon would seem to require a great weakening of the distinction between groups, here Negroes and whites, either naturally through new conceptions of each other or artificially by legal means.

In ghetto expansion the process is reduced to replacement of passive white "deserters" by active Negro migrants. Is there an alternative that would permit the integration of minorities in the overall housing market and prevent the further spread and consolidation of ghettos? Is it possible to achieve stable interracial areas, in which white purchasers, even after Negro entry,

are sufficiently numerous to maintain a balance acceptable to both? Three factors have been found crucial: proximity to a ghetto; proportions of white and nonwhite; and preparation of the neighborhood for acceptance of Negro entry.[20] Proximity to a ghetto almost forbids a stable interracial situation. Fear of inundation either panics or steels white residents. Only wealthy areas can maintain any interracial character in such a location, since few, if any, Negroes can afford to enter. Negroes entering areas remote from the ghetto are more easily accepted (after initial difficulties), because the great body of Negroes does not "threaten" neighborhood structures.

The proportion of Negroes in an area is critical for continued white purchasing. Whites are willing to accept 5 percent to 25 percent (with a mean of 10 percent) Negro

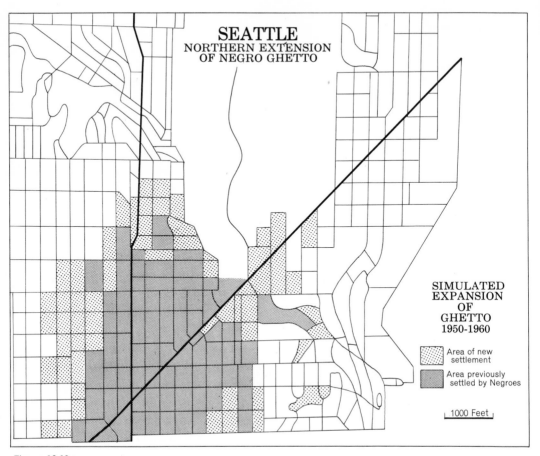

Figure 16.13

occupancy for a long time before beginning abandonment—depending on such factors as the characteristics of the Negroes moving in, the proximity of the ghetto, and the open-mindedness of the resident white population. On the other hand, although the Negro is accustomed to minority status, he usually prefers a larger proportion of his own group nearby than the critical 10 percent. Thus a fundamental dilemma arises, and there are in fact few interracial neighborhoods. For cities with low Negro ratios, say less than 10 percent, the long-run possibilities are encouraging, especially with the rise of Negro education and income, increased enforcement of nondiscrimination laws, and the more liberal views of youth today. For urban areas with high Negro ratios, such as Philadelphia, with 20 percent (40 percent in the city proper), it is difficult to imagine an alternative to the ghetto. The same con-

clusion holds for southern cities. No spatial arrangement, given present levels of prejudice, will permit so large a proportion of Negroes to be spread throughout the city without serious white reaction.

Private interracial projects have begun integration and have been successful and stable, if few in number.[21] From these experiments it has been learned that white buyers in such developments are not unusually liberal but are a normal cross section. Also, the spatial arrangement that permits the largest stable proportion of nonwhites has been found to be a cluster pattern—small, compact colonies of a few houses—rather than dispersed isolates.[22] This makes possible easy contact within the minority group, but also good opportunity for interaction with the white group, while minimizing the frequency of direct neighbors, which few whites are as yet able to accept.

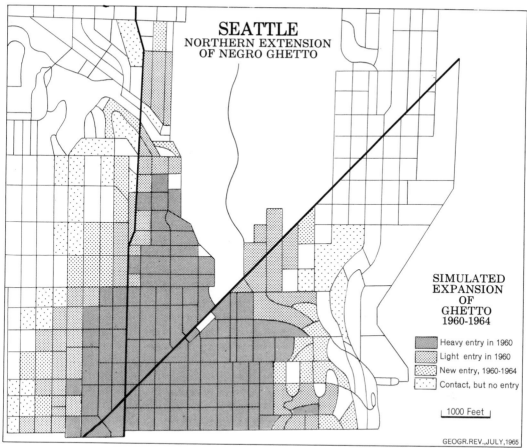

Figure 16.14

Integrated residential living will become more acceptable as Negroes achieve equality in education and employment, but housing integration will probably lag years or decades behind. At most we may expect an arrest of the extension of existing ghettos, their internal upgrading, and prevention of new ones. Experience certainly indicates a long wait for goodwill to achieve even internal improvement; hence a real reduction in ghettoization implies a governmental, not a voluntary, regulation of the urban land and housing market—that is, enforced open-housing ordinances. Everything short of that has already been tried.

The suggested model of diffusion-expansion still describes the dominant ghettoization pattern. In the future we may be able to recognize an alternative "colonization" model, in which small clusters of Negroes or other minorities break out of the ghetto and spread throughout the urban area under the fostering or protection of government.

Notes

[1]Census Tract Reports, 1960, *Ser. PHC(1)*, selected cities. Subject Reports (Census of Population, 1960, Vol. 2), 1960, *Ser. PC(2): Nonwhite Population by Race; State of Birth.* (U.S. Bureau of the Census, various dates.)

[2]Oscar Handlin: The Newcomers (New York Metropolitan Region Study [Vol. 3]; Cambridge, Mass., 1959).
[3]Charles Abrams: Forbidden Neighbors (New York, 1955), p. 19.
[4]*Ibid.*, pp. 29–43.

[5]Davis McEntire: Residence and Race: Final and Comprehensive Report to the Commission on Race and Housing (Berkeley, 1960), pp. 88–104.
[6]Nonwhite Population by Race [see footnote 1 above].

[7]Census Tract Reports [see footnote 1 above].

[8]McEntire, *op. cit.* [see footnote 5 above], pp. 148–156.

[9]Abrams, *op. cit.* [see footnote 3 above], p. 73.

[10]John C. Alston: Cost of a Slum Area (Wilberforce State College, Wilberforce, Ohio, 1948).

[11]Chester Rapkin and William G. Grigsby: The Demand for Housing in Racially Mixed Areas . . . : Special Research Report to the Commission on Race and Housing . . . (Berkeley, 1960), pp. 27–30.

[12]Nathan Glazer and Davis McEntire, edits.: Studies in Housing & Minority Groups: Special Research Report to the Commission on Race and Housing (Berkeley, 1960), pp. 5–11.

[13]McEntire, *op. cit.* [see footnote 5 above], p. 245.

[14]Luigi Mario Laurenti: Property Values and Race: Studies in 7 Cities: Special Research Report to the Commission on Race and Housing (Berkeley, 1960); [Homer Hoyt:] The Structure and Growth of Residential Neighborhoods in American Cities (Federal Housing Administration, Washington, D.C., 1939); Lloyd Rodwin: The Theory of Residential Growth and Structure, *Appraisal Journ.*, Vol. 18, 1950, pp. 295–317.

[15]Eleanor P. Wolf: The Invasion-Succession Sequence as a Self-Fulfilling Prophecy, *Journ. of Social Issues*, Vol. 13, 1957, pp. 7–20.

[16]Rapkin and Grigsby, *op. cit.* [see footnote 11 above], pp. 56–58.

[17]Herbert A. Meyer, edit.: Symposium on Monte Carlo Methods, Held at the University of Florida . . . , March 16–17, 1954 (New York and London, 1956); Everett M. Rogers: Diffusion of Innovations (New York, 1962); Warren C. Scoville: Minority Migrations and the Diffusion of Technology, *Journ. of Econ. History*, Vol. 11, 1951, pp. 347–360.

[18]Torsten Hägerstrand: On Monte Carlo Simulation of Diffusion, *in* Quantitative Geography (edited by William L. Garrison; in press); Forrest R. Pitts: Problems in Computer Simulation of Diffusion, *Papers and Proc. Regional Science Assn.*, Vol. 11, 1963, pp. 111–119.

[19]Calvin F. Schmid and Wayne W. McVey, Jr.: Growth and Distribution of Minority Races in Seattle, Washington ([Seattle] 1964); Walter B. Watson and E. A. T. Barth: Summary of Recent Research Concerning Minority Housing in Seattle (Institute for Social Research, Department of Sociology, University of Washington, 1962);

John C. Fei: Rent Differentiation Related to Segregated Housing Markets for Racial Groups with Special Reference to Seattle (unpublished Master's thesis, University of Washington, 1949).

[20]Eunice Grier and George Grier: Privately Developed Interracial Housing: An Analysis of Experience: Special Research Report to the Commission on Race and Housing (Berkeley, 1960), pp. 29–30.

[21]*Ibid*, p. 8.

[22]Reuel S. Amdur: An Exploratory Study of 19 Negro Families in the Seattle Area Who Were First Negro Residents in White Neighborhoods, Of Their White Neighbors and of the Integration Process, Together with a Proposed Program to Promote Integration in Seattle (unpublished Master's thesis in social work, University of Washington, 1962); Arnold M. Rose and others: Neighborhood Reactions to Isolated Negro Residents: An Alternative to Invasion and Succession, *Amer. Sociol. Rev.*, Vol. 18, 1953, pp. 497–507; L. K. Northwood and E. A. T. Barth: Neighborhoods in Transition: The New American Pioneers and Their Neighbors (University of Washington, School of Social Work, Seattle), pp. 27–28.

Selection Seventeen

POPULATION REDISTRIBUTION IN COMMUNIST CHINA

Leo A. Orleans

In recent centuries, China has had few major migrations other than those associated with natural, social, or political calamities, such as floods, droughts, famines, wars, or bandits. The only established exception is the movement into Manchuria, where millions of laborers and families poured into a vast new territory to work in the growing industrial and mining complexes, to build new

Reprinted from *Population Trends in Eastern Europe, the U.S.S.R., and Mainland China*, Proceedings of the Thirty-Sixth Annual Conference of the Milbank Memorial Fund, 1960, pp. 141–150, by permission of the Milbank Memorial Fund.

railroads, and to open and cultivate previously unused lands. But even here the inflows were associated with conditions of pressure and episodic catastrophes in the areas of origin. In other words, with few exceptions it has been the push rather than the pull that set people in motion, and once conditions in their villages improved, they usually returned to their homes. The result has been a relative stability in the distribution of China's population, despite the fact that most of her people are concentrated on only 10 per cent of the land which is cultivated.

There are a number of reasons why the population has not overflowed into the sparsely settled lands that surround the coastal and central provinces of China. Nature provides the most important reason. The settled areas are ringed by regions of non-productive soils with either insufficient rainfall or unsuitable topography or both; areas of intense summer heat, or of long winters with only relatively short growing seasons.

In addition, the Chinese cultural and social structures have had considerable influence in limiting long-distance migrations. Such factors as attachment to family and native village, the veneration of ancestors, and language differences, have been strong influences in grounding the people and keeping them close to their birth-place.

There is also the economic factor. The overwhelming majority of the Chinese peasants have always been close to destitution and starvation. Savings were virtually unknown; if a family did manage to improve its lot, a natural calamity or a man-made political upheaval usually wiped out anything it had accumulated. Only an unusual attraction could induce a family with little money to leave the home village with all its attachments, and to venture out into the unknown—to break up and clear new lands of marginal agricultural value. There was also the problem of subsistence in an area where transportation was either primitive or non-existent, during the long wait for the first crop. A family that managed to accumulate some money stood a much better chance of success by buying a boat ticket and heading for southeast Asia.

The result of all these factors is a density pattern that is highly unbalanced, with such extremes as the Chengtu plain in Szechwan Province, where the population density approaches 2,500 per square mile, and vast areas of Sinkiang, Tsinghai, and Tibet, which are virtually unpopulated. Another illustration of the uneven distribution of the population is the fact that if a straight line is drawn from Ai-hui in Heilungchiang Province to T'eng-chung in Yunnan Province,

40 per cent of the land area of China lies southeast of the line, but 96 per cent of the population lives there.[1] (*See* map, Figure 17.1.)

So, despite the population pressures in the coastal and central provinces, the outward flow of people was, with few exceptions, negligible. Those movements which did exist, were not the result of the pioneer-spirit of the Chinese peasant, but "... were direct or indirect consequences of the penetration of the industrial culture of the West, whether within China itself to the coastal cities where trade and industry were concentrated or to the outer regions where foreign powers had introduced industrialization and rationalized agriculture."[2]

The Communists took over power in China only a few years after the end of a war which saw some major, though generally temporary, population shifts. By 1949, most of the people who fled the Japanese occupied areas had returned to their homes. The population problem as such was not a major point of discussion either by Communist officials or by the country's press until 1954, when the results of the 1953 census-registration were published. With the disclosure that the population of Mainland China was almost 600 million and with the release of "sample" vital rates which indicated a population growth of some 12 to 13 million annually, the demographic problem became a major concern.

The Communist concern over population was further intensified by the heavy in-migration of peasants to the cities. Released figures on urban population imply that between 1949 and 1956 approximately 20 million people migrated from rural to urban areas.[3] This is equivalent to the total population of the three Benelux countries and undoubtedly constitutes one of history's largest population shifts in so short a time. The problems created by the overflowing cities were reflected in serious shortages of food, drastic lack of housing, and growing unemployment.

Partly as a result of this so-called "blind infiltration" into the cities, the Party intro-

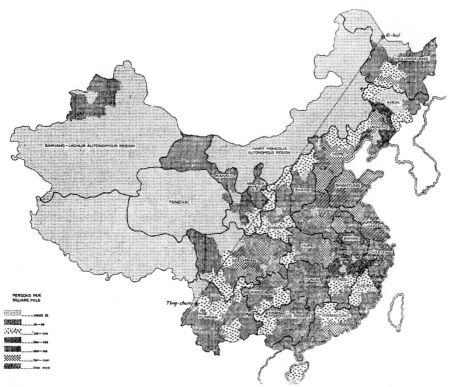

Figure 17.1 Population density of China, by special district, 1953. The Chinese Communists have not released an integrated series of population statistics for administrative units below the provincial level. The density map is therefore based on pre-Communist data which was adjusted to the 1953 figures. The 1947 hsien (county) populations (Ministry of Interior. Hsing-cheng Ch'u-yuch Chien-ts'e [Summary Tables of Administrative Territories], Shanghai, 1947) of each province were increased proportionally to correspond with the 1953 population of that province. These adjusted figures were then combined into groups, to correspond with the present boundaries of the Special Districts. Thus, the density patterns on the map are keyed to the Special Districts. Two major assumptions are implied in this method: (1) whatever errors exist in the 1947 population data are uniform throughout the country; (2) there has been no major redistribution of the rural population between 1947 and 1953 (all cities whose populations were reported at over 100,000 in 1953 have been deducted from the populations of the Special Districts). Any errors involved in these assumptions are greatly minimized by combining the hsien into groups, and by presenting the densities within fairly broad ranges. (The map was prepared by Mr. Charles Maddox.)

duced a registration system, providing for strict controls over the unplanned movement of people within China. The system was adopted by the Standing Committee of the National People's Congress on January 9, 1958.[4] As a result of these new regulations, it is virtually impossible to move from one residence to another without the knowledge and consent of the local authorities. In order to move from a rural to an urban area, a person must first obtain a certificate of employment from an urban labor agency, a certificate of acceptance from a school, or a certificate of approval for movement from an urban agency for the administration of population registers. Prior to movement to a national border defense area, which includes most of the western and northern provinces, a citizen must first obtain approval from the public security authorities of the hsien, municipality, or municipally controlled chu. When this written approval is obtained and when the individual has been accepted by an enterprise or a school, he must obtain a "removal certificate" which testifies to the fact that his name has been removed from the registration rolls of the place of departure. This certificate must then be presented at the new location within 3 days of arrival in an urban area and within 10 days of arrival in a village. The regulations are enforced by public security authorities. They seem to have effectively terminated most of the unauthorized population movements.

It is difficult to determine the volume of regional migration in China since the Communists consolidated their controls over the mainland in 1950. As is true of most quantitative data from China, statistics on migration are, in most instances, either incomplete, of dubious reliability, or non-existent. News reports frequently praise the patriotism of people who are leaving for the interior, but these migrants usually consist of small groups, precluding the possibility of obtaining any precise overall estimates. However, even prior to the above restrictions, the volume of inter-provincial migration that was not sponsored by the State could not have been significant. Collectivization and industrialization did, in fact, dislocate large numbers of people, but the overwhelming majority of them streamed into the cities from surrounding areas, while the same social, economic, and cultural factors that limited long-distance migrations in the past were still operative.

There were, however, certain state policies and goals that either directly or indirectly resulted in a deployment of people and a movement out of the densely populated coastal provinces. The Communists were committed to the industrialization and the modernization of China's backward economy. And of course they had to provide the rapidly growing population with a sufficient amount of food to sustain them, while setting aside adequate agricultural surpluses to pay some of the costs of industrialization. These were the goals that have determined the direction and the volume of regional migration in China since 1950.

Communist planners, disregarding the natural barriers that have prevented a more even distribution of China's population, have placed the blame for the irrational distribution of the country's productive forces on capitalist exploitations, political and economic control by imperialists and other reactionary classes. To correct this situation, to redistribute the productive forces and to utilize the untapped resources of the interior, they are attempting to build industrial complexes in the western half of the country.

In 1949, 77 per cent of the gross industrial product (excluding handicrafts) was derived from the coastal provinces of Kwangtung, Fukien, Chekiang, Kiangsu, Shantung, Hopei, and Liaoning; and more precisely from such cities as Shanghai, Tientsin, Peiping, and Canton.[5] This proportion reportedly decreased to 70 per cent in 1952 and to 60 per cent in 1955. The growth of the interior was not immediate. In 1952–1953, when existing industries were being rebuilt, 69 per cent of the total industrial growth still occurred in the coastal provinces. However, the First Five-Year Plan (1953–1957) stressed industrial development in new regions, and during the 1953–1955 period 55.2 per cent of all capital investment was directed toward the interior. Despite this seeming progress toward the intended goal, in 1955 the coastal provinces still produced 57 per cent of all electric power, 80 per cent of steel and iron, 54 per cent of sugar, 80 per cent of cotton cloth and 88 per cent of the machine tools in the country.

In terms of population, this phase of development naturally resulted in the growth of inland cities. Data are not available to show the differential rates of urbanization in the various provinces; however, there are figures showing a fantastic growth of individual cities in western provinces. For example, the population of Lanchou, the capital of Kansu, increased from less than 200,000 in 1950 to 680,000 in December of 1956;[6] in the Inner Mongolian Autonomous Region the population of Paotow grew from 90,000 in 1949 to 430,000 in 1957,[7] while that of Kalgan increased from 270,007 in 1949 to over 630,000 at the end of 1958;[8] the population of Sian in Shensi Province, which was less than half a million in 1949, reached 1,050,000 in 1957.[9]

Nevertheless, inter-regional migration contributed little to this urban growth, for most of it was the result of the influx of peasants from within the province. They were absorbed by the city's growing economy as unskilled construction laborers and coolies, while a few were trained in minor skills. The number of people that came from outside the province into the urban centers was limited. Unskilled labor was available locally, making it unnecessary to use the limited transport facilities to import workers from distant provinces. Groups of technical personnel have been moved into the interior, particularly from Shanghai, Tientsin, and the province of Liaoning, but they have all been small in number, for these people could not conveniently be spared by the existing plants and factories which had to release them. In 1955, of a total of 224,000 engineering and technical personnel in China, only 100,000 were located outside the seven coastal provinces,[10] while of the total number of industrial wage and salary earners in the country, 18.2 per cent were in the province of Liaoning in 1955.[11]

The precise volume of the westward migration associated with the industrial development is not known. However, it is not likely that the total would exceed one million persons. In time the movement will probably accelerate. As new mineral deposits are located, as more and more capital is invested in the development of the interior, as the number of graduates from technical and industrial schools increases, it is probable that the provinces along China's borders will require and receive an increasing number of new settlers.

The second program that has resulted in some redistribution of China's population pertains to agriculture. Despite the recent revision of past and future grain yields and goals, necessitated by statistical and natural calamities, China has, in fact, increased its agricultural output. Although most of the increase was achieved on existing agricultural lands through more intensive application of fertilizer and improved agricultural methods, a small part of the increase must be assigned to the reclamation of new agricultural lands in the west and north—particularly in the province of Heilungkiang.

Some Communist estimates of land suitable for agricultural production have undoubtedly been overly optimistic. For example, the figure of 1.5 billion mou, or almost a quarter of a billion acres, has often been quoted, and would almost double the present acreage under cultivation. More realistic observers, even in China, do not take this figure seriously. The numerous reports on the amount of land reclaimed during the past years vary, but it would seem that an annual average in the vicinity of 1.5 million acres would be an achievable, though generous, estimate of accomplishment. Whether the Communists will be able to maintain this average in the future is problematical, because the lands currently being opened to agriculture are those that are more readily accessible and adaptable. As the development reaches areas that have poorer soils and less rainfall, and that are more remote from the existing lines of communication, the investment of capital and labor will have to increase proportionately, while the expected returns will diminish.

Between 1949 and 1957, the Communists reportedly moved about 1.3 million persons to settle and work the new lands.[12] Most of the migrants came from the provinces of Hopei, Shantung and Honan—the same provinces that supplied the majority of the settlers for Manchuria during the 1920s and 1930s. Despite the living conditions and the hardships awaiting these people, many were sent in family units.[13] Some of the peasants who drifted into the eastern cities during the period of "blind infiltration" were also induced to "volunteer" their services for the development of the West. It seems unlikely that the volume of in-migration to the new land areas will increase in the near future. Based on the current reclamation rate, the number should not exceed an estimated half a million persons per year.[14]

Are there any other planned activities which have, within the past nine years, resulted in significant transfers of population? We may only guess. For example, the

Communists are explicitly trying to settle the areas populated by minority nationalities with Han Chinese, allegedly to educate the natives and modernize their economy, but primarily to consolidate political controls over these groups. Since most of the industrial and agricultural development of the interior is already taking place in these minority regions, both purposes are served by the new arrivals, and the individuals sent specifically to control the minorities are probably relatively few in number. There have been unverified reports, particularly since the recent uprisings, of several millions of Chinese entering Tibet. Although there is surely some Chinese migration into Tibet, that region, with its climate, topography, and present state of development, could not possibly support a population that doubled within a few years. Most of the Chinese in Tibet are undoubtedly military personnel rather than permanent settlers.

Road-building programs, irrigation projects, the construction of dams, and similar undertakings are utilizing millions of laborers throughout the country. It seems, though, that only a small proportion of them cross provincial boundaries, since they are usually recruited from the general area where the project is located, and they are returned to their homes when the project is completed. Other policies and campaigns, such as the "back to the land movement," have resulted in the shifting of millions of people, but these have generally been temporary in nature and limited in radius.

Thus, despite the political and economic upheavals of the past ten years, the spatial re-distribution of the Chinese population has been relatively slight. This is especially true when one views the numbers of migrants in relation to a total population of some 650 million and a natural increase that may be approaching 15 million annually. The rigid controls on unplanned migration seem to have been effective. The movement of several million people into the interior in connection with industrial and agricultural developments has made significant changes in the economy of the provinces of in-migration. However, the out-migration of these millions has not made a notable dent in the provinces from which they came. The provincial distribution of the population has changed little. As to the ever-increasing problem of China's growing population, the movement of people from the coastal provinces has not been and is not likely to be either a satisfactory or a realistic solution.

Notes

[1]Tung Chieh: Establish a Proletarian Demography. *Hsin Chien-she*, 1957, No. 4.

[2]Chia-lin Pan and Taeuber, Irene B.: The Expansion of the Chinese: North and West. *Population Index*, 1952, 18.

[3]*See* Orleans, L.A.: The Recent Growth of China's Urban Population. *The Geographical Review*, 1959, XLIX, No. 1.

[4]The complete text of the regulations was reported by the *New China News Agency* on January 9, 1958.

[5]All statistics in this discussion are from *T'ung-chi Kung-tso*, 1956, No. 21.

[6]*Jen-min Jih-pao*, 23 March 1957.

[7]*New China News Agency*, July 25, 1957.

[8]*NCNA*, January 13, 1959.

[9]*NCNA*, November 27, 1957.

[10]*T'ung-chi Kung-tso*, 1956, No. 21.

[11]*T'ung-chi Kung-tso T'ung Hsin*, 1956, No. 23.

[12]*Kuang-ming Jih-pao*, January 15, 1957.

[13]*NCNA* May 12, 1956.

[14]*See* Orleans, L.A.: The Volume of Migration in Relation to Land Reclamation in Communist China. *REMP Bulletin*, [Research Group for European Migration Problems] April–June, 1958, VI, No. 2, pp. 25–26.

A SELECTED SUPPLEMENTARY BIBLIOGRAPHY FOR PART 4

Alonzo, W., "The Form of Cities in Developing Countries," *Papers and Proceedings of the Regional Science Association*, Vol. 13, 1964, pp. 165–176.

Bogue, D. J., *The Population of the United States.* New York, The Free Press of Glencoe, 1959.

Bylund, E., "Theoretical Considerations Regarding the Distribution of Settlement in Inner North Sweden," *Geografiska Annaler*, Vol. 42, 1960, pp. 225–231.

Davis, K., "The Urbanization of the Human Population," *Scientific American*, Vol. 213, 1965, pp. 41–53.

Duncan, O. D., "The Measurement of Population Distribution," *Population Studies*, Vol. 11, 1957, pp. 27–45.

Field, N. C., "Land Hunger and the Rural Depopulation Problem in the U.S.S.R.," *Annals of the Association of American Geographers*, Vol. 53, 1963, pp. 441–464.

French, R. A., "Recent Population Trends in the U.S.S.R.," *Soviet Affairs* (St. Antony's Papers), 1965, pp. 68–95.

Hagood, M. J., and Siegel, J. S., "Projections of the Regional Distribution of the Population of the United States to 1975," *Agricultural Economics Research*, Vol. 3, 1951, pp. 41–52.

King, L. J., "A Quantitative Expression of the Pattern of Urban Settlements in Selected Areas of the United States," *Tijdschrift Voor Economische En Sociale Geografie*, Vol. 53, 1962, pp. 1–7.

Lowenthal, D., "Population Contrasts in the Guianas," *Geographical Review*, Vol. 50, 1960, pp. 41–58.

McCarty, H. H., "A Functional Analysis of Population Distribution," *Geographical Review*, Vol. 32, 1942, pp. 282–293.

Roof, M. K., and Leedy, F. A., "Population Re-

distribution in the Soviet Union," *Geographical Review*, Vol. 49, 1959, pp. 208–221.

Trewartha, G. T., "New Maps of China's Population," *Geographical Review*, Vol. 47, 1957, pp. 234–239.

———, and Zelinsky, W., "Population Distribution and Change in Korea, 1925–1949," *Geographical Review*, Vol. 45, 1955, pp. 1–26.

———, and ———, "Population Patterns in Tropical Africa," *Annals of the Association of American Geographers*, Vol. 44, 1954, pp. 135–162.

Vandermeer, C., "Population Patterns on the Island of Cebu, The Philippines, 1500–1900," *Annals of the Association of American Geographers*, Vol. 57, 1967, pp. 315–337.

Warntz, W., and Neft, D., "Contributions to a Statistical Methodology for Areal Distributions," *Journal of Regional Science*, Vol. 2, 1960, pp. 47–66.

Zelinsky, W. "Changes in the Geographic Patterns of Rural Population in the United States, 1790–1960," *Geographical Review*, Vol. 52, 1962, pp. 492–524.

———, "The Indo-Chinese Peninsula: A Demographic Anomaly," *Far Eastern Quarterly*, Vol. 9 1950, pp. 115–145.

PART FIVE

SPATIAL ASPECTS OF MORTALITY AND FERTILITY

INTRODUCTION

The obvious importance of the two major components of population growth (fertility and mortality) to problems of overpopulation, labor distribution, and national population policy and planning can hardly be exaggerated. The primary purpose of this section then is to provide some insights into spatial patterns of fertility and mortality and to sample some of the theory which relates to spatial aspects of these components.

The first two articles deal with spatial aspects of fertility and mortality decline. Chung ("Space-Time Diffusion of the Transition Model: The Twentieth Century Patterns"), in a hitherto unpublished article, presents a historical-cartographic analysis of the diffusion of demographic transition. Starting with 1905, crude rates are mapped for the nations of the world at five-year intervals, resulting in an intriguing motion picture image of the transition on a world scale. The three traditional stages of the transition model are depicted, as well as an alternate to the usually defined, explosive second stage. This alternate stage two is identified with moderate birth and moderate death rates which decline in a parallel manner rather than with the usual lag in fertility decline. A number of provocative questions are raised in the study, and three worlds are discerned in the cartographic analysis: the West, non-Western Europe which includes the U.S.S.R. and Japan, and the Latin America-Asia-Africa complex.

Carlsson ("The Decline of Fertility: Innovation or Adjustment Process") questions the validity of the predominance of the diffusion of innovation theory in explaining fertility decline. Instead, adjustment theory is posed as a more acceptable alternative. The analysis proceeds to investigate the prevalence of birth control within marriage before the secular decline in fertility, as well as the conformance of the spatial spread of the decline to the lag assumptions inherent in diffusion theory. With an examination of primarily Swedish data from 1870 to 1960, Carlsson provides a thoughtful argument which stresses the importance of time and calls for greater emphasis on study of human motivation and social situations.

The last two studies are explicitly concerned with mortality trends and the correlates of mortality in Western nations. Spiegelman's article ("Mortality Trends for Causes of Death in Countries of Low Mortality") examines general mortality trends and nine major causes of death in Western European and English-speaking countries from 1905 to 1961. The study points up a serious limitation in such research: the problem of comparability of medical information concerning cause of death among countries.

Murray's study ("The Geography of Death in the United States and the United Kingdom") is representative of a geographical study at the first level, pattern identification, with some tentative hypotheses posed to explain spatial variations. Variations in crude death rates and infant mortality rates in the United Kingdom and the United States are examined cartographically. In the United Kingdom, a cartographic association is discerned between high death rates and areas of industrialization and high population density. In the United States, such association is unclear. The difficulty inherent in the study lies in the quality of data and stresses the need for more and better information concerning mortality, especially in the United States.

Selection Eighteen
SPACE-TIME DIFFUSION OF THE TRANSITION MODEL: THE TWENTIETH CENTURY PATTERNS

Roy Chung

'The first real burst of world population growth came with the latest stage in cultural progress — the Industrial Revolution. Not only did this change, considered in its broadest sense, give an unprecedented impetus to population growth in Europe, but its rapid diffusion to other regions extended its influence around the globe. For the first time the world's entire population could be regarded as a single entity responding in varying degrees to one dynamic process."

(*Kingsley Davis, 1945*)[1]

"Since population is singularly dynamic, in that it is constantly undergoing change, the map representing change through time has unusual merit."

(*Glenn T. Trewartha, 1962*)[2]

Prepared for discussion at the annual meeting of the Population Association of America, New York, April 1966. Published by permission of Professor Roy Chung.

Introduction

It has become customary, for good reasons, to use the term "presumptuous" when attempting a global survey. There is no reason to omit the term in this study which attempts an analysis of population change on not only a synoptic global scale, but also from a diachronic perspective which is explicitly time and place specific for the first half of the century.

Since this is the first time that the space-time diffusion of the demographic transition has been mapped for any significant period of time, any inferential advantage that might accrue from synoptic map analysis through time is a distinct contribution. This paper limits itself to describing the changing patterns which emerge from the mapped data, and to exploring the implications which these findings may hold for current knowledge of world population change. The level of generalization is confined to the macro-demographic scale and the conclusions, owing to the varied degree of reliability of the data, are necessarily exploratory and tentative. Suggestions from specialists on the various regions and topics dealt with in this paper are invited.

The Demographic Transition

The demographic transition, judging from the spate of recent articles and statements relating to it, may well have superseded the Malthusian theory as the most controversial demographic theory in the mid-twentieth century. The various issues surrounding the validity and applicability of the transition prior to 1959 have been very well summed up by Hauser and Duncan.[3]

As recently as 1965, D. V. Glass wrote: "The theory of the demographic transition does not, in its present form, provide an adequate framework for the study of contemporary societies. It could hardly do so, since it is rather mechanistic and, in addition, is beset by too many apparent deviations as well as by major gaps in essential information."[4] On the other hand, van Nort wrote in 1965 ". . . even in its present embryonic form the transition theory is a fruitful guide for observation and analysis."[5] George J. Stolnitz observed in 1964: "Demographic transitions rank among the most sweeping and best-documented historical trends of modern times."[6]

It seems that while no one is entirely satisfied with the demographic transition, it "has proved valuable as a guiding generalization" as Kingsley Davis aptly puts it.[7] Frank W. Notestein made a point in 1945 which is very valid today: "The difficulty, then, is not that of making predictions in terms of the present, or a reasonably anticipated setting. Rather, it is that of taking the predictions too seriously once they are made. Having introduced assumptions concerning the governing conditions, we must constantly keep in mind the fact that they are assumptions and that a different course of events would lead to different answers."[8]

The transition theory is utilized here because it is a fruitful heuristic model and serves as a master generalizing concept which helps us to encompass the vast amount of data which is unavoidable in a comparative macro-demographic study as this purports to be. A model need not be overly complex to catch the essential "simplification that comes with expanding knowledge."[9]

The Model and Data

The transition categories used in this model (Figure 18.1) are based primarily on a three-fold typology with an alternate to stage two of the conventional transition model as a fourth sub-type. This study is dynamic and is concerned with the sequential levels of vital rates which together are the components of the direction and sequence of changes. However, it is recognized that too detailed a typology can lead to a false image of accuracy of data. Particularly at the high level of generality conditioned by the macro-scale of this study, the three-fold categories adopted here are deemed sufficient to delineate the broad patterns of the diffusion of the transition.

The Threshold points of 15 and 30 are arbitrary, but nonetheless they are a reasoned and deliberate departure from the 15 to 35 thresholds common to many models.[10] Scatter diagrams were used to minimize the error of selecting thresholds which might place units of functionally unified clusters into separate categories.

The data used are primarily reported crude rates from the United Nations Demographic Yearbooks. They vary in reliability with time and place, and there were also omissions. Where the data seemed obviously grossly distorted, I have not hesitated to use my judgment. However, for the maps as a whole the data were largely unadjusted. Stolnitz's observations on the data in his study on mortality are quite applicable here.

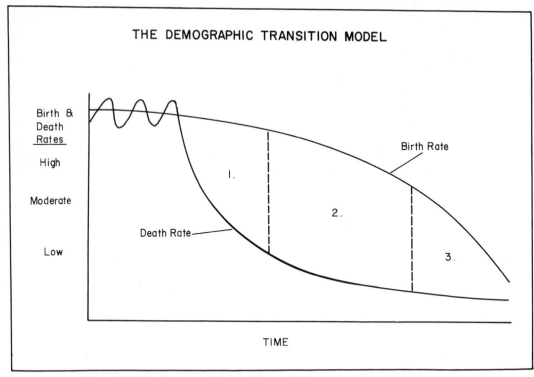

Figure 18.1 The demographic transition model
COMPONENTS OF THE DEMOGRAPHIC TRANSITION

Stage 1.	High birth rate	(Crude birth rate over 30)
	High death rate	(Crude death rate over 15)
Stage 2.	High birth rate	(Crude birth rate over 30)
	Rapidly declining death rate	(Crude death rate under 15)
Stage 3.	Low birth rate	(Crude birth rate under 30)
	Low death rate	(Crude death rate under 15)

Alternative to Stage 2 of the nodal transitional pattern above
(Show by cross-hatching on the maps)

| | Moderate birth rate | (Crude birth rate under 30) |
| | Moderate death rate | (Crude death rate over 15) |

He writes: "Fortunately there is no reason to believe that most of the major conclusions reached below would have been substantially changed if ideally accurate as opposed to complete data had been available."[11]

Because countries without census and vital registration would most likely be in stage 1, they have been so allocated rather than left blank on the map. This may do violence to some individual cases, but from the level of generalization consistent with this macro-scale, the overall pattern is still valid. Similarly, five-year intervals have been used for the maps, in order to present the general time trend and minimize annual fluctuations.

223

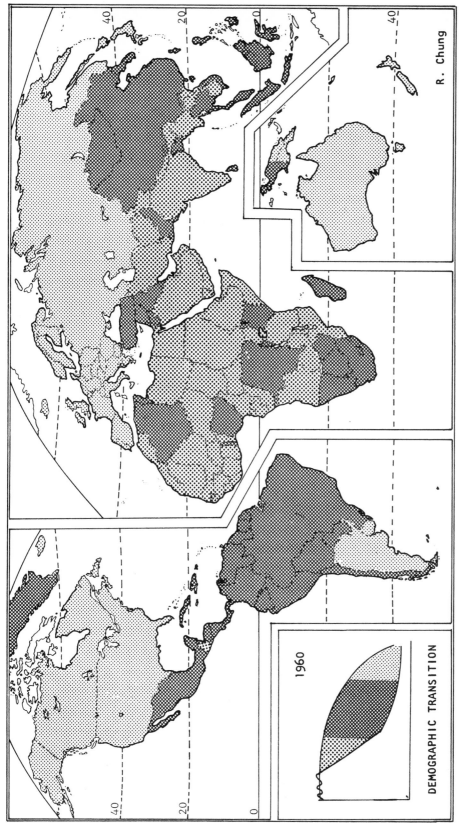

R. Chung

1960

DEMOGRAPHIC TRANSITION

Figure 18.2 — 1960

224

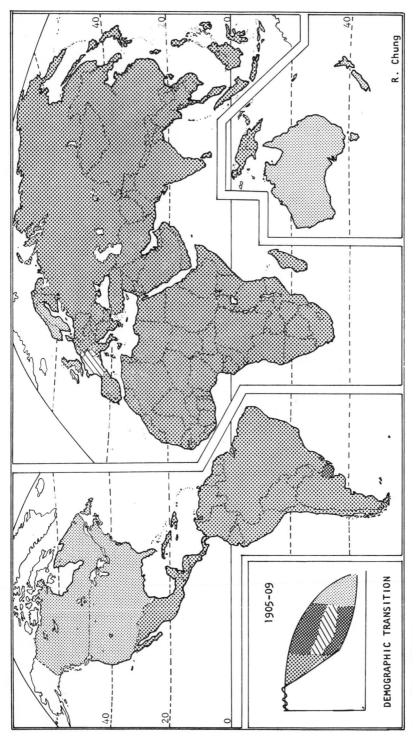

1905-09

DEMOGRAPHIC TRANSITION

R. Chung

Figure 18.3 — 1905-09

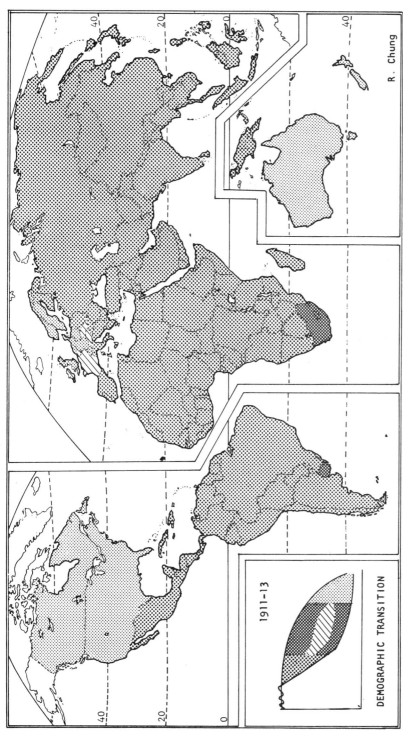

Figure 18.4 — 1911–13

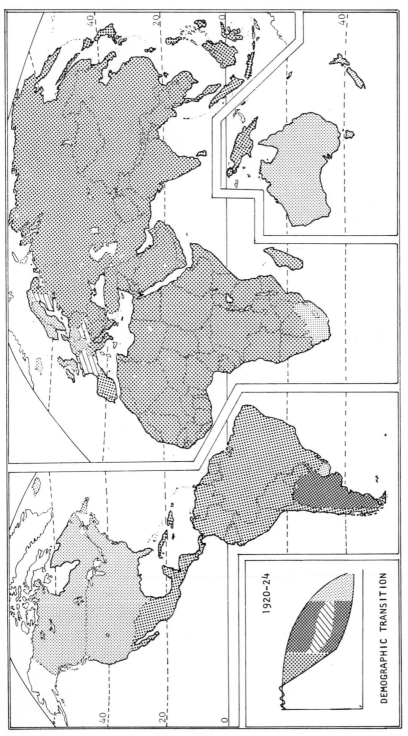

Figure 18.5 — 1920-24

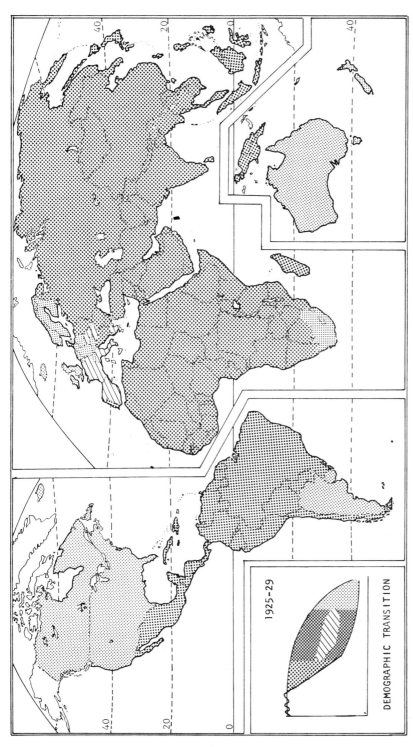

1925-29

DEMOGRAPHIC TRANSITION

Figure 18.6 — 1925-29

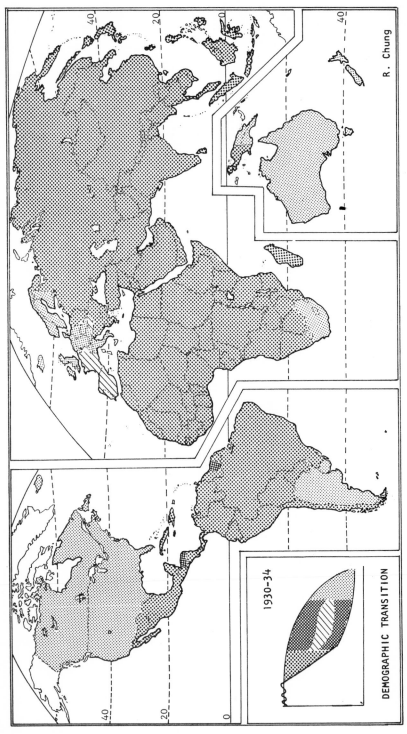

DEMOGRAPHIC TRANSITION

1930-34

R. Chung

Figure 18.7 — 1930-34

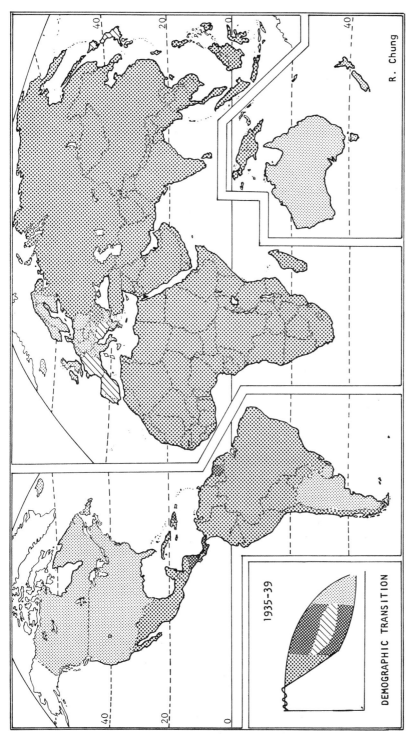

R. Chung

1935-39

DEMOGRAPHIC TRANSITION

Figure 18.8 — 1935-39

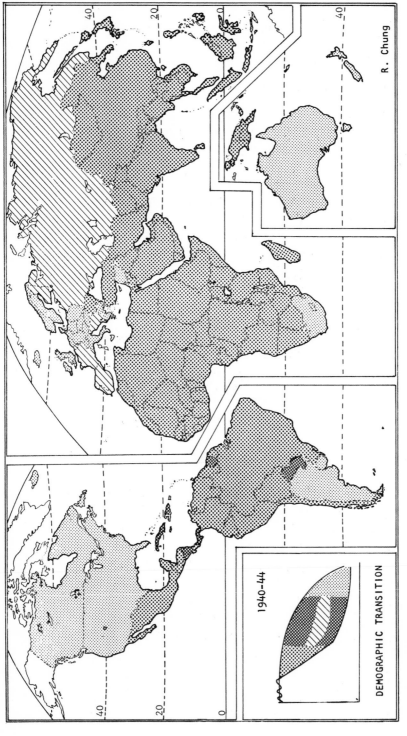

DEMOGRAPHIC TRANSITION

1940-44

R. Chung

Figure 18.9 — 1940-44

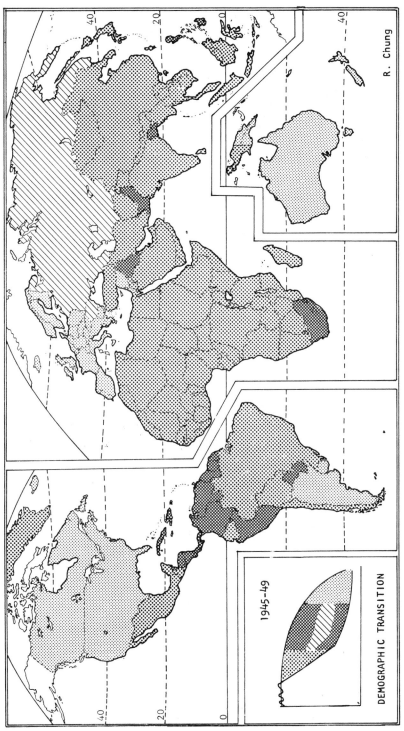

R. Chung

1945–49

DEMOGRAPHIC TRANSITION

Figure 18.10 — 1945–49

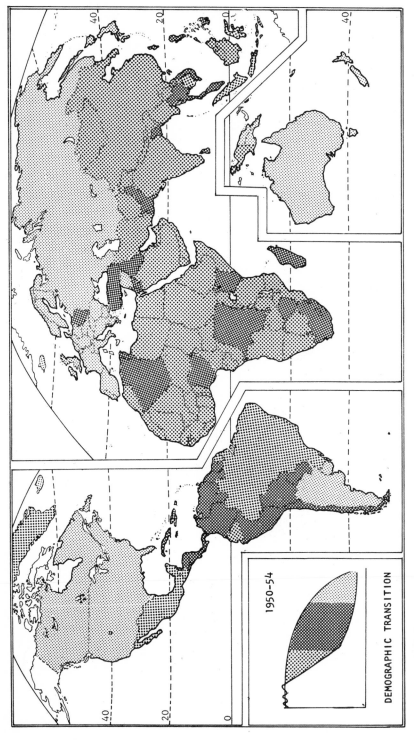

Figure 18.11 — 1950-54

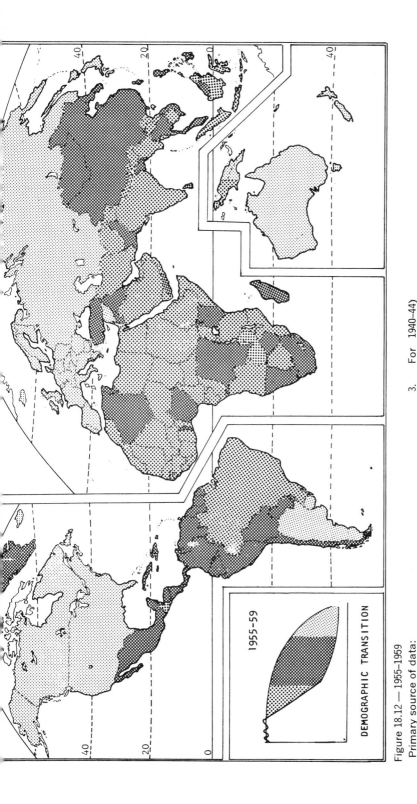

Figure 18.12 — 1955–1959

Primary source of data:

1. For 1960)
       1950–54)
       1955–59)
       1945–49)

2. For 1930–34)   U.N. Demographic Yearbook, 1963
       1920–24)
       1925–29)   U.N. Demographic Yearbook, 1955

3. For 1940–44)
       Crude birth rates: U.N. Demographic Yearbook, 1959
       Crude death rates: U.N. Demographic Yearbook, 1953
4. For 1935–39)
       Crude birth rates: U.N. Demographic Yearbook, 1959
       Crude death rates: U. N. Demographic Yearbook, 1953
5. For 1905–09)
       1911–13)   U.N. Deomgraphic Yearbook, 1951

Notes:
1. Reliability declines the farther back one goes.
2. Countries without data were included in stage 1 as an interpretational judgment by the author. Lack of registration system and data being taken as an index of premodernization.

DEMOGRAPHIC TRANSITION

1955-59

The Space-time Diffusion of the Demographic Transition–Summary Patterns

The 1960 (Figure 18.2) map shows a pattern with Europe and the Soviet Union, and the neo-European areas (Anglo-America, Australia, and parts of Southern South America) in stage 3 of the transition. Most of the underdeveloped areas of the world are in stage 2 of rapid growth, or in stage 1. Latin America is particularly dominant in the stage 2 category, and China looms large in East Asia. Japan stands out anomalously as the only stage 3 nation in the non-European areas of the world.

If we now observe the successive maps from the turn of the century onwards, it will be seen that the early maps catch a glimpse of the tail-end of northwestern Europe's transition. In one sense it is a myth to speak of a uniform Europe with respect to the transition model, since the successive levels of vital rates whose sequential patterns constitute the demographic transition are markedly different in patterns and timing for the different regions of Europe. On the other hand there is the underlying similarity of the general transitional trend from high mortality and fertility to low mortality and fertility which has been typical of all Europe, although the actual paths have been different.

1905–1909 (Figure 18.3). At the turn of the twentieth century, the demographic norm of low rates of growth, whether caused by a balance of high fertility and high mortality, or a balance of low fertility and low mortality, dominates the globe. Even the apparent structural deviation of France and Ireland does not disturb this image of low growth since the transitional phase of moderate birth rate and moderate death rate exhibited there also results in low growth. Uruguay appears anomalously unique, but one cannot make final statements here without knowing more about the historical demography of that country. T. Lynn Smith speaks of the "utter lack of dependability of the reported birth rates" for Latin America.[12]

1911–1913 (Figure 18.4). Northwestern Europe, Anglo-America and Australasia exhibit the demographic serenity of stage 3. There is a demographic stirring in Eastern Europe as Austria and Czechoslovakia depart from stage 1 of the transition model, via the alternate transitional phase of moderate birth rates and moderate mortality. In southern Europe and southeastern Europe stage 1 of the transitional model still prevails. South Africa now joins Uruguay in the explosive stage 2.

1920–1924 (Figure 18.5). Finland has now joined France, Czechoslovakia, and Austria in the intermediate alternate version of stage 2. Uruguay and South Africa have entered stage 3 of the transition model. Ireland and Switzerland have also entered stage 3 but via the intermediate path of moderate birth rates and moderate mortality. Argentina is now uniquely explosive.

1925–1929 (Figure 18.6). Argentina and Austria have made the transition to stage 3. South and southeastern Europe display marked demographic activity as Spain, Italy, Hungary and Greece now join Czechoslovakia and France in the alternate version of stage 2. Finland has moved into stage 3. This apparently was a remarkable period in the twentieth century as no "population explosion" was reported. The stirrings in South and southeastern Europe were marked by moderate fertility and moderate mortality. Since the boundaries of historical periodization are of necessity arbitrary and fragile, this period could well be viewed as the end of the nineteenth century demographically speaking.

1930–1934 (Figure 18.7). Italy completes the transition, so does Czechoslovakia. Portugal joins Spain in the alternate version of stage 2. Greece reverts to stage 1.[13] The first signs of the explosive demographic revolution that is now quite typical of much of the underdeveloped areas in the mid-twentieth century, appears like a twin-eyed specter in Surinam and Honduras in the Caribbean borderlands of Latin America. The rest of Latin America, Africa, and Asia seem to be asleep under the demographic blanket of high fertility and high mortality.

1935–1939 (Figure 18.8). Yugoslavia joins Spain and Portugal in the alternate version of stage 2. Greece, Hungary and Czechoslovakia have moved into stage 3. Poland has slipped into stage 3, without a stage 2 phase, or at least, it was not caught in the quinquennial mesh used in this study.[14]

An important apparently deviant pattern is caught on this map. Japan has departed from stage 1 of the transition model and is observed here as being in the alternate version of stage 2 with moderate birth rates and moderate death rates rather than experiencing the explosive stage 2 of the conventional transition model.

Carr-Saunders [15] in an observation which was contemporary with respect to the thirties wrote: "So far as the population position in general is concerned it is evident that Japan is to be classed with those countries in eastern Europe where the birth-rate has recently begun to decline and where medical and sanitary progress is now reducing the death-rate." He further added that (for Japan at that time) "There is no opportunity for a prolonged or dramatic fall in the death rate." If the reported rates are reasonably correct, then it is apparent that a declining birth rate caught up with a slower declining mortality in Japan in the late thirties and resulted in the alternate to stage 2, rather than the explosive stage 2. This is the pattern shared by Eastern and Southern Europe.

1940–1944 (Figure 18.9). The giant of the Slavic world is stirring as Russia enters the alternate to stage 2, resulting from birth rate declines paralleling the mortality declines. The explosive stage 2 gains a firmer foothold in mainland Latin America and the Caribbean Islands. The reported rates show Syria in Stage 3.

1945–1949 (Figure 18.10). Latin America leads the postwar explosion. Costa Rica, Venezuela, Colombia, Br. Guiana, Fr. Guiana, Peru and the Caribbean Islands have entered stage 2. Apparently South Africa, Iraq, Pakistan and the Philippines have also attained stage 2.

Romania has entered the alternate version

of stage 2 with a pattern similar to that of the Soviet Union. With the exception of Albania, all Western and Southern Europe have now moved into stage 3.

1950–1954 (Figure 18.11). The Soviet world has now moved into stage 3. Poland has shown a post-war resurgence of population. The diffusion of the explosive stage 2 is quite marked in Latin America. The Brazilian giant, however, is still in stage 1. Already Africa, the Middle East, and Southeast Asia are showing large sections with stage 2 of explosive growth. The difference in the Middle East between Lebanon and Syria with their Christian Arab orientation, and that of the Muslim Arab areas shows up clearly on the demographic map. Japan has now moved into stage 3, to become the demographic marvel of the non-Western world.

1955–1959 (Figure 18.12). Mexico has joined the stage 2 countries. A prime demographic event is the fact that China with her massive population base has moved into the explosive stage 2 phase.

1960 (Figure 18.2). Brazil and Indonesia have joined the explosive group. The diffusion of stage 2 of explosive growth is almost complete in Latin America, quite widespread in East Asia, and beginning to take on prominence in Africa and the Middle East. Nearly all the mid-latitude countries in both the northern and southern hemispheres are in stage 3.

Some Interpretational Observations

THE THREE WORLDS OF THE TWENTIETH CENTURY

Amazingly today we speak of the "Third World"—yet, at the turn of the century three worlds could be differentiated on the basis of the transition criteria. It seems that we were confronted with aspects of at least three separately identifiable, but related and interlocking transitions. The diffusion was not so much from one country to another, as from one world to another world, setting off a new cycle in that world, which in turn ran its own course at its own time and pace, and underwent modifications which were hitherto only latent in the original transition model. In any diffusion process modifications of the original are expected. Rigid conformance to the modal transitional model may have blocked recognition and identification of the latent alternatives inherent in the various phases of the transition model. Should the latent alternatives become numerous in the future, we may need a topological perspective to recognize the original transition model.

The three worlds recognized by this study are very close to those identified by George Stolnitz, who recognized "The West," "non-Western Europe," and "Latin America-Africa-Asia," and pointed out that no "clearcut basis for classification exists in the literature." The maps visibly portray these worlds, but my conceptualization includes Japan in the same world as Eastern Europe, Southern Europe and the USSR. Stolnitz was aware of the similarities but did not group Japan with the others. He writes: "A more functional classification might well have combined some of the populations in the last two groups (though hardly in all three). Certainly, Japan today is more similar to much of non-Western Europe than to most underdeveloped areas. Whether this was also true in the earlier years is uncertain, however."[16]

a The World of Northwestern Europe and its neo-European offshoot in North America, Australia, South Africa, and Southeastern South America. The 1905–1909 map barely catches a tail-end of this transition, with France, Switzerland and Ireland showing some deviations.

b The World of Southern Europe, Slavic Eurasia and Japan. In this world the transition cycle started in the 20th century rather than in the 19th, and was uniformly characterized by a movement through the alternate version of stage 2 with moderate death rates and moderate birth rates, rather than through the explosive stage 2 phase. Hatt, Farr and Weinstein[17] recognized the

category of "a balance of medium fertility and medium mortality" and said that "these countries may be thought of as modern peasant cultures, having general control over vital rates while possessing a highly agrarian economy." Stolnitz also points out: "A number of other nations, at an intermediate stage economically because development came later or was retarded, are also as a rule in an intermediate stage demographically."[18] All the countries depicted as having passed through the alternate version of the transition model and included in this second world have, or had, at the time of their intermediate transitions, what may well be called "modern peasant cultures." One may question whether Ireland ought not to be included in this cycle. Certainly, the Soviet Union and Japan are related to this cycle although they started their transitions later. France could not be classified as a modern peasant culture at that time since she probably was more advanced than the other European nations as Dudley Kirk has pointed out.[19]

c The Third World, or the world of Latin America-Africa and Asia. This world started its transition in the 1930's and is either dominantly in the explosive stage or in stage 1. The exploding areas characteristically have death rates under 15 per 1000, but the birth rates are still over 30 per 1000. It may be that with more information, and with a finer mesh, we could differentiate between sub-worlds in this world. As the section on the duration of the explosion in this world will show, there seems to be some correlation between size of country and the timing of the beginning of the transition. The second world took a path of medium fertility and medium death rate. What path will the third world take? What deviations from the first and/or second stage of the transition may be expected? The distinguished contemporary demographer, Irene Taeuber, in her reexamination of the demographic transition in Japan in 1960[20] has pointed out that "The process of demographic transition was once conceived in simple terms... As research expanded, there is increasing evidence that both fertility and mortality have been variables in the past . . . that demographic variables are not necessarily unidirectional in their change . . ." Our commitment to the "normal" transition model may have restricted or delayed our vision and stymied attempts to explore the alternatives, or recognize the beginnings of alternatives which may already be underway in this third world, but are as yet undocumented.

THE DURATION AND TIMING OF THE TRANSITION IN THE TWENTIETH CENTURY

The duration. An examination of the maps from 1930 on will reveal the astounding fact that except for the overseas neo-European areas and Japan, no area that ever entered the explosion phase 2 of the transition has emerged from it. Research needs to be focussed on the factors which tend to hold this phase of the transition model as the status quo wherever it has entered outside the dominantly non-Neo-European world.

The temporal durability of the explosive phase 2 of the Twentieth century transition should be explicitly recognized. The conventional image of the "recency" of the explosive stage of the transitional model should not prevent us from noting that operationally "recency" may actually be translated to mean 30 to 35 years in some cases. The forerunners of the modern explosion which was initiated 30 to 35 years ago—Surinam, Honduras, Panama, Nicaragua, Dominican Republic—are still in the explosive stage in the 1960's with some of the highest birth rates in the world coexisting with low modern mortality rates.

One useful operational concept that is relevant to the persistence of the explosive transition phase is the notion about ideal family-size preference which Judith Blake has developed in a recent article.[21] In the Third World today, death control often precedes modernization. It may very well be true also that a minimum kind of modernization sufficient to affect the ideal family-size preference has to precede or accompany the

acceptance of family planning for it to be optimally effective in the reduction of fertility.

The timing of the transition. An examination of the maps since 1930 reveals that until the 1950's the explosive stage 2 of the transition model was still an exotic local growth and displayed none of the gargantuan globalism typical of today's world-wide explosion. Further, there seems to be a definite correlation between time of entry into the explosive stage 2 and size of the country. The population giants of the Third World like China, Mexico, Brazil, Indonesia have only entered the explosive stage 2 within the last five or ten years, and, as late as 1960, India had not yet entered this phase. This means that the "population explosion" which started during the 1930–34 period was for twenty or thirty years primarily an explosion of small countries.

In the Third World, the transition started when death control technology was such that the achievement of a death rate of 15 per 1000 was relatively easy to attain, and so the unprecedented explosive categories of very high birth rates and low mortality became a reality. Also, in so far as the mechanism of the explosion is attributable to a dramatic mortality decline as a result of death control, then it is not unreasonable to assume that a strong causal connection would exist between the size of the national unit and the timing of the explosion phase. It was one thing for a country like say Ceylon to drop mortality overnight with DDT, but it is quite another task for countries of the magnitude of India, China, Brazil or Mexico. This lag in effective reduction of mortality in the large countries due to the sheer logistics of size and intraregional variations, seems to be one of the main reasons that explains the size differentiation in the initiation of the explosive second phase of the transition of the Third World.

In one sense, the fact that it is only within the last ten years that the population giants of the Third World have entered the explosive stage of population growth raises portents of dire population crises on an unprecedented scale. This prospect is further enhanced by the apparent durability of the explosion phase in the countries of the Third World, since none of these which entered stage 2 since the 1930's has as yet entered stage 3.

Yet, in another context, the delayed emergence of the explosion stage among these large countries has within it an optimistic note. Had the explosion occurred twenty or thirty years ago, the increment to population growth would have been enormous even for an industrial society, much less for largely peasant agrarian societies. Today the delayed mortality revolution may be their salvation. It may have given them the breathing spell necessary for the technology and sociology of fertility reduction to be sufficiently improved to a point where there is at least the possibility of an acceleration in fertility decline in these large countries in the next decade. Stolnitz has perceptively observed: "It may be also that a fertility downtrend in the underdeveloped areas, when and if it occurs, would be more rapid than precedent would suggest. This has typically been the case for the latecomers to the transition process."[22]

Summary and Conclusion

In summary, there is a rich theoretical harvest in these maps:

1 They do not necessarily furnish a new theoretical model, but a fresh look at an old concept. The diffusion of the demographic transition has never been mapped before, and so the inferential advantage of synoptic map analysis through time is a new contribution.[23]

2 The notion of alternative to stage 2, shown by cross-hatching in the earlier maps, is an explicit recognition of an alternative to stage 2 within the theoretical framework of the conventional demographic transition theory itself.

The sociologists among us will find that this hypothesis regarding the alternative to the second stage of the modal transitional pattern is in the mainstream of part of their best theoretical heritage. In structural functional terms, the transitional model does illustrate structural change, and seeing its diffusion in spatio-temporal sequence helps to understand it. The explosion stage can be seen as a kind of social disequilibrium between the equilibrium balance of stage 1 and stage 3.[24]

Moreover, if we view the conventional transitional model as a modal pattern, then the characteristic pattern of medium death rate and medium birth rate experienced in Eastern Europe and southern Europe in the twenties and thirties, and later in the Soviet Union and Japan, may be viewed as functional alternates or even as latent alternative patterns inherent in the equilibrium balance of the modal stage 1 of the transition model. In these areas, the mortality decline was paralleled by a fertility decline, rather than by the "fertility lag" which is characteristic of the conventional model of the demographic transition.

3 Presenting a comparative place-specific account of the duration and timing of the transition in the Third World, and causally relating the timing of the explosion phase to the size variation of countries, have their own intrinsic merits for present and future investigations.

4 Finally, the importance of these maps as a fruitful heuristic tool for teaching world population problems should not be overlooked.[25]

Notes

[1] Kingsley Davis: *The World Demographic Transition, The Annals of the Amer. Acad. of Political and Social Science,* Jan. 1945, p. 1.
[2] Glenn T. Trewartha: *The Geography of Population,* Abstract of paper read at the 1962 PAA meeting, *Population Index,* V. 28, 1962, p. 223. For a good summary of the advantages of map representation of dynamic relationships, see Bert F. Hoselitz's *Foreward* in Norton Ginsburg: *Atlas of Economic Development,* 1961, pp. v-vi.
[3] Hauser and Duncan: *The Study*

of Population, 1959, pp. 93–96. For some more recent views see Leighton van Nort: *Values in Population Theory, Milbank Memorial Fund Quarterly*, V. 37, 1960, pp. 387–395; Edward G. Stockwell: *Fertility, Mortality and Economic Status of Underdeveloped Areas. Social Forces* V. 4, 1963, pp. 390–395; Donald O. Cowgill: *Transition Theory as General Population Theory. Social Forces*, V. 41, 1963, pp. 270–274; A. J. Jaffe: *Notes on the Population Theory of Eugene M. Kulischer. Milbank Memorial Fund Quarterly*, Vol. 40, 1962, pp. 187–206.

[4]D. V. Glass and D. E. C. Eversley (ed.): *Population in History*, 1965, p. 6.

[5]Leighton van Nort: *Biology, Rationality and Fertility. Eugenics Quarterly* v. 3, 1965, p. 160.

[6]George J. Stolnitz: *The Demographic Transition: From High to Low Birth Rates Death Rates*, in Ronald Freedman (ed.): *Population: The Vital Revolution*, 1964, p. 30.

[7]Kingsley Davis: *The Sociology of Demographic Behavior*, in Merton and Cottrell Jr. (ed.): *Sociology Today*, 1959, p. 313.

[8]Frank W. Notestein: *Population — The Long View* in T. W. Schultz (ed.): *Food for the World*, 1945, p. 37.

[9]See Albert Szent-Gyorgyi: *Teaching and the Expanding Knowledge, Science* V. 146 (Dec. 1964), p. 1278; K. F. Helleiner, after critically examining the transition, concluded: ". . their heuristic value remains very great indeed, for it is only by taking cognizance of the universality of this phenomenon that we can hope to understand its causal mechanism." See K. F. Helleiner: *The Vital Revolution Reconsidered*, in D. V. Glass and

D. E. C. Eversley (ed.): *op. cit.*, p. 83.

[10]See Hatt, Farr and Weinstein: *Types of Population Balance, American Sociological Review*, V. 20, 1955, p. 21; and Leighton van Nort and Bertram P. Karan: *Demographic Transition Re-examined, American Sociological Review*, V. 20, 1955, p. 526, for contrasting views of the "tripartite typology." Stockwell uses 15 and 35 as thresholds in Edward G. Stockwell: *op. cit.*, pp. 391–392. For some aspects of the problem of separating functionally unified clusters see Robert T. Smith: *Method and Purpose in Functional Town Classification, Annals of the Association of American Geographers*, V. 55, 1965, pp. 539–548.

[11]George J. Stolnitz: *A Century of International Mortality Trends: Population Studies*, July 1955, pp. 25–26.

[12]T. Lynn Smith: *Latin American Population Studies*, 1960, p. 41.

[13]The patterns described in this study are always likely to do violence to the facts of particular places. For the difficulties of the demographic history of Greece, see Vasilios B. Valaoras: *A Reconstruction of the Demographic History of Modern Greece, The Milbank Memorial Fund Quarterly*, Vol. 38, 1960, pp. 116–117.

[14]Note that if the birth rate decline overtakes a moderate death rate decline rapidly enough, a country may slip into stage 3 without passing through stage 2.

[15]A. M. Carr-Saunders: *World Population*, 1936, p. 264.

[16]George J. Stolnitz: *op. cit.*, 1955, p. 26.

[17]Hatt, Farr, and Weinstein: *op. cit.*, p. 19.

[18]George J. Stolnitz: *The Demographic Transition: From High*

to Low Birth Rates and Death Rates in Ronald Freeman (ed.): *Population: The Vital Revolution*, 1964. p. 36.

[19]Dudley Kirk: *Population and Population Trends in Modern France*, in Herbert Moller (ed.): Population Movements in Modern European History, 1964, p. 93.

[20]Irene Taeuber: *Japan's Demographic Transition Re-examined, Population Studies*, V. 14, 1960, p. 28.

[21]Judith Blake: *Demographic Science and Redirection of Population Policy, Journal of Chron. Dis.*, Vol. 18, 1965, pp. 1181–1200.

[22]George J. Stolnitz: *op. cit.*, 1964, p. 45.

[23]For a plea for a comparative and historical approach to demography, see Kingsley Davis: *The Sociology of Demographic Behavior*, in Merton, Broom and Cottrell, Jr. (ed.) *op. cit.*, pp. 309–333. See also Louis Chevalier: *Towards a History of Population*, in D. V. Glass and D. E. C. Eversley, *op. cit.*, pp. 70–78; and William Petersen: *The Demographic Transition, American Sociological Review*, Vol. 25, 1960, pp. 334–346.

[24]For the terminology and methods of structural-functional analysis, see Robert F. Merton: *Social Theory and Social Structure*, 1949, pp. 49–61.

[25]The use of the Transition Model as a teaching aid is explored in Roy Chung: *An Approach to Population Change as Space-Time Diffusion of the Transition Model*, paper presented in the section on *Teaching About Problems of Population in College* at the annual conference of the National Council for Geographic Education, New York, November 26, 1965.

Selection Nineteen

THE DECLINE OF FERTILITY: INNOVATION OR ADJUSTMENT PROCESS
Gösta Carlsson

Social Change by Individual Decision

In this paper the decline in marital fertility in Sweden, and to a lesser extent in other

Reprinted from *Population Studies*, **20**, 1966, 149–174, by permission of the author and the Population Investigation Committee.

countries, will be re-examined from a sociological rather than a purely demographic point of view. The author is not a specialist in the field of population or fertility in particular, and the purposes of the study need to be clearly stated and understood.[1]

It is known that the secular decline in marital fertility, which began around 1880 in many Western European countries, was due to a change in values and attitudes and to deliberate action on the part of the married couples. It is safe to say that fertility declined because there was a spread of or more intensive use of birth control, including in this term contraception, abortion and voluntary abstinence. This is, therefore, an unusually important and interesting case of a change in mass attitudes and behavior, which may be compared with other changes in the era of industrialization. It is an instance of highly significant social change through individual or at least decentralized decision.

It is beyond this point that the real difficulty lies. Any explanation will have to acknowledge the role of industrialization and the decline of agriculture, rising levels of education, the changing status of women, and a general modernization and secularization of society although the precise nature of the causal influences is not known. But within this widely accepted framework at least two types of theory are possible, one of which, the *innovation* approach, seems to dominate the current thinking on the subject. The other, the *adjustment* approach, may at first glance not appear very different, but the author believes that the two approaches should be distinguished and that the innovation thesis has been stressed too much. The main objective of this paper is to demonstrate this, and to show that the notion of adjustment fits the fertility decline more easily.

The Spread of Birth Control

The innovation theory of birth control and the decline of fertility contains a number of specific assumptions or beliefs. They can be grouped together because they frequently occur in the literature in combination, although they are not logically dependent on one another. It is quite possible to accept some of these assumptions and to reject others, but the cluster seems important enough to be treated as a unit.

First, there is a strong tendency to regard birth control, especially contraception, as a recent invention, as something essentially new in human culture. Even if its long history is acknowledged, it is assumed that these methods were not widely used before the nineteenth century.[2] The innovation perspective will appear more natural if this was true, so that the decline of fertility started in a setting where there was no, or at most very limited, previous practice of birth control. The theory stresses the importance of the spread of information about contraception and perhaps abortion. Another and most important element is the assumption of lags and "trickle down" in the spread of skills and attitudes. Diffusion is supposed to start in metropolitan centers, and to reach other urban places with some delay, and rural areas still later. Overlapping with this is the belief that there is a regional factor; certain regions are reached before others, or are quicker to react. There is finally the firmly established belief in class differentials in the timing of the decline and the acceptance of birth control. Middle-class groups are supposed to be leading, manual workers and the farm population lagging.

The adjustment theory differs from the innovation hypothesis in most of these respects. Birth control, and especially contraception, need not be regarded as new or recent in human society. There may have been a "steady state" in which birth control was practised by part of the population, or it may have been practised with higher fertility targets. The decline in fertility is then regarded as an adjustment to a new set of forces, defining a new equilibrium level of modern or "controlled" fertility. The role of motivation and the structural factors bearing on human desires and values, is stressed more than knowledge of contraception. This type of theory is not dependent on lags or a "trickle down" pattern of spread.

Although the line between the two points

of view is sometimes blurred, the difference is nevertheless real. Much of the discussion and statistical analysis which follows will focus on the following two questions:

1 Did birth control within marriage exist on a considerable scale before the secular decline of fertility began, or did the decline end a phase in which control was not practised by married couples at all, or very rarely at most?

2 Does the pattern of spread of fertility decline, in fact conform to the lag assumptions so prominent in current theory?

Behind these questions, however, there is the more general one of the speed, characteristics and time dimensions of the process of decline. Collectively, the shift from traditional to modern fertility took some 50–70 years in Sweden, and the time taken by the transition presents an important problem with obvious implications in the study of high-fertility populations to-day.

It is not always easy to determine where a writer stands on the above issues, particularly the first. Students of Swedish development, faced with insistent evidence of birth control within marriage before 1880, have sometimes argued that contraception (mainly *coitus interruptus*) was quite widely diffused before the general decline began,[3] but they do not always seem to have stressed this possibility. The contributors to the volume on demographic history, edited by Glass and Eversley,[4] do not believe that birth control was practised widely outside Sweden before the decline began.

Neither view, however, can be regarded as firmly established and it is noticeable that different writers tend to draw somewhat different conclusions. Glass[5] believes that medical factors (health and nutrition) may have held back fertility to some extent; apparently much less importance is attached to deliberate birth control. To Eversley[6] birth control, including prolonged lactation as a conscious technique of regulating fertility, is a possible explanation of long birth intervals, to be used in combination

with the medical factors. The enormous gaps in our knowledge of pre-industrial fertility form a recurring theme in the literature on the subject.

The spread or diffusion pattern, with its assumed lags and gradients, appears to be central in the literature on fertility and its changes. That certain communities, regions or social classes were leading in the decline, and others followed with an appreciable lag, is a conclusion so often reached that it would be tedious to give quotations. The theory has recently come under fire and this criticism will be briefly touched on. In the meantime, however, it may be noted that the lag assumptions remain very important for the diagnosis and prediction of population trends.[7]

A Note on Methods

The nature and limitations of the fertility measures that will be used can more profitably be discussed in the proper context and with reference to specific research findings. However, one or two observations must be made at the outset. Part of the analysis is based on a simple period measure of fertility, the marital fertility rate (legitimate births per 1,000 married women aged 15 to 45). At times more refined (age-specific) rates will be used, but no index of true cohort behavior.

The crudeness of age-standardization is the lesser weakness; comparisons with more refined measures for the periods and populations studied suggest that the effect on results will be small. Far more serious is reliance on period rather than cohort data, an issue on which many demographers have strong feelings. The best defense for our procedure is that the cohort approach was impossible, or would have been prohibitively expensive and time-consuming. Some additional considerations may be added.

In so far as we are interested in the first of our two main questions, the prevalence of birth control before the era of general fertility decline, we are dealing with the fertility level in a reasonably stable situation as regards marriage patterns and marital fertility. There are many difficulties in this kind of analysis, but cohort effects are likely to be less important.

When considering the period of transition beginning around 1880 the risk of being misled by period measures in dating the process of decline is certainly greater. The marriage pattern did not change radically before 1930. The mean age at first marriage for women was 27.0 years in 1871–80 and 26.5 years in 1931–40. The fall in period rates cannot have been neutralized by a longer duration of married life to any considerable degree.

Finally, period measures date events at the time when they become observable. The time location of a true cohort or generation is more difficult to determine, and several solutions appear equally reasonable, by age, date of marriage, mean fertility age, etc.

Lags and Diffusion

Before the evidence on lags and diffusion gradients is examined one more preliminary remark must be made. Two regions, categories of communities, or social classes, may differ in prevalence of birth control without any lag being involved. At least, if all such relations are seen as lags, they may vary in nature. The clearest case of a lag is one in which the lagging population repeats the experience of the leading population in following exactly the same diffusion curve, differing only in starting date, a case of pure "initiation" lag. But the difference may sometimes be due to other factors; for instance, the proportion of "accessible" or "change-prone" persons. This proportion may change as fast in the lagging population as in the leading, but may be smaller in the lagging population. There are still further complications to bear in mind, and using a simple adoption or diffusion rate (the percentage showing new-style behavior) at any given time as an indicator of initiation lags

is a highly questionable procedure as will be shown below. In the case of birth control there is in addition the uncertainty about the level from which the change started.

The decline of marital fertility in Stockholm, other cities and towns ("other urban"), and the rural parts of the country is shown in Fig. 19.1. From the curves certain conclusions may be drawn if fertility is treated as an inverted measure of the spread of birth control.

In Sweden it can be said that there is little evidence of an initiation lag between the metropolis and the rest in the sense just indicated. The decline seems to have started at about the same time in Stockholm as in other parts of the country, even including the rural areas, but once under way the change proceeded at a quicker pace in the capital. There are also signs that the low-water mark of marital fertility was reached earlier in Stockholm, but the disturbances caused by the great depression of the 1930's and the subsequent swings make it impossible to be precise. It is freely admitted that minor lags, of say five years or less, would be hard to detect in this manner.

Compared with the rest of Sweden, whether urban or rural, Stockholm already had a lower fertility in 1870, and probably long before that date.[8] Lags are over-laid and partly concealed by differences in the initial level of fertility. To complicate the situation even further the Stockholm rate, though relatively low, was not appreciably lower than that of many rural areas in the same geographical region.

Whether this pattern is general cannot be determined without an exhaustive study of other cases, a task which cannot be undertaken here. Only a few parallel and confirmatory findings can be cited. In Germany the general decline in marital fertility may have started a little earlier in Berlin and Hamburg, but the lag cannot have been great.[9] The fertility rate was fairly high in the cities around 1870 (270 and 300 respectively) but fell quite rapidly thereafter. Nor is London different when compared with the rest of England if we can rely on

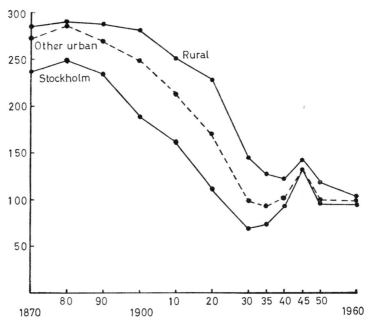

Figure 19.1 Marital fertility rates for subpopulations in Sweden. Two-year averages around census dates.

gross reproduction rates.[10] The downward movement appears to have begun at the same time as in England and Wales generally, the level was somewhat lower in London all the time and the rate of decline only a little faster. As a final and far-away example Japan[11] may be used. Here the data do not go back further than 1920; and again the measure is the gross reproduction rate rather than the marital fertility rate. As far as the evidence goes Tokyo differed more in the level of fertility (which was lower than in the rest of Japan) than in the time of onset of fertility decline.

To the extent that the picture drawn here is true and representative, metropolitan fertility rates become less useful for predicting national fertility trends. The metropolis differs from the rest of the country more with respect to the initial level of fertility, and the speed at which birth control spreads within the community, than in respect of the time at which diffusion starts.

On the subject of urban-rural lags only a few brief comments will be added. Urban areas may in general be expected to show the characteristics of the metropolis in a

weaker form, and the Swedish data as given in Fig. 19.1 do not contradict this assumption. The urban areas (excluding Stockholm) do not seem to have been reached by the diffusion wave much before the rural parts, but again once diffusion had started, it proceeded more quickly within the towns. Fertility differences before the decline are not so important here; the urban rate was somewhat lower than the rural but the difference was not large. Hence, the fertility gap between the two populations widened a great deal and did not begin to close again until the 1930's. The fact that many of the places included in the urban category in Sweden were small and unimportant in the nineteenth century, and did not differ much from villages, may have reduced demographic contrasts. It should be remembered, however, that urban-industrial regions or communities do not invariably have a lower fertility than rural-agrarian communities. In Germany, for instance, the highest marital fertility rates around 1870–80 were reached in relatively industrialized districts.[12]

Returning to the question of an urban-rural lag in the diffusion of birth control, the weakness of this hypothesis has been commented on by Grabill, Kiser and Whelpton[13] as regards fertility changes in the U.S.A. There are appreciable urban-rural differences in fertility in the expected direction, but they are manifest too early and remain too stable. If birth control had spread from cities and towns to rural areas, it must have done so very early, before 1800, and probably before any general decline in fertility had begun.

To sum up, metropolitan or urban leads, in the sense of an earlier beginning in the spread of birth control, are probably much less important as sources of variation in fertility rates than are differences in fertility levels before the period of decline began and which were sustained in that period, or unequal speed of diffusion within areas or communities.

The Regional Factor

Fertility often varies greatly between parts or regions of a country, and the differences turn out to be fairly stable over time. The regional variation has often been regarded as the result of a diffusion process even though the stability in regional differences suggests that this may be a faulty argument. The "high" regions (in terms of fertility) are assumed to have reacted later and more slowly to the spread of birth control and small-family ideals than the "low" regions. Ideally the regional factor should be separated from the metropolitan, urban and class factors by appropriate statistical controls. This is difficult or impossible if one has to rely on published statistics as is often the case in historical analyses, and the demonstration of geographical effects is therefore not always conclusive. The hypothesis would seem to apply primarily to rural districts and small towns, for here there is naturally a wide range of distances to the dominating metropolitan center.

To take one instance, sociologists and demographers have long interpreted the American data as showing a pattern of geographical spread. The most rural areas, and those furthest removed from the cities, appear to retain a high fertility longest, and explanations for these differences have been given in terms of geographical and cultural isolation.[14] Similar ideas are met in the literature on fertility differences in Sweden. More recently, doubts have been expressed on the isolation and (initiation) lag theory of American fertility differences, just as the urban-rural lag has been questioned. All geographical divisions of the United States showed a decrease in the child-woman ratio early in the nineteenth century; fertility seems to have declined on a national basis, rather than by spread from one region to the next. There is also a tendency for regions to become more alike as time passes.[15]

We shall study regional differences in Sweden on the basis of a sample of rural districts,[16] but the ground may be prepared by looking quickly at geographical variation in a few countries, and the impact of the secular decline on that variation.

There will be no detailed documentation, as the data are easily available for the reader's inspection. In England and Wales[17] the pre-existing fertility variation (gross reproduction rates) was not materially affected by the onset of the secular decline at the end of the 1870's. Nor was this the case with Japan[18] in the period 1925–50 (gross reproduction rates, variability between 46 prefectures). The Swedish development[19] at the end of the nineteenth century was similar if one considers rural population and studies the variation in marital fertility rate between the 24 counties. In all three cases there was a slight increase in variability (measured by the standard deviation) of the order of 10–20% in the beginning of the transition period and a drastic reduction at the end of this period. If the spread of birth control and the resultant decline in fertility were to take place with marked lags between regions, one would expect this to show up as a strong increase in regional variation as fertility starts to decline. Of this effect, then, there is little sign.[20]

Fertility Changes in Farm Areas:
A Swedish Sample

For several periods fertility measures are available for judiciary districts (*härad*) in Sweden. For 1891–1900 they were computed by Sundbärg,[21] for 1910–11 by S. D. Wicksell,[22] and for the period 1928–33 by S. D. Wicksell and Quensel.[23] The areas are relatively small, consisting usually of a few parishes. In all there are nearly 300 of them in rural Sweden; cities and towns fall outside this system. Though all nominally rural, they are still heterogeneous, as some contain an appreciable industrial or urban element. We therefore decided to limit the analysis

to those in which the farm element was dominant throughout the greater part of the secular decline in fertility. Accordingly only areas which had at least 70% of the economically active population in farming as late as 1930, and not more than 10% living in town-like communities in that year were included in the study.[24] There were 79 districts that met these requirements, but a few had to be abandoned because their boundaries changed, so that the final number was 73. These were grouped in nine major regions; the approximate location (but not size) of the 73 districts and the regions appear in Fig. 19.2. The regions form a simplified version of the so-called natural agricultural

Figure 19.2 Sample of rural districts

areas used in Swedish statistics.[25] In no case was the classification influenced by the fertility data.

The measure of fertility used is the marital fertility rate, the number of legitimate births (or confinements)[26] per 1,000 married women between 15 and 45 years of age. This was extracted from the sources previously quoted and for the periods mentioned. Two more values were added to the time series. A rate for 1860–61 was estimated based on the annual records of children born within each parish of the country, and the list of parishioners prepared for the 1860 census. Both sets of records are in the files of the Swedish Central Statistical Bureau. Similarly, a rate was computed for 1945–46; in this case the number of married women aged 15 to 45 was taken from the published report of the 1945 census. It should be noted that the rules for selecting the areas (at least 70% in farming, not more than 10% living in town-like communities) do not apply after 1930.

The main reason for using the simple marital fertility rate was, of course, its convenience and availability. Wicksell, and Wicksell and Quensel, rely mainly on a more refined period measure, a "fertility index" obtained through indirect standardization. Wicksell thinks this an almost indispensable precaution, but his own data hardly bear him out unless one is very demanding, for the correlation between the simple marital fertility rate and the index in the sample of 73 districts is +0.97 in both 1910–11 and 1928–33.[27]

Fertility Variations: the Parochial, the Regional and the National Pattern

The changes in fertility rates that have occurred are illustrated in Fig. 19.3, where averages for regions (unweighted averages of the district values within the region) are shown. Similar graphs can and have been prepared for each one of the 73 districts but are not reproduced here.

It appears at once that the northernmost

region (NN) stands on its own. Fertility is high and there is little sign of a decline before 1910, so the region may be called "late." It should be added that this is true of the entire county (Norrbotten) to which most of these districts belong. All this may plausibly be explained by the geographical isolation of these parts, and the continuing high fertility here has done much to create an impression of geographical spread of birth control and small-family ideals. But there are several other factors to bear in mind; a low density of population, an ethnically mixed population, and, as we shall see, a high rate of infant and child mortality.

The question, then, is whether a pattern of geographical diffusion can be discerned in the rest of the country. The regional curves on the graph tend to converge, and the differences between the regions to diminish. At the same time the regions tend to keep their relative position, though there are some changes in rank order. The northernmost region contributes to this picture of a stable rank order out of proportion, but is not solely responsible for it.

To see all this clearly, the fertility rates may be subjected to an analysis of variance, and the total variance (σ_T^2) for the 73 districts can be partitioned into a between-regions (σ_P^2) and a within-region component (σ_W^2), so that

$$\sigma_T^2 = \sigma_P^2 + \sigma_W^2. \qquad [1]$$

The aim here is not to test the statistical significance of the regional variation but to measure its size relative to the total variance. The results are shown in Table 19.1; they are given separately for the entire sample and for the sample with the northernmost region NN excluded.

Before 1910 no consistent trend appears. After that date the total variance decreases, at least if the region NN is left out. But at first this is due mostly to the sharp reduction of variability *within* regions which took place between 1910 and 1930. The variation *between* regions is much less affected at this stage; it only begins to fall after 1930 when it all but disappears if region NN is dis-

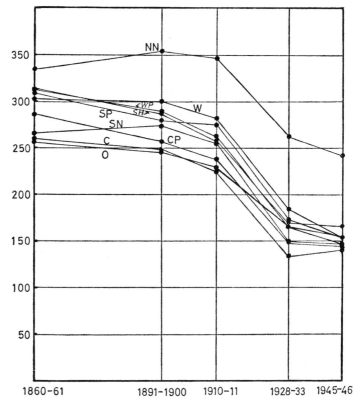

Figure 19.3 Marital fertility for regions within agricultural sample

TABLE 19.1 Analysis of variance of fertility rates[28]

PERIOD	ALL REGIONS			REGION NN EXCLUDED		
	σ_P^2	σ_W^2	σ_T^2	σ_P^2	σ_W^2	σ_T^2
1860–61	650	700	1,350	560	650	1,210
1891–1900	720	500	1,220	390	490	890
1910–11	890	610	1,510	430	630	1,070
1928–33	890	300	1,190	310	210	530
1945–46	490	460	950	60	210	270

regarded, and is much reduced if that region is included.

Perhaps the decline in fertility was part of a more general process which "ironed out" many of the former local and regional differences, and which first affected the purely local differences, the "parochial" variation. For a time this levelling effect makes the differences between remote parts of the country rather more visible than before. In this sense we have passed to a regional pattern; this is finally followed by a pattern in which national fertility standards prevail.

Fertility Variation and Birth Control

No theory of fertility and fertility change in Sweden can be regarded as satisfactory unless it accounts for the variations in marital fertility which existed before the secular decline. And Sweden is no isolated case; the variability (relative to the national mean) was about the same in England in the 1870's and in Japan in the 1920's.[29] These regional differences cannot be brushed aside as short-lived and accidental, for they are quite stable. The correlation between the 1860–61 rate and the 1891–1900 rate in Sweden for the 73 districts is +0.78, and between the

1891–1900 and the 1928–33 rates +0.72. A similar consistency appears in the English and Japanese series.

In the literature on fertility in Sweden this variation and its persistence over the period of decline is often mentioned, but no explanation has so far been offered. The data here presented allow us to follow the differences (for the sample of districts) back to 1860 but no further. It is hard to see how the variation could have been the result of spread of birth control immediately before 1860 as the national fertility rate did not change much.

This pre-industrial variation strongly suggests that fertility was in fact controlled long before 1880, not only among urban middle-class families, which are hardly represented at all in the agricultural sample. However, given a sufficiently sceptical attitude to our knowledge of human fertility and fecundity, very little is certain and therefore very little impossible. It could be argued that a marital fertility rate of 300 in the Swedish population, and a lower rate in some regions, is not necessarily an indication of deliberate birth control. A fecundity standard is needed against which observed fertility can be judged, and it is clear that this is a difficult task. Nevertheless, it seems to the author that at least a *prima facie* case for the existence of birth control on a considerable scale before the secular decline can be made out by using some other populations living in comparable conditions as standards of comparison.

Data for the Hutterite community[30] in the United States often serve as a basis, but some other cases may be more relevant. A rate around 375 was attained in German areas in the 1870's and 1880's.[31] The rate for the whole of Holland[32] was not much lower before 1880, and we have seen that the northern part of Sweden had very high rates (350 or more). In these cases the marriage patterns (age at marriage and marriage rates) were not too different from the Swedish average. A more distant example is the white population of the United States of 1800, for which the crude birth rate has

been estimated as 50–55.[33] This requires both early and nearly universal marriage, *and* a fertility within marriage not much below the level just indicated.

Admittedly no precision can be claimed for results reached in this way, but even a crude estimate will be helpful. And the conclusion is that a population where married couples make no effort whatsoever to limit the number of births, and where nineteenth-century conditions of health and nutrition prevail, ought to have a marital fertility rate not far from 375.

Because the rate is not a perfect measure little weight should be attached to moderate differences between the observed rate and the assumed fecundity limit of 375. But a rate of the order of 300 in Sweden generally before 1880, and still more of 250 as in the low-fertility regions of Sweden, seems to contradict the theory that no birth control was practised. Even a temporary departure from the fecundity level of that size takes a lot of explaining within a theory of no birth control, and the differences were not, as has been shown, temporary. The Swedish population, if not better fed than other European populations at the time, seems to have been healthier to judge from mortality data, so involuntary sterility or pregnancy wastage ought to have occurred less frequently than in Holland or German industrial areas.[34]

Before leaving the subject there is one further complication that needs to be discussed. It may be argued that prolonged lactation can be responsible for a relatively low fertility rate and that infant mortality will have an influence on lactation, and therefore on fertility. As the correlation between infant mortality and fertility will assume some importance later on in the analysis this is a point that should be cleared up as far as possible.

There are two versions of the hypothesis. The first postulates a physiological and automatic effect of infant mortality; lactation decreases the probability of a new conception—if a child dies soon after birth, lactation is interrupted and a normal conception risk is restored much earlier than in the case of a mother with a surviving child. Decreasing mortality should therefore lead to a decreasing fertility if other conditions remain constant. This possibility is mentioned by Hyrenius[35] in a study of the demography of a Swedish-Estonian population; in support he gives figures that show a shorter median interval between two births when the first child died. However, even if one accepts this difference as due to an automatic physiological mechanism (which is the real point at issue), variations and changes in infant mortality of the size that actually occur will not affect fertility by more than a few percentage points. Thus, if fertility changes in the same direction as infant mortality, the automatic effect can only explain this to a very limited degree.

In a more general manner prolonged lactation could be used as an explanation of a moderate fertility rate irrespective of infant mortality and its variations. This is a problem to which we shall have to return when we deal with the fertility of Asian populations. The extent and duration of breastfeeding within a population is usually unknown, at least in the past, nor have the precise effects of lactation on pregnancy risks been established. However, with prolonged lactation we are at least very close to contraception as usually understood, for there is evidence that many populations, at different times in history, rightly or wrongly, have believed in lactation as a means of controlling fertility.[36]

Fertility and Diffusion Rates

On the basis of the registered rates and certain assumptions it is possible to infer a *diffusion rate*, the proportion of all families or women who follow new-style ideals with respect to birth control. Let P be this proportion with the theoretical limits 0 and 1, and $1 - P$; then, the proportion of "old-style" families, meaning here non-users of birth control, with a fertility rate within marriage of 375. "New-style" families are those who completely accept birth control, though some couples may never have to

practise it because they find themselves sub-fecund, or for other reasons. Presumably even the new-style parents want some children, so the fertility rate within this element of the population will be set at 100, roughly the rate prevailing in the 1950's in Sweden. Finally, let F be the registered rate for a certain area, region or country, which then represents a mixture of the two populations. From this follows

$$F = 100P + 375(1 - P). \qquad [2]$$

By means of this equation the value of P can be found if the value of F is known. If the marital fertility rate is 300, as in rural Sweden in general, the diffusion rate becomes 0.27. With F equal to 250, as in the rural low-fertility regions, the diffusion rate becomes 0.45.

Three remarks should be added. This method cannot be expected to give more than a first approximation. It is also clear that a simple mixed-population approach is not appropriate for a situation of rapidly changing fertility, where one has to be prepared for special "dynamic effects" due to the transition.[37] But then fertility does not seem to have changed much before 1880, and the change before 1910 was quite slow in the rural areas. Finally, one may question the discontinuous, "all-or-none" nature of the theory. It could well be, for instance, that the controlling parents aimed at a somewhat higher fertility than parents in the 1950's. There are several reasons why this would be natural. Infant and child mortality is one, and will be discussed later. Also, new-style parents would still be living among neighbours whose fertility was fairly high, and might be influenced by this, so that their fertility targets were higher than to-day, or their practice of birth control less consistent and determined. The upshot of this is that the diffusion rates determined by means of Equation (2) above should be regarded as conservative or minimum estimates rather than the opposite. If the marital fertility rate in the new-style part of the population is put at 150 instead of 100, the diffusion rate becomes 0.33 for rural Sweden and

0.56 in the low-fertility areas. The more alike the behavior of new- and old-style parents is assumed to be the higher the estimated diffusion rate. The limiting case is a population in which all parents (except sterile, etc.) eventually do something to limit fertility, but with fertility targets which are high by modern standards. Equation (2) will not help us to decide between these interpretations.

A Simple Growth Model

On the basis of the "discontinuous" approach implied by Equation (2) a simple model describing the spread of birth control after 1860 can be developed. The findings reported earlier make it improbable that the spread of birth control generally started from a position of zero—spread around 1860, or 1880 in the areas included in the rural sample. One is rather led to the conclusion that at least about one-third of the population in the areas of average fertility, and about one-half in the low-fertility areas, had already been converted in 1860 to new-style behavior, that is to say, to the idea and practice of birth control. As there is little sign of change during the decades before 1860 or the two following decades, marital fertility may be regarded as being in an equilibrium state. This equilibrium was then disturbed around 1880, with an accelerating decline in marital fertility as a consequence, and therefore, according to the reasoning behind Equation (2), an accelerating growth of the proportion of new-style parents. As the term "diffusion" is more often used in connection with processes with a zero- or near-zero start (true innovations) we shall prefer terms like "growth" or "adjustment." With respect to fertility one might, of course, equally well speak of a decay process.

One hypothesis about the forces that began to act or act more strongly on fertility toward the end of the nineteenth century would be that they were impersonal and universal tendencies, not tied to local institutions or groups, or much dependent on local circumstances for their effect. Broad economic and social changes might create a "stimulus pressure" or an "infective force" resulting in a decline of fertility. This assumption can be developed and tested on the Swedish fertility data.

Only old-style, non-controlling parents remain to be converted to new-style behavior, so the rate of change ought to be proportional to the size of the old-style element, and also, of course, to the strength of the stimulus, here presented by a constant c. This leads to

$$\frac{dP}{dt} = c(1 - P) \qquad [3]$$

where P, as before, is the diffusion rate, that is to say, the proportion converted to new-style behavior. By use of (2) we get

$$\frac{dF}{dt} = -c(F - 100). \qquad [4]$$

Here F stands for the marital fertility rate, and the assumptions about new-style and old-style fertility rates are those of Equation (2). For finite time periods this can be changed to

$$D = -c(F_0 - 100) \qquad [5]$$

where D stands for the fertility difference or decrement between the rate F_0 at time T_0 and the rate F_1 at time T_1. For the purpose at hand it is not necessary to retain the somewhat artificial and implausible discontinuous postulate according to which parents are either entirely old-style or entirely new-style. Equation (5) can be interpreted in its own right, and with no regard to its derivation, as showing how fertility decreases at a rate which is proportional to its distance from the long-term equilibrium modern or new-style level. We have, in effect, a negative (decay) case of a "simple catalytic" growth model with aggregate fertility response as the dependent variable,[38] and it is no longer essential to know how fertility is distributed between new-style and old-style families.

From these definitions and assumptions it follows that F_1, fertility at T_1, can be regarded as made up of three components:

fertility F_0 at the earlier T_0, the expected decrement D between T_0 and T_1 linearly dependent on F_0, and an error or residual term u.

$$F_1 = F_0 - c(F_0 - 100) + u. \qquad [6]$$

The first and second terms together make up the systematic part of F_1, the second and third make up the observed decrement (as contrasted to the expected). The equation can also be written

$$F_1 = (1 - c)F_0 + 100c + u. \qquad [7]$$

An expected value of F_1 is thus obtained by forming a particular linear function with F_0 as the independent variable, the difference between the expected and observed value of F_1 is represented by u. The shape of the function is strictly determined by the initial hypothesis represented by (2) and (3) and the growth (or decay) model implied by it. One consequence of this is that there is only one adjustable constant, c. As a more conventional alternative a linear function with two adjustable constants, determined by the method of least squares, can be used,

$$F_1 = aF_0 + b + u. \qquad [8]$$

By virtue of the least-squares adjustment, the residual or error variance will in general be smaller than in the previous case, and the error term u will be uncorrelated with the systematic part. Equation (8) will fit the data better, but may be less meaningful.

TABLE 19.2 Error variance ($\sigma_u{}^2$) for the prediction of 1910–11 martial fertility from 1860–61 rates[39]

MODEL	DISTRICTS N = 69			REGIONS N = 8		
	$\sigma_u{}^2$	$\sigma_1{}^2$	$\sigma_u{}^2/\sigma_1{}^2$	$\sigma_u{}^2$	$\sigma_1{}^2$	$\sigma_u{}^2/\sigma_1{}^2$
Theoretical (7)	823	1,087	0.76	173	389	0.45
Regression (8)	729	1,087	0.67	158	389	0.41

When the models are tested the northern-most region NN will be excluded. This will lead to a slight bias in the results as this region shows more evidence of lags and inertia in the decline of fertility than the rest of the country. As it is atypical, and several explanations of this fact are possible, it has seemed best to treat it separately. The results above (Table 19.2) are based, then, on the remaining 69 districts and 8 regions. The error or residual variance, $\sigma_u{}^2$, has been related to the total variance $\sigma_1{}^2$ of fertility rates at time T_1, here defined as 1910–11. The 1860–61 rate is taken as F_0. The calculations have been carried out both with districts and regions as units, in the latter case the regional rates are unweighted means of district rates.

It will be seen that both models give a poor fit when applied to the variation between *districts* in 1910–11. The residual or error variance is large relative to the total variance of fertility at that date. At the same time it should be borne in mind that the regression fit, though not impressive, is equivalent to a correlation coefficient of 0.57. With *regions* the models are much more successful; the error variance (regression model) is less than half of the total variance, or the equivalent of a correlation of 0.77.

In short, a simple model of adjustment through time from an earlier and higher fertility level to a modern and lower equilibrium level explains the mean fertility rates for regions fairly well, but does not fit the data from the smaller districts nearly as well. It is thus possible that lags will apply in the districts. One way of testing this hypothesis is to look for the influence of geographical location of the districts and see whether it has any bearing on fertility change. This has been done, the results are largely negative and can be reported in a few words. Neither distance from an urban center of some importance nor the state of railway communications around 1880 turned out to be of much help in accounting for the variation between districts. With the possible exception of Region NN the evidence thus points to the conclusion that the spread of birth control after 1880 did not follow a geographical pattern. We do not know what happened before 1860, and one is therefore free to imagine a first-wave, pre-industrial adjustment or diffusion phase where geographical gradients were more important; but in the absence of data such a theory can neither be confirmed nor falsified. To infer a geographical spread pattern after 1880 on the basis of data from 1900, 1910 or 1920 seems entirely unwarranted. The regions with low rates were generally low already in 1860.

We shall return to the apparent exception, the extreme north of the country, after the role of infant and child mortality has been examined.

Birth Control as Demographic Response

It is the author's contention that the decline of marital fertility should be regarded as a shift in a stimulus balance between old-style and new-style ideals, and the consequent shift in the level of adoption, or the fertility targets of controlling parents, rather than as the spread of a new invention. However, the question remains: *what* were the forces that brought about the decline to which the parents reacted?

Davis[40] has tried to deal with this problem in a systematic manner by regarding fertility, marriage and migration as connected and interchangeable responses. A simple arithmetical identity may help to demonstrate and develop this idea. Let B_L represent the crude birth rate, counting only legitimate births,[41] M the proportion of the total population which consists of married women aged between 15 and 45, and F the marital fertility rate as previously defined (legitimate births per 1,000 married women aged 15 to 45). Then we obviously have

$$B_L = MF. \qquad [9]$$

M is a product of several factors, the age distribution, age at marriage, marriage rates, and mortality conditions. In a population of the classical Western European type, with late marriage, M will be around 0.10 or even a little lower. In an Asian population with very early and universal marriage M will be a little less than 0.20. That fertility within marriage (F) and the marriage pattern (M) offer alternative ways of limiting the fertility

of a community hardly needs demonstration; it is equally obvious that they can be used in combination. For the pre-industrial Western European populations the postponement of marriage and the lowering of M, has been held to be the only, or in any case by far the most important, of the two causes.[42] If realistic values are entered in (9) it will be seen, however, that the situation is a little less clear-cut than might be supposed.

In the following a "low M" case corresponding to the rural Swedish case of 1880 will be distinguished from a "high M" case obtained by combining the 1960 age-specific proportions married among women in the U.S.A. with the Swedish rural age distribution of 1880. The low M is 0.091, the high M 0.140. The more extreme Indian figure has not been used as it may be incompatible with maximum marital fertility.

For marital fertility three levels have been used: the "maximum F" of 375, the "rural normal F" (for Sweden) of 290, and a "rural low F" of 260. We then have

a	High M, maximum F		$B_L = 52.5$
b	Low M, maximum F		$B_L = 34.1$
c	High M, rural normal F		$B_L = 40.6$
d	High M, rural low F		$B_L = 36.4$
e	Low M, rural normal F		$B_L = 26.4$

Combination (*a*) gives a birth rate in excess of 50. Though this is high it is not beyond the bounds of possibility; rates as high or higher have been recorded for actual populations including the American population of 1800. The next case, (*b*), shows the effect of restrictions of marriage, but none on fertility within marriage. This effect is considerable, and stronger than in the next case, (*c*), where relatively early and nearly universal marriage is combined with a somewhat lower fertility within marriage. But a combination of the same marriage pattern and the rural low fertility level, combination (*d*), brings down the birth rate almost as much as postponement of marriage in combination (*b*). Finally, combination (*e*) shows the effect of marriage and fertility restrictions together; this is not far from the actual situation in Swedish rural areas.

The complete dominance of restrictions on marriage and the unimportance of birth control within marriage cannot be regarded as established for Sweden. As far as can be judged from the data, birth control within marriage may at least have been a contributory factor of some strength.

Birth Control and Child Mortality

So far the results support Davis's view that a population under pressure to limit its own growth tends to respond in more than one way ("the multi-phasic response").[43] When we return to the question, what the source of this pressure was? the most concrete and at the same time plausible answer that can be given is that the reduction of infant and child mortality provided the stimulus or motive, an explanation on which Davis relies a good deal. It is an old theory[44] which has never been quite forgotten, nor completely accepted by demographers and sociologists. We will show below that it helps to understand certain features of the fertility transition in Sweden, but some of its shortcomings and problems will also be mentioned.

If parents are bent on limiting the number of their children, then it is surviving children that should count rather than the number of children born. Hereafter the proportion surviving at the age of 15 (l_{15}) will be used as the measure of survival. This figure, in turn, will be estimated by doubling the proportion dying during the first year of life, and subtracting this figure from the number born taken as 1. Swedish life tables for several periods between 1800 and 1930 indicate that this rule of thumb holds reasonably well, though not, of course, exactly. The survival rates are only meant to be rough approximations and should be taken in this spirit. They have to be built on the life chances both of legitimate and illegitimate children.[45]

In the graph below (Figure 19.4) are shown the change in estimated survival rates for the whole of Sweden (1800–90; ten-year averages), and separate rates for rural

Sweden, the City of Stockholm and the entire county of Norrbotten (1850–1930; ten year averages).[46] Norrbotten is largely rural but includes a small fraction of urban population. To these observations linear trends have been fitted by eye.

Two things appear from the graph. First, there was a strong improvement in survival rates during the whole of the nineteenth century,[47] though the annual fluctuations here concealed were sizeable during the first decades. Secondly, after 1860, development was very different within the three populations distinguished in the graph. The Stockholm figures, appallingly bad until then, improved dramatically, and at the end of the period they were, if anything, better than the rural rate, which had also improved though not nearly so fast. The Norrbotten rate, on the other hand, shows no consistent improvement before 1900. In this case the linear trend, though it works well enough for the other populations, gives a poor fit.

If falling mortality and improving survival chances for children exerted a pressure on marital fertility, then this pressure ought to have been strongest among Stockholm parents and weakest in the northern part of the country, with the general rural population falling between these extremes. But this is also the order in terms of the speed of fertility decline of the three populations. Stockholm showed the fastest change in marital fertility; Norrbotten, and region NN in the agricultural sample, were noticeably slow to react. In short, we have the expected relation between strength of the stimulus (decline of child mortality) and strength or reaction (decline of marital fertility).

Death risks and survival rates are here treated as psychological stimuli; the purpose is not to determine their precise demographic impact. As has been emphasized by Ryder[48] the increased survival rates for adults, and the decreasing probability of a marriage being ended within the childbearing period by death of either spouse, must also be taken into account. Ryder believes there was a strong desire to limit fertility quite early in nineteenth-century Sweden, but the tradi-

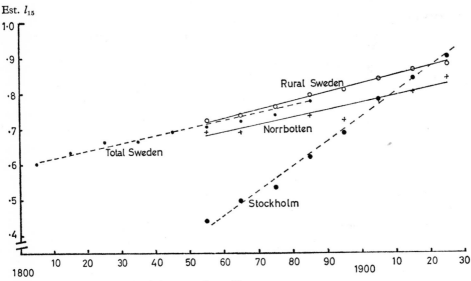

Figure 19.4 Estimated survival chances at age 15

tional technique applied, restrictions on marriage, was defeated by the continuing decline in mortality.

We do not assume that differential child mortality generally explains regional variations in marital fertility; this will have to be investigated separately. But infant mortality rates can help us on one more point where help is badly needed. Though the nineteenth-century rate was high in Sweden by modern standards, it was relatively favorable compared with other nineteenth-century populations, and this makes it more understandable why the fertility decline started at the same time in weakly industrialized, underdeveloped Sweden and the leading industrial nation, England.

However, it is not easy to see why it took parents so long to discover what was happening. Granted that one basic factor behind the decline was the falling mortality rate, why did not the decline come soon after 1800? Admittedly there are other outlets for a population surplus, but in Sweden neither industrialization, nor transatlantic emigration can have been of any importance before 1860. There was some effect on marriage patterns in the expected direction, that is to say in the direction of lower mar-

riage rates, but it was rather weak. And to continue, why did the stronger reaction, the fertility decline, come at a time when the other solutions, industrialization and emigration, had become real alternatives? A standard answer to the last query is that mobility, whether geographical or occupational, requires that people travel light, that is, with a small family. It is a convincing retort until one starts to reflect a little on the basis figures. With a mean age at first marriage for men of 30, and the reduction of marital fertility usually not very pronounced in the early phase of marriage, the influence of fertility decline on mobility chances can hardly have been great.

It is possible that parents plan their family on the basis of expectations which were well founded at some earlier period but are no longer realistic, an instance of "lagged perception." Or there could exist a predictable "threshold" so that a change in mortality and increase in survival chances is not noticed and taken into account unless it exceeds the threshold value. Presumably oscillations and temporary disturbances will mask a secular change. After all, even demographers and statisticians find the detection of recent trends no easy matter.

Such principles, if they could be found, would be of great value for diagnosis and prediction in areas where fertility is still high, and infant mortality declining. The application of perception and learning theory to this class of problems would seem to be one of the most urgent tasks for sociologists and social psochologists interested in population.

In the meantime certain conclusions can be drawn. The beliefs and opinions of parents regarding infant and child mortality are a crucial fact which should be determined in surveys and field studies of birth control and related topics. There is at least one case where this has been done with interesting results.[49] Among women in Lima, Peru, there was widespread misperception and erroneous beliefs about infant mortality which, many respondents thought, had increased.

The main conclusion is that desired family size, infant and child mortality, and fertility should be seen as three interrelated variables, and explicitly recognized as such in theoretical models or in population policy as has recently been done in an article by Tabbarah.[50] When we next turn to fertility in underdeveloped countries and regions the importance of this will become still more apparent.

The Situation in Asia To-day

If we turn to the Asian populations where birth control allegedly plays a very minor role and thus expect to find fertility near the physiological maximum, the outcome will be surprising. The crude birth rates, though high, are not nearly as high as those reported from North American populations of European stock some 200 years ago. This is even more apparent if we compare married women in Asia to-day with married women in Europe or America before the secular decline in fertility began. What leaps to the eye is the *low* marital fertility of the Asian women.

Before the evidence for this statement is examined two preliminary remarks are in order. Firstly, it is not here implied that our concern over Asian fertility is misplaced or groundless; what matters is the rate of increase of the populations in question, and therefore the relative magnitude of the birth and death rates. But if one sees a reduction in fertility as necessary or highly desirable it is surely important to determine what the present level is and what may lie behind it.

Secondly, fertility in traditional societies will here be treated only in so far as it has a bearing on the main topic of the paper, and the reader should keep in mind the limited purpose and not expect too much breadth of coverage or depth of insight. The fertility problems of countries like India are often put into the perspective of innovation theory, so it is relevant to point out the difficulties of this approach. They are similar to those noted in the study of Swedish fertility except that they may be more pronounced for certain Asian populations. Below the main stress will be on India with some reference to other countries.

The crude birth rate for India in 1961 has been estimated at 42. This may seem high, but the marital fertility rate, calculated by means of the simple relation (9) and census data on age and marital status,[51] becomes 233. For Pakistan, with an assumed birth rate of 46, a rate of 277 is indicated for the beginning of the 1960's. For Ceylon the marital fertility rate is in the neighborhood of 260. From local and regional studies more specific information is obtainable on fertility by age of wife, or the duration of marriage, or as measured by birth intervals.[52] There seems to be considerable variation between regions or localities with the high values approaching West European figures. But the general impression is one of moderate fertility and fairly long birth intervals. One of the fertility schedules from the Mysore population study ("rural plains")[53] gives a marital fertility rate of 229 when combined with the 1961 Indian age distribution among married women. This is close to the previous estimate of 233 which shows that Mysore cannot be regarded as grossly atypical of India in general, a point which will become important a little later in the argument.

Now, certain adjustments or allowances have to be made before these rates are compared with European rates from the nineteenth century. The very low age of marriage in India may call for a reduction in the expected annual birth performance of married women even without any deliberate birth control. One reason is the probable adolescent sub-fecundity of many young brides; there are also social customs that impose periods of separation between husband and wife in early marriage. If, say, half the married women between 15 and 20 were regarded as not really at risk of conceiving, this would lower the expected overall marital fertility rate by a little less than 10%. It would help to explain the low rate for this particular age group, but, having made this adjustment, the grounds for further downward adjustments are less clear.

On the other hand, the age distribution among Indian (or Pakistani) women within the childbearing period favors fertility as there is a stronger concentration in the lower part of that period, below 35, than among Swedish married women in 1880. This raises the Indian or Pakistani fertility rate by some 25–50 units. The Mysore age-specific rates give a marital fertility rate of 178 when combined with the Swedish age distribution, and the outcome is similar for other Asian fertility data.

These are awkward figures to fit into a picture of no birth control. But at this point a further set of reasons for low fertility may be invoked. For simplicity's sake they will be called "medical"; this term includes such factors as climate; disease, notably malaria; lack of medical care; malnutrition; perhaps even racial factors. Indian women, and presumably women in other Asian areas where birth control is held to be unimportant, conceive and bear children to the limit of their capacity, it may be argued, but that capacity is much lower than in Europe

or America for the medical reasons just indicated. It is a plausible line of thought, and may well contain a large element of truth. Yet it is not without its own difficulties. An interesting consequence of the theory is that early and universal marriage may once have been an indispensable trait in a society with high infant and adult mortality (regarded as independent variables). Because the fertility of women was limited by medical factors nearly every woman had to take part in the reproductive process from the earliest age, or the population could not survive. But health conditions have improved in Indian and other Asian populations, as may be seen from falling mortality rates, and one would therefore expect the medical limitations of fecundity and fertility to act less severely, with an increase in birth rates and marital fertility rates as a consequence. Of this there is little sign; if fertility *has* increased, so that it was still lower before the 1940's, one wonders how these populations managed to survive at all with the former very high mortality rates.

A variant of the medical theory has been put forward by Henry[54] who mentions the possible influence of breast-feeding on conception risks. In this connection he also refers to taboos against sexual intercourse during breast-feeding, or for some stated period after the birth of a child.

However, the last two factors, and particularly taboos against sexual intercourse (if not honored more in the breach than in observance), bring us back very closely to birth control as usually understood. The desire to space births and spare the mother too frequent pregnancies might well be one of the supporting factors behind this custom, even on the level of conscious motives. The Mysore study[55] shows that men and women within the region were concerned about fertility and that they thought that childbearing should not start too early in marriage, nor pregnancies come in too quick succession. Ideal family size, around four children, was larger than in a European population, but not very large. It agrees well, in fact, with the actual number of surviving children in the families of the region. Though admitted use of contraceptive techniques is infrequent in the rural areas, contraception is not unknown, especially in the urban population. As usual, abortion remains an unknown magnitude. Altogether, the report finds indirect evidence for family limitation in Bangalore City (the chief urban center) and perhaps also in the rural areas.[56]

With this the matter will have to rest and the reader is left to decide for himself what explanation of Indian and similar Asian fertility rates he finds most convincing. It should be stressed, again, that a theory specifically designed to fit the Indian experience may not help much in understanding, for instance, the almost equally low Japanese rate of the early 1920's.

The importance of a correct diagnosis for framing a strategy of fertility change should be obvious. A great deal will depend on the weight to attach to *information* and lack of information as opposed to *motivation* (or lack of motivation). How is a change in behavior brought about when parents, under pre-existing conditions, have as many surviving children as they deem ideal? Telling them about contraceptive techniques is hardly the answer, and to influence their attitudes may be far from easy.

Summary and Discussion

Two topics have been put in the foreground in this paper; the author believes that they are connected and that they should be discussed together. One is the spread or diffusion characteristics of the process of fertility decline, and the usefulness of the innovation approach in the study of this process. The second main question is the time taken by the decline. Although this question may have been less apparent in the bulk of the preceding analysis it is in many ways the more general and important one.

As far as Swedish fertility is concerned the author finds it hard to avoid the conclusion that a substantial proportion of families

deliberately controlled their fertility already long before the secular decline began. The decline and growth of the proportion of controlling parents should be regarded not as the spread of a new social invention but rather as a shift in a stimulus balance between old-style and new-style ideals, and the consequent shift in the equilibrium level of adoption, or in the fertility targets of controlling parents. Geographical diffusion models do not seem very helpful for the understanding of this shift, nor can the theory of the urban-rural gradient be accepted without important reservations. Social, mainly class, gradients have not here been investigated as such, but the metropolitan-urban-rural differences are strongly correlated with class distinctions, and to that extent the results throw doubt on the class lags often posited in the standard theory of the fertility transition. One suspects that these, too, will more often consist in differences of fertility levels prior to the decline, and unequal rates of change within classes rather than in the time of onset of the decline. The distinction between "old-style" and "new-style" ideals should then be understood in a highly relativistic fashion; the new-style ideals of controlled family size are not absolutely new, only stronger in modern society, or more consistently put in action.

One reason why it may be more misleading than helpful to regard the fertility decline and the wider adoption of birth control as an innovation process is that the latter designation often carries with it the idea that the process is bound to run its course to complete or near-complete adoption in a regular way. The notion of an adjustment over time to a new equilibrium level, on the other hand, keeps open the possibility of fertility staying neither fully controlled in the modern sense, nor completely uncontrolled, and this for an appreciable period. A further consequence of this line of thinking is that differences between regions, town and country, or social classes are not infallible signs of an impending general change.

The shift from innovation to adjustment

theory leads to less emphasis on information about birth control and its means, and more emphasis on motivation and social situation, and perhaps information about child mortality as decisive factors, but here it is necessary to distinguish between an individual and a collective aspect of degree of information. Information can be provided collectively through the work of governments and organizations who use channels like newspapers, the radio, lectures, or birth-control clinics. Whether the men and women exposed to this information acquire much knowledge and individually become informed is another matter. If they are indifferent or averse to the idea of birth control they may remain ignorant in spite of a barrage of information and propaganda; though much knowledge is spread, little is picked up. The other side of this is that knowledge may be supplied through oral tradition and informal contacts; the better informed pass on what they know to friends and neighbors. This, of course, assumes that a sufficiently large part of the population is already in possession of that knowledge, and in the present context it probably means that the birth control is already fairly widely practised. If this is the case, one suspects that the informal, person-to-person mechanism of information spread is, if anything, more effective than formal and contrived campaigns. Put in another way, under these conditions the organized effort to supply, or for that matter suppress information, will not make much difference.

The argument is largely speculative, though it agrees both with common sense and social-psychological theory. It also agrees well with the fact that efforts to promote birth and population control by government action have not, as a rule, been very successful either on the local or the national level; the response of parents to the "treatment" has usually been feeble.[57]

About the time taken one is tempted to say that the fertility decline in Western Europe took an astonishingly long time, at least 50 years or about three generations of childbearing women, but astonishment is impossible without prior expectations, and therefore the rudiments of theory which in this field is almost entirely lacking. That half a century or more was needed may then become perfectly understandable once we are in possession of this theory. Meanwhile there are a few explanations that can be rejected as improbable in the light of the results here presented. Delays or lags (initiation lags) when the impulse or idea spreads from the urban to the rural, or from the industrial to the farm population, or from one region to others, do not explain the length of time taken. If such lags exist at all they are quite modest in size, and too much should not be made of them. Most of the time is used for diffusion or change *within* the sub-populations just mentioned. There are some differences in the speed of this change, and the urban population changed a little faster, but even in Stockholm, to take the Swedish case, the time-span taken was about 50 years.

It is clear, both from the present study and more general experience, that the rate of decline of fertility cannot have been governed simply by the rate at which people moved into the urban or industrial sectors as defined by the census. If "urbanization" or "industrialization" are the true causes of fertility decline the terms have to be used in a much wider sense.

The gist of the matter is that the explanation and manipulation of the time factor requires that the locus or loci of time consumption are found. Much of the previous discussion could be expressed as a contrast between a *stimulus* and a *response theory* of inertia and time consumption.[58] According to the stimulus theory, mass attitude change follows a gradually changing stimulus pressure without material delays, say the decline in child mortality, or a rising educational standard. In the response theory the aggregate reaction follows changes in stimulus conditions (which may be sudden) with delays and a characteristic inertia. Obviously the basic terms "stimulus" and "response" have to be more clearly defined, but beyond the matter of terminology real and interesting questions of fact arise. If we follow the response theory we would look for the cause of time consumption in the process of communication, internal psychological processes connected with attitude change, the laws of human perception, conditioning and learning, and primary group or community structure.

The problem of mass attitude change under ill-defined and hard-to-observe stimulus pressures may or may not turn out to be a communication problem. There is, however, one final remark to be added. Almost unavoidably sociologists, following psychologists, try to solve their problems by studying *differences* in human reactions; in this case, differences between town and country, between middle and working class, Protestants and Catholics, perhaps opinion leaders and followers, etc. It is certainly natural for a sociologist to assume or hope that a good deal of the variation in human response to new ideas and practises is due to differences in position within the social and cultural framework, and that sociologists eventually will be able to establish this beyond a reasonable doubt. The sober truth is that these efforts have so far met only with limited success. Certain relations are fairly dependable, like the inverse correlation between urbanism and fertility, but even a difference as big as that between the metropolitan (Stockholm) and rural rates

in Fig. 19.1 leaves a large part of the total variance unexplained.

This is no argument against the quest for social and social-psychological correlates of response to new stimuli, but a firm commitment to the research strategy of differential behavior may blind us to certain possibilities. A society where conversion to a new practice is decided by lot would, by definition, have nothing to offer a student who was looking for determinants like class, education, residence, or religion. Yet the rate at which lots are drawn would be an extremely important variable. It would, in fact, completely govern the rate of change in time. In the real world individual change does not occur in this manner, but it remains true that there is a large element of variation which cannot be accounted for, and is in that sense random. It might still be possible to discover laws or principles behind the speed at which change takes place related among other things to frequency of contact and stimulation and similar constants of human interaction. Such a theory would almost certainly be statistical and non-deterministic in nature. Even a partial success along this line would probably advance our knowledge quite as much as the more conventional approaches. No solution is in sight, but then we have hardly even tried.

Notes

[1]The author is indebted to Professor D. V. Glass and Professor N. B. Ryder for criticism and advice; neither of them, however, is responsible for the methods and conclusions of the paper.

[2]N. E. Himes, *Medical History of Contraception* (London, 1936).

[3]See, for instance, Befolkningskommissionen, *Betänkande i sexualfrågen* (S.O.U. 1936: 59, Stockholm, 1936), pp. 27–28.

[4]D. V. Glass and D. E. C. Eversley (eds.), *Population in History* (London, 1965).

[5]D. V. Glass, "Introduction," *ibid.*, pp. 15–16.

[6]D. E. C. Eversley, "Population, economy and society," *ibid.*, pp. 46–48.

[7]Cf. A. J. Coale and E. M. Hoover, *Population Growth and Economic Development in Low-Income Countries* (Princeton, 1958), p. 47.

[8]Such estimates must be based on the estimated proportion of married women aged 15 to 45 in the Stockholm population. Direct evidence is not available for Stockholm, nor for other administrative divisions of the country.

[9]See E. A. Wrigley, *Industrial Growth and Population Change* (Cambridge, 1961), p. 133.

[10]D. V. Glass, "Changes in fertility in England and Wales," in L. Hogben (ed.), *Political Arithmetic* (London, 1938), p. 178.

[11]I. B. Taeuber, *The Population of Japan* (Princeton, 1958), p. 244.

[12]E. A. Wrigley, *op. cit.*, p. 133.

[13]W. H. Grabill, C. V. Kiser and P. K. Whelpton, *The Fertility of American Women* (New York, 1958), pp. 15–19.

[14]E.g. C. P. Loomis and Beegle, *Rural Sociology* (Englewood Cliffs, 1957), p. 70.

[15]W. H. Grabill, C. V. Kiser and P. K. Whelpton, *loc. cit.*

[16]This part of the study was sup-

ported by a grant from the Swedish Council for Social Science Research.

[17]D. V. Glass, "Changes in fertility in England and Wales."

[18]Data from I. B. Taeuber, *op. cit.*

[19]Data from G. Sundbärg, *Ekonomisk-statistisk beskrivning över Sveriges landsdelar* (Emigrationsutredningen, bil. 5; Stockholm, 1910).

[20]In Taiwan the fertility decline noticed at the end of the 1950's seems to have started simultaneously in different parts of the island. Cf. R. Freedman, "Changing fertility in Taiwan," in R. O. Greep (ed.), *Human Fertility and Population Problems; Proceedings of the Seminar sponsored by the American Academy of Arts and Sciences with the support of the Ford Foundation* (Cambridge, Mass., 1963), pp. 106–140. There is more evidence for increased variation in the German (Prussian) sample used by E. A. Wrigley, *op. cit.*, but the number of units is small and the behavior of the Berlin and Hamburg rates therefore becomes very important. In Spain there is also some evidence of lags; see J. W. Leasure, "Factors involved in the decline of fertility in Spain," *Population Studies*, 16, 3 (March 1963), pp. 271–285.

[21]G. Sundbärg, *op. cit.*

[22]S. D. Wicksell, "Till frågen om den äktenskapliga fruktsamhetens regionala fördelning i Sverige," *Ekenomisk Tidskrift*, 20 (1918), pp. 227–262.

[23]S. D. Wicksell and C.-E. Quensel, *Undersökning av de demografiska elementen i deras regionala variationer och sammanhang* (S.O.U. 1938: 24).

[24]Communities not legally considered towns or cities, but of an urban character, may be part of a judiciary district.

[25]Sveriges Officiella Statistik, *Fordbruksräkningen 1932* (Stockholm, 1936).

[26]Whenever it has been deemed important the appropriate correction was made so that confinement and birthrates are made comparable.

[27]If the northernmost region is excluded (four districts) the correlation is +0.96 also for both periods.

[28]The values have been corrected for the difference between birth and confinement rates.

[29]For English and Japanese gross reproduction rates.

[30]See J. W. Eaton and A. J. Mayer, *Man's Capacity to Reproduce* (Glencoe), reprinted from *Human Biology*, 25 (1954). The marital fertility rate in this population is around 375.

[31]Cf. E. A. Wrigley, *Industrial Growth and Population Change*, *loc. cit.*

[32]As late as 1888–91 the rate was 342 as computed from the 1889 census and the annual returns of legitimate births published in the *Annuaire Statistique des Pays-Bas*.

[33]Y. Yasuba, *Birth Rates of the White Population in the United States 1800–1860* (Baltimore, 1962), pp. 96–100.

[34]The assistance of a trained midwife could be obtained more easily in Sweden than in most other countries. It is hard to see why venereal diseases leading to sterility should have been particularly common in the Swedish farm population.

[35]H. Hyrenius, "Fertility and reproduction in a Swedish population group without family limitation," *Population Studies*, 12, 2 (November 1958), pp. 121–130. Fertility in this population was even lower than in Sweden.

[36]See N. E. Himes, *Medical History of Contraception*, pp. 16, 66, 68, 246–247, 337.

[37]On this problem see C.-E. Quensel, "Changes in fertility following birth restrictions," *Scandinavisk Aktuarietidskrift*, 1939: 3–4, pp. 177–199.

[38]Cf. H. Muench, *Catalytic Models in Epidemiology* (Cambridge, Mass., 1959), Chap. V.

[39]The entries in Table 19.2 do not agree exactly with the corresponding figures in Table 19.1 due to approximations and the different way of measuring variance between regions.

[40]K. Davis, "The theory of change and response in modern demographic history," *Population Index*, 29, 4 (October 1963), pp. 345–366.

[41]The number of children born out of wedlock is usually small compared with legitimate births, but Sweden might be considered marginal in this respect.

[42]Cf. W. Petersen, *Population* (New York, 1961), pp. 358–360. Petersen does not reject the possibility of pre-industrial birth control. On the subject of European marriage patterns, see J. Hajnal, "European marriage patterns in perspective," in D. V. Glass and E. D. C. Eversley (eds.), *Population in History*, pp. 101–143.

[43]K. Davis, *op. cit.*, pp. 349–352.

[44]Cf. R. von Ungern-Sternberg, *Die Ursachen des Geburtenrückganges im europäischen Kulturkreis;* Veroffentlichungen aus dem Gebiete der Medizinalverwaltung (Berlin, 1932), pp. 57–63.

[45]Comparison with life tables computed by Professor N. Keyfitz and kindly put at the author's disposal suggests that the survival estimates may easily be 2% off the true value for a specific short period, and sometimes more. They seem to improve towards the middle of the nineteenth century.

[46]For Norrbotten no data are available for the decade 1871–80.

[47]Infant mortality seems to have been fairly constant before 1800.

[48]N. B. Ryder, "The influence of declining mortality on Swedish reproductivity," in *Current Research in Human Fertility* (Papers presented at the 1954 Annual Conference of the Milbank Memorial Fund, New York, 1955), pp. 65–81.

[49]J. M. Stycos, "Social class and preferred family size in Peru," *American Journal of Sociology*, 70, 6 (May 1965), pp. 651–658.

[50]R. B. Tabbarah, "Birth control and population policy," *Population Studies*, 18, 2 (November 1964), pp. 187–196.

[51]Birth rate estimates from United Nations, *Provisional Report on World Population Prospects as Assessed in 1963* (New York, 1964). Census data from the appropriate volume of United Nations, *Demographic Yearbook*.

[52]Fertility schedules were published early by F. Lorimer, *Culture and Human Fertility* (Paris, 1954). See also J. R. Rele, "Some aspects of family and fertility in India," *Population Studies*, 15, 3 (March 1962), pp. 267–268; and the same author, "Fertility differentials in India," *Milbank Memorial Fund Quarterly*, 41, 2 (April 1963), pp. 183–199.

[53]United Nations: Department of Economic and Social Affairs, Population Studies, No. 34, *The Mysore Population Study* (New York, 1961) p. 84.

[54]L. Henry, "Some data on natural fertility," *Eugenics Quarterly*, 8, 2 (June 1961), pp. 81–91.

[55]*The Mysore Population Study*, Chaps. 10–12.

[56]*Ibid.*, p. 159.

[57]On this subject see J. M. Stycos, "A critique of the traditional planned parenthood approach in underdeveloped areas," in C. V. Kiser (ed.), *Research in Family*

Planning (Princeton, 1962), pp. 477–501; and D. V. Glass, "Population growth and population pol-

icy," *Journal of Chronic Diseases*, **18** (1965), pp. 1079–1094.
[58]Cf. G. Carlsson, "Time and

continuity in mass attitude change: The case of voting," *Public Opinion Quarterly*, **29**, 1 (Spring 1965), pp. 1–15.

MORTALITY TRENDS FOR CAUSES OF DEATH IN COUNTRIES OF LOW MORTALITY

Mortimer Spiegelman

For present purposes, the countries of low mortality will be identified as those that have traditionally recorded death rates which were well below those of the rest of the world. This limitation is specified, since, with the leveling of mortality throughout the world, many countries with high death rates in the not-too-distant past have now established unusually low records.[1] Discussion will therefore be restricted, as on a previous occasion, to the countries of western Europe and the English-speaking countries elsewhere.[2] The study covers nine major causes of death, in addition to the total of all causes, and the period of review runs from 1950 through 1961.

Death registration in these countries is relatively complete, according to the standard cited in the *Demographic Yearbook* of the United Nations, which is a 90 percent minimum coverage of the actual deaths. However, international comparability of records of total deaths may be affected by variations in the practice of birth registration, for some countries exclude from their totals those infants who died before their births were registered or who died within the first twenty-four hours. There are certain other differences, mostly minor, in practice among countries which relate to comparability, such as tabulation by year of registration rather than of occurrence.

Major problems in international comparisons of mortality become evident in attempts

to study specific causes of death, even in broad groupings. The factors bearing upon comparability are not only medical and otherwise technical but may also be social and economic in origin.[3] Populations may vary with respect to the stages at which symptoms are recognized and responded to, and in the kind of medical care sought, which may range from self-medication and non-professional attention to professional treatment. Such variations, it may be surmised, might have some effect upon the outcome of a morbid condition. The whole complex of a nation's system of medical care, involving not only its personnel and institutions but also its pertinent legal structure, bears upon what goes into a statement of the cause of death. The accuracy of the statement of the death record depends upon the training of the physician in attendance, whether or not he or someone else completed the death certificate, and the adequacy of the information entered on it.

Largely as a result of the aging of the populations of Western countries and the control of acutely morbid conditions, the chronic diseases, which are largely of obscure origin, have come to predominate in the mortality picture. Under such a situation, an adequate account of the train of morbid events leading to death, as required by the Sixth and later revisions of the *International Lists of Diseases and Causes of Death*, leaves much room for variation in opinion on the part of the medical certifiers, not only among countries but even within them. Opportunity is ample, then, for expression of local concepts and fashions in medical thinking in certifying

Reprinted from *Demography*, **2**, 1965, 115–125, by permission of the author and the Population Association of America.

causes of death; these are, of course, subject to change with time.

Indicative of the likelihood for an increase in difficulties with regard to medical certification are the larger proportions of the population at ages 65 and over in 1960 (*circa*) than in 1950 (*circa*) for all countries shown in Table 20.1 but New Zealand and Canada. Even more dramatic are the large and increasing proportions of all deaths that occur at ages 45 and over in all countries except New Zealand. For example, the proportion of total deaths that occurred at ages 45 and over in the United States was 80.4 percent in 1950 and 84.2 percent in 1961. On the other hand, an index of generally improved medical care is provided by the decrease in the size of population per physician in all but two countries—Switzerland and Spain—where the ratio showed only a slight rise. For the United States, the ratio of population per physician declined from 790 in 1950 to 780 in 1961. The net effect of the factors bearing upon the quality of medical certification in all countries under review but two (Union of South Africa and Spain) is apparently toward improvement, as evidenced by a decline in the proportions of deaths attributed to senility, ill-defined, and unknown causes. In 1960, these proportions were as low as 1.3 percent in the United States and 1.4 percent in England and Wales but as high as 11.4 percent in Belgium, 14.6 percent in France, and 15.6 percent in Portugal and Spain. The large proportions of deaths ascribed to the indefinite causes of death in the latter countries naturally detract from the validity of the data relating to specific causes.

Another source of variation in cause of death data among countries arises from the steps taken to process the individual death records into tabulations. Thus Table 20.2 shows that, in 1950, ten of the countries in this study were still codifying the causes on the death certificate on the basis of the Fifth Revision of the *International List* and that another ten were using the Sixth Revision; in 1951, the Fifth Revision was still used by three countries. Table 20.3 compares the ab-

breviated lists in the two revisions for the causes of death included in this study. For some causes, particularly diabetes, this change in the *International List* affected comparability over the years, in addition to comparability among countries in any one of these years. Furthermore, the classifications in the *International Lists* are themselves subject to interpretation by the cause of death codifiers. On this score, there are likely to be variations among countries in the auxiliary coding rules that have been developed and in the backgrounds and training of the personnel selected for this task.

For the most part, the death rates presented in this study are necessarily based upon estimates of populations. Also, the data are shown in the form of crude death rates, which, owing to differences in the age distributions of population among countries, hinder international comparisons of the levels of mortality. However, for most countries, the age distribution changes slowly in the course of time. Since the concern is essentially with trend, the use of crude rates in place of age-adjusted rates should have no major influence on such international comparisons.

In view of the many qualifications cited concerning international comparisons of causes of death, the following quotation from the *Demographic Yearbook* for 1951 is pertinent:[4]

> On the whole, the most that statistics on causes of death can be expected to do is to reflect average medical opinion concerning the causes of death in a population. Despite the many factors that complicate the interpretation of these data, they furnish a useful, if not a wholly accurate and consistent, record of changing patterns of mortality.

Total Mortality

Commenting on the trends of mortality in countries of the West in the century following the 1840's, Stolnitz pointed out that "The modern rise in Western life chances first be-

TABLE 20.1 Percent of population at ages 65 and over, percent of deaths at ages 45 and over, population per physician, and percent of total deaths due to senility, ill-defined and unknown causes, for selected countries of low mortality (about 1950 and about 1960)

COUNTRY	PERCENT OF TOTAL POPULATION AT AGES 65 AND OVER				PERCENT OF DEATHS AT AGES 45 AND OVER				POPULATION PER PHYSICIAN				PERCENT OF TOTAL DEATHS DUE TO SENILITY, ILL-DEFINED AND UNKNOWN CAUSES	
	ABOUT 1950		ABOUT 1960		ABOUT 1950		ABOUT 1960		ABOUT 1950		ABOUT 1960		1952	1960
	YEAR	PERCENT	YEAR	PERCENT	YEAR	PERCENT	YEAR	PERCENT	YEAR	NUMBER	YEAR	NUMBER		
United States	1950	8.1	1961	9.3	1950	80.4	1961	84.2	1950	790	1961	780	1.5	1.3
England and Wales	1950	10.9	1961	11.9	1950	87.8	1961	91.7	1951	1,100	1960	960	1.6	1.4
Scotland	1950	10.0	1961	10.4	1950	84.3	1961	90.1	1952	930	1960	760	3.1	1.2
Australia	1950	8.1	1960	8.5	1950	82.7	1961	85.2	1952	1,000	1960	860	2.1	1.0
New Zealand	1950	9.4	1960	8.7	1950	84.6	1961	84.5	1950	800	1961	690	1.0	.8
Canada	1950	7.7	1961	7.6	1950	74.8	1961	80.5	1951	970	1960	910	1.8	1.0
Union of South Africa (white)	1950	6.4	1960	6.6	1950	72.9	1960	78.0	1950	2,100[1]	1960	2,000	4.6	5.3
Ireland	1951	10.7	1956	10.9	1950	80.5	1961	88.9	1951	1,000	....	....	12.7	7.8
Netherlands	1950	7.7	1961	9.1	1950	81.5	1961	88.1	1950	1,300	1960	900	5.5	4.3
Belgium	1950	11.1	1960	12.0	1950	83.5	1960	90.2	1951	1,000	1961	740	15.3	11.9
France	1950	11.8	1961	12.1	1950	82.0	1961	88.6	1952	1,100	1960	930	18.4	14.6
Switzerland	1950	9.6	1961	10.3	1950	84.1	1961	88.2	1951	730	1961	750	2.0	1.5
West Germany	1950	9.3	1960	10.6	1950	80.0	1961	87.5	1952	750	1960	690	9.4	6.7
Denmark	1950	9.1	1960	10.6	1950	84.8	1960	89.9	1950	960	1959	830	2.1	1.5
Norway	1950	9.6	1960	10.9	1950	84.4	1960	89.6	1951	950	1960	840	8.3	6.9
Sweden	1950	10.2	1961	11.9	1950	88.1	1960	91.9	1950	1,400	1960	1,100	7.2	1.9
Finland	1950	6.6	1960	7.4	1950	72.7	1961	85.7	1950	2,000	1960	1,600	6.8	2.3
Portugal	1950	7.0	1960	7.6	1950	55.4	1961	64.7	1950	1,500	1961	1,200	17.0	15.6
Italy	1951	8.3	1960	9.2	1950	72.1	1960	82.8	1951	820	1960	610	9.5	5.0
Spain	1950	7.2	1960	8.3	1950	64.7	1959	76.7	1953	990	1961	1,000	13.3	15.6[2]

[1] Number for total population (Asiatic, white and colored).
[2] Percent for 1959.
Source: United Nations: *Demographic Yearbook.*: World Health Organization: *Annual Epidemiological and Vital Statistics.*

TABLE 20.2 "International lists" of causes of death used by selected countries of low mortality (from 1950 to 1961)

COUNTRY	5TH REVISION 1938	6TH REVISION 1948	7TH REVISION 1955
United States	....	1950–57	1958–61
England and Wales	....	1950–57	1958–61
Scotland	....	1950–57	1958–61
Australia	....	1950–57	1958–61
New Zealand	....	1950–57	1958–61
Canada	....	1950–57	1958–61
Union of South Africa (white)	....	1950–60	
Ireland	....	1950–58	1959–61
Netherlands	....	1950–57	1958–61
Belgium	1950–51	1952–60	1961
France	....	1950–57	1958–61
Switzerland	1950	1951–61	
West Germany	1950–51	1952–61	
Denmark	1950	1951–57	1958–61
Norway	1950	1951–61	
Sweden	1950	1951–57	1958–61
Finland	1950	1951–61	
Portugal	1950–51	1952–61	
Italy	1950	1951–61	
Spain	1950	1951–60	

came marked late in the nineteenth century," and then observed further that "Along with the sharp average rise in Western life chances since the beginning of this century, there has been a remarkable decline in international differences within the region."[5] He went on to say that "Many of the trends in Western life chances over the last century are unrepeatable phenomena."

The persistence of mortality reductions in the countries of the West from 1930 to 1950 and a continuing decrease in mortality differences among them was noted by Spiegelman.[6] However, some evidence of a recent slackening in mortality improvement in this area was noted in a United Nations report which stated that "the countries which had previously reached the highest levels of ex-

TABLE 20.3 International codes used for causes of death

CAUSE OF DEATH	5TH REVISION	6TH AND 7TH REVISION
Tuberculosis	A 6, 7	B 1, 2
Malignant neoplasm	A 15[1]	B 18
Diabetes	A 18[2]	B 20
Cardiovascular-renal diseases	A 22, 24, 25, 33[1]	B 22, 24 to 29, 38
Influenza and pneumonia	A 10, 27	B 30, 31
Cirrhosis of liver	....	B 37
Motor vehicle accidents	A 42	BE 47
All other accidents	A 43	BE 48
Suicide	A 40	BE 49

[1]Not strictly comparable with 6th and 7th Revisions.
[2]Not comparable with 6th and 7th Revisions.

pectation of life . . . made some further gains during the postwar period, but these gains were relatively modest."[7] In particular, Moriyama commented on the leveling of the trend of crude death rates in the decade since 1950 in the Unite States and several other countries.[8] An insight into this situation for the countries of western Europe and of English-speaking countries elsewhere is provided by Table 20.4. For convenience, the annual death rates have been averaged for the periods 1950–53, 1954–57, and 1958–61.

For all but two of the twenty countries, the average annual crude death rate was lower in 1954–57 than in 1950–53. The mortality reductions amounted to as much as 8.5 percent for Spain, 7.2 percent for Canada, and 6.9 percent for Finland. The United States recorded a modest reduction of 2.7 percent. The Netherlands had a very small rise in its crude death rate, while that for West Germany was a little more substantial. Whereas only these two out of the twenty countries failed to show an improvement in crude death rates from 1950–53 to 1954–57, there were seven such countries in a comparison of 1954–57 with 1958–61. The countries with higher average annual crude death rates for 1958–61 than for 1954–57 included the United States, England and Wales, Scotland, the Union of South Africa, and the Scandinavian bloc comprising Denmark, Norway, and Sweden. There were, in addition, five other Western countries that showed smaller rates of mortality reduction from 1954–57 to 1958–61 than from 1950–53 to 1954–57.

The pattern of a reversal or slackening in the trend in the crude death rates in these countries may not be due wholly to an aging of their populations. Although an age adjustment of death rates for the United States and for England and Wales showed a continuing decline in mortality through 1961, the rates of reduction were smaller for the later periods of comparison. It is interesting to note that a greater rate of mortality improvement during the later period was recorded by the bloc of countries comprising the Netherlands, Belgium, France, Switzerland, and West Germany.

Notwithstanding these contrary trends among the twenty Western countries since 1950, the average of their crude death rates declined from 1950–53 to 1958–61, as did the standard deviations of these rates. In other words, the range of variation of crude death rates among Western countries is continuing to diminish. However, the coefficient of variation (the ratio of the standard deviation to the average) remained unchanged.

Cardiovascular-renal Diseases

The cardiovascular-renal diseases are by far the outstanding causes of death in the countries under review.[9] They account for about one-half of the deaths from all causes in the English-speaking countries, except for the Union of South Africa, where the proportion is not quite 40 percent. The Scandinavian countries, Finland, and Ireland attribute not quite half of their deaths to this category of diseases. Considerably smaller proportions— of the magnitude of 30 percent—are reported for Belgium, France, Portugal, and Spain, each of which had relatively high proportions of their deaths ascribed to senility and ill-defined or unknown causes.[10] An improvement in cause-of-death tabulations would undoubtedly reduce the wide variations in international comparisons of cardiovascular-renal mortality.[11] The use of crude rates rather than age-adjusted rates also affects comparability.

For most countries under review in Table 20.4, the course of crude cardiovascular-renal death rates from 1954–57 to 1958–61 was not as favorable as from 1950–53 to 1954–57.[12] Of the twenty countries under review, in twelve the average annual crude death rates for 1958–61 were higher than 1954–57. Crude death rates for the United States showed little change over the three periods of comparison; England and Wales experienced only a slight upward trend. However, age-adjusted death rates for the two countries show a continuing decline, but at a lessening rate. Thus aggregate crude death rates mask variations in trend which

TABLE 20.4 Crude death rates per 100,000 from all causes, cardiovascular-renal diseases, cancer, and diabetes for selected countries of low mortality (1950–53, 1954–57, 1958–61)*

All causes

COUNTRY	AVERAGE ANNUAL DEATH RATE PER 100,000			PERCENT CHANGE		
	1950–53	1954–57	1958–61	1950–53 to 1954–57	1954–57 to 1958–61	1950–53 to 1958–61
United States	962	936	941	−2.7	.5	−2.2
England and Wales	1,172	1,154	1,169	−1.5	1.3	−0.3
Scotland	1,216	1,197	1,209	−1.6	1.0	−0.6
Australia	945	899	861	−4.9	−4.2	−8.9
New Zealand	924	910	894	−1.5	−1.8	−3.2
Canada	884	820	788	−7.2	−3.9	−10.9
Union of South Africa †	857	852	876[a]	−0.6	2.8	2.2
Ireland	1,267	1,207	1,198	−4.7	−0.7	−5.4
Netherlands	751	758	756	.9	−0.3	.7
Belgium	1,221	1,209	1,181	−1.0	−2.3	−3.3
France	1,227	1,212	1,113	−5.1	−8.2	−12.8
Switzerland	1,017	1,008	951	−0.9	−5.7	−6.5
West Germany	1,068	1,101	1,100	3.1	−0.1	3.0
Denmark	902	899	935	−0.3	4.0	3.7
Norway	863	862	905	−0.1	5.0	4.9
Sweden	979	964	973	−1.5	.9	−0.6
Finland	988	920	892	−6.9	−3.0	−9.7
Portugal	1,186	1,145	1,058	−3.5	−7.6	−10.8
Italy	1,003	971	945	−3.2	−2.7	−5.8
Spain	1,037	949	870[a]	−8.5	−8.3	−16.1

Cardiovascular-renal diseases

COUNTRY	AVERAGE ANNUAL DEATH RATE PER 100,000			PERCENT CHANGE		
	1950–53	1954–57	1958–61	1950–53 to 1954–57	1954–57 to 1958–61	1950–53 to 1958–61
United States	488	483	488	−1.0	1.0	0
England and Wales	560	568	571	1.4	.5	2.0
Scotland	597	616	623	3.2	1.1	4.4
Australia	465	451	439	−3.0	−2.7	−5.6
New Zealand	468	437	429	−6.6	−1.8	−8.3
Canada	403	384	377	−4.7	−1.8	−6.5
Union of South Africa †	320	330	338[a]	3.1	2.4	5.6
Ireland	505	550	571	8.9	3.8	13.1
Netherlands	280	311	315	11.1	1.3	12.5
Belgium	465	357	345	−23.2	−3.4	−25.8
France	384	380	359	−1.0	−5.5	−6.5
Switzerland	437	439	416	.5	−5.2	−4.8
West Germany	364	403	407	10.7	1.0	11.8
Denmark	389	406	423	4.4	4.2	8.7
Norway	331	374	421	13.0	12.6	27.2
Sweden	443	461	473	4.1	2.6	6.8
Finland	384	402	419	4.7	4.2	9.1
Portugal	299	316	307	5.7	−2.8	2.7
Italy	364	394	396	8.2	.5	8.8
Spain	303	276	262[a]	−8.9	−5.1	−13.5

	Cancer						Diabetes					
United States	142	147	148	3.5	.7	4.2	16.4[b]	15.7	16.3	-4.3[g]	3.8	-0.6[g]
England and Wales	197	207	215	5.1	3.9	9.1	7.4	7.1	7.6	-4.1	7.0	2.7
Scotland	195	207	213	6.2	2.9	9.2	9.0	9.2	10.8	2.2	17.4	20.0
Australia	128	130	130	1.6	0	1.6	12.6	12.3	11.6	-2.4	-5.7	-7.9
New Zealand	149	146	143	-2.0	-2.1	-4.0	12.2	10.8	11.8	-11.5	9.3	-3.3
Canada	128	129	129	.8	0	.8	10.9	11.0	11.5	.9	4.5	5.5
Union of South Africa†	123	132	136*	7.3	3.0	10.6	8.5	9.0	9.6[a]	5.9	6.7	12.9
Ireland	148	161	167	8.8	3.7	12.8	6.9	7.1	8.2	2.9	15.5	18.8
Netherlands	150	157	166	4.7	5.7	10.7	11.3	12.8	14.7	13.3	14.8	30.1
Belgium	159	208	220	30.8	5.8	38.4	18.6	24.0	23.7	29.0	-1.3	27.4
France	176	185	195	5.1	5.4	10.8	11.2	12.0	12.1	7.1	.8	8.0
Switzerland	187	190	191	1.6	.5	2.1	14.4	13.5	13.9	-6.3	3.0	-3.5
West Germany	179	195	205	8.9	5.1	14.5	11.1	11.3	12.9	1.8	14.2	16.2
Denmark	174	194	209	11.5	7.7	20.1	5.2	6.3	7.3	21.2	15.9	40.4
Norway	156	160	163	2.6	1.9	4.5	6.6	6.8	7.9	3.0	16.2	19.7
Sweden	155	165	181	6.5	9.7	16.8	11.5	10.4	12.9	-9.6	24.0	12.2
Finland	143	148	153	3.5	3.4	7.0	6.1	6.5	9.9	6.6	52.3	62.3
Portugal	65	82	93	26.2	13.4	43.1	5.2	6.3	6.7	21.2	6.3	28.8
Italy	115	131	146	13.9	11.5	27.0	9.8	11.5	12.5	17.3	8.7	27.6
Spain	81	99	109[a]	22.2	10.1	34.6	6.3	7.5	8.0[a]	19.0	6.7	-27.0

*See Table 20.6 for footnote and sources.

become evident when both age and sex are taken into account. For example, over the period from 1950 to 1962, the death rates for the cardiovascular-renal diseases among white females in the United States tended downward at all age groups while those for white males declined for all age groups except 65–74 years, where the rates showed little change. The improving record at the ages below 65 may be attributed to the control of infections which have residual effects on the heart and kidneys, while the situation at the older ages may be due to better medical care and the effects of a rising standard of living.

Malignant Neoplasms (Cancer)

Cancer ranks second as a cause of death in the countries under review. It accounts for about one-sixth of all deaths in each of the English-speaking countries and also in France, Italy, Norway, and Finland. High proportions—in the neighborhood of one-fifth of total deaths—are noted for Sweden and the bloc comprising Denmark, the Netherlands, Belgium, Switzerland, and West Germany.[13]

Only one country—New Zealand—presented any evidence of a reduction in the crude death rate for cancer since 1950. On the whole, in Table 20.4, there is some indication of an improving situation with regard to cancer mortality, for in most countries the percent increase in death rates from 1954–57 to 1958–61 is not as great as from 1950–53 to 1954–57. There were just three countries—the Netherlands, France, and Sweden—with greater percent changes in death rates from the second to the third period of comparison than from the first to the second.[14]

A detailed picture of the trend of cancer mortality would require analysis according to the organ or site affected and would also take age and sex into account. Age-adjusted cancer rates for England and Wales show a slowly rising trend. For the United States, the average age-adjusted rate was at about the same levels in 1950–54 and 1958–61 but

at a somewhat higher level for the intervening period. A significant factor in the upward trend in cancer mortality in general is the sharply rising rate in the death rate for cancer of the respiratory system in the countries of the West.[15]

Improved diagnosis, a factor contributing to the recorded rise in total cancer mortality, may also be an element in the reduction of death rates from cancer of the digestive system, which results from a more accurate determination and certification of the primary site of the tumor. On the favorable side is a reduction in mortality from cancer of the female genital organs.

Diabetes Mellitus

Diabetes mellitus ranks among the ten leading causes of death in the United States, Canada, Australia, New Zealand, Scotland, Italy, the Scandinavian countries, and the bloc of countries including the Netherlands, Belgium, France, West Germany, and Switzerland. About 2 percent of the total deaths is attributed to diabetes in the United States, the Netherlands, and Belgium; for most other countries mentioned, the proportions are somewhat over 1 percent.[16] However, these figures understate the importance of diabetes, since many persons with the condition have their deaths ascribed to its complications, principally those of the circulatory system. A major change, which reduced the prominence of diabetes in mortality tabulations, was introduced with the Sixth Revision of the *International List*, which was accompanied by modification in the procedure for reporting and classifying causes of death. Since some countries did not begin to use the Sixth Revision until 1952, the trend comparisons begin with that year.

Fourteen of the twenty countries under review in Table 20.2 had higher average annual crude death rates from diabetes during 1954–57 than 1952–53. Moreover, all but two of the countries showed an increase in death rates between 1958–61 and 1954–57. Although these comparisons may indicate a generally worsening situation, some favorable aspects may become evident in a study of trends by age and sex. For example, in the United States, white females showed a steady reduction in diabetes mortality since 1950, while the rates for males remained fairly stable. However, the rates for nonwhites of of each sex rose rapidly.

Tuberculosis

For twelve countries of the Western world, the crude tuberculosis death rates for 1954–57 were about half those for 1950–53, as is evident in Table 20.5. Notable exceptions were New Zealand and Italy and the area comprising Belgium, West Germany, and Switzerland, where the rates were reduced by one-third. Apparently, progress has since slackened off, for in each country but New Zealand the percent declines in death rates 1954–57 to 1958–61 are not as great as those from 1950–53 to 1954–57. Notwithstanding the marked mortality reductions, tuberculosis still remains as an important health problem, ranking among the first ten causes of death for most countries under review. The exceptions include the United States, Australia, Denmark, and the Netherlands. As much as 3 percent of all deaths in Spain and 4 percent of all deaths in Portugal are still ascribed to tuberculosis.

Influenza and Pneumonia

Influenza and pneumonia rank fourth or fifth among the causes of death for practically all countries under review. Outbreaks of influenza occurred in western Europe during 1951, followed by a more general epidemic in 1957.[17] Except for New Zealand, Sweden, and Portugal, the averages of annual crude death rates for influenza and pneumonia shown in Table 20.5 were lower in 1954–57 than those for 1950–53. This favorable situation did not continue into the next period of comparison, 1958–61, when nine countries had higher average death rates than those for

1954–57 and seven had smaller rates of decline than those from 1950–53 to 1954–57. Outbreaks of influenza may affect adversely persons in a weakened state of health, such as those with a cardiovascular condition, and thus produce an elevation in the death rate for those causes.

Cirrhosis of the Liver

Certification of cirrhosis of the liver is of very uncertain quality in the countries of the Western world. Moreover, recorded deaths are hardly a measure of the health problem that the disease occasions. A study of multiple causes of death in the United States showed that in addition to the number of deaths with cirrhosis of the liver as the underlying cause, it was mentioned as contributory to another cause in a great many instances.[18]

Cirrhosis of the liver ranked seventh among the causes of death in France, a country with a high alcohol consumption per capita. It ranked ninth in Switzerland, West Germany, Portugal, and Italy, and tenth in the United States. For most countries under consideration in Table 20.5, the crude death rate for cirrhosis of the liver rose appreciably from 1950–53 to 1954–57. This situation improved between 1954–57 and 1958–61, when twelve countries showed smaller rates of increase in their mortality and an additional four had actual decreases.

Suicide

Suicide, a major cause of death in the countries of the West, reflects the impact of cultural, social, and economic influences. It ranked sixth among the causes in Switzerland, Denmark, and Sweden; seventh in West Germany and Finland; eighth in France; and tenth in the United States, England and Wales, Australia, New Zealand, Canada, and Belgium.

Recent (1958–61) suicide rates of about 20 per 100,000 population were recorded for Switzerland, Denmark, and Finland. Not far

TABLE 20.5 Crude death rates per 100,000 from tuberculosis, influenza and pneumonia, cirrhosis of the liver, and suicide for selected countries of low mortality (1950–53, 1954–57, 1958–61)*

Tuberculosis

COUNTRY	AVERAGE ANNUAL DEATH RATE PER 100,000			PERCENT CHANGE		
	1950–53	1954–57	1958–61	1950–53 to 1954–57	1954–57 to 1958–61	1950–53 to 1958–61
United States	17.7	8.9	6.2	−49.7	−30.3	−65.0
England and Wales	28.0	13.8	8.3	−50.7	−39.9	−70.4
Scotland	38.4	17.7	10.9	−53.9	−38.4	−71.6
Australia	16.2	7.9	5.0	−51.2	−36.7	−69.1
New Zealand	17.7	11.6	6.3	−34.5	−45.7	−64.4
Canada	20.2	8.6	5.1	−57.4	−40.7	−74.8
Union of South Africa†	17.1	8.3	7.4a	−51.5	−10.8	−56.7
Ireland	61.8	28.2	17.5	−54.4	−37.9	−71.7
Netherlands	14.2	6.1	3.4	−57.0	−44.3	−76.1
Belgium	34.2	23.8	16.9	−30.4	−29.0	−50.6
France	49.6	30.1	22.5	−39.3	−25.2	−54.6
Switzerland	30.0	20.2	13.7	−32.7	−32.2	−54.3
West Germany	31.6	20.0	16.0	−36.7	−20.0	−49.4
Denmark	11.7	5.9	4.2	−49.6	−28.8	−64.1
Norway	22.3	11.8	6.5	−47.1	−44.9	−70.9
Sweden	19.1	10.5	7.5	−45.0	−28.6	−60.7
Finland	69.9	39.7	27.6	−43.2	−30.5	−60.5
Portugal	108.2	61.6	47.2	−43.1	−23.4	−56.4
Italy	34.1	22.2	17.9	−34.9	−19.4	−47.5
Spain	73.8	34.7	26.3a	−53.0	−24.2	−64.4

Influenza and Pneumonia

COUNTRY	AVERAGE ANNUAL DEATH RATE PER 100,000			PERCENT CHANGE		
	1950–53	1954–57	1958–61	1950–53 to 1954–57	1954–57 to 1958–61	1950–53 to 1958–61
United States	31.3	29.2	32.8	−6.7	12.3	4.8
England and Wales	61.1	55.2	67.1	−9.7	21.6	9.8
Scotland	48.3	43.0	49.9	−11.0	16.0	3.3
Australia	36.3	34.9	32.8	−3.9	−6.0	−9.6
New Zealand	26.0	37.4	44.3	43.8	18.4	70.4
Canada	42.2	36.8	34.6	−12.8	−6.0	−18.0
Union of South Africa†	57.3	53.0	57.8a	−7.5	9.1	.9
Ireland	67.3	50.3	59.2	−25.3	17.7	−12.0
Netherlands	35.8	28.2	26.3	−21.2	−6.7	−26.5
Belgium	50.8	37.4	35.7	−26.4	−4.5	−29.7
France	82.0	61.7	46.9	−24.8	−24.0	−42.8
Switzerland	41.5	41.0	33.1	−1.2	−19.3	−20.2
West Germany	60.7	49.9	44.8	−17.8	−10.2	−26.2
Denmark	42.4	24.9	29.6	−41.3	18.9	−30.2
Norway	51.9	45.6	50.7	−12.1	11.2	−2.3
Sweden	40.9	47.2	47.9	15.4	1.5	17.1
Finland	56.8	52.3	37.7	−7.9	−27.9	−33.6
Portugal	83.6	87.3	85.8	4.4	−1.7	2.6
Italy	71.9	57.9	47.5	−19.5	−18.0	−33.9
Spain	91.4	71.5	57.4a	−21.8	−19.7	−37.2

	Cirrhosis of the Liver						Suicide					
United States	9.9	10.6	11.1	7.1	4.7	12.1	10.5	10.0	10.6	−4.8	6.0	1.0
England and Wales	2.5	2.6	2.8	4.0	7.7	12.0	10.3	11.6	11.4	12.6	−1.7	10.7
Scotland	3.2	3.9	4.3	21.9	10.3	34.4	5.4	7.4	8.2	37.0	10.8	51.9
Australia	4.7	4.7	4.8	0	2.1	2.1	10.1	11.0	11.5	8.9	4.5	13.9
New Zealand	3.0	3.1	2.3	3.3	−25.8	−23.3	9.8	9.1	9.1	−7.1	0	−7.1
Canada	4.6	5.2	5.9	13.0	13.5	28.3	7.4	7.3	7.5	−1.4	2.7	1.4
Union of South Africa†	7.5	6.0	6.1ᵃ	−20.0	1.7	−18.7	10.2	11.4	13.0ᵃ	11.8	14.0	27.5
Ireland	2.0	2.1	2.2	5.0	4.8	10.0	2.4	2.4	2.9	0	20.8	20.8
Netherlands	2.9	3.4	3.8	17.2	11.8	31.0	6.1	6.2	6.8	1.6	9.7	11.5
Belgium	6.0ᵇ	8.2	9.1	36.7	11.0	51.7	13.3	14.2	14.3	6.8	.7	7.5
France	21.7	30.4	28.0	40.1	−7.9	29.0	15.3	16.5	16.3	7.8	−1.2	6.5
Switzerland	11.6	13.4	12.4	15.5	−7.5	6.9	22.0	21.7	19.4	−1.4	−10.6	−11.8
West Germany	8.7	13.2	17.3	51.7	31.1	98.9	18.4	18.9	18.8	2.7	−0.5	2.2
Denmark	5.3	7.0	8.1	32.1	15.7	52.8	23.5	22.8	19.9	−3.0	−12.7	−15.3
Norway	2.9	3.6	3.9	24.1	8.3	34.5	7.1	7.4	7.0	4.2	−5.4	−1.4
Sweden	3.4	4.8	5.3	41.2	10.4	55.9	16.6	18.7	17.4	12.7	−7.0	4.8
Finland	2.3	3.3	3.4	43.5	3.0	47.8	16.6	20.8	20.6	25.3	−1.0	24.1
Portugal	18.7ᵇ	23.7	20.5	26.7	−13.5	9.6	10.0ᵉ	9.1ᵈ	8.8	−9.0	−3.3	−12.0
Italy	12.7	14.6	16.7	15.0	14.4	31.5	6.6	6.6	6.2	0	−6.1	−6.1
Spain	10.4	13.6	14.4ᵃ	30.8	5.9	38.5	5.9	5.5	5.2	−6.8	−5.5	−11.9

*See Table 20.6 for footnotes and sources.

behind were the rates for France, West Germany, and Sweden. Ireland had the lowest suicide record among the countries of the West, with a rate of less than 3 per 100,000. For the United States, England and Wales, and Australia, the suicide rates were somewhat over 10 per 100,000 population.

No geographic pattern of change in the suicide rate was evident in Table 20.5 from 1950–53 to 1954–57. On the other hand, from 1954–57 to 1958–61, practically all the West of Continental Europe experienced a reduction in suicide; the Netherlands and Belgium were exceptions. The record was not as favorable for the English-speaking countries, where only England and Wales showed a reduction, and this of small dimension.

Motor Vehicle Accidents

Mortality from motor vehicle accidents, like that for suicide, is influenced by both economic and social factors. For most countries of the West, the situation has been worsening since 1950, the notable exception being the United States, where the rates have traditionally been high. Besides the United States, motor vehicle fatality rates of more than 20 per 100,000 population were experienced by Canada, Australia, Union of South Africa, Switzerland, and West Germany. Generally, Table 20.6 shows that the percent increase in the motor vehicle fatality rate from 1954–57 to 1958–61 was not as great as that from 1950–53 to 1954–57.

The rapidly growing prosperity of the West has made the automobile increasingly accessible to its peoples. Under such circumstances, control of motor vehicle accidents depends not only upon the adequacy of well-constructed roads and regulations but also upon a knowledge of the personality characteristics and attitudes of drivers and pedestrians.

All Other Accidents

Accidents—all forms, including motor vehicle—rank fourth among the causes of death in most countries under review and almost as high in the others. In all countries, a decreasing proportion of the total accident fatalities is being accounted for by injuries other than those sustained by motor vehicles. This shift reflects the reductions in death rates from nonmotor vehicle accidents in most countries. Out of the twenty countries under review in Table 20.6, fourteen showed decreases in their death rates from accidents not involving motor vehicles from 1950–53 to 1954–57 and sixteen from 1954–57 to 1958–61. For half of the countries, the percent changes between the two later periods were more favorable than between the first two periods of comparison.

The control of accidents is a complex problem, since they occur in such diverse locations as public places, on the job, and in the home. The approaches and techniques for their control must necessarily be adapted to the way of life of each nation.

Conclusion

A more detailed insight into trends of death rates for specific causes in countries of low mortality would necessarily require study according to age and sex. The surface indications furnished by an examination of crude death rates since 1950 in the countries of western Europe and English-speaking countries elsewhere show that the rate of reduction in mortality from 1950–53 to 1954–57 did not continue into the period 1958–61 for many nations. Although the major element in this situation appears to be the cardiovascular-renal diseases, the failure to show improvement, either by a reduction in mortality or by a lessening rate of increase, was shared by influenza and pneumonia.

Within the broad categories of causes of death—such as the cardiovascular-renal diseases, cancer, and accidents—the more specific conditions or injuries may not show parallel trends; some may indeed be contrary. Ordinarily, it would be expected that

TABLE 20.6 Crude death rates per 100,000 from motor vehicle accidents and all other accidents for selected countries of low mortality (1950-1953, 1954-1957, 1958-1961)*

COUNTRY	Motor Vehicle Accidents						All Other Accidents					
	AVERAGE ANNUAL DEATH RATE PER 100,000			PERCENT CHANGE			AVERAGE ANNUAL DEATH RATE PER 100,000			PERCENT CHANGE		
	1950–53	1954–57	1958–61	1950–53 to 1954–57	1954–57 to 1958–61	1950–53 to 1958–61	1950–53	1954–57	1958–61	1950–53 to 1954–57	1954–57 to 1958–61	1950–53 to 1958–61
United States	23.9	23.0	21.1	− 3.8	− 8.3	− 11.7	37.4	33.4	30.6	− 10.7	− 8.4	− 18.2
England and Wales	9.8	10.9	13.6	11.2	24.8	38.8	23.3	24.9	24.7	6.9	− 0.8	6.0
Scotland	9.8	10.9	12.6	11.2	15.6	28.6	35.1	34.7	34.0	− 1.1	− 2.0	− 3.1
Australia	23.3	23.6	24.4	1.3	3.4	4.7	33.2	31.6	27.6	− 4.8	− 12.7	− 16.9
New Zealand	13.6	16.2	16.3	19.1	.6	19.9	29.0	32.2	30.2	11.0	− 6.2	4.1
Canada	19.3	20.7	20.9	7.3	1.0	8.3	38.3	36.2	32.4	− 5.5	− 10.5	− 15.4
Union of South Africa †	17.7	20.4	27.5ᵃ	15.3	34.8	55.4	30.5	29.4	30.2	− 3.6	2.7	− 1.0
Ireland	5.8	7.5	9.0	29.3	20.0	55.2	22.5	23.6	22.2	4.9	− 5.9	− 1.3
Netherlands	9.4	13.8	15.5	46.8	12.3	64.9	25.1	21.2	21.1	− 15.5	− 0.5	− 15.9
Belgium	11.5ᵉ	12.5	17.5	8.7	40.0	52.2	29.9ᵇ	40.2	36.0	34.4	− 10.4	20.4
France	9.7	18.6	18.7	91.8	.5	92.8	47.5	42.7	41.5	− 10.1	− 2.8	− 12.6
Switzerland	14.8	19.1	21.9	29.1	14.7	48.0	40.7	37.6	38.1	− 7.6	1.3	− 6.4
West Germany	15.5	23.0	24.4	48.4	6.1	57.4	33.7	34.2	31.7	1.5	− 7.3	− 5.9
Denmark	9.9	14.8	17.0	49.5	14.9	71.7	31.8	29.3	28.3	− 7.9	− 3.4	− 11.0
Norway	5.0	7.5	8.9	50.0	18.7	78.0	38.6	38.3	37.2	− 0.8	− 2.9	− 3.6
Sweden	10.5	13.0	14.3	23.8	10.0	36.2	28.1	26.8	28.5	− 4.6	6.3	1.4
Finland	8.3ᵇ	11.0	15.3	32.5	39.1	84.3	47.1ᵉ	38.9	36.2	− 17.4	− 6.9	− 23.1
Portugal	19.1ᶠ	6.9ᵈ	9.3	−63.9	34.8	− 51.3	....	32.3ᵈ	28.1	....	− 13.0	....
Italy	10.3	16.1	17.6	56.3	9.3	70.9	22.1	21.3	23.2	− 3.6	8.9	5.0
Spain	2.9	5.3	6.7ᵃ	82.8	26.4	131.0	24.3	22.5	21.3ᵃ	− 7.4	− 5.3	− 12.3

*Footnotes
+ White population
a) average for years 1958-60
b)   "   "   1952-53
c)   "   "   1950-51
d)   "   "   1955-57
e)   "   "   1951-53
f) year 1952
g) percent change based on years 1952-53

Sources
United Nations: *Demographic Yearbook*
World Health Organization: *Epidemiological and Vital Statistics* (Annual and Monthly)

the trend patterns for these more specific conditions or injuries would be similar in countries of low mortality, since they have have ample opportunity for ready communication of advances in medical knowledge and practice.

Notes

[1]"With Special Reference to the Situation and Recent Trends of Mortality in the World," *Population Bulletin of the United Nations, No. 6, 1962* (New York, 1963), p. 10.

[2]M. Spiegelman, "An International Comparison of Mortality Rates of the Older Ages," *Proceedings of the World Population Conference, Rome, 1954* (United Nations Department of Social and Economic Affairs [New York, 1955], I, 289). Data for Spain were then omitted since a population base was not available for the computation of rates.

Related papers by the author are "Recent Trends and Determinants of Mortality in Highly Developed Countries," *Proceedings of the 1955 Annual Conference* (Milbank Memorial Fund, New York), p. 51, and "Recent Trends in Mortality at the Older Ages in Countires of Low Mortality," *International Population Conference* (New York, 1961), I, 760.

[3]*Demographic Yearbook, 1951* (United Nations [New York, 1951],) chap. ii. See also I. M. Moriyama, T. R. Dawber, and W. B. Kannel, "Evaluation of Diagnostic Information Supporting Medical Certification of Cardiovascular Disease Deaths," presented at the Annual Meeting of the American Public Health Association, November 13, 1963.

[4]*Op. cit.*, p. 26.

[5]G. J. Stolnitz, "A Century of International Mortality Trends. I," *Population Studies* (July, 1955), IX, 24.

[6]*Op. cit.*

[7]*Op. cit.*, p. 10.

[8]I. M. Moriyama, "The Change in Mortality Trend in the United States" (National Center for Health Statistics [Washington: March, 1964]).

[9]*Epidemiological and Vital Statistics Report* (World Health Organization, Geneva), XVI, No. 2, 115 (1963), and XVII, No. 4, 170 (1964).

[10]*The American Journal of Cardiology* (September, 1962), X, No. 3, has a section on "Symposium on Epidemiology of Heart Diseases," with articles on the United States, Italy, Greece, the Philippines, China, Japan, and India.

[11]An example of the limitations on analysis introduced by problems of international comparability is given by J. Yerushalmy and H. E. Helleboe, "Fat in the Diet and Mortality from Heart Disease: A Methodologic Note," *New York State Journal of Medicine* (July 15, 1957), LVII, 2343.

[12]See Table 20.2 for countries which were using the Fifth Revision of the *International List* from 1950 to 1951. For those countries, there is not complete comparability in the death rates for the cardiovascular-renal diseases with the later years.

[13]For a general discussion see A. V. Chaklin, "Geographical Differences in the Distribution of Malignant Tumours," *Bulletin of the World Health Organization* (1962), XXVII, 337, and A. J. Phillips, "Geographic Aspects of Malignant Disease," *Journal of the Canadian Medical Association* (May 9, 1964), XC, 1095.

[14]Belgium apparently introduced a change in 1953 which radically affected its classification of causes of death, as evidenced by its sharp reduction in the crude death rate for the cardiovascular-renal diseases from 1950–53 to 1954–57 and the correspondingly sharp rises for cancer and diabetes.

[15]"Trends in Cancer Mortality for Selected Sites in 24 Countries, 1950–1959" (Department of Public Health, Tohoku University School of Medicine [Japan; July, 1963]); *Epidemiological and Vital Statistics Report* (World Health Organization [Geneva, 1963]), XVI, No. 7–8, 470.

[16]*Epidemiological and Vital Statistics Report* (World Health Organization [Geneva, 1964], XVII, No. 1–2); Entmacher and H. H. Marks, "Diabetes in 1964; A World Survey" (Fifth Congress of the International Diabetes Federation [Toronto; July 20, 1964]), to be published in *Diabetes*.

[17]In this connection see the section on "Global Epidemiology," *The American Review of Respiratory Diseases* (February, 1961), LXXXIII, No. 2.

[18]H. F. Dorn and I. M. Moriyama, "Uses and Significance of Multiple Cause Tabulations for Mortality Statistics," *American Journal of Public Health* (March, 1964), LIV, 400.

Selection Twenty-one

THE GEOGRAPHY OF DEATH IN THE UNITED STATES AND THE UNITED KINGDOM[1]

Malcolm A. Murray

This paper falls within the field of medical geography.[2] Its purpose is to illustrate the

Reproduced by permission from the *Annals of the Association of American Geographers*, Vol. 57, 1967, 301–314.

spatial pattern of apparent mortality variations in the conterminous United States and in England and Wales through the medium of maps. This is done for total deaths and for infant mortality. At this level of mapping any detailed interpretation of the patterns portrayed would be both inappropriate and presumptuous. For the most part it is preferable that the reader formulate his own interpretations, keeping in mind a number of pitfalls which will be considered. A second purpose is to point out some major difficulties in working with biostatistic data in the United States in comparison to the United Kingdom.

Geography of Death in the United Kingdom

In 1962 the author published an article which illustrated, for England and Wales, the areal mortality rate variations for total deaths and for a number of categories of causes of death for the ten year period 1948–1957.[3] Since then Howe has prepared an atlas of mortality for the United Kingdom eclipsing all former efforts in medical geography for that area.[4] It illustrates mortality variations for fourteen different causes of death separately for males and females. Within the limits of its detail, this atlas has admirably fulfilled its purpose of showing the spatial patterns of variations in disease mortality.

It is apparent that for many years to come the United Kingdom offers the best laboratory for those interested in the biostatistical approach to medical geography. In relation to its size it contains enough people and consequently enough deaths to give considerable significance to studies concerned with areal mortality variations. In addition, the recording of mortality and cause of death is as accurate as can be found anywhere, and the Registrar-General's Office provides data in a convenient age and sex adjusted-death-rate form. The country is subdivided into numerous administrative units, and the mortality data can therefore easily be plotted on a base of considerable detail. Finally, in comparison to some other developed countries, the population mobility is contained enough so that relationships between disease and environment may be assessed to some degree.

The result is that maps present fairly reliable patterns of death rate variations. The

association between these variations and other distributions, both cultural and physical, is readily apparent to those familiar with the geography of the United Kingdom. Such maps are almost embarrassing in the degree to which they strongly support our intuitive preconceptions as to what the areal mortality differences should be. Referral to works previously cited should support this contention.[5]

DEATH RATE VARIATIONS FROM ALL CAUSES IN ENGLAND AND WALES

It is, of course, difficult to generalize accurately about the areal pattern of death-rate variation, since the rate varies greatly from one cause of death to another. But if we consider deaths from all causes, Figure 21.1 reveals the broader mortality patterns for England and Wales rather well.[6] This map, although similar to one published in a previous article by the author, has been updated. It represents the most detailed and up to date mortality map for England and Wales available in published form. It is included here, not only for its own interest, but also for purposes of comparison with the total mortality map of the United States (Fig. 21.3).

With some exceptions, the rates tend to be distinctly higher in the industrialized, exploitive, and densely populated areas; for example, the Lancashire-Yorkshire manufacturing area, the Birmingham and Black Country district, southern Wales, Durham, and Tyneside, and more isolated examples such as Stoke-on-Trent. The London area is about average. The more prosperous agricultural counties of the south and east generally experience lower rates than the farming and grazing counties of the north and west. On a broad basis, northern England, the Pennine area, and most of Wales experience higher rates than southern and eastern England. It is not so easy to make generalizations for Scotland, but here too the higher rates tend to be associated with the more highly industrialized and urbanized areas, and particularly the Glasgow district.[7]

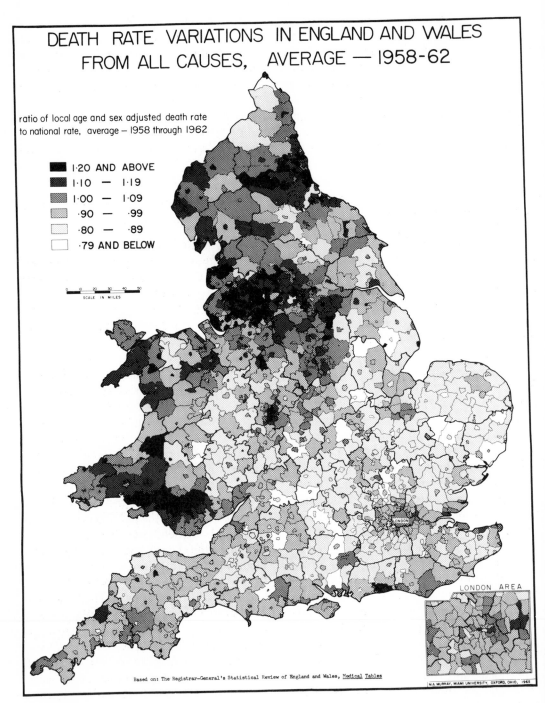

Figure 21.1

The reader will notice that the total death rate map for England and Wales (Fig. 21.1) is not directly comparable with the total death rate map for the United States (Fig. 21.3). In the case of the United Kingdom a ratio system is used in relation to a national norm of *1*. A ratio above *1* is higher than the national norm and a ratio below *1* is lower.[8] The rates for the United States are portrayed on the more usual base of deaths per thousand population. The different methods used were conditioned by the form of the available data. This factor also accounts for a five year average being used for England and Wales, whereas a ten year average is employed for the United States. For the purposes of this study it is not exigent that the span of years coincide.

The rates portrayed in Figure 21.1 and Figure 21.3 are adjusted for age and sex variations from place to place within the respective countries. For all maps in this study the data employed were based on deaths by place of residence.

At this point it should be noted that the total mortality rate is apparently somewhat higher for England and Wales (12.2 per 1000 population) than for the U.S. (9.6 per 1000 population). Infant mortality rates on the other hand, are lower for England and Wales (21 per 1000 live births) than for the U.S. (25 per 1000 live births). The figures quoted are for 1963.[9]

INFANT MORTALITY VARIATIONS IN ENGLAND AND WALES

Infant mortality rates have long been considered an excellent measure of the level of living conditions. Figure 21.2 seems to substantiate such an assumption. In the case of England and Wales, infant mortality runs two and a half times higher in the lowest social class than in the highest.[10] Since there are proportionally more people in the lower socioeconomic groups in the north and west than in the south and east, this map properly reveals that fact, as indicated by the corresponding infant mortality variations.[11] The areal pattern displayed in Figure 21.2 corresponds fairly closely with the pattern of mortality variations from all causes (Fig. 21.1).

Data for construction of the infant mortality map, however, were incomplete. For a number of administrative units data were not available for all of the five years (1958 through 1962), and in such cases it was necessary to employ an average based on less than five years. For this reason Figure 21.2 is statistically less reliable and therefore a less sensitive indicator of areal variations in level-of-living conditions than the total mortality map (Fig. 21.1).

For the most part, however, biostatistical data in the United Kingdom are fairly accurate and available in a form which the researcher can compile easily and map meaningfully.

Geography of Death in the United States

In contrast, the biostatistic approach in the United States faces some apparently insurmountable obstacles. Even under the best circumstances the accurate recording of mortality data is highly questionable. Several important factors operate against optimum success. One of these is the problem of implementing strict adherence to standard procedures in a country of such areal and socioeconomic magnitude, especially when local control is so widely variable and is not ameliorated by any sustained federal jurisdiction. Many coroners and health officers do not have the benefits of medical training, and death records suffer accordingly. It is apparent that in some sections of the country many deaths are not recorded at all. Yet no nation-wide test has ever been undertaken to determine the completeness of death registration in the United States.[12] Extreme population mobility imposes further difficulties.

These problems have been so discouraging that until now no individual, group, or agency has attempted the portrayal of areal variations of mortality rates in the United States on any kind of detailed basis. It seems however, that some attempt must be made, if only to indicate the level of sensitivity of such an approach. Even this author, however, is not naive enough to attempt this for categories of causes of deaths. Previous experience has indicated that U.S. vital statistics for deaths from specific disease groups are hopelessly inadequate at the national level.

DEATH RATE VARIATIONS FROM ALL CAUSES IN THE UNITED STATES

Expediency required that initial efforts be restricted to mapping mortality rates from all causes (Fig. 21.3), and the unit chosen was the county. Many hazards are thus elimi-

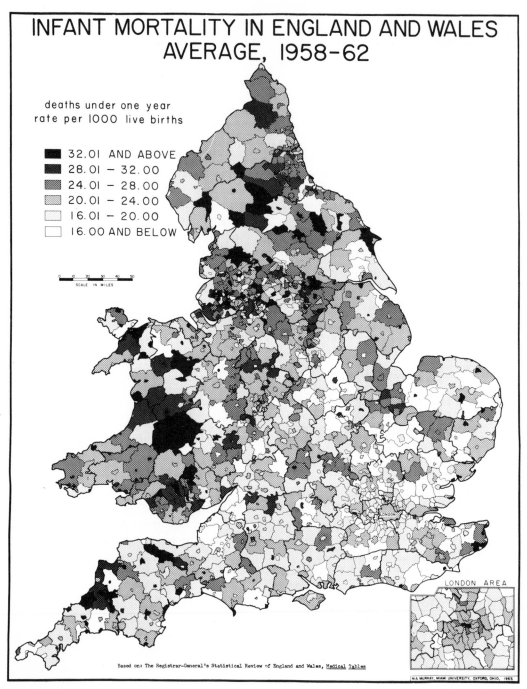

INFANT MORTALITY IN ENGLAND AND WALES
AVERAGE, 1958–62

deaths under one year
rate per 1000 live births

- ■ 32.01 AND ABOVE
- ■ 28.01 – 32.00
- ▦ 24.01 – 28.00
- ▨ 20.01 – 24.00
- ▢ 16.01 – 20.00
- ▢ 16.00 AND BELOW

0 10 20 30 40 50
SCALE IN MILES

LONDON AREA

Based on: The Registrar-General's Statistical Review of England and Wales, Medical Tables

M.A. MURRAY, MIAMI UNIVERSITY, OXFORD, OHIO, 1965

Figure 21.2

nated, but certain obstacles still prevail.

Mortality data for the administrative units of the United States are recorded as absolute figures and not as death rates. Thus for each of the 3,110 counties it was necessary to average the total number of deaths for the ten-year period 1950 through 1959.[13] A ten year average is admittedly arbitrary, but it is conditioned by several factors. Ten years include enough raw data to ensure a fairly

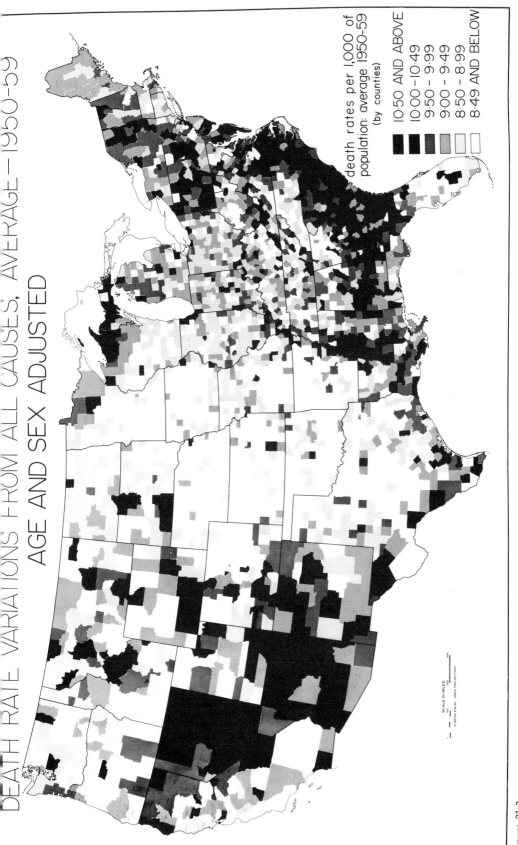

DEATH RATE VARIATIONS FROM ALL CAUSES, AVERAGE–1950-59
AGE AND SEX ADJUSTED

death rates per 1,000 of
population: average 1950-59
(by counties)

10·50 AND ABOVE
10·00-10·49
9·50 - 9·99
9·00 - 9·49
8·50 - 8·99
8·49 AND BELOW

SCALE IN MILES

ALBERS EQUAL AREA PROJECTION

Figure 21.3

high degree of statistical reliability. The span from 1950 to 1959 allows optimum use of decennial population figures for conversion of raw mortality data to death rates. After determining the intercensus population the crude death rate was computed. Since the census provides the age and sex structure for each county it was then possible to standardize for variations in age and sex composition from the national norm.[14] Finally, death rate categories and visual symbolization were selected and portrayed on a map.

Although this task is more formidable than it is sophisticated, it would have been an interminable procedure without the assistance of modern computers. The resulting map (Fig. 21.3), hopefully, is well conceived both statistically and visually. The reader is reminded that the data used for this map are based on deaths by place of residence in addition to being adjusted for areal variations in age and sex composition.

It is preferred that the observer formulate his own interpretations of the pattern portrayed, keeping in mind certain pitfalls. For many counties the portrayal is based on questionable data. Parts of the southern Appalachian region present a case in point. Many measures of level of living for this area indicate the poor socio-economic circumstances which prevail in the region, and it seems reasonable to assume that this situation would be reflected by death rates somewhat above the average. Figure 21.3, however, portrays it as a low death rate region. One is inclined to suspect that many deaths in this area are not recorded.

In large portions of the country, excessive population mobility tends to mask cause-and-effect relationships. In addition the map is visually misleading owing to wide variations in the relationship between county size and population density. Note, for example, the visual impression created by the large, sparsely populated counties of the west. This factor obviously reduces the statistical reliability for large portions of the western United States. By contrast many of the small but densely urbanized counties of the northeast, such as the New York metro-politan area, are inadequately portrayed. This, of course, is a common problem with choropleth maps. There may be other problems which are less obvious but of marked importance.

Any interpretation of the mortality pattern is obviously premature, and yet speculation is irresistible. It even may be permissible if we realize that the sensitivity limits of the mapping approach at this scale, and with the type of data available, allows for only cursory cause-and-effect conclusions.

Circumstantial evidence certainly indicates an apparent and strong association between high mortality rates and those areas of traditionally poor socio-economic circumstances in the United States. Areas of large minority group populations, such as Indian reservations, Spanish-American districts, and most particularly, the high-proportion Negro areas of the South, portray rates higher than the average.

Some of the highly urbanized counties in the Northeast also reveal above average rates, partly because of their attraction for minority and deprived groups whose longevity is jeopardized.[15] Exceptions such as Washington D.C., where the apparent rates are well below average, unaccountably prevail.

In contrast the lowest rates definitely correspond with the Great Plains and the adjacent better agricultural zones. This seems to substantiate the observation that in our culture, other factors being equal, life in rural areas and in urban places of limited industry and activity is a favorable condition for longevity.[16]

Other contrasts are readily seen but should be viewed with caution. The problem with statistical reliability in the West has already been discussed. Certain areas of Pennsylvania and New York state portray apparently high rates simply because they record their deaths in contrast, for example, to many counties in the central and southern Appalachians which may be quite perfunctory in record keeping.

In spite of obvious failings, the map does reveal a death rate pattern of some significance for the United States.

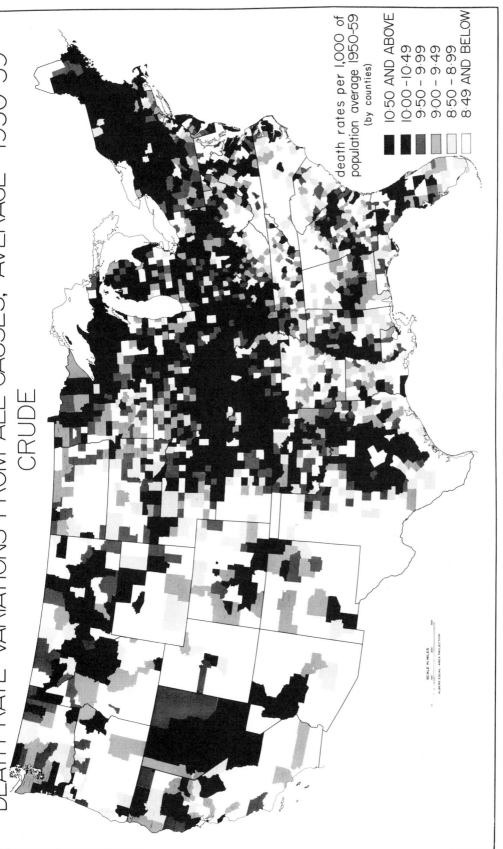

DEATH RATE VARIATIONS FROM ALL CAUSES, AVERAGE — 1950-59
CRUDE

death rates per 1,000 of
population average 1950-59
(by counties)

10·50 AND ABOVE
10·00 - 10·49
9·50 - 9·99
9·00 - 9·49
8·50 - 8·99
8·49 AND BELOW

SCALE IN MILES
ALBERS EQUAL AREA PROJECTION

Figure 21.4

CRUDE DEATH RATE VARIATIONS IN THE UNITED STATES

Figure 21.4 is included as much for interest as for value. Crude death rates reveal the actual mortality situation within the limits imposed by the accuracy of biostatistic data. The data for Figure 21.4 are not adjusted for areal variations in age and sex composition of the population. Naturally the rates will be higher in those areas containing a high proportion of older people and/or males.[17]

The age composition in the Midwest and the Northeast is considerably older than that of the South,[18] and this is reflected by the higher crude death rates for the former regions. Adjusting for age and sex composition variations helps to place all areas in a truer perspective, as a comparison between Figures 21.3 and 21.4 reveal.

Adjustment for variations in racial composition might also be done since the death rate of non-whites is higher than that of whites.[19] In this procedure, however, severe problems of statistical meaningfulness arise which cancel out any benefits derived. Race adjustment, therefore, was not incorporated into the production of Figure 21.3.

INFANT DEATH RATE VARIATIONS IN THE UNITED STATES

Figure 21.5 displays infant death rates for the year 1959.[20] Its construction was less complicated because data for only one year were employed and age and sex adjustment was not necessary. Presumably it is statistically less reliable.

In some ways, however, the pattern it displays is more definitive than that of the total mortality map. Note, for example, the more uniform gradation in intensity from the Northeast and Midwest toward the South. The large, low density gap in the central and southern Appalachians, which is so evident in the total mortality map (Fig. 21.3), is lacking in Figure 21.5. It may be that the record kept on infant deaths is better than that for total deaths. If this is the case, the map properly reflects, more accurately, the gradation in level-of-living conditions.[21]

Of some concern to public health experts is the relatively poor infant mortality position of the United States in relation to other countries. An increasing number of countries have been experiencing lower rates than the United States and the gap between the rate for the United States and the figures for these countries has widened.[22]

The general similarity in areal pattern between infant death rates and total death rates for the United States is evident. To a degree, at least, these map patterns do correspond with other criteria which reflect level-of-living variations. We may conclude that in spite of the failings of biostatistics in this country they are nonetheless of some value.

Conclusion

The maps constructed from the vital statistics of the two countries emphasize the consequent advantage that the distributional technique has in the case of the United Kingdom. Hopefully the United States can greatly improve its biostatistical data in the years ahead. Indeed a considerable advance has been made in this regard with the implementation of the National Health Survey.[23]

As with other systematic divisions of the field, the special contribution of medical geography is the mapping technique and the interpretations which potentially it allows. This study is meant to illustrate how the medical geographer can effectively use maps for pattern portrayal within the limits of the accuracy of the available data.

At the national scale the sensitivity limits of such an approach must be recognized and there can be no simple explanation of apparent mortality patterns. Such maps as these are designed to focus on areas wherein detailed studies may be of benefit in discovering or substantiating cause-and-effect relationships, particularly with respect to specific causes of death. Increasingly medical geographers are turning their attention to this task.

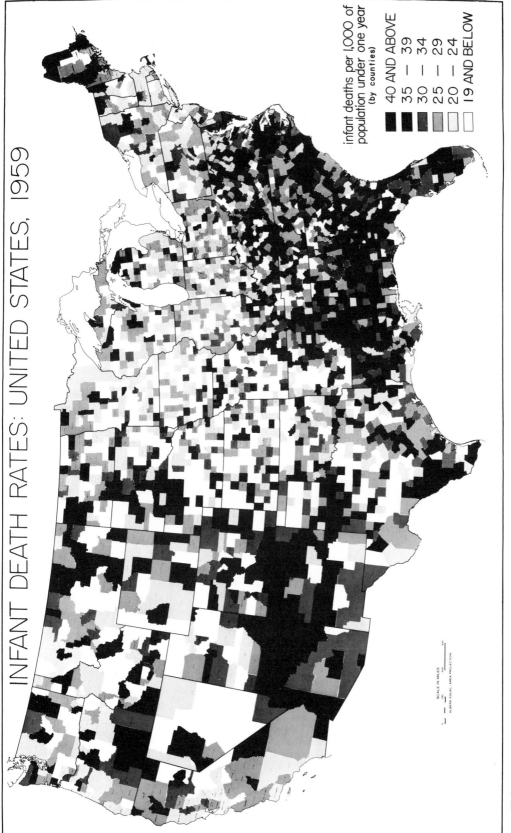

INFANT DEATH RATES: UNITED STATES, 1959

infant deaths per 1,000 of
population under one year
(by counties)

40 AND ABOVE
35 — 39
30 — 34
25 — 29
20 — 24
19 AND BELOW

SCALE IN MILES

ALBERS EQUAL-AREA PROJECTION

Figure 21.5

Notes

[1]This study was supported by a research grant from Miami University, Oxford, Ohio. A travel grant from the Social Science Research Council allowed the author to read a part of this paper at the International Geographical Congress in London, 1964.

[2]The article makes no attempt to discuss the philosophy of medical geography. For the interested reader an excellent discussion of medical geography as a discipline may be found in the first seven chapters of J. M. May, *The Ecology of Human Disease* (New York: MD Publications, Incorporated, 1958). This paper is not designed to be bibliographic in nature. Any reader, however, who is interested in acquiring a basic bibliography on medical geography in general or on more specific matters discussed in this article, is invited to correspond with the author.

[3]M. A. Murray, "The Geography of Deaths in England and Wales," *Annals*, Association of American Geographers, Vol. 52 (1962), pp. 130–49. See also G. M. Howe, "The Geography of Death in England and Wales, 1960," *The Lancet* (April 13, 1963), pp. 818–20.

[4]G. M. Howe on behalf of the Royal Geographical Society, *National Atlas of Disease Mortality in the United Kingdom* (London: Thomas Nelson and Sons Ltd., 1963). For a review of this work see M. A. Murray, "Medical Geography in the United Kingdom," *Geographical Review*, Vol. 44 (1964), pp. 582–84.

[5]See maps in references cited in footnotes 3 and 4.

[6]The data for the construction of Figure 21.1 and Figure 21.2 were derived from: Registrar-General, *Statistical Review of England and Wales*, for 1958 through 1962, Part 1, "Medical Tables" (London: Her Majesty's Stationery Office, 1960–1964).

[7]For Scotland refer to maps on pages 22 and 24 of Howe, *op. cit.*, footnote 4.

[8]The method of computing the age and sex adjusted death rate ratio is explained in: Registrar-General, *Statistical Review of England and Wales*, 1954, Part 3, "Commentary" (London: Her Majesty's Stationery Office, 1957). See especially pages 30, 32, and 57 of this volume.

[9]Office of Population Research, Princeton University; and Population Association of America, Inc., *Population Index*, Vol. 30, No. 3 (1964), Tables 2 and 3.

[10]Registrar-General, *Statistical Review of England and Wales*, 1951, "Text Volume" (London: Her Majesty's Stationery Office, 1954), p. 207.

[11]There are several reasons for this association. The north and west experience higher birth rates, and the more rapid transmission of infectious disease from one child to another in crowded households takes its toll. Moreover, inadequate prenatal care is common, and low income families often do not seek medical assistance as promptly as they should. Finally, maternal care may be less efficient and amenities such as proper sanitation tend to be poor. See B. Benjamin, *Elements of Vital Statistics* (London: George Allen and Unwin, 1959), p. 234.

[12]Personal letter of September 9, 1964 from Anders S. Lunde, Acting Chief, Mortality and Statistics Branch, Division of Vital Statistics, and Welfare.

[13]The mortality data for constructing Figures 21.3, 21.4, and 21.5 were obtained from U.S. Department of Health, Education, and Welfare, Public Health Service, National Office of Vital Statistics, *Vital Statistics of the United States*, for 1950 through 1959, Volume 11 (Washington: U.S. Government Printing Office, 1953–1961).

[14]Age and sex composition and population data for each county were extracted from U.S. Department of Commerce, Bureau of the Census, *United States Census of Population, General Population Characteristics*, for 1950 and 1960, Final Report PC (1) (Washington: U.S. Government Printing Office, 1951 and 1961).

[15]In the United States, the estimated average longevity for non-whites (63.6. years in 1963) is 6.3 years less than that of whites (69.9 years in 1963). See sources cited in footnote 16.

[16]Quite aside from the possible effects of stress in the megalopolis, there is much to indicate that longevity is jeopardized by air pollution, an environmental factor which the metropolitan dweller cannot easily escape. See, for example, H. F. Dorn, "The Increasing Mortality from Chronic Respiratory Diseases," *Biometrics*, Vol. 18 (1962), p. 260; F. J. Massey, et al., "Air Pollution and Mortality in Two Areas of Los Angeles County," *Biometrics*, Vol. 18 (1962), p. 263. In the United Kingdom, the strong association between high mortality rates and air pollution has been recognized for many years.

[17]Since the latter part of the nineteenth century the average life span for males in the United States has been significantly less than that of females, and the gap is widening. Whereas in 1900 the average life span for females was two years longer than for males, by 1963 it was 6.8 years longer. For 1963 the estimated average length of life for males was 66.6 years and for females 73.4 years. See U.S. Department of Health, Education, and Welfare, Public Health Service, National Center for Health Statistics, *Vital Statistics of the United States*, 1963, Volume 2, Section 5, "Life Tables" (Washington: U.S. Government Printing Office, 1964), pp. 5–12, Tables 5–6.

[18]For example, the 1960 median age in the Middle Atlantic States (New York, New Jersey, Pennsylvania) was 32.6 years, in contrast to 27.5 years for the South Atlantic States. See U.S. Department of Commerce, Bureau of the Census, *Statistical Abstract of the United States*, 1964 (Washington: U.S. Government Printing Office, 1964), p. 23, Table 18.

[19]In 1963 the estimated average length of life for "non-whites" and "whites" was 63.6 years and 70.8 years respectively.

[20]This map is adapted from one in an unpublished M.A. thesis by Patricia S. Cortright, *Infant Death Rates in the United States*, 1959, Miami University, Oxford, Ohio (1963), p. 2. The map was constructed on the basis of the number of deaths under one year of age in relation to each thousand of the population under one year of age. Thus the designation "infant death rates" rather than "infant mortality" is used. The latter term (as used in Fig. 21.2 for example) refers to deaths under one year of age in relation to each thousand live births. For purposes of this study the results obtained by the

two methods are essentially comparable.

[21]There is recent evidence, however, that infant mortality is no longer the extremely sensitive index of differences in socio-economic status that it was in the past. See E. G. Stockwell, "Infant Mortality and Socio-Economic Status," *Milbank Memorial Fund Quarterly*, Vol. 40 (1962), pp. 101–11.

[22]S. Shapiro and I. M. Moriyama, "International Trends in Infant Mortality and Their Implications for the United States," *American Journal of Public Health*, Vol. 53 (1963), pp. 747–60.

[23]The National Health Survey was established by Congress in 1956. It is a program of the National Center for Health Statistics, Public Health Service. From the viewpoint of the medical geographer the two most important aspects of it are the Health Interview Survey and the Health Examination Survey. These continuing surveys are based on sample population interviews and examinations in different parts of the United States. The information derived is recorded systematically, accurately, and in detail. Publications and data pertaining to the Survey began to appear in the early 1960's. For an interesting account of some of the findings of the Survey to date see F. E. Linder, "The Health of the American People," *Scientific American*, Vol. 214, No. 6 (1966), pp. 21–29.

A SELECTED SUPPLEMENTARY BIBLIOGRAPHY FOR PART 5

Adelman, I., and Morris, C., "A Quantitative Study of Social and Political Determinants of Fertility," *Economic Development and Cultural Change*, Vol. 14, 1966, pp. 129–157.

Carleton, R., "Fertility Trends and Differentials in Latin America," *Milbank Memorial Fund Quarterly*, Vol. 43, 1965, pp. 15–29.

Cook, R. C., *Human Fertility: The Modern Dilemma*, New York: W. Sloan Associates, 1951.

Davis, K., "Institutional Patterns Favoring High Fertility in Under-Developed Areas," *Eugenics Quarterly*, Vol. 11, 1955, pp. 33–39.

Freedman, R., Whelpton, P. K., and Campbell, P. K., *Family Planning, Sterility, and Population*. New York: McGraw-Hill Book Company, 1959.

Gille, H., "An International Survey of Recent Fertility Trends," National Bureau of Economic Research, *Demographic and Economic Change in Developed Countries* (Pt. 1). Princeton, N.J.: Princeton University Press, 1960 pp. 17–35.

Hauser, P. M., and Kitagawa, E. M., "Social and Economic Mortality Differentials in the United States, 1960: Outline of a Research Project," *Proceedings of the Social Statistics Section:* 1960, Washington, D.C., 1960.

Heenan, L. D. B., "Rural-Urban Distribution of Fertility in South Island, New Zealand," *Annals of the Association of American Geographers*, Vol. 57, 1967, pp. 713–735.

Horst, O., "The Specter of Death in a Guatemalan Highland Community," *The Geographical Review*, Vol. 57, 1967, pp. 151–167.

Morris, J., "New Patterns in U.S. Fertility," *Population Bulletin*, Vol. 20, 1964, pp. 113–117.

Murray, M., "The Geography of Death in England and Wales," *Annals of the Association of American Geographers*, Vol. 53, 1963, pp. 130–147.

Spiegelman, M., "Mortality Trends and Prospects and Their Implications," *The Annals of the American Academy of Political and Social Science*, Vol. 315, 1958, pp. 25–33.

U.S. National Center for Health Statistics, *The Change in Mortality Trends in the United States*, Vital and Health Statistics Series, No. 1, Washington, D.C., 1964.

PART SIX

SPATIAL PATTERNS AND POPULATION FLOWS

INTRODUCTION

The most complex component of population change and growth is migration, or the flow of people from place to place. Any attempt to define migration inevitably leads to a set of definitions or a typology based on such criteria as change of residence, journey to work, types of boundaries crossed, and many others. The importance of each movement is obvious also in that it provides an important network for the diffusion of ideas and information, indicates symptoms of social and economic change, and can be regarded as a human adjustment to economic, environmental, and social problems. In addition, migration is the component of change most difficult to project because of the uncertainty associated with the decision to change one's place of residence, not to mention the unavailability and unreliability of data.

The process of migration should be of particular interest to the geographer because of its inherently spatial character. Questions of differential rates of movement between individual source areas and places of destination, changing migration networks, spatial perception of opportunities, and many others are, or should be, of major importance to the economic, social, and cultural geographer.

The group of articles in this section are intended to point up some of the principal aspects of migration as they have been treated by researchers specifically interested in the spatial dimension. The first article by

Lee ("A Theory of Migration") attempts to provide a general theoretical framework for the spatial movements of the populations. The migration process is divided into four parts. The first two of these are the factors related to the area of origin and those related to the destination. Origin and destination are, of course, very different in that the former is familiar to residents (or potential migrants), and therefore the effect of inertia is significant. Individuals, on the other hand, rarely have complete information or an accurate perception of possible destinations. As Lee indicates, migration may be the result of a comparison of advantages and disadvantages associated with origin and destination as perceived by the migrant, an admittedly complex process to unravel. The third part of Lee's schema deals with intervening obstacles such as distance, physical barriers, and boundaries. The final component is a set of personal factors, which ties together a number of variables such as intelligence and rationality of individuals, their perceptions and stage in the life cycle. Such a conceptualization of the migration process leads to the formulation of a series of hypotheses related to the volume of migration, migration streams, and characteristics of migrants.

Wolpert ("Behavioral Aspects of the Decision to Migrate") proposes a model of migration based on behavior theory and the premise that most migration models emphasize distance and ecological characteristics of place rather than the behavioral parameters of the migrants. Three basic concepts of migration behavior are brought together to form the model: (1) place utility, in which migration is viewed as an adaptation to perceived change in one's surrounding: (2) field theory approach to search behavior, which relates to the potential migrant's sources of information about his action space; and (3) a life-cycle approach to threshold formation.

Kirk's study ("Major Migrations Since World War II") is a discussion of problems of forced migration, free migration, and overseas movements of European and Asian populations in the postwar period. In addition, the significance of internal migration, especially in the United States, is assessed. This world view of movement captures some of the major trends, such as migration from less to more developed areas, from smaller to larger population centers, and highlights some of the important problems of recent population displacement in Asia.

The analysis of Soviet migration by four Soviet geographers (Pokshishevskiy et al., "On Basic Migration Patterns") is a regional study selected for its Leninist-Marxist viewpoint. The emphasis on population as one of the productive forces and its importance in economic planning clearly reflect this viewpoint. The study examines interregional and intraregional trends in migration from prerevolutionary periods to the present. Attention is focused upon recent migration patterns in the Soviet Union, and migration balances are calculated for regions of the country by a residual method. Most interesting is the negative migration balance for Siberia and the Far East which the authors attribute, in part, to poor living conditions in these areas.

The final selection (Akers's "Immigration Data and National Population Estimates for the United States") is concerned with sources of immigration data and methods of estimation of immigration for the United States. Akers reviews the importance of immigration information as a source of error in population estimates and demonstrates the relevance of such data in the determination of ethnic changes, population growth, and policy formation. The author attempts also to measure unrecorded immigration as well as the age, sex, and race of immigrants.

Selection Twenty-two

A THEORY OF MIGRATION*

Everett S. Lee

It was a remark of Farr's to the effect that migration appeared to go on without any definite law that led Ravenstein to present his celebrated paper on the laws of migration before the Royal Statistical Society on March 17, 1885.[1] This paper was based upon the British Census of 1881, but in 1889 Ravenstein returned to the subject with data from more than twenty countries.[2] Finding corroboration for his earlier views in this broader investigation, he also entitled his second paper, "The Laws of Migration," though he noted that it was ambitiously headed and warned that "laws of population, and economic laws generally, have not the rigidity of physical laws." An irreverent critic, Mr. N. A. Humphreys, immediately retorted that "After carefully reading Mr. Ravenstein's former paper, and listening to the present one, [I arrived] at the conclusion that migration was rather distinquished for its lawlessness than for having any definite law."[3] Mr. Stephen Bourne's criticism was less devastating but logically more serious: "that although Mr. Ravenstein had spoken of 'Laws of Migration,' he had not formulated them in such a categorical order that they could be criticized."[4] Nevertheless, Ravenstein's papers have stood the test of time and remain the starting point for work in migration theory.

As found in the first paper and extended or amended in the second, Ravenstein's laws are summarized in his own words below. The first five of these items include the laws

as they are usually quoted, while items 6 and 7, though taken from the general conclusions of his second paper, are not ordinarily included. This, however, is due more to Ravenstein's way of numbering the laws and to his somewhat tentative statement of the dominance of the economic motive than to his own estimate of the importance of his conclusions.

1   *Migration and distance.* (*a*) "[T]he great body of our migrants only proceed a short distance" and "migrants enumerated in a certain center of absorption will . . . grow less [as distance from the center increases]" (I, pp. 198–99).[5]

(*b*) "Migrants proceeding long distances generally go by preference to one of the great centers of commerce and industry" (I, p. 199).

2   *Migration by stages.* (*a*) "[T]here takes place consequently a universal shifting or displacement of the population, which produces 'currents of migration,' setting in the direction of the great centers of commerce and industry which absorb the migrants" (I, p. 198).

(*b*) "The inhabitants of the country immediately surrounding a town of rapid growth flock into it; the gaps thus left in the rural population are filled up by migrants from more remote districts, until the attractive force of one of our rapidly growing cities makes its influence felt, step by step, to the most remote corner of the kingdom" (I, p. 199).

(*c*) "The process of dispersion is the inverse of that of absorption, and exhibits similar features" (I, p. 199).

3   *Stream and counterstream.* "Each main current of migration produces a compensating counter-current" (I, p. 199). In modern terminology, stream and counterstream have been substituted for

*Presented at the Annual Meeting of the Mississippi Valley Historical Association, Kansas City, April 23, 1965 ("Population Studies Center Series in Studies of Human Resources," No. 1). This paper has benefited greatly from discussions with Professor Surinder K. Mehta.

Reprinted from *Demography*, 3, 1966, 47–57, by permission of the author and the Population Association of America.

Ravenstein's current and counter-current.

4 *Urban-rural differences in propensity to migrate.* "The natives of towns are less migratory than those of the rural parts of the country" (I, p. 199).

5 *Predominance of females among short-distance migrants.* "Females appear to predominate among short-journey migrants" (II, p. 288).

6 *Technology and migration.* "Does migration increase? I believe so! ... Wherever I was able to make a comparison I found that an increase in the means of locomotion and a development of manufactures and commerce have led to an increase of migration" (II, p. 288).

7 *Dominance of the economic motive.* "Bad or oppressive laws, heavy taxation, an unattractive climate, uncongenial social surroundings, and even compulsion (slave trade, transportation), all have produced and are still producing currents of migration, but none of these currents can compare in volume with that which arises from the desire inherent in most men to 'better' themselves in material respects" (II, p. 286).

This century has brought no comparable excursion into migration theory. With the development of equilibrium analysis, economists abandoned the study of population, and most sociologists and historians are reluctant to deal with masses of statistical data. A crew of demographers has sprung up, but they have been largely content with empirical findings and unwilling to generalize. Indeed, Vance, in his presidential address to the Population Association of America, entitled "Is Theory for Demographers?" contends that demography, for lack of theory, remains unstructured and raises the question, "Is there room [in demography] for the bold and audacious?"[6]

In the three-quarters of a century which have passed, Ravenstein has been much quoted and occasionally challenged. But, while there have been literally thousands of migration studies in the meantime, few additional generalizations have been advanced. True, there have been studies of age and migration, sex and migration, race and migration, distance and migration, education and migration, the labor force and migration, and so forth; but most studies which focused upon the characteristics of migrants have been conducted with little reverence to the volume of migration, and few studies have considered the reasons for migration or the assimilation of the migrant at destination. So little developed was the field in the 1930's that Dorothy Thomas and her associates concluded that the only generalization that could be made in regard to differentials in internal migration was that migrants tended to be young adults or persons in their late teens.[7] Later Bogue and Hagood trenchantly summed up the current state of knowledge under the heading "An Approach to a Theory of Differential Migration,"[8] and Otis Durant Duncan contributed a valuable essay on "The Theory and Consequences of Mobility of Farm Population,"[9] but both were restricted to the United States and both were hampered by a lack of data which has since been partially repaired. Most essays in migration theory have dealt with migration and distance and advance mathematical formulations of the relationship. Perhaps the best known of recent theories of migration is Stouffer's theory of intervening opportunities.[10]

Except for Dudley Kirk,[11] Ravenstein seems to have been the last person to make a detailed comparison of the volume of internal migration or the characteristics of migrants within a goodly number of nations. Generally speaking, considerations of internal migration have been divorced from considerations of immigration and emigration, and very short moves, such as those within counties in the United States or within *Kreise* in Germany, have not been considered along with the longer distance movement that is labeled migration. Also, such forced migration as the refugee movements of World War II and its aftermath have not been grouped with the so-called free migration.

It is the purpose of this paper to attempt the development of a general schema into which a variety of spatial movements can be placed and, from a small number of what would seem to be self-evident propositions, to deduce a number of conclusions with regard to the volume of migration, the development of streams and counterstreams, and the characteristics of migrants. As a starting point for this analysis, a definition of migration is introduced which is considerably more general than that usually applied.

Definition of Migration

Migration is defined broadly as a permanent or semipermanent change of residence. No restriction is placed upon the distance of the move or upon the voluntary or involuntary nature of the act, and no distinction is made between external and internal migration. Thus, a move across the hall from one apartment to another is counted as just as much an act of migration as a move from Bombay, India, to Cedar Rapids, Iowa, though, of course, the initiation and consequences of such moves are vastly different. However, not all kinds of spatial mobility are included in this definition. Excluded, for example, are the continual movements of nomads and migratory workers, for whom there is no long-term residence, and temporary moves like those to the mountains for the summer.

No matter how short or how long, how easy or how difficult, every act of migration involves an origin, a destination, and an intervening set of obstacles. Among the set of intervening obstacles, we include the distance of the move as one that is always present.

Factors of the Act of Migration

The factors which enter into the decision to migrate and the process of migration may be summarized under four headings, as follows:

1 Factors associated with the area of origin.
2 Factors associated with the area of destination.
3 Intervening obstacles.
4 Personal factors.

The first three of these are indicated schematically in Figure 22.1. In every area there are countless factors which act to hold people within the area or attract people to it, and there are others which tend to repel them. These are shown in the diagram as $+$ and $-$ signs. There are others, shown as 0's, to which people are essentially indifferent. Some of these factors affect most people in much the same way, while others affect different people in different ways. Thus a good climate is attractive and a bad climate is repulsive to nearly everyone; but a good school system may be counted as a $+$ by a parent with young children and a $-$ by a houseowner with no children because of the high real estate taxes engendered, while an unmarried male without taxable property is indifferent to the situation.

Clearly the set of $+$'s and $-$'s at both origin and destination is differently defined for every migrant or prospective migrant. Nevertheless, we may distinguish classes of people who react in similar fashion to the same general sets of factors at origin and destination. Indeed, since we `can never specify the exact set of factors which impels or prohibits migration for a given person, we can, in general, only set forth a few which seem of special importance and note the general or average reaction of a considerable group. Needless to say, the factors that hold and attract or repel people are precisely understood neither by the social scientist nor the persons directly affected. Like Bentham's calculus of pleasure and pain, the calculus of $+$'s and $-$'s at origin and destination is always inexact.

There are, however, important differences between the factors associated with the area of origin and those associated with the area of destination. Persons living in an area have an immediate and often long-term acquaint-

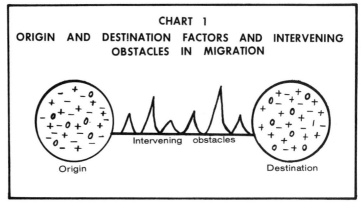

CHART 1

ORIGIN AND DESTINATION FACTORS AND INTERVENING
OBSTACLES IN MIGRATION

Intervening obstacles

Origin

Destination

Figure 22.1

ance with the area and are usually able to make considered and unhurried judgments regarding them. This is not necessarily true of the factors associated with the area of destination. Knowledge of the area of destination is seldom exact, and indeed some of the advantages and disadvantages of an area can only be perceived by living there. Thus there is always an element of ignorance or even mystery about the area of destination, and there must always be some uncertainty with regard to the reception of a migrant in a new area.

Another important difference between the factors associated with area of origin and area of destination is related to stages of the life cycle. For many migrants the area of origin is that in which the formative years have been spent and for which the general good health of youth and the absence of annoying responsibilities create in retrospect an overevaluation of the positive elements in the environment and an underevaluation of the negative elements. On the other hand, the difficulties associated with assimilation in a new environment may create in the newly arrived a contrary but equally erroneous evaluation of the positive and negative factors at destination.

While migration may result from a comparison of factors at origin and destination, a simple calculus of +'s and −'s does not decide the act of migration. The balance in favor of the move must be enough to overcome the natural inertia which always exists.

Furthermore, between every two points there stands a set of intervening obstacles which may be slight in some instances and insurmountable in others. The most studied of these obstacles is distance, which, while omnipresent, is by no means the most important. Actual physical barriers like the Berlin Wall may be interposed, or immigration laws may restrict the movement. Different people are, of course, affected in different ways by the same set of obstacles. What may be trivial to some people—the cost of transporting household goods, for example—may be prohibitive to others.

The effect of a given set of obstacles depends also upon the impedimenta with which the migrant is encumbered. For some migrants these are relatively unimportant and the difficulty of surmounting the intervening obstacles is consequently minimal; but for others, making the same move, the impedimenta, among which we must reckon children and other dependents, greatly increase the difficulties posed by intervening obstacles.

Finally, there are many personal factors which affect individual thresholds and facilitate or retard migration. Some of these are more or less constant throughout the life of the individual, while others are associated with stages in the life cycle and in particular with the sharp breaks that denote passage from one stage to another.

In this connection, we must note that it is not so much the actual factors at origin and destination as the perception of these factors which results in migration. Personal sensitivities, intelligence, and awareness of conditions elsewhere enter into the evaluation of the situation at origin, and knowledge of the situation at destination depends upon personal contacts or upon sources of information which are not universally available. In addition, there are personalities which are resistant to change—change of residence as well as other changes—and there are personalities which welcome change for the sake of change. For some individuals, there must be compelling reasons for migration, while for others little provocation or promise suffices.

The decision to migrate, therefore, is never completely rational, and for some persons the rational component is much less than the irrational. We must expect, therefore, to find many exceptions to our generalizations since transient emotions, mental disorder, and accidental occurrences account for a considerable proportion of the total migrations.

Indeed, not all persons who migrate reach that decision themselves. Children are carried along by their parents, willy-nilly, and wives accompany their husbands though it tears them away from environments they love. There are clearly stages in the life cycle in which the positive elements at origin are overwhelmingly important in limiting migration, and there are times in which such bonds are slackened with catastrophic suddenness. Children are bound to the familial residence by the need for care and subsistence, but, as one grows older, ages are reached at which it is customary to cease one stage of development and begin another. Such times are the cessation of education, entrance into the labor force, or retirement from work. Marriage, too, constitutes such a change in the life cycle, as does the dissolution of marriage, either through divorce or the death of a spouse.

Many more or less random occurrences can also greatly reduce the hold of an area upon a person and increase the attractiveness of other areas. Victims of injustice as well as

the perpetrators of crime may be forced to leave the area in which they are living. These and other events which affect but a few persons in the total community may nevertheless bulk large in the motivation of the migrant group.

This conceptualization of migration as involving a set of factors at origin and destination, a set of intervening obstacles, and a series of personal factors is a simple one which may perhaps be accepted as self-evident. It is now argued that, simple though this is, it provides a framework for much of what we know about migration and indicates a number of fields for investigation. It is used below to formulate a series of hypotheses about the volume of migration under varying conditions, the development of stream and counterstream, and the characteristics of migrants.

Volume of Migration

1. *The volume of migration within a given territory varies with the degree of diversity of areas included in that territory.* If migration, as we have assumed, results in part from a consideration of positive and negative factors at origin and destination, then a high degree of diversity among areas should result in high levels of migration. These we find in countries which are being opened up for settlement, as was the United States in the nineteenth century, eastern Europe during the twelfth and thirteenth centuries, and Siberia in the twentieth century. Under such conditions, opportunities arise which are sufficient to attract to them persons whose dissatisfaction with their places of origin is little more than minimal. Very great attractions spring up suddenly, as, for example, the discovery of gold in California, of silver in Colorado, and the opening up of Indian Territory for white settlement. The servicing of such a movement, in terms of providing transportation, protection, supplies, and the niceties as well as the necessities of life, creates highly specialized but often very lucrative oppor-

tunities. Thus, pioneers and settlers are accompanied by soldiers and merchants and ladies of fortune, who indeed may push ahead of the wave of settlement to establish outposts and nodal points.

The end of the period of settlement does not necessarily imply a decrease in areal diversity. On the contrary, the industrialization, which has traditionally followed settlement, is a great creator of areal diversity. In a dynamic economy, new opportunities are continually created in places to which workers must be drawn, and old enterprises are ruthlessly abandoned when they are no longer profitable.

2. *The volume of migration varies with the diversity of people.* The diversity of people also affects the volume of migration. Where there is a great sameness among people—whether in terms of race or ethnic origin, of education, of income, or tradition —we may expect a lesser rate of migration than where there is great diversity. A diversity of people implies the existence of groups that are specially fitted for given pursuits. Thus, we find throughout northern Europe, where land has been reclaimed from the sea or marshes drained, villages which still bear the stamps of their Dutch origin. The settlement of the American West would have been more difficult had it not been for the Jewish merchant who came with or even preceded the rush of migrants, and the conditions which attended Irish and Chinese immigration made them especially responsive to the demands for railroad laborers. Indeed, it is a common finding that immigrant groups specialize in particular occupations and become scattered throughout the country wherever the need for such work is found. Thus, Chinese laundry operators and Greek restaurant owners in the United States had their counterparts in the widely spread German and Jewish craftsmen of eastern Europe.

A diversity of people inevitably implies that the social statuses of some groups will become elevated above those of others. Discrimination among racial or ethnic groups is the rule rather than the exception, and the degree of discrimination varies from place to place, often in as extreme a manner as in the United States. Though discrimination leads to the establishment of ghettos, it also operates to bring about vast movements of people from one area to another—witness the recent migration of the American Negro.

Ethnic diversity may disappear as minorities become assimilated, but a major aim of modern civilization is to inaugurate other kinds of diversity among people. The aim of prolonged education is to create specialists, for many of whom the demand is small in any one place but widespread. For them migration is a concomitant of their vocations. Thus, engineers and professors have become peripatetic, but so have business executives and actors.

3. *The volume of migration is related to the difficulty of surmounting the intervening obstacles.* This hypothesis hardly needs elaboration. One of the most important considerations in the decision to migrate is the difficulty of the intervening obstacles. To tunnel under the Berlin Wall is a hazardous task not to be undertaken lightly; nor was sea passage to the Americas in the seventeenth and eighteenth centuries. The removal of immigration restrictions within the Common Market countries has been accompanied by large migrations of workers from one of these countries to another. There are many other instances in history where the removal of obstacles has set in motion large flows of migrants, and others in which the imposition of new obstacles or the heightening of old ones has brought about the sharp diminution of a long continued flow.

4. *The volume of migration varies with fluctuations in the economy.* Business cycles affect the volume of migration in many ways, but a crucial consideration is the manner in which they affect the comparison of positive and negative factors at origin and destination. During periods of economic expansion, new businesses and industries are created at a rapid rate, and old industries begin to recruit workmen from afar. Such opportunities, however, are by no means evenly spread, and parts of the country

remain in a state of relative stagnation. The contrast between the positive factors at origin and destination is therefore heightened, and the negative factors at origin seem more distressing. During depressions, however, some of the newly created businesses fail and others cease to expand. A leveling of opportunities occurs, and sheer familiarity with the place of residence (which in itself constitutes an element of safety) militates against moving to places where positive factors no longer so heavily outweigh those at home. Many tests of this hypothesis have been made, but among them the most revealing and confirming are the studies of Jerome in relation to immigration to the United States[12] and of Thomas in relation to migration within the United States.[13]

5. *Unless severe checks are imposed, both volume and rate of migration tend to increase with time.* The volume of migration tends to increase with time for a number of reasons, among them increasing diversity of areas, increasing diversity of people, and the diminution of intervening obstacles. As indicated above, industrialization and Westernization, the explicit or implicit goals of most countries, increase the diversity of areas. It is also true that in both developed and developing countries the differences between areas, both in terms of economics and of amenities, become heightened. On an international scale, the economic differences between advanced and backward countries are increasing rather than diminishing, and within all countries the differences between agricultural and urban areas are becoming more pronounced.

Other factors which tend to bring about an increase in the volume of migration are both the increasing differences among people and the view taken of these differences. In a primitive or agricultural society, specialization is limited and the development of differences among people tends to be discouraged. In an advancing society, however, specializations multiply, and there is an increased realization of both the existence and the need for special aptitudes or training. Thus, even in an agricultural area children are trained for urban pursuits, and an increased variety of developed aptitudes renders the population more susceptible to the appeal of highly special positive factors in scattered places.

Increasing technology plays an important role in diminishing intervening obstacles. Communication becomes easier, and transportation relative to average income becomes cheaper. Even if there were no change in the balance of factors at origin and destination, improving technology alone should result in an increase in the volume of migration.

Also operating to increase migration is migration itself. A person who has once migrated and who has once broken the bonds which tie him to the place in which he has spent his childhood is more likely to migrate again than is the person who has never previously migrated. Furthermore, succeeding migration lowers inertia even more. Once a set of intervening obstacles has been overcome, other sets do not seem so formidable, and there is an increasing ability to evaluate the positive and negative factors at origin and destination.

6. *The volume and rate of migration vary with the state of progress in a country or area.* As Ravenstein remarked, "Migration means life and progress; a sedentary population stagnation."[14] The reasons why this is true are similar to those advanced above under item 5. In an economically progressive country, the differences among areas are accentuated by industrial development and the differences among people by education. At the same time, intervening obstacles to migration within the country are lessened by improving technology and by political design.

We should, therefore, expect to find heavy immigration to developed countries where this is permitted and within such countries a high rate of internal migration. On the other hand, in the least developed countries we should find a largely immobile population which usually changes residence only under duress and then en masse rather than through individual action. In the United States, economically the most advanced of nations, rates of migration are unbelievably high, one in five persons changing his residence each year. In other economically advanced countries, like Sweden, Canada, or West Germany, we find this repeated at a somewhat lower level. We may argue that a high rate of progress entails a population which is continually in a state of flux, responding quickly to new opportunities and reacting swiftly to diminishing opportunities.

Stream and Counterstream

1. *Migration tends to take place largely within well defined streams.* It is a common observation that migrants proceed along well defined routes toward highly specific destinations. This is true in part because opportunities tend to be highly localized and in part because migrants must usually follow established routes of transportation. Perhaps just as important is the flow of knowledge back from destination to origin and, indeed, the actual recruitment of migrants at the place of origin. The overcoming of a set of intervening obstacles by early migrants lessens the difficulty of the passage for later migrants, and in effect pathways are created which pass over intervening opportunities as elevated highways pass over the countryside.

Thus the process of settlement tends to be a leapfrogging operation in which military outposts or trading centers become the focus of migration streams and the filling-up of the passed over territory is left to a later stage of development. From this point of view, the real frontiersmen are not the famers but the merchants, the missionaries, and the military. It was in this fashion that German colonization east of the Elbe was accomplished, and it was in this fashion that the American West was won.

In many cases, large movements take on the form of streams which are highly specific both in origin and destination. For example, Italians from Sicily and southern Italy migrated chiefly to the United States and

within the United States to a few northern cities, while high proportions of their countrymen from Lombardy and Tuscany went to South America and, in particular, to Buenos Aires. There are many examples of even more specific streams. Goldstein has noted that high proportions of Negroes resident in Norristown, Pennsylvania, in 1950 had come from Saluda, South Carolina, where a small contingent of Negroes had been recruited by the Pennsylvania Railroad as laborers and sent to Norristown during World War I.[15] At the present time, a small stream of miners is proceeding from Appalachia to copper-mining centers in the West, and this movement has been paralleled in the past by the movement of British mechanics to New England and British potters to Ohio.

2. *For every major migration stream, a counterstream develops.* A counterstream is established for several reasons. One is that positive factors at origin may disappear, or be muted, as during a depression, or there may be a re-evaluation of the balance of positive and negative factors at origin and destination. The very existence of a migration stream creates contacts between origin and destination, and the acquisition of new attributes at destination, be they skills or wealth, often makes it possible to return to the origin on advantageous terms. Migrants become aware of opportunities at origin which were not previously exploited, or they may use their contacts in the new area to set up businesses in the old. Accompanying the returning migrants will be their children born at destination, and along with them will be people indigenous to the area of destination who have become aware of opportunities or amenities at the place of origin through stream migrants. Furthermore, not all persons who migrate intend to remain indefinitely at the place of destination. For example, many Italian immigrants to the United States intended to stay only long enough to make enough money to be comfortable in Italy.

3. *The efficiency of the stream (ratio of stream to counterstream or the net redistribu-*

tion of population effected by the opposite flows) is high if the major factors in the development of a migration stream were minus factors at origin. Again, this point is so obvious that it hardly needs elaboration. Few of the Irish who fled famine conditions returned to Ireland, and few American Negroes return to the South.

4. *The efficiency of stream and counterstream tends to be low if origin and destination are similar.* In this case, persons moving in opposing flows move largely for the same reasons and in effect cancel each other out.

5. *The efficiency of migration streams will be high if the intervening obstacles are great.* Migrants who overcome a considerable set of intervening obstacles do so for compelling reasons, and such migrations are not undertaken lightly. To some degree, the set of obstacles in stream and counterstream is the same, and return migrants are faced with the necessity of twice negotiating a nearly overwhelming set of obstacles. For example, migrants from Pennsylvania to California are deterred from returning by the very expense of the journey.

6. *The efficiency of a migration stream varies with economic conditions, being high in prosperous times and low in times of depression.* During boom times the usual areas of destination, that is, the great centers of commerce and industry, expand rapidly, and relatively few persons, either return migrants or others, make the countermove. In times of depression, however, many migrants return to the area of origin, and others move toward the comparatively "safer" nonindustrialized areas. In extreme instances stream and counterstream may be reversed, as was the case with movement to and from rural areas during the worst years of the Great Depression. More recently, the mild recession in 1949 seems to have reversed the usual net flow from Oklahoma to California.

Characteristics of Migrants

1. *Migration is selective.* This simply states that migrants are not a random sample of the population at origin. The reason why migration is selective is that persons respond differently to the sets of plus and minus factors at origin and at destination, have different abilities to overcome the intervening sets of obstacles, and differ from each other in terms of the personal factors discussed above. It would seem impossible, therefore, for migration not to be selective. The kind of selection, however, varies, being positive in some streams and negative in others. By positive selection is meant selection for migrants of high quality and by negative selection the reverse.

2. *Migrants responding primarily to plus factors at destination tend to be positively selected.* These persons are under no necessity to migrate but do so because they perceive opportunities from afar and they can weigh the advantages and disadvantages at origin and destination. For example, highly educated persons who are already comfortably situated frequently migrate because they receive better offers elsewhere. Professional and managerial people are also highly mobile, and often because migration means advancement.

3. *Migrants responding primarily to minus factors at origin tend to be negatively selected; or, where the minus factors are overwhelming to entire population groups, they may not be selected at all.* Examples of the latter are political expulsions like that of the Germans from Poland and East Prussia or the Irish flight which followed the failure of the potato crop. On the whole, however, factors at origin operate most stringently against persons who in some way have failed economically or socially. Though there are conditions in many places which push out the unorthodox and the highly creative, it is more likely to be the uneducated or the disturbed who are forced to migrate.

4. *Taking all migrants together, selection tends to be bimodal.* For any given origin, some of the migrants who leave are responding primarily to plus factors at destination and therefore tend to be positively selected, while others are responding

to minus factors and therefore tend to be negatively selected. Therefore, if we plot characteristics of total migrants along a continuum ranging from poor to excellent, we often get a J-shaped or U-shaped curve. Such curves are found, for example, where the characteristic is either occupational class or education.

5. *The degree of positive selection increases with the difficulty of the intervening obstacles.* Even though selection is negative or random at origin, intervening obstacles serve to weed out some of the weak or the incapable. Thus, the rigors of the voyage to America in the seventeenth and eighteenth centuries eliminated many of the weak, and the same kind of selection is apparent among the German refugees from eastern Europe during and after World War II. It is also commonly noted that as distance of migration increases, the migrants become an increasingly superior group. At the other extreme, we have the milling-around in restricted areas of persons who, by any definition are less capable; for example, uneducated slum dwellers often move round and round within a few-block radius. Such short distance movements were also characteristic of sharecroppers in the pre-World War II days in the United States.

6. *The heightened propensity to migrate at certain stages of the life cycle is important in the selection of migrants.* To some degree, migration is a part of the *rites de passage.* Thus, persons who enter the labor force or get married tend to migrate from their parental home, while persons who are divorced or widowed also tend to move away. Since some of these events happen at quite well defined ages, they are important in shaping the curve of age selection. They are also important in establishing other types of selection—marital status or size of family, for example.

7. *The characteristics of migrants tend to be intermediate between the characteristics of the population at origin and the population at destination.* Persons with different characteristics react differently to the balance of plus and minus factors at origin and destina-

tion. Even before they leave, migrants tend to have taken on some of the characteristics of the population at destination, but they can never completely lose some which they share with the population at origin. It is because they are already to some degree like the population at destination that they find certain positive factors there, and it is because they are unlike the population at origin that certain minus factors there warrant migration. Many studies have shown this intermediate relationship. The fertility of migrants, for example, tends to fall between that of the population at origin and the population at destination, and the education of migrants from rural areas, while greater than that of nonmigrants at origin, is less than that of the population at destination. Thus, we have one of the paradoxes of migration in that the movement of people may tend to lower the quality of population, as expressed in terms of some particular characteristic, at both origin and destination.

Summary

In summary, a simple schema for migration has been elaborated, and from it certain hypotheses in regard to volume of migration, the establishment of stream and counterstream, and the characteristics of migrants have been formulated. The aim has been the construction of a related set of hypotheses within a general framework, and work is proceeding toward further development in regard to the assimilation of migrants and in regard to the effect upon gaining and losing areas.

Where possible, the hypotheses have been put in such form that they are immediately testable with current data. For others the necessary data are not now available, and others require restatement in terms of available data. It is to be expected that many exceptions will be found, since migration is a complex phenomenon and the often necessary simplifying condition—all other things being equal—is impossible to realize. Nevertheless, from what is now known about migration, encouraging agreement is found with the theory outlined in this paper. Full testing depends, of course, upon the amassing of materials from different cultures. Fortunately, recognition of the importance of internal migration in social and economic development has spurred research, and more and more countries publish detailed migration data from their censuses or population registers.

Notes

[1]E. G. Ravenstein, "The Laws of Migration," *Journal of the Royal Statistical Society*, XLVIII, Part 2 (June, 1885), 167–227. Also Reprint No. S-482 in the "Bobbs-Merrill Series in the Social Sciences."

[2]Ravenstein, "The Laws of Migration," *Journal of the Royal Statistical Society*, LII (June, 1889), 241–301. Also Reprint No. S-483 in the "Bobbs-Merrill Series in the Social Sciences."

[3]"Discussion on Mr. Ravenstein's Paper," *Journal of the Royal Statistical Society*, LII (June, 1889), 302.

[4]*Ibid.*, p. 303.

[5]In the quotations from Ravenstein, "I" refers to the 1885 paper and "II" to the 1889 paper.

[6]Rupert B. Vance, "Is Theory for Demographers?" *Social Forces*, XXXI (October, 1952), 9–13.

[7]Dorothy Swaine Thomas, *Research Memorandum on Migration Differentials* (New York: Social Science Research Council, Bulletin 43, 1938).

[8]Donald J. Bogue and Margaret Marman Hagood, *Subregional Migration in the United States, 1935–1940*, Vol. II: *Differential Migration in the Corn and Cotton Belts* (Miami, Ohio: Scripps Foundation Studies in Population Distribution, No. 6, 1953), pp. 124–27.

[9]Otis Durant Duncan, "The Theory and Consequences of Mobility of Farm Population," *Oklahoma Agriculture Experiment Station Circular No. 88* (Stillwater, Okla., May, 1940). Reprinted in Joseph J. Spengler and Otis Dudley Duncan, *Population Theory and Policy* (Glencoe, Ill.: Free Press, 1956), pp. 417–34.

[10]Samuel A. Stouffer, "Intervening Opportunities: A Theory Relating Mobility and Distance," *American Sociological Review*, V (December, 1940), 845–67, and "Intervening Opportunites and Competing Migrants," *Journal of Regional Science* II, (1960), 1–26.

[11]Dudley Kirk, *Europe's Population in the Interwar Years* (Princeton, N.J.: Princeton University Press, 1946).

[12]Harry Jerome, *Migration and Business Cycles* (New York: National Bureau of Economic Research Inc., 1926).

[13]Hope T. Eldridge and Dorothy Swaine Thomas, *Population Redistribution and Economic Growth, United States, 1870–1950*, Vol. III: *Demographic Analyses and Interrelations* (Philadelphia: American Philosophical Society, 1964), 321 ff.

[14]Ravenstein, "The Laws of Migration," *Journal of the Royal Statistical Society*, LII (June, 1889), 288.

[15]Sidney Goldstein, *Patterns of Mobility, 1910–1950: The Norristown Study* (Philadelphia: University of Pennsylvania Press, 1958), p. 38.

Selection Twenty-three

BEHAVIORAL ASPECTS OF THE DECISION TO MIGRATE

Julian Wolpert

During the decade 1950–60, there were sufficient changes from previous patterns of migration streams in the United States to warrant some reexamination and reevaluation of model building attempts in migration analysis. It must be admitted that the gravity model and its elaborations appear to lose

Reprinted from *Papers and Proceedings of the Regional Science Association*, **15**, 1965, 159–169, by permission of the editor.

explanatory power with each successive census. When flows are disaggregated, the need becomes greater selectively to determine unique weights for areas and unique distance functions for subgroups of in- and out-migrants. The Stouffer model of "competing migrants" (34) provided a rather poor prediction of migration streams for the 1955–60 period. Perhaps the most successful of spatial interaction models, which does take into consideration the spatial arrangement of places of origin and destination, is sufficiently rooted in the 1935–40 depression-period movements so as to present serious deficiencies when applied to recent streams. Plots of migration distances defy the persistence of the most tenacious of curve fitters.

The defenders of the wage theory of economic determinism find some validity for their constructs, so long as net, and not gross, migration figures are used and regional disaggregation does not proceed below the state level, thereby neglecting much of the intrastate heterogeneity (2), (3), (5), (24), (31).

The extremely scanty empirical evidence of the "friends and relatives effect" in directing migration has given birth to a generation of models which, although offering the solace of a behavioral approach, provide little explanation of the actual process involved (13), (21). Perhaps the most serious gap occurs in the transition from micro- to macro-model and in the selection of appropriate surrogates for testing. Here, the inadequacy of published data in the United States appears to have its most telling effect. Though almost every conceivable method of combining existing data into useful indicators has been tried, explanation through surrogates hardly provides an analysis which is independent of the bias which is introduced.

A good deal of useful information has come from the analysis of migration differentials by categories of occupation, income, race, and, especially, age (3), (10), (37), (40). However, predictive models have not been designed to include these findings and to consider the interdependence of these characteristics in migration behavior. Demonstrating the potential usefulness of the migration differential approach is one of the objectives of this paper.

A composite of interesting ideas about migration behavior has been incorporated within Price's ambitious proposed simulation model (23). On the basis of selected characteristics of individuals and of places of origin and destination, migration prob-

abilities are generated reflecting empirically observed regularities. As far as is known, the model has not become operational—the task for simulating United States migration would overtax the most modern computer. The only successful attempt in this direction has been Morrill's study of the emerging town development in south central Sweden (19).

The use of Monte Carlo simulation models in migration analysis does offer a viable and promising approach, especially considering the rather persistent tendencies for critical elements or parameters to remain stable over time. Thus, although the streams show considerable variation over time, and the characteristics of the population and of places continuously change, stability persists in migration behavior.

To illustrate this observation it may be noted that Bogue, Shryock, and Hoermann (3), in their analysis of the 1935–40 migration streams, summarize with the following statements that could as well be applied to the 1955–60 streams:

1 Basic shifts in the regional and territorial balance of the economy guided the direction and flow of migration streams.
2 The two factors that seem to contribute most to the mobility of the population are above average educational training and employment in white collar occupations.
3 Any theory of economic determinism in migration is inclined to be incomplete.

It appears, therefore, that understanding and prediction of migration streams require determining of the constants in migration behavior and distinguishing these from the variables with respect to population composition and place characteristics which evolve differentially over time.

As indicated, attempts at model building in migration research have largely focused on variables and surrogates such as distance and ecological characteristics of places exerting "push and pull" forces (3), (7) to the exclusion of behavioral parameters of the migrants. The model suggested here is of doubtful usefulness as an exact predictive tool. It borrows much of its concepts and terminology from the behavioral theorists, because of the intuitive relevance of their findings to the analysis of mobility. Verification will be only partial because of the general absence in this country of migrational histories. Instead, greater reliance will be placed upon evidence from a variety of sources and special studies. The framework of the analysis must be classified as descriptive or behavioral and partially dynamic.

Clearly, the focus must remain with the process of internal migration, i.e., a change of residence which extends beyond a territorial boundary. Some attempt will be made, however, to relate this process of "long distance" movement to the more general topic of mobility which encompasses not only shifts within areal divisions but also movement between jobs and social categories. This larger zone of investigation is referred to as the "mover-stayer" problem (11).

Central Concepts of Migration Behavior

The central concepts of migration behavior with which we shall be concerned are: 1. the notion of place utility, 2. the field theory approach to search behavior, and 3. the life-cycle approach to threshold formation.

Before translating these concepts into an operational format within a proposed model, some attempt will be made to trace their relevance to migrational decisions.

PLACE UTILITY

Population migration is an expression of interaction over space but differs in certain essential characteristics from other channels of interaction, mainly in terms of the commodity which is being transported. Other flows, such as those of mail, goods, telephone calls, and capital also reflect connectivity between places, but, in migration, the agent which is being transported is itself active and generates its own flow. The origin and destination points take on significance only in the framework in which they are perceived by the active agents.

A degree of disengagement and upheaval is associated with population movements; thus, households are not as readily mobile as other phenomena subject to flow behavior. Yet, it would be unrealistic to assume that sedentariness reflects an equilibrium position for a population. Migrational flows are always present, but normally the reaction is lagged and the decision to migrate is non-programmed. Thus, migration is viewed as a form of individual or group adaptation to perceived changes in environment, a recognition of marginality with respect to a stationary position, and a flow reflecting an appraisal by a potential migrant of his present site as opposed to a number of other potential sites. Other forms of adaptation are perhaps more common than change of residence and job. The individual may adjust to the changing conditions at his site and postpone, perhaps permanently, the decision to migrate. Migration is not, therefore, merely a direct response or reaction to the objective economic circumstances which might be incorporated, for example, within a normative transportation model.

In designing the framework for a model of the migration decision, it would be useful at the outset to enumerate certain basic descriptive principles which have been observed to have some general applicability and regularity in decision behavior. To a significant degree these principles have their origin in the studies of organizational theorists.

We begin with the concept of "intendedly rational" man (30) who, although limited to finite ability to perceive, calculate, and predict and to an otherwise imperfect knowledge of environment, still differentiates between alternative courses of action according to their relative utility or expected utility. Man responds to the perception of unequal utility, i.e., if utility is measured broadly enough to encompass the friction of adaptation and change.

The individual has a threshold of net utility or an aspiration level that adjusts itself on the basis of experience (8), (14), (18), (28), (30), (33). This subjectively determined threshold is a weighted composite of a set of yardsticks for achievement in the specific realms in which he participates. His contributions, or inputs, into the economic and social systems in terms of effort, time, and concern are rewarded by actual and expected attainments. The threshold functions as an evaluative mechanism for distinguishing, in a binary sense, between success or failure, or between positive or negative net utilities. The process is self-adjusting because aspirations tend to adjust to the attainable. Satisfaction leads to slack which may induce a lower level of attainment (8). Dissatisfaction acts as a stimulus to search behavior.

Without too great a degree of artificiality, these concepts of "bounded rationality" (30) may be transferred to the mover-stayer decision environment and a spatial context. It is necessary, only, to introduce a place subscript for the measures of utility. *Place utility*, then, refers to the net composite of utilities which are derived from the individual's integration at some position in space. The threshold reference point is also a relevant criterion for evaluating the individual's place utility. According to the model, the threshold will be some function of his experience or attainments at a particular place and the attainments of his peers. Thus, place utility may be expressed as a positive or negative quantity, expressing respectively the individual's satisfaction or dissatisfaction with respect to that place. He derives a measure of utility from the past or expected future rewards at his stationary position.

Quite different is the utility associated with the other points which are considered as potential destinations. The utility with respect to these alternative sites consists largely of anticipated utility and optimism which lacks the reinforcement of past rewards. This is precisely why the stream of information is so important in long-distance migration—information about prospects must somehow compensate for the absence of personal experience.

All moves are purposeful, for an evaluation process has preceded them, but some are more beneficial, in an *ex post* sense, because of the objective quality of search behavior, the completeness of the information stream and the mating of anticipated with realized utility. If migrations may be classified as either successes or failures in a relative sense, then clearly the efficiency of the search process and the ability to forecast accurately the consequences of the move are essential elements.

Assuming intendedly rational behavior, then the generation of population migration may be considered to be the result of a decision process which aims at altering the future in some way and which recognizes differences in utility associated with different places. The individual will tend to locate himself at a place whose characteristics possess or promise a relatively higher level of utility than in other places which are conspicuous to him. Thus, the flow of population reflects a subjective place-utility evaluation by individuals. Streams of migration may not be expected to be optimal because of incomplete knowledge and relocation lag but neither may we expect that individuals purposefully move in response to the prospect of lower expected utility.

The process of migration is conceived in the model as: 1. proceeding from sets of stimuli perceived with varying degrees of imperfection, and 2. involving responses in a stayer-mover framework.

The stayers are considered lagged movers postponing the decision to migrate for periods of time extending up to an entire lifetime. Thus, the mover-stayer dichotomy may be reduced to the single dimension of time—when to move.

Distinction must clearly be made between the objective stimuli which are relevant for the mover-stayer decision and the stimuli which are perceived by individuals and to which there is some reaction. The stimuli which are instrumental in generating response originate in the individual's action space which is that part of the limited environment with which the individual has contact (14). Thus, the perceived state of the environment is the action space within which individuals select to remain or, on the other hand, from which to withdraw in exchange for a modified environment.

FIELD THEORY APPROACH TO SEARCH BEHAVIOR

Though the individual theoretically has access to a very broad environmental range of local, regional, national, and international information coverage, typically only some rather limited portion of the environment is relevant and applicable for his decision behavior. This immediate subjective environment or action space is the set of place utilities which the individual perceives and to which he responds. This notion of the action space is similar to Lewin's concept of life space—the universe of space and time in which the person conceives that he can or might move about (14). Some correspondence may exist with the actual external environment, but there may also be a radical degree of deviation. The life space is a surface over which the organism can locomote and is dependent upon the needs, drives, or goals of the organism and upon its perceptual apparatus (29). Our concern is with man in terms of his efficiency or effectiveness as an information collecting and assimilating organism and thus with his ability to produce an efficient and unbiased estimation or evaluation of the objective environment. It is suggested that the subjective action space is perceived by the individual through a sampling process whose parameters are determined by the individual's needs, drives, and abilities. There may not be a conscious and formal sampling design in operation, but, nevertheless, a sampling process is inherently involved in man's acquisition of knowledge about his environment.

Both sampling and nonsampling errors may be expected in the individual's perceived action space—a spatial bias induced by man's greater degree of expected contact and interaction in his more immediate environment, as well as sampling errors introduced because of man's finite ability to perceive and his limited exposure and observation. The simple organism which Simon describes has vision which permits it to see, at any moment, a circular portion of the surface about the point in which it is standing and to distinguish merely between the presence or absence of food within the circle (29).

The degree to which the individual's action-space accurately represents the physically objective world in its totality is a variable function of characteristics of both man and the variability of the environment. Of primary emphasis here are the consequences of man's fixity to a specific location—the spatial particularism of the action space to which he responds.

What is conspicuous to the individual at any given time includes primarily information about elements in his close proximity. Representing the information bits as points, the resulting sampling design most closely resembles a cluster in the immediate vicinity of the stationary position. The individual may be considered at the stationary position within the cluster of alternative places, each of which may be represented by a point on a plane. The consequences of this clustered distribution of alternatives within the immediate vicinity of the individual is a spatially biased information set, or a mover-stayer decision based upon knowledge of only a small portion of the plane.

Cluster sampling may be expected to exhibit significantly greater sampling bias for a given number of observations than random sampling; its most important advantage is in the reduction of the effort or cost in the collection of information. In the absence of a homogeneous surface, however, the difference in cost may be more than outweighed by the loss in representativeness of a given cluster.

The local environment of the individual may not, of course, be confined purely to his immediate surroundings. The action space may vary in terms of number and intensity of contacts from the limited environmental realm of the infant to the extensive action space within which diplomats, for example, operate. The degree of contact may perhaps be measured by the rate of receipt perception of information bits (16). Mass communications and travel, communication with friends and relatives, for example, integrate the individual into a more comprehensive spatial setting but one which is, nevertheless, still biased spatially. Mass communications media typically have coverage which is limited to the service area of the media's transmission center. Here a hierarchy of nodal centers exists in terms of the extent of service area and range of coverage. Thus the amount of transmission and expected perception of information by individuals is some function of the relative position of places within the network of communication channels. The resident in the area of a primary node has an additional advantage resulting from his greater exposure to information covering a relatively more extensive area of choice. His range of contact and interaction is broader, and the likelihood of an unbiased and representative action space is greater.

THE LIFE CYCLE APPROACH TO THRESHOLD FORMATION

Another significant determinant of the nature and extent of the individual's action space (i.e., the number and arrangement of points in the cluster) consists of a set of factors which may be grouped under the heading of the "life cycle." Illustrative of this approach is Hägerstrand's analysis of population as a flow through a system of stations (12). Lifelines represent individuals moving between stations. The cycle of life almost inevitably gives rise to distinct movement behavior from birth, education, and search for a niche involving prime or replacement movements. Richard Meier also has examined this notion of the expanding action space of the individual from birth through maturity (15), (16). The action space expands as a function of information input—and growth depends on organization of the environment so that exploration becomes

more efficient. Associated with the evolution of the individual's action space through time is a complex of other institutional and social forces which introduce early differentiation. Differences in sex, race, formal education, family income, and status are likely to find their expression early in shaping the area of movement and choice. Although the action space is unique for each individual, still there is likely to be a good deal of convergence into a limited number of broad classes. The congruity and interdependence of the effects of race, family income, education, and occupation are likely to result in subgroups of individuals with rather homogeneous action spaces.

In Lewin's concept, behavior is a function of the life space, which in turn is a function of the person and the environment (14). The behavior-influencing aspects of the external (physical and social) environment are represented through the life space. Similarly, but in a more limited fashion, the action space may be considered to include the range of choice or the individual's area of movement which is defined by both his personal attributes and environment. Most prominent among the determinants of the alternatives in this action space which are conspicuous to the individual in his position on one of divergent life cycles and location in terms of the communication networks linking his position to other places. His accumulated needs, drives, and abilities define his aspirations—the communication channels carry information about the alternative ways of satisfying these aspirations. To illustrate this structure in terms of the simple organism, we may turn to Simon's model of adaptive behavior (29). The organism he describes has only the simple needs of food getting and resting. The third kind of activity of which it is capable is exploration for food by locomotion within the life space where heaps of food are located at scattered points. In the schema, exploration and adaptive response to clues are necessary for survival; random behavior leads to extinction. The chances of survival, i.e., the ability to satisfy needs, are dependent upon two parameters describing the organism (its storage capacity and its range of vision) and two parameters describing the environment (its richness in food and in paths). Of course, with respect to the human organism, aspirations require the fulfillment of many needs, and thresholds are higher. Exploratory search is aided by clues provided by the external environment through communication channels which extend the range of vision.

OTHER BEHAVIORAL PARAMETERS

The discussion was intended to develop the concept of action space as a spatial parameter in the mover-stayer decision. Thus the action space of the individual includes not only his present position but a finite number of alternative sites which are made conspicuous to him through a combination of his search effort and the transmission of communications. The action space refers, in our mover-stayer framework, to a set of places for which expected utilities have been defined by the individual. A utility is attached to his own place and relatively higher or lower utility has been assigned to the alternative sites. The variables here are the absolute number of alternative sites and their spatial pattern or arrangement with respect to his site. The sites may consist of alternative dwellings within a single block, alternative suburbs in a metropolitan area, or alternative metropolitan areas. The alternatives may not all present themselves simultaneously but may appear sequentially over time.

There are other components of behavioral theories which are relevant in the analysis of migration, especially with respect to the problem of uncertainty avoidance. We have already mentioned the sequential attention to goals and the sequential consideration of alternatives (8). The order in which the environment is searched determines to a substantial extent the decisions that will be made. In addition, observations appear to confirm that alternatives which *minimize uncertainty* are preferred and that the decision maker *negotiates for an environment of relative certainty* (8). Evidence shows also that there is a tendency to *postpone decisions* and to rely upon the *feedback of information*, i.e., policies are reactive rather than anticipatory (8). Uncertainty is also reduced by imitating the successful procedures followed by others (8).

The composite of these attempts to reduce uncertainty may be reflected in a lagged response. A lapse of time intervenes in a cause and effect relationship—an instantaneous human response may not be expected. As with other stimulus-response models, events are paired sequentially through a process of observation and inference into actions and reactions, e.g., unemployment and outmigration. As developed in economics, a lag implies a delayed, but rational, human response to an external event. Similarly, with respect to migration, responses may be measured in terms of elasticity which is in turn conditional upon factors such as complementarity and substitutability. A time dimension may be added to measures of elasticity, and the result is a specific or a distributed lag—a response surface reflecting the need for reenforcement of the perception of the permanence of change.

Framework of a Proposed Operating Model

The model which is proposed attempts to translate into an operational framework the central concepts with which we have been concerned: the notion of place utility, the field theory approach to search behavior, and life cycle approach to threshold formation.

The model is designed to relate aggregate behavior in terms of migration differentials into measures of place utility relevant for individuals. The objective is a prediction of the composition of in- and out-migrants and their choice of destination, i.e., by incorporating the stable elements which are involved in the changes in composition of population of places.

Inputs into the system are the following set of matrices:

1 Matrix A, defining the migration differentials associated with the division of the population by life cycles and by age, represented respectively by the rows and columns.
2 Matrix B, representing the distribution of a place's population within the life cycle and age categories.
3 Matrices C, D, E, and F, representing respectively the gross in-, out-, and net-migration and "migration efficiency"[1] for each of the cell categories corresponding to Matrix B.

The rates for the A matrix are determined on an aggregate basis for the United States population by means of the "one in a thousand" 1960 census sample. These rates are then applied to the B matrix entries for specific places to predict the expected out-migration rates of profile groups at these places. The differences between the expected rates and those observed in the C, D, E, and F matrix tabulations are then used to provide a measure of the relative utility of specific places for the given profile groups which may be specified as a place utility matrix. The net migrations, whether positive or negative for the given cell, represent the consensus of cell members of the utility which the place offers relative to other places which they perceive. The migration efficiency measures not only the relative transitoriness of specific subgroups of the population but also the role of the specific place as a transitional stepping stone or station for certain groups.

There is an additional matrix, Matrix G, representing the parameters of search behavior which are characteristic of the subgroup populations. These are specified in terms of the number of alternatives which are perceived and the degree of clustering of these alternatives in space. The destination of the out-migrants predicted by means of the G matrix entries are tested against the observed migration flows in order to derive measures of distance and directional bias.

The concepts of place utility, life cycle, and search behavior are integrated, therefore, within the classification of the population into subgroups. Preliminary testing has revealed a significant degree of homogeneity of migrational behavior by subgroup populations in terms of differential rate of migration, distance, and direction of movement. The classification procedure, involving the use of multivariate analysis, is designed to provide a set of profile or core groups whose attributes may be represented by prototype individuals. The differential migration rates of Matrix A are assumed, therefore, to be parameters in the migration system, at least for the purposes of short-term forecasting. Individuals move along each row as they grow older and, to some extent, move in either direction along age columns as socioeconomic status changes over time, but the migration rates for the cells remain relatively constant.

Similarly, the utility to the population subgroups of the specific places of origin and destination shift over the long-term but remain relatively constant in the short-run. For long-term forecasting, exogenous measures of economic trends in specific places would be necessary inputs.

Notes

[1] Migrational efficiency refers to the ratio of net migration to total gross migration (27).

References

1. Ajo, Reino. "New Aspects of Geographic and Social Patterns of Net Migration Rate," *Svensk Geografisk Årsbok* (1954) Lund, Sweden.
2. Blanco, Cicely. "Prospective Unemployment and Interstate Population Movements," *Review of Economics and Statistics*, XVLI (1964), pp. 221–22.
3. Bogue, Donald J., Shryock, Henry S., Hoermann Siegfried. "Streams of Migration between Sub-

regions," *Scripps Foundation Studies in Population Distribution* (1957), No. 5, Oxford Ohio.

4. Bogue, Donald J. "Internal Migration" in Hauser, P. M. and Duncan, O. D., eds, *The Study of Population*. Chicago: The University of Chicago Press, 1959.

5. Bunting, Robert L. "A Test of the Theory of Geographic Mobility," *Industrial and Labor Relations Review*, **15**, (1961), pp. 76–82.

6. Bunting, Robert L. "Labor Mobility in the Crescent," in Chapin, F. Stuart, Jr., and Weiss, Shirley F., eds, *Urban Growth Dynamics in a Regional Cluster of Cities*. New York: Wiley, 1962.

7. Burford, Roger L. "An Index of Distance as Related to Internal Migration," *Southern Economic Journal*, XXIX (1962), pp. 77–81.

8. Cyert, R. M. and Marsh, J. G. *A Behavioral Theory of the Firm*. Englewood Cliffs, N.J.: Prentice-Hall, 1963.

9. Eldridge, Hope T. "A Cohort Approach to the Analysis of Migration Differentials," *Demography* 1 (1964), pp. 212–19.

10. Eldridge, Hope T. and Thomas, Dorothy Swaine. *Population Redistribution and Economic Growth, United States 1870–1950*. Philadelphia: American Philosophical Society, 1964.

11. Goodman, Leo. "Statistical Methods for the Mover-Stayer Model," *Journal of the American Statistical Association*, **56** (1961), pp. 841–68.

12. Hägerstrand, Torsten. "Geographical Measurements of Migration," *Entretiens de Monaco en Sciences Humaines*, 1962.

13. Kerr, Clark. "Migration to the Seattle Labor Market Area, 1940–42," *University of Washington Publications in the Social Sciences*, **11** (1942), p. 129–88.

14. Lewin, Kurt. *Field Theory in Social Science*. New York: Harper and Row, 1951.

15. Meier, Richard L. "Measuring Social and Cultural Change in Urban Regions," *Journal of the American Institute of Planners*, XXV (1959), pp. 180–90.

16. Meier, Richard L. *A Communications Theory of Urban Growth*. Cambridge: Massachusetts Institute of Technology Press, 1962.

17. McGinnis, Robert and Pilger, John E. "On a Model for Temporal Analysis" and "Internal Migration as a Stochastic Process," (mimeo). Department of Sociology, Cornell University, 1963.

18. McGuire, Joseph W. *Theories of Business Behavior*. Englewood Cliffs, N.J.: Prentice-Hall, 1964.

19. Morrill, Richard L. "The Development of Models of Migration," *Entretiens de Monaco en Sciences Humaines*, 1962.

20. Morrill, Richard L. and Pitts, Forest R. *Marriage*, "Marriage, Migration and the Mean Information Field," *Annals*, Association of American Geographers, forthcoming.

21. Nelson, Phillip. "Migration, Real Income and Information," *Journal of Regional Science*, **1** (1959), pp. 43–74.

22. Oliver, F. R. "Inter-Regional Migration and Unemployment, 1951–61," *Journal of the Royal Statistical Society*, Series A, **127** (1964), pp. 42–75.

23. Price, D. O. "A Mathematical Model of Migration Suitable for Simulation on an Electronic Computer," *Proceedings, International Population Conference*, Vienna, 1959, pp. 665–73.

24. Raimon, Robert L. "Interstate Migration and Wage Theory," *Review of Economics and Statistics*, XLIV (1962), pp. 428–38.

25. Rosen, Howard. "Projected Occupational Structure and Population Distribution," *Labor Mobility and Population in Agriculture*. Ames: Iowa State University Press, 1961.

26. Rossi, Peter. *Why Families Move*. The Free Press of Glencoe, Illinois, 1955.

27. Shryock, H. S., Jr. "The Efficiency of Internal Migration in the United States," *Proceedings, International Population Conference*, Vienna, 1959, pp. 685–94.

28. Siegel, S. "Level of Aspiration and Decision Making," *Psychological Review*, **64** (1957), pp. 253–63.

29. Simon, Herbert A. "Rational Choice and the Structure of the Environment," *Psychological Review*, **63** (1956), pp. 129–38.

30. Simon, Herbert A. "Economics and Psychology," in Koch, Sigmund, ed., *Psychology: A Study of a Science*, **6** New York: McGraw-Hill, 1963.

31. Sjaastad, Larry A. "The Relationship Between Migration and Income in the United States," *Papers and Proceedings, Regional Science Association*, VI (1960), pp. 37–64.

32. Sjaastad, Larry A. "Occupational Structure and Migration Patterns," *Labor Mobility and Population in Agriculture*. Ames: Iowa State University Press, 1961.

33. Starbuck, William H. "Level of Aspiration Theory and Economic Behavior," *Behavioral Science*, **8** (1963), pp. 128–36.

34. Stouffer, Samuel A. "Intervening Opportunities and Competing Migrants," *Journal of Regional Science*, **2** (1960), pp. 1–26.

35. Taeuber, Karl E. and Taeuber, Alma F. "White Migration and Socio-Enonomic Differences between Cities and Suburbs," *American Sociological Review*, **29** (1964), pp. 718–24.

36. Ter Heide, H. "Migration Models and Their Significance for Population Forecasts," *Milbank Memorial Fund Quarterly*, XLI (1963), pp. 56–76.

37. Thomas, Dorothy S. "Age and Economic Differentials in Internal Migration in the United States: Structure and Distance," *Proceedings, International Population Conference*, Vienna, 1959, pp. 714–21.

38. Thomas, Dorothy S. "Age and Economic Differentials in Interstate Migration," *Population Index*, 1958, pp. 313–24.

39. Webber, Melvin M. "The Urban Place and the Non-place Urban Realm," *Explorations into Urban Structure* Philadelphia: University of Pennsylvania Press, 1964.

40. Wilber, George L. "Migration Expectancy in the United States," *Journal of the American Statistical Association*, **58** (1963), pp. 444–53.

Selection Twenty-four

MAJOR MIGRATIONS SINCE WORLD WAR II

Dudley Kirk

Eleven years ago an earlier conference of the Milbank Fund was devoted to "Postwar Problems of Migration."[1] The purpose of this paper is to give a brief conspectus of the major migratory movements since that time.

In 1946 the dust was just beginning to settle after the war, and our thinking on migration, as in so many fields, was much influenced by the problems created by that conflict. These problems led us to think in terms of a new basic classification for analyzing migration—a distinction between "forced" migrations imposed by fear or force and "free" migrations undertaken by individual choice, usually for economic motives.

In the following discussion we shall refer first to the problems of forced migration, whether the legacy of World War II or the creation of postwar upheavals; second to free migrations and especially the overseas movements affecting Europe and Asia; and finally to the significance of internal migration in the postwar period.[2]

Forced Migrations:
The Legacy of the Second World War

Just after World War II the most obvious problem of migration was how to cope with the masses of displaced persons, expellees, and refugees. Heaviest on our conscience was the plight of the 600,000 displaced persons on the rolls of the international refugee organizations in 1946. But the war had left a much larger residue of 25–30 million people in Europe permanently uprooted. On the very day the earlier Mil-

bank Conference met, on October 29, 1946, a census was taken in Germany that recorded almost 10 million German expellees from Eastern Europe and from German territories lost in the war. Nor was the movement then complete. Many hundred thousand more Germans were later expelled or migrated from the East.

The vast wanderings of World War II were recorded in detail by Joseph Schechtman and by the late Eugene Kulischer.[3] The movements were extraordinarily complex and at the time seemed to be a random shuffling back and forth across the face of Europe with the tide of battle and military force.

But whatever their motivation—and in most cases it was fear or force—the lasting displacements of population were primarily in the direction of historical movements, the pressure of population from the less developed East toward the more developed areas of Central and Western Europe and overseas; and from areas of high natural increase to areas of lower natural increase.

Politically the great displacements of population from East to West are a part of a historical revolt of the East that began in nationalistic movements against German and Austrian domination in Central Europe long before the First World War. The revolt was strengthened by the larger natural increase of the Eastern European populations.

In many respects it was a rural-urban movement. The forced migrations ousted the Germans and Jews, and in some areas Italians and Hungarians, who formerly were disproportionate segments of the urban, industrial, and governing populations of Eastern Europe. Their displacement created expanded opportunity for the eastern nationalities, whether Polish, Czech, Serb, Rumanian, or Russian, and helped to absorb large agrarian surpluses of popula-

Reprinted from *Selected Studies of Migration Since World War II*, Proceedings of the Thirty-Fourth Annual Conference of the Milbank Memorial Fund, 1958, 11–28, by permission of the Milbank Memorial Fund.

tion in Eastern Europe. As a result of these migrations Poles and Czechs for example, are far more urban and industrial than they were before the war.[4]

Thus the great displacements of European populations in World War II swam with powerful historical trends. Perhaps for this reason resettlement of the survivors has proved to be generally stable and economically successful.[5] I am not here attempting to evaluate the justice or strength of political irredentism which inevitably exists among persons expelled from their homelands.

Probably most surprising has been the integration of some 12 million German refugees and migrants from the East. There were many who predicted that the German economy would be swamped and permanently weakened by this enormous movement into a reduced territory shattered by war and defeat.

The pessimistic predictions regarding the future of Germany and its truncated economy were not realized. By 1950 industrial production in Western Germany had reached 1936 levels in the same territory. By 1955 this figure had been doubled, and it has continued progressively higher.

The refugees have not necessarily fully shared the results of this progress. Many older refugees never made a satisfactory economic adjustment. The refugees are still at a disadvantage in some ways, notably in housing. But in general they came from areas that before the war had lower per capita incomes than Western Germany. Their present economic situation is only relatively disadvantageous, and this with regard to their West German neighbors more than to their own prewar condition. On the whole the refugees are now prosperous in Germany even by their own prewar standards.

I will not dwell on the reasons for German revival and the relatively successful absorption of refugees.[6] The West German industrial plant was not nearly so much destroyed by the war as was first supposed. With ingenuity and hard work the Germans were able to restore it rapidly. This achievement was promoted at first by Allied aid and later by the stable German government, by its sound economic policies, and by the strong foreign demand for the products of heavy industry that Germany could supply.

Less is known about the success of millions of Poles, Czechs, and other nationalities who replaced the Germans in former German territory east of the Oder-Neisse line, in the Sudetenland, and in the former German colonies scattered throughout Eastern Europe. These migrants and their governments appear to have been generally successful in restoring the cities and the industries abandoned by the Germans, and in achieving an economic level of living superior to what they previously enjoyed. More difficulty seems to have been encountered in restoring the agriculture and agricultural efficiency of the Germans in the rural areas. But it is fair to say that the countries concerned have been able to take advantage of the greater "living space" and opportunities for economic progress afforded by the departure of the Germans.

But what of the political refugees of Eastern European nationality, the hard core of displaced persons? There were about a million of these left after the war.

Now, a decade later, even the most difficult cases have largely been resettled, chiefly in overseas countries. I would not argue that the psychological and economic adjustment of these people has in all cases been ideal. But, as Mr. Davie predicted at the Conference in 1946, the economic, social, and cultural adjustments of the displaced persons have generally been very good.[7]

I think it is fair to say that the wartime legacy of displaced persons, expellees, and political refugees in Europe has been effectively liquidated. There were helpful actions of governments such as our own; there were fortuitous circumstances such as the creation of Israel in 1948. There were splendid achievements by international agencies dedicated to the solution of the refugee problem. But much of the success is also attributable to the fact that the great displacements of population generally moved in the directions of economic opportunity, whether from East to West in Europe or from Europe overseas.

New Forced Migrations

It would be a happy circumstance if we could at this point close the book on forced migrations. Unhappily, these did not come to an end with the reestablishment of peace. Postwar political turmoil has been reflected in the new uprooting of peoples and the setting in motion of repeated forced migrations. Partition of India in 1947 generated mass migrations on a vast scale. The total movement is estimated to be about 17 million, about half of Muslims into Pakistan and about half of Hindus from Pakistan into India.

The establishment of the State of Israel resulted, on the one hand, in bringing over 600,000 Jews from Europe, North Africa, and the Arab world. About the same number of Arabs fled or were dislodged from their ancestral homes in territory incorporated in the new state.

The victory of the Communists in China sent millions of Chinese into exile in Formosa and Hong Kong and drove out the European community, some members of which were already refugees from the first World War.

The Korean conflict has left a legacy of hundreds of thousands of refugees; more recently the defeat of the French and partition of Vietnam in Indochina set in motion a flight of hundreds of thousands of refugees from north to south.

By contrast with the refugee movements of Europeans, the immediate problems created by these Asian movements remain. The flotsam and jetsam are only too readily observable in Karachi, in Calcutta and in Hong Kong, in Seoul and in Saigon. For many of the refugees there has been no effective resettlement and little alleviation of their misery. Ten years after the strife between Israel and the Arab countries Israel has made great strides in integrating Jewish immigrants but there are more Arab

refugees under international care than there were immediately after the conflict.

By contrast one year after the revolt in Hungary, 90 per cent of the 191,000 Hungarians who sought temporary asylum in Austria and Yugoslavia have been resettled in new homes. Only 12,000 still require international assistance, and this number is falling rapidly.[8]

There remain major problems of resettlement expecially in Asia where these blend into the still larger problems of agrarian underemployment and overpopulation.

Overseas Migration from Europe[9]

Let us turn from "forced" migrations to the developments in "normal" international migration. Overseas migration from Europe is presented in Figure 24.1 and Table 24.1. The figures presented almost certainly understate the actual totals owing to the fact that information is lacking for some areas.

In the first postwar decade 1946–1955 there was a net outmigration from Europe of about four and one-half million, a not inconsiderable movement. About one million of these were from the Soviet orbit and, of course, largely displaced persons. There has been very little free migration from Eastern Europe since the war. The remainder, about three and one-half million, were from Western and Southern Europe. The British Isles furnished 860,000, many of whom went to the Dominions and other parts of the Commonwealth. For these migration did not involve sacrifice of either citizenship or language—in many respects it was an internal migration. Half a million left Germany and relatively small numbers came from the Netherlands, Scandinavia, and other Western European countries. Overseas migration from these countries is substantially free. American quotas usually can accommodate those desiring to come and migrants from these countries are generally favored by the other major overseas countries of immigration.

In relation to population size, the largest

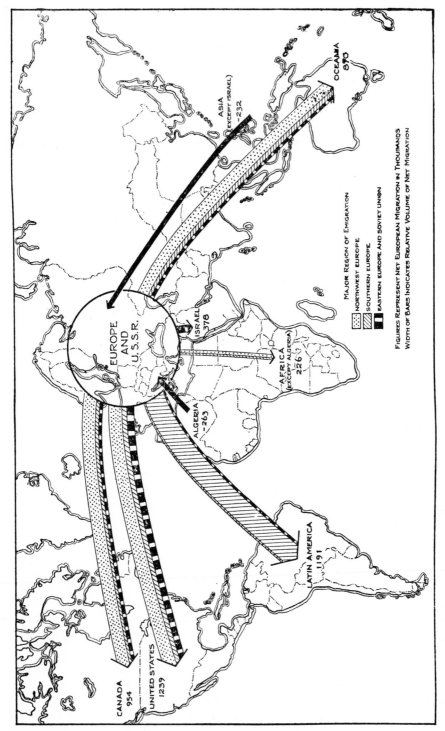

Figure 24.1 Net immigration from Europe, 1946–1955 (in thousands).

contributions were from Southern Europe. Italy led with a net overseas emigration of close to a million. Portugal contributed a net emigration of almost 300,000 from a population of about 8 million. Emigration from Spain was of comparable size but from a substantially larger population.

The net outward movement from Europe in the postwar period was the largest since the United States imposed severe restrictions in the early 1920s. In volume it compares with European emigration in the period 1880–1900.

The destinations of postwar European migration are less concentrated than in the great migrations before the first World War. In 1930 over 60 per cent of all Europeans (i.e., born in Europe) living overseas were resident in the United States, ten per cent were in Canada, 23 per cent were in Latin America and only seven per cent were in Australia and South Africa.[10] As illustrated by Figure 24.1 the four major destinations now claim much more equal shares of the total.

The migration from Northern and Western Europe went almost entirely to Canada, the United States, and to Oceania. Less than 100,000 went to Latin America. This is natural in view of the fact that the British Isles and Germany contributed so heavily to the movement.

Southern Europeans also first sought areas in which their languages, customs and religion are predominant. Over half of the migration from the Southern countries went to Latin America. Spanish emigrants went to Spanish-speaking countries, Portuguese emigrants to Portuguese-speaking Brazil. Italians went in greatest numbers to Latin America. Eastern Europeans, chiefly displaced persons, were widely dispersed though there was a heavy complement to Israel.

The International Refugee Organization in 1947–1951 and the Intergovernmental Committee for European Migration from 1952 to the present have sponsored very substantial migration. They have organized the very difficult cross-cultural migrations

that often required special financial assistance and, on the part of the United States, special legislation. Almost half of the net migration into the United States in this period came under special legislation incorporated in the Displaced Persons Act of 1948 (341,000) and the Refugee Act of 1953 (214,000).

There has been some resurgence of the older pattern of individual migration. Individual migration, by contrast with organized migration, responds with great sensitivity to the immediate opportunities for employment, often brought to the potential migrant's attention by sponsoring relatives and countrymen in the countries of destination.

What is the significance of this continued immigration from Europe? Historically, overseas migration has served Europe in two fundamental ways. First, it has offered an escape both from political oppression and from population pressures. Second, it has been part and parcel of the expansion of Europe.

The resumption of overseas emigration made possible the resettlement of the displaced persons; it also provided some outlet for agrarian population in Southern Europe. In Portugal, which is by some measures the most overpopulated country of Western Europe, emigration removed about 30 per cent of the natural increase in the population in the postwar decade. Such emigration has contributed to the reduction of unemployment and underemployment in the region.

The great free migrations provided the human skills and the sinews for European colonization and empire. Where these were not directly an instrument of political expansion, they promoted European trade, capital movements and cultural ties.

The colonization of new lands is no longer a major aspect of European migration unless Jewish settlement of Israel can be so regarded. The vast majority of European migrants go now to areas already occupied by persons of European race. This is true

TABLE 24.1 Net emigration from Europe, 1946–1955 (in thousands)

| | AREA OF EMIGRATION | | | | | | | | | | |
| | NORTHWEST | | | | | | SOUTH | | | | |
AREA OF IMMIGRATION	BRITISH ISLES	SCANDINAVIA	GERMANY	NETHERLANDS	FRANCE	OTHER[1]	ITALY	PORTUGAL	SPAIN	GREECE	YUGOSLAV
NORTH AMERICA	512	61	397	129	55	127	246	12	7	41	63
Canada	281	19	132	101	26	70	127	3	2	14	19
United States	231	42	265	28	29	57	119	9	5	27	44
LATIN AMERICA	−33	4	24	22	6	26	571	205	294	4	16
Argentina	—	—	10	—	1	7	362	9	161	—	11
Brazil	3	—	12	4	5	7	76	173	35	4	1
Venezuela	—	—	—	—	—	3	109	21	61	—	2
Other[2]	−36	4	2	18	—	9	24	2	37	—	2
AFRICA	112	2	12	26	−261	10	1	60	—	1	—
Algeria	—	—	—	—	−263	—	—	—	—	—	—
Union of South Africa	77	1	12	22	2	6	6	—	—	1	—
Other[3]	35	1	0	4	—	4	−5	60	—	—	—
ASIA	−82	—	8	−148	3	6	2	1	—	3	8
Israel	1	—	8	1	3	6	2	1	—	3	8
Other[4]	−83	—	—	−149	—	—	—	—	—	—	—
OCEANIA	351	2	46	88	3	43	119	—	—	34	27
Australia	269	2	46	71	3	30	119	—	—	34	26
New Zealand	82	—	—	17	—	13	—	—	—	—	1
WORLD TOTAL	860	69	487	117	−194	212	939	278	301	83	114

General Note. This table summarizes and carries through the year 1955 detailed compilations given in Department of State, Office of Intelligence Research, *Survey of Overseas Emigration from Europe, 1946–51*, and *Overseas Emigration from Europe, 1952*, Intelligence Reports Nos. 6054 and 6054S, May 8 and August 19, 1953. The data are derived from numerous national and international sources which are often incomplete and inconsistent. Since there is generally better reporting of arrivals than of departures, this table is in principle based on statistics of the receiving country, i.e., for out-bound movements the overseas country of immigration and for return migration the European country concerned. In practice there are many exceptions where it is necessary to piece together information from any sources available. The

even in Latin America. Three-fourths of European migration to Latin America goes to Argentina and to the predominantly European areas of southern Brazil.

Aside from Israel there is only a small exception and this is in Africa. I refer to the influx of British settlers into Rhodesia and to a less extent in neighboring territories just after the war. Nowhere in Africa was there sufficient immigration to create a European majority in even a local area. And this movement has died since the Mau Mau

revolt and the emergence of native African nationalism as a political force.

The large British migration to the Commonwealth has undoubtedly strengthened the ties that hold together this loose association. It has also presumably provided a better distribution of population within the Commonwealth. But it is interesting to note that those departing England were numerically replaced by British repatriates from India and other parts of Asia, and by Poles, by Irish, and now increasingly by West

	EAST					TOTALS			
BULGARIA	CZECHO-SLOVAKIA	HUNGARY	POLAND	RUMANIA	U.S.S.R.	NORTHWEST	SOUTH	EAST	EUROPE & U.S.S.R.
2	47	36	271	26	161	1,281	369	543	2,193
1	13	12	88	10	36	629	165	160	954
1	34	24	183	16	125	652	204	383	1,239
—	3	8	23	2	16	49	1,090	52	1,191
—	1	3	13	1	7	18	543	25	586
—	1	2	4	1	1	31	289	9	329
—	1	2	3	—	4	3	193	10	206
—	—	1	3	—	4	−3	65	8	70
—	—	—	—	—	—	−99	62	—	−37
—	—	—	—	—	—	−263	—	—	−263
—	—	—	—	—	—	120	7	—	127
—	—	—	—	—	—	44	55	—	99
39	22	19	122	134	9	−213	14	345	146
39	22	19	122	134	9	19	14	345	378
—	—	—	—	—	—	−232	—	—	−232
1	11	13	72	3	57	533	180	157	870
1	11	13	71	2	56	421	179	154	754
—	—	—	1	1	1	112	1	3	116
42	83	76[5]	488	165	243	1,551	1,715	1,097	4,363

table shows only *recorded* migrations and hence almost certainly understates the actual movements in many instances [1] Including Austria, Belgium, Finland, Luxembourg, and Switzerland. [2] Chiefly the following: West Indians to the United Kingdom; Dutch to Surinam, Italians to Uruguay and Peru; and Spaniards to Cuba, Uruguay, and the Dominican Republic. [3] Chiefly British to Rhodesia and Portuguese to Angola and Mozambique. [4] Chiefly British repatriation from India and Pakistan and Dutch repatriation from Indonesia. [5] Does not include 190,000 Hungarian refugees following the revolt of 1956.

Indians and Africans. The net postwar loss of population to the United Kingdom has been statistically negligible.[11]

France has had an inward balance of migration, particularly from North Africa, first of Arabs and now increasingly of French.

What has been the effect of the migration on the receiving countries? This movement has generally been profitable to them if for no reason other than that they have acquired workers, usually of good quality and skills, without bearing the cost of their up-bringing and education. In Canada, Australia, and New Zealand the migrants entered countries lightly populated in relation to their resources and where economic opportunities were great. The movement to the United States was not in sufficient numbers to have any great effect on the economy but the immigrants provided certain skills, whether in trades and services or in scientific advances of critical value for purposes of defense.

In Latin America the relatively small numbers of European immigrants have played a disproportionately large role in economic development of that area. At the 1946 Conference Kingsley Davis said, "The region cannot attract the kind of immigrants it wants and does not want the kind it can attract; and also it does not need mass immigration anyway."[12]

Latin America has not in fact experienced very large mass migration. But European migration has contributed a type of person of which it is much in need—an urban entrepreneurial and skilled labor class. Unhappily most of the migration has been channeled to the countries where these skills are already more common, such as Argentina. In two countries, Brazil and Venezuela, recent European immigrants are of great importance in economic development. In Venezuela particularly the 200,000 European immigrants since the war are playing an indispensable part in the economic renaissance of the country. Of course it required the earnings from great oil and iron deposits to create a situation that would attract this volume of immigration. Other Latin American countries are less fortunate.

Nowhere in Latin America was the volume of European migration too large to absorb. Only in Australia and Israel was it sometimes too large to digest. In these countries it has been necessary to slow up and absorb before taking more. In Australia and particularly Israel the volume of immigration in relation to population has been as great or greater than occurred in this country in the peak periods of immigration.

The chief conflicts connected with immigration have tended to be social and cultural rather than economic. The xenophobic fears of cultural inundation that exist in overseas countries and which are reflected in rigid controls of immigration far exceed the factual dangers. Actually the great bulk of European migrants moved to areas where their language and customs were understood.

The problems of assimilation were greatest in the cross-cultural movements of refugees, especially the political refugees who came from countries that had no colonies of similar language and customs overseas. The assimiliation problems of Israel with its Jews of many languages and customs were among the most interesting and complex.

Overseas migration from Europe continues on a sizable scale. Since the war it has averaged an amount equal to that of the decade 1921–1930 and exceeded only by the period 1900–1914. To Americans its importance may be somewhat obscured by the fact that the destinations of European emigrants are more dispersed than in the heyday of overseas migration when this country absorbed most of the movement. The Intergovernmental Committee for European Migration in its six years of existence has actively promoted this dispersion and it will continue to do so barring further liberalization of American immigration restrictions.

Asian Migrations since the Second World War

Asia has participated little in the international migrations of the decade. The decade has certainly borne out Irene Taeuber's prediction in 1946 that international migration holds no promise as a solution for Asian problems of population pressure.[13]

A study conducted by the author at the State Department several years ago reached the conclusion that by European (not American) average levels of agricultural productivity per farm worker Asia has a rural surplus population of 600 million people. Any international migration sufficient to remove even a small fraction of this overwhelming mass is almost unthinkable in a peaceful world. The total net overseas migration of Europeans over a century and a half has been only about one-tenth of this rural surplus.

Nevertheless overseas and international migration were formerly of some importance in Asia. The quantitative significance of such migration is suggested by the estimate that in

1940 over eight million Chinese were living outside of China, chiefly in Asian countries; three and one-half million Japanese were living outside the home islands, many of these of course in the Japanese empire; and four million Indians were estimated to be living outside India and Pakistan. In the interwar period there were very sizable migrations from China to Southeast Asian countries, and especially to Malaya where net Chinese immigration reached a peak of 181,000 in 1937. In the 1920's there was a net emigration of a million from India, chiefly to Burma, Ceylon, and Malaya.[14]

Since the war most of these movements have been stopped or reversed by political developments. In this period the main Asian countries of immigration achieved independence and then, if not earlier, imposed severe restrictions on immigration. In some cases there were active efforts to force the repatriation of earlier migrants. Voluntary international migration in Asia has essentially come to a standstill, unless we consider under this head the continuing exchange of populations between India and Pakistan and the movement of Jews from Arab countries to Israel.

Nor has internal settlement and colonization been important. For example, in Indonesia one third of the hard-won budget for economic development has been spent on "transmigration" from crowded Java to the relatively empty outer Islands of the archipelago. Despite these efforts the actual balance of movement since independence has been into, not out of, Java. The numbers settled in the outer Islands were more than offset by a movement from the outer Islands to the cities of Java. The efforts of land settlement in the Philippines and other countries of Asia have met with similar difficulties in the organization and in the high cost of colonization and settlement.

Not that internal migration has been unimportant in Asia. There is probably no country in Asia, nor for that matter in the world, that has not experienced some degree of urbanization since World War II. Rural-urban migration is one of the most powerful and consistent forces in the world today. In numbers this movement is vastly more than international migration, and international migration itself is more often than not to the cities of the receiving countries.

Internal Migration

The experience of the United States may illustrate the relative importance of international and internal migration. It also may illustrate the difficulties of obtaining accurate data on both types of movement.

In demographic convention the influence of migration is commonly discussed as the migration component in population change. In this country we lack sufficiently accurate direct measures of migration to justify direct computation. So migration is usually estimated as a residual, that is to say the difference between population growth and natural increase.

This procedure gives a minimum statement of the importance of migration. Thus in 1940–1950 the population of the continental United States (including Armed Forces overseas) increased 19.6 million, of which 17.7 was from natural increase, and only about two million from net immigration. By this measure net immigration accounted for only about 10 per cent of the population growth in the United States between 1940 and 1950.

There is no accurate measure of the migration balance since 1950, nor do we know with any precision what were the components of net immigration in the decade 1940–1950. We of course know that the net balance is the residue of a much larger movement to and from the United States. There is statistical coverage of overseas migration from foreign countries and in the last few years from Puerto Rico, but control of the movement across land boundaries with Canada and Mexico is still inadequate to provide accurate statistics on permanent migration.

Migration is of course much more important in determining the growth, composition, and characteristics of the population within states and local areas. Postwar migrations within the United States have matched in volume the wartime movements described by several participants in the 1946 Milbank Conference and have exceeded the cautious projections then made by Hauser and Eldridge.[15]

Fortunately we now have means of estimating at least the gross volume of internal migration in the United States. In the decade 1946–1955 there were 37.2 million births, 14.7 million deaths and over 100 million migrations.[16]

In the first postwar decade some 48 million migrants moved from one state to another and an approximately equal number moved from one county to another within the same state. About six and one-half million residents came from abroad, and an unknown number went to foreign countries.

As the regional and interstate differences in birth and death rates tend to level off, migration has become the decisive factor in determining differences in the rates of population change. The influence of migration will become even more definitive if there is a trend toward greater and greater mobility of our people.

To suggest the importance of internal migration I will refer to three major movements within the continental United States, each with vital implications for the future of the country: (1) the continued westward movement, or, more properly speaking, the attraction of areas with favorable climates such as California, the Southwest, and Florida; (2) rural-urban migration; (3) the movement from the central cities to the suburbs and, beyond, to exurbia.

The first of these is modifying the regional distribution of population, which is of course not new in American history. If present trends continue California will within a few years replace New York as the first state of the Union and Nevada will lose its historical position as the smallest.

The second involves a flight from the land that in some areas has reached drastic proportions. To cite an extreme example, over half of the farm population of Oklahoma alive in 1940 migrated from the farms in the succeeding decade. The impact of this flight from the land was further accentuated by the fact that out-migrants included disproportionate numbers of young people. About two-thirds of the Oklahoma farm population 10–19 in 1940 and 20–29 in 1950 left the farms in the decade.[17] Much of the interregional migration (i.e., from South to North) is at the same time rural-urban.

Finally, it is scarcely an exaggeration to say that migration to the suburbs is creating a new American way of life comparable in its way to the changes historically wrought first by the westward movement of the 19th century and then by urbanization of the country in the first half of the 20th.

Important changes in the composition of the population may be involved even where the net balance of migration may be small. Thus in Connecticut, which has had a relatively small balance of internal migration over the past generation, close to half of the population was born in other states or abroad. Close to a quarter of the population born in Connecticut now lives elsewhere.

Unfortunately we know very little about the effect of such movements on the character of state populations. What is the effect on the composition and characteristics of the population of California of the fact that almost two-thirds of its population was born elsewhere? Conversely, what is the effect on Arkansas of the fact that 43 per cent of the people born in that state have left its territory? What selective elements may have been involved? What was the effect on the quality of leadership and the political and social institutions of that state?

Much of the answer is to be found in the detail of the Census publications but it often remains unanalyzed partly because we lack adequate methodology to reduce it to manageable rates and ratios, partly because we have no adequate theoretical structure of migration "laws," generalizations and hypotheses.

Summary

The above review is far from a complete history of significant migrations in the postwar decade, but it may serve as a background for the several generalizations that follow.

The first postwar decade has witnessed the successful liquidation of the huge legacy of displaced persons and refugees directly caused by World War II. In Europe this success is the result of intensive national and international efforts and of the fact that these displacements moved in the direction of the greater underlying economic opportunity in the more industrial and developed areas. Political and military influences were dominant but the lasting movements were also usually in the direction of economic pressures.

Unhappily there have been vast new postwar forced migrations, particularly in Asia, that have been less satisfactorily resolved.

Overseas migration from Europe has been resumed. This renewed migration was partly connected with overseas settlement of displaced persons and partly induced by the continuing pressures of population, especially in Southern Europe. But European colonization is at an end. Almost all European emigration went to overseas areas already occupied by Europeans, and within these to the cities rather than the countryside. Migration is closely controlled in the overseas countries and a large part of it is sponsored by international organizations. Numerous postwar proposals for revision of American immigration restrictions have been unsuccessful except for temporary and emergency legislation.[18]

Overseas migration within Asia, once quite considerable, has come to a standstill owing to restrictions on migration imposed by the Asian countries of immigration, most of which have gained independence since the war.

Political and ethnic frontiers are replacing geography as the chief barriers to international migration. In general free international migration is less than in the past. In Europe there has been no postwar counterpart to the great influx of workers into France from Italy, Spain, and Eastern Europe. In Asia there has been no postwar counterpart to the earlier Chinese migrations to Malaya and Southeast Asia and of Indian migration to Ceylon, Burma, and Malaya. In North America, Mexican immigration into the United States is more rigidly controlled than in the comparable period of prosperity in the 1920s.

By contrast, within national boundaries population is everywhere becoming more mobile. It is doubtful if there is any country in the world where there has not been some rural-urban migration and growth of urbanization since World War II.

Everywhere we see the centripetal forces of migration dominant in the world, from the less developed to the more developed areas, from the smaller to the larger population aggregates. The most important migrations today are the internal and largely unrecorded migrations from rural to urban areas and within metropolitan areas. In the United States great mobility is leading to rapid changes in the population distribution and composition. Other countries in the world are less mobile but mobility is an integral part of economic and social development, and as yet there is no end in sight of the trend towards greater and greater mobility. The scientific analysis of migration is a matter of rapidly growing importance in the world today.

Notes

[1]Postwar Problems of Migration. Papers presented at the Round Table on Population Problems, 1946 Conference of the Milbank Memorial Fund, October 29–30, 1946, New York, Milbank Memorial Fund, 1947.

[2]Unfortunately these several categories of migration are not always either sharply distinguished or mutually exclusive. In practice one must rely on the frequently in-

consistent administrative definitions used by governments in the collection of migration data. The statistics of international migration are notoriously defective; more often than not statistics of internal migration simply do not exist. *Cf.* United Nations, Department of Economic and Social Affairs: Problems of Migration Statistics. Population Studies No. 5. New York, 1949.

[3]Schechtman, Joseph B.: European Population Transfers, 1939–1945. New York, Oxford University Press, 1946; and Kulischer, Eugene M.: Europe on the Move: War and Population Changes, 1917–1947. New York, Columbia Univ. Press, 1948.

[4]Systematic analyses of the demographic changes resulting from these movements are given in the International Population Statistics Reports of the United States Bureau of the Census, especially The Population of the Federal Republic of Germany and West Berlin by Paul F. Myers and W. Parker Mauldin, 1952; The Population of Czechoslovakia by Walter Wynne, Jr., 1953; The Population of Poland by W. Parker Mauldin and Donald S. Akers, 1954; and The Population of Yugoslavia by Paul F. Myers and Arthur A. Campbell, 1954.

[5]This thesis is presented more fully by the present author in Hans W. Weigert and others, Principles of Political Geography. New York, Appleton-Century, 1957. Pp. 350–355 and 365–367.

[6]These are more fully analyzed by the present author in an article on "Economic and Demographic Developments in Western Germany" in *Population Index*, January, 1958, pp. 3–21.

[7]Davie, Maurice R.: Recent Refugee Immigration from Europe. In Postwar Problems of Migration, op. cit., pp. 110–123.

[8]Intergovernmental Committee for European Migration *Press Release* #228, New York, October 23, 1957.

[9]The following discussion of this topic summarizes and brings up to date materials in the author's article (with Earl Huyck) on Overseas Migration from Europe since World War II in *American Sociological Review*, August, 1954, **19**, No. 4, pp. 447–456.

[10]From the author's Europe's Population in the Interwar Years. League of Nations, 1946, p. 281.

[11]Isaac, Julius: British Postwar Migration. National Institute of Economic and Social Research, Occasional Papers xvii. Cambridge University Press, 1954, Pp. 203–210.

[12]Future Migration into Latin America. *In* Postwar Problems of Migration. Op. cit., p. 48.

[13]Taeuber, Irene B.: Migration and the Population Potential of Monsoon Asia. In Postwar Problems of Migration. Op. cit., pp. 7–29.

[14]*Cf.:* International Migrations in the Far East During Recent Times: The Countries of Emigration *In* United Nations *Population Bulletin*, December, 1951, No. 1, pp. 13–41; and The Countries of

Immigration in *Ibid.*, October, 1952, No. 2, pp. 27–58.

[15]*Cf.* papers by Conrad Taeuber, Henry S. Shryock, Jr., Ira De. A. Reid, and Philip M. Hauser and Hope T. Eldridge in Postwar Problems of Migration, op. cit.

[16]The mobility of the population of the United States has been determined each year since 1947 from Current Population Surveys conducted by the Bureau of the Census in March or April of each year. These figures, plus an estimate for 1946 based on average figures for 1947–1950, provide an estimated total of 96 million migrants in the decade, approximately equally divided between interstate migrants and migrants between counties in the same state. These estimates are subject to considerable error since they are based on sample enumerations which actually covered years from March to March and April to April rather than calendar years. Cf. Bureau of the Census: Mobility of the Population of the United States: March 1955 to 1956 in *Current Population Reports*, March 12, 1957, P-20, No. 73, Washington, D.C.

[17]Tarver, James D.: Population Change and Migration in Oklahoma 1940–50. Oklahoma A. & M. College, Division of Agriculture, Bulletin No. B-485, January 1957.

[18]*Cf.* papers contributed by Carter Goodrich, E. P. Hutchinson and Warren Thompson in Postwar Problems of Migration, op. cit.

Selection Twenty-five

ON BASIC MIGRATION PATTERNS

**V. V. Pokshishevskiy
V. V. Vorob'yev
Ye. N. Gladysheva
V. I. Perevedentsev**

The Marxist-Leninist concept of population, of the working people, as the main productive force makes data about the numbers,

Translated by Theodore Shabad from *Materialy K IV S'yezdu Geograficheskogo obshchestva S.S.S.R.* (Materials of the Fourth Congress of the Geographical Society of the U.S.S.R.) [mimeographed], Leningrad, 1964.

distribution, and structure of the population (taken over time) basic for an understanding of the economic geography of a country. This is especially evident in the case of the USSR and other socialist countries, where cities have no unemployment and rural areas do not suffer from overpopulation, two phenomena that often darken the direct and principal relationship between the manpower continents and their productive potential under the conditions of capitalism.

In terms of mobility, population occupies an intermediate position among all productive forces, between natural resources, which are territorially "immobile," and the tools of labor and the already extracted objects of labor, which, in principle, have "absolute" mobility (although they vary in transportability). At the same time, live labor can be utilized in the production process only where it is localized, a fact that distinguishes it from all materalized labor. (This excludes commuting to work within limited areas; see V. V. Pokshishevskiy, "The geography of population and its tasks," *Izv. AN SSSR, ser. geogr.*, 1962, No. 4, p. 8.)

Territorial redistributions of population and manpower are determined in the final analysis by shifts of production, but require a substantial amount of time. At any given period, therefore, the existing geography of population constitutes one of the main factors in the "current" location of production. This is especially true in the case of a socialist economy, which in principle assures full employment in any region; the concept of a population "surplus" in this case has a relative meaning, namely that the manpower in a "surplus" region can be used with less effectiveness than in other regions. The phenomenon of "depressed areas," which under capitalist conditions became areas of out-migration, is unknown in a socialist economy. (The present "depressed areas" of the United States, the French departments of the Massif Central that are losing population, and the depressed agrarian areas of northeastern Brazil had an analogue in pre-revolutionary Russia in the guberniyas of the middle belt of European Russia, which suffered from an acute agrarian depression. Lenin wrote about these areas: "The colonization problem in Russia is subordinated to the agrarian question in the center of the country" [*Works*, in Russian, 3rd edition, Vol. XII, p. 225]. This Leninist formulation uncovers an important

economic law of migration under the capitalist mode of production, namely the predominance of the role of the "expellant factor" in migrations, rather than the principle of equilibrium between "push and pull factors" favored by bourgeois scholars. Lenin's law also holds true in explaining related processes, such as urbanization in many underdeveloped countries, which is proceeding at a scale far from commensurate with the real economic potential of the cities of these countries.) The driving forces of the migration process in the USSR are not related to unemployment and overpopulation in the areas of origin—these phenomena now exist only on the pages of Soviet textbooks—but to the positive aims of resource development and to the realization that the use of a high level of socialist technology combined with live labor will yield a higher effect when applied to the rich resources of newly settled areas.

The geographic redistribution of population, reflecting shifts in the geography of a growing economy, has been one of the key features of economic development of our country, both before the revolution and in Soviet times.

Aside from migration, this redistribution has been distinguished by another important factor: territorial differences in the rate of natural increase of the population. (The importance of this factor was first stressed in general terms by Soviet specialists on the history of population geography; see: A. G. Rashin, *Naseleniye Rossii za 100 let, 1811–1913* [The Population of Russia for 100 Years, 1811–1913], Moscow, 1956; and "Shifts in the territorial distribution of population of Russia in the nineteenth and early twentieth centuries," *Voprosy geografii*, No. 20, 1950; and V. K. Yatsunskiy, "Changes in the distribution of population of European Russia, 1724–1916," *Istoriya SSSR*, 1957, No. 1.) The relative importance of the migration factor and of differences in the rate of natural increase has varied at different stages in history. In the period of development of capitalism in Russia, a higher rate of natural increase was evident in the colonization areas whose economy was on the rise at that time, the steppe guberniyas of New Russia and Siberia; these areas were also the destinations of the principal migration flows. During this period the area of peasant out-migration expanded as the territorial extent of the agrarian depression increased. (See: V. V. Pokshishevskiy, *Zaseleniye Sibiri* [The Settling of Siberia], 1951; and "Essays on the settling of the wooded-steppe and steppe regions of the Russian Plain," *Ekonomicheskaya geografiya SSSR*, No. 5, published by the Geography-Biology Faculty of the Moscow State Pedagogic Institute named for Lenin, Moscow, 1960. The second study contains, for 1863–1913, the following balances of the principal inter-regional migration flows, in millions of people; Siberia, +4.2; Far East, +0.7; Urals, mostly southern Urals, +0.8; Central Asia and Kazakhstan, except northern Kazakhstan which was included in Siberia, +1.3; steppe guberniyas of New Russia, +3.6; Northern Caucasus, +1.5; Chernozem and Non-Chernozem Center, −4.5; Ukrainian wooded steppe, −3.2; Volga, −0.8; European North, −0.5. There was also a substantial out-migration from the Baltic region and the Polish territories that were then part of Russia, but it represented mainly emigration to other countries. This study also contains migration data for the preceding period, starting in the seventeenth century, in the tabular appendices.)

In the Soviet period, the spread of socialist conditions throughout the country eliminated the social hardships that produced low rates of natural increase in some areas in the past. The gap between rates of natural increase in urban and rural areas was reduced. Only in periods of intensification of the class struggle do we find a temporary decline of the growth rate in areas where that struggle was particularly intense. For example, while the total population of the USSR rose by 16 per cent between 1926 and 1939, the increase was only 1.2 per cent in Kazakhstan, despite in-migration. (In Kazakhstan, intensification of the class struggle coincided with the breakup of the previously

dominant nomad herding economy; this led to the loss of much livestock and a temporary decline in living standards. Some of the former nomads settled on neighboring lands of Uzbekistan.)

Inter-regional migrations assumed a large scale in connection with industrial construction of the five-year plans. Between 1926 and 1939, about 3 million people moved to Siberia and the Far East, and more than 1.7 million to Central Asia and Kazakhstan (*Trudovyye resursy SSSR* [Manpower Resources of the USSR], Moscow, 1961, p. 209). A big percentage of the new settlers settled in cities: the share of urban population rose from 18 to 32 per cent, with the growth especially marked in large cities. The total population of the twenty-five largest cities (1939) rose from 8.77 million in 1926 to 18.12 million in 1939, chiefly as a result of inter-regional migrations, especially to Moscow, which grew by more than 2 million, Leningrad (by 1.5 million), Novosibirsk, Gor'kiy, Sverdlovsk, Volgograd, and Zaporozh'ye (three- to fivefold).

The years of the Great Patriotic War (1941–45) were marked, together with large absolute population losses (from military losses, extermination of civilians by the Fascist invaders, higher mortality, and a lower birth rate), by major territorial population shifts. Most important was the temporary eastward migration from territories occupied by the Hitlerite invaders and from the frontline zone (evacuation of civilians and of industries). Between June 1941 and February 1, 1942, 10.4 million people were evacuated (*Istoriya Velikoy Otechestvennoy voyny* [History of the Great Patriotic War], Vol. II, pp. 548–49). This figure is based on a survey conducted by the railroads. According to a survey conducted by local authorities, almost 6 million found refuge by the spring of 1942 in oblasts of the RSFSR (mainly in the Volga, Urals, and Western and Eastern Siberia), and more than 1.5 million in Kazakhstan, Central Asia, and Transcaucasia. These data are apparently less complete because some of the evacuated people settled in the new areas without passing through organized evacuation centers). The evacuation of 1941 was followed by the second evacuation wave of 1942. During the period of maximum eastward advance by the invaders, the population of nonoccupied territories did not fall below 130 million (N. Voznesenskiy, *Voyennaya ekonomika SSSR v period Otechestvennoy voyny* [The War Economy of the USSR in the Period of the Patriotic War]. Moscow: 1948, p. 26. Voznesenskiy also says [p. 157] that the occupied territories held 45 per cent of the Soviet population before the war); we can therefore conclude that the total evacuation, from June 1941 to October 1942, was close to 20 million.

Although it was temporary in principle, this huge migration resulted in the partial settling of the evacuated population in the eastern areas, especially in the Urals, Western Siberia, and Kazakhstan. For example, in 1947, when the last count of evacuated population was made in Irkutsk Oblast, fifteen per cent of the original arrivals were still there. Re-evacuation extended over many years.

Territorial differences in the natural rate of increase of the population also played a role in the war years. The eastern areas were able to compensate in part for their human losses by natural population growth. A "net" population loss applied mainly to the European part of the country, where the occupied territories accounted for three-fourths of the total loss (including displaced persons).

In the post-war years, the natural population increase was consistently higher in the eastern and southern areas than in the western areas that had suffered especially from war destruction. Even by the time of the 1959 census, the pre-war population level had not been reached in some formerly occupied western areas—Belorussian SSR, Lithuanian SSR, Pskov, Novgorod, Smolensk, and Kalinin oblasts of the RSFSR, and some oblasts of the Ukrainian SSR. (The recovery of the Moldavian SSR resulted from a combination of a high rate of natural increase and in-migration of Russians and Ukrainians in connection with industrialization; the share of Russians and Ukrainians in the population of the Moldavian SSR rose from 16–17 per cent in 1941 to 24.8 per cent in 1959. In the case of Estonia and Latvia, where the rate of natural increase was low, the recovery was related to an influx of Russians, Ukrainians, and Belorussians, whose share in the population of Estonia reached 22.3 per cent by 1959, and of Latvia 30.9 per cent. This influx was related to the industrial rebirth of the Baltic region as its ports assumed a key role in the geographic division of labor.) In the east and south, consistent population increases were insured by a high rate of natural increase and, in some areas, by continuing in-migration.

The absence from the 1959 census questionnaire of questions that would permit distinguishing between the migration factor and the natural rate of increase in over-all population growth makes it difficult to judge the relative importance of these two factors in the redistribution of the population both in the first post-war five-year plans and subsequently. The two factors can be distinguished only indirectly by comparing the actual population growth with the rate of natural increase, but this method at least yields an order of magnitude. (Current registration data of new arrivals also do not yield the answer because registration in rural areas began only in 1960, having been limited previously to cities; furthermore one would have to assume incompleteness of registration, the fact that registration does not take account of the length of stay in the previous place of residence, etc. Available data on territorial differences in the rate of natural increase were recently generalized for major regions by G. S. Nevel'shteyn ["Territorial differences in the natural increase of population of the USSR," *Materialy po geografii naseleniya* (Materials on Population Geography), No. 1. Leningrad: Geographical Society USSR, 1962]. The author used more than eighty statistical handbooks published in republics, krays, and oblasts in 1956–60. He notes that fluctuations in the rate of natural increase depend mainly on birth-rate levels "which vary to a much greater extent in individual regions than death rates" [p. 8].)

An over-all picture of the territorial redistribution of population over the last four years as a result of migration is shown in the cartograms. (These have been compiled on the basis of the migration balance, the difference between the actual population growth and the natural rate of increase.) The redistribution of population by migration in the last four years apparently amounted to as much as one-seventh of the natural increase. The first cartogram (Fig. 25.1) suggests the approximate scale of both out-migration and in-migration in various regions of the USSR. In 1959–62, for example, Kazakhstan had an in-migration of almost one million people (representing the main inter-regional migration flow). In-migration was also substantial in Central Asia and in the Northern Caucasus, and was relatively noticeable in the Baltic republics and in Transcaucasia. Contrary to the general impression there was no "net" in-migration in Siberia and the Far East, where the migration balance is now negative. (This change in the direction of migration, which it is hoped is temporary, was demonstrated in the last few years in the work of V. I. Perevedentsev, for example, in: "Basic aspects of Western Siberia's external migration links, "*Materialy I soveshchaniya po geografii naseleniya* [Proceedings of the First Conference on Population Geography], No. 2, 1961; "Problems of territorial redistribution of manpower resources," *Voprosy ekonomiki*, 1962, No. 5. This material was then generalized in the dissertation *Sovremennaya migratsiya naseleniya Sibiri* [Present-Day Migration of the Population of Siberia], Moscow: Institute of Economics, Academy of Sciences USSR, 1963.)

The main source of out-migration still is the central areas of the European part of the RSFSR (especially the Volga-Vyatka region, where out-migration is almost equal to the natural increase; out-migration is also high in several oblasts of the Central Region,

although for the region as a whole this is compensated in part by the continuing attraction of population to the Moscow agglomeration). During this period more than one million people from the central European RSFSR moved to other parts of the country. Another major source of out-migration is Belorussia, whose contribution to the replenishment of manpower reserves elsewhere is quite substantial compared with the modest size of the population of the republic itself. On the other hand, the contribution of the Ukraine is unexpectedly small. Although the Ukraine itself is well supplied with manpower, and even has a surplus in the western part, out-migration from the Ukraine was lower than from Belorussia, whose population is five times smaller. (The low level of out-migration from the Ukraine can be explained in part by the fact that in the migration exchange with Siberia, in the period 1956–60, arrivals in the Ukraine exceeded departures: for every 100 departures from the Ukraine for Siberia, 143 moved from Siberia to the Ukraine [V. I. Perevedentsev, *Sovremennaya migratsiya . . . , op. cit.*, dissertation summary, p. 12].) The Urals, once a region of net in-migration, now also records an excess of departures over arrivals.

The second cartogram (Fig. 25.2) gives a picture of the relationship between the migration factor and natural increase in over-all population growth. The sum of the differences between regional rates of natural increase and the national average is somewhat smaller than the volume of migrations, but works out quite closely.

It is interesting to note that, except for the Belorussians, Russians take a far more active part in migrations than the indigenous peoples of national republics. This has been borne out, for example, by a special study of the influence of the ethnic factor on the intensity of migrations, made by Perevedentsev at the Institute of Economics in Novosibirsk. The study investigated the participation in the migrations to various parts of Siberia of ethnic groups originating in areas with similar natural and climatic

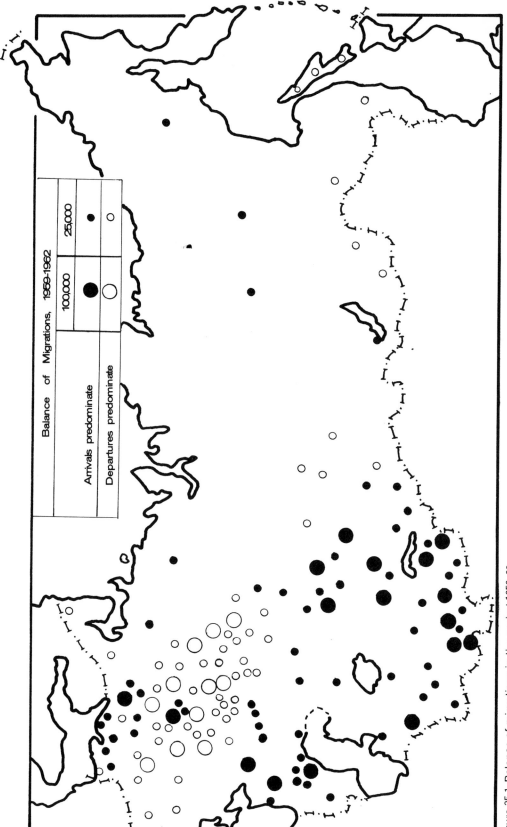

Figure 25.1 Balance of migrations in the period 1959–62

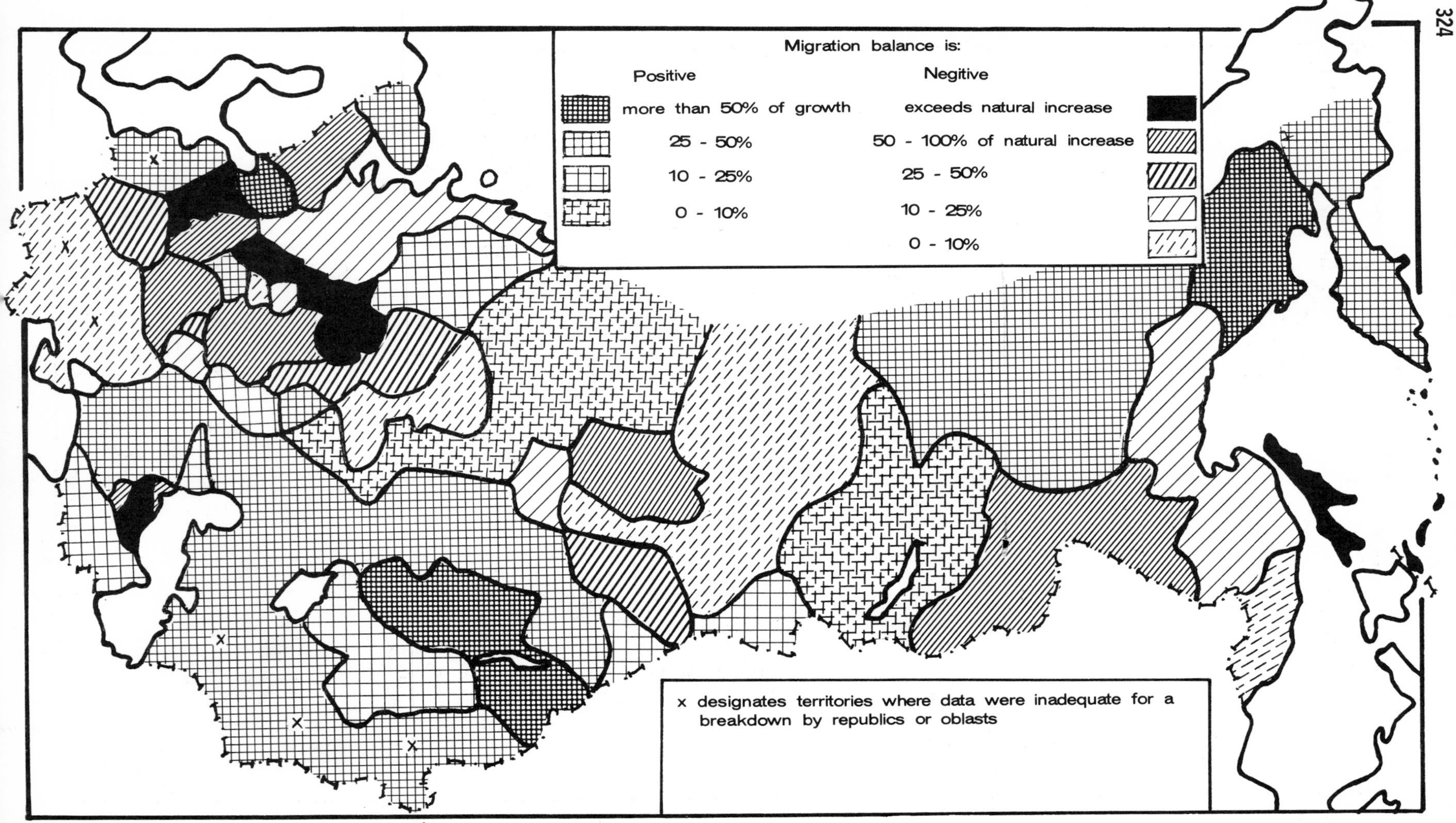

Figure 25.2 The migration factor and natural increase in population growth

conditions. (For example, among migrants from the Ukraine who arrived in Novosibirsk in 1959, 65 per cent were Russians and 31 per cent were Ukrainians, although Ukrainians far outnumber Russians in the Ukraine itself; Russians also accounted for 65 per cent of the migrants from Transcaucasia, 86 per cent from Central Asia, 78 per cent from Kazakhstan and 82 per cent from the Baltic republics. Only Belorussia supplied more Belorussians (54 per cent) than Russians (36 per cent). The share of indigenous peoples was also quite high among migrants from the Volga region, Russians accounting for two-thirds and indigenous groups for one-third of the migrants.)

Study of the geography of migrations should take account of the existence of several types of migrations (which are closely interwoven in practice): (a) Migration within rural areas (mainly from smaller rural places to larger ones, such as central settlements of collective and state farms). This type is motivated both by the consolidation of agricultural enterprises, requiring in turn a consolidation of settlements, and by the desire of people to live in larger and more comfortable settlements. A lack of data makes it impossible to analyze this process in quantitative terms; it can be followed indirectly in terms of the number of rural population centers and their size groups. (For example, in Irkutsk Oblast, the number of rural places declined from 5,000 to 3,220 in the period 1926–59, and their average size rose from 130 to 230 people [V. V. Vorob'yev, "Changes in the distribution of population of Eastern Siberia," in the book *Geografiya naseleniya Vostochnoy Sibiri* (Geography of Population of Eastern Siberia), Moscow, 1962, p. 15.) The population of smaller rural places is usually limited to those who are essential for work in associated livestock and crop sectors of the large farms. (b) Migration from rural areas to towns (of the same region)—the principal source of growth of urban population. This type of migration, related to the rapid expansion of industry and the need for manpower, takes place in all regions of the USSR, although with varying degrees of intensity. The reverse flow, from town to countryside, is far smaller. (c) Migration between urban places (within a region), usually from small urban places to more diversified, multi-functional cities and industrial centers. Small urban places often serve as an intermediate stopping point in the movement of rural population to urban centers (including urban centers of other regions) that are constantly experiencing an influx of population from the countryside. (This tendency, characteristic of many parts of the USSR, was illustrated by the example of Krasnoyarsk Kray in the study by Zh. A. Zayonchkovskaya and V. I. Perevedentsev, "On the question of the present-day migration links of the population of Krasnoyarsk Kray," in the book *Geografiya naseleniya Vostochnoy Sibiri, op. cit.*)

All these types of migration are intra-oblast or intra-regional. They are being investigated less frequently than inter-regional migrations although they also deserve attention in terms of volume and their role in changes in population geography. The migration type that is most commonly being studied is (d) the exchange of population between regions. The traditional picture of migration from regions with surplus manpower to regions with a manpower deficit arose, as we noted above, from the migration experience of the capitalist era, although even for that period such a generalization was too mechanistic. Under conditions of a socialist economy, in addition to the "consciousness" factor, territorial differences in conditions and living levels play an important part. We do not mean here any single indicator, but the entire complex of living conditions. In addition to natural conditions, this complex includes housing with its "quality" (availability of utilities, such as gas, water, baths, and central heating), public health institutions, schools, children's institutions, consumer services (repair shops, public baths, etc.), and availability of durable consumer goods and food. Inter-regional migration has two forms: (1) organized migration (government hiring for work in distant areas, planned rural resettlement, assignments of young graduates, resettlement as a result of public appeals); (2) individual (unorganized) migration. The first form now accounts for 15 to 20 per cent of the total, so that individual movements greatly predominate. But even these differ from the haphazard migrations customary under capitalism. Under Soviet conditions, individual migration is regulated indirectly by the state through the planned development of specific industries, the "guided" training of personnel and other measures.

Many economic-geographic problems that are of practical importance and are related to all these migration types can be traced in regions that suffer from a constant manpower shortage, namely Kazakhstan and Siberia with the Far East.

Kazakhstan is the Soviet region with the most rapid population growth. (The following figures are mainly from the statistical handbook *Narodnoye khozyaystvo Kazakhskoy SSR v 1960 i 1961 gg.* [The National Economy of the Kazakh SSR in 1960 and 1961], Alma-Ata, 1963.) Between the 1939 and 1959 censuses, the population of Kazakhstan rose by more than 50 per cent (average growth in the USSR as a whole was 9.5 per cent). From the 1959 census until July 1, 1963 (a period of four and one-half years), a further growth of 25 per cent was recorded. An important factor in the growth is a high rate of natural increase, almost double the average rate for the USSR (in 1961, respectively 29.1 and 16.7 per 1,000). Natural increase alone accounted for 1.3 million people in the last four and one-half years; the rest (more than one million) resulted from in-migration.

Even before the revolution, the vast, sparsely populated lands of Kazakhstan were among the principal areas of mass settlement of peasants, mainly from the Chernozem Center, the Volga, the Ukraine and Belorussia. This migration flow has continued in Soviet times, varying in intensity at different stages under the in-fluence of changing factors. As the industrialization of Kazakhstan proceeded in the 1930's, demand was greatest for industrial workers and trained personnel at construction projects of the republic, which lacked its own industrial labor force. There was also some planned settlement of peasants, especially in northern Kazakhstan. Cities grew rapidly. From 1926 to 1939, urban population increased from 519,000 to 1,690,000. (In this period, many large villages, rayon seats, and railroad settlements were transformed into urban places.) More than 321,000 people moved to the cities of Kazakhstan in 1939–40. During World War II, when Kazakhstan became one of the arsenals in the eastern part of the Soviet Union and received many evacuated industrial plants with their labor forces, the population of the republic's cities increased by 30 per cent (by the beginning of 1945) despite mobilization into the armed forces and a low rate of natural increase.

Toward the end of the war, starting in 1944, re-evacuation resulted in out-migration from Kazakhstan. A large in-migration in 1946–47 and a high rate of settlement of the arrivals (48 to 51.6 per cent of them remained in Kazakhstan) were related to mass demobilization. Subsequently the movement to Kazakhstan cities remained high until the opening up of the virgin lands (for example, in 1950, more than 100,000 people moved to the cities).

In 1955 a stage began of unprecedentedly intensive migration processes related to the opening up of the virgin lands and an increased rate of industrial development. A chronic manpower-deficit region, Kazakhstan would have been unable with its own human resources to plow up 22 million hectares of virgin and idle lands and at the same time to develop its extractive industries and other branches of the economy and culture.

In subsequent years, the cities of Kazakhstan recorded a drop in the net in-migration balance, not because of a decline in arrivals but because of an increase of departures as a lower percentage of arrivals settled down.

	REGION'S SHARE OF ALL IN-MIGRATION	PERCENTAGE DISTRIBUTION OF ARRIVALS BY:		PERCENTAGE OF PERMANENT SETTLERS (1):	
		URBAN PLACES	RURAL AREAS	URBAN PLACES	RURAL AREAS
RSFSR (2)	51.6	62	38	30	23
Ukrainian SSR (3)	28.3	50	50	38	42
Belorussian SSR	9.7	42	58	42	50
Moldavian SSR	1.9	16	84	17	51
Others	8.5	—	—	—	—
Total	100.0	59	41	29	31

[1]Percentage of arrivals who settled down.

[2]The principal regions of origin in the RSFSR were Siberian oblasts bordering on Kazakhstan (connected by the Turksib and Trans-Siberian railroads) and the Urals as well as the Volga-Vyatka region. The areas with a net out-migration to Kazakhstan in 1962 were: Altay Kray, Sverdlovsk, Kemerovo, Perm', Novosibirsk, Chelyabinsk, Omsk, Irkutsk, Gor'kiy and Kirov oblasts.

[3]The principal areas of origin were the coal oblasts of the Ukraine — Donetsk and Lugansk; compare with the relatively high share of migrants from Kemerovo Oblast in Note 2; this reflects the manpower needs of the Karaganda coal basin.

(In 1955, 44.1 per cent of the arrivals settled down; in 1963, 18.5 per cent.)

The following table shows the regions of origin of migration to Kazakhstan in 1960–62:

Out of the total number of arrivals and departures in Kazakhstan in the period 1960–62, almost half made up movements within Kazakhstan. Of these, one-third represented city-to-city migration, mostly residents of smaller urban places moving to larger cities (especially to republic and kray capitals) and from slower-growing to faster-growing places. (In addition there was a migration flow from the cities of Kazakhstan to other large cities of the Soviet Union, especially the capitals of nearby oblasts— Omsk, Novosibirsk, Sverdlovsk, Chelyabinsk, and Tashkent.) Second in importance (25 per cent of all movement within the republic) were migrations from the countryside to towns. The reverse flow, from urban to rural areas, accounts for 22 per cent; migration between rural areas for 18 per cent.

Migration processes vary in different parts of Kazakhstan in terms of size, intensity, percentage of permanent settlement, and composition of the migrants. A distinctive role in intra-Kazakhstan migrations is played by the Virgin Lands Kray, which in 1962 accounted for almost one-half of all migration in rural areas and one-third of all migration in urban areas. Here the population evidently has not yet "settled down." Up to 90 per cent of the migrations from countryside to towns took place within the kray.

The low rate of permanent settlement in Kazakhstan is due primarily to the lag in housing construction. The still lower rate of permanent settlement in urban areas results both from the fact that the cities contain a substantial grouping of skilled workers who cannot always find work in their field, not only in the countryside, but even in the cities also, and from the fact that organized government's hiring of industrial workers often brings rather unqualified people to Kazakhstan. Being used to life in comfortable large cities, these migrants cannot accept the relatively lower standards of services in Kazakhstan villages and towns. The higher rate of permanent settlement of migrants originating in rural areas, on the other hand, is explained by the fact that they want to advance their technical training in city institutions and therefore settle down to a permanent job and home. Migrants from rural areas of Belorussia, the Ukraine, and especially the neighboring RSFSR oblasts of Kazakhstan also find their customary surroundings in Kazakhstan rural areas. As government-sponsored rural settlers, they get a government loan for acquiring livestock and for construction of a home, or even a finished home. Migrants originating in rural areas, in contrast to the more mobile city people, usually move with their entire family and "forever." For example, in Kokchetav Oblast, almost 90 per cent of the government-sponsored rural settlers who arrived in the period 1956–60 stayed to settle down. The results of government hiring of industrial workers in other parts of the Soviet Union have been far less satisfactory.

Replenishments of the labor force from outside areas are expected to continue in the future, amounting to one-half or more of the planned labor-force growth; this points up the importance of studying in Kazakhstan the entire problem of migratory processes, including the composition of the migrants and factors influencing their settling down in the new areas. Some of the measures that would help stabilize the permanent settlement of new arrivals are: expansion of vocational training facilities in labor-deficit areas, more housing construction, better consumer services, improved urban planning that would insure employment for other family members, and expansion of child-care institutions.

Siberia and the Far East are also short of population. It has been estimated that the development of these regions alone in the foreseeable future will require an influx of 5 to 15 million people (V. V. Pokshishevskiy, "Prospects of population migrations in the USSR," in the book *Geografiya naseleniya Vostochnoy Sibiri, op. cit.*, p. 75).

Despite such prospects, these regions have been characterized in the last few years (1956–62) by: (a) a net westward trend of population movement, which constitutues a dangerous paradox in areas of labor-deficit; (b) a very high out-migration from the countryside, mainly to local cities, but also to cities of other regions; (c) a high over-all population mobility, two to three times greater than in the Center; (d) a substantial westward migration of city dwellers, and their replacement by migrants from the countryside. In some areas resettlement has resulted in a net in-migration (Irkutsk Oblast, Yakut ASSR), but in others the migration balance has been consistently negative since 1956 (Chita and Tomsk oblasts, and, partly, Altay Kray). In the Far East, out-migration has been most pronounced in Sakhalin and Amur Oblast. (For Sakhalin, see L. L. Rybakovskiy, "On the creation of permanent settlement in Sakhalin," in the volume *Voprosy trudovykh resursov v rayonakh Sibiri* [Manpower Problems in the Siberian Regions], Novosibirsk: Siberian Division of the Academy of Sciences USSR, 1961.)

A peculiar feature in Siberia is the step-like pattern of migrations. Siberia is the place where migration flows to the Far East and the Far North originate. Migrants arriving in Siberia from the west settle mainly along the more developed southern railroad belt, to which part of the population from northerly areas of Siberia has also been moving; this has resulted in a concentration of population and, at the same time, an expansion of the southern railroad belt. The Far North and equivalent areas (Bodaybo, Aldan, etc.) have an especially high mobility of population, as many migrants remain for only three to five years. In the last few years, increasing mechanization in the mining industry has insured a steady or even higher level of output with fewer workers, so that these areas also have begun to show a net out-migration.

The outflow of population from the Siberian countryside is far greater than the actual manpower surplus. Among those who are leaving are farm specialists, machine operators, and educated youths who have not yet had specialized training.

The principal factors in the present predominance of the westward movement and the outflow of population from the countryside are differences in living conditions, including those between the cities of the eastern regions themselves. (The living-standard differential has been repeatedly pointed out in the economic literature, for example, in *Trudovyye resursy SSSR, op. cit.*, pp. 220–22; D. D. Moskvin,

"The effect of the living standard on the location of manpower resources and population stability," in the book *Problemy razmeshcheniya proizvoditel'nykh sil v period razvernutogo stroitel'stva kommunizma* (Problems of Location of Productive Forces in the Period of Full-Fledged Construction of Communism), Moscow, 1960, etc. Very persuasive material has now been published in the handbooks of the Central Statistical Administration RSFSR titled *Zhilishchnyy fond v gorodakh i rabochikh poselkakh RSFSR* [Housing in the Cities and Workers' Settlements of the RSFSR], Moscow, 1963 showing that Siberia and the Far East are far below the RSFSR average in housing per capita and in the share of housing that is equipped with running water, sewers, or central heating, and *Bytovoye obsluzhivaniye naseleniya* [Consumer Services], Moscow, 1963, which also shows that the eastern regions lag, especially behind the Central Region, in many important indicators.)

The westward movement from Siberia and the outflow from the countryside have had negative economic consequences. In particular, the constant replacement of city dwellers with migrants from the countryside has held back the level of skilled labor in the cities; some industries, notably lumbering and construction, have suffered acute labor shortages; agriculture has lagged because of a shortage of manpower in general and of skilled labor in particular; great losses were incurred in the direct cost of organized mass movements to Siberia as well as in other types of organized and non-organized migrations.

A rationalization of migratory processes will require the provision of optimal relationships between the living standards of the following population groups: (a) city dwellers of various regions; (b) urban and rural population within regions; (c) various occupational and skilled-labor groups; (d) new settlers and old settlers. The basic principles of inter-regional and intra-regional regulation of living standards should be: (1) establishment of a higher living standard for workers of given occupations and skills

in labor-deficit as compared with labor-surplus regions; (2) reduction of the gap in living standards between urban and rural population in areas with a farm-labor shortage compared with areas with a farm-labor surplus; (3) provision of living conditions for new settlers that would enable them to match the living comfort of old settlers within a relatively short period. All this can be done only if natural and social-economic regional characteristics are taken into account and if the necessary living conditions are assured in the light of those characteristics.

The migratory processes of Sakhalin have been quite specific in character. The population of Sakhalin was 100,000 in 1939 (northern part only), and reached almost 650,000 in 1959 (including the southern part of Sakhalin and the Kurile Islands). Since 130,000 people lived in the northern part of Sakhalin in 1959, the difference (520,000) was made up by new settlers and their children; the actual volume of migration is estimated at 400,000. Direct in-migration took place mainly in the period 1946–54; later, as the economy became organized, mechanization increased, and the need for manpower declined, the reverse trend began. In 1955–57, out-migration was still compensated by natural increase, but since 1957, the population of Sakhalin has been declining (L. L. Rybakovskiy in "On the creation . . . ," *op. cit.*, speaks of a high turnover in the labor force, in addition to the negative migration balance. "The specific aspect of the Far East, that a large part of the population consists of migrants from other parts of the country, has assumed a classic character in Sakhalin" [p. 157]. A survey of eight enterprises in southern Sakhalin, conducted by Rybakovskiy in 1960, showed that 97 per cent of the workers were not born in Sakhalin [p. 159].)

In addition to the principal migration theaters discussed above, there are some secondary theaters that also were significantly affected by migration in the post-war period.

The settling of the lumbering areas and

mining centers of the northern part of European Russia was mainly the result of migration within the vast Northwest region. It was most intensive in the post-war boom areas of the Komi ASSR and Murmansk Oblast (where the Pechenga Rayon, returned to the USSR, was also settled), and in the Karelian ASSR, which had suffered heavily during the war. The population changes of these areas are shown in the following table (in thousands):

	1939	1956	1959	1963
Komi ASSR	319	670	806	902
Murmansk Oblast	291	474	567	648
Karelian ASSR	469	615	651	673

In the case of the two autonomous republics, the large volume of in-migration can also be judged from the ethnic make-up of the population: in the Komi ASSR, Russians now make up 48.4 per cent, Ukrainians and Belorussians 12.7 per cent; in the Karelian ASSR, the share of Russians (who, incidentally, made up half of the population even earlier) rose to 63.4 per cent, and there are also many Belorussians (11.0 per cent) and Ukrainians (3.6 per cent).

Another area in the Northwest that had to be settled was Kaliningrad Oblast (northern part of former East Prussia— Editor). The mass-migration stage (mainly from the central and western oblasts of the RSFSR, and partly from the Belorussian SSR) was completed by 1954; by that time, more than 50,000 workers' and farmers' families had been settled; a certain number of demobilized servicemen were also settled in the oblast. Additional in-migration continued, especially in the cities (for example, the population of the city of Kaliningrad rose from 188,000 in 1956 to 204,000 in 1959 and 232,000 in 1962, i.e., faster than would be possible simply on the basis of natural increase), but in the last few years the migration balance has been slightly negative. It can be assumed that out of the present oblast population of more than

600,000, as many as 400,000 are "first-generation" migrants.

Migrations that were local in character but quite sizeable in volume moved from mountain areas of Central Asia to the plain, mainly to newly irrigated lands (such as the Golodnaya Steppe and the Vakhsh valley). We lack generalized studies of these migratory processes, but a large amount of information about them can be found in regional monographs.

Another local development was the repatriation of Armenians from abroad, which started shortly before the war; in the post-war period about 100,000 persons came to the USSR and settled almost entirely in Armenia (especially in the late 1940's) (*Atlas Armyanskoy SSR*, Yerevan-Moscow, 1961, sheet 59).

A rather large, but unrepeated migration was the repatriation of Poles to Poland, mainly from the Western Ukraine, Belorussia, and Lithuania; their number was about 1.5 million and most were repatriated in 1945–46 (L. Kosinski, *Procesy ludnosciowe na Ziemiach Odzyskanych w latach 1945–60* [Population Processes in the Recovered Lands in the Years 1945–60], Warsaw: Institute of Geography of the Polish Academy of Sciences, 1963).

Finally there is the continuing attraction of large urbanized agglomerations, for example, the redistribution within the Ukraine in favor of the Donets-Dnieper region. The attractive power of the Moscow agglomeration must also be mentioned. There the population flow was mainly to the cities of Moscow Oblast (except Moscow proper) since the rural population in the oblast declined and the growth of the city of Moscow was limited. The net in-migration into Moscow Oblast has been about 40,000 a year since 1950.

An examination of migration processes of the last few years suggests a certain decline in intensity; in any case, it is far from meeting the manpower needs of the economy. In many areas, production shifts create serious manpower shortages. Differences in natural increase, which have been playing a significant role in the post-war period in the territorial redistribution of population, are too slow in their effect to "respond" promptly enough to increasing labor needs resulting from the rapid concentration of industry in new projects.

The observed "hitch" in the unfolding of migrations, which are supposed to insure a more even distribution of population (at least in the zone that is sufficiently favorable for habitation; the more difficult Far North, arid desert, and high mountains will undoubtedly continue to be spottily settled), can be explained in terms of two factors. On the one hand, the very economic-geographic nature of the industries that developed most rapidly in the new areas was oriented toward low labor requirements; and, being located in labor-deficit areas, these industries were rapidly mechanized. Economic development in the seven-year plan (1959–65) was marked by a desire to gain time and therefore to expand production as much as possible on the basis of existing facilities; this in turn held back movements into new areas in the case of many industries. All these aspects had the objective effect of reducing the social need for migrations.

The second factor was the lag of the "new" (especially the eastern) areas in consumer services, housing, and living comfort. This resulted in a stoppage of migrations (and a reverse trend from labor-deficit areas) even when there was an objective need for migrations. Not until the last few years have the character and magnitude of this slowdown of migration been analyzed (previously, under the continuing influence of the personality cult, these phenomena were hidden by a kind of veil of shame). Only on the basis of such an analysis can effective measures be taken to overcome the slowdown. A certain change is already noticeable; the housing construction plan for 1964–65, for example provides for a higher construction rate in the eastern regions (P. F. Lomako's speech at the Third Session of the 6th Supreme Soviet USSR, *Pravda*, December 17, 1963).

N. S. Khrushchev's statement at a meeting in Vladivostok still holds true as a means of insuring the needed rate and direction of migration. He said: "You must attract new people not by higher wages compared with other cities, but by good living conditions" (*Pravda*, Oct. 8, 1959; see also Khrushchev's comment about the importance of living conditions in insuring migration, made at the 22nd party congress [*Materialy XXII s'yezda KPSS* (Materials of the 22nd Congress of the Soviet Communist Party,), Gospolitizdat, 1961, p. 180]).

Selection Twenty-six

IMMIGRATION DATA AND NATIONAL POPULATION ESTIMATES FOR THE UNITED STATES

Donald S. Akers*

Specialists engaged in making estimates of any kind must concern themselves with the quality of the basic data underlying the

*The interpretations made in this paper are the author's own and do not necessarily represent the position of the United States Bureau of the Census. Elayne J. Urban assisted with the calculations.

Reprinted from *Demography*, **4**, 1967, 262–272, by permission of the author and the Population Association of America.

estimates and with applicability of the data to the estimating procedures. If they are engaged in making population estimates, they must concern themselves with census counts and with data relating to the components of population change between the census and the date of estimate. These components include births, deaths, the net balance of immigration, and, unless the estimates are of national totals, internal migration.

Immigration has received less attention

than the other components of change because it contributes only a small fraction of total change. In recent years, immigration has contributed only 10 percent of national growth, the rest being natural increase (excess of births over deaths), and immigrants account for only 7 percent of all intercounty migration within the United States. But even if the immigration component is comparatively small, it is not insignificant and may indeed be an important source of error in the estimates. Therefore, it warrants the consideration of those concerned with population estimates.

Hutchinson has recently reviewed the sources of immigration data and the problems of coverage and definition in adapting them to the requirements of national population estimates.[1] This paper will consider alternative methods for deriving estimates of immigration from the raw data. It presents estimates of net immigration from 1950 to 1965 (Table 26.1) by the method which the author believes affords the best estimates. They are based on estimates previously published by the Bureau of the Census but differ at some points at which new data have become available or a review of the data has led to a change in judgment on how best to use them.[2]

Immigration is defined for policy purposes as the arrival of aliens with permanent visas. For the purpose of population estimates, however, immigration may best be defined in terms of net rather than gross movement and and should include all groups who transfer their residence into or out of the United States (residence as defined in the census). Therefore, net immigration should include the movement of aliens with temporary visas and those without visas (of whom the Cuban "parolees" are now the most important group) who established residence, net arrivals of civilian citizens from abroad, net arrivals from Puerto Rico and other outlying areas, and net movement of Armed Forces to overseas posts. That these other categories of migrants are an important element in total movement may be seen by examining the summary of estimated immigration shown in Table 26.1. Since the movement of Armed Forces has previously been discussed by Siegel and Zitter,[3] only civilian immigration will be considered here.

According to these estimates, civilian immigration added 4.6 million people to the population of the United States between 1950 and 1965. Of these, 3.8 million were aliens entering through normal channels, 250,000 were refugees (mostly Cubans) not afforded permanent residence, 500,000 were from Puerto Rico, and about 50,000 were returning citizens. The annual average of net immigration was 301,000 for the period. It has varied markedly from year to year, but on balance it has been increasing. The average was 252,000 for 1950–55 and 371,000 for 1960–65 (Table 26.2). The peak year was 1963, with 406,000.

Contributing to the rise was the arrival of refugees from Cuba, the admission of a number of other refugee groups under special legislation, increased immigration from a number of areas in the West Indies and Central America, and the immigration of children born abroad to the wives of American servicemen. Puerto Rican immigration, however, dropped from an average of 51,000 in 1950–55 to 9,000 in 1960–65. Net immigration is expected to continue to increase somewhat under the provisions of the Immigration Act of 1965—perhaps to something like 400,000 a year.

Census-Based Estimates

Immigration may be estimated from the recording of entries and departures, from the registration of aliens, or from census counts and surveys of population. The Immigration and Naturalization Service records entries and departures and registers aliens,[4] and the Bureau of the Census is the principal source of the relevant census counts and surveys.

There are several ways in which census counts and surveys may be used to estimate immigration. One is from questions on previous residence. Each spring, the Current Population Survey asks for the residence of

TABLE 26.1   Estimated net immigration by category, 1950–1965[1]

PERIOD (JULY 1 TO JUNE 30)	NET TOTAL IMMIGRATION	NET CIVILIAN IMMIGRATION					NET MOVEMENT OF ARMED FORCES
		TOTAL	ALIEN IMMIGRANTS	REFUGEES NOT ACCORDED PERMANENT RESIDENCE[2]	CITIZENS FROM ABROAD	PUERTO RICANS	
1950 to 1965[3]	4,146,690	4,571,835	3,759,652	252,467	55,615	504,101	−425,145
1960 to 1965[3]	1,850,231	1,945,830	1,520,590	184,311	192,310	48,619	−95,599
1950 to 1960[4]	2,296,459	2,626,005	2,239,062	68,156	−136,695	455,482	−329,546
1964–1965	300,276	331,515	296,697	5,119	18,941	10,758	−31,239
1963–1964	365,544	353,332	292,248	8,272	48,446	4,366	12,212
1962–1963	412,528	406,212	306,260	44,224	50,930	4,798	6,316
1961–1962	314,943	383,520	283,763	75,019	13,375	11,363	−68,577
1960–1961	376,055	381,731	271,344	44,040	52,585	13,762	−5,676
1959–1960	280,868	279,846	235,901	52,098	−31,895	23,742	1,022
April 1 to June 30	(80,885)	(89,520)	(70,278)	(7,637)	(8,033)	(3,572)	(−8,635)
July 1 to March 31	(199,983)	(190,326)	(165,623)	(44,461)	(−39,928)	(20,170)	(9,657)
1958–1959	298,359	262,236	205,731	23,695	− 4,402	37,212	36,123
1957–1958	280,074	218,217	239,834	....	−47,573	25,956	61,857
1956–1957	318,903	302,883	338,703	....	−84,104	48,284	16,020
1955–1956	377,017	332,108	292,048	....	−21,587	61,647	44,909
1954–1955	530,614	254,999	197,318	....	26,499	31,182	275,615
1953–1954	331,302	250,360	180,281	....	25,870	44,209	80,942
1952–1953	97,035	178,044	122,848	....	−19,407	74,603	−81,009
1951–1952	25,343	294,318	254,451	....	−21,775	61,642	−268,975
1950–1951	−212,753	280,332	194,637	....	43,775	41,920	−493,085
1950: April 1 to June 30	(50,582)	(62,182)	(47,588)	....	(5,937)	(8,657)	(−11,600)

[1]A minus sign denotes outward movement
[2]Cubans, Hong Kong Chinese, and refugee-escapees.
[3]April 1 to June 30.
[4]April 1 to March 31.

the previous year. The count of those who had previously been living abroad is a fair estimate of gross immigration to the United States. However, the survey cannot discover the number who had left the country because their departure carries them beyond the scope of the survey. The Current Population Survey shows that from 1950 to 1964 11.7 million people moved to the United States,[5] as compared with the estimated net immigration of 4.6 million for the period in Table 26.1.

A second method for estimating net migration—the vital statistics method—is the subtraction of natural increase from the net change in population between two censuses. The method places net civilian immigration[6] between 1950 and 1960 at 2,972,000. However, the method is unreliable because it incorporates the net error in the estimators of change, including census underenumeration, into the estimated migration. The net error might well be a million or more.

A third approach is the census survival rate method.[7] Census survival rates for the native population of the United States are the logical product of a survival rate, reflecting mortality, and a relative change in the percent of net census undercount between the two censuses. These rates may be used to

TABLE 26.2 Average annual net civilian immigration by category, 1950–1965[1]

CATEGORY	1960 to 1965	1955 to 1960	1950 to 1955
Total civilian imigration	371,000	279,000	252,000
Alien imigrants	290,000	262,000	190,000
Refugees not accorded permanent residence[2]	35,000	15,000	
Citizens from abroad	37,000	−38,000	11,000
Arrivals from Puerto Rico	9,000	39,000	51,000

[1]Periods are from July 1 of initial year to June 30 of terminal year.
[2]Cubans, Hong Kong Chinese and refugee-escapees.

derive estimates of net immigration of the foreign-born between censuses in which the effect of census errors has been discounted, at least in theory. Estimates of net immigration of the foreign-born by age and sex between 1950 and 1960 by this method are shown in Table 26.3.[8]

Eldridge believes that the census survival rate method seriously underestimates the immigration of the foreign-born to the United States.[9] Her conclusion is reinforced by the comparison of these estimates with the estimates of net immigration for the decade by sex and age cohort based on the visa data of the Immigration and Naturalization Service, shown in Table 26.3. The estimates by the census survival rate method are 80,000 less for the decade than those based on the visa data. The former estimates show less immigration than do the visa data for most ages up to age 60 and a heavy outward movement for ages 60 and over. There was a net outward movement of 500,000 foreign-born aged 60 and over, according to these estimates, as compared with an indicated net arrival of 100,000 aliens at these ages. Such factors as the under-reporting of departing aliens in the visa data and the return of elderly naturalized citizens to their native land may explain the differences in part, but the principal difference must be the misreporting of nativity in the census.

Alien Immigration

It must be concluded, after reviewing the ways in which survey and census counts

might be used to estimate immigration, that they are less reliable methods for estimating the over-all amount of net immigration than is the recording of entries and departures, useful as it may be to estimate the immigration of special categories or the characteristics of immigrants. The estimates in Table 26.1 start with estimates of alien immigration based on data obtained by the Immigration and Naturalization Service. The secondary categories of net arrivals of civilian citizens from abroad and from Puerto Rico were estimated as separate categories.

The Immigration and Naturalization Service compiles data from the visa forms surrendered by aliens at the port of entry (Forms FS-510 and FS-511), from the annual registration of the addresses of aliens in January (same forms), and from the Arrival/Departure Record (Form I-94) filled out by passengers on ships and planes. The principal source of information is the visa data.

The Immigration and Naturalization Service identifies two categories of aliens entering the United States with visas: (*a*) immigrants are either aliens entering the United States for the first time with permanent visas or aliens already in the United States with temporary visas who have their status changed to permanent residence, and (*b*) non-immigrants are aliens entering the United States either with temporary visas or with permanent visas but re-entering the United States after a temporary stay abroad. There are other categories of aliens entering the United States legitimately but without

TABLE 26.3 Estimates of net immigration, by age cohort and sex, 1950–1960, based on the census survival rate method and on visa data[1]

AGE OF COHORT IN 1960	ESTIMATES BASED ON THE CENSUS SURVIVAL RATE METHOD[2]		ESTIMATES BASED ON VISA DATA	
	MALE	FEMALE	MALE	FEMALE
Total, all ages	708,200	699,200	1,013,200	1,225,100
Under 5 years	54,600	52,800	30,100	27,600
5 to 9 years	90,100	86,100	79,700	77,500
10 to 14 years	84,700	81,600	89,500	86,600
15 to 19 years	66,900	72,300	70,800	78,600
20 to 24 years	110,000	140,300	89,500	151,100
25 to 29 years	125,400	167,100	117,700	201,600
30 to 34 years	109,200	142,100	130,100	177,800
35 to 39 years	94,300	101,700	119,300	127,500
40 to 44 years	62,500	59,300	81,300	77,300
45 to 49 years	60,400	49,900	71,900	66,000
50 to 54 years	36,100	28,600	53,900	53,100
55 to 59 years	17,000	300	36,100	40,200
60 to 64 years	− 6,900	− 1,900	23,400	28,700
65 to 69 years	− 22,500	− 31,900	12,400	16,600
70 to 74 years	− 31,300	− 44,700	5,000	8,600
75 to 79 years	− 50,700	− 74,400	1,800	4,200
80 to 84 years	− 35,100	− 52,000	700	1,300
85 years and over	− 56,500	− 78,100	100	700

[1]Estimates by the census survival rate method relate to the foreign born; estimates based on visa data, collected by the Immigration and Naturalization Service, relate to aliens. A minus sign denotes net outward movement.
[2]By the reverse procedure.

visas. These include temporary border-crossers, crews of merchant vessels, foreign laborers admitted by special treaties and agreements, and aliens admitted at the direction of the Attorney General. Most of this last category are political refugees, the Cubans being the most prominent example.

Both the arrival and departure of aliens were recorded until 1956. Then, the recording of departures was discontinued[10] because it was proving a burden in the administration of immigration and because the reporting of departures was thought to be very deficient, particularly at the land borders. The estimates of the immigration of aliens up to the 1960 Census shown in Table 26.1 represent principally the net balance of aliens traveling with visas.[11] Since then, the estimates of the immigration of aliens represent the sum of immigrant aliens and refugees not accorded permanent residence,

as reported by the Immigration and Naturalization Service. The category of refugees in Table 26.1 includes 231,553 Cubans, 13,657 Chinese residents of Hong Kong, and 7,257 "refugee-escapees" who arrived either as non-immigrant aliens or parolees and have not yet been accorded permanent residence. The argument supporting this procedure is that the migration of non-immigrant and non-visa aliens should largely balance out over a period of several years except for those who have their status changed to permanent residence (when they are reported again as immigrants) and for the refugees. Few Cubans have been permitted to adjust their status so far. The departures of resident aliens are treated as negligible.

There are several features of the visa data which may limit the validity of the estimates of alien immigration derived from them. The visa data include arrivals at the ports of San

Juan, Puerto Rico; Charlotte Amalie, Virgin Islands; and Agana, Guam; as well as of the United States proper. However, the small increase in the foreign-born in these areas between 1950 and 1960 suggests that most immigrants arriving at these ports continue on to the United States mainland.

Another feature is the reduced coverage of the immigration data after 1956. As a consequence, they no longer reflect annual changes as well as they might. They do not include non-immigrant aliens, many of whom establish residence in the United States as defined by the census even though their stay is temporary. The data do include those non-immigrant aliens who change their status to permanent residence, but these immigrants are assigned to the year in which the adjustment was made rather than to the year they entered the United States. Some of these aliens had been in the country for only a year or two when their status was adjusted, but others had been here for a generation. The number of adjustments has been increasing recently (from 17,000 in 1961 to 27,000 in 1964). If some shift in policy should permit larger numbers of adjustments (say, of some of the 200,000 Cuban refugees), the annual estimates of immigration would be distorted. It would be helpful if there were some way of ascertaining when aliens who adjust their residence status first entered the country.

The estimates of immigration are biased upward by the failure to allow for resident aliens who depart. The reported outward movement of resident aliens was running about 25,000 in the years before the reporting was stopped, and the Immigration and Naturalization Service believes that the reported number was an understatement. Thus, the estimates of alien immigration for recent years in Table 26.1, being gross rather than net figures, are somewhat overstated.

The other two sources of immigration data—alien registration and passenger data—might provide information that cannot be obtained from visa data. Aliens must register with the Immigration and Natural-

ization Service every January. The change in the number registering is the net result of net immigration, mortality, naturalization, and changes in coverage. If changes in coverage were disregarded, net immigration could be estimated by subtracting mortality and naturalization from net change. The number of naturalizations is reported by the Immigration and Naturalization Service. However, mortality would have to be estimated, for deaths of aliens are not identified separately in vital statistics. Reasonable estimates of mortality require some knowledge of the age composition of the alien population, for mortality is largely a function of age. Unfortunately, there are no age data for aliens. Only the total number of aliens is reported from the registration count. If citizenship were to be restored to the general list of questions in the 1970 Census, it might provide the necessary age detail to make the alien registration data usable for estimating immigration. Without the assurance of consistent coverage, however, the method would not be too reliable.

Passenger data offer another possibility for estimating net immigration. The data are obtained by the Immigration and Naturalization Service from the Arrival/Departure Record filled out by each passenger, alien or citizen, on a ship or plane traveling between the United States and a foreign port (except for planes going to Canada). The excess of passengers arriving over passengers departing represents an estimate of net immigration. Since most passengers are not immigrants, each arrival should be balanced by a departure within the year unless the passenger is in fact changing residence.

The passenger data do not include arrivals and departures by way of the Canadian and Mexican borders. An allowance may be made for the arrival of immigrant aliens across the land borders (but not their departures) by adding in the visa data for entries at the Canadian and Mexican ports of entry. Such estimates from 1950 to 1964 are as follows:

	NO.
Alien passengers arriving	13,916,041
Alien passengers departing	10,735,963
Alien immigrants by way of Canadian ports of entry	624,515
Alien immigrants by way of Mexican ports of entry	506,025
Net alien immigration	4,310,618

There were 3,623,264 immigrant aliens recorded for the same period. Thus, the net figure for alien immigration exceeds the gross figure by 700,000, although logically it ought to be smaller. Hence, the passenger data do not give reasonable estimates of net alien immigration.

The passenger data might still be used to estimate the outward movement of resident aliens if the data on departing aliens were tabulated by residence status. The difference between the number of alien residents of the United States leaving the country and the number of alien residents returning should be a fair estimate of the alien residents leaving the country for good. Returning resident aliens are already tabulated separately. It should also be possible to count those departing either from the Arrival/Departure Record (Form I-94) or from the Permit To Reenter the United States (Form I-418). Net alien immigration would then be estimated by subtracting the estimated outward movement of resident aliens from immigrant aliens as tabulated from the visa data.

Unrecorded Immigration

The estimates make no allowance for unrecorded immigration. It is possible that the number not recorded is large. Between 1950 and 1964, 3.9 million aliens were apprehended for being in the United States illegally. Perhaps three-fourths of them were Mexicans apprehended between 1950 and 1955, at the height of the entry of Mexican "wetbacks." Most of those apprehended

were in the United States for a matter of weeks, but some undoubtedly had established residence.

The census counts are one possible source for measuring unrecorded immigration, but not a very promising one. They cannot even be used to estimate reliably the total amount of immigration, as has been seen, and furthermore aliens in the country illegally are likely to evade enumeration or misreport their status. Still, the number of Canadians and Mexicans entering the country without being recorded might conceivably be so large that their presence would show up in the census. The entry of these two nationalities into the United States is most likely to go unrecorded because of the ease by which the land borders are crossed.

Accordingly, estimates have been made here of net immigration from 1950 to 1960 from counts of (1) natives of Canada and Mexico, by the census survival rate method; (2) the population with Spanish surname in five southwestern states, again by the census survival rate method, assuming all migrants to the area of Spanish ethnic stock are from Mexico; and (3) the residents of Mexico, from Mexican census and vital statistics data, assuming that all Mexican migration is to or from the United States. The estimates of net immigration from Mexico and Canada, 1950–60, as a result of these calculations, as well as the immigration shown by visa data, are shown in the accompanying tabulation.

SOURCE	CANADA	MEXICO
Visa data:		
Country of birth	272,000	313,000
Country of last residence	372,000	293,000
U. S. Census		
Country of birth	141,000	205,000
Spanish surname	......	350,000
Mexican census and vital		
statistics	......	473,000

The American census data do not suggest that there is any unrecorded immigration, but the Mexican data suggest that it may have amounted to 150,000 for the decade. The latter figure, because it was made by the vital statistics method, is subject to large error. However, the most likely sources of error in the figure are an underregistration of births or poorer coverage in the 1950 Census than in 1960. Both of these biases would minimize the estimated migration to the United States. Thus, the evidence as to whether there has been a substantial amount of unrecorded immigration is inconclusive.

Citizens Abroad

To complete the estimates of immigration, estimates must be made of the net arrivals of citizens from abroad and of migrants from outlying areas. The only recording of the movement of civilian citizens to and from foreign countries is that of the passenger data collected by the Immigration and Naturalization Service. However, they will serve poorly as estimators if they have the same degree of bias as those for alien passengers. Furthermore, it is difficult to credit the persistent excess of returning citizens found in the data—amounting to 393,000 from 1950 to 1964.

The immediate reaction that there cannot be a persistent excess of citizen arrivals must be tempered by consideration of the migratory cross-currents of the period. There were many departures of Americans becoming expatriates, of foreign-born citizens returning to their native countries, of Americans taking foreign assignments with private firms or the government, and of wives of servicemen joining their husbands at overseas posts. But many of these wives and other young American women of childbearing age chose to bear their children abroad, so that there were 481,000 births to Americans abroad reported from April, 1950, to July, 1964. Their arrival in the United States would lend a positive weight to net immigration.

Estimates may be made of the movement of selected categories of citizens from 1950 to 1960 which, when taken collectively, may represent an alternative to the estimates based on passenger data. The United States census attempts to count the United States population living abroad as an adjunct to the decennial census. The count is incomplete and not included in the official census. If, however, we may assume that the children who were counted abroad are also those whose parents would see that their birth was registered with the United States consular service, we can estimate the migration of young children as follows:

	NO.
Births to Americans abroad, 1950–60	332,474
Expected survivors, 1960	318,413
Enumerated population abroad under age 10, 1960	295,452
Net movement, 1950–60	22,961

Hence, there was a return migration of 23,000 to the United States.

Coverage is fairly complete for the counts of Americans abroad who are federal civilian employees, their dependents and dependents of the Armed Forces, and crews of merchant vessels. These categories may be termed "Americans abroad under government auspices." The movement abroad under government auspices of American civilian citizens[12] aged 10 and over in 1960, from 1950 to 1960 may be estimated as follows:

	NO.
Enumerated population, all ages, 1950	171,437
Expected population, aged 10 and over, 1960	166,639
Enumerated population, age 10 and over, 1960	301,040
Net movement, 1950–60	134,401

Statistics from foreign countries might serve to estimate the migration of other categories of citizens. The only data so far exploited are the statistics from the Canadian census on population born in the United

States. There was a net movement of 25,255 Americans aged 10 and over to Canada from 1951 to 1961.

The composite estimate of net movement of American citizens from 1950 to 1960 from these three sources was as follows:

	NO.
Net arrivals of citizens under age 10	22,961
Net arrivals of citizens abroad under government auspices, aged 10 and over	− 134,401
Net arrivals of citizens from Canada	− 25,255
Net migration of citzens, 1950–60	− 136,695

The passenger data show a net arrival of 280,000 citizens during the decade as compared with the composite estimate above of 137,000 departures. The latter reckoning does not cover all citizen migration, but it is not likely that there could be an excess of 417,000 arrivals among other categories of citizens—the difference between the two statistics. The composite estimate has been accepted as the more reasonable of the two estimates.

The estimates of net citizen arrivals since 1960 have been derived by carrying forward estimates of civilian citizens abroad under government auspices. The series has been developed from data on citizens employed by the federal government who are assigned to overseas posts as reported by the Civil Service Commission, from data on dependents of the Armed Forces and civilian citizen employees abroad as reported by the Department of Defense, and from data on births occurring at hospitals and medical facilities of the Department. These data are not available for the years before 1960, so the estimated total for the decade has been distributed by year according to the pattern of migration indicated by the passenger data.

Outlying Areas

The alien and citizen immigration so far discussed relates mostly to the movement between the United States and foreign countries. Yet to be considered is the movement between the United States proper and Puerto Rico and the outlying areas of the United States—the Virgin Islands, the Canal Zone, American Samoa, Guam, and the Trust Territory of the Pacific Islands. There is a substantial movement of federal employees and their families to and from these areas. In Table 26.1, their movement has been included after 1960 in the category of net arrival of citizens from abroad. There has also been a migration of natives of these areas to the United States in recent years. Their departure is an important element in the equation for population growth for each area, but the amount of migration from each of the smaller areas is so small relative to total immigration to the United States that the extra work in estimating it is not warranted.

Puerto Rico, on the other hand, is well known for its contribution to the immigration of the United States. In the last fifteen years, there has been a net migration of 500,000 Puerto Ricans to the United States, amounting to 11 percent of all civilian immigration here. For this category of migration, the various estimates are in fair agreement, obviating the need to debate which estimate is the better. Estimates of net departures from Puerto Rico have been made (1) from passenger data collected by the Puerto Rico Planning Board, (2) by the vital statistics method using the census counts and vital statistics from Puerto Rico, and (3) by the census survival rate method applied to natives of Puerto Rico resident on the mainland and natives of the United States mainland resident in Puerto Rico.

The estimates of net departures from Puerto Rico from 1950 to 1960 are as follows:

	NO.
Passenger data	455,482
Vital statistics method estimate	491,127
Census survival rate method estimate	369,201
Puerto Ricans to mainland	408,627
Mainlanders to Puerto Rico	39,426

The estimate of Puerto Rican migration based on passenger data has been accepted here simply because it is the middle one of the three estimates and is the only one that has an annual series.

The Puerto Rico Planning Board has observed that some travel to Puerto Rico is circular. Some travelers go from the mainland to Puerto Rico, on to foreign countries, and then directly back home. The passenger data also include aliens who arrive by way of San Juan and are already counted with the alien immigrants. It seems best, then, to take as the estimate of net migration to the United States from 1950 to 1965, not the number destined for the mainland (511,761) but the total number of departures from Puerto Rico (495,444).

Characteristics of Immigrants

Population estimates are generally not limited to the over-all total but are distributed by various characteristics. The determination of age and sex characteristics is nearly universal, but estimates by color and nativity are also common. For estimating purposes, immigrants must be estimated in like detail. Immigrant aliens are tabulated by age and sex, thus accounting for the composition of the major portion of immigrants. However, there is no information on the age and sex compositon of Cuban refugees. Some notion of their composition could have been gleaned from a tabulation of the 70,000 refugees who had already arrived by the time of the 1960 Census. The group could easily have been identified and tallied in a special tabulation of previous country of residence. However, no one was alert to the possibility, and the opportunity was missed. As a substitute, the characteristics of Cuban refugees have been estimated from tabulations of the population of Florida who had been living abroad five years previously.

The estimates of net citizen arrivals from 1950 to 1960 were made in such a way as to provide estimates of the distribution of the

movement by sex and age cohort.[13] The migrants from Puerto Rico for the decade were also distributed by sex and age cohort by the vital statistics method. It was a requirement of the estimating procedure that the migrants be further distributed over the decade by age at entry, by year of entry. This was done by a computer program.

The estimated age composition of citizen arrivals from abroad since 1960 made use of the assumption that the net result of the large turnover in this population was a stable age distribution from one year to the next. The computations implied a large return migration at ages 5–14. The estimated age composition of arrivals from Puerto Rico was based on a sample drawn by the Puerto Rican Department of Labor of passengers to and from Puerto Rico.

There is an increasing demand for estimates of the non-white and the Negro population by federal agencies concerned with civil rights and economic opportunity, by civil rights organizations, and by university research personnel. At the same time, problems in estimating color or race have increased because of the decision of some agencies to discontinue detail on race in their statistics. Information on the race of immigrant aliens has not been obtained since 1961, when Congress repealed the statutory requirement that a question on race be included on the visa application form. Country of origin provides a basis for estimating the race of immigrants, but a weak one in the case of the West Indies and Central America.

Conclusion

The conclusion to be drawn from this involved account of estimate-making must be that major gaps are to be found in our immigration accounts which no amount of ingenuity can close. The two principal categories omitted are the departure of resident aliens and the movement of those citizens going abroad who are not going under government auspices.

There is little likelihood of extending the collection of data on immigration. Hutchinson states:

> The Immigration and Naturalization Service, unlike the agencies responsible for census and registration data, is not a statistical or information collecting agency. It is a law-enforcement and operating agency engaged in carrying out its responsibilities as set forth by the laws and federal regulations relating to international migration. Its statistics are a byproduct and a record of its operations.

He adds:

> With the volume of movement, most of it over land borders, it would be impossible to enforce individual inspection and strict data collection without interfering seriously with travel.

And finally:

> Whatever shortages or gaps exist in immigration and emigration statistics for the purpose of computing net immigration arise from insufficient information collected under present procedures for the control and recording of arrivals and departures, rather than from failure to utilize fully the information that is collected.[14]

There are additional tabulations, however, which would aid materially in improving immigration estimates. They have been suggested above in describing estimating procedures. There are opportunities for improving the estimates of immigration if the need for improvement is felt.

Immigration estimates are of importance not only for population estimates but for policy purposes and for an understanding of population growth and ethnic changes. One may speculate as to whether the change in the limitation of immigration enacted in the Immigration Act of 1965 might have been different if the legislative committee had had more complete information on which to base its decision. Immigration has risen again to one-third of what it was at the turn of the century, yet research on the topic remains negligible. Demographers might consider reviving immigration as a field of inquiry.

Notes

[1]E. P. Hutchinson, *Our Statistics of International Migration: Comparability and Completeness for Demographic Use* (report to the Committee on Population Statistics of the Population Association of America, July, 1965). See also E. P. Hutchinson, "Notes on Immigration Statistics of the United States," *Journal of the American Statistical Association*, Vol. LIII, No. 284 (December, 1958).

[2]The paper is an elaboration of procedures already outlined in the following articles of the United States Bureau of the Census: *Current Population Reports: Estimates of the Population of the United States and Components of Change, 1940 to 1966*, Series P-25, No. 331 (March, 1966); Jacob S. Siegel, Donald S. Akers, and Ward D. Jones, *Estimates of the Population of the United States and Components of Change: By Age, Color, and Sex, 1950 to 1960*, Series P-25, No. 310 (June, 1965); *Estimates of the Population of the United States: By Age, Color, and Sex: July 1, 1960 to 1965*, Series P-25, No. 321 (November, 1965). The estimates are based on the cumulative experience and judgment of members of the staff of the National Estimates and Projections Branch, Population Division, Bureau of the Census under the supervision of Jacob S. Siegel, Chief.

[3]Jacob S. Siegel and Meyer Zitter, "Demographic Aspects of Military Statistics" (paper presented at the annual meetings of the American Statistical Association, Chicago, December, 1958).

[4]The Immigration and Naturalization Service releases its statistics primarily through its *Annal Report*. An additional source is the *and I N Reporter*, published quarterly. See the article in that journal by Gertrude D. Krichefsky, "International Migration Statistics as Related to the United States," XIII, Nos. 1 and 2 (July and October, 1954).

[5]United States Bureau of the Census, *Mobility of the Population of the United States: March, 1963, to March, 1964, Current Population Reports*, Series P-20, No. 41 (September, 1965), Table 1.

[6]Bureau of the Census, P-25, No. 331; Conrad Taeuber and Morris H. Hansen, "A Preliminary Evaluation of the 1960 Censuses of Population and Housing," *Demography*, Vol. I, No. 1, 1964.

[7]Donald S. Akers and Jacob S. Siegel, *National Census Survival Rates, by Color and Sex, for 1950 to 1960* (United States Bureau of the Census, *Current Population Reports*, Series P-23, No. 15, July, 1965).

[8]For the application of a survival rate method to historical data, see Simon Kuznets and Ernest

Rubin, *Immigration and the Foreign Born* (Occasional Paper 46 [National Bureau of Economic Research, 1954]).

[9]Hope T. Eldridge, *Net Intercensal Migration for States and Geographic Divisions of the United States, 1950–1960: Methodological and Substantive Aspects* (Analytical and Technical Reports, No. 5; [Philadelphia: University of Pennsylvania, Population Studies Center, May, 1965]), pp. 91–94.

[10]The tabulation of non-emigrant aliens was discontinued after June, 1956. The tabulation of emigrant aliens was reduced after June, 1957, and discontinued entirely after June, 1958.

[11]The net movement of non-immigrants was adjusted for seasonality by a moving average. Components dropped after 1956 were estimated up to the 1960 Census. The category of immigration by a change of status to permanent residence appeared in the data only after 1957. Up to 1960, they were reassigned to a possible year of entry. An estimate was added of 68,000 Cuban refugees arriving without visas from January, 1959, to March, 1960.

[12]The citizenship of Americans abroad was estimated.

[13]An age cohort is the population born in the same year or group of years. Their age will vary from census to census.

[14]Hutchinson, "Our Statistics of International Migration. . . ."

A SELECTED SUPPLEMENTARY BIBLIOGRAPHY FOR PART 6

Elizaga, J. C., "Internal Migrations in Latin America," *Milbank Memorial Fund Quarterly*, Vol. 43, Pt. 2, 1965, pp. 144–165.

Hannerberg, D., Hägerstrand, T., and Odeving, B. (eds.), *Migration in Sweden; a Symposium*, Lund Studies in Geography, Series B, Human Geography; No. 13. Lund, Sweden: C. W. K. Gleerup, 1957.

Kariel, H. G., "Selected Factors Areally Associated with Population Growth Due to Net Migration," *Annals of the Association of American Geographers*, Vol. 53, 1963, pp. 210–223.

Kulldorf, G., *Migration Probabilities*, Lund Studies in Geography, Series B, Human Geography; No. 14. Lund, Sweden: 1957.

Lowenthal, D., and Comitas, L., "Emigration and Depopulation: Some Neglected Aspects of Population Geography," *Geographical Review*, Vol. 52, 1962, pp. 195–210.

Lowry, I., *Migration and Metropolitan Growth: Two Analytical Models*, Institute of Government and Public Affairs, University of California at Los Angeles. San Francisco: Chandler Publishing Co., 1966.

Olsson, G., "Distance and Human Interaction: A Migration Study," *Grografiska Annaler*, Vol. 47B, 1965, pp. 3–39.

Peterson, W., "A General Typology of Migration," *American Sociological Review*, Vol. 23, 1958, pp. 256–266.

Porter, P. W., "Approach to Migration Through Its Mechanism," *Geografiska Annaler*, Vol. 38, 1956, pp. 317–343.

Shryock, H. S., *Population Mobility Within the United States*. Chicago: Publication of the Community and Family Study Center, University of Chicago, 1964.

Stewart, C. T., "Migration as a Function of Population and Distance," *American Sociological Review*, Vol. 25, 1960, pp. 347–356.

Stouffer, S., "Intervening Opportunities: A Theory Relating Mobility and Distance," *American Sociological Review*, Vol. 5, 1940, pp. 1–26.

Wendel, B., *A Migration Schema: Theories and Observations*, Lund Studies in Geography, Series B, Human Geography; No. 9. Lund, Sweden: 1955.

Zipf, G. K., The P_1P_2/D Hypothesis: On the Intercity Movement of Persons," *American Sociological Review*, Vol. 11, 1946, pp. 677–685.

PART SEVEN

GEOGRAPHIC ASPECTS OF SELECTED POPULATION CHARACTERISTICS

INTRODUCTION

Aside from the purely demographic characteristics of populations, there are other traits which frequently play a profound role in the problems of economic and social development that emerge within territorial units of varying size. The set of characteristics which will be described in the following articles are most often termed *ascribed* or *achieved*, depending upon their level of permanency. The spatial dimension of these attributes has been largely ignored by geographers, as it was not traditionally thought to represent items appropriate for geographic study.

The following articles treat, either singly or in combination, attributes of ethnicity, language, age-sex structure, religion, race, and occupational chracteristics. Instead of attempting to provide specific regional coverage, a topical presentation has been adopted to illustrate the significance of these attributes in the study of population geography.

Both the Zelinsky article ("An Approach to the Religious Geography of the United States . . .") and the Hart article "The Changing Distribution of the American Negro,") represent pioneer treatments by American geographers of religion and race respectively. This does not imply that previous work had not been conducted, rather that only minimal attention had been previously focused on these attributes within a spatial context. Although almost a decade has transpired since the appearance of Hart's contribution and a slightly shorter interval since Zelinsky's, there has been only minor evidence of interest, in terms of number of items published, in either of these topics. At present, however, interest in the spatial dimension as it relates to race, especially with regard to the Negro population, has increased. The difficulty encountered in securing religious information has no doubt worked against the development of major studies in this area.

There have been few previous attempts by geographers to investigate spatial variations in the age structure of a population as a single overriding interest. Coulson's "The Distribution of Population Age Structures in Kansas City" differs from those of his predecessors, both in scale and methodology. His treatment of age variations over a spatial surface is cast in an analytical mode as a means of explaining the existing variations. Similarly, his analysis focuses on the internal variations in age within the context of a specific metropolitan system, thereby permitting the labeling of his effort as microscale analysis in contrast to macroscale or aggregate analysis (so often pursued by other

researchers with a demonstrated interest in the age variable as one of many items for consideration within a specific regional setting).

The last two contributions in this section (Neville's "Singapore: Ethnic Diversity and Its Implications" and Scott's "The Population Structure of Australian Cities") place heavy emphasis upon the spatial patterns attributed to the existence of cultural pluralism or, as some have referred to it, area pluralism. As used here, pluralism is related to the social and economic attributes associated with the ethnic variable. In both instances, the role of the nationality mix and its associated consequences are considered (in terms of variations in the presence of social and economic characteristics of the population growing out of multiethnic populations).

Attributes of any given population can frequently be related to the decision-making process, which, in turn, affects the spatial arrangement of population and its social and economic institutions. Thus, it seems that contributions focused upon characteristics by geographers should gain greater currency.

Selection Twenty-seven

AN APPROACH TO THE RELIGIOUS GEOGRAPHY OF THE UNITED STATES: PATTERNS OF CHURCH MEMBERSHIP IN 1952[1]

Wilbur Zelinsky

Almost all human geographers will accept the truism that among the phenomena forming or reflecting the areal differences in cultures with which they are so intimately concerned, few are as potent and sensitive as religion. In seeking to grasp the identity, conformation, and implications of such cultural regions as may exist in the United States, we

Reproduced by permission from the *Annals of the Association of American Geographers*, Vol. 51, 1961, 139–193 (pages 172 through 191 have been omitted here).

must inevitably approach the areal patterns of religious characteristics and their interactions with other human activities and cultural traits. The immediate inspiration for this study is a simple curiosity concerning the nature of these patterns, for it is abundantly clear from the available evidence that this nation has a startling profusion of denominations, considerable variation in their relative strength from place to place, and altogether more than enough complexity through time and space in the relationships between religion and other factors to challenge the ingenuity of the geographer. A larger purpose is implicit, however. It is hoped that this paper may provide not only a first approximation of the nation's religious regions and an introductory statement of the shape and meaning of areal variations in American religious characteristics, but that it may also contribute some material toward our still quite shadowy delineation of the general cultural regions of Anglo-America and stimulate some thought as to the variety of ways in which religious data might be used in other kinds of geographic work.

In spite of the clear logic of granting religion a prominent place on the geographer's agenda, a review of the literature indicates surprisingly little discussion of the subject, whether for the United States or for other parts of the world. A perusal of five of the larger and more important general treatises on human geography discloses the fact that two do not directly confront the topic of religion at all,[2] two others limit their treatment to a single paragraph,[3] and only one deals with religion in more than cursory fashion.[4] Similarly, two major surveys of significant recent research[5] contain no references to work on the geography of religion. There can be little doubt that a wider search of the literature would yield equally disappointing results. Only one book-length attempt to deal with the geography of religion has been published, one that is, by the author's admission, an experimental effort based on inadequate materials.[6] Four shorter—and, again, rather provisional —treatments of the subject merit attention, even though they are intentionally limited in purpose and accomplishment.[7] There are innumerable instances in the geographic literature of passing references to the religious situation in discussions of the human geography of various regions, but only a few serious efforts to delve deeply into the relationships between religious and other geographic phenomena.[8] In the case of the United States, only a single pair of highly tentative discussions, both so-

ciological, can be recommended to the student interested in the contemporary geography of religion on a national scale;[9] the available geographical literature on the more limited aspects of the American religious scene consists of two doctoral dissertations, one on religious institutions in Cincinnati and the other treating the historical geography of Roman Catholicism in the Atlantic Seaboard states.[10]

All this would be a matter of interest largely for the specialist in geographic bibliography or the history of ideas were it not that the factors that have generally inhibited work on the geography of religion also operate to circumscribe sharply the possible compass of this paper. There is, first of all, the simple inadequacy of the available statistics and other fundamental data. As is the case with demographic materials in general, the collection of the basic information is a task beyond the capacities of the individual scholar, who must look to national and international agencies. These agencies have either neglected to assemble any data or have done so in ways that make their interpretation difficult, especially for international comparisons.[11] Secondly, there is the intractability of the material itself. Unlike some other demographic or cultural traits, religion is a many-sided phenomenon; some of its more important aspects are extremely difficult to define or measure, and others, such as personal attitudes on religious matters, are possibly beyond the scope of direct observation. Among the multiple definitions of religion we must include: a mental complex accessible only to the anthropologist, theologian, or psychologist; a highly diversified body of customs, some only quite indirectly related to theological concerns; a formal institution, i.e., church or denomination; and a group of persons sharing some degree of religious identity by virtue of tradition or common observance. This wide range of meanings leads, in turn, to a number of serious methodological problems. Should the geographer confine his interest to formal adherence to the various creeds? Or if he rejects this approach, how does he measure and study the intensity of religious belief and observance in all their endless ramifications? Is religion cause or effect in the cultural landscape, or somehow both? Should the geographer simply note the material manifestations of religion, as in the settlement landscape, economic processes, or political relations, or should he concentrate on the inward, spiritual aspects of what is essentially an incorporeal phenomenon?

Largely because of the difficulty of obtaining adequate data on other phases of religion or of making direct observations on its nonmaterial aspects, most of those geographers who have pioneered in the study of religion have had to restrict their attention to the effects of religious faith and practice on the cultural scene, especially architecture, urban and village morphology, and other phases of the settlement landscape.[12] In the present instance, lack of adequate background studies or good alternative sources of statistics have meant a study limited almost wholly to the analysis of the membership data reported by the various American religious denominations.

Nature and Limitations of the Data[13]

The great bulk of our statistical data on religion in the United States has been collected and published by the Bureau of the Census. Beginning with the Seventh Census in 1850, information on churches was compiled in connection with each of the decennial enumerations until 1890, although the 1880 material never reached the publication stage. In 1906, the Bureau inaugurated a special Census of Religious Bodies which was continued at ten-year intervals until 1936.[14] It is generally believed that the 1926 Census was the most complete and successful in the series. The 1850, 1860, and 1870 enumerations resulted in the publication of information on the number and seating capacity of church edifices, as well as a variety of facts about finances, educational, missionary, and other activities of the denominations, but

no statistics on membership. The earliest figures on number of members (for each denomination, on a county basis) appeared in the reports of the 1890 Census; and this material was published for all the subsequent Censuses of Religious Bodies.

In every instance, the Census canvass involved the procurement of information from the local congregation, at first by direct interrogation by an enumerator and later by means of mailed inquiries. No effort was ever made to ascertain the church affiliation or preference of individuals by including a religious query in the regular census schedule. A single attempt to do so on a sample basis in 1957 proved to be abortive.[15] The constitutional doctrine of the separation of church and state has come to be interpreted in many quarters as even prohibiting the collection by a government agency of any information concerning churches, much less any facts regarding the religious status of individuals.[16] It was apparently a growing sensitivity on this issue that led to a marked deterioration in the response to the 1936 canvass and the failure to publish the partial results of the 1946 Census of Religious Bodies or even to initiate one in 1956. With the withering away of the decennial Census of Religious Bodies and the failure, despite a concerted campaign, to have a question on religious preference included in the 1960 enumeration schedule, it is highly unlikely that any additional religious statistics will be issued by the Bureau of the Census until 1970, if then.

Critics of the various Census efforts to tally church membership have unanimously appraised them as seriously defective in terms of completeness, reliability, and comparability. These shortcomings stem from the highly variable responses of the thousands of local church officials involved and the many different criteria of church membership used by the various denominations. An additional factor, for which the Census officials are completely blameless, is the frequency with which religious bodies in the United States splinter, merge, change their names, simply vanish, and otherwise make it difficult to keep track of their identity from one enumeration to another. Since the latest official data, those for 1936, hardly seemed adequate in terms of quality or timeliness for a useful study of contemporary patterns of church membership, it was decided to utilize the results of a major private effort to collect comprehensive statistics on American church membership, the National Council of Churches of Christ in the U. S. A.'s *Churches and Church Membership in the United States: an Enumeration and Analysis by Counties, States, and Religions.*[17] Our complete reliance on this source makes it essential to understand the methods used to assemble the data and their virtues and limitations before we can proceed with any geographical analysis.

Churches and Church Membership in the United States is a compilation of statistics on number of churches and church members, by county, submitted by the national headquarters of the various participating religious bodies listed in the 1953 *Yearbook of American Churches*[18] for the year 1952 or the nearest practicable date.[19] Out of the 251 religious bodies reported in the *Yearbook*, accounting for 92,546,000 members in 285,277 local churches, 112 bodies, with 74,125,462 members in 182,856 churches, were able and willing to participate. Most of the non-participating bodies are relatively small or were unable to supply information because of the lack of centralized records.[20] The largest block of missing members, an estimated 9,392,694 persons, is accounted for by five important, but loosely organized Negro groups—two Baptist and three Methodist bodies—in the Southern states, which include a large majority of all Negro church members in the United States. The subsequent discussion is thus largely, but not entirely, confined to the white church membership of the nation. Another predominantly Southern group, the Churches of Christ, with an estimated 1,500,000 members, was not reported; and since less than one percent of the estimated 2,720,739 members of the various Eastern Orthodox, Old Catholic, and Polish National Catholic

churches were tabulated, they are omitted from further consideration here. The Church of Christ Scientist, whose 1936 membership was estimated at 268,915 has a regulation that forbids "the numbering of people and reporting of such statistics for publication." In the case of the Church of Jesus Christ of Latter-day Saints, some 230,956 of the 1,077,285 members reported for 1952 could not be assigned to any geographic "stakes" and hence are omitted from the tabulations. Nearly half the Roman Catholic county figures were estimated on the basis of a formula derived from known diocesan totals, and are substantially less reliable than the balance of the county data.

The count of members was reported to the National Council of Churches under the several definitions of the participating bodies; and the variety of these definitions is the major source of the non-comparability of the denominational groups employed in this study. Here we cannot do better than to quote from the introductory material in *Churches and Church Membership in the United States:*

> For those bodies having several membership categories (e.g., baptized, confirmed, communicant), the most inclusive category was generally reported. . . . The Roman Catholics count all baptized persons, including infants. The Jews regard as members all Jews in communities having congregations. . . . Most Protestant bodies count only the persons who have attained full membership, and previous estimates have indicated that all but a small minority of these are over 13 years of age. However, many Lutheran bodies and the Protestant Episcopal Church now report all baptized persons, and not only those confirmed. It is also known that the Church of Jesus Christ of Latter-day Saints includes in its membership children of about eight years of age.

Comparison or correlation of membership statistics with 1950 Census data is hampered by the fact that the place of membership is established by the location of the church and not by the actual residence of the member. Although there is no way of ascertaining their location or the effects of this situation in a cartographic analysis, there are undoubtedly numerous cases where a significant number of members are reported for counties in which they do not reside.

In addition to the problems created by the omission of a good many religious bodies, the variety of membership criteria used, and the lack of complete correspondence between place of membership and place of residence, we also have the fact that the data are not entirely simultaneous, but range from 1951 to early 1954 with a heavy concentration in 1952 and that a significant, but undetermined degree of undercounting and overcounting occurred in the coverage of some localities and groups in spite of careful checking and editing of the raw data. Nevertheless, a comparison of the material provided by *Churches and Church Membership in the United States* with that in the 1936 Census of Religious Bodies leads to the firm conclusion that the former is superior in terms of both completeness and quality of data. Although the later study lacks the wide range of subject matter covered by the 1936 canvass, the use of centralized sources and other methodological refinements eliminated much of the variability and incompleteness of response. Local analysis is facilitated by the publication of county data for all religious groups, whereas county figures were made available only for the major denominations in the tables published by the 1936 Census of Religious Bodies.

Plan of Study

Since it is obviously impractical to deal individually with each of the 112 religious bodies for which data are furnished in *Churches and Church Membership in the United States*, it was decided to combine various bodies of common origin or close affinity into a relatively small number of denominational groups.[21] In performing this operation, I have followed the system employed in the statistical tabulations of the *Yearbook of American Churches*, which

involves a combination of historical and theological factors. Twenty-two groups, comprising 80 religious bodies, were selected for further analysis: those twenty denominational groups having a total reported membership in excess of 100,000 each and two smaller groups—the Friends and the Moravian Bodies—of especial historical and geographical interest (the first 22 groups listed in Column 1 of Table 27.1).[22] The remaining 32 religious bodies, which have an average membership of less than 12,000 and are of marginal interest at best, have been omitted from further discussion. In spite of their recent merger, the Congregational Christian Churches and the Evangelical and Reformed Church are so distinctive in terms of origin, geographical pattern, history, and ethnic affiliation that little would have been gained and a great deal lost, for the purposes of this study, by combining them into a single denominational group. On the other hand, the Unitarian and Universalist bodies would have been combined into a single group because of their pronounced similarities even if their recent union had not taken place.[23] The subsequent discussion will show that it has proved profitable, for purposes of geographical analysis, to arrange the 22 major denominational groups into three broad classes in terms of provenience: those of British colonial origin, groups introduced by immigration from the European continent, and those bodies originating in the United States.[24] The classification is as follows:

I. British Colonial Groups

Protestant Episcopal	Congregational Christian
Presbyterian Bodies	Baptist Bodies
Methodist Bodies	Friends

II. Immigrant European Groups

Roman Catholic	Reformed Bodies
Jewish Congregations	Bretheren Churches
Lutheran Bodies	Mennonite Bodies
Evangelical and Reformed	Moravian Bodies

III. Native American Groups

Disciples of Christ	Church of the Nazarene
Unitarian and Universalist Churches	Assemblies of God
	Churches of God
Latter-day Saints	Evangelical United
Adventist Bodies	Brethren

TABLE 27.1   United States, reported membership in religious bodies

RELIGIOUS BODY	NATIONAL COUNCIL OF CHURCHES SURVEY— "CHURCHES AND CHURCH MEMBERSHIP" (1952)[1]	MEMBERSHIP REPORTED FOR 1952 IN "YEAR- BOOK OF AMERICAN CHURCHES"[2]	CURRENT POPULATION SURVEY, MARCH, 1957[3] (PERSONS 14 YEARS OLD AND OVER)
Roman Catholic	29,688,058	30,253,427	30,669,000
Baptist Bodies	9,795,782	17,470,111	23,525,000
Methodist Bodies	8,892,869	11,664,978	16,676,000
Lutheran Bodies	6,418,269	6,313,892	8,417,000
Jewish Congregations	5,112,024	5,000,000	3,868,000
Presbyterian Bodies	3,532,176	3,535,171	6,656,000
Protestant Episcopal	2,544,320	2,482,887	
Disciples of Christ	1,836,104	1,815,627	
Congregational Christian	1,263,472	1,269,466	
Latter-day Saints (Mormons)	953,588	1,210,336	
Evangelical & Reformed	750,463	751,003	
Evangelical United Brethren	722,966	724,055	
Assemblies of God	459,256	370,118	
Reformed Bodies	349,164	373,780	
Adventist Bodies	283,516	290,898	
Church of the Nazarene	249,033	243,152	
Churches of God	241,966	305,043	
Brethren Churches	232,569	256,525	
Unitarian & Universalist	159,904	158,402	
Mennonite Bodies	100,925	142,513	
Friends (Quakers)	96,451	114,119	
Moravian Bodies	48,843	54,505	
Eastern Churches	13,169	2,353,783	
Churches of Christ	—	1,500,000	
Christian Unity Science Church	—	1,112,123	
Church of God in Christ	—	328,304	
Pentecostal Assemblies	41,555	300,070	
Church of Christ Scientist	—	268,915 (1936)	
Polish National Catholic Church	—	265,879	
Salvation Army	—	232,631	
International General Assembly of Spirtualists	—	157,000	
Old Catholic Churches	1,471	101,077	
Federated Churches	—	88,411	
International Church of the Foursquare Gospel	66,191	78,471	
Apostolic Overcoming Church of God	—	75,000	
Other Bodies	261,358	593,017	25,223,000
Total	74,125,462	92,546,000	115,034,000

[1]Includes only those groups reporting membership by county.
[2]Includes all groups reporting total national membership.
[3]Reports religious affiliation or identification rather than formal membership.

An explanatory note concerning the maps* that are the principal means for analyzing the denominational data may be useful to the reader. It was immediately apparent that the statistics on church membership are of much greater geographic, cultural, and demographic significance than those on the number of churches; and there was no difficulty in deciding that the limitations in the completeness and quality of the data precluded the possibility of any useful series of maps showing the relative strength, i.e., percentage within total population or of total church membership, of the various denominational groups. Consequently, the best cartographic expedient was clearly a set of maps showing the distribution of absolute numbers of reported members of the various denominational groups on the basis of counties and Standard Metropolitan Areas. It is interesting to note that the only two previous efforts to map the religious composition of the American population in any detail adopted quite different techniques. In *The Atlas of the Historical Geography of the United States*, the distribution of churches, i.e., congregations, is shown for the leading denominations in 1775—1776, 1860, and 1890, for lack of any alternative data in the case of the first two dates and for the sake of consistency in the case of the last.[25] A statistical atlas published by the U.S. Census Office in 1898 has a series of choropleth maps depicting the proportion of the members of the eight leading denominations to the aggregate population by county and state in 1890 and shows the same ratio for eight lesser denominations by state only.[26] In spite of the great differences in kinds of data and methods of representation, comparisons between the earlier and the present series of maps are most instructive.

For all their shortcomings, the statistics presented in *Churches and Church Membership in the United States* have been accepted at face value in constructing the maps,

except in two cases where major gaps in the data would have caused serious distortion in the resultant map patterns. The Roman Catholic membership in several counties, including Webb (Laredo), within the Corpus Christi Diocese, which was grossly underreported in the National Council of Churches' tables, has been estimated on the basis of information supplied by the diocesan chancery; and the omission of figures on the members of the Protestant Episcopal Church in its Sacramento (Northern California) Diocese has been rectified by reference to the *Episcopal Church Annual*. There are many other obvious lesser discrepancies in the statistics, as for example the reporting of only 502 members of Methodist bodies in Lucas County (Toledo), Ohio, or only 48 Methodists in Wake County (Raleigh), North Carolina; but it was felt that any tampering with the figures without a thorough investigation involving extensive correspondence and field work might well have done more harm than good.

The choice of the symbols used in the maps and their quantitative equivalents involved a considerable amount of experimentation. The extremely uneven distribution of human populations, and specifically the heaping up of great masses of persons within relatively minute urban areas and the thin dispersion of small numbers in many extensive rural areas, poses a problem for the cartographer for which there seems to be no truly satisfactory solution. In the present instance, it was decided to use shaded three-dimensional symbols to represent the larger values and open circles for the lesser ones. For the ten smallest denominational groups, the number of reported members in each county or SMA with a total of 1,000 or more is shown by means of a cube,[27] the volume of which is proportional to the value in question, while the area of the open circle is scaled to values ranging from one number through 999. The numerical equivalents of the symbols were doubled for all the larger denominational groups, except the Roman Catholic, so that the smallest cubical symbol represents 2,000 members and the others

---

range proportionately higher. In the case of Roman Catholics, the uniquely large volume of membership necessitated much higher equivalents for the symbols—five times those used for the smaller denominational groups, or two and one half times those used for the others. The final choice of values for the symbols represents an attempt to reconcile three rather contradictory purposes: to render legibly the number and location of members in thinly occupied areas; to avoid excessive congestion and overlapping of symbols in areas of concentrated membership; and to make possible realistic comparisons among the various maps using the same values for their symbols.[28]

Historical Considerations

It is neither feasible nor necessary here to chronicle the complex histories of all the denominations with which we are concerned. But it is essential to sketch some of the broader historical conditions and trends governing the evolution of America's religious life if we are to appreciate the place of the church in our cultural landscape or make much sense of the contemporary distribution of denominations. During the first two centuries of settlement, the overwhelming majority of the immigrants who entered the United States were drawn from the United Kingdom. The remainder of the white settlers were largely derived from German-speaking areas, principally the Rhine-land, or the Netherlands, with only trifling additions from other sections of the European continent.[29] It is hardly surprising, then, to discover that all the principal British sects had made the trans-Atlantic journey and were liberally represented during the later phases of American colonial history, or that several denominations of German and Dutch origin were firmly established in various corners of British North America. It is almost certain, however, that there was no faithful reproduction of the British religious scene in the New World. Although

it is quite easy to exaggerate the influence of religious nonconformity in generating movement to America, it is still undoubtedly true that dissenters from the established churches of Great Britain and certain continental countries accounted for a disproportionately large share of the arrivals. This fact clearly stands out in the following tabulation of congregations existing in the United States in 1775–76 that Paullin was able to identify and locate geographically in his remarkable analysis of colonial documents:[30]

Congregational	668	Moravian	31
Presbyterian	588	Congregational-	
Episcopalian	495	Separatist	24
Baptist	494	Mennonite	16
Friends	310	French Protestant	7
German		Sandemanian	6
Reformed	159	Jewish	5
Lutheran	150	Rogerene	3
Dutch Reformed	120	Others	31
Methodist	65		
Catholic	56	Total	3,228

Unfortunately, we have no comparable statistics for the contemporary religious composition of the British population to set alongside these figures; but it is unquestionable that the "Established," i.e., Episcopal, Church was much feebler on the western side of the Atlantic than in Great Britain. Indeed, one of the central facts of American religious history is the failure of any genuine established church to appear, in spite of tentative efforts on the part of the British Crown and some of the colonial administrations. As a consequence of this, we can note not only the early appearance of a strong denominational diversity but also a freedom to experiment with new modes of religious experience and organization—or to abstain entirely from formal religious adherence. The Great Awakening that reached American shores after bursting forth in mid-eighteenth century England may well have planted some of the seeds that were later to blossom into a spectacular profusion of denominations; but there were already signs of great ferment among various German and Dutch Protestant congregations. The unsettling effects of the English Civil War, the great difficulty of effectively controlling American congregations across a distance of 3,000 miles, the sharply disruptive effects of the War of Independence, the establishment of the doctrine of the separation of church and state, and, above all, the completely novel social and economic conditions of a rapidly moving frontier all played their part in giving a new coloration and pattern to imported creeds and in spawning the abundance of native American denominations that have never left off their fissiparous way since the last quarter of the eighteenth century. The same factors that favored variety in religious affiliation also permitted a high incidence of dissociation from formal religious ties or simple lack of interest in spiritual affairs. We are on exceedingly shaky statistical grounds in estimating the ratio of church members to non-members in the early days of the Republic; but most scholars agree that a low point was reached in that period and that the trend has been rather steadily upward ever since.[31] Whatever their origin, a large multitude of the unchurched abounded in the United States at the end of the 1700's and provided a fertile missionary field during the Second Great Awakening in the opening years of the nineteenth century not only for the traditional denominations but for a variety of new ones as well.

The maps of the 1775–76 distribution of American churches furnished by Paullin distinctly foreshadow later regional concentrations. The Congregationalists were powerful in New England, but were infrequently found elsewhere; the Episcopalians, though occurring over a wide area, were most strongly entrenched in Virginia, Maryland, Connecticut, and New York; the Friends, also widely dispersed, were centered primarily in southeastern Pennsylvania and adjacent sections of New Jersey; the Presbyterians were well represented almost everywhere except southern New England, but were most prominent in the newly settled western fringes of the Atlantic Seaboard states; the Dutch Reformed and the various Teutonic churches were strong and even dominant in various sections of New York, Pennsylvania, and the Maryland and Carolina Piedmont. Only the Baptists, who were well nigh universally, if thinly, distributed, had failed to show the regional gravitation that was to become so well marked in their subsequent history. Methodism was still too young and weak in America to have achieved any real regional pattern, but incipient clusters in Maryland and New Jersey faintly reveal the shape of things to come. The minute Roman Catholic population—only an estimated 32,500 in 1784[32]—was confined to relatively libertarian Maryland, Pennsylvania, Delaware, and New Jersey; the few isolated Jewish congregations bear little relevance to later developments.

After the Atlantic Seaboard had been fully occupied and the principal denominations had begun to sort themselves out regionally, four major processes were to shape the present-day areal patterns of religious allegiance in the United States: (1) the westward thrust of the frontier and the differential fortunes of the colonial British and Teutonic churches in claiming the vast, ecclesiastically virgin territories of the central and western states; (2) the rise, growth, and wide dispersion of a number of native American denominations; (3) the great new flood of immigration beginning in the 1830's with Irish Catholics and both Catholic and Protestant Germans and followed soon after by adherents of numerous denominations from Scandinavia, Eastern Europe, and Southern Europe; and, finally, (4) the great tides of internal migration that have constantly re-grouped the inhabitants and, hence, the religious map of perhaps the most mobile nation of modern times. These are themes that can be most fruitfully pursued in our subsequent discussion; but it is interesting to note the common element of swift movement. There are persistent, relatively stable features in the spatial disposition of some religious bodies, but more important is the phenomenon of constant and rapid change, the restless shifting of forces, the transmutation and re-shaping of regions, and thus the provisional configuration of current patterns. Although critics of American civilization may, with considerable justice, accuse it of being grossly secular, we may note the parodoxical fact, too little studied by cultural historians, of those of our native churches and some revitalized groups of European vintage which have generated especially great momentum, carrying their missionary message not only to the non-Christian sections of the world but to the British Commonwealth and Europe as well. We have, then, a religiously dynamic and complex United States functioning as a hearth area for elements of non-material culture, i.e., new forms of religious worship and concepts of salvation, in addition to the many advanced forms of material technology, for which the nation has received vastly more publicity.

Incidence of Church Membership

One of the significant background facts to be borne in mind during the subsequent discussion is the great variation among states and counties in the percentage of population reported as members of religious bodies. Although we are exposed to the vagaries of inconsistent and incomplete statistics, certain broad generalizations can be sustained. The incidence of church membership is highest in those areas, particularly in the Northeast, where settlement is old, dense, and stable and where strongly organized denominations, especially the Roman Catholic, are well represented (Table 27.2). It is lowest in those places with heavy in-migration—and thus a temporary loosening of church associations—such as California, Washington, Oregon, Nevada, or Florida—or those areas which are relatively inaccessible, thinly settled, or characterized by low incomes. The low ranking of the Mountain states—except for strongly Catholic New Mexico and strongly Mormon Utah—is readily explained in these terms. The poor

TABLE 27.2 Reported church membership as percentage of total population

UNITED STATES	49.2		
New England	62.5	*South Atlantic* (cont.)	
Maine	41.2	Virginia	38.5
New Hampshire	53.0	West Virginia	32.8
Vermont	52.7	North Carolina	39.9
Massachusetts	67.1	South Carolina	40.0
Rhode Island	75.7	Georgia	38.3
Connecticut	60.5	Florida	36.4
Middle Atlantic	59.3	*East South Central*	38.6
New York	60.1	Kentucky	44.8
New Jersey	57.6	Tennessee	40.2
Pennsylvania	58.9	Alabama	34.2
East North Central	49.2	Mississippi	33.9
Ohio	46.4	*West South Central*	49.0
Indiana	43.6	Arkansas	31.3
Illinois	53.6	Louisiana	53.7
Michigan	42.3	Oklahoma	42.4
Wisconsin	63.8	Texas	53.6
West North Central	53.6	*Mountain*	50.4
Minnesota	61.6	Montana	46.7
Iowa	53.6	Idaho	44.1
Missouri	48.9	Wyoming	43.6
North Dakota	63.0	Colorado	41.6
South Dakota	58.4	New Mexico	64.9
Nebraska	53.4	Arizona	44.9
Kansas	46.6	Utah	73.3
South Atlantic	39.5	Nevada	37.6
Delaware	44.3	*Pacific*	37.7
Maryland	47.7	Washington	30.5
District of		Oregon	27.7
Columbia	46.6	California	40.7

Source: *Churches and Church Membership in the United States*, Series A, No. 3, Table 4.

showing of the Southern states in Table 27.2 is, in large part, the result of excluding the great bulk of Negro church members from the reckoning. Church members account for 53.9 percent of the white population of the South, only slightly less than the corresponding statistic—54.6 percent—for the nation as a whole. The state figures do, however, mask an interesting differential between lowland and upland tracts that appears in such states as Virginia, Kentucky, Tennessee, West Virginia, Georgia, Alabama, and Arkansas.[33] The low percentages reported for the poor, remote, and often thinly occupied areas of high or rugged terrain doubtless reflect the difficulties for actual or potential congregations; but they also quite probably indicate the relative importance in such areas of autonomous, rather tentatively organized groups, largely oriented toward the fundamentalist theology and largely unreported in our statistics.

Urban-rural Differentials

Another major distributional phenomenon that does not appear in our map series is the difference in the strength of membership in the various denominational groups as between urban and rural areas. Our statistical source indicates that 60.8 percent of the reported church members of the nation in 1952 were accounted for by the 168 Standard

Metropolitan Areas in which 56.8 percent of the population resided in 1950. It is not at all clear whether church membership in the United States is actually more urbanized than the population in general or whether these figures simply reflect under-enumeration of church members in rural tracts and the absence from our statistics of several important, essentially rural religious bodies. There are, however, emphatic differences in the degree to which the membership of the individual denominational groups is urban or rural (Table 27.3). If we accept our figures at face value, 97.5 percent of the American Jewish population is to be found within metropolitan areas, 2.5 percent in intermediate counties (those containing one

TABLE 27.3 Denominational groups by percentage of reported members in metropolitan and non-metropolitian areas, ca. 1952.

| | | NON-METROPOLITAN COUNTIES | |
| | | | |
DENOMINATIONAL GROUP	METROPOLITAN COUNTIES	INTERMEDIATE COUNTIES	RURAL COUNTIES
Jewish Congregations	97.5	2.5	0
Roman Catholic	74.5	23.0	2.4
Reported members of all Protestant Groups	45.6	45.3	9.0
Unitarian and Universalist Churches	74.4	25.6	
Protestant Episcopal	72.8	25.1	2.1
Moravian Bodies	70.3	29.7	
Congregational Christian Churches	59.9	34.9	5.1
Evangelical and Reformed	59.5	37.0	3.5
Presbyterian Bodies	58.1	37.6	4.3
Reformed Bodies	54.9	45.1	
Assemblies of God	54.5	45.5	
Adventist Bodies	52.1	47.9	
Lutheran Bodies	51.1	40.5	8.4
Latter-day Saints	45.8	44.5	9.8
Friends	44.8	55.2	
Church of the Nazarene	43.8	56.2	
Evangelical United Brethren	42.0	50.6	7.4
Methodist Bodies	40.1	49.8	10.1
Mennonite Bodies	37.9	62.1	
Disciples of Christ	36.0	53.3	10.7
Brethren Churches	35.7	64.3	
Baptist Bodies	34.9	52.2	12.9
Churches of God	34.6	65.4	
Total Reported Church Members	60.8	33.5	5.8
United States population, 1950	56.8	36.4	6.8

Source: *Churches and Church Membership in the United States*, Series D, Nos. 3 to 6, Tables 136 to 139 and Series E, No. 1, Table 140.

or more urban places, but not constituting part of a metropolitan area), and none at all in the purely rural counties.[34] The members of the Roman Catholic and Protestant Episcopal churches are also highly urbanized, with 74.5 and 72.7 percent, respectively, in metropolitan areas and only 2.4 and 2.1 percent in rural counties; and the much smaller membership in the Unitarian-Universalist group shows the same predilection for cities.[35] At the opposite extreme the Disciples of Christ, Churches of God, Brethren, Baptist, and Mennonite bodies look to non-metropolitan counties for more than 60 percent of their membership. Five other groups—Lutheran bodies, Latter-day Saints, Friends, Church of the Nazarene, and Evangelical United Brethren—are essentially rural with metropolitan counties making up only 40 to 50 percent of the membership. The remaining six groups—the Congregational Christian Church, Evangelical and Reformed Church, Presbyterian bodies, Reformed bodies, Assemblies of God, and Adventist bodies—approach the national average in the residential composition of their membership. These national averages should be interpreted with caution since there are such significant local departures from the national

pattern, as for example, substantial rural Catholic populations in various parts of the Middle West, strong rural concentrations of Episcopalians in Virginia, or a largely urban Baptist population in California. It should also be noted that despite their considerable absolute magnitude and decidedly urban character, the Catholic and Jewish groups nowhere dominate the population of metropolitan areas as overwhelmingly as do the Protestant groups in most urban areas in the Southeast (Table 27.4).

Other General Distributional Characteristics

We have already touched on the fact that the number and diversity of denominations in the predominantly Protestant United States is unmatched in any other nation. This diversity is apparent even within a small rural county or urban community where it is not uncommon for a dozen or more denominations to be represented by formal congregations; and in the larger cities the number of distinct religious bodies may run to several score. This rampant "over-churching" may, incidentally, be one of the by-products of an unusually produc-

TABLE 27.4   Leading Protestant, Roman Catholic, and Jewish standard metropolitan areas, as ranked in terms of total reported church members, ca. 1952

PROTESTANT		ROMAN CATHOLIC		JEWISH	
1. Winston-Salem, N. C.	98.2	Laredo, Texas (est.)	93.1	New York–Northeastern New Jersey	33.1
2. Gadsden, Alabama	97.6	Fall River–New Bedford, Mass.	80.2	Miami, Florida	29.2
3. Knoxville, Tenn.	97.3	Dubuque, Iowa	78.7	Los Angeles, Calif.	18.0
4. Greenville, S. C.	97.0	Manchester, N. H.	78.6	Atlantic City, N. J.	16.5
5. Greensboro-High Point, N. C.	96.6	Providence, R. I.	78.5	Philadelphia, Pa.	12.8
6. Raleigh, N. C.	96.5	New Orleans, La.	76.9	Baltimore, Maryland	11.8
7. Ashville, N. C.	96.2	Springfield-Holyoke, Mass.	75.4	Chicago, Illinois	11.4
8. Charlotte, N. C.	95.8	Albuquerque, N. M.	73.9	Cleveland, Ohio	10.8
9. Durham, N. C.	95.6	El Paso, Texas	73.2	Hartford–New Haven–Bristol, Conn.	9.3
10. Columbus, Georgia	95.0	Green Bay, Wisconsin	72.9	Boston–Lowell–Lawrence, Mass.	8.4

Source: *Churches and Church Membership in the United States,* Series D, Nos. 1 and 2, Tables 133 and 134.

tive economy, since it is difficult to see how a less prosperous nation could afford to support such an obvious surplus of religious accommodations.[36] One of the surprising facts about the American religious scene, one that does not necessarily follow from the multiplicity of denominations, is the extent which most of the major groups tend to be national in distribution. No two of the areal patterns closely resemble each other, and each of the denominational groups does have one or more regional concentrations; but each of the larger groups tends to reach into every corner of the land, however unevenly. Thirteen of the 22 groups studied here (including the Roman Catholic and Jewish) are established in each of the 48 states,[37] and the remaining nine are among the smallest in terms of membership. How ever, even the latter groups are dispersed quite widely, so that we find the most areally limited of all—the Moravians—in no less than fourteen states. There has evidently been unusual mobility of people and of religious ideas, with no successful creed limited to a single minor segment of the national territory. Even the Latter-day Saints, who are so nearly synonymous with Utah and some adjacent areas and dominate their region to a degree unparalleled else-where, are present in moderate numbers in many other sections of the country.

This strong tendency toward national occurrence among most of the denomina-tional groups is given quantitative expression in Tables 27.5 and 27.6. The coefficient of geographic association (g),[38] which has been computed by denominational group and by state, is the total church membership of a state or a denominational group less the percentage who would have to be shifted to other states or other groups in order to have the distribution of the group within the nation or the state conform with the national average. Most states and denominational groups have rather high g values. Only Utah, kindred Idaho, and the states of the Deep South deviate widely from the national pattern; and among the denominations, the more divergent groups are rather small in

membership except for the Baptist bodies, with their powerful concentration within the South, and the strongly localized Latter-day Saints. Four denominational groups rank exceptionally high, and thus most nearly approach a uniform and fully national distribution—the Roman Catholic, Meth-odist, Presbyterian, and Episcopalian. The primacy of the Roman Catholics is, in good part, due to the fact that by accounting for more than 40 percent of reported church members, this group contributes greatly toward the definition of the norm from which deviations are being measured. Another factor is the choice of the areal unit; Cath-olics would probably score much lower and some Protestant groups much higher if g

TABLE 27.5 Coefficient of geographic association (g) between distribution of members of denom-inational groups and total reported church mem-bership, by state, ca. 1952

DENOMINATIONAL GROUP	g
Roman Catholic	80.8
Presbyterian Bodies	80.1
Protestant Episcopal	78.7
Methodist Bodies	72.7
Church of the Nazarene	64.8
Adventist Bodies	64.0
Unitarian and Universalist Churches	62.9
Assemblies of God	61.6
Lutheran Bodies	61.3
Congregational Christian Church	57.5
Jewish Congregations	57.0
Churches of God	55.8
Disciples of Christ	54.9
Evangelical and Reformed Church	50.4
Friends	49.6
Baptist Bodies	48.7
Evangelical United Brethren Church	46.2
Reformed Bodies	42.2
Brethren Churches	41.3
Mennonite Bodies	40.8
Moravian Bodies	36.3
Latter-day Saints	22.0

$$g = 100 - \frac{\Sigma(m - m_s)}{2}$$

Where $m = \dfrac{\text{total, all church members in state}}{\text{total, all church members in U. S.}}$

$m_s = \dfrac{\text{members of denominational group in state}}{\text{national membership of denominational group}}$

were calculated for counties or some other areal category below the state level. The wide and rather even dispersion of Episcopalians, despite their strong affinity for urban locations, is striking on the map as well as in Table 27.5; and Presbyterians are even more uniformly distributed, relative to both urban and rural population, than the Episcopalians.

Neither a simple distributional map nor any known statistical index can, however, do justice to the extraordinary position of Methodism in the United States. Although far outnumbered by both Roman Catholics and Baptists and not quite as evenly distributed as the Presbyterians or Episcopalians, the Methodists more closely approach the status of a "national" denomination in a geographical and statistical sense than any other group. This fact is brought out in Figure 27.6 which shows those counties in which Methodists represent a plurality of reported church membership, those in which they are outnumbered only by Roman Catholics, and those in which they are the second largest Protestant group. Although Methodism is dominant in a smaller area than is claimed by either the Baptists or the Catholics (cf. Figs. 27.5, 27.3),[39] the total area in which it ranks first, second, or third among the 22 denominational groups is much larger and is, indeed, well over 50 percent of the national territory. In fact, the only areas of conspicuous Methodist weakness are southern New England, east-central North Carolina, a portion of eastern Kentucky, and scattered sections of the Rocky Mountain states.

The distribution of each of the groups covered in this study could be readily analyzed and explained if we had adequate statistical data on the six demographic processes governing their growth: births, deaths, in-migration, out-migration, conversion (including church mergers), and apostasy (including the division of religious bodies). Unfortunately, we have very little reliable information on the fertility and mortality of the various denominations or the number of their converts or apostates.

TABLE 27.6 Coefficient of similarity (*g*) between incidence of reported members, of denominational groups in each state and for the United States, ca. 1952

STATE	*g*	STATE	*g*
1. Colorado	87.2	26. Minnesota	66.2
2. Ohio	85.0	27. South Dakota	65.7
3. Illinois	84.6	28. Vermont	65.3
4. Maryland	82.6	29. Wisconsin	65.1
5. Washington	81.3	30. Iowa	63.6
6. District of Columbia	80.7	31. Nevada	63.5
7. Missouri	80.5	32. Massachusetts	60.5
8. Michigan	78.8	33. North Dakota	60.1
9. California	78.8	34. New Hampshire	60.0
10. Pennsylvania	78.5	35. Rhode Island	58.4
11. Montana	76.4	36. Delaware	58.1
12. Wyoming	75.8	37. West Virginia	57.2
13. Arizona	75.0	38. Oklahoma	48.1
14. Texas	74.4	39. Virginia	47.9
15. Oregon	72.4	40. Florida	47.9
16. Indiana	71.0	41. North Carolina	46.0
17. Louisiana	70.8	42. Idaho	43.8
18. New Mexico	70.7	43. South Carolina	43.5
19. New Jersey	70.1	44. Arkansas	42.8
20. Kansas	70.0	45. Tennessee	42.4
21. Nebraska	69.5	46. Alabama	41.7
22. Kentucky	67.9	47. Georgia	40.8
23. Maine	67.3	48. Mississippi	37.9
24. New York	67.2	49. Utah	10.7
25. Connecticut	66.2		

$$g = 100 - \frac{\Sigma(m - m_s)}{2}$$

Where $m = \dfrac{\text{national membership of denominational group}}{\text{total, all church members in U. S.}}$

$m_s = \dfrac{\text{members of denominational group in state}}{\text{total, all church members in state}}$

We do have an abundance of material concerning the organizational history of American churches; but since nearly all the mergers and divisions took place within the boundaries of our denominational groups, little of this information is relevant to our purpose. We must, then, rely heavily on such information as we have on the migration of church members—most of it quite indirect—along with some general facts about the human geography of the United States and items drawn from general observation in our attempt to explain the larger aspects of the present-day areal patterns of the denominational groups. Many of the minor distributional details can be easily dismissed by pointing out the existence of certain seminaries, denominational schools, hospitals, homes for the aged, publishing firms, or military camps. Such special nuclei of church members are particularly conspicuous on the maps of smaller denominations, such as the Adventists or Friends, but can occasionally be invoked even for the larger groups.[40]

JEWISH PATTERNS

The traditional division of the American population into members of three major faiths, Roman Catholic, Jewish, and Protestant, provides a convenient approach to a discussion of the geography of the leading denominational groups. The least numerous of the three and the one whose areal pattern is easiest to describe and explain, by virtue of its recency and extreme urban character, is the Jewish group (Fig. 27.4). Adherents of Judaism formed an infinitesimal fraction of the American population until the 1840's when a sizeable contingent of German Jews appeared on the scene, and it was not until the 1880's that substantial Jewish immigration, originating largely in Eastern Europe, gave the United States a large non-Christian minority. Jewish immigration has continued, but at a greatly reduced scale, since the general slackening of movement to the United States in the early 1920's.[41] Most of the Jewish newcomers chose to reside in the major ports of entry and the other leading metropolises of the Northeast, pre-eminently New York City, but also Philadelphia, Boston, Baltimore, Chicago, Detroit, Pittsburgh, and Cleveland. As Table 27.4 and Figure 27.2 indicate, the Jewish group comprises a large proportion of the total church membership reported for these larger cities (no less than 33.1 percent in the New York-Northeastern New Jersey metropolitan area), and so could, incidentally, play a pivotal role in those elections or other policy decisions in which Catholic and Protestant blocs are nearly evenly balanced.

There would seem to be a strong positive correlation between size of metropolis and percentage of Jews among total church membership, so that the great bulk of the American Jewish community is confined to a relatively few places. Still there are small, but significant Jewish groups in most of the lesser cities of the nation. In the smallest of these, Jewish economic activity is largely restricted to retail sales; but in the medium-sized city Jews are attracted to certain wholesale, petty manufacturing, and professional opportunities, in addition to retailing. In fact, there is an interesting correspondence, outside the primary concentration in the urban Northeast, between the importance of a city as a wholesaling center and the size of its Jewish population. There are, of course, major departures from such a pattern of crude economic determinism. The rather larger than expected size of the Jewish groups in Savannah, Charleston, and Norfolk may, in good part, be attributed to the stability and early start of Sephardic (i.e., Iberian Jewish) settlement in those cities. Jewish migrants have followed national trends in moving to Washington, D. C., Florida, and, in especially large numbers, to the Pacific Coast cities. There has been the predictable outward surge to the suburban counties of the larger metropolitan areas; and the amenities would appear to play a greater role in Jewish internal migration than is observed among gentile groups in view of the unusually strong Jewish representation in the Catskill counties, Atlantic City, the larger Florida communities, and such Western centers as Denver, Tucson, and Phoenix.

ROMAN CATHOLIC PATTERNS

The historical geography of American Catholicism has been a great deal more complex. Before the annexation of the Louisiana Territory and the acquisition of a substantial French-speaking Catholic population in southern Louisiana, Catholics had been conspicuous by their general rarity in the American population. The great influx of Irish and German Catholic immigrants that began arriving in the 1830's was predominantly urban in destination, the Irish almost wholly so. But many German and Swiss Catholics elected to settle in rural tracts, particularly in the lower Ohio Valley, the eastern Ozarks, the Texas prairies, and various sections of Michigan, Wisconsin, and Minnesota. Except for the movement to Texas, both the earlier and later Catholic immigration tended to shun the Southern states, as did most other immigrant groups. In the latter decades of the Nineteenth Century and the first quarter of the Twentieth, the Irish and German streams were reinforced by substantial Catholic immigration from Italy, Poland, Lithuania, Hungary, Croatia, Austria, Czechoslovakia, Portugal, and French Canada and lesser contributions from such areas as Great Britain, the Low Countries, and the Philippines. Currently, the trickle of incoming European Catholics is probably exceeded by entrants from Puerto Rico and French Canada and those crossing the Mexican border legally or otherwise to add their numbers to the descendants of the substantial Spanish-American population acquired by annexation in 1845, 1848, and 1853. Most of the more recent European Catholic immigrants settled in cities; but significant numbers also gravitated to the agricultural frontiers of the northern Great Plains or to various small mining settlements.

As has been the case with all immigrant communities, the initial areal patterns of Catholic settlement have been considerably modified by later internal migration. The great majority of the numerous Catholic church members on the Pacific Coast or those in peninsular Florida can be traced to sources in the Eastern and Central states rather than to direct European origins; and it is likely that most of the small, scattered Catholic groups in the Southeast are derived from points in the Northeast. It is also quite plausible, even in the absence of direct evidence, that the Catholic population of many of the larger cities of the Northeast and Middle West has been bolstered by in-migration from rural areas. Nevertheless, even though the details of Catholic distribu-

tion may have been greatly modified through the years and the total number of communicants has increased enormously, the basic pattern, established as early at 1860,[42] has remained remarkably stable for the past century.

The relative numbers of Catholics and non-Catholics have been plotted by county in Figure 27.1; and since Jews form only a small portion of the non-Catholic population and are numerically significant in only a few counties, the non-Catholic church membership may be interpreted for general purposes as aggregate Protestant membership. Because of the inclusion of baptized infants as members of the Roman Catholic Church and the generally more restrictive criteria of membership and frequent under-enumeration of members among many Protestant groups, this map significantly overstates the relative size of Catholic membership and understates Protestant strength. Using the results of the March, 1957 *Current Population Reports* sample survey as a guide to the actual number of professed Catholics and Protestants in the United States, the probable percentages of Catholics and non-Catholics have been indicated parenthetically in the map legend. In spite of the obvious weakness of the assumption that Protestant church membership is uniformly understated throughout the nation, the parenthetical figures probably approach the truth more closely than those derived directly from the National Council of Churches' data.

A study of Figures 27.1, 27.2, and 27.3 discloses the existence of several distinct regions in which Roman Catholics either predominate or form a strong minority of total church membership. Perhaps the most impressive aspect of the geography of American Catholics is the fact that they form the largest group in fourteen of our sixteen largest metropolitan areas (Washington and Minneapolis–St. Paul are the two exceptions), with more members than either the Protestant or Jewish faiths, and that they are predominant in many of the lesser as well as the larger cities of the Northeast. Thus although Roman Catholics constitute only a very large minority of the American population as a whole (40.1 percent of total church membership according to *Churches and Church Membership in the United States*, or 26.7 percent according to *Current Population Reports*), they form a substantially larger, even dominant part of the population of the highly urbanized, industrialized, and economically advanced Northeastern states (69.1 percent of total reported church membership in New England, 50.8 percent in the Middle Atlantic States, and 45.2 percent in the East North Central States[43]) which can, in turn, be considered as the "heartland" of Anglo-America.

The great Catholic concentration in the Northeast can be divided into three major sub-regions. First and most decidedly Catholic, by virtue of the convergence of several strong streams of immigration from Catholic sources, is the New England sub-region. The early, powerful Irish movement was followed by large numbers of French-Canadians, Italians, Poles, and other Eastern Europeans, with Portuguese immigrants appearing in noticeable numbers in some localities. This Catholic population is, of course, primarily urban; but there has been significant penetration of the villages and countryside, and only eastern Maine retains something of its original Protestant exclusiveness. Even greater in terms of absolute numbers is the sub-region taking in the huge coastal metropolises from New York southwest to Baltimore—and now, by recent extension, Washington—and reaching inland to include northeastern Pennsylvania, nearly all of upstate New York, western Pennsylvania, northern Ohio, and southeastern Michigan. Southeastern and central Pennsylvania (exclusive of Philadelphia) is the only large Protestant island interrupting the continuity of this area. Catholicism is relatively weak in Indiana and western Michigan, but a third large subregion commences on the western shores of Lake Michigan to include northern Illinois, much of Wisconsin, and major portions of Minnesota and Iowa. Certain lesser concentra-

tions lying on the outskirts of this primary region date back to the early years of settlement. Thus the remarkably persistent Catholic population of Charles and St. Marys counties, Maryland bears witness to the initial character of the colony; the sizeable communities in Marion and Nelson counties, Kentucky may be related to the fact that Bardstown was the first suffragan see west of the Appalachians;[44] the clusters of Roman Catholics in Cincinnati and at points further down the Ohio and in east-central Missouri largely originated with pioneer settlement.

Quite distinct in origin is the French Catholic region of southern Louisiana, which extends in considerably attenuated form eastward as far as Mobil Bay. The only other significant Catholic concentration in the South is the predominantly Mexican community in the lower Rio Grande Valley and other sections of southern Texas. This region adjoins and overlaps a portion of central Texas in which Catholics of German extraction are a prominent demographic element. The south Texas area might be considered a fragment of a larger Mexican Catholic region which reaches its greatest development in the upper Rio Grande Valley and other portions of New Mexico, south-central Colorado, and southern Arizona. The major Catholic agglomeration located in the southern two-thirds of California contains only a moderate number of persons of Mexican descent and is principally the result of the recent massive migration from the eastern portions of the United States. Except for a few immigrant communities of farmers and miners in Idaho, Montana, and North Dakota, the relative strength of Catholicism is not impressive in the northwestern quadrant of the nation.

There are two extensive portions of the United States in which Catholics are rarely found: the South, and the Mormon region of Utah and adjacent states. Aside from French Louisiana, those portions of Texas with sizeable Mexican or German communities, the moderately large Catholic population of peninsular Florida, the Catholic areas of

Kentucky and Maryland noted above, and some of the larger commercial and manufacturing cities, Catholics are quite scarce in the overwhelmingly Protestant South. The Mormon hegemony over a vast section of the Intermontane section of the West has meant feeble representation for almost all non-Mormon groups, whether Catholic, Protestant, or Jewish. It is also important to note that there are many basically rural tracts in the southern Middle West and, as already stated, in central and southeastern Pennsylvania where Catholics form an inconspicuous minority.

THE   BRITISH   COLONIAL   DENOMINATIONAL GROUPS

Very nearly two-thirds (66.4 percent) of the reported Protestant church membership of the United States is accounted for by six denominational groups, the Protestant Episcopal, Quaker, Congregational, Presbyterian, Methodist, and Baptist, which have in common a British Colonial origin but are otherwise quite divergent in their history and geography. A considerable proportion of the pre-Revolutionary immigrants in the United States were Congregationalists and Friends from the British Isles, approximately 31 and 9 percent, respectively, if the Paullin tally of congregations in 1775–76 can be applied to the composition of the immigrant group. But at the present time these two groups, which ranked first and fifth among the church groups of 1775–76, have dropped to seventh and nineteenth place among the Protestant denominational groups. There is evidence to indicate that the Friends had already spent most of their initial missionary fervor by the end of the Seventeenth Century, well before the crest of their migrational movement to America and that they attracted few converts in the United States. Indeed, the current small size of the group indicates not only a feeble missionary program but also the strong probability that many persons born into Quaker families have left the faith, possibly because this form of worship may not be particularly congenial to the American ethos, and have joined other churches or are

unchurched. There are now only three significant clusters of Quakers outside the original nucleus of settlement in southeastern Pennsylvania: that in the North Carolina Piedmont, the community in central Indiana and neighboring portions of Ohio and Illinois, and the much smaller group scattered through southeastern Iowa. It may be assumed that all three represent colonies derived from southeastern Pennsylvania.

The colonial nucleus of Congregationalism in New England persists as the major center for adherents of this creed; but despite a general unaggressiveness in winning converts similar to that observed among the Friends, the Congregationalists were much more successful in maintaining their numbers and in extending, through migration from New England, the area in which they are a significant population element. The only major exception to the strong westward thrust responsible for widespread Congregational representation in the northern third of the United States is the movement to the North Carolina Piedmont. The relative weakness of Congregationalism west of the Appalachians, as compared to the Methodist, Baptist, or Presbyterian showing, may well be attributed to the "Plan of Union" in effect among the Presbyterians and Congregationalists during much of the critical period of settlement. This rather informal agreement on a division of labor was effective in preventing Presbyterian inroads in New England, but it worked greatly to the disadvantage of Congregationalists in the winning of frontier areas.[45]

The Episcopalians, who were apparently outnumbered by the Congregationalists in colonial times, have been able to overtake them both quantitatively and areally. After a period during and just after the American Revolution when the Episcopal Church underwent serious difficulties because of the suspicion of pro-British leanings, it managed to recover much of its importance and extend its membership over the entire territory of the United States. But even now the major grouping of Episcopalians lies within the only region where they figure importantly in the rural population, the primary area of colonial concentration from Connecticut southward to Virginia. From this original cluster we can trace a significant migrational stream to western New York and the northern Middle West. There has not been much deliberate missionary work (except among the Indians of the northern Great Plains[46]); but the contemporary distribution and composition of the Episcopalian population cannot be accounted for by natural increase and migration alone. It appears that, partly for reasons of prestige and social status, a significant number of persons of middle and upper class position and urban residence throughout the country have gravitated to the Protestant Episcopal Church. This fact is particularly striking if membership statistics for certain suburban counties, which are distinctly upper-income in character, are compared with other counties within the same metropolitan areas.[47] We have, then, a distributional pattern much of which can be accounted for more readily by referring to current socioeconomic factors than by the historical geography of the denomination.

The Presbyterians, who migrated to the United States in considerable numbers both before and after the American Revolution, have not only augmented their ranks through natural increase but have also succeeded in attracting large numbers of converts, particularly during their westward progress across the continent.[48] Once again, the primary initial cluster lingers on as the major modern concentration: the "staging area" in western Pennsylvania and New York and eastern Ohio from which Presbyterians thrust vigorously westward and southward. There is no particular pattern in the distribution of this group outside this area of maximum strength and a secondary concentration in the Carolina Piedmont, which might well be anticipated from a study of early routes of settlement; Presbyterians form a strong minority almost everywhere, and occasionally account for a plurality of church membership—except in New England.

Only a small number of Methodists and Baptists migrated to America during or after the colonial period. The spectacular success of these two leading Protestant denominations is almost wholly a matter of the conversion of the unchurched and members of other denominations by zealous bands of preachers who began fanning out into almost all portions of the nation around 1800. Church historians advance the highly plausible thesis that both the theology and polity of these churches were unusually well adapted to the social conditions of the frontier and other recently settled districts.[49] We have already noted the nearly universal prevalence of Methodists as a prominent religious minority and, frequently, as the largest single group. What remains unexplained is their particularly heavy concentration in a wide band reaching westward from New Jersey, Delaware, and Maryland across the southern Middle West to the foot of the Rocky Mountains. It may be assumed that this east-west belt is simply an extension of the colonial beachhead of Methodism in the Middle Atlantic region; but since the genesis of this early cluster has not yet been accounted for, the problem remains open.

One of the most provocative questions confronting the student of American cultural geography is the close affinity between Baptism and Southern culture during the past several decades (Fig. 27.5). The areal distribution of members of Baptist bodies in the Southern states so closely mimics that of aggregate population that it is disconcerting to encounter the occasional gaps, such as those in the Kentucky Bluegrass or a group of counties in Appalachian Virginia or eastern North Carolina. Nonetheless, this powerful dominance of Baptism within the South is evidently rather recent in origin. If we can trust the earlier census enumerations, Baptist congregations were less numerous than those of Methodist affiliation in Southern states as late as 1860; and it was only in 1890 that the current pattern plainly emerges. The great multitude of Baptist members in the South tends to obscure the fact that Baptism is one of the most widely disseminated creeds in the United States. Its adherents form a significant minority and even occasionally a plurality of total church membership in most non-Southern regions. An example of particular interest is the New England concentration dating from the Eighteenth Century.[50]

THE IMMIGRANT EUROPEAN CHURCH GROUPS The migrational factor readily accounts for the principal distributional features of those Protestant denominational groups considered here which can be traced to the European continent.[51] Among these groups— predominantly German, Dutch, Swiss, and Scandinavian in derivation—religion has remained strongly identified with ethnic origin. Relatively few converts have been made among Americans born into other churches, certainly far fewer than the number of persons who have drifted away from the traditional faith. These denominations tend to be more localized than most of the British Colonial or native American churches and their chief strength lies within the Middle Atlantic and Middle Western states. Conversely, they are weak in New England (which did, however, attract many Catholic immigrants) and most of the South, an area which failed to draw many of the Nineteenth and Twentieth Century arrivals from Europe. All of these groups, or their antecedent denominations, appeared in Eighteenth Century Pennsylvania and the Dutch Reformed group even earlier in Seventeenth Century New York and adjacent sections of New Jersey. As soon as the western territories were opened to settlement, they attracted a strong flow of the church members in question, partly from the older nuclei on the Atlantic Seaboard, but in greater numbers from overseas. Thus we now have sizeable clusters—and even an occasional case of local dominance—of members of the Evangelical and Reformed, Brethren, Reformed, and Mennonite churches within western Pennsylvania, Ohio, Indiana, Illinois, Iowa, southern Michigan, and southern Wisconsin.

The largest such migration was that of members of the various Lutheran bodies who have come to be the leading group over much of the territory west of the Hudson and north of the 40th Parallel. A secondary, but unusually interesting movement, beginning in the Eighteenth and apparently continuing well in to the Nineteenth Century, was that of Brethren, Moravians, Lutherans, and members of the groups that were to become the Evangelical and Reformed Church southwestward from Pennsylvania and Piedmont Maryland down the Great Valley and the upper Piedmont route to various localities in western Virginia, eastern Tennessee, and, most significantly, into central North and South Carolina. The only other important entry into the South was that of Lutherans and members of the Evangelical and Reformed Church into portions of central Texas, probably directly from Europe. More recently, some members of immigrant European church groups have moved into Great Plains localities or to the Pacific Coast, notably the Lutherans who are a major element in the population of the northern Great Plains and the Pacific Northwest.

By studying and comparing the maps of all the groups thus far discussed, two broad statements can be ventured concerning their migrational behavior. Firstly, we can readily detect three stages of migration, though not equally well for each denominational group: (1) the consolidation of one or more clusters of immigrants or locally converted church members in the Atlantic Seaboard during the colonial period; (2) a streaming inland of migrants, some from the older centers near the Atlantic, others from European sources, throughout the century during which the vast trans-Appalachian regions were occupied; and (3) a re-distribution of church members after the close of settlement frontiers that followed much the same patterns as can be observed for the general population—toward the Pacific Coast and the southwestern states, toward peninsular Florida and a few other favored localities on the Gulf of Mexico, and toward the large metropolises in the Northeastern quarter of the nation. Secondly, there is also a rather clear latitudinal zonation in the westward movement of Protestant church members from the Atlantic Seaboard, so that we can define three broad east-west belts—a northern zone in which denominations of Scandinavian, North German, and New England provenience (including the Unitarian) are of particular importance; a central zone in which there is a heavy concentration of groups firmly established in the Middle Atlantic area at an early date; and a large southern zone in which Baptism prevails, apparently through both migration and conversion. These zones are most sharply defined toward their eastern termini; but even though they are blurred in the West, at least the first and third are still discernible on the Pacific Coast. It is interesting to note the persistence of patterns established by early migration. Even extensive out-migration from places initially settled by Catholics or members of non-British Protestant groups has not erased their denominational distinctiveness. Thus modern religious data may serve as tracers of early movements long after Census publications cease to offer information on the national origin of a given local population.

THE NATIVE AMERICAN DENOMINATIONAL GROUPS

The religious bodies of American origin represent the culmination of a trend toward a special New World identity that is apparent in most other denominations. The Protestant groups of British origin have all been strongly Americanized, in some cases almost totally transformed, and the process has gone quite far with most of the denominations originating on the European continent, in spite of stubborn rearguard actions. Even among English speaking Catholics and Jews, who apparently will indefinitely retain Latin and Hebrew (at least among those Jews of Orthodox persuasion) as their liturgical languages, the form and spirit of religious life depart considerably from Old World practice. In some cases the new American sects patterned themselves closely after traditional models, but in numerous instances both theology and style of devotion are quite original.

We are badly handicapped in accounting for the areal patterns in the membership of most native American denominations by two basic facts: only one (the Evangelical United Brethren) of the eight groups that have been mapped for this study can be associated with an immigrant group and so tied in with known migrational currents; and there is good reason to suspect that the underreporting of membership is more serious among most of these groups than for American denominations in general. The relatively poor statistical situation can be attributed to the loose, uncentralized structure and frequent shifts in alliance that characterize the congregations affiliated as the Assemblies of God, Churches of God, Disciples of Christ, or Church of the Nazarene and make it impossible for the National Council of Churches to gather data on some other equally important bodies. The regionalization of the Evangelical United Brethren, a body formed in 1946 by the union of two essentially Teutonic groups of Eighteenth Century Pennsylvania origin and Methodist affinity, follows the familiar pattern already observed for immigrant groups with an initial base in Pennsylvania.[52] There is the marked clustering in southeastern Pennsylvania and the adjacent segment of Maryland, an important, evidently derivative belt to the westward in the lower Middle West, and a scattering further west in the Great Plains and along the West Coast.

We are on fairly solid ground in interpreting the distribution of two other groups, the Unitarian and Universalist and the Latter-day Saints. The former pair are strongly rooted in New England, the Unitarians as a late Eighteenth Century offshoot of Congregationalism and the Universalists as a group whose philosophy can be traced to European sources but who found New England during the early 1800's their most congenial rallying ground. Although there is a persistent dominance of the natal area, Unitarianism and Universalism now reach into all sections of the land. The pattern is, in some ways, quite reminiscent of the Episcopalian, for the Unitarians and Universalists are strongly urban in residence, middle and upper class in social orientation, and rather indifferent toward missionary activity. There is one interesting difference, however. Unitarianism seems to have a particular appeal for well-educated persons of a certain libertarian and philosophical bent; and it is not surprising to find a membership symbol wherever a major university community appears on the map.

The Mormons are unique in theology, geographical implications, and the close attention they have received from the historian.[53] The historical facts are familiar enough so as not to call for recapitulation. For the geographer, the salient points concerning Mormonism are its spectacular achievements, after many early vicissitudes in the Middle West: the penetration of the Great Basin region during the 1840's well in advance of regular settlement, the development of workable methods for utilizing arid lands, the attraction of considerable members of overseas proselytes to the "Land of Zion" during the initial years in Utah, and the subsequent success in missionary work and re-settlement elsewhere in the United States and in other countries. The advantages of an early start and particularly effective ecclesiastical and economic organization are reflected in the unique degree of dominance the Mormons have gained in their stronghold within Utah, southern Idaho, and portions of other Western states. A second substantial Mormon group, presumably containing both converts and migrants from Utah, is found along the Pacific Coast, with special strength in the Central Valley and the Los Angeles Basin. There are also numerous groups of Latter-day Saints in the eastern half of the nation, and particularly the Middle West, who may be explained, in part, by the persistence of early splinter groups or by the missionary efforts of the principal denomination operating out from Salt Lake City. In addition, there is a steady

migration of Mormons eastward from Utah and in other directions[54] that has been generated by high fertility[55] and the limitations of the local economy.

The remaining native American denominational groups have several elements in common, aside from a tendency toward local autonomy. The Churches of God, Assemblies of God, Disciples of Christ, and Church of the Nazarene may be described as pentecostal, holiness, or evangelical groups that tend to be decidedly fundamentalist and "enthusiastic" and to lay particular stress on individual salvation through a strong personal relation with the Deity. The Adventist bodies stand somewhat aside by virtue of their rather distinctive theology. The Adventist and Mormon movements originated almost simultaneously in the same aptly styled "Burned-over District" of western New York;[56] and, strikingly enough, both denominations are rather poorly represented today in their original habitat. Adventism is now widely distributed throughout the country in both urban and rural areas; but its strongest concentration, that along the West Coast, is unique among all our denominational groups and one for which there is no ready explanation. The other groups are also widely dispersed, but each with a distinct regional emphasis. The largest and oldest is the Disciples of Christ, who first appeared in Kentucky and western Pennsylvania between 1810 and 1830 and are now most numerous in the lower Middle West and Upper South, with significant outliers in eastern North Carolina, the Pacific Northwest, and central Texas. The Church of the Nazarene finds its principal strength in Ohio and Indiana, the Assemblies of God in the West South Central states, and the Churches of God in those counties in and near the Southern Appalachians. All four groups have two locational aspects in common: a strongly rural orientation[57] and a negative correlation with regions in which the foreign-born are numerous. On the basis of the map data and cursory observation, these church members might be characterized as lower or lower middle-class native whites residing chiefly on farms and in small towns. The defects of our data may well conceal other significant facts, such as the possibility, suggested by travel in the region, that this group of fundamentalist bodies, along with others not included in this study, may be much more strongly represented in the upland than in the lowland sections of the South. Any attempt to explain the areal patterns of these denominations must fall back upon the facts of their place of origin, the careers of especially forceful individuals, the almost random events of church history and diplomacy, and, possibly, certain common social and cultural tendencies about which we have no information.

The Religious Regions of the United States

In view of strong variations in denominational strength from place to place in the United States that are clearly evident in spite of serious shortcomings in our data, it is most desirable to hazard some delineation of religious regions. There is little doubt that any number of regional systems could be worked out on a quantitative basis which would satisfy various sets of logical, but arbitrary, statistical assumptions. Such an exercise would not, however, answer the question of whether such regions really exist or are just a figment of the geographic imagination. If we accept the inherently reasonable notion that regions truly exist within the cultural landscape when their residents are aware of their existence and find them significant in some manner, it is not too hard to demonstrate religious regions in many parts of the Old World—in the Near East or Eastern and Central Europe, for example. The case of the United States is much less simple. The Mormon realm is an admirable example of a human geographic region in which religion is the chief genetic factor as well as a reason for the persistent distinctiveness of the area; and, on a lesser scale, a good case can

be made out for southeastern Pennsylvania having acquired a unique geographic personality mainly because of its large quota of "peculiar people" and other staunch church members to whom religion has been a dominant force. On a miniature scale, there are scattered about the nation a number of small colonies of pietistic church members —notably those within the Mennonite fold— who have gone to some lengths to shun the worldly ways of their neighbors and have created microregions strikingly different in form and function from the encompassing culture.[58]

The special regional character of New England might also be attributed in part to its quasi-theocratic past and the unique blend of denominations housed within the area. Religion is certainly a significant element in the maintenance of cultural identity within the French- and Spanish-speaking Catholic areas; but, strictly speaking, it is subordinate to the ethnic factor, as can be seen if we consider the contrasts with the strong English-speaking Catholic populations which adjoin or overlap these groups at various points. A much less convincing argument could be advanced for the role of religion in the creation and preservation of the South as a distinct geographic region. There are no peculiarly Southern religious practices or denominational groups; and even though the particular combination of churches found within the region is not even distantly approached elsewhere, few, if any, Southerners are conscious of religion as an item setting them apart from the non-Southern population. Thus, with the possible exceptions of the areas listed above, most Americans do not regard religious affiliation as a factor making one locality markedly different from another and are, in fact, only dimly aware of areal variations in the relative strength of major denominations.

This indifference is reflected and reinforced by the relatively minor contribution of the religious life to the visible landscape of the nation. Outside the Mormon and certain of the older Spanish-American areas, the church has played a rather inconspicuous part in shaping the form and content of settlement, whether urban or rural. In New England, the church building often does dominate the village green; but elsewhere the anomalous status of religion in American life is painfully clear in the relegation of churches to sites generally outside the urban core. Aside from church buildings, the only tangible evidence of spiritual concern is found in burial grounds, parochial school buildings and the quite occasional nunnery or monastery—a wholly different situation from that documented in great detail by Deffontaines for much of the Old World. Furthermore, there are some religious bodies, such as the Friends, which are assiduously invisible; and even the connoisseur of ecclesiastical architecture is often hard pressed to distinguish the churches of one Protestant denomination from those of another.[59]

Most of the seven major regions and five sub-regions shown in a general and tentative way in Figure 27.7 can be justified neither by rigorous statistical logic nor by any obvious manifestations in the works or non-religious ways of men, but only by a certain loose areal association among certain groupings of church members, i.e., some moderate degree of areal homogeneity apparent to the map analyst if not to the majority of inhabitants,[60] and the little we know of the configuration of the general culture areas of the United States.[61] It is not at all clear whether their particular religious composition is a genetic factor in the emergence of these general areas, whether it is one of the by-products of the larger culture, or whether there has been a more complex interplay of forces at work; but, in any event, this areal coincidence between religion and other cultural phenomena does call for further investigation into their mutual relations. It is, then, in the hope of illuminating the larger problems of the cultural regionalization of the nation that the following, quite provisional scheme is offered.

Two other prefatory comments are necessary. Although the huge Catholic population

of the Northeast is recognized on the regional map by the use of a special pattern showing its principal concentrations, this population appeared too recently to have been effective in shaping the enduring cultural personalities of the Northeastern states. Consequently, regional boundaries were drawn solely upon the basis of earlier Protestant groupings. Elsewhere, in the Spanish Catholic region and the French Catholic sub-region, Catholicism was a decisive early force and is so acknowledged in locating regional boundaries. It was impossible, without making the map altogether too complex, to recognize the religious uniqueness of many of our larger cities. It is hoped that the reader will realize that such cities as New York, Miami, Detroit, or Pittsburgh do form areally minute subregions standing quite apart from the larger regions in which they are situated.

New England, the first of our major religious regions, is one in which Roman Catholicism is widely dominant, but its distinguishing characteristic is the strength of its Congregationalist population and, to a lesser extent, the large contingents of Unitarians, Universalists, and Episcopalians. There are substantial Jewish populations in some of the larger cities and rather more Baptists in the region than are found in most of the remainder of the American Northeast. Conspicuous by their rarity are Methodists and Presbyterians (except in northern New England) and members of the various Teutonic denominations (except for a modest number of Lutherans in southern New England).

A second, much larger region denoted as the Midland reaches westward rather irregularly from the Middle Atlantic shore to the Central Rockies. Methodism is the branch of Protestantism most strongly represented, but religious composition varies greatly from place to place. Many cities and some rural tracts are dominated by Catholics, while the Jewish element is prominent in the larger metropolises. Large numbers of Presbyterians, Baptists, Episcopalians, Disciples of Christ, and various native American and Teutonic groups appear in many localities. A major sub-region, the Pennsylvania German, can be delimited in Pennsylvania and portions of Maryland, West Virginia, and Virginia, within which churches of Teutonic provenience are clearly in the majority or form a large minority and Catholicism is inconspicuous.

The Upper Middle Western Region is one in which Lutheranism frequently shares dominance with Catholicism, but it is still recognizable as the westward extension of New England in the strong showing of Congregationalists and, in some cities, Unitarians. Large minorities of Methodists, Episcopalians, and Presbyterians are in evidence. Locally, Baptists and members of various native American and Teutonic churches may be important.

The large Southern Region is readily identified as one in which Baptists are strongly dominant and Methodists form persistently large minorities. Presbyterians and Episcopalians are also well represented, while such native American churches as the Disciples of Christ, the Church of the Nazarene, or Churches of God show some strength locally. The uniformly British and native Protestant character of most of the Southern Region is interrupted by islands of Catholics—German and Spanish-speaking in Texas, French-speaking in Louisiana, and Catholics of Northern origin in southern Florida. Each of these sub-regions is clearly set apart from the remainder of the South by important non-religious factors. A sub-region of peculiar interest is that located in the Carolina Piedmont, an area whose cultural distinctiveness has not been fully appreciated in the geographical literature. This sub-region is decidedly a portion of the South; but the significance of Presbyterians, Friends, Congregationalists, and various Teutonic groups suggests a divergence in general demographic, cultural, and historical development from, say, Virginia or South Carolina that even the causal student would have little trouble in detecting. The common boundary between the Southern and Mid-land Regions shown in Figure 27.7 corresponds surprisingly well with what is known about the northward extent of the more general Southern culture area, except possibly for the exclusion of part of the Kentucky Bluegrass from the South.[62] I believe it is safe to state, from personal observation and discussion, that there is a closer identification in the Southern Region between religious denomination on the one hand and caste and class on the other than is to be found elswhere in the United States, although something of the same situation seems to prevail in rural and small-town society in a good many parts of the Middle West. This correlation between religious and social status is distinct from, though not unrelated to, the lowland-upland dichotomy already noted in the religious structure of the South.

The Mormon Region is the most easily mapped and described of all seven, for within it only negligible numbers of Catholics, Jews, or other Protestant church members appear. The almost equally distinctive Spanish Catholic Region is centered primarily in New Mexico, Arizona, and southwestern Texas, but extends northward into Colorado and overlaps the Western Region in southern California. Members of various British and native Protestant denominations, particularly the Baptist and Methodist, form sizeable minorities alongside the Catholic plurality.

The last of the regions, the Western, has the least recognizable personality. As the recipient of steady streams of migrants from all other sections of the nation, this region has substantial numbers of members in almost all the denominational groups, but is not the major center for any, with the doubtful exception of the Adventists. Neither do we find any clear patterns of dominance by any single church, if we except the Catholic situation in portions of California; but there is a tendency for the groups that are best developed in the New England and Upper Middle Western regions to be well represented in the Pacific Northwest and for the denominations that are firmly based in the Southeastern states to gravitate to central and southern California.

Some Conclusions

After analyzing recent church membership data which, for all their shortcomings, constitute the best set of statistics yet to appear on the religious composition of the American population, it is possible to offer several significant, but highly general, observations on the distributional aspects of the major denominational groups:

(1) The great multiplicity of denominations in the country as a whole is matched by the heterogeneity of religious composition within smaller areas. The major exceptions are to be found in the Mormon Region and much of the South.

(2) As a corollary to (1), we must note that while no two denominational groups have strongly similar distributional patterns and each does have one or more major regional concentrations, most denominational groups do tend, to a striking degree, to be national in distribution.

(3) The system of religious regions and sub-regions tentatively postulated in this study contains only two or possibly three cases of regions whose religious distinctiveness is immediately apparent to the casual observer and is generally apprehended by their inhabitants. The other regions in this set are suggested on the basis of their possible correlation with general culture areas and/or on the basis of the areal association of church membership patterns of various denominational groups as observed on a rather coarse scale.

(4) There is a great deal of heterogeneity within the postulated religious regions in terms of the lesser details of the areal patterns of individual denominational groups (but, as indicated in (3), much less variability on the macroregional scale). This heterogeneity has been partially recognized in the establishment of the sub-regions. Although

there are many sharp contrasts among small rural tracts, the most important contrasts are those between rural and urban patterns. These rural-urban differentials can, indeed, be said to transcend the limits of all the regions and present a national dichotomy, the understanding of which is basic not only for the study of religion and demography but for most of the phenomena of concern to the human geographer as well.

(5) It is possible to offer only partial, rudimentary interpretations of the areal patterns of the individual religious regions and the various denominational groups, mainly in terms of migrational history and, to a much lesser degree, vital trends and the processes of conversion and apostasy.

(6) It is apparent from general observations and from such scanty information as has been brought into evidence in this study that there is almost certainly some sort of areal correlation between religious adherence on the one hand and length, stability, source and type of settlement, rural-urban residence, social class, economic status, and certain cultural and psychological characteristics on the other, both for individual denominational groups and for the religious regions. Unfortunately, we lack the information or the research techniques to state the precise nature and significance of such interrelationships. Thus it would not be prudent to search further at this time for the answers to the questions that have motivated this study: What kinds of religious regions and how many exist in the United States; how did they happen to originate; and how has religion interacted with other phenomena in imparting regional differences to the land and people of the nation?

The temptation to speculate on the interrelationships between religious affiliation and political, social, and economic behavior is admittedly almost irresistible; but the data are hopelessly inadequate not only for purposes of explanation but even for satisfactory basic description. In pursuing such research, it would be foolhardy to rely solely on membership data, the only sort we have or are likely to be given for some time, even assuming their completeness, accuracy, and comparability; but it may be profitable to see, in retrospect, why we have leaned as heavily as we have on such a seemingly slender reed. Each of our denominational groups—in fact almost every one of the individual religious bodies—is a haven for persons of widely differing theological, social, and cultural attitudes. There is usually a characteristic and strongly defined cluster of traits, a mode or stereotype which adequately defines much of the membership; but significant minorities of members may be strewn along the entire range of the theological or social gamut. A brief consideration of the Methodists, whom we have described as perhaps the most nearly national in distribution of all the major denominational groups, would bear out this contention, but any other group would do as well. Even the Roman Catholic Church is much less monolithic in structure and behavior than many persons believe; there are many distinct and semi-autonomous foreign-language groups within the Church, each jealously guarding its particular set of cultural characteristics, and beyond the basic religious life of the English-speaking parish there lies a great array of monastic orders, social and cultural lay groups, and educational institutions catering to a broad variety of tastes. The ascription of a common cultural and historical background to the Jewish population is possible, although an experiment fraught with hazard. In actuality, American Jewry is deeply cloven not only along the lines separating the Orthodox, Conservative, and Reformed sectors but by political, national, and class barriers as well. The heterogeneity of most of the Protestant denominations finds expression in the constant emission of new splinter groups.

What we need, then, are not only tabulations of formal adherence to a given creed but also some adequate measures of intensity of religious belief, frequency or regularity in religious observances, locus on the liberal-fundamentalist spectrum, and statistics that will enable us to relate religious behavior with social, demographic, and economic characteristics. If denominational affiliation is so poor an indicator of the religious or social identity of an individual, and hence, by implication, of a locality, why should geographers concern themselves at all with the topic? Simply because, despite a general looseness in structure and willingness to be as miscellaneous as possible which we find among most American church groups, they do have central tendencies. They are not only convenient receptacles for people of common national origin, spiritual aspiration, or socioeconomic attitudes, but they can also at least partially re-mould the personalities and actions of the persons born or adopted into the fold. It is unquestionable that individuals born within Catholic, Jewish, Mormon, Mennonite, or a number of other Protestant groups will inherit an ineradicable set of cultural differences from their families and co-religionists. Those who elect to transfer their allegiance to a faith to which they are not native but toward which they feel a strong affinity may frequently find themselves carried along faster and further than they had originally intended as they comply with the group norms. We may have trouble in detecting contrasts in the appearance, behavior, or material works of American denominations, for this is a nation in which religious feeling tends to run shallow despite the luxuriation of creeds; but the sense of religious difference—as distinct from religious feeling *per se*—is a powerful and often highly emotional element in the minds of Americans that works to bind together or separate groups of people and thus to create areal resemblances or contrasts.[63] Of central importance to geographers is this fact that religious institutions seek out, accentuate, and preserve differences among men and that differences, not only in the land but in the people who occupy it, whether they be real or imagined, are the meat and drink of geographers. Religious denominations have certainly been among the factors in the creation and perpetuation of some American cultural regions. In the case of the Mormon realm, it has been a phenomenon of overwhelming importance; and in New England and eastern Pennsylvania less decisive, but certainly significant. Elsewhere, as in the South where Baptism was apparently adopted as the creed most compatible with the genius of the region long after its personality had become clearly defined, a given blend of denominations may well have helped to crystallize a region or at least served to prevent its obliteration. From the scanty evidence available, we have reasonable grounds for proposing the hypothesis that religion is a significant element in the population geography of the United States, in the geography of a number of economic, social, and cultural phenomena, and in the genesis and persistence of general cultural regions; but we have too little knowledge of the precise ways in which religion operates in these various directions. Devising ways to collect and interpret information for testing this hypothesis may prove to be one of the most difficult, but also potentially one of the most rewarding tasks awaiting the student of American cultural geography.

An adequate discussion of the more promising methods that might be tested in approaching the geography of religion in the United States would require a rather lengthy statement. In closing the present study, however, a few tentative suggestions, briefly stated, would seem to be in order. If we assume, as we regrettably must, that there is scant likelihood of any marked improvement in the quantity and quality of our religious data in the foreseeable future, the geographic investigator might gain valuable insights into the role of religion in shaping the individuality and variability of our land by pursuing any of these five, not necessarily exclusive, avenues of research: (1) Intensive local studies; (2) detailed study of the histor-ical geography of individual denominations; (3) the statistical analysis of areal association on a national or regional scale involving such religious statistics as we have and relevant demographic, economic, and social statistics; (4) the careful search for relevant material in both the methodological and substantive writings of scholars in other fields touching on religion—theology, demography, sociology, social psychology, political science, and history (including the history of ideas, art history, and other topics beyond the more conventional limits of historical scholarship; and (5) comparative studies involving the United States, or substantial sections thereof, and other portions of the world.

The first approach would take any region of convenient size and character and subject its religious characteristics past and present to the most rigorous analysis possible. All aspects of religion of possible relevance to the geographer would be explored in depth both in the field and through the study of documents. The second method would follow much the same course as the first; and in examining a given group rather than a fixed area would scrutinize all phases of its historical geography, going beyond the national boundaries when necessary. The next approach, though beset by many statistical pitfalls occasioned by the feebleness of much of the basic information, is greatly to be commended to those who are amply supplied with both technique and caution. After the accumulation of a significant store of information through one or more of these methods, the results of research in corollary disciplines and by geographers in other nations could be exploited most fruitfully in framing a new, more nearly satisfactory statement of the geography of religion in the United States.

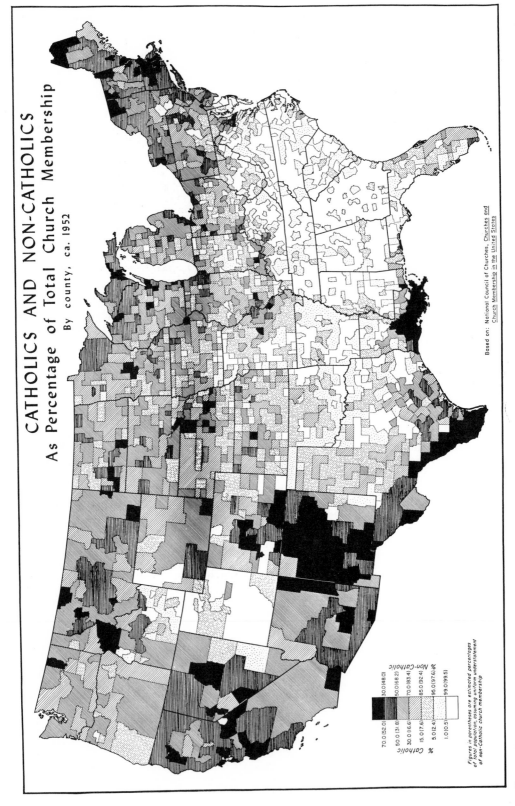

CATHOLICS AND NON-CATHOLICS
As Percentage of Total Church Membership
By county, ca. 1952

Based on: National Council of Churches, Churches and
Church Membership in the United States

Non-Catholic %
30.0 (48.0)
50.0 (68.2)
70.0 (83.4)
85.0 (92.4)
95.0 (97.6)
99.0 (99.5)

Catholic %
70.0 (52.0)
50.0 (31.8)
30.0 (16.6)
15.0 (7.6)
5.0 (2.4)
1.0 (0.5)

Figures in parentheses are estimated percentages
of total population, assuming uniform understatement
of non-Catholic church membership

Figure 27.1

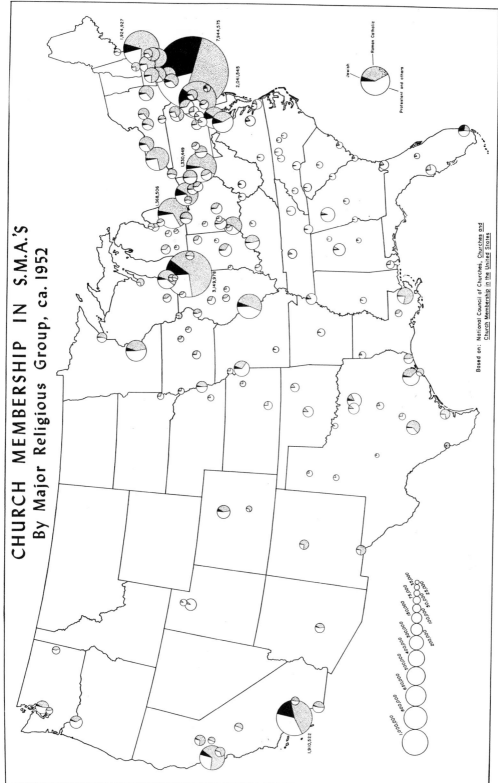

CHURCH MEMBERSHIP IN S.M.A.'S
By Major Religious Group, ca. 1952

Based on: National Council of Churches, Churches and
Church Membership in the United States

Figure 27.2

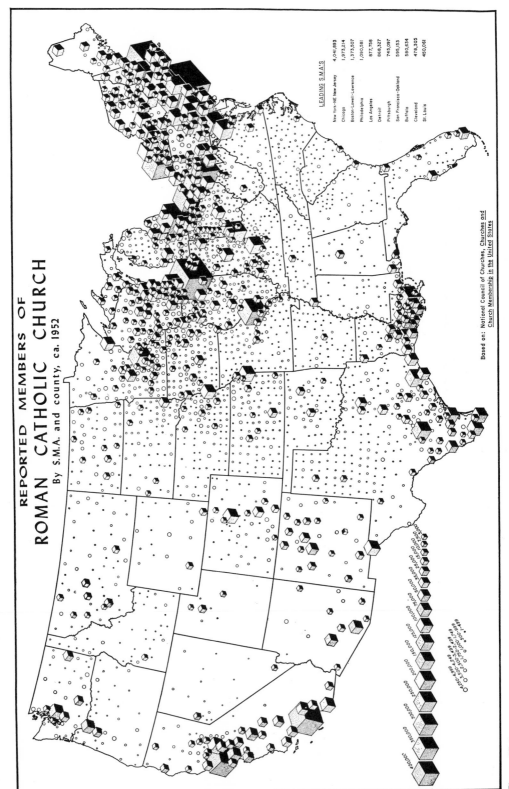

REPORTED MEMBERS OF
ROMAN CATHOLIC CHURCH
By S.M.A. and county, ca. 1952

LEADING S.M.A'S

New York-NE New Jersey	4,041,893
Chicago	1,973,214
Boston-Lowell-Lawrence	1,373,507
Philadelphia	1,090,581
Los Angeles	877,758
Detroit	868,327
Pittsburgh	745,097
San Francisco-Oakland	595,153
Buffalo	580,634
Cleveland	478,305
St. Louis	450,061

Based on: National Council of Churches, Churches and
Church Membership in the United States

Figure 27.3

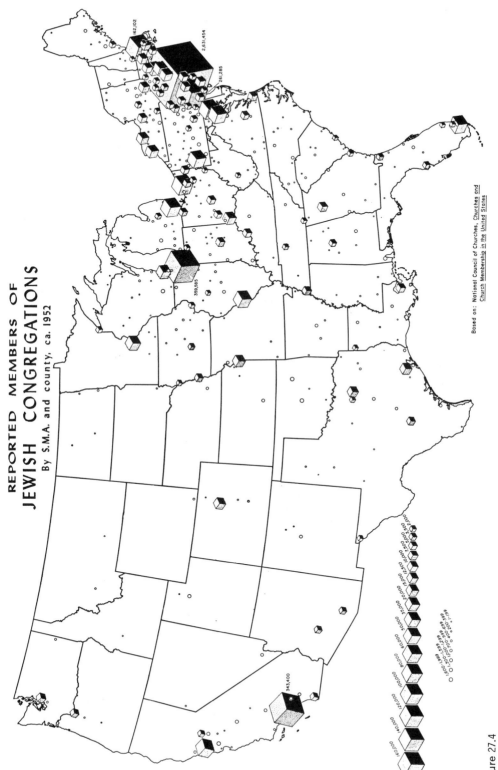

REPORTED MEMBERS OF
JEWISH CONGREGATIONS
By S.M.A. and county, ca. 1952

Based on: National Council of Churches, Churches and
Church Membership in the United States

Figure 27.4

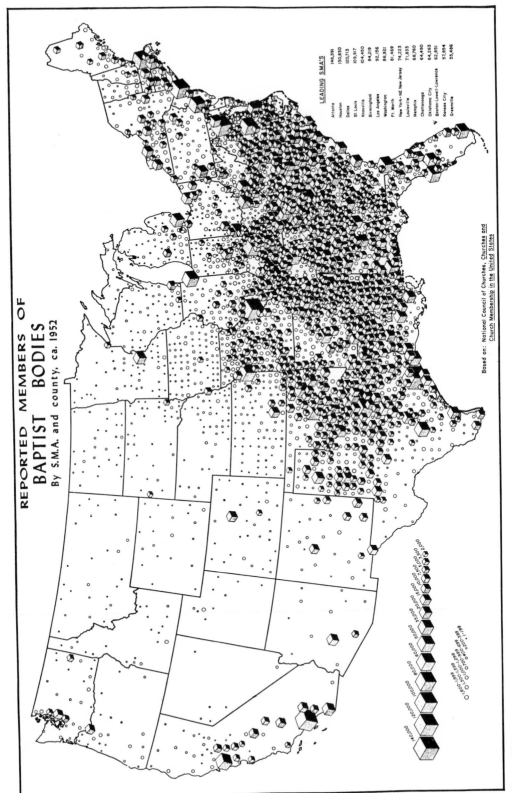

REPORTED MEMBERS OF
BAPTIST BODIES
By S.M.A. and county, ca. 1952

LEADING SMA'S

Atlanta	146,391
Houston	130,830
Dallas	120,713
St. Louis	109,917
Knoxville	104,450
Birmingham	94,219
Los Angeles	92,156
Washington	86,921
Ft. Worth	81,469
New York-NE New Jersey	74,223
Louisville	71,833
Memphis	68,760
Chattanooga	64,490
Oklahoma City	64,263
Boston-Lowell-Lawrence	62,851
Kansas City	57,854
Greenville	55,486

Based on: National Council of Churches, Churches and
Church Membership in the United States

Figure 27.5

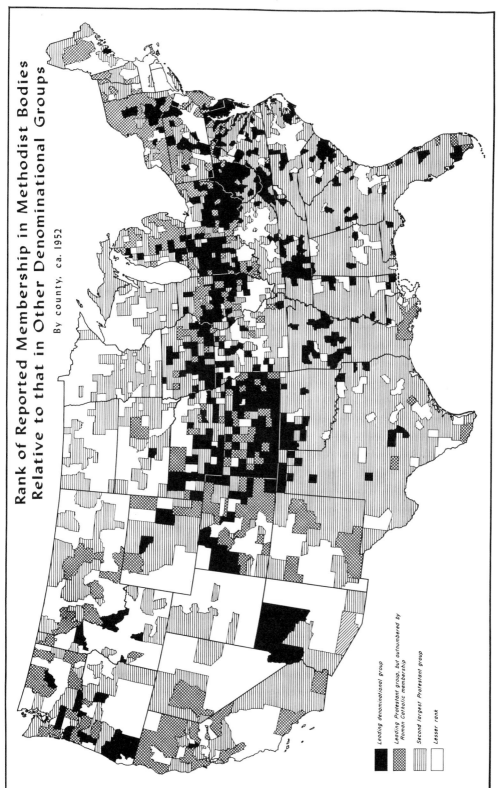

Rank of Reported Membership in Methodist Bodies Relative to that in Other Denominational Groups

By county, ca. 1952

Leading denominational group

Leading Protestant group, but outnumbered by Roman Catholic membership

Second largest Protestant group

Lesser rank

Figure 27.6

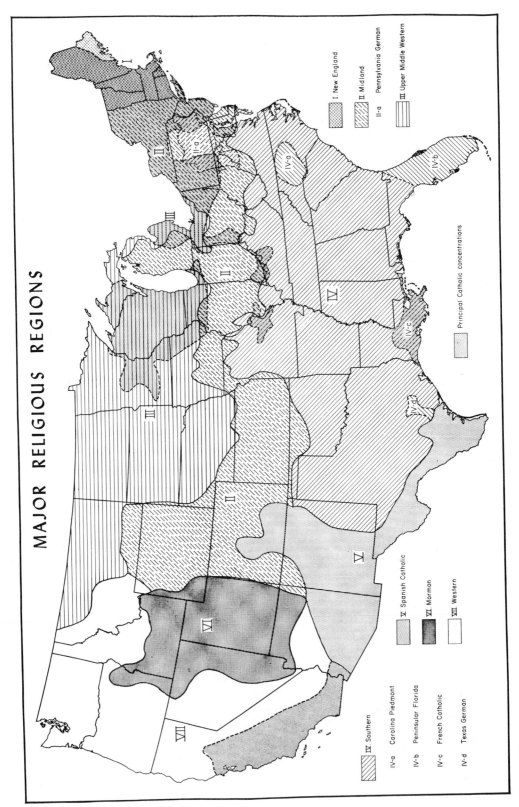

MAJOR RELIGIOUS REGIONS

I New England
II Midland
II-a Pennsylvania German
III Upper Middle Western

Principal Catholic concentrations

IV-a
IV-b
IV-c
IV-d

V Spanish Catholic
VI Mormon
VII Western

IV Southern
IV-a Carolina Piedmont
IV-b Peninsular Florida
IV-c French Catholic
IV-d Texas German

Figure 27.7

Notes

[1]This study was supported by a research grant from Southern Illinois University. I also wish to express my gratitude to John E. Brush, Rutgers University, J. Fraser Hart, Indiana University, and Philip W. Porter, University of Minnesota for the opportunity to examine notes, maps, and seminar papers relevant to the geography of religion in the United States that were produced under their supervision.

[2]P. Vidal de la Blache, *Principes de Géographie Humaine* (Paris, 1941) and Maximilien Sorre, *Les Fondements de la Géographie Humaine*, 3 vols. (Paris, 1947–52).

[3]Alfred Hettner, *Allgemeine Geographie des Menschen, I. Band. Die Menschheit, Grundlegung des Geographie des Menschen* (Stuttgart, 1947), pp. 146–147 and V. C. Finch, G. T. Trewartha, A. H. Robinson, and E. H. Hammond, *Elements of Geography, Physical and Cultural*, 4th ed. (New York, 1957), p. 534.

[4]Roberto Almagià, *Fondamenti di Geografia Generale*, 2 vols. (Roma, 1945–46), II, pp. 578–581. Figure 24, pp. 588–589 is one of the better world maps of religious adherence.

[5]Griffith Taylor, ed., *Geography in the Twentieth Century*, 3rd ed. (New York, 1957), and Preston E. James and Clarence F. Jones, eds., *American Geography: Inventory and Prospect* (Syracuse, 1954). In a briefer survey, Jan O. M. Broek, "Progress in Human Geography," pp. 34–53 in Preston E. James, ed., *New Viewpoints in Geography; Twenty-Ninth Yearbook National Council for the Social Studies, 1959* (Washington, 1959), does enter a plea for the study of religion as a major element in cultural geography; but there is no reference to any published studies.

[6]Pierre Deffontaines, *Géographie et Religions* (Paris, 1948). This erudite volume, which leans heavily on anthropological literature, deals almost exclusively with the impact of religion on settlement features and various aspects of human behavior as a one-way process; it is limited in scope, so that it never sorts out the various religions or discusses their geography *per se* nor attempts to explore the multidirectional interplay among religion, non-religious phases of culture, history, and the physical environment.

[7]Paul Fickeler, "Grundfragen der Religionsgeographie," *Erdkunde*, Vol. 1 (1947), pp. 121–144 (presents a valuable critical bibliography of German-language materials relevant to the geography of religion as well as a discussion of some of the methodological problems of the field); H. J. Fleure, "The Geographical Distribution of the Major Religions," *Bulletin, Société Royale de Géographie d'Egypte*, Vol. 24 (1951), pp. 1–18; Eric Fischer, "Some Comments on a Geography of Religion," an unpublished paper read at the 1956 meeting of the Association of American Geographers and abstracted in *Annals*, Association of American Geographers, Vol. 46 (1956), pp. 246–247; and, by the same author, "Religions, their Distribution and Role in Political Geography," pp. 405–439 in Hans W. Weigert, *et al.*, *Principles of Political Geography* (New York, 1957). The last item does exceed the limits implied in its title and, in addition to providing a valuable survey of the distribution of the major faiths, indicates some interesting points of departure for future research on the non-political, as well as political, aspects of the geography of religion.

[8]The outstanding examples are: E. Friedrich, "Religionsgeographie Chiles," *Petermanns Mitteilungen*, Vol. 63 (1917), pp. 183–186; Ludwig Mecking, "Kult und Landschaft in Japan," *Geographischer Anzeiger*, Vol. 30 (1929), pp. 1–10; Herman Lautensach, "Religion and Landschaft in Korea," *Nippon. Zeitschrift für Japanologie*, Vol. 8 (1942), pp. 204–219; Wilhelm Credner, "Kultbauten in dem Hinterindischen Landschaft," *Erdkunde*, Vol. 1 (1947), pp. 48–61; John E. Brush, "The Distribution of Religious Communities in India," *Annals*, Association of American Geographers, Vol. 39 (1949), pp. 81–98; Etienne de Vaumas, "La Répartition Confessionnelle au Liban et l'Equilibre de l'État Libanais," *Revue de Géographie Alpine*, Vol. 30(1955), pp. 511–604; Helmut Hahn, "Konfession und Sozialstruktur; Vergleichende Analysen auf Geographischer Grundlage," *Erdkunde*, Vol. 12 (1958), pp. 241–253 (dealing with the Hunsrück district in Western Germany); Angelica Sievers, "Christentum und Landschaft in Sudwest-Ceylon," *Erdkunde*, Vol. 12 (1958), pp. 107–120; and Andrew H. Clark, "Old World Origins and Religious Adherence in Nova Scotia," *Geographical Review*, Vol. 50 (1960), pp. 317–344. Perhaps the most ambitious of the regional treatments of the geography of religion is Xavier de Planhol, *The World of Islam* (*Le Monde Islamique; Essai de Géographie Religieuse*) (Ithaca, N. Y., 1959); but it must be considered a brilliant sketch rather than the definitive statement on a huge and complex subject.

[9]T. Lynn Smith, "Religious Composition," pp. 175–189 in *Population Analysis* (New York, 1948) and Donald J. Bogue, "Religious Affiliation," pp. 678–709 in *The Population of the United States* (Glencoe, Ill., 1959). Two items by an American geographer which have religious overtones are also basically sociological in approach: Walter M. Kollmorgen, *Culture of a Contemporary Rural Community; the Old Order Amish of Lancaster County, Pennsylvania*, USDA, Bureau of Agricultural Economics, Rural Life Studies No. 4 (Washington, 1942), and "The Agricultural Stability of the Old Order Amish and Old Order Mennonites of Lancaster County, Pennsylvania," *American Journal of Sociology*, Vol. 49 (1943), pp. 233–241.

[10]Wesley Akin Hotchkiss, *Areal Patterns of Religious Institutions in Cincinnati*, University of Chicago, Department of Geography, Research Paper, No. 13 (Chicago, 1950), and Sister Mary Ursula Hauk, "Changing Patterns of Catholic Population in Eastern United States (1790–1950)," Doctoral Dissertation, Clark University, 1958.

[11]The best recent compilation of statistics for religion on a world scale is United Nations, Department of Economic and Social Affairs, *Demographic Yearbook, 1956* (New York, 1956).

[12]This is the prevailing theme in Deffontaines, *op. cit.* and also, for

example, in Credner, *op. cit.* and Fickeler, *op. cit.* The best recent exposition of this concept is Erich Isaac, "Religion, Landscape and Space," *Landscape*, Vol. 9 (Winter, 1959–1960), pp. 14–18.

[13]There is no single comprehensive bibliography of the statistical data and general literature on religion in the United States, but the best general guides are Benson Y. Landis, "A Guide to the Literature on Statistics of Religious Affiliation with References to Related Social Studies," *Journal of the American Statistical Association*, Vol. 54 (1959), pp. 335–357 and Dorothy Good, "Questions on Religion in the United States Census," *Population Index*, Vol. 25 (1959), pp. 3–16. Valuable bibliographical material on immigrant religious communities can be found in Stanley J. Tracy, ed., *A Report on World Population Migrations, as Related to the United States of America* (Washington, 1956).

[14]The basic tabulations appear in the following publications:

Seventh Census of the United States: 1850, Table XIV, "Church Property, etc.," 1853.

Eighth Census of the United States: 1860. Statistics of the United States (Including Mortality, Property, etc.) in 1860, 1866.

Ninth Census of the United States: 1870, Vol. I, Tables XL, XLI, XLII, 1872.

Eleventh Census of the United States: 1890, Vol. IX, Report on Statistics of Churches in the United States, 1894.

Religious Bodies: 1906, Part I, Summary. Part 2, Separate Denominations, 2 vols., 1910.

Religious Bodies: 1916. Part I, Summary. Part 2, Separate Denominations, 2 vols., 1919.

Religious Bodies: 1926. Vol. I, Summary, Vol. II, Separate Denominations, 2 vols., 1929–1930.

Religious Bodies: 1936. Vol. I, Summary. Vol. II, Statistics, History, Doctrine, Organization, and Work, 2 vols. in 3, 1941.

[15]Only a portion of the material that had been collected and analyzed had appeared ("Religion Reported by the Civilian Population of the United States: March, 1957," *Current Population Reports*, Series P-20, Population Characteristics, No. 79, Washington, Feb. 2, 1958) before the Bureau decided to suspend further publication.

[16]For strong arguments against this interpretation, see Smith, *op. cit.*, pp. 175–176, Good, *op. cit.*, Bogue, *op. cit.*, pp. 688–689, and Otis Dudley Duncan, "Report of the Committee on the 1960 Census, Population Association of America, *Population Index*, Vol. 23 (1957), pp. 293–305.

[17]Published in New York (1956–1958) in a total of 80 bulletins arranged in the following series: Series A, Major Faiths by Regions, Divisions, and States; Series B, Denominational Statistics by Regions, Divisions, and States; Series C, Denominational Statistics by States and Counties; Series D, Denominational Statistics by Standard Metropolitan Areas; and Series E, Analysis of Socio-Economic Characteristics. This survey is briefly described in Wilbur Zelinsky, "The Religious Composition of the American Population," *Geographical Review*, Vol. 50 (1960), pp. 272–273. It should also be noted that for some years the National Council of Churches has also been publishing figures on the total membership of all religious bodies making such data available. The latest such compilation appears in *Yearbook of American Churches . . . 28th Issue, Annual Edition for 1960*, edited by B. Y. Landis (New York, 1959).

[18]New York, National Council of Churches, 1953.

[19]The purposes, methodology, and problems involved in the survey are described in Series A, Bulletin No. 1 in *Churches and Church Membership in the United States*.

[20]These 251 religious bodies do not necessarily comprise the totality of religious groups in the United States. It is quite likely that there existed in the United States in 1952 an additional several score of small, ephemeral, local, or poorly organized groups which were not reported in the *Yearbook of American Churches*.

[21]At this point a bibliographical note on the major descriptive and historical surveys of American denominations may be in order. The *Yearbook of American Churches* contains brief historical and organizational notes on each religious body, in addition to the statistics already mentioned. The best general guide is probably Frank S. Mead, *Handbook of Denominations in the United States*, rev. ed. (New York,

1956); but it can be usefully supplemented by F. E. Mayer, *The Religious Bodies of America*, 2nd ed. (St. Louis, 1956). Valuable essays on the leading Protestant denominations are to be found in Vergilius Ferm, ed., *The American Church of the Protestant Heritage* (New York, 1953). Four of the most useful histories and general analyses of the religious situation in the United States are: Kenneth Scott Latourette, *A History of the Expansion of Christianity. Volume IV. The Great Century, A. D. 1800—A. D. 1914, Europe and the United States of America* (New York, 1941); Willard L. Sperry, *Religion in America* (Cambridge, 1946); Anson Phelp Stokes, *Church and State in the United States*, 3 vols. (New York, 1950); and William Warren Sweet, *The Story of Religion in America* (New York, 1950).

[22]The following is an alphabetical listing of the denominational groups and their component religious bodies. It should be noted again that many religious bodies that would have been included within these groups do not appear because of the unavailablity of statistical data.

Adventist Bodies.—Seventh Day Adventists, Advent Christian Church, Life and Advent Union.

Assemblies of God.

Baptist Bodies.—American Baptist Convention, Southern Baptist Convention, Baptist General Conference of America, Christian Unity Baptist Association, North American Baptist General Conference, Seventh Day Baptist General Conference, United Baptists.

Brethren.—Church of the Brethren, Brethren Church (Ashland, Ohio), Brethren Church (Progressive), Church of God (New Dunkards), Plymouth Brethren, Brethren in Christ.

Churches of God.—Church of God (Cleveland, Tenn.), Church of God (Anderson, Ind.), Church of God in Christ.

Congregational Christian Churches.

Disciples of Christ, International Convention.

Evangelical and Reformed Church.

Evangelical United Brethren Church.

Friends.—Religious Society of Friends (Conservative), Religious Society of Friends (General Conference), Five Year Meeting of

Friends, Religious Society of Friends (Philadelphia and Vicinity), Central Yearly Meeting of Friends, Oregon Yearly Meeting of Friends Church, Pacific Yearly Meeting of Friends.

Jewish Congregations.

Latter-day Saints.—Church of Jesus Christ of Latter-day Saints, Reorganized Church of Jesus Christ of Latter-day Saints, Church of Jesus Christ (Bickertonites), Church of Jesus Christ (Cutlerites).

Lutheran Bodies.—American Lutheran Church, Augustana Evangelical Lutheran Church, Evangelical Lutheran Church, Lutheran Church-Missouri Synod, Evangelical Lutheran Joint Synod of Wisconsin and Other States, United Lutheran Church in America, United Evangelical Lutheran Church, Slovak Evangelical Lutheran Church, Negro Missions (Lutheran), Church of the Lutheran Brethren of America, American Evangelical Lutheran Church, Evangelical Lutheran Church in America (Eilsen Synod), Finnish Apostolic Lutheran Church of America, Finnish Evangelical Lutheran Church (Suomi Synod).

Mennonite Bodies.—Conference of the Evangelical Mennonite Church, Conservative Mennonite Conference, Hutterian Brethren, Mennonite Brethren Church of North America, Mennonite Church, Old Order Amish Mennonite Church, Old Order (Wisler) Mennonite Church, Reformed Mennonite Church, Stauffer Mennonite Church.

Methodist Bodies.—The Methodist Church, Free Methodist Church of North America, Holiness Methodist Church, Lumber River Annual Conference of the Holiness Methodist Church, Primitive Methodist Church, U.S.A., Reformed Zion Union Apostolic Church, Wesleyan Methodist Church of America.

Moravian Bodies.—Bohemian and Moravian Brethren, Moravian Church in America.

Presbyterian Bodies.—Presbyterian Church in the U.S., Presbyterian Church in the U.S.A., United Presbyterian Church of North America, Associated Presbyterian Church of N.A., Cumberland Presbyterian Church.

Protestant Episcopal Church.

Reformed Bodies.—Christian Reformed Church, Reformed Church in America.

Roman Catholic Church.

Unitarian-Universalist Church.—Unitarian Churches, Universalist Church of America.

[23]During the early stages of this study, serious consideration was given to the possibility of extending the study area northward to include Canada and its excellent census statistics on religious preference. This idea was discarded because of the problem caused by the different dates of the American and Canadian statistics, the completely different methods used in defining religious affiliation and gathering data, and the lack of identity, in some instances, between denominations separated by the international boundary. The reader may, however, find it worth his while to examine the maps of the six leading Canadian denominations (Roman Catholic, Anglican, Baptist, United Church of Canada, Presbyterian, and Lutheran) appearing in the *Atlas of Canada* (Ottawa: Department of Mines and Surveys, Geography Branch, 1957) alongside those accompanying this study. There is much less to be gained by comparing the religious patterns of the United States and Mexico, since the latter's 1950 census indicates that more than 98 percent of the population adheres to the Catholic faith.

[24]A classification based on theological orientation, such as the eleven categories utilized by Mayer, *op. cit.*, was briefly considered and abandoned.

[25]Charles O. Paullin, *Atlas of the Historical Geography of the United States* (Washington and New York, 1932), pp. 49–51 and Plates 82 to 88

[26]U.S. Census Office, *Statistical Atlas of the United States, Based Upon the Results of the Eleventh Census* (Washington, 1898), Plates 34 to 40. Additional maps and graphs, of less general utility, appear in U.S. Census Office, *Statistical Atlas of the United States Based on the Results of the Ninth Census of 1870* (Washington, 1874), in which Plate XXXI contains a series of graphs showing "Ratio of Church Accommodations to the Total Population over 10 Years of Age," by state and territory for the eleven leading denominations, and U.S. Bureau of the Census, *Statistical Atlas of the United States* (Washington, 1914), in which Plates 479 to 492 contain graphs and maps

showing the characteristics and distribution, by state, of the major denominations in 1906. Maps of the Roman Catholic population in the Atlantic Seaboard states in 1790, 1820, 1860, 1890, 1920, and 1950 appear in Hauk, *op. cit.*, pp. 53–58.

[27]The cube offers two major advantages as compared to the rather more popular sphere. Its drafting is much less difficult, and its measurability, whether casually by eye or precisely by means of a rule, is considerably greater.

[28]In some of the more congested maps, particularly the Baptist and Methodist, a number of smaller symbols have been omitted from extremely crowded areas where their inclusion would have seriously impaired legibility without adding much useful information.

[29]If we ignore the substantial influx of Negro slaves into the United States, it is only because this movement had little, if any, direct impact upon the religious scene during the earlier periods of American history and because the limitations of our statistical source oblige us to bypass almost completely the topic of Negro religious affiliation.

[30]Paullin, *op. cit.*, p. 50.

[31]Latourette, *op. cit.*, p. 177, states church membership at 5.0 percent of total population in 1790 and 6.9 percent in 1800, but without citing any authority. These figures seem unacceptably low, even allowing for a great dropping off in church membership during the Revolutionary period. If we apply the current average of about 387 members per church, a not unreasonable figure for the late colonial period, to the admittedly incomplete total of 3,228 churches counted by Paullin and Wright for 1775-76, we obtain 1,249,000 church members or some 48.6 percent of the estimated total population of that time. A progressive rise in church membership during the past hundred years is quite plausible. Latourette estimates that some 15.5 percent of the American populations were church members in 1850. Census statistics indicate a gradual rise in this index, from 32.7 to 43.6 percent between 1890 and 1936. The latest available figure on total church membership is 109,557,741 for 1958 (1960 edition of *Yearbook of American Churches*), or 63.0 percent of the total population. It is only fair to state that many

acute observers of the current religious scene do not equate this boom in church membership with a genuine revival in religious fervor.

[32]Hauk, *op. cit.*, p. 34.

[33]The bulletins in Series C of *Churches and Church Membership in the United States* contain maps showing "Reported Church Membership of Major Faiths as Percent of Total Population," by county for each state.

[34]In actuality, there are a small number of Jews, almost certainly well below one percent of the national total, who reside in rural counties, principally as rural nonfarm persons, but are unreported, largely because there is no organized congregation in the vicinity.

[35]The high incidence of urban residence indicated for the Moravians is a statistical fluke. Most of the members of this small group happen to reside in the outer, strictly rural sections of five SMA's.

[36]The relatively small number of denominations with significant contingents in the Southern states may, in part, reflect the less advanced condition of the Southern economy; but it is also the result of defects in the data collected by the National Council of Churches and of the general weakness of migratory movement into the region.

[37]Two of these more restricted groups, the Disciples of Christ and the Latter-day Saints, are missing in only three and five states, respectively.

[38]This index is defined and discussed in Harold H. McCarty, John C. Hook, and Duane S. Knos, *The Measurement of Association in Industrial Geography* (State University of Iowa, Iowa City, 1956), pp. 30–31.

[39]A series of manuscript maps was prepared in the course of this study showing the ranking of the leading denominational groups by counties. Only the Methodist map displayed sufficient divergence from the patterns discernible in the maps of absolute membership to merit reproduction.

[40]For example, the unexpectedly large Catholic group in Onslow County, North Carolina, is explained by the presence there of Camp Lejeune. Most of this is transitory and not properly counted as such in N.C.

[41]Our immigration and census statistics, which classify arrivals by nation of origin rather than by cultural group or religion, make it difficult to estimate the religious composition of immigrant groups except in the roughest terms.

[42]Paullin, *op. cit.*, Plate 85.

[43]Or 45.1 percent of the population of the Census "Northeast," i.e., New England and the Middle Atlantic States, according to *Current Population Reports*.

[44]Latourette, *op. cit*,. p. 233.

[45]Latourette, *op. cit.*, pp. 203–214; Sperry, *op. cit.*, pp. 112–113.

[46]For a map of Indian missions in the United States, see James S. Dennis, Harlan P. Beach, and Charles H. Fahs, eds., *World Atlas of Christian Missions* (Student Volunteer Movement for Foreign Missions, New York), 1911, Plate 18.

[47]Actually there is no solid proof for the notion that persons who have risen on the social ladder have deserted other denominations for the Protestant Episcopal Church. It is simply part of the folklore of American sociology. On the other hand, it is hardly credible that the numerous well-to-do Episcopalians populating the better residential sections of the nation should all be lineal descendants of members of the colonial Church of England or of more recent Anglican immigrants. For a concise survey of what is known of the sociology of religion in the United States, see Bogue, *op. cit.*

[48]Thereby cancelling, in good part, the rather close identification between Presbyterianism and a Scotch-Irish origin that was valid during an earlier period.

[49]For a concise and illuminating statement of church history on the American frontier, see Latourette, *op. cit.*, pp. 175–223.

[50]And the Baptist contingent in neighboring New Brunswick and Nova Scotia. Cf. Clark, *op. cit.*

[51]One of the identifying features of these groups is the fact that they retained the mother tongue for church services long past the time when it was dropped as the customary household language.

[52]The Brethren, or German Baptist, bodies might also have been classified as native American, since the current polity is so strongly American in character and origin; but their Old World connections were strong enough to confer immigrant status on the group.

[53]Perhaps the most objective and penetrating account in the large Mormon literature is the work of a Catholic scholar, Thomas F. O'Dea, *The Mormons* (Chicago, 1957).

[54]Some American Mormons have re-settled in Canada. The Albertan groups are discussed in D. W. Buchanan, "The Mormons in Canada," *Canadian Geographical Journal*, Vol. 2(1931), pp. 255–270.

[55]Here, for once, we can speak of differential fertility with some assurance. The vital statistics for Utah's aggregate population may be taken as a valid approximation of the Mormon situation.

[56]The remarkable religious ferment in western New York during the early 1800's has been described and analyzed in an admirable historical study, Whitney R. Cross, *The Burned-Over District; the Social and Intellectual History of Enthusiastic Religion in Western New York, 1800–1850* (Ithaca, N.Y., 1950). One of Cross' principle theses, and an idea that will bear further investigation, is the suggestion that the religious malaise and inventiveness of an area settled largely by New Englanders was basically a series of variations upon the earlier New England religious syndrome.

[57]Quite possibly, much of this strength in the larger metropolitan areas is based on recent migration from the countryside; but this is, of course, pure speculation.

[58]A Manitoba example is examined in John Warkentin, "Mennonite Agricultural Settlements of Southern Manitoba," *Geographical Review*, Vol. 49 (1959), pp. 342–368.

[59]This is not to deny the existence of some interesting denominational, regional, and chronological differences in American church buildings. The stylistic features of Catholic, Christian Scientist and Jewish structures are easily recognized and widely known, as are the New England colonial, the Georgian, and the Greek Revival schools of church architecture. There are also other genres, such as the Southern rural Negro church, which, unfortunately, no architectural historian has yet undertaken to study.

[60]Figure 27.7 was drawn after a study of both the maps showing absolute numbers of church members and the manuscript maps

showing relative ranking of denominational groups.

[61]An approach to the delimitation of these areas is attempted in Glenn T. Trewartha, "Types of Rural Settlement in Colonial America," *Geographical Review*, Vol. 36 (1946), pp. 568–596, Wilbur Zelinsky, "Where the South Begins: the Northern Limit of the Cis-Appalachian South in terms of Settlement Landscape," *Social Forces*, Vol. 30 (1951), pp. 172–178 and "Some Problems in the Distribution of Generic Terms in the Place-Names of the Northeastern United States," *Annals*, Association of American Geographers, Vol. 45 (1955), pp. 319–349, and Hans Kurath, *A Word Geography of the Eastern United States* (Ann Arbor, 1949).

[62]Cf. Kurath, *op. cit.*, and Zelinsky, "Where the South Begins." The northern limits of the South tend to blur west of the Mississippi, a fact indicated in a study of a rather anomalous area in central and north-eastern Missouri, Robert M. Crisler, "An Experiment in Regional Delimitation: the Little Dixie Region of Missouri," *Summaries of Doctoral Dissertations XVII (1949), Northwestern University*, pp. 352–356.

[63]There may be a little overt difference in the behavior of most Protestants, Jews, and Catholics; but even if he is religiously indifferent, the sense of belonging to an endogamous group is a strong one for a member of any of the three major faiths, and he realizes that he may suffer serious psychological and social disabilities should he marry outside the faith.

Selection Twenty-eight

THE CHANGING DISTRIBUTION OF THE AMERICAN NEGRO[1]

John Fraser Hart

The changing distribution of its Negro population has been one of the most dramatic aspects of the population geography of the United States over the last half century. In 1910 the Negroes of the United States were concentrated mainly in rural areas on the plains of the southeastern part of the nation, but by 1950 most of the nation's Negroes had left the rural areas, and many of them had left the South as well. In 1910 only one Negro in four lived in an urban place, and Negroes comprised only 6.3 percent of the urban population; by 1950 two thirds of the nation's Negroes lived in urban areas, and 9.7 percent of the urban population was Negro.

It is the purpose of this paper to examine and describe the changing patterns of Negro distribution in the United States. Insofar as possible these patterns are analyzed and interpreted, but they are so complex, both temporally and areally, that no one person could be fully competent to analyze them adequately, and in some instances the paper has had to be limited to descriptions of patterns rather than attempt interpretation.

In describing the redistribution of Negroes, this paper treats four separate but closely interrelated aspects of this redistribution: (1) the widely varying regional trends of growth and decline in the Negro population; (2) changes in the distribution of Negroes between 1910 and 1950, with a delimitation of the Negro area of the United States; (3) areal variations in the date of maximum Negro population; and (4) patterns of Negro migration in the decade 1940–50, with a discussion of techniques for measuring migration.

Major Trends by Census Regions

The steady increase of the Negro population of the United States, from 757,208 persons in 1790 to 15,042,286 in 1950, has actually been the composite of widely varying regional trends. Only once, and in only one[2] of the nine census divisions, has there ever been an actual decline in the Negro population, but the rates and amounts of increase in the different divisions have shown considerable divergence.

Reproduced by permission from the *Annals of the Association of American Geographers*, Vol. 50, 1960, 242–266.

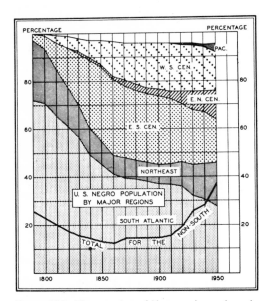

Figure 28.1   The number of Negroes in each major region of the United States as a percentage of the national total, 1790–1950. The regions are essentially the geographic divisions used by the Bureau of the Census, except that the Northeast includes Delaware, Maryland, and the District of Columbia in addition to the New England and Middle Atlantic divisions, and the South Atlantic region includes only Virginia, the Carolinas, Georgia, and Florida.

For ready comparison, the number of Negroes in each division at each census has been calculated as a percentage of the national total at the time of the census (Fig. 28.1).[3] When examining this graph, one must remember that the 504,392 Negroes in the Pacific states in 1950 (only 3.3 percent of the national total) form a group almost as large as the total Negro population of the nation (757,208) in 1790. Similarly, although it has increased almost eightfold in actual size, the Negro population of the five South Atlantic states had declined from more than 70 percent of the national total in 1790 to less than 30 percent in 1950.

The regional redistribution of American Negroes occurred in three rather distinct periods, with major breaks at the censuses of 1860 and 1910. Between 1790 and 1860 the Negro population was expanding westward in the South, with a relative decrease in the Seaboard states. The period from 1860 to 1910 is one of relative stability in the Negro population distribution, with all census divi-

sions increasing at approximately the same rate. In terms of interregional Negro migration this half century was essentially a slack tide between the great westward surge which had preceded it and the great northward diaspora which was to follow.

The years since 1910 have witnessed considerable relative increases in the Negro population of the Northeastern and East North Central states, and sharp relative decreases in the South. Although this trend is apparent in the regional curves, it is emphasized by the heavy trend line across the lower part of the graph, which represents the total Negro population of all states outside the South. Since 1910, but only since 1910, the South's share of the nation's Negroes has declined strikingly.

This graph also indicates the existence of an interesting reciprocal relationship—insofar as the Negro population is concerned—between three pairs of regions, with one member of each pair in the South and the other outside (Fig. 28.1). The percentage of the nation's Negroes in each pair of regions has remained surprisingly constant, but the share of the region in the South has declined as the share of the nonsouthern region has increased. Since 1890, for instance, 47 percent of the Negroes of the United States have lived in the combined Northeastern and South Atlantic states, and the relative increase of the Negro population of the Northeast has exactly balanced the relative decrease in the South Atlantic states. The East North Central states have a similar relationship with the East South Central states, and the Pacific states with the West South Central states.

Although this graph illustrates important trends in the Negro population of the South in relation to the nation as a whole, it does not adequately emphasize divergent Negro population trends within the South. These trends are shown quite clearly, however, when data for the Negro population of various areas within the South are regrouped in terms of the date of maximum Negro population (Fig. 28.2). Although it anticipates material to be discussed in detail later in this

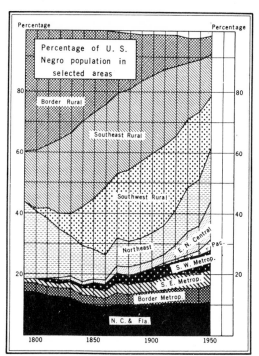

Figure 28.2 Percentage of the Negro population of the United States in selected areas at each census, 1790–1950. The Border includes Virginia, Kentucky, Tennessee, and Missouri; the Southeast includes Mississippi, Arkansas, Louisiana, Texas, and Oklahoma; the Northeast includes the New England and Middle Atlantic divisions plus Delaware, Maryland, West Virginia, and the District of Columbia; the East North Central and Pacific divisions are as defined by the Bureau of the Census.

paper, the graph itself must be considered here because of the light it casts on gross patterns of Negro redistribution within the South.

First, North Carolina and Florida should be separated from the remaining states of the Southeast, because the Negro population of these two states has grown at the same rate as the Negro population of the nation since 1860. Then the four border states of Virginia, Kentucky, Tennessee, and Missouri should be separated from their respective census divisions and grouped together, because the majority of rural counties in each of these states attained their maximum Negro population at an early date. Finally, throughout the South metropolitan counties should be separated from their respective states and grouped together because of the divergent Negro

population trends in metropolitan and nonmetropolitan counties in the South.

Although this second graph fails to show the reciprocal relationships between pairs of regions at the national level, it emphasizes two major aspects of Negro redistribution within the South: (1) the northern margin was the first part of the South to lose a significant proportion of its Negro population, and (2) the Negro population of metropolitan areas in the South continues to increase, both relatively and absolutely, whereas the Negro population in most other parts of the South is declining.

The rural portions of the border states did not reach their maximum Negro population until 1880, but the relative importance of their Negro population has declined steadily since 1790, when they had almost two fifths of the nation's Negroes, until 1950, when they had only 6 percent (Table 28.1, Fig. 28.2). The rural portions of the Southeastern states had 17 percent of the nation's Negroes in 1790, increased steadily until 1850, when they reached a peak of 28.5 percent, and subsequently have decreased just as steadily, until in 1950 they had only 14 percent. Their maximum Negro population was reached in 1910; since then their Negro population has declined absolutely as well as relatively. The rural portions of the Southwestern states had their maximum Negro populations in 1940, but their percentage of the national total has been on the wane since 1910. In all three areas the effects of underenumeration in rural areas at the census of 1870 are quite apparent.

The Negro population of the Northeastern and East North Central states has grown steadily, both absolutely and in percentage, since the Civil War, and the Pacific states, which had had only 0.3 percent of the nation's Negroes in 1910, had mushroomed to 3.3 percent by 1950. Unlike adjacent rural areas, the metropolitan areas of the Southwest, Southeast, and border states have been increasing in Negro population steadily ever since the first censuses. The share of the nation's Negroes has also increased steadily in the metropolitan areas of the Southwest and Southeast, but the share of metropolitan areas in the border states grew somewhat erratically until 1870; subsequently it also has increased steadily. In North Carolina and in Florida the Negro population has been increasing at almost exactly the national rate for the last hundred years.

Distribution of Negroes in 1910 and 1950

The distribution of the Negro population in 1910 is of considerable importance. On the regional level it was essentially where it had been for some fifty years, albeit thicker on the ground. The massive northward migration was about to start, but had not yet gotten under way. In short, the census of 1910 records the high tide of the rural Negro in the South, and any comprehension of the subsequent redistribution must be based on an understanding of the situation in 1910.[4]

The distribution of Negroes in 1950 provides a useful basis for comparison with the 1910 distribution, and also, despite the more recent data of the 1960 census of population,

TABLE 28.1 Number of Negroes in selected areas of the United States, 1790–1950[1] (thousands of persons)

YEAR	U.S. TOTAL	NORTHEAST	EAST NORTH CENTRAL	PACIFIC	BORDER NON-METROP.	BORDER METROP.	SOUTHEAST NON-METROP.	SOUTHEAST METROPOLITAN	SOUTHWEST NON-METROP.	SOUTHWEST METROPOLITAN	NORTH CAROLINA AND FLORIDA
1950	15,042	2,844	1,804	504	906	858	2,098	767	2,487	931	1,650
1940	12,866	2,013	1,069	134	938	690	2,226	656	2,800	700	1,328
1930	11,891	1,701	930	90	959	619	2,224	586	2,696	595	1,226
1920	10,463	1,149	515	48	1,026	530	2,480	492	2,565	433	1,092
1910	9,828	905	301	29	1,101	462	2,498	423	2,615	379	1,007
1900	8,834	781	258	15	1,180	407	2,293	351	2,306	297	855
1890	7,489	623	207	14	1,154	330	1,947	279	1,896	225	727
1880	6,581	551	183	7	1,200	251	1,730	199	1,548	190	658
1870	4,880	439	130	5	977	198	1,282	155	1,035	148	484
1860	4,442	363	64	4	1,070	117	1,213	103	997	84	425
1850	3,639	349	45	1	975	109	1,032	92	612	68	356
1840	2,874	328	29	–	858	80	811	64	365	46	296
1830	2,329	312	16	–	787	72	615	47	171	26	281
1820	1,772	285	8	–	635	50	430	28	94	21	220
1810	1,377	272	3	–	515	40	288	20	47	12	179
1800	1,002	226	1	–	393	28	196	13	4	–	140
1790	757	191	–	–	299	23	129	10	–	–	106

[1]Definition of areas: The East North Central area and the Pacific area are the geographic divisions used by the Bureau of the Census.

The Northeast includes the New England and Middle Atlantic geographic divisions plus the states of Delaware, Maryland, West Virginia, and the District of Columbia.

The Border includes the states of Virginia, Kentucky, Tennessee, and Missouri. The Border Metropolitan area includes Jackson County, St. Louis County, and St. Louis City in Missouri, Fayette and Jefferson counties in Kentucky, Davidson, Hamilton, Knox, and Shelby counties in Tennessee, and Arlington, Fairfax, Henrico, Norfolk, Princess Anne and Roanoke counties in Virginia, in addition to the independent cities of Alexandria, Norfolk, Portsmouth, Richmond, Roanoke, and South Norfolk in Virginia.

The Southeast includes the states of South Carolina, Georgia, and Alabama. The Southeast Metropolitan area includes Greeneville and Richland counties in South Carolina, Bibb, Chatham, De Kalb, Fulton, Muscogee, and Richmond counties in Georgia, and Etowah, Jefferson, Mobile, and Montgomery counties in Alabama.

The Southwest includes the states of Mississippi, Arkansas, Louisiana, Oklahoma and Texas. The Southwest Metropolitan area includes Hinds County in Mississippi, Pulaski County in Arkansas, Caddo, East Baton Rouge, Jefferson, and Orleans parishes in Louisiana, Oklahoma and Tulsa counties in Oklahoma, and Bexar, Dallas, Galveston, Harris, Jefferson, McLennan, Tarrant, and Travis counties in Texas.

it merits consideration in its own right. The turbulent decade of 1940–50 witnessed the greatest Negro redistribution, both relatively and absolutely, that has ever been recorded in the United States. Existing trends were intensified by wartime mobilization and industrialization, and by 1950 every major metropolitan area had a sizable Negro population.

When considering the distribution of Negroes—or any other minority group—in the United States, neither density per square mile nor percentage of Negroes in the total population is a completely satisfactory index, if used alone.[5] Some urban areas, for example, have almost astronomical Negro densities; yet the percentage of Negroes in the total population is quite low. Conversely, Negroes comprise an extremely high percentage of the total population in some sparsely settled areas; yet there may be less than one Negro person square mile. It is necessary, therefore, to consider both indices in order fully to comprehend the distribution of Negroes.

The major area of Negro population in the United States in 1910 was a belt some two hundred miles wide which spanned the plainsland South[6] from the Black Prairies of Texas to Virginia, and then tapered to a narrow tip in Megalopolis (Fig. 28.3). This belt widened perceptibly where it crossed the Mississippi River bottomlands, sent a finger curling into northern Florida, and had outliers in the middle Tennessee River Valley–Nashville Basin–Pennyroyal Plain area and in the Kentucky Bluegrass. The greatest rural densities within the belt were in the Mississippi Delta country, in the Black Belt, on the Piedmont of Georgia and South Carolina, and on the Inner Coastal Plain of South Carolina. Relatively few counties had urban densities of more than 70 Negroes per square mile, and urban Negro communities in the Middle West were still relatively small.

Southern Florida and the Appalachian uplands had few Negroes in 1910, but there was more than one Negro per square mile in western Tennessee, western Kentucky, and the part of southwestern Ohio which centers on the old Virginia Military District. There were two or three Negro families per square mile along the lower Missouri River, in the eastern part of the new state of Oklahoma, and along the Gulf Coast. Farther afield only Chicago and Pittsburgh had more than 33 Negroes per square mile, but there was a hint of things to come in the increasing Negro population of many northern cities, especially those in the Pittsburgh-Cleveland area.

Two major changes are apparent in 1950: the shrinkage of the major belt and the increased number of counties with urban densities (Fig. 28.3). The number of urban Negroes increased notably in the Middle West and the trans-Mississippi South, and the Negro population also increased in parts of the High Plains of Texas, western Oklahoma, peninsular Florida, and the Inner Coastal Plain of the Carolinas. But there were fewer Negroes in much of eastern Texas, in the southern Appalachians, and in three areas which had a dense rural Negro population in 1910: The Mississippi Delta, the Black Belt, and the Piedmont of Georgia and South Carolina.

The same broad patterns are revealed by maps of Negro intensity (Fig. 28.4). In 1950 the counties which were more than half Negro were concentrated in the Mississippi Delta, in the Black Belt, on the Piedmont of Georgia and South Carolina, on the South Carolina Coastal Plain, and in areas centering on the peanut country of Virginia–Carolina and Georgia–Florida. The large number of counties which dropped out of this category between 1910 and 1950 are scattered throughout the South, but the greatest losses were in areas isolated from the main belt, or along its fringes.

The counties in which at least one-third of the population was Negro tend to fill the interstitial areas of the preceding pattern (Fig. 28.4). The largest additional areas are in eastern North Carolina, northern Florida, southern Arkansas, Louisiana, and eastern Texas. The counties which dropped below this percentage between 1910 and 1950 are almost entirely peripheral, with the largest number in the Piedmont, northern Florida, Louisiana, and Texas.

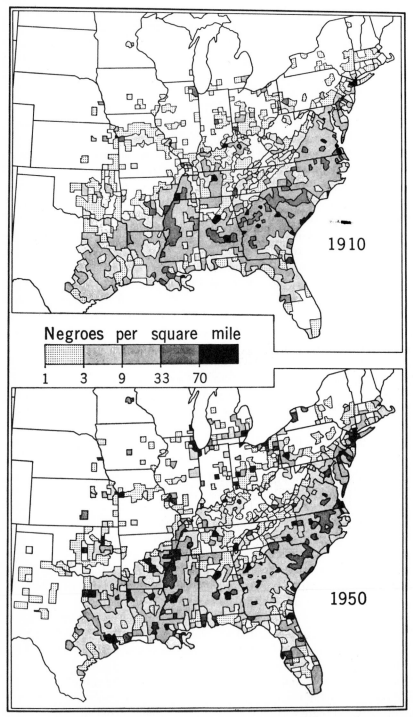

Figure 28.3   Negroes per square mile in 1910 and 1950. A density of more than 70 per square mile indicates a major Negro community in an urban area; contiguous counties with more than 33 per square miles have dense rural Negro population, whereas isolated counties with this density are urban, for the most part; a county with a density of less than 9 will have fewer than three Negro families per square mile; and one with a density of less than 3, less than one family.

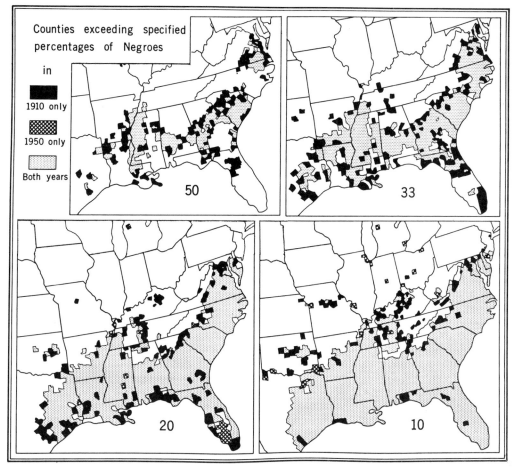

Figure 28.4 Counties in which more than 50, 33, 20, and 10 percent of the total population were Negroes in 1910, in 1950, and in both years

Virtually the entire plainsland South, from Texas to southern Maryland, had at least one Negro for every five persons in 1910 (Fig. 28. 4). The small outlying areas in which Negroes comprised at least 20 percent of the total population included the Kentucky Bluegrass, the Middle Tennessee River Valley–Nashville Basin–Pennyroyal Plain area, and east central Oklahoma, but these areas had shrivelled considerably or even completely disappeared from the map by 1950. Otherwise, as in the two higher percentage categories, the counties whose Negro intensity dropped below the 20 percent mark between 1910 and 1950 were strung along the margins of the main area. This is the highest percentage category, however, to which counties were added between 1910 and 1950, with the major area of accre-

tion in southern Florida. It is also noteworthy that, with the exception of Lake County, Michigan, and Howard County, Missouri, there has been no county outside the traditional South in which more than 20 percent of the population is Negro.[7]

Apart from the upland areas, in virtually every county in the South in 1910 at least one person in ten was a Negro (Fig. 28.4). There was little change on the plains between 1910 and 1950, but along the margins of the uplands the Negro intensity dropped below 10 percent in many counties. It is much more significant, however, that in the same period, between 1910 and 1950, the number of Negroes exceeded 10 percent of the population in many northern cities, including Chicago, Detroit, Indianapolis, Cincinnati, Columbus,

TABLE 28.2 Negro population in selected states, 1950

STATE[1]	NEGRO POPULATION	
	IN SELECTED URBANIZED AREAS	ELSEWHERE IN STATE
California (7)	402,281	59,891
Washington (2)	19,870	10,821
Arizona (1)	13,406	12,568
Colorado (1)	15,611	4,566
Nebraska (1)	17,011	2,223
Oregon (1)	10,664	865
Minnesota (1)	12,561	1,461
New Mexico		8,408
Nevada		4,302
Utah		2,729
Wyoming		2,557
Montana		1,232
Idaho		1,050
South Dakota		727
North Dakota		257
Total	491,404	113,657

[1]Numbers in parentheses indicate the number of urbanized areas included in the calculation.

Cleveland, Philadelphia, and Newark. Parenthetically it might be noted that in 1950 Negroes comprised exactly 10.0 percent of the population of the United States.

Approximately half the counties of the United States had two or more Negroes per hundred persons in 1910 or in 1950, if not in both years (Fig. 28.5). The South is so solid that the main interest lies in those counties whose Negro numbers have climbed above or dropped below the 2 percent level. Most of the losses are in the border area, and they call attention to the early role of the Missouri and Ohio rivers in the distribution of American Negroes. Although the Negro population has declined along the Ohio, at one time that river was lined, as the lower Missouri still is, by counties in which at least one person in fifty was a Negro.

The great majority of counties whose Negro population surpassed the 2 percent level between 1910 and 1950 are in the North and in the southern part of the West. North of the Ohio River and the Mason-Dixon line all but a few of these counties contain a major urban center. In the West, however, the pattern is

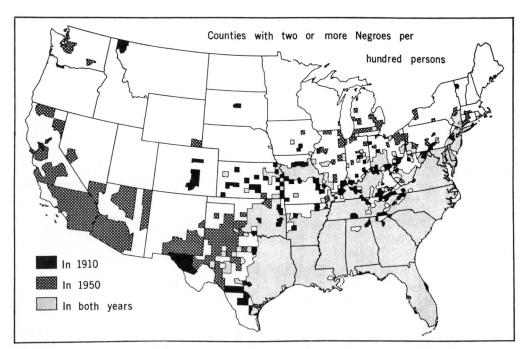

Figure 28.5 Counties in which at least 2 percent of the population were Negroes in 1910, in 1950, and in both years

complicated by the large size and sparse population of many counties. In western Texas, for instance, many counties have fewer than 10,000 people, and 2 percent of the population is only 200 persons.

Despite the appearance of the map, to the north and west of a line from San Antonio through Kansas City to Milwaukee the Negro population actually is highly localized (Table 28.2). Fifteen states in this area had a total Negro population of more than 600,000 persons in 1950, but over four-fifths of the total number lived in only thirteen urbanized areas, and well over half lived in the Los Angeles and San Francisco urbanized areas. Outside the thirteen urbanized areas the total Negro population of these fifteen states is far less than half the Negro population of the eleven counties between the Mississippi and Yazoo rivers in the Mississippi Delta country.

But whereas the percentage of Negroes has been increasing in other parts of the nation, the Negro population intensity has been decreasing in the South (Table 28.3). Fewer counties had extremely high percentages of Negroes in 1950 than in 1910, but at the lower percentage levels there were about the same number. For example, the number of counties in which more than half the population was Negro dropped from 285 to 163, but the number of counties with more than three Negroes per hundred persons rose from 1211 to 1244.

The Negro Area in 1950

Combining density and intensity criteria into a single index provides a better understanding of the relative importance of the Negro population of the United States than can be gained by the use of either criterion alone. From the previous discussion one may conclude that the Negro area of the United States includes those counties which meet two criteria: (1) a density of at least one Negro per square mile, and (2) an intensity of at least 2 percent. Negroes patently are of minimal importance in counties which fail to meet both these criteria.

Within the Negro area one must recognize a core of counties in which the density is at least nine Negroes per square mile, and in which at least 20 percent of the people are Negroes. Furthermore, there are two types of counties intermediate between the core of the Negro area and those outlying areas which barely meet the criteria for inclusion. Many highly urbanized counties have a density of more than nine Negroes per square mile, but an intensity of less than 20 percent; conversely, numerous sparsely settled counties have an intensity greater than 20 percent but fewer than nine Negroes per square mile.

The core of the Negro area in 1950 swings in a great arc across the plainsland South from eastern Maryland to eastern Texas (Fig. 6). There are scattered outliers in Texas, Florida, and the area extending north and south through Nashville, but the core consists of a group of impressively contiguous counties. The sparsely settled counties of the Negro area—those with low densities and high intensities—are largely in eastern Texas, Florida, and along the Gulf Coast near Mobile Bay. Conversely, the counties with high densities and low intensities, which are the highly urbanized portions of the Negro area, lie north of the core area. The largest concentration is in Megalopolis, but there are smaller clusters in the Pittsburgh–Cleveland area, in the Detroit–Chicago area, in southwestern Ohio, and on the Piedmont of Georgia and North Carolina.

Some counties of the lowest category are scattered through the core of the Negro area, but for the most part the counties of this category lie around the margins of the area or are completely separated from it. They are strung along the Great Valley, from Hagerstown to Birmingham, and festoon the eastern front of the Blue Ridge from Virginia to Georgia. They cover much of northern Alabama, middle Tennessee, and western Kentucky, and extend northward into the old Virginia Military District of Ohio. Farther west they are found along the lower course of the Missouri River, in central Oklahoma, in eastern Texas, and scattered over the High Plains. And there are a number of counties in this lowest category on the West Coast.

For the most part, those counties which were in a lower category in 1950 than in 1910 are those which were in the lowest category in 1950, or had dropped completely out of the Negro area (Fig. 7). There was a decline throughout the uplands; the Blue Ridge Mountains, the Appalachian Hills, the Highland Rim–Pennyroyal Hills, and the Ozark–Ouachita borders are all areas in which the Negro population was of less importance in 1950 than in 1910. Interestingly enough, however, the Great Valley held its own, as did several other more favorable areas in the hill country. There was also a decline in many counties of the western South, and along the Gulf Coast, with concentrations in south central Texas, the marshlands of southern Louisiana, and the flatwoods country east of Mobile Bay and in southeastern Georgia and northern Florida.

The Negro area of 1910 lay almost entirely to the south and east of a line from New York City to Kansas City, and thence to San Antonio, and the Negro redistribution after 1910 might almost be described as an eruption across this line. The analogy is strengthened by the way in which counties of a higher category in 1950 than in 1910 are splattered across the map; they are on the West Coast, in the western part of the South, in the North, and in Florida. There is a cluster in southern Missouri, several in coal-mining areas of Kentucky and West Virginia, and one on the industrial Piedmont of North Carolina.

But most impressive of all, perhaps, is the fact that such a large proportion of the counties of the Negro area were in the same categories in 1950 as they had been in 1910. Although there was some attrition of counties along its northern fringes, the core area in particular remained remarkably stable, and so did the sparsely settled areas of eastern Texas and northern Florida. This is not to say, quite obviously, that there were no changes, because there were many and they

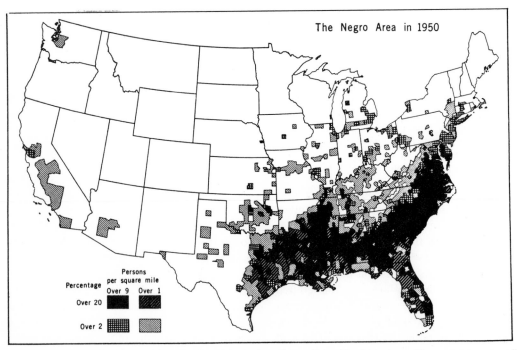

Figure 28.6   The Negro area, as here defined, includes all counties with at least one Negro per square mile in which Negroes comprise at least 2 percent of the total population. The core of the Negro area includes only those counties in which there are at least nine Negroes per square mile and in which Negroes comprise at least a fifth of the total population.

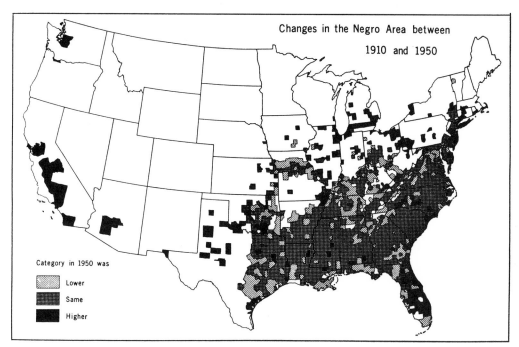

Figure 28.7   Changes in the Negro area between 1910 and 1950. This map must be compared with Fig. 28.6, which shows the distribution, as of 1950, of the counties in the high category, the two intermediate categories, and the low category.

were far-reaching, but it does indicate that the Negro area as here defined, and its core in particular, had a considerable degree of stability between 1910 and 1950.

Censal Year of Maximum Negro Population

Although 1910 is a critical year for any general consideration of Negro redistribution in the United States, it would be foolhardy not to assume that other years might be equally critical in various parts of the nation. It seems logical, therefore, to discover whether there actually is any great variation in the censal year in which various counties attained their maximum Negro population, and if so, to determine whether these variations have any areal significance.

Deciding the areal extent of the area to be investigated poses an immediate problem. Although the Negro area has shown a surprising degree of areal stability between 1910 and 1950, there still have been enough changes to warrant extension of the investiga-

tion beyond its outer limits. On the other hand, there seems little point in extending the the investigation to the entire nation, as the Negro population of a large number of counties has always been small and subject to fairly great fluctuations; the censal year of maximum Negro population for these counties would be almost meaningless.[8] After some experimentation, it became evident that the requirements of this study would be satisfied if the investigation included all counties which at some time have had a Negro population density of at least one person per square mile.

The question of the censal year in which to begin the investigation was easily answered by the notorious differential under-enumeration of Negroes in the South in the ninth census in 1870. Some years afterward Francis A. Walker, who had been superintendent of the ninth census, told a legislative committee:

When the appointments of enumerators were made in 1870 the entire lot was taken from the Republican Party, and most of those in the South were Negroes. Some of the Negroes could not read or write, and the enumeration of the Southern population was done very badly. My judgment was that the Census of 1870 erred as to the colored population between 350,000 and 400,000.[9]

The first step in investigating the censal year of maximum Negro population, therefore, was the preparation of a map of the maximum Negro population density attained by each county in any census between 1880 and 1950 (Fig. 28.8). This map holds relatively few surprises. A few counties are added in New England, and there are minor accretions all along the upland margins. There are also a number of marginal counties with higher

densities than they had in 1910 or in 1950, but no large blocks of counties are added to the areas already considered previously. Furthermore, the counties west of the 100th meridian were so uniform in attaining their peak Negro population in 1950 that they were omitted from further consideration, and the investigation was restricted to the eastern portion of the country.

It soon became apparent that the maximum Negro population was attained almost simultaneously in large contiguous groups of counties with an impressive degree of regional concentration (Fig. 28.9). The peak was reached at a surprisingly early date in the four border states of Missouri, Kentucky, Tennessee, and Virginia, where large numbers of counties had their maximum Negro

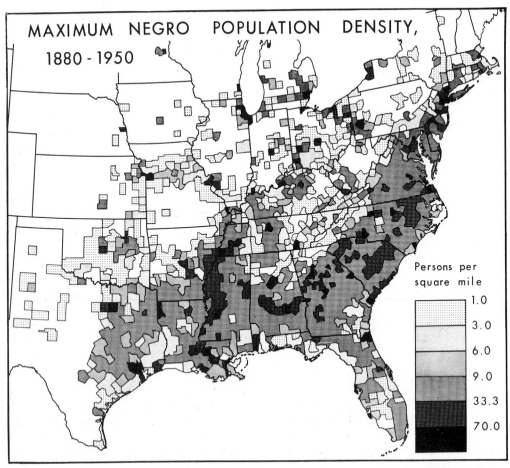

Figure 28.8 Density of Negro population in the year of maximum Negro population at any census between 1880 and 1950

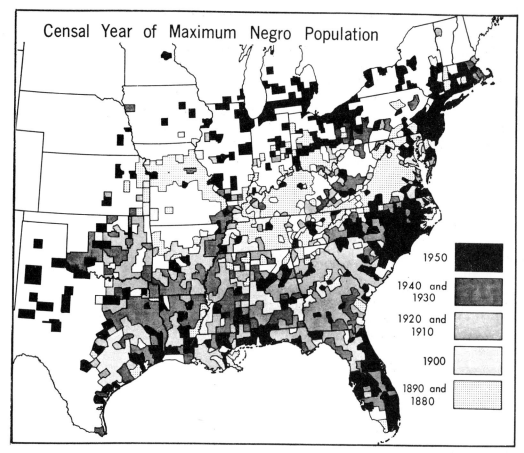

Figure 28.9 Censal year of maximum Negro population. Each county which has had a Negro population of at least one person per square mile at the census of 1880 or at any subsequent census is shaded according to the date of the census at which its maximum Negro population was attained.

population in 1880 or in 1890. These counties are concentrated in the lower Missouri valley, in middle Tennessee and middle and western Kentucky—including most of the Bluegrass and Nashville Basins—in southwestern Ohio, in the Great Valley, and on the Virginia Piedmont. This period was the Negro high tide in the central hilly belt of the eastern United States, and by 1950 Negroes had almost disappeared in many of these counties.

In 1900 many additional counties around the margins of the hills attained their maximum Negro population, but this year is more notable because a few plainsland counties also reached their peaks. They are strung along the Fall Line in Georgia, a dozen are in the Alabama Black Belt, a few are along the lower Mississippi River, and some sixteen are

in southern East Texas. But in 1900 the Negro population of most of the Cotton South was still growing.

The tide turned in 1910 and in 1920. Perhaps the boll weevil was pushing Negroes off the farms; perhaps wartime labor shortages in northern cities were pulling them off; in any event, three-fifths of the counties of South Carolina and Georgia, half in Arkansas and northern Florida, a third in Alabama, and a quarter in East Texas had more Negroes in 1910 or in 1920 than they have ever had before or since. North Carolina counties held their own, but throughout the rest of the Cotton South, from South Carolina to Oklahoma and Texas, the Negro population of many counties reached its peak at this period.

The years 1930 and 1940 were the heyday

of the Negro population in the western parts of the South, with heavy concentrations in central Oklahoma, on the sandy lands of Texas–Arkansas–Louisiana and of southern Mississippi, and on the alluvial lands along the Mississippi River. In this same period the Negro population curve reached its apex in coal-mining areas of Pennsylvania and West Virginia, in Piedmont and mountain areas of western North Carolina, and in parts of the Georgia–Florida flatwoods.

At this point attention needs to be called to the relationship between peak Negro population and the regional trends which have already been discussed. The sharp drop in the percentage of the Negro population in the South Atlantic states after 1920 corresponds with the fact that so many South Carolina and Georgia counties had their peak Negro population in 1910 or in 1920 (cf. Figs. 28.1 and 28.9). The steady decline in the East South Central region's share between 1920 and 1950 is mirrored in the counties of Alabama, which had their peak years in 1920 or 1930, and in the counties of Mississippi, which had theirs in 1930 or 1940. The sharp decline in the West South Central region's share after 1940 is closely related to the fact that so many counties in Texas, Louisiana, and Arkansas had their peak Negro population in 1930 or 1940.

The counties whose Negro population was at its zenith in 1950 are rather less concentrated than those counties whose Negro population crested earlier. True enough, there are some quite obvious concentrations of counties with a 1950 peak—in the tier of states from Illinois to the Atlantic Seaboard, in eastern North Carolina, and in peninsular Florida—but a large number of such counties are scattered through the South.

Outside of North Carolina and Florida the counties which had their maximum Negro population in 1950 are urban, for the most part, and their distribution is closely related to the distribution of major urban centers (Fig. 28.10). Some city counties—especially north and west of Chicago—lacked the one Negro per square mile necessary for inclusion in this investigation, and some city counties

in the South had fewer Negroes in 1950 than in some previous census year. By and large, however, one may conclude that those counties which contain a major city also attained their major Negro population in 1950.

This conclusion, of course, led to the refined grouping of areas used above in discussing regional trends in the Negro population, because in the South the trends of the metropolitan and nonmetropolitan Negro populations quite obviously are diverging (Fig. 28.2). Furthermore, the trend of the Negro population in Florida and in North Carolina differs from other parts of the South.

A number of factors presumably contribute to the fact that such a large part of peninsular Florida recorded its maximum Negro population in 1950. The absolute increase in the Negro populations between 1940 and 1950 was not large, and the Negro density in Florida is still sparse (Fig. 28.3). Counties are comparatively large, and many have urban centers which have retained the natural increase of their Negro population and even attracted immigrants. These urban centers have rather large numbers of retired persons, representing an unusually good opportunity for Negro employment in personal services, and presumably the influx of people from the North has created a social climate rather more acceptable to Negroes than in other parts of the South.

The concentration of counties with a 1950 peak Negro population in eastern North Carolina is more puzzling, and thus far no completely satisfactory explanation for it has been discovered. It has been suggested that a more enlightened political climate might have played a role in providing more acceptable conditions for Negro life, but this concentration is in the politically more conservative part of the state; furthermore, it includes eight counties in South Carolina, a state not especially renowned for the excellence of its race relations. Later in this paper it will be suggested that the agricultural system and demographic history of the area might provide some explanation, but the unique character of the rural Negro popula-

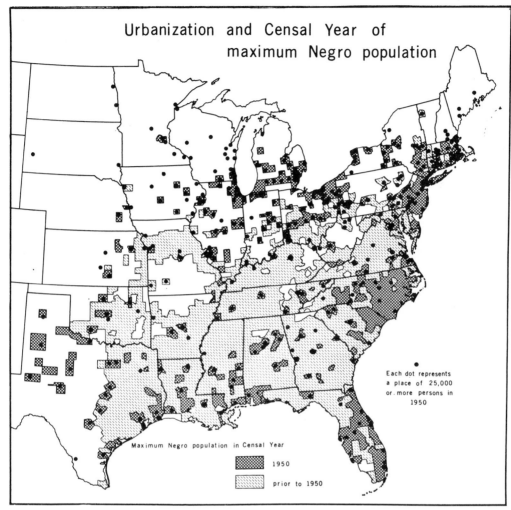

Figure 28.10   Relationship between urbanization and census year of maximum Negro population. The darker shading shows those counties which had their maximum Negro population in 1950, and the black dots represent cities of 25,000 or more in 1950; their relationship is striking. The more lightly shaded counties had fewer Negroes in 1950 than they had at some previous time.

tion trend in eastern North Carolina unquestionably warrants further investigation.

To what extent has the Negro population declined since its peak year in those five of every six southern counties which had fewer Negroes in 1950 than in some previous year? Although the relationship is not as close as might have been suspected, there is general correspondence between the length of time since the peak was reached and the amount of subsequent decline (Fig. 28.11). The simplest rule of thumb, which has almost as many exceptions as instances, is that the decline has been approximately 10 percent per decade in those counties whose Negro population was at its maximum before 1950.

One is immediately tempted to wonder about the extent to which Negro depopulation has continued, and about where Negroes go when they leave. Our attention thus far has been focused on changes in the numbers of Negroes living in specific areas, with little mention of migration. Before we can discuss Negro migration in the United States, however, we need to consider the various techniques by which it can be measured, the types of data which are available, and the pitfalls to heed.

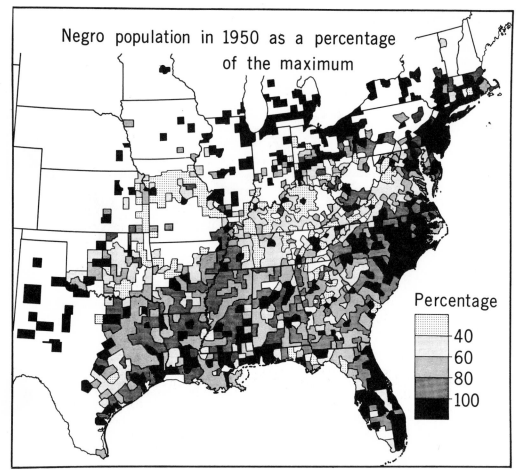

Figure 28.11 Negro population in 1950 as a percentage of the maximum Negro population attained in each county which had at least one Negro per square mile at the time of maximum population.

Techniques of Measuring Migration

Four more or less standard techniques might be used for measuring migration in the United States during the decade 1940–50. Each of these techniques makes use of a different set of data, and each has its own strong points and weaknesses. These techniques consist in an analysis of four criteria:

Mobility A representative 20 percent sample of persons one year old and over at the time of the 1950 census were asked their place of residence one year previously. On the basis of their responses, data have been published on the numbers and some selected characteristics of nonwhite migrants for State Economic Areas.[10] It can be argued, how-

ever, that the State Economic Area is not an especially satisfactory unit of area for geographic purposes. Furthermore, these data pertain only to a single year, and unfortunately it was a year in which mobility appears to have been relatively low for the postwar years because of the mild economic recession of 1949 and 1950. A final minor objection is the difficulty of distinguishing the specialized migration of college students. For these reasons it was concluded that this measure of migration would contribute little or nothing to the present study, and consequently it has not been used.

Census Survival Ratio The prime exemplar of the census survival ratio as a measure of migration is the monumental work of

Everett S. Lee in estimating migration data for each state for each decade since 1870.[11] A survival ratio for each age-sex group is calculated by dividing the number of persons in the age-sex group by the number of persons in the age-sex group ten years younger at the previous decennial census. This ratio is calculated for the entire population of the nation; if it is assumed that age-specific mortality rates are uniform throughout the nation, then this ratio represents the intercensal change which would occur in the age-sex group within each unit of area if there were no migration. The actual population of the younger age-sex group at the earlier census is multiplied by the survival ratio to provide an estimate of the number of persons in the group who would have lived to be enumerated in the older age-sex group at the succeeding census. The difference between this estimate and the population actually enumerated in the age-sex group is attributed to migration.

For instance, the number of nonwhite males aged 20–24 in the United States in 1950 (603,511) is divided by the number of nonwhite males aged 10–14 in the United States in 1940 (693,322) to give a survival ratio of 0.8703. When the number of nonwhite males aged 10–14 in Sunflower County, Mississippi, in 1940 (2,302) is multiplied by the survival ratio of 0.8703, one obtains an estimate that 2,003 nonwhite males in this group should have lived to be enumerated in the age-sex group aged 20–24 in 1950. In 1950, 1,539 nonwhite males aged 20–24 were actually enumerated in Sunflower County, and it is assumed that the difference represents a loss of 464 persons from this group by migration. The process is repeated for each age-sex group to determine the total gain or loss by migration.

Although they are obligatory under this method, any geographer would wince at the assumptions (1) that there are no areal variations in the age-sex pyramids of states and counties in the United States, and (2) that there are no areal variations in age-specific mortality rates of states and counties in this country. Lee himself points out that "there are considerable differences in relative sur-

vival ratios among the states,"[12] and it is only logical to assume that there are even greater differences between counties. There is the further objection that this technique yields estimates only for persons ten years old or older, and further complicated calculations are necessary to estimate the migration of persons born during the intercensal period.

For these reasons the census survival ratio technique of measuring migration has not been used in the present study, despite its very great value for certain types of investigation.[13] If adequate age data are available the survival ratios are easily computed and applied to provide a wealth of information on the age-sex composition of migrants. It should also be noted that estimates obtained by the survival-ratio technique are not affected by the migration of previous decades, as are those obtained by the state-of-birth technique. Lee concludes, however, that correspondence between data obtained by these two methods is remarkably good for major migrations, although there may be discrepancies on small movements.[14]

State of birth In the census of 1950 a representative 20 percent sample of the population were asked their state of birth, and the resulting data have been published with a complete cross-tabulation of state of birth by state of residence.[15] For any state, therefore, it is possible to determine the states of which all of its residents are natives, and the states in which all of its natives are resident.

Unfortunately, albeit for understandable reasons of economy, data on state of birth—and also on vital statistics, which are discussed below—are published only for nonwhite population, without separate tabulation for Negroes, Indians, Japanese, Chinese, and others. The Taeubers suggest, however, that "since the Negroes are such a large portion (95.5%) of all nonwhites, the trends in numbers, structure, and distribution in the nonwhite population are essentially those of the Negro,"[16] and demographers generally appear to find no fault with this assumption. It is not precisely correct, however, to equate the nonwhite and Negro populations, especially at the county level,[17] and in this paper the terms "Negro" and "nonwhite" are specifically differentiated. Data for the Negro population are used whenever possible, but when data for Negroes alone are not available in published form, data for the nonwhite population are used, and the population is referred to as "nonwhite" rather than as "Negro."

Data on state of birth must be used with a certain degree of caution, because they indicate only the net resultant of migration during the widely variant lifetimes of the persons enumerated, and give no information on intermediate or intra-state moves. They also tend to be heavily weighted toward adjacent states because of the ease with which persons move their residences across state lines, especially when the state line transects a metropolitan area.

State of birth data have been published for every census from 1850, however, and it is possible to circumvent some of the difficulties described above by computing intercensal change. For instance, if the 34,653 nonwhite natives of Georgia residing in New York in 1940 are subtracted from the corresponding 62,605 in 1950, it would appear that 27,952 nonwhite natives of Georgia had moved to New York in the decade of 1940–50. A problem of indeterminate proportions is created, however, by the intercensal deaths of migrants from previous decades. In 1940, for example, Arkansas residents included 2,166 nonwhite natives of South Carolina, whereas the number had declined to 1,315 in 1950. The loss of 851 persons may be attributable either to back-migration or to deaths of earlier migrants.

Nevertheless, despite the defects which require that they be used and interpreted with the greatest caution, state of birth data are indispensable to any study of migration, for they are the only available source of information on the direction of movement, and even of the very existence of migration streams. Furthermore, the user can take considerable comfort in Lee's conclusion, cited above, that data obtained by the census survival ratio and the state of birth computations are

reasonably comparable insofar as major movements are concerned.

Natural increase   The number of people in any given area can be changed only by births, deaths, and migration. The technique of using natural increase to measure migration assumes that any intercensal population increase greater than the natural increase—the surplus of births over deaths—must result from in-migration, and that a population increase less than the natural increase must result from out-migration.

TABLE 28.3 Nonwhite natural increase in two selected counties, 1940–1949[1]

	MARSHALL COUNTY, MISS.		PEACH COUNTY, GA.	
YEAR	DEATHS	BIRTHS	DEATHS	BIRTHS
1940	201	605	85	165
1941	165	572	83	166
1942	193	654	89	187
1943	158	626	83	172
1944	155	594	88	180
1945	167	588	81	174
1946	160	616	86	154
1947	165	710	59	171
1948	146	714	67	219
1949	145	734	75	211
Total	1,655	6,413	796	1,799
Natural increase	4,758		1,003	

[1]Source of data: *Vital Statistics of the United States*, Births and Deaths by Place of Residence, for appropriate years.

The amount of natural increase is determined easily enough from data contained in the annual volumes of *Vital Statistics of the United States*, which give the number of births and deaths each year, by place of residence, for every county in the United States and for every city with a population of at least 10,000 persons at the preceding census. In the years 1940–49, for example, Marshall County, Mississippi, had 6,413 nonwhite births and 1,655 nonwhite deaths for a natural increase of 4,758 nonwhite persons; Peach County, Georgia, had 1,799 nonwhite births and 796 nonwhite deaths for a natural increase of 1,003 nonwhite persons (Table 28.3). Unhappily, the vital statistics data, like the state of birth data, make no distinction between Negroes and other nonwhite persons, and even separate nonwhite data are published only for those counties and places in which the nonwhite population formed at least 10 percent of the total population or numbered 10,000 or more persons at the last census. Where published, however, they are the best available source for measuring migration at the county level.

The number of migrants from any given county is determined by subtracting the natural increase from the population increase; it is necessary to perform this operation algebraically, because either quantity may actually represent a decrease rather than an increase, and hence must be treated as a negative quantity. The result indicates in-migration if positive, out-migration if negative. The population increase must be corrected, where appropriate, for the change

TABLE 28.4 Nonwhite migration from two selected counties, 1940–1950

	MARSHALL CO., MISS.	PEACH CO., GA.
1940 population	17,966	6,366
Number of students in 1940[1]	118	225
Total in 1940	18,084	6,591
1950 population	17,730	7,173
Population increase	−354	582
Less natural increase	−4,758	−1,003
Number of migrants	−5,112	−421
Migration rate	−28.5%	−6.6%

[1]Data on resident college enrollment during the regular session, 1939–40 in Rust College (Holy Springs, Miss.) and Fort Valley State College (Fort Valley, Ga.) from Table 18, "Faculty, Students, and Graduates, 1939–40," in U.S. Office of Education, *Biennial Surveys of Education in the United States, 1938–40 and 1940–42*, Vol. II, Chap. IV, "Statistics of Higher Education, 1939–40 and 1941–42."

in place of enumeration of college students, who in 1950 were enumerated in the college community rather than in the community of parental home, as in 1940. As there is no pos-

sibility of "restoring" college students to the home community in 1950, this correction is best made by adding the resident college enrollment during the regular session, 1939–40, to the 1940 population of the college community.

In 1940, for instance, Marshall County, Mississippi, had a nonwhite population of 17,966 persons, plus 118 students in Rust College at Holly Springs, for a total population of 18,084 (Table 28.4). The nonwhite population in 1950 was only 17,730 persons, a loss of 354 persons, whereas the natural increase, as we have seen in Table 28.3, was 4,758 persons. Algebraic subtraction of the natural increase shows that there were 5,112 nonwhite migrants from Marshall County in the decade 1940–50. Peach County, Georgia, illustrates the calculation of migration when the population has increased. The migration rate is calculated by dividing the number of migrants by the 1940 population, and is given the same sign as the number of migrants; in-migration is indicated by a plus sign, out-migration by a minus.

Nonwhite Interstate Migration, 1940-50

Both state of birth and natural-increase measurements must be used to develop a clear picture of nonwhite migration patterns in the decade 1940–50. State of birth data reveal the dominant patterns of interstate movement, but give no indication of source or magnet areas within states. The magnitude of migration in each county can be computed from the natural increase, but this gives no indication of the origin or destination of migrants. Comparison of the patterns revealed by the two sets of data, however, appear to justify conclusions which are not warranted on the basis of either set of data alone.

As measured by the state of birth data, Mississippi was the leading producer of nonwhite migrants in the decade 1940–50 but was not far ahead of the other seven states from North Carolina to Florida (Fig. 28.12). Smaller numbers were produced by Oklahoma, Tennessee, and Florida, and even

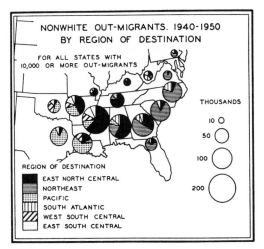

Figure 28.12 Region of destination of nonwhite migrants, 1940–1950, calculated from intercensal change in state of birth data. Regions are identical with the geographic divisions used by the Bureau of the Census, except that the Northeast includes both the New England and the Middle Atlantic division.

fewer by the four border states from Virginia to Missouri. Pennsylvania was the lone state outside the South to produce more than 10,000 out-migrants.

Interstate nonwhite migration is highly selective regionally; that is, a large percentage of the migrants from each region select the same region of destination. In each of the South Atlantic states except Georgia, for instance, more than three-quarters of the nonwhite migrants went to the Northeast, which also attracted just over half of the nonwhite migrants from Georgia. The Northeast attracted less than a quarter of the nonwhite migrants from Alabama, however, and had virtually no attraction for migrants from other states.[18]

In similar fashion, the largest proportion of nonwhite migrants from the East South Central states went due northward. The majority of nonwhite migrants from Mississippi, Alabama, Tennessee, and Kentucky, as well as almost half of those from Arkansas, were attracted into the East North Central states. The pull of the Pacific states was felt slightly in Mississippi, somewhat more strongly in Arkansas and Oklahoma, and most strongly of all in Louisiana and Texas; to a lesser degree the westward surge from the West South

Central states is indicated by the extent of intra-regional migration, which is directed almost entirely into Texas.

The other side of the coin reveals the same high degree of regional selectivity in nonwhite migration; just as each source region has a dominating region of destination, so each migration magnet region pulls primarily from a single region of origin (Fig. 28.13). Three-fourths of the nonwhite migrants to the Pacific states hailed from the four West South Central states. Illinois and Indiana received almost three-fourths, and Wisconsin, Michigan, Ohio, and Missouri rather more than half their nonwhite migrants from the four East South Central states. And three of every four migrants to Megalopolis had come up the Atlantic Seaboard from the South Atlantic states.

These data indicate that there were three great streams of nonwhite migration in the United States in the decade 1940–50. One moved westward from the trans-Mississippi South toward the Pacific Coast. A second flowed northward from the middle South into the Middle West. The third moved up the Atlantic Seaboard from the South Atlantic states into the Northeast. The existence of these three streams reinforces our earlier con-

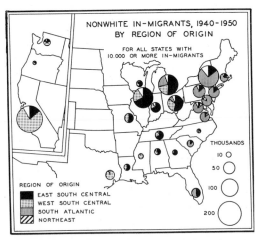

Figure 28.13 Region of origin of nonwhite migrants, 1940–1950, calculated from intercensal change in state of birth data. Regions are identical with the geographic divisions used by the Bureau of the Census, except that the New England and the Middle Atlantic divisions are combined as the Northeast.

clusion about reciprocal trends in the Negro population of pairs of regions, one in and one outside the South (Fig. 28.1). This reciprocal relationship quite obviously is based on the flow of migrants, and the length of time over which these trends have existed gives some indication also that the streams of migration follow relatively old routes; it has even been pointed out that the streams fairly closely follow the old route of the Underground Railway!

If we wish to trace the origin and destination of nonwhite migration streams with greater geographic precision, on a county rather than a state basis, we must turn from state of birth data to natural increase data. In varying degree, nonwhite out-migration characterized the large majority of counties for which data could be computed in the decade 1940–50 (Fig. 28.14). The largest number of migrants came from the counties with the densest rural Negro population. The leading migrant producing area was the Delta country of Mississippi, with the Black Belt fairly close behind. Large numbers of migrants also came from the sandy lands of Louisiana and Texas, and the Inner Coastal Plain and Piedmont of Georgia and South Carolina.

At least three areas of apparently heavy out-migration—Iredell County, North Carolina, Jefferson County, Alabama, and East Baton Rouge Parish, Louisiana—seem to be simply a product of changes in city boundaries.[19] On the other hand, nonwhite overspill from cities or migration into cities of less than 10,000 persons—for which data are not available—appears to account for some

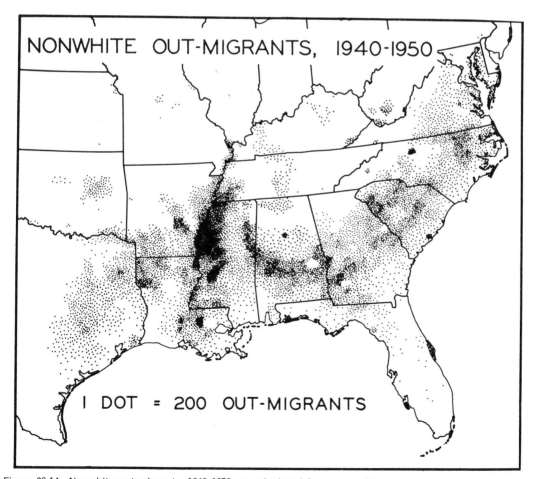

Figure 28.14   Nonwhite out-migrants, 1940–1950, as calculated from natural increase

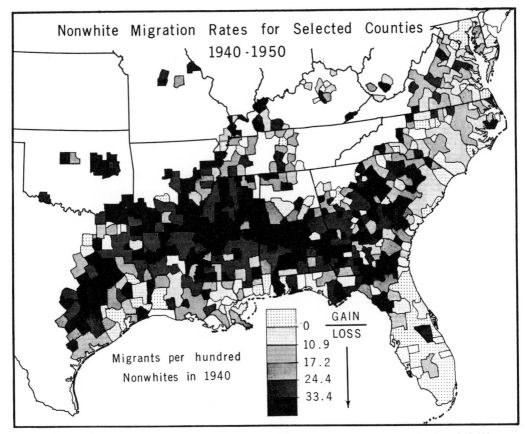

Figure 28.15 The nonwhite migration rate for counties (excluding the population of cities of 10,000 or more persons) in which the nonwhite population in 1940 exceeded 10,000 persons or 10 percent of the total population. The migration rate is the number of migrants (calculated from natural increase) in the decade 1940–50 expressed as a percentage of the 1940 population.

counties of anomalously light out-migration, such as Macon County in Alabama or Dougherty, Bibb, Baldwin, and Richmond counties in Georgia.

There is a relatively close areal relationship between those areas with large numbers of out-migrants and those areas with the heaviest rates of out-migration, although the rates in sparsely settled eastern Texas are higher than might have been suspected from the total number of migrants (Fig. 28.15). A large number of counties lost more than one-third of their nonwhite population by migration between 1940 and 1950, and the majority of counties from South Carolina to eastern Texas lost more than a quarter of their nonwhite population. The impressive implications of this figure, when it is remembered that the majority of migrants are in the younger age groups, are best realized by consideration of counties farther north which had much lower rates of out-migration in the decade 1940–50.

In the rural areas of ten Kentucky Bluegrass counties, for instance, there were 24,490 Negroes in 1940 and only 20,736 in 1950, a loss of 3,724 persons. More than a fifth of the loss, however, can be attributed to the fact that these counties had 796 *more nonwhite deaths than births.* The explanation lies in the age structure which has been produced in these counties by long-continued out-migration. The migrants are most commonly young people, in the reproductive ages, and their departure by removing part of the reproductive potential of the county reduces the number of births. The number of births is reduced still farther as the remaining population ages and passes the reproductive years. In 1950, for example, 34 percent of the Negroes of the rural Bluegrass were aged 45 or older, as compared with 22 percent of the total Negro population of the nation. The migration rate from the aging and dying Negro population of the rural Bluegrass was low because, quite literally, there was no one left to migrate! The same is true for other counties along the northern fringes of the South, especially in Virginia. And if the 1940–50 migration rates are maintained, it is reasonable to expect that similar demographic conditions will characterize much of the rural South within a generation or so.

Paradoxically, the low migration rates of the eastern Carolinas appear to be attributable to a youthful population which has not been artificially aged by migration. For some reason (perhaps related to the difficulties involved in mechanizing various cultivational and harvesting operations required by such labor-hungry crops as peanuts, cotton, and flue-cured tobacco) the counties of this area appear not to have experienced heavy out-migration in the past, and the population is still young. In twenty counties selected at random from this area, only 16 percent of the Negro population was aged 45 or older, as compared with 22 percent in the nation, and 34 percent in the Bluegrass. It would appear that a youthful Negro population with a high rate of reproduction accounts for the low migration rate, despite the fact that relatively large numbers of migrants have left the area. It is further suggested that the age structure of the population might be a clue to the problem of why this area should have attained its maximum population in 1950 (Fig. 28.9).

On the urban side, many southern cities had negative or only very low positive migration rates for the decade 1940–50 (Fig. 28.16). Nonwhite migration from urban areas was especially pronounced in the Border states and on the Piedmont, but every southern state had at least one city whose nonwhite population declined as a result of migration. Furthermore, relatively few southern cities had high rates of in-migration, although there were exceptions in the Norfolk area,

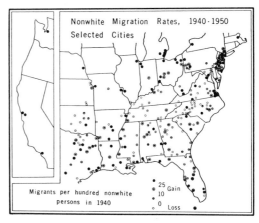

Figure 28.16   The nonwhite migration rate for cities of 10,000 or more persons in 1940 in which the nonwhite population exceeded 10,000 persons or 10 percent of the total population. The migration rate is the number of migrants (calculated from natural increase) in the decade 1940–50 expressed as a percentage of the 1940 population.

along the Gulf Coast, and in the western South. As a general rule, it appears safe to conclude that cities in the South had surprisingly little attraction for Negro migrants, whereas cities outside the South typically had high rates of in-migration.

Unfortunately, these data give only the net resultant of migration, and it is therefore impossible to tell whether cities in the South act as "staging points" for Negro migrants. It would be interesting to know, for instance, whether the Negro migrant from the rural South goes straight from the cotton fields to the asphalt jungle of the metropolis, or whether he first spends an acclimatization period in a smaller city. It is possible that a southern city could experience considerable in-migration which would not appear here if it had been balanced by migration "up the ladder" to a larger town on the part of natives or in-migrants of an earlier decade.

There is no question that the major metropolitan areas were the major magnets for Negro migrants in the decade 1940–50 (Fig. 28.17). The Houston area, greatest magnet in the South, attracted less than fifty thousand nonwhite persons during the entire decade, greater Norfolk attracted only thirty-seven thousand, Memphis, Atlanta, and New Orleans only twelve thousand each, and Bir-

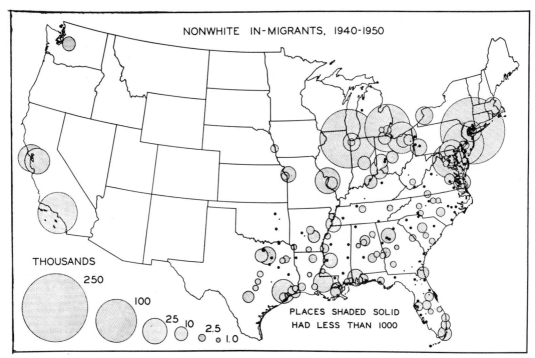

Figure 28.17 Nonwhite in-migrants, 1940–50, as calculated from natural increase. Circles are proportional to the number of migrants.

mingham only eight thousand. These six metropolitan areas, combined, attracted fewer nonwhite persons than did metropolitan Detroit alone, and only half as many as metropolitan New York. Metropolitan Los Angeles attracted almost as many nonwhite persons during the decade as the three most attractive metropolitan areas in the South.

The vast bulk of Negro migrants, in short, are moving to cities outside the South. South of a line from Norfolk through Cincinnati and St. Louis to Los Angeles only a very few cities attracted as many as a thousand nonwhite migrants a year over the decade. But Baltimore and St. Louis averaged four thousand a year, Washington six thousand, San Francisco eight thousand, Los Angeles nine thousand, Philadelphia ten thousand, Detroit thirteen thousand, and Chicago twenty thousand a year. And metropolitan New York attracted an average of two thousand nonwhite migrants each *month* for the entire decade.

Within the South only the towns and cities are attracting Negro migrants, and the Negro

population increase of the South is concentrated almost entirely in the cities. Virtually all nonmetropolitan counties in the South had a smaller Negro population than at some previous census, whereas the majority of the metropolitan counties had more Negroes than they ever had before (Fig. 28.10). As noted earlier, these divergent trends within the South suggested the desirability of refining the areas originally used in discussing regional trends in the Negro population (Fig. 28.2).

Conclusion

The American Negro is becoming increasingly urbanized, and largely as a result of migration from the rural South to metropolitan areas outside the South. In light of the information here presented, the three major streams of Negro migration in the United States can be defined more precisely. Natural increase data indicate that the great majority of Negro migrants from the South Atlantic states come from the Inner Coastal Plain and the Piedmont of Georgia, the Carolinas, and Virginia; state of birth data show that the vast majority of migrants from these states move to the Northeast; and natural increase data indicate that migrants to the Northeast settle almost entirely in the metropolitan areas of Megalopolis.

In the same fashion, we may conclude that the second major stream consists of migrants from the Delta, the Black Belt, and virtually the entire state of Mississippi who are moving toward Chicago, Detroit, and the other urban centers from Cleveland to St. Louis. This stream, like the first, is fed partially from the Georgia-Alabama Coastal Plain, which also appears to send migrants to peninsular Florida. The third stream of Negro migration originates in the sandy lands of southern Arkansas, northern Louisiana, and eastern Texas, and flows westward toward Los Angeles, San Francisco, and Seattle; some migrants from the Delta also appear to join this stream.

Examination of Negro population trends by regions shows a reciprocity between regions which would seem to indicate that these streams of migration have existed for at least half a century, although their volume was not so great in the earlier years. Migration has nonetheless decimated the Negro population of many areas, as is revealed by the study of peak years. First, Negroes left the hills, which had reached their peak by 1900; then they left the South Atlantic states, where 1910–20 peaks are most common; next came heavy migration from the central South, where most counties have peaks between 1910 and 1940; more recently heavy migration from the trans-Mississippi South has been associated with peaks in 1930 and in 1940. But the cities—the major magnets for Negro migrants—had more Negroes in 1950 than they had ever had before, and are increasing their share of the nation's increasing Negro population.

Urbanization for the American Negro has come more belatedly than it came for his white neighbor, but now that it has started it is proceeding with a rush. Negroes have almost disappeared in some rural areas where once they were numerous. Virtually every nonmetropolitan county in the South had fewer Negroes in 1950 than in some previous year, whereas metropolitan areas throughout the nation had their maximum Negro population in 1950. But Negro migrants are attracted mainly to cities outside the South. In short, the American Negro, who was a rural Southerner two generations ago, is rapidly becoming an urban Northerner or Westerner.

Notes

[1] Appreciation is expressed to Miss Helen Lightfoot, Documents Librarian at Indiana University, for the readiness with which she made out-of-print public documents available; to George F. Jenks, University of Kansas, for cartographic suggestions; and to Robert C. Kingsbury, Indiana University, for editorial advice and assistance.

[2] The East South Central, which dropped from 2,780,635 Negroes in 1940 to 2,698,635 in 1950 for a loss of 82,000. It should also be noted, however, that the West South Central division's increase of 6,907 Negroes between 1940 and 1950 was only 0.3 percent of the division's 1940 Negro population.

[3] As their Negro population trends are essentially similar, Delaware, Maryland, and the District of Columbia have here been combined with the New England and Middle Atlantic divisions as the Northeast, and the curve for the South Atlantic region represents only the Negro population of Virginia, the Carolinas, Georgia, and Florida.

[4] With almost uncanny prescience, after completion of the census of 1910, the Bureau of the Census sponsored a monumental study of the Negro: John Cummings, *Negro Population, 1790–1915* (Washington: Government Printing Office, 1918).

[5] Although the term "density" is universally accepted for describing the concept of number of units per unit of area, there appears to be no equally suitable and generally accepted term for the concept of proportionality, such as the percentage of Negroes or of older persons. It is suggested, therefore, that the term "intensity" might be used in describing the concept of the percentage of components of a population. Hereafter in this paper the term "Negro intensity" will be considered synonymous with "percentage of Negroes in the total population."

[6] "Plainsland South" appears preferable to the more common "deep South" or "lower South," and is rather less cumbersome than "Piedmont and Atlantic and Gulf Coastal Plain Physiographic Provinces" as a name for that part of the South in which level to rolling topography, a sizable rural Negro population,

and an agricultural economy dominated by production of cotton or tobacco are more or less coextensive. The plainsland South is quite different from the "hill-land South" of the Blue Ridge, Ridge and Valley, Appalachian Plateau, Interior Low Plateau, Ozark, and Ouachita Physiographic Provinces, in which a predominantly native white population practices "general farming" in areas of hilly topography.

[7] For a discussion of the Negro population of Lake County, Michigan, see John Fraser Hart, "A Rural Retreat for Northern Negroes," *Geographical Review*, Vol. 50 (April 1960), pp. 147–68.

[8] An excellent illustration is provided by Chittenden County, Vermont, whose Negro population soared from 153 in 1900 to 1,114 in 1910, then dropped abruptly to 175 in 1920, and has never exceeded 208 persons at any other time. The explanation apparently has to do with the stationing of Negro troops at Fort Ethan Allen.

[9] As quoted in James P. Munroe, *A Life of Francis Amasa Walker* (New York: Henry Holt, 1923), p. 113. Although great improvements have been made since 1870, partisan considerations still play too large a role in the appointment of enumerators.

[10] *U. S. Census of Population: 1950*. Vol. IV, *Special Reports*, Part 4, Chapter B, "Population Mobility—States and State Economic Areas" (Washington: Government Printing Office, 1956).

[11] Everett S. Lee, "Migration Estimates," pp. 7–361 of Everett S. Lee, Ann Ratner Miller, Carol P. Brainerd, and Richard A. Easterlin, *Population Redistribution and Economic Growth: United States, 1870–1950*. Vol. I, *Methodological Considerations and Reference Tables* (Philadelphia: American Philosophical Society, 1957).

[12] *Ibid.*, p. 34.

[13] For instance, see Gladys K. Bowles, *Farm Population: Net Migration from the Rural-Farm Population, 1940–50*, U.S. Department of Agriculture Statistical Bulletin No. 176 (Washington: Government Printing Office, 1956).

[14] Lee, *op. cit.*, p. 95.

[15] *U.S. Census of Population: 1950.* Vol. IV, *Special Reports*, Part 4, Chapter A, "State of Birth" (Washington: Government Printing Office, 1953).

[16] Conrad Taeuber and Irene B. Taeuber, *The Changing Population of the United States* (New York: John Wiley & Sons, 1958), p. 71.

[17] Wesley C. Calef and Howard J. Nelson, "Distribution of Negro Population in the United States," *Geographical Review*, Vol. 46 (January 1956), pp. 82–97.

[18] West Virginia has highly complicated patterns of nonwhite interregional migration primarily because the state is contiguous with four geographic divisions, and a considerable part of the nonwhite migration from the state may well consist merely of short shifts of residence across nearby state lines. To some extent this is also true of Arkansas.

[19] It is impossible to estimate compensating corrections for changes in city boundaries because population and vital statistics data are not available for the annexed area *alone*. Thus one cannot compute the decennial population change or the amount of natural increase within either the old or the new boundaries. The simple and admittedly unsatisfactory technique used here is utilization of data actually reported for both population and vital statistics. This has the effect of treating the entire 1940 population of the annexed area as migrants from the county to the city (which, in a sense, perhaps they were), thus producing high out-migration rates in the county and high in-migration rates in the city.

Selection Twenty-nine

THE DISTRIBUTION OF POPULATION AGE STRUCTURES IN KANSAS CITY[1]

Michael R. C. Coulson

The age structure of a population is a description of that population according to the age of each of its members. For practical purposes, five year age groups are usually used: each member of the study population is assigned to the appropriate age group. The age structure of that population then becomes a description of the relative size of the

Reproduced by permission from the *Annals of the Association of American Geographers*, Vol. 58, 1968, 155–176.

various age groups. Age structure will vary from one population to another, and also will vary for one population over the course of time. It is possible, therefore, to compare age structures of different populations.

Age structure is, potentially, a very powerful planning tool. The potential, however, is largely unrealized in practical planning and indeed virtually nothing is known about within-city age structure distributions and their meaning. If efficient services are to be

provided for the inhabitants of a neighborhood, then a knowledge of their age structure
is essential. A park with swings and slides in
an area of retired couples would look foolish:
public ornamental gardens hardly suit the
needs of young families. From a different
perspective, what will happen to a neighborhood's age structure over the course of time?
Are we building schools in new suburbs to
serve a single generation of children? Should
we build such services to last or should we
gear them for later adaptation? Present
knowledge scarcely scratches the surface of
these questions. Yet how many of the
necessary community services are dependent
more on the age structure of the population
than on any other single criterion?

Is it possible to account for the spatial
distribution of age structure within cities? If
correlations could be established between age
structure and the distribution of other urban
phenomena, such as race, sex, or socio-economic status, then the potential of age
structure in practical studies could begin to
be realized.

In demographic writings the age structure
of a population is presented in a position of
basic importance.[2]

> The characteristic groupings which make
> up the peculiar structure of a population at
> any particular time or its changing struc-
> ture over a period are known as its *com-
> position*. Of these groupings, none are
> more important than age and sex.
> . . . for the social scientist, the age struc-
> ture of the population is of paramount
> importance, because in a great many ways,
> some of them extremely subtle, age con-
> ditions practically (control) every aspect of
> social phenomena.

In demographic analysis, however, the
techniques applied to age-structure data
remain crude and superficial. The general
conclusion is based upon an investigation of
a comprehensive selection of studies involving age structure. Included were works
on methods of demographic analysis, plus
studies on a world, national, regional, and
individual city scale.[3]

The Literature

From the literature studied, it is deduced that
the most common approach to the analysis
of age structure features either a table
showing population size by age group, or the
graphic population pyramid, together with a
descriptive text.[4] Variations occur from the
number of age groups used in the analysis
(0–4, 5–9, 10–15 . . . 80–84, 85+; 0–14,
15–44, 45–64, 65+) or the placing of emphasis upon one age group (65+).[5] Alternatively, the Median Age is sometimes
used to describe a population.[6] Other
variations at a somewhat more sophisticated
level occur where the size of the labor force
(15–64 years) is compared to that of children
(0–14 years) and retired persons (65 + years)
to give a Dependency Ratio.[7] A further
technique, Index Numbers of Age, measures
the deviation from the norm of the population universe for each age group.[8] The index
numbers are then combined in a deviation
graph to give a population profile.

In the present study it is desired to describe
the age structure of each of the two hundred
and twenty-four census tracts that comprise
the tracted portion of the Kansas City Standard Metropolitan Statistical Area (SMSA).
Further, this description, or classification,
should allow comparison between the various census tract populations and should
allow them to be ranked from oldest to
youngest. None of the techniques investigated were considered adequate for the
present study. The various numerical techniques examined do not accurately describe
the age structure of populations. With
tables or graphic means it is just not practical
to classify a large number of populations. In
view of the unsatisfactory nature of previous
work, a new method of classification, the
age-structure index, has been developed.

The Age Structure Index

The age-structure index provides a single
quantitative measure of the age structure.
Using an ideal age-structure histogram, we

find that the size relationships between age groups can be generalized as a straight line (Fig. 29.1). When the histogram for a young population is so generalized, a steeper slope results. Similarly, an old population produces a flatter line. The angle of slope of the line changes according to the distribution of the population among the various age groups. Thus, by measuring the angle of the line which generalizes the histogram, we may obtain a quantitative measure of the total age structure: such is the age-structure index.

The mechanics of computing the age-structure index are found in the equation describing a linear least squares trend line:

$$Y = a + bX$$

For each census tract, the percentage of the population in each age group (Y) was plotted against the middle age of each age group (X). The a is a constant representing the value of Y, when X equals zero. The b is the regression coefficient and is a measure of the angle of the slope of the least squares trend line. Thus the value of b is the age-structure index for each census tract.

When index values were assembled for all two hundred and twenty-four tracts, a range was found from $+0.09141$ (for the oldest population) to -0.19062 (for the youngest population).[9] The great majority of cases lay on the minus side of the range. Although one desired criterion of a numerical description for each tract has been met, the form of the index, particularly differing signs, detracts from utility. Certain adjustments, therefore, have been made to the index numbers, prior to their use in analyses.

Fortunately, very simple mathematical adjustments can eliminate the awkward characteristics of the regression coefficients. First, -0.10000 was added to each index number, bringing the range to -0.00859 to -0.29026. The sign could then be disregarded and, finally, the decimal point was dropped. Thus, the index used in statistical computations was a five digit number with a range 00859 to 29026, in which the larger the number, the younger the age structure of the population.

The distribution of age-structure values over the range of the index is portrayed in

POPULATION AGE STRUCTURES

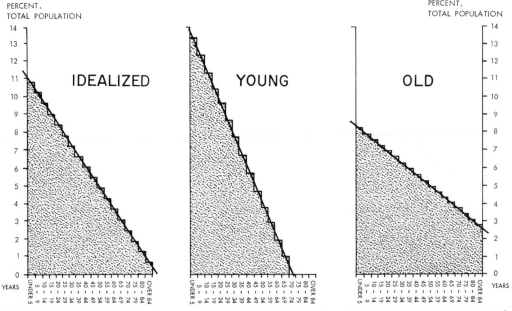

Figure 29.1   Using ideal age-structure histograms, the size relationships between age groups can be generalized as straight lines. The angle of slope of the line changes according to the distribution of population among the age groups.

GRAPHIC ARRAY OF THE AGE STRUCTURE INDEX VALUES

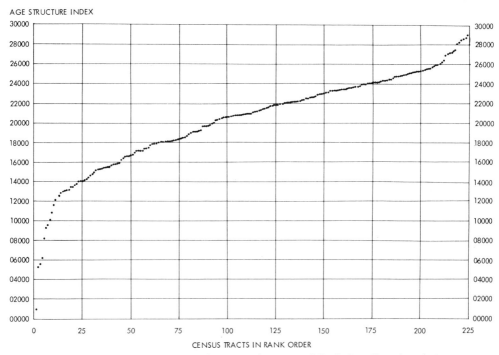

Figure 29.2   The distribution of age-structure values over the range of the index. Note the regular arrangement of values between 12,000 and 26,000 on the index scale.

Figure 29.2, and a striking feature of this graphic array is the regular arrangement of values between 12000 and 26000 on the index scale. Within these bounds, it is impossible to identify distinct groups, for the change is very gradual throughout. Since eighty-nine percent (two hundred) of the 224 tracts lie between 12000 and 26000, it is a reasonable conclusion that no system of natural classes exists: further, that the present index is preferable to any classification based on a system of classes.[10]

INTERPRETING   THE   AGE-STRUCTURE   INDEX

How may we describe an index value in verbal terms? Since no system of natural classes exists it is not reasonable to divide up the age structure, either into a number of inclusive classes, or into type-age structures, which implies transitional zones. There are features of histogram form, however, which are characteristic of each index value. They may be seen visually and described verbally.

The following index values represent not classes of age structure, therefore, but steps across the range of the continuum.

The four index values selected to exemplify the range of the age-structure index are graphically portrayed in Figures 29.3 and 29.4.[11] The upper part of each figure is the traditional population pyramid. In the lower section, the graph has been turned on its side as a histogram and percent of the total population is graphed. In addition, the least squares trend line which determines the index value is shown.

The number 00859 is a value on the index scale representative of the small number of unbalanced age structures and is the index value for census tract 002. The age structure in tract 002 is described as unbalanced because the greater proportion of the population is above forty years of age and almost fifty percent is above sixty years of age. As a result, the least squares trend line which generalizes the age structure, suggests that the older the age group, the higher the pro-

412

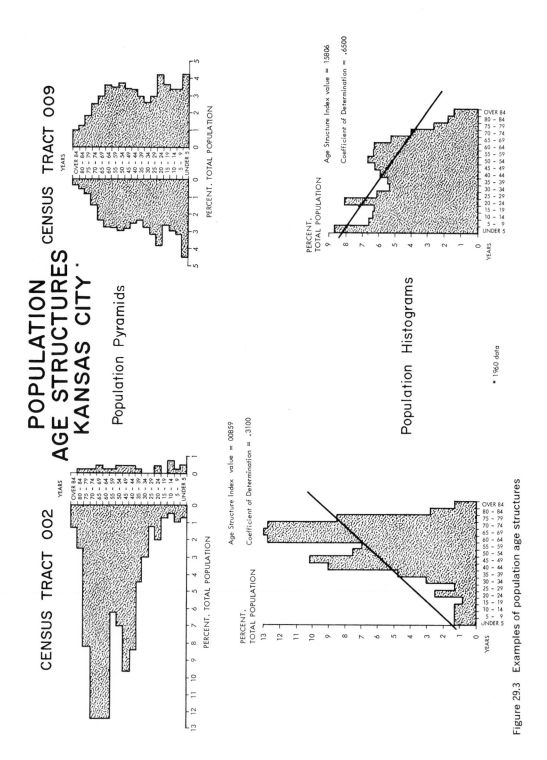

Figure 29.3 Examples of population age structures

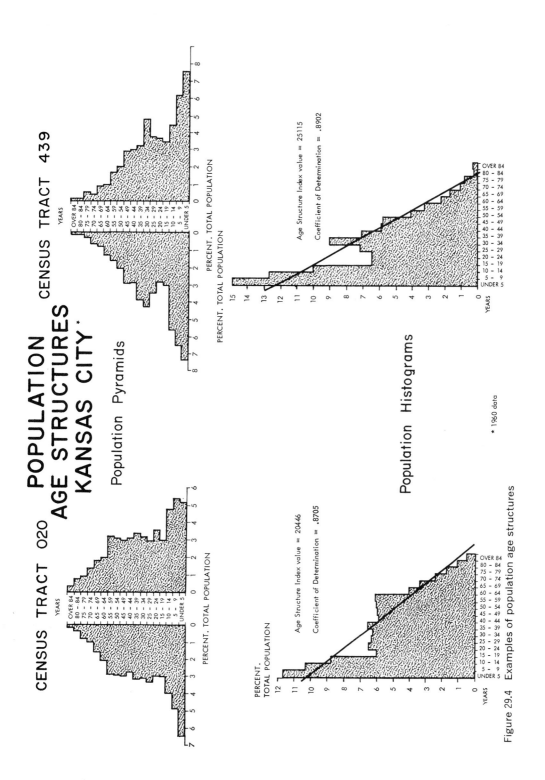

Figure 29.4 Examples of population age structures

portion of the total population that will be found within it. This is clearly not what one would expect in normal populations. Census tract 002 lies between the Missouri River on the north and Independence Avenue on the south, Broadway on the west and Locust Street-trafficway (Highway 71) on the east. It has a non-residential character, with a total population of 403. The southern section is now dominated by the inter-city freeway which replaced old, mainly slum, dwellings. Also within tract 002 lies the Municipal Market with commercial premises and many cheap hotels around it. From the population pyramid, we may further note that only 5.5 percent of the population is female. Clearly no semblance of family life is possible in this area and the population may be summarily described as male transient. The age structure of such a population may be expected to change quite radically over a short period of time and the index value describes the age structure in only very gross terms.

The number 15806 is a value on the index scale representative of old but normal age structures. It is the index value for tract 009, which has twenty-one percent of its population over sixty years of age. There is, however, enough representation in the younger age groups to give the least squares trend line a normal, if slight, slope. Census tract 009 lies on the edge of the southern bluffs of the Missouri River. Official boundaries are the Missouri-Pacific Railroad tracks to the north and Independence Avenue to the south; Chestnut Parkway on the west and Monroe Avenue on the east. It has a residential character with mainly older (pre-1939) buildings. Many of these have been converted to apartments; newer apartment buildings adjoin Independence Avenue. The population is based on family life, but must be near the extreme age structure for a stable (contrast tract 002) population. There is a high rate of depletion from the older age groups by death. It is reasonable to speculate that the character of the area may change. Young adults have already entered the area (note the size of the twenty to twenty-four years age group). Presumably these new-comers are occupying the apartment buildings and converted old family houses.

The number 20446 is a value on the index scale representative of the mean age structure (20353). Moreover, the tract has a population (3,632) very close to the ideal 4,000 desired by the census bureau. This is the population age structure for census tract 020, which lies across the northern portion of the Big Blue River Valley and includes part of the Blue Valley industrial district. The official tract boundaries are Independence Avenue to the north and Twelfth Street to the south; Topping Avenue to the west and Skiles Avenue to the east. A considerable proportion of the tract's area is given over to industrial land uses, and the residential section of tract 020 lies mainly to the west of the Big Blue River. It is an area of older, small family homes and this physical character is reflected in the age-structure histogram. People of all ages are well represented. There is a slight preponderance in the older adult age group (forty-five to fifty-nine years) at the expense of the younger adult groups. The result of this adult age pattern is that children of all ages are found, including the fifteen to nineteen years group which is well above the metropolitan average in size.

The number 25115 is a value on the index scale representative of youthful age structures and is that for tract 439 which is a large, suburban census tract immediately west of Kansas City, Kansas, and north of the Kansas River. The official tract boundaries are Parallel Avenue to the north and the Kansas River to the south; Turner Expressway and 69th–70th Streets to the west and a variety of streets representing the Kansas City, Kansas, boundary as of 1960 to the east. Tract 439 has a large area and includes developments from the last ten to fifteen years. In addition, there are many scattered older houses. Whereas development has continued over a period of time, the majority of building occurred in the period 1955–1960 and is continuing. The physical character of the area is mirrored in the age-structure histogram. The youthful character of the population is spread across all three child-

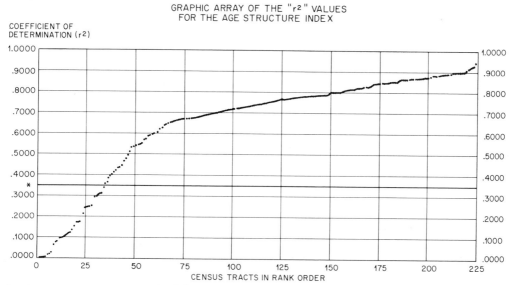

* 99% Level of confidence, Student's t "t" test, where n = 18, m = 2.

Figure 29.5   The coefficient of determination was used to test the efficiency at the index in describing population age structures

hood age groups; thus, whereas fifteen percent of the population are under five years of age, 37.6 percent are under fifteen years of age.

TESTING THE AGE-STRUCTURE INDEX

With a great variety of population age structures classified, a question naturally arises as to the degree of descriptive accuracy which the index attains. In practice, few census tracts have age-structure histograms which give a perfect fit to a straight line generalization (compare Figs. 29.3 and 29.4 with Fig. 29.1). The age-structure index is, therefore, an approximation and tests were run to determine how approximate.

The testing of the age-structure index was based on the coefficient of determination (r^2), as calculated for each census tract. The coefficient of determination measures the proportion of the variation among the age groups which is accounted for by the least squares trend line. Thus, 1.0000 would represent a perfect fit, the situation in Figure 29.1. Testing is particularly important as it is well known that identical least squares trend lines can generalize very different distributions.

However, with high coefficients of determination, there is very little chance for contrasting age structures to have similar trend lines, and the resultant similar index values.

The results of the test of efficiency on the age-structure index values are shown in Figure 29.5, which is a graphic array. A range in values of r^2 was found between .0004 (tract 011) at the low end of the scale and .9450 (tract 301) at the high end of the scale. The mean value was .6567 with a standard deviation of .2470. The median value was .7370. A test of randomness was derived from Students' "t" test. Census tracts recording coefficients of determination below .3481 may be assumed to be very unreliable (thirty-six census tracts).

Further examination revealed that tracts recording coefficients of determination below the ninety-nine percent level of confidence (.3481) were mainly those with extremely old values of the age structure index. All twenty-six values of the age structure index older than 14200 were below the confidence limits.[12] One assumption involving the age-structure index is that there will be regularity in the distribution of population among age groups as a result of family relationships (children-parents). It appears that in very old age structures this familial relationship no longer holds. As a result, there is no interdependence among age groups and a linear least squares trend line fails to describe adequately the population age structure. The age structure of tract 002 reflects this situation (Fig. 29.3). The second example, tract 009, also shows an old population but one where age groups remain interdependent as a result of family relationships.

In summary, we may say that the age-structure index adequately reproduces age group trends for the greater number of census tracts in the Kansas City SMSA. Problematical weaknesses of the index appear to be confined to the very old values of the index, which themselves reflect highly unstable, non-integrated populations. The age-structure index is particularly efficient for populations with index values of 15000 or larger (younger), and therefore has been adopted as a valid technique for identifying age structure.[13]

The Spatial Distribution of Age Structure

The spatial distribution of the age-structure index is portrayed in Figures 29.6 and 29.7. These illustrations give at once a vivid visual impression of the distribution, but yet obscure the subtleties of variation between tracts. Figure 29.6 is a choropleth map of the distribution of age-structure index values. Practical considerations limit the number of values which can be shown to seven. Considerable care has been exercised in selecting the class limits to generalize in the most realistic manner. As no natural classes exist, divisions have been made from the rank order graph (Fig. 29.2). This graph reveals a straight line relationship across the greater part of the range of the values. Thus, regular class intervals have been chosen.

Figure 29.7 seeks to portray the general pattern of the distribution. It is an isometric block diagram and the surface has been developed from an isoline map of the spatial age structure data. From Figure 29.7, it is impossible to deduce the index value for any one tract. The general pattern of spatial distribution, however, is clearly shown.

What may we determine from Figures 29.6 and 29.7? First, the spatial distribution of age structure is far from random. It exhibits great regularity with the older age structures in the older parts of the city and a sharp decline to very young age structures out in all directions towards the suburbs. Moreover, the separate, well-established towns of Kansas City, Kansas, and Independence, Missouri, break the regularity of the surface with their own older core areas. The main grouping of older age structures lies in a compact area stretching north-south through the core of Kansas City, Missouri. Its boundaries may be listed roughly as the Missouri River to the north, Prospect Avenue to the east, 79th Street to the south, and the state line to the west. Within the area lie all the tracts having abnormally old, unbalanced age structures (less than 10000).

Relationships between Age Structure and other Demographic Measures

The main analytical body of the research seeks to explain the spatial variations in age structure which have been shown to exist within the study area. In the present investigation, relationships have been sought between age structure and twenty other demographic measures. Selection of each measure was based on an ability to develop a common-sense hypothetical relationship between the measure and age structure.

The study design required operational definitions suitable for parametric methods of statistical analysis. In short, this necessitated a quantitative value for each factor for each census tract. Thus, for example, whereas occupational structure may be related to age structure, analysis will measure the relationship between the age-structure index and a single measure of occupation structure. The analysis is valid to the degree

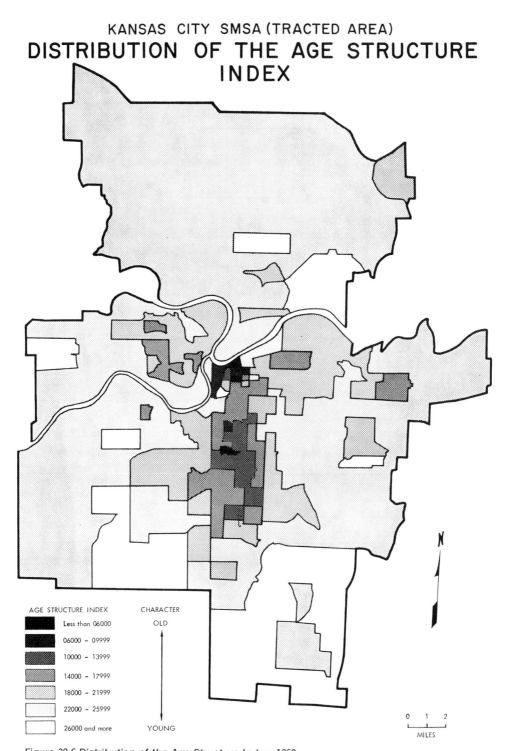

Figure 29.6 Distribution of the Age Structure Index, 1960

KANSAS CITY SMSA (TRACTED AREA)
ISOMETRIC DISTRIBUTION OF THE AGE STRUCTURE INDEX

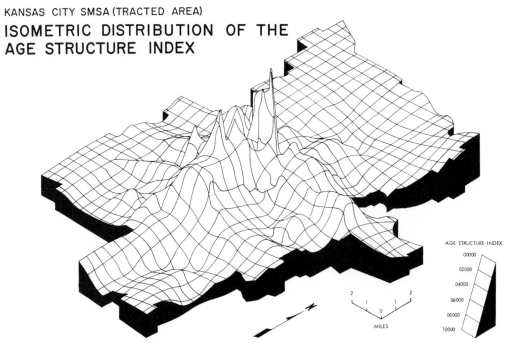

Figure 29.7   Isometric Distribution of the Age-Structure Index, 1960

that the measure (operational definition) truly reflects occupation structure. As with occupation structure, so also with the other nineteen factors. A good operational definition is essential to the validity of the analysis. A complete list of the operational definitions developed for the independent variables is given in Table 29.1.

The operational definitions must be practical as well as valid measures of the demographic factors. A comprehensive body of available statistical data is necessary to implement twenty definitions with quantitative forms. *The United States Census of Population and Housing* provides such a source.[14] It was the basis of all twenty measures defined. Use of the national census has many advantages. The data are comprehensive and have a high degree of completeness and reliability. The data are available by census tract, the study unit adopted for this investigation. Further, as similar data are published for all major cities, it would be possible to extend techniques and to compare cities.

INTERRELATIONSHIPS AMONG THE INDEPENDENT VARIABLES

Prior to the detailed development of the hypothetical framework, interrelationships among the twenty independent variables were examined. This was done by means of Elementary Linkage Analysis which divides variables into mutually exclusive groups on the basis of coefficients of correlation.[15]

Table 29.2 is a matrix which includes the coefficients of linear correlation of each of the twenty variables with all other independent variables. In the column of each variable the highest coefficient of correlation was underlined. The process of linkage was begun with the highest correlation coefficient in the matrix, -0.9047, between percent Single Family Housing ($X17$) and percent Renter Occupied Housing ($X18$). Rows $X17$ and $X18$ were then investigated for any other underlined coefficient. A total of ten variables fall into Group I and their relationships are indicated in the upper part of Figure 29.8.

TABLE 29.1 Operational definitions of the independent variables

*X*01 The number of Negroes in each census tract expressed as a percentage of the total population in that tract.

*X*02 The number of Irish Foreign Stock in each census tract expressed as a percentage of the total population in that tract.

*X*03 The number of Polish Foreign Stock in each census tract expressed as a percentage of the total population in that tract.

*X*04 The number of Italian Foreign Stock in each census tract expressed as a percentage of the total population in that tract.

*X*05 The number of Mexican Foreign Stock in each census tract expressed as a percentage of the total population in that tract.

*X*06 The number of Children, 0–4 years, in each census tract per thousand Females, 15–44 years in that tract.

*X*07 The number of Persons Per Acre for each census tract.

*X*08 The number of Females in each census tract expressed as a percentage of the total population in that tract.

*X*09 The number of persons Married in each census tract expressed as a percentage of the total population over 14 years in that tract.

*X*10 The number of persons Widowed in each census tract expressed as a percentage of the total population over 14 years in that tract.

*X*11 The number of Married Women in the Labor Force for each census tract expressed as a percentage of the total number of Females in the Labor Force.

*X*12 The number of Males in the Labor Force for each census tract expressed as a percentage of the total number of Males over 14 years in that tract.

*X*13 The number of Craftsmen, Operatives, and Laborers for each census tract expressed as a percentage of the total population over 14 years in that tract.

*X*14 The Median Family Income for each census tract.

*X*15 The Median School Years completed for all persons over 25 years in each census tract.

*X*17 The number of Single Family Housing Units in each census tract expressed as a percentage of the total number of Housing Units in that tract.

*X*18 The number of Renter-occupied Housing Units in each census tract expressed as a percentage of the total number of Housing Units in that tract.

*X*19 The number of persons, 5 years and over, in each census tract who have moved their residence within the SMSA since 1955, expressed as a percentage of the total population 5 years and over in that tract.

*X*20 The number of persons, 5 years and over, in each census tract who have moved their residence into the SMSA since 1955, expressed as a percentage of the total population 5 years and over in that tract.

*X*21 The number of Housing Units with 1.01 or more persons per room in each census tract expressed as a percentage of the total number of Housing Units in that tract.

Source: Compiled by author.

Of the remaining variables, the highest intercorrelation was between occupation ratio and overcrowding index which, therefore, formed the basis of Group II. Additional variables were added as with Group I, giving Group II a final complement of six (Fig. 29.8). The remaining four variables proved to fall into a single Group III (Fig. 29.8).

The hypothetical framework was developed for all twenty variables. By referring to the linkage groups, however, it was also possible to hypothesize about the impact of multiples of these measures upon age structure.

TESTS OF SIMPLE LINEAR CORRELATION

The standard statistical technique of correlation analysis was used to test the hypotheses, and linear relationships were assumed in all cases. The initial stage was the testing of the simple associations between age structure and each of the independent variables. The result for the variables in Group I are shown in Table 29.3.

It was hypothesized that the higher the proportion of single family housing units (*X*17), the younger the age structure (*Y*). The coefficient of correlation ($r = 0.5856$) is well above the confidence level we have

LINKAGE GROUPS FOR THE INDEPENDENT VARIABLES

Group I

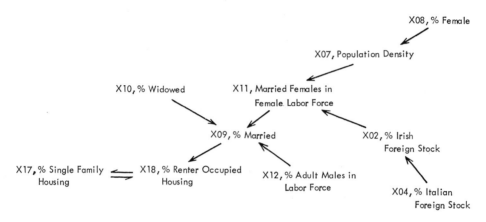

Group II

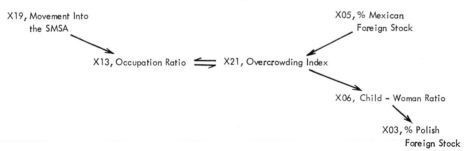

Group III

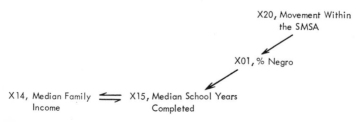

Figure 29.8

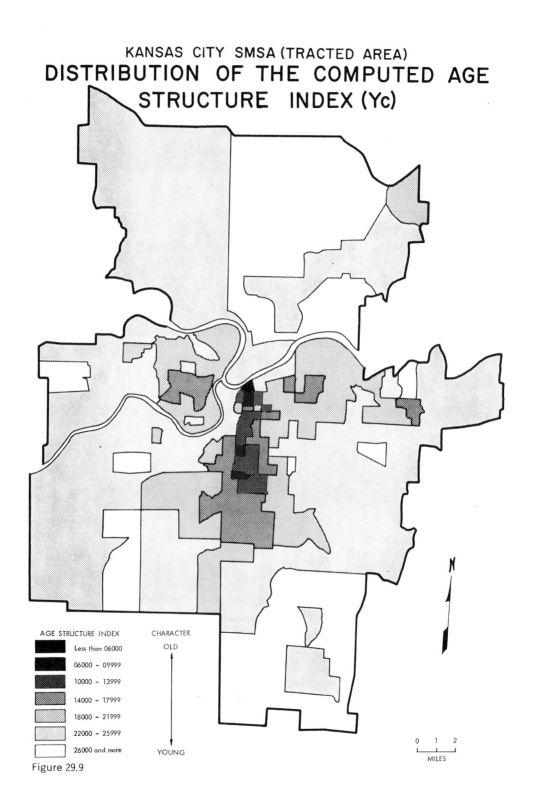

KANSAS CITY SMSA (TRACTED AREA)
DISTRIBUTION OF THE COMPUTED AGE STRUCTURE INDEX (Yc)

AGE STRUCTURE INDEX

- Less than 06000
- 06000 – 09999
- 10000 – 13999
- 14000 – 17999
- 18000 – 21999
- 22000 – 25999
- 26000 and more

CHARACTER

OLD

YOUNG

0 1 2
MILES

Figure 29.9

TABLE 29.2　Matrix of correlation coefficients for the independent variables

	X01	X02	X03	X04	X05	X06	X07
X01, % Negro		−.2185	−.1193	−.1239	.0060	.3143	.4253
X02, % Irish Foreign Stock	−.2185		.1247	.1859	.0112	−.4009	.2678
X03, % Polish Foreign Stock	−.1193	.1247		−.0215	−.0473	−.2869	.0138
X04, % Italian Foreign Stock	−.1239	.1859	−.0215		−.0351	−.0341	.1353
X05, % Mexican Foreign Stock	.0060	.0112	−.0473	−.0351		.2634	.0223
X06, Child — Woman Ratio	.3143	−.4009	−.2869	.0341	.2634		−.1893
X07, Population Density	.4253	.2678	.0138	.1353	.0223	−.1893	
X08, % Female	.0368	.1700	−.2622	.0805	−.0495	−.1569	.3306
X09, % Married	−.3054	−.3562	−.2471	−.0525	−.1393	.4548	−.5521
X10, % Widowed	.3555	.2294	.2542	.0484	.0525	−.3450	.4758
X11, Married Females in Female Labor Force	.3125	.4046	−.0149	.1024	.1372	−.4275	.6436
X12, % Adult Males in Labor Force	−.4364	−.2054	.0074	−.1445	−.2172	.0617	−.3936
X13, Occupation Ratio	.1688	−.2888	.1237	−.0389	.3103	.4851	−.1188
X14, Median Family Income	−.4293	.0349	.0632	−.0487	−.1601	−.1869	−.3234
X15, Median School Years Completed	−.4782	.0843	−.0647	−.0849	−.3497	−.2633	−.2824
X17, % Single Family Housing	−.2989	−.2305	−.1001	−.1781	−.0417	.3588	−.6372
X18, % Renter Occupied Housing	.3188	.2430	.0328	.1677	.1607	−.2405	−.6313
X19, Movement Into the SMSA	−.1985	−.0392	−.0400	−.0041	−.1230	−.0513	−.0445
X20, Movement Within the SMSA	.2652	−.2475	−.1556	−.0469	−.0731	.2393	.0994
X21, Overcrowding Index	.3721	−.3154	−.2242	.0029	.4604	.6546	.0316

adopted and the hypothesis may therefore be considered substantiated. The coefficient of determination, $r^2 = 0.3430$ however, reveals that this variable accounts for only 34.30 percent of the total variation of age structure. For renter occupied housing ($X18$) an inverse relationship was hypothesized. That is, the lower the proportion of renter occupied housing units, the younger the age structure. The coefficient of correlation is −0.5790, which is again well above the confidence limit and this second hypothesis has been substantiated. Once again, however, the independent variable accounts for only about one-third of the variation of age structure.

Five of the other hypotheses in Group I are substantiated. Direct relationships exist between age structure and percent married ($X09$) and male participation in the labor force ($X12$). Inverse relationships are confirmed with percent widowed ($X10$), married female participation in the female labor force ($X11$) and population density ($X07$).

It has been hypothesized that the higher the proportion of Irish foreign stock ($X02$), the younger the age structure and, indeed, we obtain a highly significant coefficient of correlation. The direction of the association,

however, is opposite to that hypothesized. Thus, the argument advanced does not hold in fact. Concentrations of Irish foreign stock are associated with old, rather than young, age structures. An explanation appears to lie in the time period of the major Irish immigration, which was prior to 1930.[16] Thus, the great majority of Irish immigrants and their children have passed the childbearing period.

In the case of the two remaining hypotheses, the coefficients of correlation are very low. Thus, the hypotheses that the higher the proportion Italian foreign stock ($X04$), the younger the age structure, and the higher the proportion female ($X08$), the younger the age structure are not substantiated by the evidence.

Six variables were considered within Group II, and the results are shown in Table 29.4. The hypotheses for direct relationships between age structure and the occupation ratio ($X13$), the overcrowding index ($X21$), and the child-woman ratio ($X06$) are substantiated. The measure of Polish foreign stock ($X03$) also records a significant coefficient, but the direction of association is the reverse of that hypothesized. An explanation similar to that for Irish foreign stock appears logical.[17] Direct

X08	X09	X10	X11	X12	X13	X14	X15	X17	X18	X19	X20	X21
.0368	−.3054	.3555	.3125	−.4364	.1668	−.4293	−.4782	−.2989	.3188	−.1985	.2652	.3721
.1700	−.3562	−.2294	.4046	−.2054	−.2888	.0349	.0843	−.2305	.2430	−.0392	−.2475	−.3154
−.2622	−.2471	.2542	−.0149	.0074	.1237	.0632	−.0647	−.1001	.0328	−.0400	−.1556	−.2242
.0805	−.0525	.0484	.1024	−.1445	−.0389	−.0487	−.0849	−.1781	.1677	−.0041	−.0469	.0029
−.0495	−.1393	.0525	.1372	−.2172	.3103	−.1601	−.3497	−.0417	.1607	−.1230	−.0731	.4604
−.1569	.4548	−.3450	−.4275	.0617	.4851	−.1869	−.2633	.3588	−.2405	−.0513	.2393	.6546
.3306	−.5521	.4758	.6436	−.3936	−.1188	−.3234	−.2824	−.6372	.6313	−.0445	.0944	.0316
	.2044	−.0610	−.2474	.2368	−.2046	.1493	.2832	−.0168	−.0204	−.1502	−.0886	−.0785
.2044		−.7797	−.7931	.7195	.0651	.4240	.4974	.8007	−.8212	−.0048	.0833	−.0768
−.0610	−.7797		.6264	−.5640	.0037	−.3888	−.4598	−.6763	.6538	−.1159	−.0218	−.0441
−.2474	−.7931	.6264		−.6722	−.1654	−.2268	−.3392	−.7144	.7143	−.1104	−.1204	−.0999
.2368	.7195	−.5640	−.6722		−.1596	.4325	.6431	.5648	−.6244	.2146	.0749	−.1718
−.2046	.0651	.0037	−.1654	−.1596		−.5636	−.6651	.0007	.0864	−.2231	.1507	.7540
.1493	.4240	−.3888	−.2268	.4325	−.5636		.7360	.5005	−.5627	.0559	−.1842	−.4983
.2832	.4974	−.4598	−.3392	.6431	−.6651	.7360		.4599	−.5379	.2187	−.0649	.5986
−.0168	.8007	−.6763	−.7144	.5648	.0007	.5005	.4599		−.9047	−.1074	−.1162	−.0031
−.0204	−.8212	.6538	.7143	−.6244	.0864	−.5627	.5379	−.9047		.1024	.0308	.1580
−.1502	−.0048	−.1159	−.1104	.2146	−.2231	.0559	.2187	−.1074	.1024		−.0331	−.1391
−.0886	.0833	−.0218	−.1204	.0749	.1507	−.1842	−.0649	−.1162	.0308	−.0331		.1118
−.0785	−.0768	−.0441	−.0999	−.1718	.7540	−.4983	−.5986	−.0031	.1580	−.1391	.1118	

TABLE 29.3 Results of simple linear correlations of group I variables with age structure

	VARIABLE	r	r^2	SIGNIFICANT AT 1% LEVEL*
X17	Percent Single Family Housing	0.5856	0.3430	Yes
X18	Percent Renter Occupied Housing	−0.5790	0.3352	Yes
X09	Percent Married	0.8338	0.6952	Yes
X10	Percent Widowed	−0.6668	0.4446	Yes
X11	Married Females in Labor Force	−0.7134	0.5089	Yes
X12	Male Participation in Labor Force	0.5425	0.2943	Yes
X07	Population Density	−0.4427	0.1960	Yes
X02	Irish Foreign Stock	−0.4782	0.2287	Yes
X04	Italian Foreign Stock	−0.0518	0.0027	No
X08	Percent Female	0.0712	0.0051	No

*The least highly significant value for "r," where $n = 224$ and $m = 2$, is approximately 0.175.
Source: Compiled by author.

relationships with age structure were hypothesized for Mexican foreign stock (X05) and movement into the SMSA (X19). In both cases, the coefficients of correlation are very low and the hypotheses are, therefore, not substantiated.

The remaining four hypotheses were developed within Group III, and test results are shown in Table 29.5. Highly significant coefficients of correlation are found for the direct relationship hypothesized between age structure and median school years completed (X15) and movement within the SMSA (X20). Direct relationships hypothesized between age structure and percent Negro (X01) and median family income (X14) have coefficients well below the confidence level adopted and are, therefore, considered to be not proven.

Twenty hypotheses have been tested, which relate age structure to single demographic variables. In fourteen cases, the

TABLE 29.4   Results of simple linear correlations of group II variables with age structure

	VARIABLE	r	r^2	SIGNIFICANT AT 1% LEVEL*
$X13$	Occupation Ratio	0.3269	0.1069	Yes
$X21$	Overcrowding Index	0.4680	0.2190	Yes
$X06$	Child-Woman Ratio	0.7150	0.5112	Yes
$X03$	Percent Polish Foreign Stock	−0.2856	0.0816	Yes
$X05$	Percent Mexican Foreign Stock	0.0684	0.0047	No
$X19$	Movement Into SMSA	0.0646	0.0042	No

*The least highly significant value for "r," where $n = 224$ and $m = 2$, is approximately 0.175.
Source: Compiled by author.

TABLE 29.5   Results of simple linear correlations of group III variables with age structure

	VARIABLE	r	r^2	SIGNIFICANT AT 1% LEVEL*
$X14$	Median Family Income	0.1138	0.0130	No
$X15$	Median School Years Completed	0.1830	0.0335	Yes
$X01$	Percent Negro	−0.0369	0.0014	No
$X20$	Movement Within SMSA	0.2439	0.0595	Yes

*The least highly significant value for "r," where $n = 224$ and $m = 2$, is approximately 0.175.
Source: Compiled by author.

coefficient of correlation recorded a highly significant relationship. At the same time, the amount of variation in age structure accounted for is normally quite small. Percent married records the highest coefficient of determination (69.52 percent) and only two other variables (married females in the female labor force and child-woman ratio) are above fifty percent.

It is possible that higher values of the r^2 might be obtained if several variables were considered simultaneously in relation to age structure. This, we may assume, is nearer the real world situation, where many factors are simultaneously influencing most situations. For example, the hypothesis between age structure and percent married does not allow for areas of older married couples where the children have left home. In such areas, high values for percent widowed may be expected. Thus, the addition of the measure of widows into the analysis should

increase the explained proportion of variation in age structure. The testing of relationships between age structure and the twenty demographic factors, therefore, proceeds to analyses where combinations of variables are considered simultaneously. The method of testing is multiple correlation analysis.

TESTS OF MULTIPLE CORRELATION

The initial test of multiple correlation was made between age structure and all twenty independent variables. The twenty basic variables were thus, in a sense, combined and considered simultaneously. The six hypotheses found non-significant in the simple correlation were retained in this section. It was considered possible that some of the variables involved might add considerably to the study when considered in association with more basic variables.

The results of the initial multiple correla-

TABLE 29.6 Multiple correlation between age structure and twenty variables

VARIABLE	PARTIAL REGRESSION COEFFICIENT "B"	"F RATIO"	SIGNIFICANT AT 1% LEVEL[1]
X01, % Negro	9.6083	2.1845	Yes
X02, % Irish Foreign Stock	−130.0702	0.7351	No
X03, % Polish Foreign Stock	161.8419	2.9219	Yes
X04, % Italian Foreign Stock	37.6348	0.4956	No
X05, % Mexican Foreign Stock	34.1460	1.0730	No
X06, Child-Woman Ratio	6.4150	31.5983	Yes
X07, Population Density	−49.9403	8.9723	Yes
X08, % Female	8.2714	0.0583	No
X09, % Married	226.3155	54.1187	Yes
X10, % Widowed	−58.9147	4.1163	Yes
X11, Married Females in Female Labor Force	1.1475	0.0052	No
X12, Male Participation in Labor Force	35.5808	1.1784	No
X13, Occupation Ratio	−6.1165	0.2029	No
X14, Median Family Income	−0.0844	1.4153	No
X15, Median School Years Completed	462.3895	8.7959	Yes
X17, % Single Family Housing	−48.1843	29.2843	Yes
X18, % Renter Occupied Housing	−41.2827	11.0185	Yes
X19, Movement Into the SMSA	42.3730	10.8990	Yes
X20, Movement Within the SMSA	37.2603	9.2034	Yes
X21, Overcrowding index	336.8381	77.1663	Yes

Coefficient of multiple correlation   = 0.9618
Coefficient of multiple determination = 0.9251
Standard error of estimate = 1327.85
"a" = 6256.2680

[1]The least highly significant value for "F," where $n = 224$ and $m = 21$, is approximately 1.97.
The least highly significant value for "R," where $n = 224$ and $m = 21$, is approximately 0.390.
Source: Compiled by author.

tion and regression analysis are set out in Table 29.6. All twenty variables were included, and a linear relationship was assumed in all cases. A test for significance showed the coefficient of multiple correlation ($R = 0.9618$) to be statistically highly significant. Further the multiple analysis with twenty variables explains 92.51 percent of the variation of age structure.

Although these results represent a high level of accuracy, some of the variables may not be making any real contribution in the analysis and indeed, only twelve are significant at the ninety-nine percent level of confidence, as measured by means of the F ratio.

REDUCING THE NUMBER OF INDEPENDENT VARIABLES

What is the smallest number of variables necessary to retain a high level of predictive accuracy? The next step of the investigation sought to answer this question by reducing the number of variables in the analysis to a minimum without significantly reducing the level of the association. This may be called the development of the most efficient equation. The importance of the concept of an efficient equation becomes apparent in any application of the study results. A practical application of the regression equation would call for a high degree of predictive accuracy, yet it is also desirable to make generalizations as simple as possible. Every additional variable adds to the complexity of the generalization and, moreover, increases the time necessary for computation. The point of diminishing returns must, therefore, be identified.

The reduction in the number of variables considered in the analysis was achieved in two steps. First, an ordering of the variables, and second the building up of a regression equation by adding variables. As each variable was added, it was tested for the significance of its contribution. The establishment of an order for adding variables is important because of the complex pattern of interrelationships. The method employed was a sequential deletion of the variable with the lowest F ratio.

The process was begun with a full multiple correlation of twenty variables. The variable with the lowest F ratio was married female participation in the female labor force ($X11$). This variable was therefore deleted and a multiple correlation reworked with nineteen independent variables. In this case, percent female ($X08$) had the lowest F ratio and was deleted. The process was repeated until only one variable remained (percent married ($X09$)). The deletion method used allowed separate consideration of each variable's contribution at each stage. This detailed reevaluation proved important. The F ratio values changed considerably both in size and in relative position in the deletion process. Such changes mark the adjustment of remaining variables as interdependencies are removed with each deletion.

The second stage in developing the most efficient grouping of variables was the actual selection of the essential variables. This was achieved by making use of the order of variables previously established. Starting with percent married, variables were added, one at a time, to the correlation analysis and the significance of their contribution measured by means of the "Adjusted R."[18]

The concept of the "Adjusted R" test is to consider the magnitude of coefficients of correlation when adjusted for changes in

TABLE 29.7 Addition of variables and tests with "adjusted R"

NUMBER OF VARIABLES	VARIABLE ADDED	r^2	r	ADJUSTED R
1	9	0.6952	0.8338	0.8338
2	21	0.8594	0.9270	0.9277
3	20	0.8771	0.9365	0.9371
4	19	0.8936	0.9453	0.9712
5	6	0.9031	0.9503	0.9740
6	17	0.9056	0.9516	0.9749
7	18	0.9114	0.9547	0.9767
8	15	0.9165	0.9573	0.9782

Source: Compiled by author.

degrees of freedom. When a variable is added into the analysis, it may be expected to raise the coefficient of correlation. However, it also decreases the degree of freedom. The "Adjusted R" answers the question, is an increase in the coefficient significant in the light of the loss of degree of freedom? The resultant "Adjusted R" is compared with the preceding "Adjusted R." If it is larger, the variable is retained. If it is smaller, the variable does not add significantly to the explanation and is deleted.

Table 29.7 shows the results of applying the "Adjusted R" to the study. Up to a total of eight as each variable was added, the "Adjusted R" itself increased. With variables $X06$, $X09$, $X15$, $X17$, $X18$, $X19$, $X20$, $X21$, included, the "Adjusted R" reached 0.9782. When the ninth variable was added ($X07$), the "Adjusted R" fell to 0.9606. Variable $X07$ does not add significantly to the analysis and was deleted. The process of comparing "Adjusted R's$" was carried on by adding, in turn, each of the remaining variables to the basic eight. This produced a series of adjusted "R's," all based on nine variables (Table 29.8). All of them are substantially below that for the eight variables.

Eight variables have been distilled from the original twenty. Together they represent the smallest number of variables which account for the highest proportion of the variation in age structure. With these eight variables, 91.65 percent of the variations of

TABLE 29.8 Addition of variables and tests with adjusted "R"

BASIC EIGHT VARIABLES	R^2	ADJUSTED R
6, 9, 15, 17, 18, 19, 20, 21	0.9165	0.9782

VARIABLE ADDED TO THE BASIC EIGHT		
1	0.9165	0.9591
2	0.9173	0.9595
3	0.9178	0.9598
4	0.9165	0.9591
5	0.9167	0.9592
7	0.9195	0.9606
8	0.9172	0.9594
10	0.9174	0.9595
11	0.9178	0.9597
12	0.9176	0.9596
13	0.9165	0.9591
14	0.9169	0.9593

Source: Compiled by author.

age structure can be explained, a loss of less than one percent from the full correlation with twenty variables. Further, these eight variables adequately represent the influences exerted by all twenty independent variables considered in the study. The original hypothetical framework was developed from three groups of variables established by linkage analysis. It is interesting that all three groups are represented in the final selection of variables.

Group I	*Group II*	*Group III*
X_{09}, Per Cent Married	X_{06}, Child-Woman Ratio	X_{15}, Median School Years Completed
X_{17}, Per Cent Single Family Housing	X_{19}, Movement into SMSA	X_{20}, Movement Within SMSA
X_{18}, Per Cent Renter Occupied Housing	X_{21}, Overcrowding Index	

Not surprisingly, all eight variables in the final analysis have highly significant partial associations with age structure when tested

with the F ratio (Table 29.9). The relative contribution of each variable is also shown in Table 29.9 by Beta coefficients. The measure of fertility (child-woman ratio) is found to be by far the most important contributer, with percent married second. The other variables make much smaller contributions in comparison.

REGRESSION ANALYSIS

One product of the analysis is a regression equation, which reads: $Y_c = 5702.56 + 6.28 X_{06} + 246.23 X_{09} + 405.42 X_{15} - 44.34 X_{17} - 51.06 X_{18} + 55.24 X_{19} + 41.44 X_{20} + 357.262 X_{21}$, where Y_c = age structure index (computed), and the independent variables are as listed in Table 29.9. The regression equation has been utilized in Figure 29.9 to give a visual picture of the degree of accuracy attained.

When the computed age structure is compared with the actual distribution a strong similarity is evident, reflecting the high coefficient of determination (Fig. 29.2). Discrepancies do exist, however, and as a final step in the study, a map of residuals was constructed (Fig. 29.10).

RESIDUAL ANALYSIS

The Accuracy of Estimate map divides residuals into five classes according to their size which is measured in terms of standard errors of estimate. Wherever a discrepancy between the real and computed age structure is less than the average size of residual, or one standard error of estimate (1402.184), the map is grey. A larger residual is darker (estimated too old) or lighter (estimated too young).

The accuracy of estimate map reveals an intricate distribution of large residuals across wide areas of predictive accuracy. It is noticeable that very large residuals are clustered along the core of older age structure running north-south within Kansas City, Missouri. They present, moreover, a highly discontinuous pattern and very large residuals—both plus and minus values, occur in close proximity. It is probable that at least a

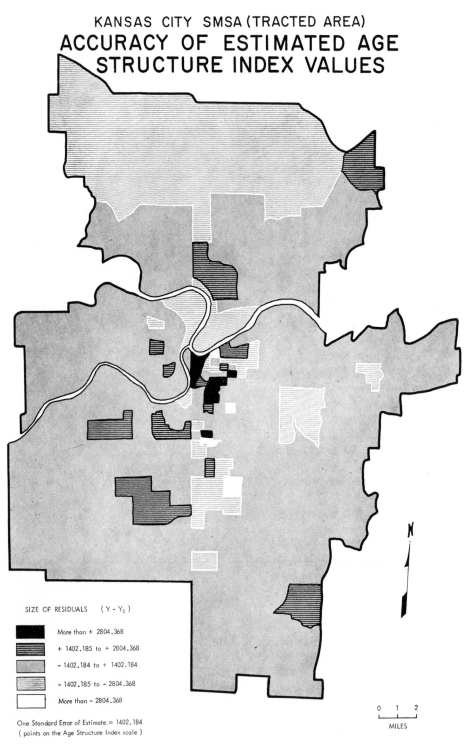

KANSAS CITY SMSA (TRACTED AREA)
ACCURACY OF ESTIMATED AGE STRUCTURE INDEX VALUES

SIZE OF RESIDUALS $(Y - Y_c)$

■	More than + 2804.368
▨	+ 1402.185 to + 2804.368
▨	− 1402.184 to + 1402.184
▨	− 1402.185 to − 2804.368
□	More than − 2804.368

One Standard Error of Estimate .= 1402.184
(points on the Age Structure Index scale)

0   1   2
MILES

Figure 29.10

partial explanation of these large residuals in the core area lies in the scale of the study. The heart of the metropolis is characterized by great diversity of land use and population. Thus, although census tracts are designed for homogeneity, their mesh is almost certainly too coarse to separate out the complexities of the spatial pattern. A second important area of large residuals appears to lie on the northern borders of the tracted area. Actually, very few census tracts are involved, but since they lie in suburban areas, we have a very coarse census tract network which contrasts greatly with that in the central parts of the city.

TABLE 29.9 F ratio and beta values for the eight basic variables

		F RATIO*	BETA
X06,	Child-Woman Ratio	42.40	1.4883
X09,	Percent Married	201.44	0.5238
X17,	Single Family Housing	26.52	0.1644
X21,	Overcrowding Index	131.24	0.1444
X18,	Renter Occupied Housing	18.35	0.0679
X19,	Movement Into SMSA	23.47	0.0423
X20,	Movement Within SMSA	13.42	0.0255
X15,	Median School Years Completed	13.14	0.0039

*The least highly significant value ($p = 0.01$) of F where $n = 224$ and $m = 9$ is 2.60.
Source: Compiled by author.

A further, more detailed analysis of residuals was made by focusing on individual census tracts. As a result, some insights were gained which may aid future work in this field. First, it was found that the direct linear relationship hypothesized between percent married and age structure, did not allow for those areas where married couples continued to live in their family homes, although their children had grown up. In view of the fundamental position of the measure of marriage in the analysis, it seems reasonable to suggest that a curvilinear relationship would be more appropriate in spite of its complexities. Further, the measures of mobility should be modified to eliminate the effect of recent housing construction.

A second line of suggestions concerned additional measures that should be investigated with relation to age structure. The census includes suitable data for the definition of measures of dislocated family life, mean value of owner occupied housing, percent of apartments in apartment buildings, and age of housing structures. Finally, certain measures beyond the scope of census data, such as religious affiliation, appear promising. Such suggestions are of potential value only, however, until they have been tested within the context of the tracted area as a whole.

Conclusion

The results of this investigation should have important general significance for the study of cities. The age-structure index is a flexible, operational definition which allows age structure to be measured, mapped, and incorporated in a wide variety of methods of statistical analysis. Further, it has been demonstrated that age structure varies spatially within cities and that this variation is related to many other attributes of the population. At the same time, considerably more research is needed before a general body of knowledge concerning age structure can be developed.[19]

With the results of this present analysis, we may be bold enough to speculate on which avenues of future research may be most profitable to the understanding of age structures:

1 A widespread program of testing for the age-structure index itself;

2 The associations between age structure and demographic variables need testing for a wide variety of urban areas;

3 The search for associations should be broadened beyond demographic factors. For example, is age structure related to age of housing, date of first development, distance from downtown, or some other focus, traffic arteries, patterns of non-residential land-use?

4 How do population age structures

change through time? Are there such things as stable age structures? Moreover, how are changing age structures related to the trends of other urban phenomena?

5 The development of predictive techniques by which age structure data can be incorporated in the decision-making processes of planning.

Notes

[1] Research supported with a University Fellowship for Doctoral Research from Community Studies, Inc., Kansas City, Missouri. In addition, the Computing Center of The University of Kansas awarded a grant of computer time. The author also wishes to acknowledge the guidance of Dr. Duane S. Knos, dissertation adviser, the assistance of Carl Zimmerman and Gordon Jones, computing assistants, and the sustained encouragement of Dr. George F. Jenks, Dr. J. Gordon Nelson, and all my colleagues at The University of Kansas and The University of Calgary.

[2] The first quotation is from R. E. Chaddock, "Age and Sex in Population Analysis," in J. J. Spengler and O. D. Duncan (Eds.), *Demographic Analysis, Selected Readings* (Glencoe, Illinois: The Free Press, 1956), p. 443; the second quotation is from T. L. Smith, *Population Analysis* (New York: McGraw-Hill, 1948), p. 88.

[3] Methodological studies are those by G. W. Barclay, *Techniques of Population Analysis* (New York: John Wiley, 1958); J. Beaujeu-Garnier, *Geographie de la Population* (Paris: Librairie de Médicis, 1956); P. R. Cox, *Demography* (Cambridge, England: Cambridge University Press, 1959). Worldwide studies include Political and Economic Planning, *World Population and Resources* (London: Allen and Unwin, 1955); C. C. Kuczynski, *Demographic Survey of the British Colonial Empire* (London: Oxford University Press, 1948). National studies are illustrated by D. J. Bogue, *The Population of the United States* (Glencoe, Illinois: The Free Press, 1959); I. B. Taeuber, *The Population of Japan* (Princeton, New Jersey: Princeton University Press, 1958). Among the regional studies are those by J. W. House

and B. Fullerton, *Tees-side at Mid-Century* (London: Macmillan, 1960) A. W. Lind, *Hawaii's People* (Honolulu: University of Hawaii Press, 1955). Studies of individual cities are represented by E. M. Hoover and R. Vernon, *Anatomy of a Metropolis* (Cambridge: Harvard University Press, 1959); E. Jones, *A Social Geography of Belfast* (London: Oxford University Press, 1960); L. Kuper, H. Watts, and R. Davis, *Durban, A Study in Racial Ecology* (London: Jonathan Cape Ltd., 1958).

[4] An age group study is that of E. Solomon and Z. G. Bilbija, *Metropolitan Chicago: An Economic Analysis* (Glencoe, Illinois: The Free Press, 1959), pp. 34–35; the population pyramid has been discussed by C. Newcomb, "Graphic Presentation of Age and Sex Distribution of Population in the City," in P. K. Hatt and A. J. Reiss, Jr. (Eds.), *Cities and Society* (Glencoe, Illinois: The Free Press, 1961), pp. 382–92.

[5] For the first series, see Bogue, *op. cit.*, footnote 3, p. 103; for the second series see A. H. Le Nereu, "Regional and Ethnic Differences in the age composition of Canada's population," *Proceedings of the World Population Conference, 1954* (New York: United Nations Organization, 1955), Volume III, pp. 499–511; and the single age group was used by H. L. Browning, "Methods for Describing the Age-Sex Structure of Cities," in P. Gibbs (Ed.), *Urban Research Methods* (New York: Van Nostrand, 1961), p. 136.

[6] N. McArthur, *Introducing Population Statistics* (Melbourne: Oxford University Press, 1961).

[7] Browning, *op. cit.*, footnote 5, pp. 135–36.

[8] Smith, *op. cit.*, footnote 2, p. 102.

[9] Based on population data by five-

year age groups from U.S. Bureau of the Census, *U. S. Censuses of Population and Housing: 1960 Census Tracts* Final Report PHC (1)-70 (Washington, D.C.: Government Printing Office, 1962), Table P 2.

[10] Compare with Newcomb, *op. cit.*, footnote 4, p. 390.

[11] For a precise location of these census tracts see the map in U.S. Bureau of the Census, PHC (1) -70, *op. cit.*, footnote 9.

[12] The least highly significant value of r when $n = 18$, $m = 2$, is 0.590.

[13] Seventy-two census tracts record coefficients of determination of more than 0.8000.

[14] U.S. Bureau of the Census, *op. cit.*, footnote 9.

[15] L. L. McQuitty, "Elementary Linkage Analysis for Isolating Orthogonal and Oblique Types and Typal Relevancies," *Educational and Psychological Measurement*, Vol. 17 (1957), pp. 207–29.

[16] U.S. Bureau of the Census, *Historical Statistics of the United States, Colonial Times to 1957* (Washington, D.C.: Government Printing Office, 1960).

[17] U.S. Bureau of the Census, *op. cit.*, footnote 16.

[18] The Adjusted

$$R = 1 - \frac{1 - R^2(N - m)}{N - 1}$$

Where N = number of cases (census tracts)

m = number of partial regression coefficients (b) plus the constant a.

[19] For additional information regarding this study see M. R. C. Coulson, *The Spatial Distribution of Population Age Structure Within the 1960 Tracted Area of the Kansas City SMSA* (Unpublished Ph.D. Dissertation, Lawrence: University of Kansas, 1966).

Selection Thirty
SINGAPORE: ETHNIC DIVERSITY AND ITS IMPLICATIONS
Warwick Neville

Most large cities of the world contain diverse populations, and their human heterogeneity is evident not only in the diversity of the ethnic element, but also in the variety of language, religion, social structure, and occupational patterns which in the main follow ethnic divisions. Such disjunctive factors frequently combine to bring about areal concentrations of sections of the total population into enclaves of relatively homogeneous composition. In this way, the internal heterogeneity of a large city may, in a sense, divide it into several sub-cities when the whole is judged from human and cultural criteria. Although subdivided on several levels, the large city must also operate as a partially integrated common population, sharing in the activities which form part of the functional unity of the whole city. This variety of subdivision and integration may introduce particular kinds of problems to specific sectors of the total population, problems which become of major political and economic significance, especially when differences are permanent or strongly resistant to change.

Recent studies of large cities have concentrated upon particular themes, thereby tending to ignore the internal human composition of the city, and producing an implication that all cities are alike in this respect. Such recent studies have examined the areal spacing of particular economic activities, have analyzed the functional roles of cities, have dealt with population in terms of size and rank, or have examined the economic and political roles of cities within political states. In such studies the city is thereby often treated as though it contained a homogeneous population, so far as broad elements of culture are concerned.

Internal composition is a variable held fixed in order to examine in detail some particular urban criterion. However, the internal composition of a large city may well have a significant bearing upon the development of the particular criterion examined in such detail. There is evidence that the large city in a long-established and developed political state is likely to display internal human variety of a sort significantly different from that to be found in a large city in a country having a colonial history and only a very short development of national economic and political institutions. The examination of the human composition of large cities is an important aspect of human and urban geography which has received only scant attention, usually as an aside in the development of a quite different theme. In the few instances in which specific studies have been made, human differences have generally been focused in the public eye as a significant aspect of the political scene: The case of ethnic differences in South African cities provides a notable instance.[1] This paper concerns the human diversity which derives basically from ethnic differences and its implications in the urban milieu of a newly independent state undergoing rapid economic and social change, thereby depicting one aspect of human heterogeneity in an urban context. The example is that of Singapore, a modern city–state in Southeast Asia.

The most distinctive features of the present-day population of Singapore are its ethnic diversity, its rapid rate of natural increase, and the consequent youthfulness of the population. Ethnic diversity is symptomatic of fundamental cultural differences most clearly demonstrated in the contrasts of language, religion, and custom. This paper examines the most outstanding demographic, economic, and social aspects of this diversity and the immensity of the problems involved.

Reproduced by permission from the *Annals of the Association of American Geographers*, Vol. 56, #2, 1966, pp. 236–253.

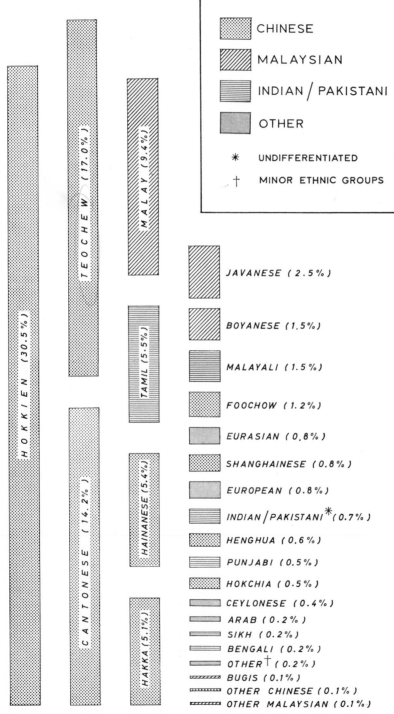

Figure 30.1 Specific communities as percentage of total population, 1957

Ethnic Composition

Almost since its inception Singapore has had a predominantly Chinese population, with Malaysians and Indians–Pakistanis comprising substantial minority groups:[2] by 1957, Chinese numbered 1,090,596, Malaysians numbered 197,059, and Indians–Pakistanis numbered 124,084. The three major ethnic groups comprised 75.4 percent, 13.6 percent, and 8.6 percent respectively (altogether 97.6 percent) of the total population of 1,445,929.[3]

The simple division of the population into three ethnic groups obscures its highly heterogeneous character. There are five main communities within the Chinese population in Singapore, the three largest each more numerous than the whole Malaysian ethnic group. The Indian–Pakistani group is similarly heterogeneous in composition including peoples of widely differing language, religion, and custom. Even the Malaysian group, most homogeneous of all, is comprised of several specific communities. Figure 30.1 illustrates the relative importance of the main specific communities identified in the 1957 census of population. Smaller communities of Jews, Nepalese, Filipinos, Koreans, Japanese, and other mainly Asian peoples introduce a truly cosmopolitan element into the already diverse composition of this plural society.

The heterogeneous ethnic composition of Singapore is a product of the national and international pressures which were operative in Southeast Asia during the nineteenth century. The modern settlement was founded by British commercial interests but owed much of its early rapid growth to the advent of transients from China and later from India. Push factors in countries of origin probably accounted for most of the early movement, pressure on the land, political upheaval, unemployment, and low levels of living; but with the growth of the entrepôt and associated commercial function of Singapore, pull factors were also operative, new opportunities for the small businessman, employment, and access to the tin and developing plantation industries of Malaya. The resultant influx was largely male, transient, without capital, often in debt for passage money, and frequently disillusioned because of the oversupply of labor and the mirage of easy fortune-making. These factors produced a rather unstable society which was demographically, economically, and socially unbalanced.

Demographic Characteristics

Because Singapore's population was predominantly immigrant and transient, sex ratios were extremely unbalance. Large-scale movement of Chinese and Indian–Pakistani women was precluded by prejudices against women migrating, against uprooting the whole family from localities of ancestral significance, and lack of finances, thus perpetuating the relatively minor role of natural increase in population growth. In the decade prior to the Second World War large numbers of Chinese women entered the country, but there was no comparable influx of Indian–Pakistani women. The contrasting pattern between ethnic groups is illustrated Figure 30.2.

Similar factors account for the main differences in age structure between ethnic groups. The tendency for migrants to be males in the middle age groups produced a marked impact on the age structure in 1931 (Fig. 30.2). By 1957, however, the emphasis had been completely reversed and natural increase, supported by legislation prohibiting nearly all immigration, had assumed the role of chief contributor to population growth. Only the Indian–Pakistani group retained the immigrant pattern and even in that group natural increase provided a larger child population and more balanced sex ratio than previously.[4]

Trends in mortality were highly significant in bringing about the change from immigration to natural increase as the chief determinant in population growth. Present-day natural increase rates are substantially higher amongst Malaysians despite a relatively high crude death rate and the highest infant mor-

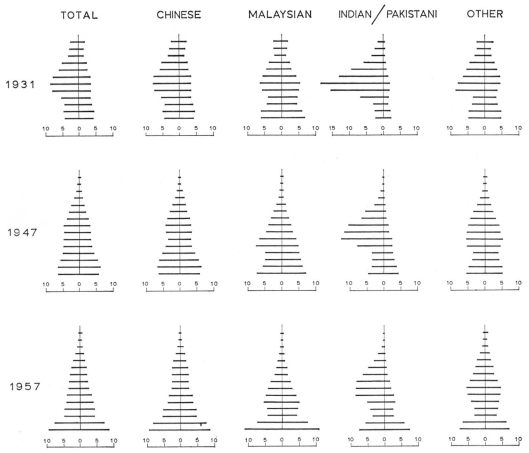

Figure 30.2 Sex and age composition by ethnic groups, at the 1931, 1947, and 1957 censuses. Age groups are for five-year intervals, with males represented on the left and females on the right. The scale indicates the percentage of the total population in each group.

tality rate. The low Indian–Pakistani crude death rate is resultant upon the large-scale exodus among the older age groups. Although current natural increase rates reflect a substantially reduced ethnic differential, life expectancy varies considerably between groups (Table 30.1).

For all ethnic groups, the increasing youthfulness of the population has contributed very substantially to the overall lowering of the mortality rate.[5] Lowered infant mortality rates were particularly significant but the lessened hazard of childbearing, because of improved health facilities and ante- and postnatal care, greatly depressed the rate in the reproductive ages. Reasons for the high Malaysian rates stem mainly from conservative attitudes and traditional observances

which still encourage confinement at home under supervision of a *bidan* (untrained midwife), although professional care by qualified nurses has reduced the rate even in these circumstances. Owing to the outlying locations of many *kampongs* and fishing villages such as those of the southern islands, adequate facilities and hygienic conditions are often lacking. Nutritional deficiencies of the Malaysian diet traceable to custom or poverty lower resistance, and the early childbearing age of Malaysian women subjects both mothers and infants to higher mortality rates. The low Indian–Pakistani crude death rates are due to the transient nature of the population and the custom for the older men to return home to their wives and children in India and Pakistan.

TABLE 30.1 Population and vital statistics by ethnic group, 1961

CRUDE RATES PER 1,000 MIDYEAR POPULATION

CRUDE RATE	TOTAL	CHINESE	MALAYSIAN	INDIAN-PAKISTANI
Natural increase	29.6	28.1	38.9	28.6
Births	35.5	33.9	46.5	33.6
Deaths	5.9	5.8	7.6	5.0
Infant mortality[1]	32.3	26.3	56.8	33.4
Life	males	61.1	57.0	63.2
expectancy[2]	females	68.2	58.8	62.1

[1]Per 1,000 live births.
[2]At birth, 1956–58, in years.
Sources: State of Singapore, *Report on the Registration of births and deaths, marriages, and persons for 1961* (Singapore Govt. Printer, Singapore, 1963). Saw Swee Hock, *The population of Singapore and its social and economic implications* (unpublished M.A. thesis, University of Malaya in Singapore, 1960).

The youthfulness of the population is also of importance in the interpretation of the crude birth rate figures as indicators of fertility. The birth rate has fallen very largely because of the declining proportion of women in the reproductive age groups. General fertility rates, referring only to women of childbearing age, indicate that there has been a small overall increase in fertility since the Second World War. However, the crude birth rates indicate the very high proportion of births to total population of each ethnic group, a product of the widespread tradition of the large family as socially desirable and economically essential. The high Malaysian rates are related to the early age of marriage and beginning of childbearing, and deep-rooted reluctance to seek advice on family planning and birth control.

Economic Characteristics

The simplest method of demonstrating the broad economic differences between ethnic groups is by examination of industrial and occupational structure.[6] Three basic features

should be noted.[7] First, the Chinese dominate the labor force and greatly outnumber other groups in seven of the eight industries listed and in all nine occupational categories. Secondly, because of their large male component in the economically active age groups, Indians–Pakistanis comprise a much larger proportion of the labor force (13.2 percent) than of the total population (8.6 percent) and reduce the Malaysian labor force to third in rank order (11.7 percent of the total labor force). Thirdly, a breakdown of the economically active into sexes and ethnic groups indicates a basic difference in female participation in their respective labor forces between Chinese (22.4 percent), Malaysians (6.2 percent), and Indians–Pakistanis (2.3 percent); the large proportion of Chinese females reflects the significant percentage of females amongst unskilled laborers, the relative emancipation of Chinese women and middle-class approval of the "working wife," and the tendency for Chinese boys to remain longer in educational institutions than girls who become economically active sooner.[8]

Composition by Industry

The importance of the entrepôt function to the economy of Singapore is reflected in the large proportion of persons earning a living in tertiary industry (71.9 percent of the total labor force), particularly trade, commerce, and allied servicing industries. The metropolitan character of Singapore is further emphasized by the proportion employed in secondary industry (19.3 percent) and the minor role of primary industry (8.8 percent).

Because Chinese comprise over 72 percent of the total labor force and are distributed through all industries, their predominance varies only in degree in all but the utility services (Fig. 30.3). In this context, the significance of the industrial composition lies rather in the pattern of employment by industry within each ethnic group (Fig. 30.4).

For all ethnic groups the largest proportions occur in "services" which include administrative, educational, health, military

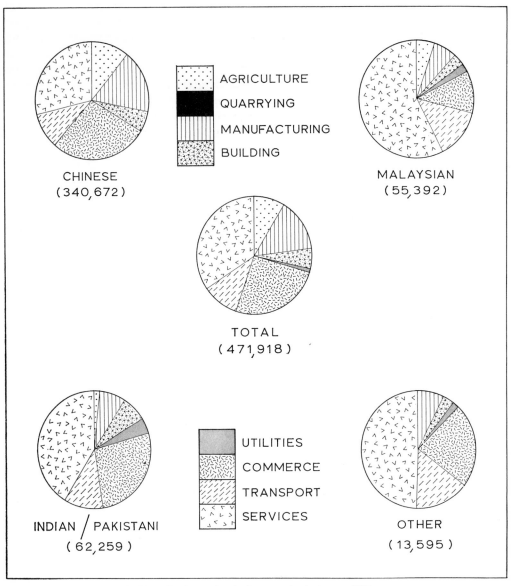

Figure 30.3 The economically active in each ethnic group by industry, 1957

and, most numerous of all, personal services. Apart from this basic feature in common, the Chinese are chiefly active in commerce and manufacturing; the Malaysians in transport–storage–communication and commerce; and the Indians–Pakistanis and others in commerce and transport–storage–communication. Thus after services, commerce provides the main sector of employment for all groups but Malaysians, and ancillary activities also rank high; only Chinese are involved to a major degree in manufacturing.

Primary industry in Singapore is of only minor importance; 10.7 percent of the Chinese labor force falls in this category and amongst Malaysians, the traditionally rural people of Malaya, farming and fishing play a subordinate role. Chinese predominate in secondary industry, and 22.2 percent of economically active Chinese are in this category; but manufacturing, building, and construction employ much smaller proportions of both the Malaysian and Indian–Pakistani labor forces. In tertiary industry,

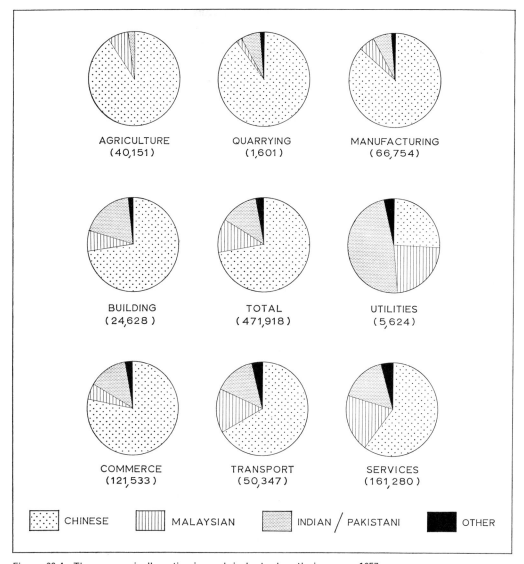

Figure 30.4   The economically active in each industry by ethnic group, 1957

services employ a much smaller proportion of Chinese than of Malaysians and Indians–Pakistanis. The relative importance of commerce in the industrial structure of the Malaysians (more than double the proportion in agriculture) is not generally recognized chiefly because of their relatively small contribution to the total numbers employed in commerce and the nature of their occupations within this industry.

The broad generalizations of the eight industrial categories conceal considerable specialization by ethnic groups. For example, in agriculture Chinese are market gardeners, and raise all the pigs and most of the poultry; buffalo, cattle, and goat rearing is mainly in the hands of Indians–Pakistanis; and fishing is apportioned between Chinese and Malaysians. In manufacturing, Chinese are mainly employed in manufacture of footwear, wearing apparel, and made-up textile goods, the food manufacturing industries, manufacture of furniture, fixtures, and all types of wood products, and in general engineering. Malaysians are mainly employed in the manufacture of nonmetallic mineral products, the beverage and tobacco industries, general engineering, and the printing and publishing

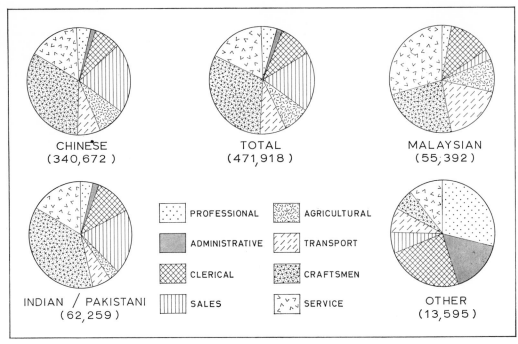

Figure 30.5   The economically active in each ethnic group by occupation, 1957

industries. Within commerce, it is Chinese who are retailers in furniture, clocks and watches, and bicycles; and who operate in pawnbroking and deal in smallholders' produce. In transport–storage–communication, Indians–Pakistanis predominate on the railway, Chinese in road transport; all three ethnic groups are active in water transport and Malaysians predominate in communications.

Composition by Occupation

The economic characteristics of the population can also be presented on the basis of occupation, in contrast to classification on the basis of industry in which the occupation is pursued. On this basis, craftsmen–production process workers–general laborers comprise the main occupational category in Singapore followed by sales workers, service–sport–entertainment–recreation workers, and clerical workers (Fig. 30.5).

Every category has a large majority of Chinese and this dominant group, comprising 72.2 percent of the labor force,

exceeds this proportion amongst sales workers, agricultural workers, quarrymen, and craftsmen–process production workers–laborers. Malaysians exceed their average (11.7 percent) amongst clerical workers, agricultural workers, workers in transport–communication, and service–sport–entertainment–recreation. Indians–Pakistanis exceed 13.2 percent in clerical, sales, and craftsmen–process production worker–laborer occupations. Others contribute disproportionately large numbers in administrative–executive–managerial, professional–technical, and clerical occupations.

The variation in the occupational structure within each ethnic group is also significant (Fig. 30.6). Nearly one-third of the Chinese labor force and an even larger proportion of Indians–Pakistanis fall in the category of craftsmen–production process workers–laborers. In both instances (and also for the smaller Malaysian group) laborers constitute the largest component and mechanics–fitters–turners the next main element. But whereas half the Indians–Pakistanis are laborers, less than one-third of the Chinese are laborers, and significant proportions of Chinese are

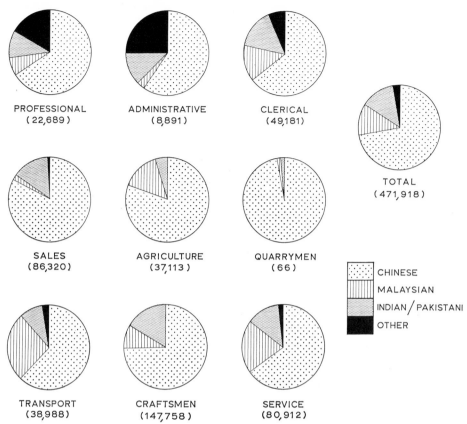

Figure 30.6   The economically active in each occupation by ethnic group, 1957

classified in production processing (packing and grading), as carpenters–cabinet makers, and tailors–dressmakers; Indians–Pakistanis work as engine–excavating–lifting equipment operators; and overseers–*mandores* (foremen); and amongst Malaysians, electricians rank third after laborers and mechanics.

The service category is important to all the ethnic groups, but considerable diversity occurs within this occupation. The Chinese are mainly workers in domestic service–hospitals –hotels–clubs–restaurants, especially amahs (female house servants) and cooks–waiters, but also hairdressers and launderers–dry cleaners. The Malaysians are members of the armed forces, firemen–policemen–watchmen, and workers in domestic service. The Indians–Pakistanis are mainly *jagas* (watchmen) and policemen, but are also cooks–waiters, and hairdressers. Most others are policemen–wardens, workers in domestic

service, and members of the armed forces.

Malaysians diverge from the general pattern (set by the Chinese labor force and closely followed by the Indians–Pakistanis) in the relatively large proportion of the labor force occupied in transport–communication, and the relatively small proportion occupied as sales workers. In transport–communication further specialization on the basis of ethnic group is evident; Malaysians comprise 28 percent of drivers but 75 percent of *syces* (chauffeurs); trishaw pedallers are 97 percent Chinese; and postmen and messengers are 65 percent Malaysians.

Malaysians also have the highest proportion of any labor force in agriculture and fishing, although this amounts to less than 10 percent. This designation is misleading, however, as 58 percent of these are gardeners–grass cutters; 25 percent are fishermen, and 12 percent are rubber tappers. The Indians–

Pakistanis in this category are also mainly gardeners–grass cutters (69 percent) but next are chiefly occupied with livestock and on smallholdings (22 percent); only 4 percent of those in agriculture are rubber tappers. Chinese are chiefly workers on smallholdings (including livestock) and market gardeners (80 percent); 10 percent are fishermen, and 5 percent are rubber tappers.

An occupational category with a special relationship to ethnic group is that of priests and related members of religious orders; these are generally persons whose ethnic groups comprise the bulk of adherents, the Muslim *kathis*, *imams*, and *bilals* are predominantly Malaysians and Indians–Pakistanis; Buddhist monks, priests, and nuns are almost wholly Chinese; Hindu priests are nearly all Indians–Pakistanis; Christian clergy and related workers are predominantly others but over one-third are Chinese.

Occupational specialization relates to the varied economic and social practices and prejudices not only by ethnic group but also amongst specific communities; for example, Hokkiens comprise the major element of Chinese merchants; Cantonese are frequently artisans of all kinds; and Hainanese specialize in domestic service, and as cooks and waiters.[9]

In instances where certain practices are confined exclusively to one group, specialization in associated occupations can readily be accounted for: these include religious activities; highly specialized food and drink preparation (e.g., toddy, and Indian drink); Chinese medicine (herbalists) and burial ceremony (professional mourners).

Traditionalism also influences participation in certain activities. Job vacancies are frequently filled by family relatives or on the recommendation of an employee, often regardless of achievement or experience; but in making crucial (e.g., managerial) appointments business acumen is not subordinated to kinship obligation and a son-in-law or nephew may be preferred to a less capable son. In manufacturing, many skills were brought from countries of origin (especially China) and these are learned mainly by on-

the-job training which, combined with the method of employee selection, perpetuates the exclusive element of the occupation. This process is sometimes taken a stage further. With technological advancement a group may continue as the dominant element in a new but related activity: for example, Malaysians once predominated in grooming horses and driving gharries; today they continue to predominate amongst employed drivers of private cars. Also, in an increasingly urban environment, Malaysians and Indians–Pakistanis in agricultural occupations are gardeners–grass cutters, contrasting with the more characteristically agricultural occupations of rural Malaya where these groups are predominantly small farmers and plantation workers.

Some occupations are dominated by one group as a result of deliberate government policy: this is operative chiefly within the government service or where important resources, such as land, come directly under government control. The employment of Malaysians in government services and particularly in administration, communications, police, and the armed forces is directly attributable to such policies.

Social Characteristics

The heterogeneous patterns of the social milieu in Singapore are difficult to assess and cannot readily be summed up by an analysis of any single aspect. Literacy provides one indicator of overall social development, educational achievement, and adjustment to modern living; and mutual intelligibility of language, as a basic element in social intercourse, reflects the fragmentation and relative isolation of groups within society as a whole.

LITERACY

Just over 52 percent of the nonchild population was recorded as literate at the 1957 census, with a substantial discrepancy between male and female rates. There is also a correlation of literacy with age: the older the age group the lower the rate of literacy.

By ethnic group, others are the most literate. Of the three main ethnic groups, Indians–Pakistanis have the highest average literacy rate and Chinese the lowest. Taking the sexes separately, Malaysians have the highest male rate, and Indian–Pakistani females greatly exceed the other female rates. The greatest discrepancy between the sexes occurs in the Malaysian group. Despite the relatively low rate of literacy amongst Chinese, this group is so large that Chinese comprise over 66 percent of those literate in any language, a significant fact in accounting for the dominant role of the Chinese and their impact on society as a whole.

The high literacy rate amongst Malaysians is a reflection of the British policy of providing free primary education for Malays since the late nineteenth century; the discrepancy between the sexes is due mainly to the conservative attitude which persisted towards the education of girls and the belief that the place of a daughter was at home and the arts she needed could best be learned there. Education in Chinese, by contrast, was left largely to the initiative of the Chinese themselves and operating without significant government assistance prior to 1956, associations, societies, and committees of management did their best to recruit staff from China and to provide an adequate education, in their own dialects, for the largest ethnic group in Singapore. A proportion of all groups received an education in English, the Indian–Pakistani group particularly benefitting since vernacular schools (Tamil only) have never been of major importance in Singapore. Most English schools have been either government schools or government aided and have thus had the resources to provide for a large sector of the population receiving any schooling.

Of the total school enrollment of 397,005 in September 1962, 50 percent were receiving an education in English, 39 percent in Chinese, 6 percent in Malay, and a negligible number in Tamil; the remaining 5 percent at school were in multi-lingual integrated, technical–vocational and other specialized schools.

LANGUAGE

The intrinsic heterogeneity of the population (in contrast to differences in achievement as demonstrated by literacy rates) is indicated by the diversity of language. Mother tongue, defined as the language spoken at home during early childhood, varies widely both between and within ethnic groups. Hokkien, Teochew, and Cantonese have by far the highest rates, followed by Malay, Hainanese, and Tamil. The general dissimilarity of the languages introduces a degree of complexity uncommon in the language structure of even much larger societies.

Other noteworthy features include the diversity of mother tongues spoken by small but significant minorities; the small percentage of Chinese speaking Mandarin as their mother tongue (English is spoken as the mother tongue of a larger number); and the complete dominance of Malaysian dialects among Malaysians. This classification does not provide an accurate assessment of proficiency in the various languages, particularly amongst Chinese: many educated young people speak Mandarin or English more fluently than their mother tongue, and even amongst the uneducated the mother tongue may be spoken less frequently than another dialect, depending on the immediate circumstances.

Unlike dialectal differences in many parts of the world, most Chinese dialects are not mutually intelligible, although a fair degree of understanding is possible between Hokkien–Teochew; Cantonese–Hakka; Shanghainese–Mandarin; and Foochow–Henghua–Hokchia. For this reason the adoption of one dialect has been encouraged and Mandarin, the national language of China,[10] has been introduced into the Chinese schools as the medium of instruction and is the official Chinese dialect for most purposes.

Similar diversity occurs among the Indian-Pakistani group of languages but in this instance the dominant language, Tamil, and not the official language of India (Hindi) or Pakistan (Bengali and Urdu), has tended to become the standard language for the group as a whole.

The contact between ethnic groups can be gauged roughly by the numbers able to speak one or more of the four "official" languages whether or not it is their mother tongue. On this basis less than half the total population were able to converse in Malay, the most widely spoken of the four languages; and less than one-quarter in either English or Mandarin. However, some are able to speak more than one of these languages: this indicates a considerable potential for intergroup contact and highlights the important role of the educated in bridging the gap between mutually unintelligible groups; it also implies that knowledge of these languages is more restricted than at first appears and that many people are unable to speak even one. Absence of an "official" language occurs particularly amongst the Chinese: only those with an advanced education, or who have come from China relatively recently, or who have passed through the school system since Mandarin was introduced are able to speak Mandarin. Most Chinese speak only the provincial dialects, but this alone (particularly when dialects are mutually intelligible or when more than one dialect is known, as amongst the smaller dialect groups) may be sufficient to allow conversational access to substantial proportions of the population; and despite the limited adoption of Mandarin so far, more Chinese speak Mandarin than speak either Malay or English.

The role of the English-educated is particularly significant since the people involved are drawn from all ethnic groups. This enables much more than simple verbal intercourse of one group with another: for by about the third generation the English-educated are likely to have a greater affinity with each other (whether Chinese, Malaysian or Indian–Pakistani) than with their own ethnic group. For this linguistically and culturally hybrid group, ties with a remote country of family origin are minimal and permanency of residence and loyalty to the new nation are

generally taken for granted. Furthermore, it is from the intellectual elite of this group that most members of the government (including the civil service) have been drawn.

Malay is widely spoken not only by Malaysians but also by Indians–Pakistanis and others; and (exclusive of others) English is most widely spoken by Indians–Pakistanis. Mandarin and Tamil are little spoken outside their respective ethnic groups.

Lack of a single language intelligible to all is a product of traditional usage and lack of incentive to learn other languages. English has been used as the language of commerce and, until recently, of most higher education, and has therefore been learnt to gain access to associated occupations. But small businessmen, predominantly Chinese and Indians–Pakistanis, negotiate mainly in their own languages, in "bazaar" Malay or in a form of "pidgin" English. However, Malay is the national language and strong official support is accelerating its use for official purposes, especially as a minimal knowledge of the language is a prerequisite to employment in certain positions; with official sanction and facilities for learning the language, Malay is rapidly becoming the lingua franca.

Areal Distribution

The main ethnic groups are not evenly distributed throughout the settled areas.[11] However, segregation is not highly developed and except for a short period soon after the settlement's foundation, separation on the basis of ethnic group has never formed a direct part of official policy.[12] Figure 30.7 illustrates the distribution of each ethnic group: the dots represent percentage values of the ethnic groups taken separately.

The main concentrations of Chinese occur in Chinatown and in the Rochore area (sometimes referred to as the "old town" and the "new town," respectively), the two nuclei towards the historical and functional core of the island. The Malaysians are most heavily concentrated in the Geylang Serai district where the main nucleus of settlement occurs

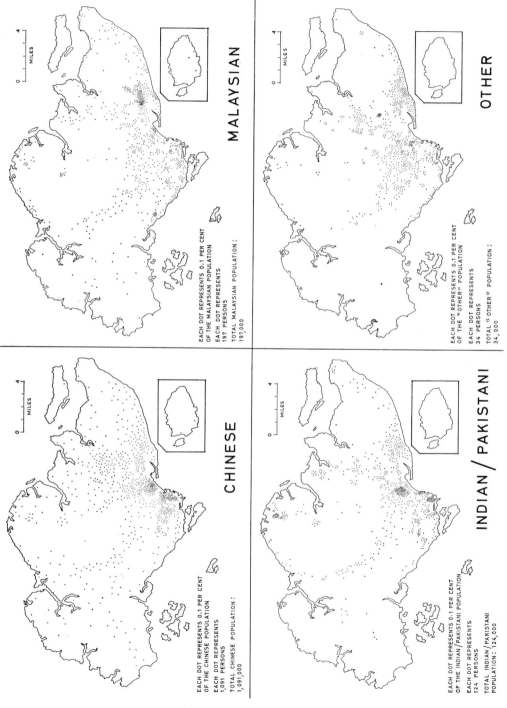

Figure 30.7 Areal distribution of the main ethnic groups, 1957

outside the administrative city limits. The Malaysian population is almost wholly lacking in Chinatown and only minor nuclei occur in the northern section of the Rochore area; a significant proportion of the Malaysian population is located in the Southern Islands.

The pattern of distribution of the Indian–Pakistani population lies between the extremes of the Chinese and Malaysian populations. As with the Chinese, two main groupings occur towards the central core of the city, both of them on the outer periphery of the main Chinese nuclei, notably in the Kandang Kerbau and Tanjong Pagar districts. The other population is less dispersed than the main ethnic groups but lacks any focus of concentration. The main areas of occupance are north of the city in Tanglin, Mount Sofia, Serangoon, and Katong. Owing to the exclusion of foreign military and associated civilian personnel from the statistical data,[13] heavy concentrations of others to be expected in the naval and air bases and in other British military establishments do not appear on the maps.[14]

Government policy has played an increasingly significant role in designating areas for settlement and resettlement particularly under large-scale schemes to provide high density housing. Most significant instance influencing the existing ethnic distribution was the reservation of land for Malaysian settlement in the Paya Lebar–Geylang Serai area.

Many examples of economic and social factors influencing the distribution of ethnic groups could be cited. The commercial interests of the Chinese and large numbers employed in this and associated industries have sustained high densities in central localities near the Singapore River, warehouses, offices, and in the main retail areas. The large proportion of dock and railway labor provided by Indians–Pakistanis has encouraged the heavy concentrations of that group in the dock area near Tanjong Pagar; merchants are concentrated in the lower Serangoon area and considerable skilled and unskilled Indian–Pakistani labor is employed by military

forces based in peripheral areas. The Malaysian group, largely divorced from small business and trading activities avoids the necessity of living in the shophouse unit favored by both Chinese and Indians–Pakistanis, and prefers the traditional style of single-storied detached house in a suburban setting. Away from the dense nuclei of each ethnic group, where ethnic composition tends to be relatively static and predictable, social levels are more varied and class rather than ethnic groupings tend to develop, as in the districts of Katong and Tanglin.

Implications and Problems

Singapore is subject to most of the problems of a plural economy operating within a plural society developed under a colonial regime. Many of the features characterizing a developing country appear, but where serious discrepancies and unevenness occur in levels of economic and social development these are perpetuated and greatly intensified because they frequently correspond to differences in ethnic and community composition.

Singapore's demographic character raises several problems. The problem of dependency in a society with a relatively small proportion of persons in the economically active sex and age groups is a recurrent one in developing countries. In Singapore the economic differences between ethnic groups result in an unequal sharing of the predominantly youthful dependency burden. The Malaysians, with the largest proportion of children under fifteen years of age, have the smallest proportion of economically active, employed mainly in the less remunerative occupations. The Indian–Pakistani population, being predominantly male and adult, has a very small dependency burden within Singapore, a position which is greatly modified by the substantial numbers of dependents in India and Pakistan who benefit from remittances and the eventual return of men and capital to their homelands.

The youthfulness of the population raises the problem of adequate educational facilities and opportunities; this too is a problem common to all developing countries. In Singapore, where the problem is more than usually acute because of the sustained high natural increase rate, the situation is greatly complicated by the necessity for schools in four language media. This increases the difficulty of providing teachers and suitable teacher training, standardizing syllabuses, providing teaching material suited to each cultural group and recognizing the group's mores and values, reaching similar standards of achievement regardless of language medium, and coordinating administration in the various languages.

The large numbers of school children and young adults pose a serious problem in providing adequate employment opportunity. Substantial unemployment already exists (variously estimated at around ten percent) and only very rapid diversification into non-entrepôt activities can prevent the situation worsening. Again, ethnic diversity plays a complicating role: with a trend in many occupations and industries for ethnic specialization the perpetuation of the status quo by the selection of members of one's own group or community is a common occurrence. In technical, professional, or other skilled occupations this may occur where applicants have similar abilities or achievement levels; but at the level of unskilled, semi-skilled, or on-the-job-trained personnel both the job vacancy and the desire for employment are made known through personal contacts, and selection may take little or no account of aptitude, achievement, or experience.

In Singapore, as in many developing societies, the economy is less unified and coordinated than in many industrialized countries and three systems may be recognized within the economy as a whole, giving rise to a plural economy. These are:

1 an imported system influenced by Western techniques and capitalistic methods of production in which economic development is relatively advanced;
2 an indigenous system where production is at a pre-capitalistic stage, techniques are relatively retarded, and levels of economic welfare relatively low, operating mainly in the rural sector (and thus relatively minor in metropolitan Singapore); and
3 an intrusive system introduced by the immigrant Asian groups, the Chinese and Indians–Pakistanis, differing from the indigenous system in its capitalistic organization based on exchange, and from the imported western system in that the economic organization is usually small-scale and less capital intensive.

In most societies the alien group exists as a minority. In Singapore the Chinese immigrant group has an absolute majority, and among the economically active the Indian–Pakistani immigrant group is second in numerical size. The Malaysian population, regarded as indigenous for most purposes, is greatly out-numbered and plays a relatively minor role in Singapore's economy. The Chinese, supported by the Indians–Pakistanis, comprise not only the greater proportion of economically active in the economy as a whole but also the influential entrepreneurial group; they have provided most of the initiative, skills, and adaptive ingenuity, and supplied much of the capital; but their dominant economic role and the economic status of their most successful minority do not enhance inter-group relations. In addition, large numbers from all three main ethnic groups, and particularly Malaysians, have taken regular employment in less remunerative but more secure jobs such as government employment of all types.

Despite the significance of the diverse demographic and economic attributes of the main ethnic groups, such disjunctive characteristics might be substantially negated if other fundamental social elements were common to all. Religion and language are the two main factors potentially capable of creating a sense of community or nationhood. The multiplicity of both of these in Singapore, as in many parts of Asia, presents a formidable obstacle in the path of economic, social, and political development.

In Singapore, no precise enumeration of religions has been undertaken. Malaysians are almost invariably Muslims. Among the Chinese, the majority are Buddhists, Taoists, and Confucianists or followers of folk-religions derived in part from these religions, and there is a very small Christian minority. Most Indians are Hindus but among Indians –Pakistanis there are also Muslims, Sikhs, and a few Christians. Almost all Europeans and Eurasians are adherents of Christianity; and numerous other small groups occur including Jews, Parsees, and a significant cross-cultural group (comprising mainly those with advanced education in either Chinese or English) who are essentially agnostic although frequently deferential to parental wishes in the observance of religious festivals. Religious differences form one of the main barriers to fraternization between groups, preclude extensive intermarriage, and minimize opportunities for cooperation or common ground for mutual trust and understanding. Islam is particularly strict in this respect and marriages contracted between Muslims and non-Muslims are negligible in modern Singapore. Even attitudes toward religion differ considerably between groups: for example, whereas among Muslims it is the right and privilege of the man to pray, amongst many Chinese the day-to-day religious rites tend to be delegated to the women. Although religious beliefs and ritual are not equally significant to all groups (on the whole, less compelling to the Chinese and most important to the Malaysians), religious and superstitious elements permeate most aspects of society including customs of food, dress, behavior, and even whether a shop remains closed each week on Friday or Sunday.

Establishing tolerance, understanding, and sympathy between ethnic groups and specific communities is difficult under circumstances where cultural backgrounds are as divergent as in Singapore. These factors create problems not only at the face to face and individual level but also reduce the effectiveness of mass media of communication; official or other printed propaganda must appear in several scripts and even then will be intelligible to only a proportion of the public. Even audio and audio-visual media must take account of language differences. On radio, four medium-wave stations provide for the four official language streams and the main Chinese dialects. On television, resources are more restrictive and programs are broadcast on one main channel (with a restricted service on another) in all the main languages and dialects. Important items must be relayed four times on the same channel, so that a fifteen-minute news bulletin, for example, lasts an hour. But the widespread use of television in particular is contributing substantially to the breakdown of these language barriers as a large number of indiscriminate viewers gain, informally, an understanding of other languages.

Although of utmost significance in retarding the immediate realization of the concepts of community and nationhood, religious and linguistic differences are themselves symptomatic of broader cultural contrasts which influence the values and attitudes of each of the component groups. In Singapore, the greatest divergence in outlook occurs between the Chinese and the Malaysians. To the Chinese as a group, acquisition of wealth is one of the most important aims in life and they are, therefore, indefatigable workers and keen businessmen. To the Malaysian, work is a necessity but not a virtue; he is much more concerned with easy and graceful living. In Singapore, he is undoubtedly attracted by the sophistication and advantages of suburban living, but he is not prepared to forego his established values to obtain them. The difference in outlook between Chinese and Malaysian revolves around contrasting attitudes to wealth, saving, and leisure; the economic incentive, so effective with the Chinese (and others) is less successful with the Malaysians.

The problem of contrasting values and goals is being perpetuated in the socioeconomic structure of Singapore because of the dominant role of traditionalism. The adoption of universalistic value patterns is taking place very gradually. But for the greater proportion of the population the social structure emphasizes particularism; the Chinese, and to a lesser extent Indians–Pakistanis, tend to combine achievement values with particularism, whereas ascriptive values tend to be more significant among the Malaysians. The continuing emphasis on traditionalism thus tends to perpetuate substantial cultural differences, maintain economic and social specialization on an ethno-cultural basis, and retard the difficult process of fusing such a cosmopolitan population into a single co-ordinated and intradependent society deriving its unity from more than mere locational contiguity.

The recency of arrival and maintenance of close connections with countries of origin makes suspect the personal and political loyalties of some sectors of each of the main ethnic groups. This derives from the declining but substantial numbers of nonlocally born (greatest for Indians–Pakistanis and Others, moderate for Chinese and least for Malaysians), from the substantial amounts still remitted to India in particular and also to China, from the significantly large proportion of Javanese and Boyanese (Indonesians) in the Malaysian population, and from the transience and outside affinities of Others (except Eurasians) and the interests they represent.

However, other trends indicate consolidation within each ethnic group in Singapore. These include the ready acceptance of Indonesian settlers by the Malays, the decline in the importance of the caste system amongst Indians–Pakistanis, and the acceptance of Mandarin as the lingua franca of the Chinese. But as a concomitant of this consolidatory trend and owing partly to external circumstances (such as the favored status of Malays in Malaysia and the increased solidarity with the growth of national consciousness in China and Taiwan, India and Pakistan) the major groups have tended to draw farther apart from each other and there is now a predisposition to approach almost any issue from a communal viewpoint. This trend is strongly opposed by the government which recognizes and constantly reiterates that although ethnic groups have co-existed amicably in Singapore for nearly 150 years, mainly under colonial rule, mere co-existence is an inadequate basis for the creation of a self-governing state; greater cohesion and unity are essential, and divided loyalties can no longer be countenanced.

Clearly the problem of Singapore is not only one of general economic development and expansion but of resolving, as part of a program of planned economic growth, the imbalance and inequalities which exist between ethnic groups; inevitably economic maturity is both dependent upon and contributory to demographic and social maturity. In Singapore, the realization of advanced levels of living within a unified and stable society is possible only if accompanied by a high degree of intercultural cooperation and fraternization.

Notes

[1]For example, H. C. Brookfield and M. A. Tatham, "The Distribution of Racial Groups in Durban," *Geographical Review*, Vol. 47 (1957), pp. 44–65; L. Kuper, H. Watts, and R. Davies, *Durban: a Study in Racial Ecology* (New York: 1958), 239 pp.; P. Scott "Cape Town: a Multi-Racial City," *Geographical Journal*, Vol. 121 (1955), pp. 149-57.
[2]Recent political changes have resulted in several ambiguities in the established terminology: demographically the term "Malaysian" refers to peoples of Malay, Indonesian, and aboriginal stock, and this use of the term is followed here; however, all citizens of Malaysia may now be considered "Malaysians" and, in this political context, the term includes Chinese, Indians–Pakistanis, and all other permanently domiciled groups. In August, 1965, Singapore ceased to comprise part of the Federation of Malaysia and in the present context the distinction between political and demographic usages has, therefore, become less crucial.
[3]By the end of 1964, the total population was officially estimated to number 1,844,200, but in the absence of significant migration the ethnic breakdown was considered to have changed little: Chinese 75.0 percent, Malaysians 14.2 percent and Indians–Pakistanis 8.3 percent. The 1957 census data have been retained throughout this paper (with additional details added where possible) because statistics other than vital statistics are available only from census sources and under conditions of rapid but uneven demographic, economic, and social change cannot be projected satisfactorily to provide more up-to-date data.

[4]R. J. W. Neville, "Singapore: Recent Trends in the Sex and Age Composition of a Cosmopolitan Community," *Population Studies*, Vol. 17 (1963), pp. 99–112.

[5]P. S. You, "The Population Growth of Singapore," *Malayan Economic Review*, Vol. 4 (1959), pp. 56–69.

[6]Industry refers to the activity of the firm, establishment, or department in which the person was employed or to the kind of business the person operated. The occupation of a person is defined as the trade or profession followed or the type of work performed.

[7]S. H. Saw and R. Ma, "The Economic Characteristics of the Population of Singapore, 1957," *Malayan Economic Review*, Vol. 5 (1960), pp. 31–51.

[8]In this paper, data describing the economically active population exclude 8,349 persons who had never worked, and all children under ten years of age. Primary industries

are defined to include agriculture (including rubber processing), forestry, hunting, fishing, and mining; secondary industries include manufacturing, building, and construction; and tertiary industries include electricity, gas, water and sanitary services, commerce, transport, storage and communication, and government, community, business, personal, defense and other services.

[9]B. W. Hodder, "Racial Groupings in Singapore," *Malayan Journal of Tropical Geography*, Vol. 1 (1953), pp. 25–36.

[10]Mandarin is also referred to as Kuo-yu, literally national language. In Singapore this term has recently become ambiguous as Malay is now the national language and, therefore, the term Kuo-yu is used to refer to Malay and not to Mandarin.

[11]R. J. W. Neville, "The Areal Distribution of Population in Singapore," *Journal of Tropical Geog-*

raphy, Vol. 20 (1965), pp. 16–25.

[12]Raffles specified certain areas for Europeans, Chinese, Malays, Bugis, Arabs, and Chuliahs; the designations were chiefly ethnic but also mentioned occupational and social status: Merchants to be given preferential treatment, lower laboring classes to be restricted to the western side of the town, and so on, "Notices of Singapore," *Journal of the Indian Archipelago*, Vol. 8 (1854), pp. 101–09, Vol. 9 (1855), p. 453; although greatly modified, this pattern can still be traced in areas of early settlement.

[13]All data in this paper exclude nonlocally domiciled service personnel (including United Kingdom based civilians employed by the services) and their families, who totalled 27,299 in 1957.

[14]R. J. W. Neville, "The European Military Population in Singapore," *Pacific Viewpoint*, Vol. 5 (1964), pp. 205–10.

Selection Thirty-one

THE POPULATION STRUCTURE OF AUSTRALIAN CITIES
Peter Scott

Since the Second World War Australia, which ranks after the United Kingdom as the second most highly urbanized country in the world, has experienced the greatest urban expansion in its history. This expansion has been made possible in no small measure by immigration not only from the British Isles but more especially from continental Europe. Accordingly "New Australians," as the immigrants from continental Europe are known in Australia, now outnumber those from the British Isles. Among the combined populations in the thirty largest cities—that is, those having in 1961 at least 20,000 inhabitants—one in every twelve persons was born in the British Isles (hereinafter designated "British-born") and one in every ten on the European

Reprinted from *The Geographical Journal*, **131**, 1965, 463–478, by permission of the author and the Royal Geographical Society.

continent. Yet the ratios of the British-born and the continental Europeans vary greatly from city to city. In particular, continental Europeans are far less evenly distributed both among and within cities than are the British-born.

In this paper the populations of Australian cities are examined with special reference to the impact that immigration has had on selected demographic and social attributes. Inter-city variations are considered in respect of the thirty largest cities and intra-city variations in respect of each of the five mainland State capitals; census definitions of cities and metropolitan areas are adopted. In 1961 the thirty largest cities together housed 67 per cent of the Australian population, 78 per cent of the British-born, and 80 per cent of the New Australians; the five largest housed 55, 64 and no less than 69 per cent respectively. However, the use of census data on which a large-scale comparative analysis must necessarily be based precludes consideration of much significant movement of population. Such movement is therefore exemplified from the more intensive investigations we are pursuing in Hobart by questionnaire and interview survey.

Immigration and Population Change

A basic feature of the urban distribution of immigrants as revealed by the 1961 census is that all cities in the three peripheral states—Queensland, Western Australia, Tasmania—contain more British-born than continental

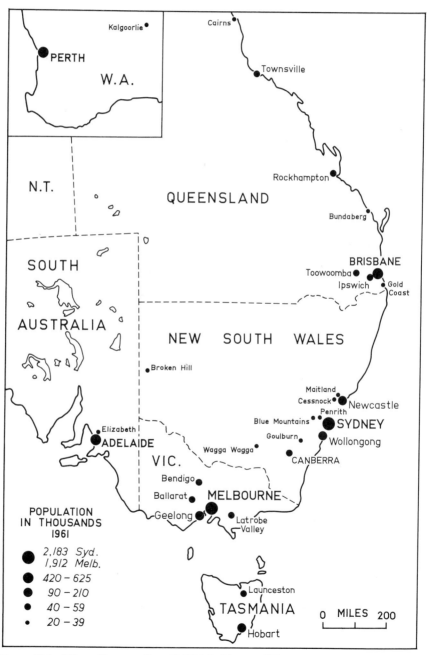

Figure 31.1 Cities with more than 20,000 inhabitants, 1961

Europeans, while the great majority of cities in Victoria and New South Wales have more New Australians than British (Fig. 31.1 and Table 31.1). In this regard South Australia ranks with Victoria, for Elizabeth, which was inaugurated in 1955 as a self-contained New Town, functions also as a dormitory satellite of Adelaide; if its population, despite the massive component of British immigrants, is added to that of the capital, then Adelaide still has many more continental Europeans than British. This tendency for the British to be relatively more prominent on the periphery with continental Europeans more confined to the south-east derives not only from the scale and character of post-war employment opportunities in the south-east (Rose, 1958b, 515) but also from the much greater importance among continental Europeans than among the British-born of migration chains linking local communities in Europe and Australia and even within Australia over long periods (Lochore, 1951, 24).

Aside from the capital cities, the pull of employment opportunities is readily apparent in respect of many centres of rapid post-war growth. Woolmington (1958a) has demonstrated that continental Europeans have played a critical role in the post-war expansion of Australian basic industries. Their over-representation in the work force of the heavy and noxious industries has resulted in part from the contract system under which assisted non-British immigrants are required to spend their first two years in specified employment. But it has also stemmed from the preference of native-born Australians for employment in the lighter industries and in the tertiary sector, a preference shared by British immigrants. Continental Europeans are therefore relatively more prominent in the mining and industrial center of Wollongong, the brown coal region of the Latrobe Valley, industrial Geelong and the federal capital of Canberra, where they are engaged mainly in building and construction than in any of the State capitals. In the Latrobe Valley, which is not a city but a statistical concept embracing six

townships, the high proportion of British immigrants stems largely from the Victorian State Electricity Commission recruiting independently employees in the United Kingdom, though latterly the number of British immigrants in the Latrobe Valley has been declining relatively to continental Europeans. On the Gold Coast, which again is not a city but a succession of townships, the low ratio of continental Europeans despite spectacular post-war growth derives simply from its function as a tourist resort. For all its pretentious, precious-metallic sophistication the Gold Coast is Suburbia- rather than Soho-on-Sea.

Throughout Australian history centers of rapid population growth have not only attracted European immigrants but have developed as nuclei from which secondary migration chains have emanated. Price (1963, 168–84) has shown that during the period 1880–1919 the proportion of the southern European population of Australia which moved each year either inter-state or intra-state averaged at least one-tenth. At Broken Hill, where southern Europeans have never bulked large in the work force partly because of the power of the industrial union (Wilson, 1962, 128), the proportion who entered or left the town each year in the period 1892–1921 averaged between one-third and one-half. Thus from Broken Hill to Sydney, from the cane-fields of the Queensland coast to Brisbane and Melbourne, from the goldfields of Western Australia to Perth, and from countless other centers to the capital cities continental European immigrants have forged secondary migration chains.

Since the Second World War the communities already established in the capital cities have been the foci of large-scale chain immigration as well as secondary internal movements. The importance of chain settlements among continental Europeans is borne out by the contrasting proportions of the British-born and the continental Europeans in the five major cities. All the cities except Perth are remarkably uniform in their relative share of British immigrants; the high ratio for Perth may be due to the simple but impressive fact that Fremantle is the first port of call from Europe and the city, though not its port, is delightfully attractive. Yet in their intakes of continental Europeans the major cities vary considerably. In Melbourne and Adelaide the non-British immigrants make up one-eighth of the population, in Sydney and Perth one-twelfth, and in Brisbane less than one-twentieth. Even Hobart has a higher percentage than

Brisbane, though both cities are situated away from the main shipping route and both have comparatively low ratios.

Within each of the major cities, irrespective of the scale of immigration experienced, two main concentrations of continental Europeans are discernible: a core area consisting chiefly of southern Europeans and a suburban zone in which other Europeans predominate (Fig. 31.2). The core areas comprise mostly Italians (Jones, 1964) and

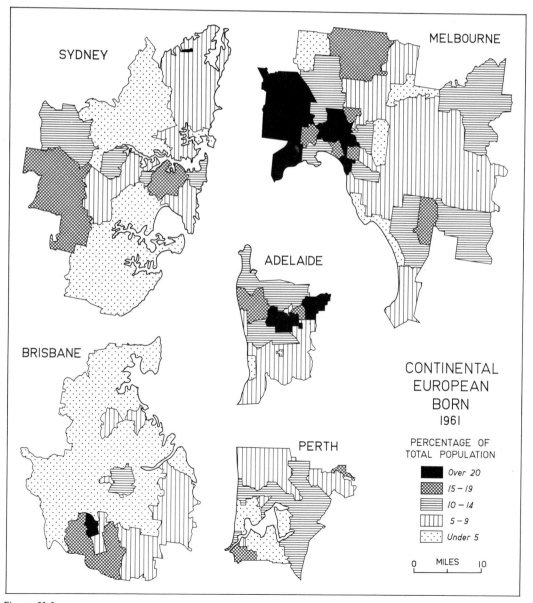

Figure 31.2

to a lesser extent Greeks with a small admixture of numerous other European groups, notably Maltese. Italians occur throughout these areas and among continental Europeans are generally predominant but Greeks tend to be the more highly segregated. Greeks are largely confined to the eastern part of central Melbourne, to the east and south-east in central Sydney, to the south in central Brisbane, and to the west in central Adelaide. In surburban concentrations, aside from anomalies resulting from migrant camps as a Darra in south-western Brisbane and Bankstown and Liverpool in western Sydney, there is much greater ethnic diversity. Populations comprise mostly Germans, Poles and other central and eastern Europeans together with some southern Europeans. The chief reasons for these concentrations are the prevalence of low land values and the absence of local government regulations prohibiting the building of low-grade housing (Jeans and Logan, 1961, 31). A secondary factor is the proximity of industrial job opportunities. Locally on the fringe are communities of Italian, Maltese and Dutch market gardeners, as in western Sydney, western Melbourne and southern Brisbane respectively.

For Perth, however, Figure 31.2 differentiates neither the core area nor the principal suburban concentration. The two areas of high incidence shown are Fremantle, a secondary inner concentration comprising mainly a long-established Italian fishing community (Borrie, 1954, 130 and 132), and Midland Junction, where most continental Europeans are employed in the railway workshops. In the case of Perth the use of local government areas, which in all Australian cities vary significantly in number and size (Table 31.2), is particularly disadvantageous. The City of Perth is only one of nineteen local government areas within the metropolitan region but it alone accounts for nearly one-quarter of the population; within its boundaries are clustered one-third of the continental Europeans, mostly Italians and Greeks. Similarly the strong suburban concentration of Italian, Dutch, German, Polish and Greek immigrants to the north is engulfed within another extensive local government area containing one-fifth of the metropolitan population. In Brisbane the use of local government areas necessitates the inclusion of much rural land within the metropolitan region, though this limitation at least carries the bonus of disclosing the presence of Dutch market gardeners in the south.

In each of the major cities continental Europeans are also scattered through the lower-income suburbs and tend to be but poorly represented in suburbs of above-average income. In Sydney few are to be found, except in a migrant camp, in the high-income areas north-west of the harbor, though Dutch and Italian horticulturalists boost the proportion to the north. In Melbourne the correlation with income tends to be even more apparent: the low-income industrial areas to the west and in the south-east have an above-average share of continental Europeans while the more favored residential districts east of the center have disproportionately few. Similarly the Adelaide pattern evokes the contrast between the hill suburbs to the south-east and the industrial suburbs to the north-west. In Perth the south-western suburbs of middle and high income contain few continental Europeans. Since it is the central and north-western Europeans who are the most widely dispersed they yield lower segregation indices than the Italians who in turn are less segregated than either the Greeks or the Maltese (Zubrzycki, 1960, 82–4; cf. Rose, 1958a, 68–9).

Hobart, in spite of its comparatively small total population and its low ratio of non-British immigrants, resembles the major cities in having an inner concentration mainly of southern Europeans and a suburban concentration mainly of central and eastern Europeans. In 1963–4, in order to determine how these clusters had emerged and the extent to which the inhabitants confined their activities to these areas, the residents were interviewed in one-fifth of the homes selected by random sampling. The survey areas were chosen by an analysis of census data for collectors' districts. An inner district at North Hobart was found to have one-fifth of its population continental European and an outer district at Springfield one-third; no other district had a ratio approaching these values. The survey areas were defined to overlap the boundaries of these two districts. Although all residents, immigrant and native-born Australians alike, were interviewed only the non-British respondents are discussed here. They numbered 67 in North Hobart, including 34 Italians and 12 Greeks, and 118 at suburban Springfield, including 27 Poles, 13 Germans, 12 Lithuanians and 11 Italians. Australian wives and the children born to European parents in Australia are excluded. Birthplaces for the North Hobart sample relate to twelve countries and for the Springfield sample fourteen.

Small and heterogeneous though these samples undoubtedly are, they shed some light on how these concentrations have developed. In Figure 31.3 the pattern of in-movement shows the suburbs from which the migrants have been drawn. At Springfield 55 per cent of the respondents had moved in from other suburbs, chiefly from the inner areas, though a secondary origin had been nearby industrial Moonah where many Springfield residents are employed. Yet the journey-to-work pattern reveals that at least as many Springfield residents work in the central area as at Moonah. That Springfield should have attracted from the inner suburbs residents who work at the center, and even from Claremont those employed in the Cadbury factory nearby, illustrates the importance of cheap land and low rates as residential determinants. At North Hobart only 45 per cent come from the metropolitan area, and then almost exclusively from the inner city. However three-fifths of the North Hobart respondents work locally, mainly in small shops along the principal thoroughfare, and one-quarter are employed in the central

area. The other one-third have to travel not inconsiderable distances to work but prefer to do so in order to enjoy residence in a fairly closely-knit ethnic community.

Almost one-half the respondents at Springfield and more than one-half at North Hobart had not resided previously in the metropolitan area; these are depicted by circle in Figure 31.3 (top left). At Springfield most were displaced persons from eastern Europe who had arrived in Tasmania between 1947 and 1952; they had moved in either from a migrant hostel north of the built-up area or from the Central Plateau at the expiry of their contracts with the Hydro-Electric Commission. Since 1957 all the new arrivals at Springfield who had not lived previously in Hobart had come from overseas; all have relatives or friends already resident in southern Tasmania. These included Italians, Yugoslavs and Germans. As a consequence, one-quarter of the Springfield sample had relatives in the metropolitan area, though not many of the relatives lived in Springfield itself. In North Hobart there were few displaced persons, and chain immigration had had a longer history. One-half the respondents, including Italians, Greeks, Germans and Dutch (cf. Taft, 1961), had relatives in the metropolitan region, mostly in close proximity, some even in the same dwelling. Only two-thirds of the Hobart respondents stated they had friends whom they visited at least once a month; most of these lived locally. At Springfield, on the other hand, almost all residents claimed to have friends whom they regularly visited, only a third of them locally (cf. Murphy, 1952). In short, the two communities present a notable contrast in the extent to which their residents have economic and social links with the rest of the metropolitan region.

Other survey data might have been invoked, had space permitted, to demonstrate that British immigrants in Hobart are even more integrated in the metropolitan community than the central and eastern Europeans at Springfield. For just as British immigrants are more evenly distributed than

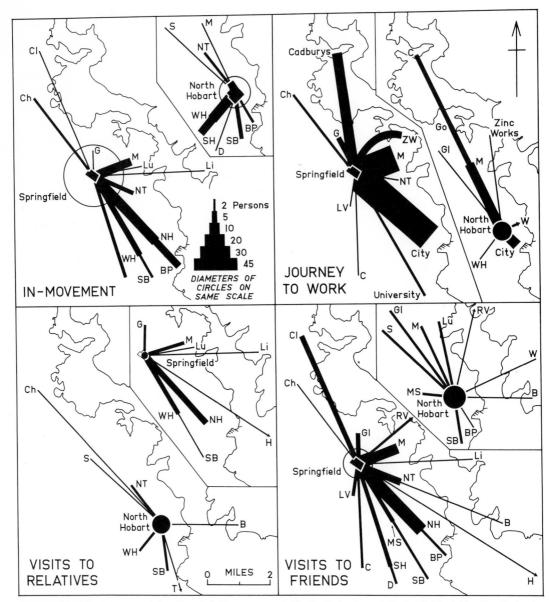

Figure 31.3 Movements of Continental Europeans at North Hobart and Springfield within the Hobart metropolitian region. The names of most suburbs may be identified by reference to Fig. 31.11.

continental Europeans among cities of more than 20,000 inhabitants (cf. Woolmington, 1958b, 93) so they are more evenly distributed within each of the capital cities (Fig. 4). Zubrzycki (1960, 82) has shown that in the four largest cities the metropolitan segregation indices for British immigrants are conspicuously low, far lower indeed than for any other immigrant group including New Zealanders. But even within Perth, which relatively to the cities has

50 per cent more British and a greater size variation in local government areas, almost all areas approximate closely to the average. In western Sydney the high ratio of British immigrants at Liverpool is partly attributable to the migrant camp and in south-western Melbourne to the establishment of an oil refinery and other industrial development involving a strong component of British labor.

All other areas of above-average occur-

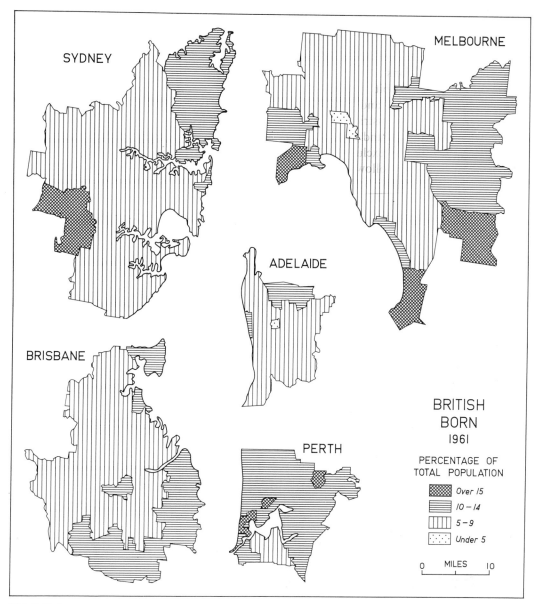

SYDNEY

MELBOURNE

ADELAIDE

BRISBANE

PERTH

BRITISH
BORN
1961

PERCENTAGE OF
TOTAL POPULATION

Over 15
10 – 14
5 – 9
Under 5

0   MILES   10

Figure 31.4

rence of the British-born are, with but few exceptions, either coastal or part of the urban-rural fringe. In Brisbane the preference for the coast is related not only to the subdivision that has taken place at Redcliffe in the north but also to the cooler climate than prevails inland. Yet even in Hobart, which has a cool temperate climate and a fairly even spread of the British through the built-up area, two minor concentrations are evident: one is at coastal Taroona and the other at rural Claremont. It is tempting to

conclude that, in so far as British immigrants in Australian cities betray a predilection for residential location, their choice is for the seaside or the countryside rather than for suburb or city. But, as Figure 31.4 suggests, only a puny minority manifests such sensitivity toward what Robin Boyd has described as "the Australian ugliness"; the rest, if this be so, exude typical British tolerance.

Since the British-born are for the most part evenly distributed, and continental Europeans show a strong tendency to segregate, one might expect the pattern of recent population change to bear some relationship to that of non-British rather than British immigrants. Certainly the main suburban concentrations of central and eastern Europeans exhibit typically high growth rates (cf. Fig. 31.2 and 31.5). But so also do many suburban districts where the British tend to cluster and many other districts occupied almost exclusively by the Australian-born. This follows from the fact that for the major cities the net contribution of continental Europeans to intercensal growth was only 28 per cent and of the British-born less than 8 per cent, though such figures seriously understate by excluding children born to immigrants in Australia. As in most Western cities the inner areas, despite the outward encroachment by cultural invasion and succession, are characterized by population decline.

All the major cities, but particularly

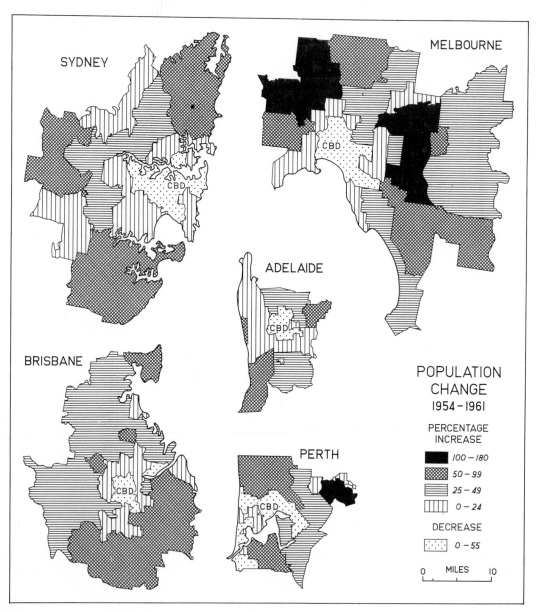

Figure 31.5

Sydney, disclose some tendency toward concentric zonal patterns of population change, but the tendency is modified by topographical, political and other factors. In Sydney for example the direction of the outward sprawl has been determined largely by the availability of cheap land in the low-lying Cumberland Plain west and south of the center (Logan, 1962). Similarly in Brisbane irregular terrain north-west of the river has confined the most rapid growth to the more easily developed land in the south-east. In Adelaide the Mount Lofty Ranges have channelled growth toward the north-east and the south-west, while in Perth the location of poorly drained land and the coastal limestone hills have influenced development north-ward from the pre-existing built-up area and south of the river. In Melbourne the high growth rate east of the center has been due to the availability of reasonably accessible, undulating land and represents the city's principal suburban development of middle-income housing, while the west is flat, wind-swept and occupied mainly by low-income housing.

Age and Sex Composition

Growth rates are, of course, closely related to the age and sex composition of the population. In general Australian cities with high growth rates and large immigrant communities—Wollongong, Canberra, Latrobe Valley, Penrith, Elizabeth—have populations that are typically youthful and predominantly male (Table 31.3). Incidentally, the sex ratio is expressed in a form alien to the British who defer to the female even demographically; Australian usage nevertheless appears appropriate both demographically and socially to Australia. The only city with a high growth rate but few continental Europeans as well as an ageing and predominantly female population is the Gold Coast. There the demographic traits derive from the substantial provision of tourist accommodation facilities—the census classifies

one-eighth of the work force as "employers"—and the high ratio of retired persons.

At the other end of the scale are cities with slow growth rates and few immigrants, chiefly central places such as Launceston, Bendigo, Goulburn and Toowoomba, which have ageing and predominantly female populations. Such cities owe their demographic features not only to their limited job opportunities but also to the influx of young unmarried girls seeking employment and retired persons from surrounding rural districts. Two outstanding exceptions are the inland mining centers of Broken Hill and Kalgoorlie, which have recently lost population but understandably remain youthful and predominantly masculine.

Age structure and the sex ratio are not always related to total growth rates, as the cities of near average growth exemplify. Blue Mountains, a center of tourism and retirement, has the oldest population of any Australian city, being considerably older even than that of the Gold Coast. However, as if to compensate for this depressing condition, those women who are of child-bearing age carry an above-average burden of children. Sydney, Melbourne, Adelaide and Brisbane, despite varying rates of population change, have the lowest proportions of children—Sydney displays exceptionally low fertility—and yet they have only an average share of the aged. Consequently their populations include a disproportionately large number of persons aged 15–64. To no small extent this reflects the age and sex composition of immigrants. Over the last intercensal period the number of continental Europeans grew more rapidly in Sydney and Melbourne than in the other capital cities. Thus in 1961 the million cities not only contained two-fifths of all Australians but of all Australian cities they furnished the highest proportions of people of working age. The economic advantages accruing to such population structure need no under-scoring.

Figure 31.6 attempts to summarize a few salient distributional features of the age structure of the major cities. It classifies local government areas according as to whether the proportions of the population aged 0–14, 15–64 and 65 and over (therein designated young, mature and old respectively) exceed the averages for the five cities. Old people are present in above-average proportions principally in the inner areas, including not only the zones of population decline but also the adjoining zones where growth rates are slowing

down. But the aged also return an above-average incidence in many high-income suburbs, in a few tracts on the rural-urban fringe of Melbourne, Brisbane and Perth, and in many waterfront suburbs to which the more affluent tend to retire. There is, in fact, a noteworthy concomitance between areas designated "old" and the main occurrences of flats, home units and luxury apartments. Inner areas are also characterized by a mature population while almost all suburbs

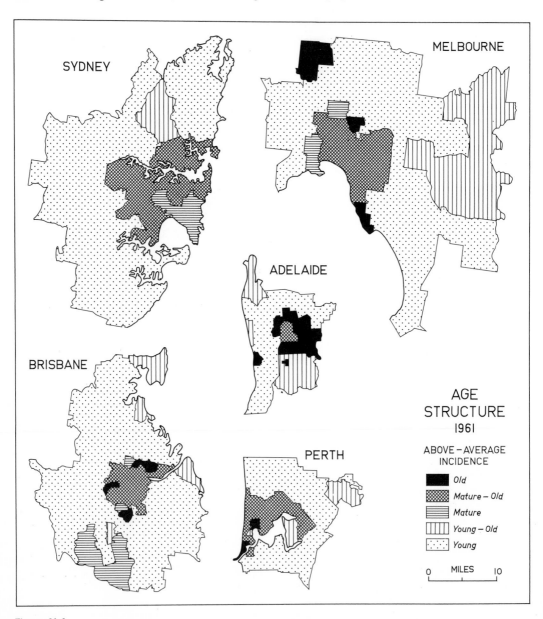

Figure 31.6

have populations that are typically young. In their age structure therefore Australian cities are basically very little different from cities in Europe and North America.

That each city nevertheless displays in detail an individuality of its own is borne out by the pattern of the child–woman ratio (Fig. 31.7). Although the contrast typical of Western cities between the inner and outer districts is readily identifiable the suburbs present a complex pattern related

in varying degrees to age structure, geographical origins, socio-economic status and religious affiliation. In general, areas of recent rapid growth, particularly in Melbourne and Adelaide, have high fertility ratios but there are many suburbs of moderate growth with equally high fertility. Some of these suburbs contain large tracts of government housing occupied almost exclusively by young married couples with children. Examples include Blacktown in

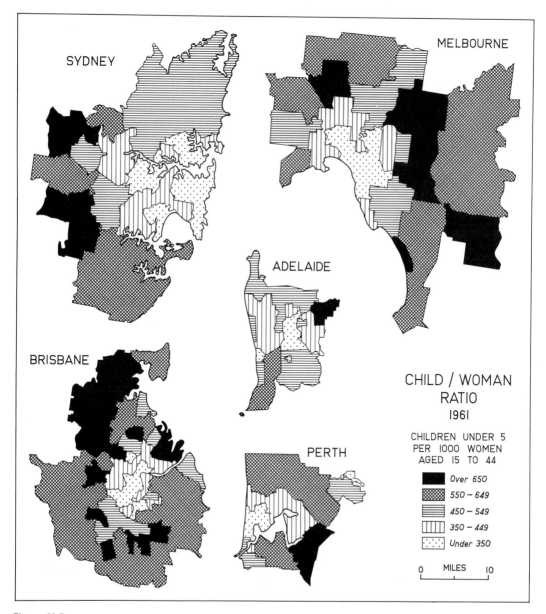

Figure 31.7

north-western Sydney, Inala in southern Brisbane, Geebung in northern Brisbane, Berwick and Fankston in south-eastern Melbourne, Altona in south-western Melbourne and Canning in south-eastern Perth. In Adelaide where government housing is widely dispersed this factor is far less evident. In Melbourne and Sydney areas with some concentration of British immigrants exhibit high fertility but generally there is no strong correlation of fertility with the distribution of immigrants, especially of continental Europeans (cf. Borrie, 1959, 12). Some high-income suburbs, notably in Sydney, Melbourne and Brisbane, have at best average ratios while high ratios are found in some outer, markedly Catholic suburbs, notably in southern and western Sydney and north-eastern Brisbane. Unfortunately, the census sheds no light on the proportion of rural migrants, who in Australia, as in the United States (Goldberg, 1959), contribute significantly to differential urban fertility.

Intra-city patterns of sex ratios are also related to the selectivity of migration and to socio-economic status (Fig. 31.8). Some of the highest ratios, particularly in Sydney and Melbourne, coincide with the main concentrations of continental Europeans. But because young unmarried workers in industry tend to seek accommodation near their place of work many other industrial suburbs also display high masculinity. In Brisbane, as in parts of eastern Perth, the rural periphery is largely responsible for a high ratio. By contrast areas of high social status are graced with prominent femininity.

Religious Affiliation

Perhaps the most pervasive cultural influence of post-war immigration has been in respect of religious affiliation. Although Australian urban life cannot be described as otherwise than overwhelmingly secular, religious affiliation has long been a separatist influence in the political, social and even economic spheres. In the nineteenth and

early twentieth centuries a sharp cleavage existed between Roman Catholics and Protestants but since the thirties the position has ameliorated considerably, though mutual distrust tends to persist. In some cities mutual distrust is much more pronounced than in others: in Sydney, for example, a Church of England predominantly evangelical is a far remove from a Catholic Church which is distinctively Irish; but in Brisbane, where the Church of England is essentially Anglo-Catholic, Anglicans and Roman Catholics enjoy unusually close relations.

In general, the urban pattern of religious affiliation in Australia is one of State regionalism indicative of a much higher degree of migration intra-State than inter-State. This holds for each of the four major affiliations but it is more marked among Anglicans and Presbyterians than among Catholics and Methodists. The Church of England, which in Australia is not established but simply a voluntary body in status, is particularly prominent in Tasmania and New South Wales (Table 31.4). Significantly, New South Wales even displays pronounced intra-State regionalism: the cities of the Sydney region have higher Anglican ratios than those of the Hunter Valley or the southern part of the State. By contrast, Presbyterians are disproportionately numerous in all Queensland and Victorian cities but disproportionately few in almost all other cities. Catholics reach their greatest prominence in southern New South Wales and decline in relative importance southward along the Queensland coast. Methodists are present in very similar average proportions in the coastal cities of Queensland and in very similar below-average proportions in central and southern New South Wales. Incidentally Hobart and Launceston lend support to the popular image of Tasmania as the most English of the states in having the highest ratios of Anglicans and among the lowest ratios of Catholics among Australian cities.

Inter-State migration has nevertheless been an important factor shaping the

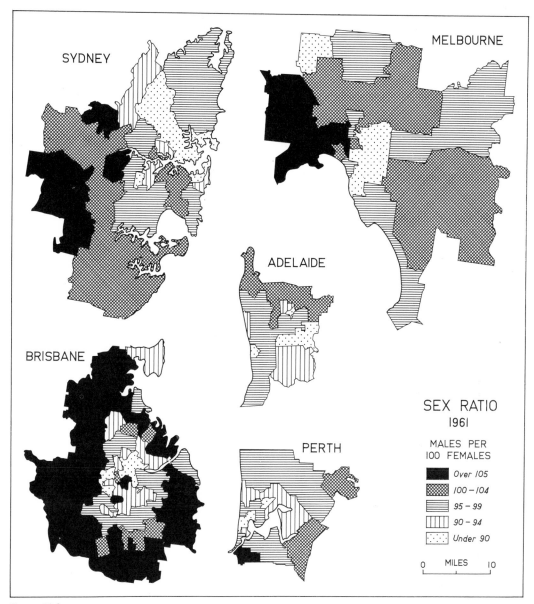

Figure 31.8

religious structure of many cities which deviate markedly from this general pattern. It is far from coincidental that Broken Hill and Adelaide should have the highest ratios of Methodists and the lowest ratios of Presbyterians, for the population of "the Hill" has been drawn mainly and selectively from Adelaide. In the past Methodists appear to have loomed large in the migrations to other mining centers as well. But the high ratios for most of the mining centers included in Table 31.4 are also attributable, at least in part, to local in-migrations from mixed-farming areas which throughout south-eastern Australia are typified by proportionately numerous Methodists. This also largely explains, together with the influx from declining mining towns, the high Methodist ratio for Launceston. Similarly the high Anglican ratio for the Gold Coast may be ascribed to the selective in-migration of persons engaged in the service industries and of elderly, presumably affluent persons, both groups probably to no small extent from New South Wales.

The contribution of post-war immigration to these religious patterns has been highly complex but, because the chief source of non-British immigrants has been Italy and other immigrant groups have included large numbers of Catholics, the major effect has been to boost the growth rate of Catholics relative to the other main affiliations (cf. Price, 1957). During the 1954–61 intercensal period the number of Catholics in Australia rose by 27 per cent, of Presbyterians by only 12 per cent, of Methodists by 10 per cent and of Anglicans by less than 8 per cent. The Catholic growth rate was especially high in Melbourne and Adelaide, where Catholic numbers increased by two-thirds and one-half respectively, and to a lesser extent in Sydney, Newcastle and Wollongong. But the highest growth rates among religious affiliations have been those of the Lutheran and Greek Orthodox Churches which in the number of adherents in Australia now rank fifth and sixth respectively.

Within the major cities the pattern of Anglicanism reflects both the impact of post-war immigration and more especially social status (Fig. 31.9). Many areas with a low incidence of Anglican adherence have a high incidence of New Australians while some, but by no means all, of the areas with more British immigrants than the average have above-average ratios of Anglicans. More significant is the relationship between high *per capita* income and the prevalence of Anglican affiliation. Witness in particular northern Sydney, Kogorah on Botany Bay, Walkerville in north-eastern Adelaide, and south-western Perth. Less pronounced but equally relevant are the east-central areas of Melbourne, south-eastern Adelaide, and the small inland tracts of St. Lucia and Ascot in Brisbane. In trend post-war immigration has weakened the position of Anglicanism in the lower-income areas and strengthened thereby its more distinctive association with the more prosperous suburbs.

Not all areas of middle or even high incomes, however, exhibit high ratios of Anglicans. Here it is necessary to note the contribution of Methodists and Presbyterians to the metropolitan patterns. Aside from a low incidence in the inner areas Methodists tend to be fairly evenly distributed, markedly so in Sydney; but they also reveal some tendency to be over-represented in districts of predominantly middle, particularly lower-middle income. This suggests a partial explanation for the relatively low ratio of Anglicans in south-eastern Melbourne, in the tiny enclave of Colonel Light Gardens in southern Adelaide, and in tracts of northern and western Brisbane. Presbyterians are likewise under-represented in the inner areas and display elsewhere a fairly even spread, notably in Adelaide; but they become conspicuous in districts enjoying a high social status. They therefore reduce the margin of Anglican supremacy in northern Sydney, in areas east of central Melbourne, and at Kenmore and St. Lucia in south-western Brisbane.

By contrast with Anglicanism, Roman Catholicism has increased its strong associations with areas of low socio-economic status (Fig. 31.10). The pattern of Roman Catholicism in Sydney for instance, corresponds impressively—far more so than any other pattern of Sydney's population considered in this study—with Congalton's map of the status ranking of Sydney suburbs (Congalton, 1961). Likewise the patterns in the other cities may be broadly interpreted in socioeconomic terms. Barcan has claimed that "since 1945 Roman Catholicism's social pattern has become assimilated to the general Australian pattern," though he added that Catholics "have never been, and still are not, strong in the most important . . . sections of society" (Barcan, 1962, 56 and 61). While there is abundant evidence of increasing Catholic penetration into certain middle-class professions, Barcan fails to note the relatively greater expansion of Roman

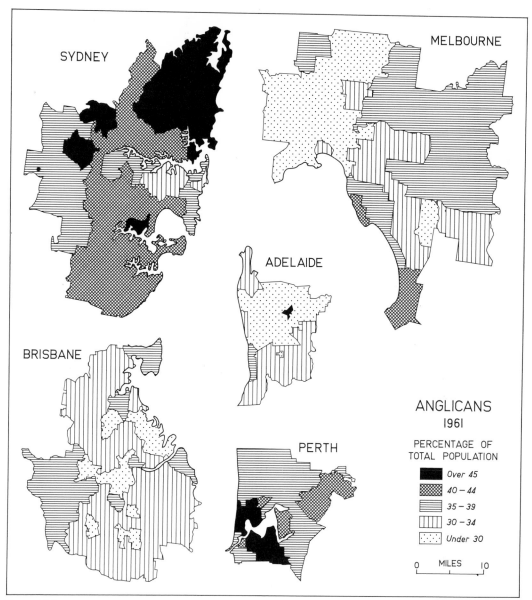

Figure 31.9

Catholicism among the lower-income groups. This expansion has resulted since the war in an increasingly rapid outward spread of Catholic predominance in the four largest cities. In Melbourne and Adelaide, where no local government area was predominantly Catholic in 1947, Catholic supremacy now extends from the core northwestward and northeastward respectively to the fringe.

Yet a spatial analysis of census data on religious affiliation has limited significance, for a voluntary assertion on the census schedule made usually in domestic comfort is appreciably less exacting than the rigors of church-going. In Hobart we have undertaken a series of questionnaire and interview surveys to determine in detail the pattern of church attendance. This project was initiated in part response to a request from the Church of England Synod in 1962 to carry

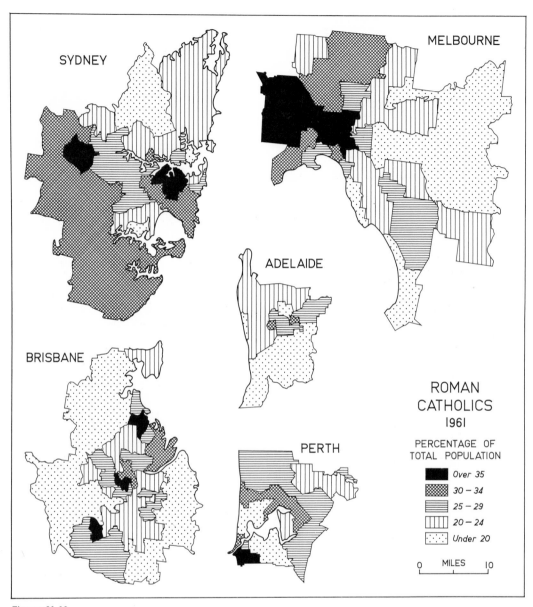

Figure 31.10

out a demographic survey of the Diocese of Tasmania. Subsequently we have extended our enquiries to embrace both the Roman Catholic Church and the Methodist Church. According to the 1961 census these three churches together claimed 77.3 per cent of Hobart's population or 86.5 per cent of those who professed Christianity.

Some index to church attendance is furnished by the proportions of those professing affiliation who go to church on the occasion of special festivals or on the average Sunday. Of professing Anglicans the proportion who attended Holy Communion at either Easter or Christmas in 1961 was only 10.7 per cent and of professing Methodists only 6.7 per cent while of professing Roman Catholics those who partook of Paschal Communion in 1961 amounted to 36.9 per cent. On an average Sunday church attendance among Anglicans was 6.7 per cent, among Methodists 7.3 per cent and among

Catholics 21.7 per cent. Consequently active membership would seem to be very much higher among Catholics than among either Anglicans or Methodists. Even though Anglicans make up one-half of the Hobart metropolitan population and Catholics only one-fifth more Catholics go to church at Easter or even on the average Sunday than Anglicans. It should be added that the Catholic Church has as many priests engaged in pastoral duties within metropolitan Hobart as the Church of England, even two ministering well-nigh exclusively to a small Italian immigrant community. Nevertheless these findings highlight the current decline in Protestantism evident in all Australian cities and give added significance to the growing predominance of Roman Catholicism over extensive intra-city areas.

Fascinating or salutary though such findings may be, the geographer is more concerned with the extent of church catchment areas and with the variation in church attendance by parish or circuit. The definition of catchment areas is made somewhat difficult by the degree of interparochial or intracircuit movement which in Hobart is particularly marked in the inner areas. In Figure 31.11 the number of active members at, for instance, a specific Anglican Church is expressed as a ratio of total Anglican parishioners minus those who are active members of other Anglican Churches and together with Anglicans from other parishes who attend the church in question; territorial boundaries have been omitted. For parishes or circuits with two or more closely integrated churches or stations the data for the subsidiary centers have been incorporated with those for the main church. This procedure was necessitated by the inclusion of the Methodist Church where a single circuit

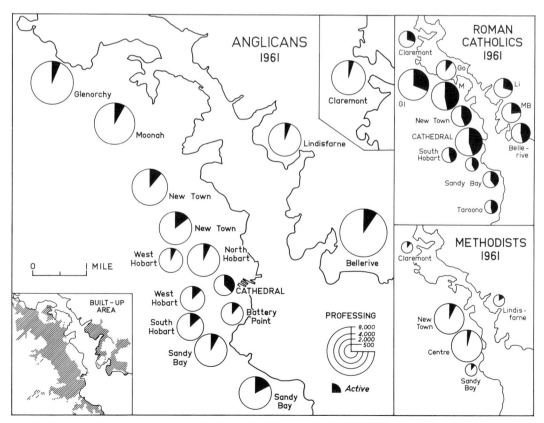

Figure 31.11 Active membership of the Church of England, The Roman Catholic Church, and the Methodist Church expressed as a proportion of those professing affiliation to the respective churches in 1961

comprises from three to seven centers and the determination of the tributary population for each center proved to be excessively arbitrary. "Professing" Christians are those self defined in the census; "active" Christians are those who attend church regularly—at least once a year!

At first glance the extent of church attendance by suburb would appear to be strikingly consistent within each religious group but like so much of the Australian social scene the superficial sameness belies a subtle but meaningful variation. Among Anglicans the Cathedral overshadows the inner parishes which are broadly conterminous with the extent of nineteenth century and early twentieth housing. Nevertheless the Cathedral's pull is weakest for South Hobart where the prevalence of Anglo-Catholicism furnishes the most distinctive Anglican churchmanship in the city. Beyond this inner region the active percentage of professing Anglicans declines steadily northward from New Town (14.3 per cent) to Claremont (4.7 per cent), a haven of British immigrants. On the eastern shore, Bellerive and Lindisfarne provide a similar contrast in church attendance, here between a sub-center and the periphery (cf. Zimmer and Hawley, 1961, 90–91). Yet seemingly the most active congregation is in southern Sandy Bay, a high-grade hillside suburb commanding excellent views of the heavens and earth. But its pre-eminence in church attendance is not sustained from Christmas to the average Sunday. In fact Sandy Bay has not only the largest proportion of Anglicans within any Hobart suburb and the wealthiest parishioners but the largest proportion of those who merely pay an annual fire-insurance premium.

Roman Catholics and Methodists are probably each more homogeneous socially and their patterns of church attendance are correspondingly somewhat less diversified. This is particularly so with Catholics who attend church in much the same proportions throughout the built-up area south of Moonah and at Bellerive. Sandy Bay even has a slightly lower ratio than the rest,

attributable perhaps to the greater built-in resistance of Sandy Bay residents to a fairly intensive pastoral ministry. Otherwise it is the residents of the inner low-income core who attend church the least frequently. But notwithstanding these minor variations all the suburbs south of Moonah display ratios about 50 per cent higher than those characterizing the low-density fringe at Claremont, Glenorchy, Lindisfarne and Montagu Bay. Significantly the poorest attendance of all is manifest by Goodwood, a government-housing area whose residents have mostly moved out from the center.

In marked contrast to the Anglican and Roman Catholic patterns the level of Methodist participation in church life tends to increase rather than decrease northward from the center. It may well be that as Methodists prosper and move out to the suburbs they tend more readily to conform by going to church. Certainly the lower-middle income suburbs of Hobart in which Methodists are especially numerous show marked social and economic aspirations. It is symptomatic that church attendance ranks high at Sandy Bay, for the congregations are drawn not so much from the high-income district to the south as from the lower-middle income areas of early twentieth century housing to the north. No inference can be drawn from the high ratio for Lindisfarne since the church is favored by Presbyterians and Congregationalists and it proved impossible to separate them entirely from the Methodist total.

Our field surveys have indicated that immigrants are more punctilious in attending church than are native-born Australians. This probably reflects not so much greater religious fervor as the role played by certain churches in the social adjustment of immigrants. That this might be so follows from our findings that British immigrants and the Australian-born appear to be indistinguishable in the proportions who attend church regularly though there are proportionately many more British immigrants than Australian-born who go to church occasionally. Among continental Europeans the Italians

TABLE 31.1 Population of cities with more than 20,000 inhabitants and the proportion born in Europe

CITY	POPULATION 1961	PERCENTAGE CHANGE 1954–1961	PERCENTAGE OF BRITISH-BORN 1961	PERCENTAGE OF CONTINENTAL EUROPEANS 1961
Sydney	2,183,388	17.2	8.2	8.7
Melbourne	1,911,895	25.4	8.1	12.8
Brisbane	621,550	23.7	8.4	4.7
Adelaide	587,957	21.6	8.2	12.5
Perth	420,133	20.5	12.4	9.2
Newcastle	208,630	17.1	6.4	5.1
Wollongong	131,754	44.5	11.4	15.7
Hobart	115,932	21.8	5.9	5.1
Geelong	91,777	26.4	7.3	13.5
Launceston	56,721	19.9	5.9	4.0
Canberra	56,449	99.6	9.6	14.2
Ballarat	54,880	14.3	3.9	5.4
Townsville	51,143	26.4	5.4	2.8
Toowoomba	50,134	16.2	5.5	1.5
Latrobe Valley	49,473	48.8	12.8	13.6
Ipswich	48,679	25.0	6.2	3.4
Rockhampton	44,128	8.5	4.1	1.1
Bendigo	40,327	9.2	3.1	1.6
Cessnock	35,281	−12.1	9.4	1.9
Gold Cost	33,715	70.2	8.9	2.7
Penrith	31,969	78.4	9.2	11.9
Broken Hill	31,267	−0.3	1.9	4.0
Blue Mountains	28,119	21.8	11.6	3.9
Maitland	27,353	6.6	2.4	4.2
Cairns	25,204	19.9	6.1	5.2
Elizabeth	23,326	—	42.3	7.6
Bundaberg	22,799	14.3	4.5	2.1
Wagga Wagga	22,092	14.9	2.9	3.2
Kalgoorlie	21,773	−4.7	6.9	7.5
Goulburn	20,544	7.1	3.3	2.5

TABLE 31.2 Variation in population size of the local government areas in the major cities, 1961

CITY	NUMBER OF L.G.A.'s	MEAN POPULATION	STANDARD DEVIATION
Sydney	35	61,775	36,350
Melbourne	46	33,699	27,034
Brisbane	57	10,904	5,830
Adelaide	21	27,998	21,727
Perth	19	22,112	25,032

TABLE 31.3   Age and sex ratios of the population in cities with more than 20,000 inhabitants, 1961

CITY	0–14	PERCENTAGE OF POPULATION AGED 15–64	OVER 64	CHILDREN 0–4 PER 1000 WOMEN 15–44	MALES PER 100 FEMALES
Sydney	26.3	64.3	9.4	425	97.5
Melbourne	27.8	63.4	8.8	468	98.7
Brisbane	29.2	61.2	9.6	481	96.2
Adelaide	28.9	61.3	9.8	470	97.0
Perth	30.5	60.8	8.7	495	95.4
Newcastle	29.1	62.6	8.3	488	100.7
Wollongong	31.6	63.5	5.0	541	112.9
Hobart	31.4	60.3	8.3	536	97.9
Geelong	31.8	60.4	7.4	534	100.8
Launceston	30.5	60.8	8.7	497	93.8
Canberra	35.1	61.9	3.0	594	110.3
Ballarat	30.6	58.6	10.8	540	94.8
Townsville	30.6	61.4	7.9	557	105.1
Toowoomba	31.1	58.9	10.0	497	93.7
Latrobe Valley	38.3	58.3	3.3	669	111.3
Ipswich	32.0	59.7	8.2	583	101.3
Rockhampton	30.4	59.9	9.7	515	96.2
Bendigo	29.7	58.4	11.9	542	92.4
Cessnock	30.0	60.2	9.8	497	99.1
Gold Coast	29.0	60.2	12.8	481	94.3
Penrith	36.8	58.5	4.8	436	105.5
Broken Hill	33.3	60.1	6.6	612	101.5
Blue Mountains	29.6	55.2	15.2	4	90.3
Maitland	31.7	60.2	8.1	533	99.2
Cairns	31.0	62.5	7.5	498	105.6
Elizabeth	43.9	55.3	0.8	778	104.1
Bundaberg	30.7	58.5	10.8	541	93.9
Wagga Wagga	31.9	60.1	8.0	536	95.0
Kalgoorlie	34.0	59.2	6.7	627	105.5
Goulburn	30.4	60.8	8.8	506	100.8

seem to be pre-eminent in good attendance, closely followed by the Polish Catholics and adherents to the Greek Orthodox and the Dutch Reformed Churches; groups seemingly very remiss are the Germans and especially the Lithuanians. Yet the North Hobart and Springfield samples, for instance, observed the same distinction in attendance levels as the inner and outer areas generally. Springfield residents attend church less frequently than North Hobart residents, the difference holding in varying degrees for Catholics and Protestants alike.

This lecture has outlined some of the salient features of the population structure of Australian cities. Foremost among these features have been many reflecting the impact of post-war immigration from con-

tinental Europe, an impact perhaps more pronounced economically and culturally than demographically. Yet many important facets of urban populations have perforce been excluded from review through the paucity of source data available and of research findings. These aspects include net residential density, occupational structure, the journey to work, social status, voting habits and the effects of governmental policy. However, the population census to be held next year may well furnish standard tabulations for the first time on the journey to work and on education and even perhaps income. Meanwhile research currently under way in Australian universities will throw much-needed light on the social areas of Canberra, Melbourne and Brisbane, and on

TABLE 31.4 Percentage of population by principal religious affiliations in cities with more than 20,000 inhabitants, 1961

CITY	CHURCH OF ENGLAND	ROMAN CATHOLIC	METHODIST	PRESBYTERIAN
Sydney	40.9	27.2	5.0	7.1
Melbourne	30.9	27.0	7.8	10.2
Brisbane	31.8	24.8	10.2	10.6
Adelaide	28.3	21.2	19.2	3.2
Perth	39.2	24.5	9.1	6.3
Newcastle	37.0	21.4	15.9	8.1
Wollongong	35.3	28.2	8.0	8.9
Hobart	48.3	21.1	7.7	3.7
Geelong	25.1	28.0	11.7	13.8
Launceston	44.3	16.9	13.6	7.3
Canberra	34.5	31.7	5.7	9.2
Ballarat	26.8	25.4	16.6	11.8
Townsville	31.5	27.8	12.8	10.7
Toowoomba	32.6	27.6	7.0	12.8
Latrobe Valley	30.6	26.0	8.8	13.9
Ipswich	27.4	20.4	13.3	10.3
Rockhampton	30.5	26.0	11.6	13.0
Bendigo	32.0	22.4	19.3	9.3
Cessnock	37.6	17.0	17.9	9.5
Gold Coast	40.3	18.5	9.8	11.9
Penrith	42.5	26.1	6.0	6.5
Broken Hill	19.5	27.3	31.1	2.9
Blue Mountains	42.5	21.8	7.5	9.3
Maitland	37.5	31.4	10.5	8.1
Cairns	30.8	29.9	10.3	12.0
Elizabeth	39.2	17.6	13.3	6.3
Bundaberg	31.9	17.9	12.5	16.4
Wagga Wagga	35.3	32.2	7.8	13.2
Kalgoorlie	33.3	28.3	13.9	6.3
Goulburn	39.9	36.2	5.2	4.9

the occupational structure of all Australian cities. Similarly research undertaken in connection with comprehensive transportation studies in most of the capital cities is yielding a wealth of new material, particularly on the daily movements of people. That the scope for research remains vast is evidenced by the numerous relationships posited in this lecture but requiring detailed quantitative testing

Some indication has also been given as to the nature and direction of our research on Hobart, though it has not been possible within the present context to pursue in depth the findings of the two surveys cited. Against a background analysis of census data—and on Hobart we have analyzed statistically most of the 1961 census by collectors'

districts—we are probing selected areas with restricted specific goals. In time we hope thereby to understand in depth the subtle patterns of selective differentiation and the economic, social and political links that make up the spatial interactions of a metropolitan community. For even though the population of Australian cities offers vast scope for large-scale geographical research, particularly at this time of rapid growth and cultural change, the need is to know more about those who make decisions as well as the sum effect of countless decisions on the demographic and cultural scene. Side by side with the statistically sophisticated study of the dynamics and attributes of population aggregates we need to know how selected groups of families as well as individuals live and move and have their being.

Acknowledgments

The writer's thanks are due to the following for kindly furnishing information: the residents of North Hobart and Springfield who responded to the home interview survey, particularly those displaced persons at Springfield who understandably responded with reluctance; Mr. D. Ryder-Turner who undertook the North Hobart survey; and the Hobart leaders of the Church of England, the Roman Catholic Church, and the Methodist Church in Tasmania.

References

Barcan, A. 1962 Education and Catholic social status. *Aust. Quart.* **34**: 47–61.

Borrie, W. D. 1954 *Italians and Germans in Australia: A study of assimilation.* Melbourne.

———1959 The growth of the Australian population with particular reference to the period since 1947. *Popul. Stud.* **13**: 4–18.

Congalton, A. A. 1961 Status ranking of Sydney suburbs. *Univ. N.S.W. Stud. Sociol.* **I**.

Goldberg, D. 1959 The fertility of two-generation urbanites. *Popul. Stud.* **12**: 214–22.

Jeans, D. N. and M. I. Logan 1961 The problems of growth in Sydney's new suburbs, *Aust. J. soc. Issues* **I**: 40–48.

Jones, F. L. 1964 Italians in the Carlton area: the growth of an ethnic concentration. *Aust. J. pol. Hist.* **10**: 83–95.

Lochore, R. A. 1951 *From Europe to New Zealand: an account of our continental European settlers.* Wellington.

Logan, M. I. 1962 Population changes in the Sydney metropolitan area. *Geography* **47**: 415–418.

Murphy, H. B. M. 1952 The assimilation of refugee immigrants in Australia. *Popul. Stud.* **5**: 179–206.

Price, C. A. 1957 The effects of post-war immigration on the growth of population, ethnic composition and religious structure of Australia. *Aust. Quart.* **29**: 28–40.

———1963 *Southern Europeans in Australia.* Melbourne.

Rose, A. J. 1958a Some social aspects of Australia's immigrant population. *Aust. Quart.* **30**: 56–70.

———1958b The geographical pattern of European immigration in Australia. *Geogr. Rev.* **48**: 512–27.

Taft, R. 1961 The assimilation of Dutch male immigrants in a Western Australian community: a replication of Richardson's study of British immigrants. *Hum. Relat.* **14**: 265–81.

Wilson, M. G. A. 1962 Some population characteristics of Australian mining settlements. *Tijdschr. econ. soc. Geogr.* **53**: 125–32.

Woolmington, E. H. 1958a Post-war immigration and industrial development in Australia. *Aust. Quart.* **30**: 77–8.

———1958b The distribution of immigrants in the Newcastle region of N.S.W. *Aust. Geogr.* **7**: 85–96.

Zimmer, B. G. and A. H. Hawley 1961 Suburbanization and some of its consequences. *Land Econ.* **37**: 87–93.

Zubrzycki, J. 1930 *Immigrants in Australia: a demographic survey based upon the 1954 census.* Melbourne.

A SELECTED SUPPLEMENTARY BIBLIOGRAPHY FOR PART 7

Augelli, J., "Cultural and Economic Change of Bastos, a Japanese Colony on Brazil's Paulista Frontier," *Annals of the Association of American Geographers*, Vol. 48, 1958, pp. 3–19.

Baum, S., "The World's Labour Force and Its Industrial Distribution, 1950 and 1960," *International Labour Review*, Vol. 95, 1967, pp. 96–112.

Davies, R. J., "Social Distance and the Distribution of Occupational Categories in Johannesburg and Pretoria," *The South African Geographical Journal*, Vol. 46, 1964, pp. 24–39.

Duncan, O. D., and Reiss, A. J., *Social Characteristics of Urban and Rural Communities*, 1950. New York: John Wiley and Sons, Inc., 1956.

Franklin, S. H., "The Age Structure of New Zealand's North Island Communities," *Economic Geography*, Vol. 34, 1958, pp. 64–79.

Isaac, E., "Religious Geography and the Geography of Religion," *Man and the Earth*, The University of Colorado Studies, Series in Earth Sciences, No. 3. Boulder: University of Colorado Press, 1965, pp. 1–14.

Keyfitz, N., "Age Distribution as a Challenge to Development," *American Journal of Sociology*, Vol. 65, 1965, pp. 659–668.

Lall, A., "The Age and Sex Structure of Cities in India," *Geographical Review of India*, Vol. 24, 1962, pp. 7–29.

Lowenthal, D., "Population Contrasts in the Guianas," *Geographical Review*, Vol. 50, 1960, pp. 41–58.

Preston, D. A., "Negro, Mestizo and Indian in an Andean Environment," *The Geographical Journal*, Vol. 131, Pt. 2, 1965, pp. 220–234.

Rose, H. M., "The All-Negro Town: Its Evolution and Function," *Geographical Review*, Vol. 55, 1965, pp. 362–381.

Schwartzberg, J. E., "The Distribution of Selected

Castes in the North Indian Plain," *Geographical Review*, Vol. 55, 1965, pp. 477–495.

Smith, T. L., "The Racial Composition of the Population of Columbia," *Journal of Inter-American Studies*, Vol. 7, 1966, pp. 213–235.

United Nations, Department of Economic and Social Affairs, "Demographic Aspects of Manpower, Report 1, Sex and Age Patterns of Participation in Economic Activities," *Population Studies*, No. 33, New York, 1962.

Wagner, P. L., "Remarks on the Geography of Language," *Geographical Review*, Vol. 48, 1958, pp. 86–97.

Wayland, S., and Brunner, E. de S., *The Educational Characteristics of the American People*. New York: Teachers College Bureau of Publications for the Bureau of Applied Social Research, Columbia University, 1958.

PART EIGHT

POPULATION AND RESOURCES

INTRODUCTION

The interest of geographers in the study of population most often manifests itself, directly or indirectly, in their investigations of the population-resource dichotomy. Numerous studies of this general type can thus be found in the geographic literature. Geographers, perhaps more than those from other disciplines, have had a long and abiding interest in the problems of population growth and resource adequacy. Such interest is a reflection of the breadth of geography which, although becoming more closely associated with the social sciences, maintains necessary ties with the biological and physical sciences. The outstanding contributions by geographers to the literature on the conservation of natural resources, rather implicitly within the population-resources nexus, serve to underscore the place of geography among the various sciences.

The contributions appearing in this volume represent an attempt to portray population-resource relationships within a limited number of pages. It is obvious from the selection of articles that the term "resources" is employed in its broadest context and is not confined to those aspects of the natural environment from which human needs and sustenance are directly extracted. While the several authors have focused their attention upon quite different aspects of the problem and have likewise chosen to do so at different scales, the many ramifications of the problem are brought into focus.

The questions to which these contributors address themselves are the same as those to which persons concerned with population problems in general are addressing themselves. This implies that geographers are beginning to study problems which have more nearly universal interest and practical application. The question of the role of technology in resource development, the impact of developing nations, and the kinds of problems which emerge as a result of rapid population growth at different scales, are all treated in this series of essays.

Blyn, in the first article in this section ("Controversial Views on the Geography of Nutrition"), differentiates between the terms "undernourishment" and "malnourishment." This accomplished, he proceeds to a brief discussion of the connection between population growth and hunger, and concludes by attempting to answer the question—what is the geography of hunger?

Ackerman, Zelinsky, and Gonzalez focus their investigations upon segments of the earth's surface of various size, moving from a view of population-resource problems in world perspective to those characterizing a single continent. Ackerman ("Population, Natural Resources, and Technology") has developed a population-resource typology, enabling him to specify and delineate a set of population-resource regions based on level of technological development and man-land ratio. He describes the interaction necessary to provide adequate food resources for each of the four elements in his model through the choice of certain strategies, thus highlighting the role of spatial processes.

Whereas Ackerman treats resource problems on a world scale, Zelinsky confines his comments on population pressure to the underdeveloped parts of the earth. "The Geographer and his Crowding Planet . . ." presents a well-organized, logically conceived set of arguments designed to refute, as Zelinsky says, the ". . . expectation that somehow, however late in the game it may be, the 'experts' will save the day. . . . The main burden of this essay is that there is as yet little grounds for such faith." The similarity of viewpoint between this article and some of those in Part 2 of this book is explicit and serves to emphasize the significance of the population-resource imbalance.

Gonzalez' timely article ("Some Effects of Population Growth on Latin America's Economy") investigates the principal dimensions of the problems arising from the population-resource disequilibrium in Latin America. After describing the changes taking place in the various sectors of the Latin American economy, vis-à-vis population growth, the author states that the people of Latin America must come to a decision regarding the path they wish to follow. That decision will certainly revolve around the following strategies: population control and technological development.

Selection Thirty-two

CONTROVERSIAL VIEWS ON THE GEOGRAPHY OF NUTRITION

George Blyn

This article deals with certain of the views expressed in J. De Castro's *Geography of Hunger*, 1952; M. K. Bennett's *The World's Food*, 1954; and the FAO *Second World Food Survey*, 1952.

Reprinted from *Economic Geography*, **37**, 1961, 72–74, by permission of the editor.

The effects of nutrition, or food intake, on the body may be divided between two aspects, its energy-yielding aspect, as measured by calories, and its health-protecting aspects, such as measured by vitamins and minerals. When the former aspect is deficient the condition may be called undernourishment; when the latter aspect is deficient the appropriate term is malnourishment. In place of such drab terms the emotion-quickening term, hunger, which combines, or confuses, both undernourishment and malnourishment, has come to be used in some recent literature in this field.

Thus when De Castro speaks of the geography of hunger he is not always, in fact he is not usually, referring to starvation in the sense of people with empty bellies. If he were, then perhaps his self-avowed revolutionary boldness, ranking himself with Freud, in bringing taboos out in the open, would be deserved. What De Castro calls hunger may in fact either be undernourishment, inadequate intake of calories, or malnourishment, which may be the absence of any of about forty food constituents needed to maintain health. Ohers connected with FAO, as is De Castro, also use the term hunger in this manner.

Bennett on the other hand reserves the use of the term hunger for the sensation which most people associate with it, and defines it, as it had been used in the League of Nations, as a condition in which calorie food intake is less than that required to maintain normal body weight when activity is normal. This is a critical concept which would appear to merit a distinct term to describe it, whether it be undernourishment or hunger.

The consequences of deficient levels of nutritional intake are far-reaching in their implications. Here De Castro's interpretations are at least interesting for their suggestiveness. It would seem, however, that at least some of the broad claims he makes for social consequences of dietary deficiencies are inextricably bound up with a variety of other forces so that proof may not be possible. Is malnourishment really the reason why the starving Latin-American allows his fields to be idle while he goes hungry? Is sex-play really the national sport of India, and is it because hunger-induced lack of energy, and scanty resources, have left them no alternative? Is the Chinese peasant hungry because he lacks the energy to make his fields more productive, rather than because of over-population?

Other supposedly significant aspects of hunger may be questioned, as has Bennett. The latter scoffs at De Castro's view that size of human body is a function of quantity and quality of diet rather than of genetics and race. De Castro says Chinese are small because they have been starved for past ages; Bennett says that it may simply be because they are a given variety of man, and the latter vary in size just as, for instance, the various kinds of dogs. Moreover, Bennett suggests, the interpretation of the statistical correlation between diet and size might well be the opposite of what De Castro claims. Bigger size, genetically caused, may have brought about the better and bigger diet of the larger peoples.

Of great importance is De Castro's claim concerning the connection between population growth and malnourishment. His view completely reverses the Malthusian concept. Population pressure does not cause hunger, but rather it is hunger that causes population pressure. This is explained by fertility allegedly varying inversely with protein intake. According to De Castro this is proved by animal experiments, although these do not seem to necessarily support his conclusion, and by a statistical correlation of 14 countries showing perfect inverse order of rank in birth rates and protein intake. Statistical correlation at best "proves" nothing with respect to cause. These statistics are, moreover, hardly the best. The number of countries is quite narrow. Fecundity would probably be a more meaningful measure than fertility. Neither the reliability of the statistics, and their range of error, nor the possible other causes for the ranking are considered.

The significance of hunger appears to depend on what is meant by hunger. Most of the world is said to be hungry. If this is a hunger of empty bellies, deficient calories, then the prospects are frightening in terms of potential political and military consequences. It would seem that the power given to FAO and such organizations would have to be drastically increased. This state of hunger is said to exist according to Boyd-Orr and FAO. But if the world's hunger is not one of empty bellies, but rather one of improperly balanced diets, then the urgency is of quite a different order.

What then is the geography of hunger? According to the FAO Second World Food Survey, all of Africa, Asia, and Latin America (outside the Plata countries) have deficient caloric intake. This is about two-thirds of world population. If, as Bennett insists, caloric deficiency must mean emaciation, then incredulity is not surprising concerning this vast claim of hunger. Bennett argues that the FAO underestimates caloric intake and overestimates caloric requirements in underdeveloped areas. When allowance is made for differences in body size and activity, and accurate account is taken of age and sex distribution, as well as climate, Bennett believes that the data would show intake at least equalling requirements. Sporadic deficiencies do occur but these are irregular in time and space.

Whether there is a geography of hunger in the sense of caloric deficiency may be disputed. But there is no disagreement that a geography of malnourishment certainly exists. This is the geography that De Castro describes. To describe this geography, however, requires more than merely classifying countries as between hungry or not on the basis of any evidence of malnutrition in the country. For on such a basis there becomes virtually no geography. All the world is hungry; there is no difference in this respect between national regions. Yet this broadside approach is used by De Castro; he says, for instance, "A few cases will suffice to prove that no nation or geographic area on the American continent is entirely free from the perils of hunger and malnutrition."

Some discrimination as to degree of malnutrition is needed in describing the geography. In many, if not most, countries, especially those likely to be ranked low in nutrition, there is insufficient direct evidence of nutritional intake to be able to establish this degree. Much of the classification is based on indirect evidence obtained by examining one ratio, the proportion of calories obtained from starchy staples, pre-

sumed to be low in health-protecting nutrients, in the total calorie intake. Inference of malnutrition appears safe when the ratio is very high, at least two-thirds, but this cannot be considered wholly adequate evidence.

The geography of both caloric deficiency, if there is any, and vitamin-mineral deficiency suffer from lack of regional discrimination within the national units. Whole nations are classified on a calorie basis according to the national average. However low that average is, there must be substantial elements of population with an intake below that average, as well as some above, and these are not apt to be uniformly distributed throughout a country. This geography, and demography, may be of equal or greater importance than that on the national average unit.

De Castro professes to a rosy view of the future despite the stark geography he draws. But if the conditions of achieving this happy state are as he sees them, then many others of us may be far from being so optimistic. National, or colonial, specialization in production of certain raw materials must be ended, according to his view. But such a change in economies will only partially remedy the present world "hunger." The economic system of present civilization, except perhaps in socialist or communist countries, is said to be rooted in hunger, and would also have to change. Even economics as a science must be revamped, from being a science of human misery, as he puts it, to becoming an instrument for balanced distribution of the good things of the earth.

Bennett's view is more conservative. He says that over a 50-year period, but scarcely in less time, the most glaring deficiencies could be eliminated. In that time there would be, however, no possibility of geographically equalizing nutrition at the present level of the advanced countries. The limited advance would depend on freedom from war and from economic "autarky."

While it is likely that economic development will improve nutrition conditions, Bennett suggests that it will not necessarily do so. It is not ponly overty that makes for malnutrition but also ignorance as well as people's preferences between foods. For the latter reason even wealthy countries may show nutritional deficiency. When income rises the consumption of sugar, fats, and highly refined grains rises; caloric intake increases but the quality of nutrition may decline. The intake of starchy food has declined

as income has risen in the United States; this is a favorable feature. One may wonder, however, what the change in diet composition will be in a country like India; as income rises will diet composition include more starches, from highly refined grains, as well as more fat and more sugar?

Selection Thirty-three

POPULATION, NATURAL RESOURCES, AND TECHNOLOGY

Edward A. Ackerman

L'ère du monde fini commence.
— Paul Valéry

The principal objective of this article is a portrayal of the role that technology may be expected to play in the future capacity of natural resources to support increasing numbers of people. "Natural resources" will be considered to include food-producing resources, the first concern of most human beings. We shall be interested in answers to two questions: (1) Can technology alleviate problems of population "pressure" existing in several regions of the world in the near future, and, if so, under what conditions? (2) What hope can technology provide for the support of the world's population over the long run, that is, indefinitely into the future?

Technology-source and Technology-deficient Regions

Nearly every literate person today is familiar with a journalistic distinction between the *developed* and the *developing* countries. This crude classification calls attention to technology. Resources become productive to men mainly through the medium of culture. The comparative state of a country's technology,

therefore, tells us something about the availability of its resources. The more advanced the technology, the greater will be the country's capacity to support people from the resources it has. But in addition to this, one must take account of the existing density of population and its potential natural resources.

Instead of *developed* and *less developed*, one may classify the world into *technology-source* and *technology-deficient areas*.[1] In addition there are areas with high population-resource ratios and areas with low population-resource ratios.[2] To complete the simple criteria of classification we should distinguish between the unproductive natural environments, like the deserts and arctic regions, and the actually or potentially productive, comprising the remainder of the earth's land area.

With these few criteria we can produce a simple but useful classification of the countries and regions of the world that reflects their population-resource relations and technology status: (1) technology-source areas of high population-potential resource ratios (European type); (2) technology-source areas of low population-potential resource ratio (United States type); (3) technology-deficient areas of low population-resource ratios (Brazil type); (4) technology-deficient areas

Reprinted from *The Annals of the American Academy of Political and Social Science*, **369**, 1967, 84–97, by permission of the author and the Academy.

of high population-resource ratio (India-China type); and (5) the arctic-desert type, technology-deficient and with few potential food-producing resources (Figure 33.1).[3]

On the basis of these simple distinctions some interesting observations can be made about the regional attributes of the world's population-resource relations. The most striking single observation is that more than one half of the world's people live in the technology-deficient areas with a high ratio of population to potential resources. Among the countries in this classification are China, India, Java and some of the other islands of Indonesia, Korea, Egypt, Pakistan, and Iran. Although data are incomplete, the best available observations leave no doubt that many millions of people in these areas are malnourished, particularly because of protein shortages, but also because of inadequate caloric intake. The probable daily average for most people in these countries is 2,100 calories or fewer, compared with the estimated minimum of 2,400 calories needed for health. Many of the 300–500 million people considered seriously undernourished by the Food and Agriculture Organization's Third World Food Survey live in these countries.[4] For all, there is the problem of resource adequacy, and the equilibrium that is kept between population and resources would appear to have a strong Malthusian element.

At least two-thirds of the total population of the technology-deficient countries live under natural conditions where vagaries of weather, particularly drought, cause notable fluctuations in the productivity of food-producing natural resources. These lands have little "cushion" to protect them against the inevitable fluctuations in natural productivity found in varying degrees throughout the world.

The remaining half of the world's population is divided about evenly among three of the other population-resource types. About one sixth live in the technology-deficient countries of low population-potential resource ratios. They are exemplified by much of Africa and Latin America. The principal problem of this group is the lack of immediate adequacy of employed resources, a condition from which they generally suffer because of technical deficiencies. Many people in these countries live near potentially productive resources, but they still exist close to the subsistence living level of the technology-deficient densely settled lands.

Another sixth of the world's population live in countries or regions where industrial organization and technology permit them to extend their resource base through world trade, thus effectively meeting the deficiency of their low domestic per capita resource production. These are the technology-source areas with a high population-resource ratio. The western European countries and Japan are illustrative of this group. Although their present position is relatively secure for available resources, they are vulnerable over the long run to competing demands from other lands for resources they now draw upon outside their own territory.

A final sixth of the world's population live in countries that are technically advanced and have territory that permits relatively low ratios of population to potential resources. The United States, important sections of the Soviet Union, Canada, Australia, and others come within this group.

Technology Transfer: the Case of a World System of Food Resources

If one starts with the simplest and most basic of all human needs, that of food, one finds a world in want, where a major part of the world's population lacks both adequate food and the technology that could promise to produce more food in the future. Furthermore, the problem of adequacy of present supplies is not limited to those countries that have a high ratio of population to resources. If one examines a map of comparative food intakes (Figure 33.2) he will see that low per capita intakes are spread throughout the technology-deficient area with little relation to population density-resource ratios. Every country with daily caloric intakes of less than 2,700 calories per person may be assumed to

478

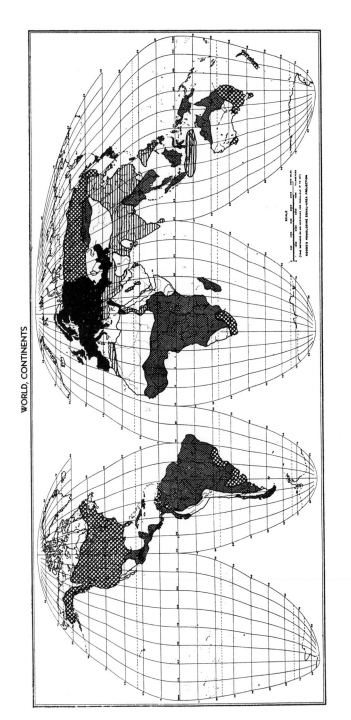

WORLD, CONTINENTS

1 European type (Technology-source; high population-resource ratio.)

2 United States type (Technology-source; low population-resource ratio.)

3 India-China type (Technology-deficient; high population-resource ratio.)

4 Brazil type (Technology-deficient; low population-resource ratio.)

5 Arctic and desert type (Technology-deficient; few food producing resources.)

Figure 33.1

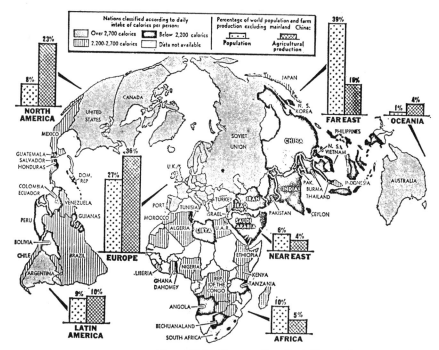

Figure 33.2 (Source: New York Times, January 24, 1966)

have a resource adequacy problem in supporting all or a major part of its population. Technology deficiency and adequacy of *employed* resources as distinguished from *potential* resources thus appear to be covariant.

What hope, if any, can improved technology offer to the technology-deficient lands, whose deficiency is reflected in unacceptably low living levels for large sections of their populations? For the time being we shall confine our discussion to the basic matter of food-producing resources.

There are four general ways in which technology can increase the output of food-producing resources: It can promote (1) an increase in yields of all food-producing resources now under exploitation, (2) the future employment of resources that are not now used, (3) conditions that permit adequate exchange of foodstuffs between surplus countries and deficit regions, and (4) the development of nutritional value from materials not presently serving as human food.

For the purpose of examining our first question—the capacity of technology to

alleviate problems of population pressure in the immediate future—it will be helpful to model the world roughly as a four-element system based on the types of countries identified above (Figure 33.3). The modeling of such a system would seem to be valid because some degree of responsibility has been recognized on a world-wide basis for the nutrition of all people. An accepted objective for the "system" is the production and distribution to each person in the world of enough food to permit a 2,700-calorie or greater daily intake, with an adequate share of the calories in protein form and adequate vitamin and mineral content.[5]

To simplify discussion of the model we shall assume that the technology-source countries of both low population-resource ratio and high population-resource ratio will provide sufficient food for their populations for an indefinite period in the future, either through domestic production or through foreign trade.

Achieving a minimally adequate diet for everyone may be viewed roughly as a communications problem. The food-producing resources of the technology-deficient coun-

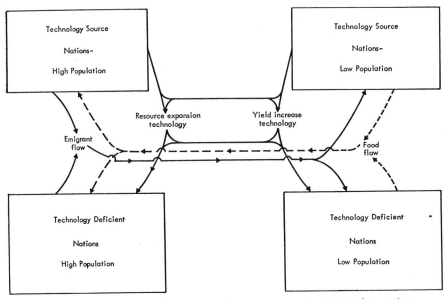

Figure 33.3   A sketch model of the world food production and consumption system

tries, with few exceptions, give yields far below standards set in the technology-source areas, and most of them lack adequate technical organizations to increase that productivity. Achieving food adequacy for every consumer is a matter of increasing the flow in four channels: (1) a flow of yield-improvement technology from the technology-source areas to the technology-deficient areas; (2) a flow of resource-expansion technology (cultivated-land addition and the like) from the technology-source areas to the technology-deficient areas with low population-resource ratios; (3) an increase in the flow of food from both of the low population-resource areas to the technologically deficient high population-resource regions; and finally (4) an increase in the migrant flow from the technology-deficient areas of high population-resource ratios to those of low ratios.

It is generally agreed that by far the most hopeful direction for increasing food production is to improve agricultural yields. The heart of yield improvement, in turn, is to raise the output of cultivated cereals, other grasses, and other plants.

The productivity of agricultural plants can be influenced basically in four ways: (1) manipulation of the genetic character of the plant, as in hybrid corn; (2) protection of the plant against diseases and pests; (3) improvement of water supplied to the plant, by manipulating natural soil moisture sources and by providing exotic supplies; and (4) addition of mineral nutrients to the soil.

For all of these, technical knowledge exists that can effect dramatic increases in the output of every major food crop in every technology-deficient country. For example, the yield of rice per acre in India in 1963 was only about 27 per cent that of Japan.[6] Furthermore, the rice output of India in the years 1960–1963 was only about 5 per cent greater than in the years 1936–1939. The yield trend for all grains in India is only slowly upward. Thus far, Indian yields are a long distance from the "yield takeoff" point shown in the agricultural history of the technologically advanced countries[7] (Figure 33.4). It is one of a number of ironies in the present-day world that the agricultural productivity of the technology-source areas is increasing more rapidly than that of some of the more populous technology-deficient areas. The "yield gap" between the developed and developing countries has been steadily widening.[8]

The technology flow from the source areas

CURRENT RICE YIELDS IN SELECTED COUNTRIES RELATED TO JAPAN'S HISTORICAL TREND

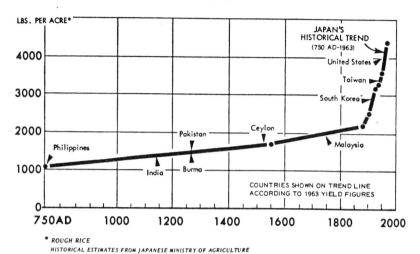

* ROUGH RICE
HISTORICAL ESTIMATES FROM JAPANESE MINISTRY OF AGRICULTURE

U.S. DEPARTMENT OF AGRICULTURE   NEG. ERS 3559–65(3) ECONOMIC RESEARCH SERVICE

CURRENT WHEAT YIELDS IN SELECTED COUNTRIES RELATED TO UNITED KINGDOM'S HISTORICAL TREND

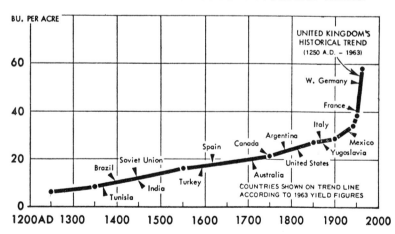

U.K. HISTORICAL ESTIMATES FROM H.I.. RICHARDSON IN OUTLOOK ON AGRICULTURE VOL. III NO. I. 1960

U.S. DEPARTMENT OF AGRICULTURE   NEG. ERS 3558–65(3) ECONOMIC RESEARCH SERVICE

Figure 33.4 Two examples of "yield takeoff" curves (Brown, op. cit., pp. 78, 81)

to the deficient areas thus must be termed generally disappointing in spite of sincere, consistent, and occasionally very effective efforts on the part of technologically advanced nations like the United States. In a way it has been remarkable, considering the sheer mass of the problem of improving the lot of two billion people, that even more serious deficiencies have not appeared. But the total flow of yield-improvement technology in the present system is still slow.

The reasons yield-improvement technology has moved slowly into the technology-deficient countries are found in conditions within these countries. Although every technical innovation involves an adaptation to national, regional, or local culture, the adaptations in agriculture are particularly difficult because of the enormous number of entrepreneurs (farmers) who must be reached in order to transfer the new techniques, and the great variety of local, cultural, and natural conditions in which they live. For the technology-deficient countries as a whole there are literally hundreds of millions of farmers.[9]

The problem of the large number of farmers in the developing countries is compounded by the level of literacy. An illiterate farmer is more difficult to reach and more limited in response than the literate man. About 1960 the level of literacy in India, for example, was only about 24 per cent, for Pakistan it was 15 per cent, and for some African countries it was even lower.[10] Literacy and at least some elementary education may be considered important prerequisites to any notable change in agricultural productive capacity. If we can estimate the time when the farm population of a country is more than two-thirds literate, we also have an estimate of the first date when important changes in agricultural productivity will be favored.

Other important determinants of the flow of yield-improvement technology in any country are production motivation for farmers, availability of capital for land improvements and equipment, and supply sources for equipment and fertilizers priced within the farmers' means. There is little point in introducing the farmer to ways of improving his production if he does not own his land or share in its ownership, or if he cannot obtain goods in return for surplus production. This, of course, is a many-faceted factor that runs from landownership reform to the efficiency of the country's economic distribution system. Like literacy and education it has universal applicability.

Fortunately, two of the important ways of increasing food production—improvement in

seed and plant stock, and protection of plants against diseases and pests—require relatively little capital.[11] On the other hand, capital requirements are heavier for food-supply increases through irrigation and other land improvement and for the provision of equipment and fertilizers. The most important single opportunity for increasing food production is through added fertilization, although it is most effective when added to improved plant stock. Parker and Nelson estimate that the food supply for one additional person can be provided through a capital investment of about four dollars in fertilizer plant.[12] This is not large in American terms, but considered in the light of population increases of billions over the next few decades it is a gigantic task in capital formation for countries where annual per capita incomes are $100 or less.

We might summarize the outlook for yield improvement in the technology-deficient countries in this manner: (1) The technology exists for vast improvements in the agricultural production of the technology-deficient countries; (2) there are few obstacles, if any, to the export of needed technology from the technology-source areas; and (3) the main obstacles to flow of technical improvements to the farmers of the technology-deficient areas lie within those countries. A higher level of literacy, economic systems that give farmers incentives to produce, and adequate capital formation appear to be keys to the situation.

Development of Additional Food-Producing Resources

The second important general means of increasing food production is to expand the food-producing resources of the world. This may occur through additions to cultivated land and pasture, through extension of marine and other aquatic cultivation, and through the development of synthetic plant environments (algae or other hydroponic cultivation) or of "chemical" foods. Of these, there is space to discuss only extension of the land area under cultivation.

There is little land left for the expansion of cultivation in all of the regions with a high ratio of population to resources, including both the technology-source and the technology-deficient countries. Indeed, a large proportion of the world's highest-quality agricultural lands adapted to the most productive farming is now in use. Nevertheless, important extensions of the cultivated land area are still possible in the United States, in Australia, in Canada, and in middle-latitude South America, through cereal production and other techniques of Western middle-latitude agriculture. Whether or not these lands are to be used will depend on the organization of the world's economy and political structure for the purpose of making the lands useful, through either foreign trade or migration.

There are other lands that might be made available for cultivation in middle-and low-latitude desert regions throughout the world, as adequate water supplies are discovered, developed, and applied to the land. At present they are limited by the extremely small water supply that may be expected for any of the desert and semiarid regions. Even an oasis like that of Egypt (population about 25 million) is modest in comparison with world totals of population.

The remaining land types within which potential extensions of cultivation may be considered are the podsolized soils of Canada and the Soviet Union, and the rain forest and savanna (wet-and-dry) environments of South America, Africa, Indonesia, and the southeast Asian peninsula. All suffer from low natural soil fertility, except in alluvial ribbons or pockets, where there are often drainage problems. The northern regions also suffer from a short growing season. Surveys and agronomic experimentation are needed to determine which lands are likely to be usable economically under known technology, and the capital demands for development appear huge. With some local exceptions, like the development of the Mekong Valley in Laos, Cambodia, and Vietnam, the best hopes for expanding production to meet the domestic needs of the technology-deficient low-population countries lie more immediately in improved yields than in land-use extensions. This opinion is corroborated by the recent experience of Mexico, which quadrupled its wheat yields with the use of the phenomenal new dwarf wheats between 1943 and 1963.[13]

The possibilities for extension of cultivation may be summarized thus: (1) Middle-latitude technology-source low-population areas—some tens of millions of acres are available in the near future if either migration or world trade can be so organized as to stimulate their use. Under present world trade and migration outlooks, however, few of these lands appear scheduled for use within this century. (2) Desert and semiarid areas of the middle latitudes and tropics—modest land extensions will be possible in the near future, depending on the availability of capital. The technology for development exists and is easily exportable, and new techniques for discovery and assessment of water supplies have materially expanded the prospect of development, but in world terms the potential additions to cultivated areas are very modest. (3) The lands of the podsolized areas of the North, and the rain forest and savanna lands of the tropics—except for some alluvial oases, these must be generally regarded as longer-range possibilities for expansion and cultivation in any great amount, probably beyond the turn of the century. A vast task of local exploration and of agronomic experimentation appears to be prerequisite if expensive failures and dislocations are to be avoided, particularly in tropical areas. Among the interesting aspects of developing the tropics is application of technology to extracting leaf protein.[14]

Technology and Food-Producing Resources: The Next Fifty Years

Those who seek exact projections of the capacity of resources to produce food to match the expanding population of the world in the future must inevitably be disappointed in the state of our knowledge. In many ways our existing data are filled with unknowns and imponderables. Furthermore, the very nature of technology, dependent as it is upon unforeseeable events in science, makes it one of the largest imponderables of all. The preceding discussion has deliberately eschewed an extensive presentation of statistical data. Can we then give any helpful answer to the first of the two general questions posed at the beginning of this chapter? Can technology alleviate problems of population pressure existing in several regions of the world in the near future?

Among the few relatively firm quantitative data we have are those on comparative yields of major food-producing crops throughout the world. The differences between technology-source and technology-deficient countries and the past rates of increase in yield in the technology-source areas suggest that a tripling or possibly a larger multiple increase of world food production from yield increases alone is not an impossible goal.

In 1962 the range between the highest and the lowest national average yields (major producing countries) was 8 to 1 for wheat, 6 to 1 for corn, and 4 to 1 for rice.[15] We know that the average yields of the leading countries are much below the yields obtained by the most expert farmers or the most progressive farming communities within the same nations. We know also that some developing countries have achieved striking increases in food production since the end of the Second World War; Mexico, Yugoslavia, the Sudan, Taiwan, and Thailand are examples. Theoretically, then, it should be possible to produce food for a sevenfold increase in world population upon the basis of improved production techniques.

But the *rate* of increase is probably more important than the range of total increase possible. Can technology in this instance keep up with the present 2 per cent per year rate of population increase? Superficially the experience of the past decade suggests that technology can keep up with the rate of increase of population. However, food production increases have not been in the same

places as the greater part of the population increases. The technology-source areas gained in per capita production during the past decade, whereas many of the technology-deficient countries, particularly in the Far East and Latin America, now have a lower per capita food production than before the Second World War.[16] The present trend is to place heavier and heavier dependence on the technology-source low-density countries for the food supplies of the high-population technology-deficient areas. The deepening food gap of the technology-deficient areas suggests that the rate of transfer of technology is not rapid enough.

It is instructive to look at the result of the only case history in agricultural development that seems a valid analogue for the technology-deficient countries. Since about 1880, soon after its modernization commenced, Japan has managed to maintain an increase in yield per unit area between 1.0 and 1.5 per cent per year. As will be readily noticed, this is below the 2 per cent annual population increase of the world, and far below the 3 per cent annual population increase of some of the technology-deficient countries. Can any of the latter countries be expected to improve the Japanese record of yield increases by 30 to 100 per cent? Among countries of this type the best record thus far has been that of Taiwan, which averaged 2.9 per cent gain per year in its crop yields between 1948 and 1963.[17] On the other hand, India and Pakistan averaged less than 1.0 per cent. Interestingly, the literacy rate in Taiwan is 57 per cent, and that in Pakistan and India 20–24 per cent.[18]

In candor it must be said that the outlook for yield increases of this order seems dim. Japan had achieved a 95 per cent literacy as early as the year 1900, and rapidly developed a domestic industrial capacity in response to opportunities in world trade. Furthermore, the tight cultural organization of the nation operated as a favorable institutional factor, promoting capital formation, among other things. There is no country among the high-density technology-deficient group today in which all of these conditions that favored

Japan are to be found, and some important countries have none of them.

We can only conclude that neither the record of Japan since 1880 nor the record of the technology-deficient countries during the last ten years should give us any high degree of optimism about organizing the flow of technology to support a yield increase of 2 per cent per year or greater in the most important technology-deficient high-population countries. Until formidable problems of raising the level of literacy have been surmounted, until capital formation is much increased in comparison with the present, until many institutional changes have been made, or until rates of population natural increases have declined, the flow of technology to increase yields is not as much favored as population growth.

An interesting test case is pending in the proposed wheat improvement program in Pakistan. It was hoped in 1966 that the introduction of the Mexican dwarf wheats and increased fertilization could make West Pakistan self-sufficient in this important food crop by 1970.[19] Such a dramatic change in the flow of technology, if achieved, will indicate that the literacy barrier has been successfully by-passed for the time being. However, other extraordinary alterations of factors influencing technology flow also seem to be required before the capacity of the technology-deficient nations to increase their production can be the principal stabilizing element in the world food supply.

Nonfood Resources

Within the space permitted in this article, food-producing resources were chosen for comment because of their obvious critical importance in the future history of the world. No other single natural resource or set of resources has the same critical significance. The distinction between the technology-source and the technology-deficient lands also applies to the use of other natural resources. However, there is a basic difference for nonfood resources as compared with agriculture. The outlook for the flow of new technology from the technology-source areas to the technology-deficient areas is more favorable for nonfood resources than for food-producing resources. The more concentrated nature of entrepreneurial organization for mineral and forestry production facilitates the technology exchange. In part for this reason, the capacity to export forestry and mineral products is increasing more rapidly in the technology-deficient countries than it is in the technology-source lands.

On the world-wide basis we should not anticipate any shortages in production from the nonfood resources that cannot be counteracted within a reasonable time by technology. Regional and local deficiencies of water supply in the deserts and drier parts of semi-arid regions must be excepted from this generalization. Techniques of recycling, substitution, and other devices for manipulating the flow and utilization of materials efficiently to match demand with supply, now seem to have a sound scientific backing. We can expect them to meet the challenges presented to them by a severalfold increase in world population. It is even possible that present nonfood resources will be able to supplement the present world sources of food output.

We now have completed a report on the first of two questions posed at the beginning of this article, even though it may not be an answer. The report was made in terms of a projection of standards of living prevailing in the world today, or modest increases thereof. Even under this assumption we have suggested that the outlook for technological improvement in food production at the same rate as the present rates of population increase is uncertain. If rates of population increase were nearer 1.0 or even 1.5 per cent rather than 2 per cent or more, the likelihood of a world food crisis within this century would be much lessened.

Outlook for the Longer-range Future

It is obvious that the world's population cannot go on increasing indefinitely even if the twentieth-century crisis is taken care of. The capacity of resources (including mere space) to support people must eventually come to an end. This is more than an academic question. Projecting the present 2 per cent rate of population increase could result in sixteen hundred billion people on the earth's surface at the end of a little more than two and one half centuries. This would be more than twelve thousand for every square kilometer of land surface on the nonpolar continents, a density greater than the central part of most Western cities. We may doubt that twenty square meters of the earth's surface would be enough to maintain the psychological health of an individual, even if there were adequate nourishment for him.[20] Thus, at that or some earlier point, the world would be faced with a definite deterioration in the level of living available to its inhabitants.

Yet, even today the tendency of the world's people is toward higher living levels for each individual wherever that is possible, and there can be little doubt that the much discussed "revolution of rising expectations" is touching a majority of the world's people. If the habits of past economically favored members of the human race are any clue, levels of living representing incomes many times those now available would be eagerly sought as soon as they were in the realm of reality. It is then even more obvious that resources cannot indefinitely support increases in levels of living of continually increasing numbers of people. The point at which the limit is approached ultimately, or at any given time, depends on the objective. During the last ten years, part of the world, almost entirely within the technology-source areas, has opted for increased levels of living. The other, and by far the larger part, the technology-deficient areas, has opted by force of circumstances for large numbers of people.

We conclude that although technology promises ultimate support of a world population several times that of today, the present rate of improvement in the flow of technology to the deficient areas must be greatly accelerated if critical problems of food supply are to be surmounted during this generation. We conclude also that resources, even in the hands of the most ingenious technology conceivable, have limits over the long term in their capacity to support people in increasing numbers and at high levels of living. Both the shorter-run situation and that of the longer term therefore have important elements in common. Action appropriate to the alleviation of shorter-run problems will also be compatible with long-range interests.

The capacity of resources and technology to support the world's people and improve their level of living now seems to depend significantly upon a number of ethical and political decisions, which leaders of political and social thought will do well to consider. Among them are:

Is a "natalist" doctrine ethically preferable to the "good life" for a nation or for a society?

Is the present commitment of technology-source nations to increase the flow of technology to the deficient nations deep enough?

How large a differential in level of living between nations is ethically and politically tolerable? A direct corollary question is: What proportion of investment funds available in the advanced nations should be dedicated to increasing the technology flow to the deficient areas?

How far is it the responsibility of surplus producers of food to support food export to hunger regions? How far is the market place the proper arbiter for world trade in food to meet minimum requirements of deficient areas? What *are* per capita minimum requirements?

How long are institutional obstacles to technologic change, like resistance to land reform, to be tolerated in deficient areas?

It is the answers to questions like these that will determine the future adequacy of technology and resources just as much as the progress of science and engineering.

Notes

[1]One indicator of technologic state is the number of patents granted for inventions. All but a very small percentage are to persons or organizations in the technology-source areas. Agricultural yields are another indicator.

[2]One available indicator of the population-resource ratio is the ratio of people to agricultural land. A rough dividing line between the low population-resource and high population-resource countries is about 0.6 person per acre of agricultural land in use. Most East Asian countries have one person per acre or more. See data in U.S. Department of Agriculture, *World Food Budget 1970*, Foreign Agricultural Economic Report No. 19 (Washington, D.C.: U.S. Government Printing Office, Table 6); and V. M. Dandekar, "Role of Food Aid Under Conditions of Rapid Population Growth," Meeting A-7, Table 1, *Second United Nations World Population Conference*, Belgrade, 1965.

[3]Classifications shown on Figure 33.1 are intended as generally illustrative. The boundaries of regions are generalized.

[4]P. V. Sukhatme, V. Schule, and Z. M. Ahmad, "Demographic Factors Affecting Food Supplies and Agricultural Development," Background Paper, Meeting A-7, *Second United Nations World Population Conference*, Belgrade, 1965, p. 13. See also U.S., Department of Agriculture, Economic Research Service, *Changes in Agriculture in 26 Developing Nations, 1948 to 1963*, Foreign Agricultural Economic Report No. 27 (Washington, D.C.: U.S. Government Printing Office, 1965), p. 3.

[5]The exact amount of caloric intake, even national averages, may vary somewhat according to climatic, physiological, and possibly other conditions. The minimum needed for health also is subject to some professional dispute. The 2,700-calorie intake may be slightly above the minimum adequate for health, but it cannot be counted as a diet with much excess food in it.

[6]303 kilograms as compared with 1450 kilograms (Lester R. Brown, *Increasing World Food Output*, Foreign Agricultural Economic Report No. 25, U.S. Department of Agriculture [Washington, D.C.: U.S. Government Printing Office, 1954], pp. 126, 128).

[7]*Ibid.*, pp. 78, 81, 126.

[8]*Ibid.*, p. 114.

[9]The United States, by comparison, has only a few million.

[10]Brown, *op. cit.*, p. 36; *Changes in Agriculture in 26 Developing Nations, op. cit.*, p. 15.

[11]F. W. Parker and L. B. Nelson, "More Fertilizers for More Food," *Symposium on Prospects of the World Food Supply*, 103rd Annual Meeting of National Academy of Sciences, Washington, D.C., April 25, 1966, p. 5.

[12]*Ibid.*, p. 3.

[13]Ignacio Narvaez and Norman E. Borlaug, "Accelerated Wheat Improvement in West Pakistan, and the Resolution of Agriculture," Office of the Secretary of Agriculture, West Pakistan, Lahore, 1966, p. 20.

[14]N. W. Pirie, "Leaf Protein as Human Food," *Science*, 152 (1966), pp. 1701–1705.

[15]Brown, *op. cit.*, p. 102.

[16]*The State of Food and Agriculture, 1965 (Review of the Second Postwar Decade)* (Rome: Food and Agricultural Organization, United Nations, 1965), p. 7.

[17]*Changes in Agriculture in 26 Developing Nations, op. cit.*, p. 15.

[18]*Idem.*

[19]Narvaez and Borlaug, *op. cit.*

[20]E. A. Ackerman, "Population and Natural Resources—Moderator's Statement," *Second United Nations World Population Conference*, Section B-10, Belgrade, September 1965.

Selection Thirty-four

THE GEOGRAPHER AND HIS CROWDING WORLD; CAUTIONARY NOTES TOWARD THE STUDY OF POPULATION PRESSURE IN THE "DEVELOPING LANDS"

Wilbur Zelinsky

If anything is safely predictable for the final third of this most complex, dynamic, and crucial of mankind's many centuries, it is that the management and consequences of rapid, massive population increase will engross the attention of more and more of

Reprinted from *Revista Geografica*, No. 65, 1966, 7–28, by permission of the author and the Comissão De Geografia, Instituto Panamericano de Geografia e Historia.

our best minds. Parallel with that ominously steepening arc graphing the total accumulation of human beings, there has been a recent upsurge of interest in such matters not only among social scientists but also among statemen and the public at large. For anyone who recalls with chagrin the apathy concerning matters demographic in places both high and low a mere twenty years ago, the current general consternation over the

"Population Explosion" is scarcely credible, and even a bit disconcerting. What is implied thereby is an expectation that somehow, however late in the game it may be, the "experts" will save the day with some brilliant panacea or technical legerdemain. The main burden of this essay is that there is as yet little grounds for such faith. The enormity and uniqueness of the huge Twentieth Century proliferation of human numbers has caught population scientists unawares, or at least technically and methodologically unequipped. I can say this with some assurance for the still rather underdeveloped field of population geography; but I suspect that the situation is not much better among demographers in general.

The basic argument can be stated quite simply: We are about to confront practical decisions of the utmost gravity in our social, economic, ethical, political, and ecological affairs brought about, in large part, by very great population increments in recent years in most inhabited areas and by the even greater growth forecast for the immediate future. Furthermore, theoretical problems of major interest and importance are being posed by the radically novel situations now coming into being. Unfortunately, our existing body of population doctrine was distilled from the experience of past or vanishing epochs of decreasing relevance to this strange new "crowded" world. Indeed, the inertia of ideas being what it is, we may find ourselves positively hindered in the scientific study of developing population pressures by some of our scholarly legacy or the related folk wisdom of the literate. As a contribution toward the more realistic, meaningful, and utilitarian theoretical framework still to be erected—a ground-clearing operation so to speak—I propose to examine eleven important ideas that are either explicit or implicit in recent statements and thought on population matters, and are also of some interest to geographers. It will be argued that all can be classed as either fallacies or unproved assumptions, the latter to be used with caution awaiting the time they can be either certified or discredited. The casual reader may infer congenital pessimism or malicious mischief in this approach. In actuality, the mood is one of painful self-scrutiny and the intent that of breaking through to deeper levels of understanding and ultimately to truly constructive approaches to the long-term welfare of our species and its habitat. In this process, it is necessary to concede that a lively appreciation of one's ignorance is the beginning of true wisdom.

Attention is confined to the so-called "underdeveloped" world, or "developing lands," more for the sake of convenience than through conviction. It is quite possible that the arithmetically less alarming rates of population growth in the advanced nations, combined as they are with virtually unlimited expansion of economic production and consumption and by more mischievous manipulation of the environment, may ultimately engender crises more pernicious and insoluble than those so visibly looming over less affluent countries. It is also arguable that both the ultimate causes and cures for the population/resource afflictions of the underdeveloped world are to be found in the advanced nations. Currently, neither proposition is so nearly generally accepted as the imminence of trouble in the former class of areas. And since a separate essay would be needed to validate these theses, the question of the advanced nations is bypassed reluctantly for the time being.

Before this review of dubious propositions can be begun, two premises must be stated: that a critical situation is indeed being produced in the developing lands by the amount and rate of population growth; and that, quite aside from the sheer magnitude of this expansion, the new sets of man-earth and man-man relationships that are linked to this growth are qualitatively distinct from anything that has preceded them historically.

Scientists are obliged to be skeptical creatures, by virtue of temperament and their professional charge. The sheer raucousness of some of the Neo-Malthusian canon and the fear-mongering of various journalistic approaches to the population problems of developing lands will automatically induce some students to assume that so much sound and fury may well signify nothing. Unfortunately, though the shriller criers of havoc may be doing their cause more harm, than good, the simple facts are incontrovertible.

There are many ways to indicate the severity of the approaching crisis, even, though, admittedly, we are still quite uncertain as to exactly what forms it will take or what the outcome will be. One device, as effective as any, is to consider the probable change in total population of the developing lands during the expected lifetime of children already born. For the following six, randomly chosen nations, I have projected the aggregate population that will reside in each at the time the average female inhabitant born in 1964 can be expected to die. These projections, based on 1964 population figures, the most reliable estimates of annual rate of increase for the same date, and the most recent data on female expectation of life at birth, are somewhat conservative. The indicated rate of change for 1964 may understate the true rate in some instances; in addition, mortality rates are susceptible to lowering, or are actually declining in some of these countries; and almost certainly the 1964 life expectation value in every case well exceeds that given here.

Thus we must quite soberly contemplate the prospect that an Egyptian girl born in 1964 will breathe her last in a nation containing over 132 million inhabitants. Given Egypt's present social and physical resources,

I find it impossible to imagine how so many individuals could live in reasonable material comfort without some truly revolutionary remodeling of the social and economic structure of the country. Such a development is, of course, not necessarily undesirable or impossible, but would be quite a feat during the next 54 years. The same argument applies to the other nations, although the immediate environmental constraints upon demographic growth are not nearly as great in Brazil, Costa Rica, or (outer) Indonesia. The dilemmas of large populations pressing upon limited immediately exploitable resources could be circumvented by a rapid reduction in fertility; but this too (unless implemented by brute force) would imply a rather implausible degree of skill in social engineering or incredibly good luck. The more probable alternative is a serious depression of level of living and a return to the former pattern of high mortality rates and low expectation of life. In any event, the status quo cannot be maintained; difficult, painful, and even disastrous alternatives must be pondered.

The argument that the present or impending population/resource situation of the developing lands is historically unique could be sustained quite firmly on quantitative grounds. Never before in human history has there been so rapid and persistent an increase in population involving so large a percentage of mankind; and, although there is little comfort in this fact, it seems highly unlikely that the experience can ever be

	POPULATION[1] 1964 (MILLIONS)	ANNUAL RATE[2] OF INCREASE 1964	EXPECTATION OF[2] LIFE AT BIRTH, FEMALE	PROJECTED POPULATION, YEAR OF DEATH OF AVERAGE FEMALE BORN 1964 (MILLIONS)
Brazil	78.8	+2.81%	45.5 (1940–50)	289.2
Costa Rica	1.4	3.82	57.0 (1949–51)	12.3
Egypt	28.9	2.73	53.8 (1960)	132.4
Jordan	1.9	4.08	50.0 (est.)	13.7
Indonesia	102.2	2.2	50.0 (est.)	302.5
South Korea	27.6	2.76	53.7 (1955–60)	125.9

[1]Population Index, 32:1 (1966).
[2]Population Index, 31:4 (1965).

repeated during a later epoch. The sheer mass and rapidity of this change would in itself induce major qualitative social and geographic innovations. But there are more fundamental reasons for the uniqueness of the developing situation. There is growing evidence that the current extraordinary demographic situation is but a single phase of a larger unique episode in human history —the phenomenon that has received the unfortunate, but probably indelible, designation "underdevelopment." Poverty, in many forms and degrees, has always been with us; and there have been earlier large, rapid, localized spurts of population. But the existence of large, impoverished masses of people undergoing rapid numerical increase for several decades is indeed quite unprecedented; and the profound disequilibrium between demographic growth and a relatively slow expansion or exploitation of physical and social resources appears to be symptomatic of some quite deep structural changes—possibly of a pathological character—in the nature and organization of human society. Thus the so-called "Population Explosion" is both a symptom of and a contributing factor to a much larger process, of which "Underdevelopment" is another relatively visible manifestation. This observation leads logically to the first of the ideas to be scrutinized:

1. **The fallacy that the population/resource disequilibrium of the developing lands is an isolated phenomenon, and the unproved assumption that it constitutes their single most important problem.**

The first portion of this statement is one that few thoughtful scholars would endorse, since it collapses the moment the real world is examined. Nonetheless, it merits our attention since this is a notion that much recent non-academic literature would tend to convey. There is also the ever-present danger that the population student may unconsciously slip into this fallacy when, as he often must, he disaggregates the fearsome complexities of social reality into manageable fragments. In any event, the image of a simple, stable underdeveloped community, idyllically undisturbed and unchanging for centuries, suddenly erupting demographically with the arrival of a few physicians, nurses, wonder drugs, and DDT is patently misleading. In almost every instance, the community had, for some time, been experiencing radical changes, either under the direct impact of the advanced nations or through endogenous processes initiated by such contacts. Thus a great many new things had been going on; and the rather abrupt onset of a decidedly lower death rate (and possibly also a significantly higher birth rate) came as the culmination of a whole series of changes, not as a whimsical trick of fate. Furthermore, the new demographic regime is associated with major revisions in socioeconomic and psychological patterns and with innovations in transportation, communications, education, and many aspects of technology. The interactions among all these are real and important; and this functional interrelatedness, which may frequently find spatial expression, is a quality that should endear the study of population change to the geographer.

A major reason for belief in this fallacy— or allegiance to the unproved assumption that population/resource disequilibrium, i.e. the "Population Problem," is the most urgent of problems in the underdeveloped world— is its exceptional statistical visibility. The number of inhabitants is probably the most widely available statistic for underdeveloped countries taken as a whole. Rapid change in this index can be detected quickly and easily even by the most amateurish of observers. On the other hand, it is reasonable to suggest, at least for the sake of argument, that even more momentous upheavals have been going on in the basic socioeconomic structure, in ideas, values, and attitudes, in the nature of the relations among communities, among individuals, and between man and the land, or even in the essential psychological makeup of the people—and that, in fact, one or more of these sets of changes comprise the truly central and decisive problem. If such is the case, then we are faced with problems of observation, measurement, and analysis that will tax our most resourceful social scientists. The more radical transformations that may underlie an abrupt demographic change could involve entities not easily quantifiable and, in any case, ones not immediately rising to any statistical surface. Least of all are they likely to reveal themselves in the visible landscape; and in much of the underdeveloped world revolutionary new generations of social and economic geographies may have reached an advanced embryonic stage and be ready for hatching within the shell of old, traditional vistas.

In brief, then, recent population growth in underdeveloped countries at a pace well beyond the demonstrated capacity of social and economic systems to provide adequately for human needs is a phenomenon inextricably bound to other less well observed, or poorly understood, ongoing processes. Until we learn the true nature and interrelations of this complex of processes, the chain of causes and effects, and the hierarchy of forces among them, there is no sound basis for claiming that excessive population growth is the most crucial problem confronting these areas.

2. The fallacy that any consensus exists concerning the kind of resolution to be sought for the population/resources problems of the developing lands (disregarding the means to be employed to attain this desideratum).

The discovery that the foregoing notion is indeed a fallacious one is probably more unsettling philosophically and more suggestive of future practical difficulties than any of the other negative or cautionary statements offered in this essay. Virtually every writer and social scientist who has been responsive to the demographic distress of the underdeveloped world has instinctively adopted the idea that he, or the people concerned, clearly visualizes the sort of normalcy, the demographic or economic good health to which the community must

be restored. In actual fact, almost no methodical thinking has been done on this crucial issue.

A rough medical analogy may be in order. Imagine that some students of natural history had acquired in a young, immature form the only known specimen of some rare animal species, one that had never been observed in its adult stage, and were attempting to rear and study it in captivity. During this process, this unique organism has contracted a serious chronic disease, one which finally becomes acute, produces serious malformations, and threatens the life of the creature. All the attending veterinarians agree that everything possible must be done to save it. They have succeeded in describing the symptoms and are able to speculate intelligently on probable diagnoses and causes. Several possible courses of treatment suggest themselves. They have, of course, never previously been applied to this particular animal; and although it is not certain whether any of the possible therapies will be efficacious, it is agreed to try the most promising one. At this juncture, one of the more reflective veterinarians points out that during the course of his illness their patient has apparently entered the adolescent stage and may, in fact, be on the verge of full adulthood. How are they to tell just when the treatment has succeeded, i.e. when the creature begins to look and act like a healthy, normal adult of its species? How can they be sure that, although the therapy may save its life, it may not also produce a permanently crippled, abnormal organism and, incidentally, spoil forever their earlier plans for studying its behavior and biological characteristics?

As we leave our imaginary friends with their unresolved quandary, it must be admitted that this is a defective analogy. Strictly speaking, no discussion of either immediate action or ultimate results is absolutely necessary in the case of "runaway" population growth in the underdeveloped lands. It is simple to demonstrate mathematically that the problem is self-limiting, that within a very few generations the current rate of growth must come to an end because of the finiteness of terrestrial mass and space and the existence of certain basic physical laws. And the patient will not necessarily die if left unattended. Even though the final results may be most unpleasant, the prognoses are, in order of declining plausibility, an arresting or reversal of growth through (a) a death rate rising well above present levels, (b) a spontaneous decline in fertility, or (c) any of the many possible combinations of the two foregoing changes. The countries passing through this experience of letting their population crises run its course may find themselves subsisting under wretched conditions; but the population will have survived somehow.

Many of the affected countries still remain at the stage where the problem is unrecognized or where, through disinterest, indecision, or positive choice, a laissez-faire policy is being followed. But more and more—and eventually possibly all—will agree that it is desirable and urgently necessary to avoid major catastrophe. And that, finally, returns us to the main point of this discussion: Is it possible to adhere to a policy that limits itself to the purely negative objective of substantially reducing rates of population growth? It seems much more intelligent, more commonsensical tactically, to recognize that, willy-nilly, such a policy will result in a country basically different from what it has been, or that the negative program is more likely to be consummated if it is combined with a positive push toward useful and desirable goals. The status quo ante cannot possibly be patched together again. And so what sort of world are we getting in its stead? Or what sort of world **can** or **should** we strive for?

We are, in fact, being coerced by the huge, inexorable mechanism of the "modernization" process into thinking seriously about which utopias, or sub-utopias, or reasonable facsimilies theoreof, we can put on the drawing boards. It is even conceivable that this compulsory review of means and ends may be a blessing in disguise. Gone are the leisurely days when history took care of

itself. Until recently, one could hopefully contemplate the autonomous forces of social and economic change propelling mankind forever forward and upward along the erratic, but ascending, paths of Progress toward some glorious, if rather indistinct, destiny. Now it is abundantly clear that active, skillful human intervention is mandatory for survival or for the qualitative enhancement of human existence.

No agreement has been reached, and none is possible without great difficulty, over the goals—the signs of returning health—that might be striven for in any campaign to deal with extremely rapid population growth. Or perhaps the issue has already been settled tacitly. Many writers claim that the underdeveloped countries have been undergoing a "Revolution of Rising Expectations" (though without much specificity as to what is being expected). It is not really clear, and certainly has not been verified by any rigorous research, that any truly fundamental revision of material appetites or life-goals has taken place; but if it has, these new values must be reckoned with in any demographic programs. In any case, what aspirations can be proclaimed concerning the size, composition, dynamics, economic status, environmental ecology, or any of a variety of relationships between man and physical and social resources in the populations that will have survived their period of trauma? Even more basically, which (or whose) values—cultural, philosophical, or whatever —are to be preserved and strengthened? What of our obligations to other species of life or to the quality of the inanimate environment? For whose benefit are plans to be made and implemented—for that of the locality, the nation, or all of mankind? Or for which segment of the population— the business community, the military, the administrative bureaucracy, the intelligentsia, or the "common people"? And for which generation—those who are now alive, or their children or grandchildren? Or do we think in terms of perpetuity? These are profound questions of intent to be debated, questions of scale, duration, conflict of interest, and philosophic bias. I would suggest that the time has arrived when we should begin asking them.

3.   The preoccupation with population numbers as items of essential importance per se.

Population scientists are so accustomed to dealing with statistics as a useful surrogate for the reality with which they are, in fact, truly concerned that they may impute to them an importance not actually inherent in them. More specifically, scholars, and many laymen as well, may tend to view population/resource problems in the light of numerical indices rather than the grosser, and partly unmeasurable, world that underlies them. It is self-evident that for any given area or community a particular population size is not absolutely good or bad in itself as long as it stands somewhere above the minimum needed for biological and cultural survival and below that maximum where sheer physical congestion inhibits the movement or physical and mental health of individuals. The statistic is important, of course, but only takes on meaning in the context of specific conditions and specific value systems (even though, incidentally, it is extremely difficult to assign hard numerical values to the concepts of "underpopulation," "overpopulation," or "optimum" population even when all the facts and assumptions are open to inspection). In the same vein, no specific rate of population change is necessarily good or evil—unless it is prolonged to the point where the population either disappears or expands to calamitous dimensions. Thus, during a limited time span, population growth or decline, or stasis, or a complex cycle of change may be good, bad, or indifferent, depending on the character of the place and the period. An annual net reproductive increase of $+4.0\%$ or thereabouts in Kentucky in 1790 was an occasion for rejoicing; in El Salvador in 1990 it could be disastrous.

Excessive preoccupation with population counts may lead to treatment of symptoms rather than causes. We may find ourselves worrying over how to slow down the annual population increment in some area from 3% to 1% or less, while omitting any real concern about gains or losses in human and social values. Conversely, the absence of any perturbations on the demographic fever chart may lead to a false sense of well-being. A stable population is not necessarily happy or a fundamentally healthy one. Just as we can delude ourselves into believing that all is well with the body politic if the citizens are not actively rioting in the streets, so too it is possible to postpone dangerously any serious investigation of the population/resource situation in a region that seems stationary in its behavior.

4.   The fallacy of demographic predestination—the belief that mankind is moving teleologically toward a happy resolution of its population problems or, conversely, directly toward demographic doom.

This is a fallacy that is much more likely to be implicit, or sometimes even subconscious, rather than explicitly avowed by the student. It may be the result of belief in supernatural forces or simply a matter of temperamental outlook. The scholar is, of course, entitled to harbor his own private credo, whether it be melioristic or fatalistic, but should guard against letting it warp his judgment when attempting to deal in systematic, scientific fashion with the facts at hand. In particular, there is genuine danger that this kind of innate bias may predispose the population scientist to write as though man were either utterly impotent or else all-powerful in grappling with his demographic destiny. As it happens, no very convincing evidence is yet visible in the pattern of history or the innate logic of current facts to support belief in either brand of teleology—the inevitable ascent of mankind to higher levels of social and geographic grace or the imminence of Doomsday. Is it not the better part of wisdom for the population scholar to take nothing for granted, but rather proceed to test the limits of the necessary and the possible through careful observation and analysis and through the design of action programs that are not circumscribed by unproved, a priori assumptions?

5. The fallacy that the population/resource problem in developing lands is simply one of adequate food production.

This is a fallacy that is widely and explicitly current in both the scholarly and popular literature on demographic problems. And since food production is a favorite subject for geographic investigation, geographers may be particularly vulnerable to it. It is, of course, axiomatic that the day-to-day problem of feeding most of the low-income citizens of low-income lands is a matter of large, lasting concern. During the millenia when most communities were small, self-contained, non-monetary economic units operating outside any large regional or world market, local food production could indeed be the paramount problem in survival: and insofar as population/resource crises appeared, food shortages might be cause or effect. But it does not follow, now that all the world's peoples are more or less integrated into the world market economy, that either the population/resource problem or the phenomenon of underdevelopment can be defined solely, or even primarily, in terms of the calories people consume or how much food they can grow. To see them as such, even at the rudimentary level of immediate human needs, is a gross distortion of reality, a sort of alimentary determinism.

For his animal survival, man everywhere requires food, potable liquids, and breathable air and, in those areas with winters or cold nights, clothing, shelter, and domestic fuel. But even the most primitive communities have other needs; and in those lands that can be realistically called "developing," there is an imposing inventory of necessities. Industrial fuel and energy requirements must be met; a wide range of industrial raw materials is called for; various services— among them, transportation, education, and administration—must be supplied; and the amenities are in ever increasing demand.

Indeed, as the country climbs up the developmental scale, the problem of producing and supplying food recedes as other problems come to the fore; yet population/resource crises may still occur. Indeed, I believe it is possible for even the most advanced of nations to anticipate severe population/resource situations in which the issue of food supply may be totally irrelevant. And the irrelevance of food production as the critical element in population/resource imbalances may also be demonstrated in those various countries, past or present, that have produced food surpluses but, nonetheless, have displayed acute symptoms of "underdevelopment" or of an incapacity to provide for the wants of rapidly increasing populations.

A country may be said to have mastered its population/resource problems when it is living within its own technical, institutional, and ecological means and at the same time offering its inhabitants the wherewithal for acquiring all the goods and services they regard as basic for a decent existence. This "wherewithal" simply means purchasing power. And money, in turn, implies the existence of reasonably well-paying jobs for all, or nearly all, the labor force, and a labor force with a reasonably high level of productivity, or, more precisely, the capacity for producing in abundance goods and services other people wish to buy. Where a market demand exists, in the form of would-be purchasers willing and able to spend money, food or any other commodity can be furnished to the inhabitants of either underdeveloped or advanced countries from either external or internal sources.

It is quite inaccurate to characterize an area as suffering from "population problems" if it does not produce all the foodstuffs it consumes. (Most advanced nations would fall into this class.) It is equally erroneous to believe that an underdeveloped land experiencing food shortages will shed its status as an area undergoing population/resource problems simply by importing or producing more food—unless the augmented production yields a marketable, transportable surplus that will generate capital for the developmental process. This is not the solving of a problem, but simply the temporary staving off of starvation or malnutrition. In any case, it is unfair to expect the underdeveloped lands to be what nearly all the advanced nations are not—self-sufficient in the basic raw materials for human existence.

Even on a planetary scale, the availability of food cannot be said to be an essential issue in present or impending population/resource crises, at least for the next few generations. If consumers in the underdeveloped areas were, through some magic, to acquire instantaneously large amounts of cash for food purchases or, better still, the negotiable goods and services which such cash represents, the nations possessing advanced agricultural techniques could probably double, or perhaps triple, their output of foodstuffs within the next few years, using currently known techniques and capital equipment already on hand or readily obtainable. And it is quite thinkable that this brisk demand might also induce farmers in the less developed countries to extend and upgrade their activities and vastly increase their output. It has been estimated that if all the world's present and potential food-producing surfaces were exploited to maximum capacity, using current technologies or those that can be reasonably anticipated for the future, it should be possible to feed as many as 50 billion persons. We are ignoring, of course, the supply of other physical and social needs or the quality of human existence that would result from such singleminded agricultural zeal.

Thus, until a genuine impasse in agricultural expansion is reached, the real problem is employment and productivity, how an underdeveloped society can rearrange and revolutionize its socioeconomic structure so that its citizens can produce enough goods (including edibles, but certainly much else besides) and services that can be exchanged with other peoples for other goods and services and thus also, one hopes, make life comfortable, purposeful, and interesting. Unfortunately, the steps whereby these revolutionary changes are initiated are still rather mysterious; and there is no guarantee that any country can enjoy such a transformation just by wanting and struggling for it. However, anything else, including the simple expansion of food production for subsistence within the traditional economy, will not provide a way out of the economic dilemma faced by such areas; at best, it would merely postpone the crucial period. In summary, then, population/resource problems in developing lands can be neither defined nor solved solely in terms of food production.

6. The unproved assumption that processes already in operation will rid the developing countries of their population/resource problems.

Under this dubious proposition, we can group several rather different notions, but ones that all imply strong faith in some deus ex machina or in the long-term rightness and equilibrium induced by the autonomous workings of basic geographic, social, economic, and political processes. They are thus not unrelated to the teleological dogma discussed above as Item 4. Perhaps the most interesting and attractive of these various sub-assumptions is:

(a) The unproved assumption that rapid, massive population growth under contemporary conditions will of itself trigger major economic advance or, at least, contribute materially to its success.

The chief inspiration for this notion is, of course, the fact that among the advanced nations both phenomena—rapid growth and qualitative change in the economy; and a great expansion in the population—have been roughly concurrent. Furthermore, under certain conditions, within these same countries, it is clear that population growth is a positive stimulant to the economy. But it would appear that this is a dangerous analogy as applied to the underdeveloped countries. Although the two events do much overlap in time, the evidence indicates that it was significant economic innovation that tended to precede the demographic revolution, not the other way around. An even greater difficulty is the fact that the preconditions for both demographic and economic growth in the advanced nations were so strikingly different from those prevailing in the currently "developing" lands. In brief, then, there is as yet no well-authenticated instance in modern demographic history of rapid demographic growth in any sort of country preceding, or becoming one of the significant reasons for, basic improvements in the economy. It is true enough that such might seem superficially to have happened in Hong Kong, Taiwan, Puerto Rico, Jamaica, Mexico, and Venezuela; but I believe that the facts indicate quite the contrary in each case—that large population increments have been economic hindrances or, at best, of neutral value.

It is not impossible that rapid population growth may become the main instrument for significant economic advance in some underdeveloped land in the future; but for the moment we have no proof that this has ever happened or that it is likely to happen. It is, of course, also possible that an awareness of rapid population growth may precipitate a course of action leading to economic progress; but this is quite another matter.

There are persuasive arguments, as put forward by Ester Boserup [**The Conditions of Agricultural Growth; the Economics of Agrarian Change under Population Pressure** (Chicago, 1965)] for a related hypothesis— that sustained, relatively slow population growth may have been the prime genetic factor in bringing about the intensification of agricultural output per unit of land and, ultimately, radical changes in land-use systems and a complex train of consequences in the spheres of social and political behavior. There may be much truth in this argument (although I suspect that the actual situation has been rather more complicated and ambiguous than such a simple one-way cause-and-effect formula would indicate); but the author is careful to refrain from any claim that her idea is valid for places currently undergoing rapid rural population increases.

(b) A mystic belief in national salvation through the more or less spontaneous development of "great, untapped natural riches."

This amounts to a visceral feeling rather than any coherent doctrine, and is simply faith in the prospect that somehow through the exploitation in some unspecified ways of natural resources, whose nature and extent are at best quite approximately surveyed, the nation will arrive at some unspecified answer to its demographic, social, and economic worries. A careful inventory of possibilities and a detailed set of working plans for their realization may or may not be necessary eventually; but they are incidental to the central article of this faith: the transcendent goodness and wonder-working nature of these as yet untouched gifts of Nature. Although this sort of feeling will not withstand logical analysis, it is influential among large sections of the general population, as well as the governing élite, at least in Indonesia, Mexico, Guatemala, Brazil and other nations sharing the Amazon Basin, and in several African nations.

(c) Present and future pioneer settlement as the way out of the demographic dilemma.

This notion is, of course, closely related to the preceding one. And it is also a most appealing option in the diminishingly few underdeveloped countries that do still have any considerable amount of land suitable for pioneer settlement—particularly in the light of the historical experience of Anglo-America, Siberia, Australia, Argentina, and a few other areas where rapid frontier advance seems to have had a salutary effect upon the national welfare. Unfortunately, only a few realistic observations will quickly deflate one's confidence in the frontier as the great hope of underdeveloped nations suffering from population pressure upon available resources. Recent experience indicates that the supply of empty land meriting any sort of capital input under present conditions is quite finite and likely to be exhausted rapidly, that (with the one, quite temporary, exception of Costa Rica) the frontierward migration removes only a minor fraction of the redundant population from overcrowded areas, that these frontier zones contribute little, if anything at all, to the net worth of the national economy of underdeveloped lands, and that where, as so often happens, unplanned or unsupervised settlement occurs the effects may be most deleterious to the habitat and to its agricultural and general biotic productivity. However, this is not to deny the possibility that pioneer settlement may be a most useful and profitable device as part of a larger, well-organized national development plan.

(d) The continuing export of permanent or temporary emigrants to foreign lands as a demographic "safety valve."

There is little doubt that this device has worked well to alleviate population pressures in a number of smaller nations or dependencies. Among those that come readily to mind are Jamaica, Puerto Rico, several of the Lesser Antilles, the Azores, the Canary Islands, Algeria, Malta, Syria, Lebanon, Greece, and Western Samoa. In these cases and others, there are two obvious advantages: the immediate reduction in the ranks of the unemployed or the underemployed; and the return flow of remittances from abroad. But there is one major drawback. Those most likely to leave are usually those who are also the least expendable—the skilled, well-educated, and ambitious—precisely the persons most needed to man the growth points in the national economy and infrastructure. Mass emigration is, in any case, not a valid general solution, and least of all in those countries with more than a very few million inhabitants. It is ludicrous even to think of it in connection with the Chinese, Indians, or Pakistani, or even the much smaller Egyptian population. And it is the most irresponsible, pseudoscientific sort of folly to suggest extraterrestrial outlets for potential emigrants.

Even the maintenance of the **status quo** may be difficult for the various smaller areas that are postponing a basic solution to their population/resource difficulties through vigorous emigration. The historic trends of the present century point clearly to further restrictions on international movements of migrants not to their relaxation. Even where the channels are left open for small, but crowded, lands enjoying a privileged political or economic relationship with a larger, more affluent patron, the relative demand for unskilled labor is likely to shrink, while the flow of the skilled and semi-skilled may quicken, to the benefit of the latter and detriment of the former.

(e) The transfer of redundant population from rural tracts to urban centers as a major contribution toward the solution of population/resource problems.

The urbanization process is well begun and rapidly accelerating in nearly all underdeveloped lands. Thus, if this cityward movement does indeed offer much hope as a way of eliminating population pressures, it has the added advantage of calling for little artificial encouragement. Largely for lack of sufficient research, we know much too little about the economic and demographic conquences of rapid urbanization in the underdeveloped world. The few broad generalizations that can be offered, however, do little to support the stated assumption. In virtually every instance, the removal of migrants from countryside to town or city is much less rapid than the natural increase of rural populations. Although the availability of social services and amenities may be greater in the cities, it has yet to be demonstrated that, as a general rule, the chances for full employment are greater or that real incomes are significantly higher in an urban milieu. There may be certain cost-saving advantages for the national economy in the centralization of skills and markets; but there are also severe strains upon poorly developed supply systems. Thus we may be rapidly approaching the danger point in the logistics of water, food, fuel, and raw materials in several large metropolises, not to mention grave difficulties in waste disposal and the provision of vital social services.

Another disappointment is the finding that the depression of fertility rates has been much less in the metropolises of developing lands than in their counterparts in advanced nations. The urban birth rates, though appreciably lower than in the countryside, are still high enough so as to ensure a vigorous growth of city population even without further recruitment of rural migrants. Thus, as with pioneer settlement, the urbanization process is far from a complete answer, even though it may well play a significant role in a larger, more effective program.

(f) The belief that many demographically distressed underdeveloped lands can survive indefinitely through charitable contributions from the richer nations.

This is a doctrine seldom proclaimed publicly, but one implicit in the actions of the client countries. In a sense this notion underlies all the various aid programs in the developing lands financed by a few rich nations, but with the critical distinction that most of such programs are intended to be catalytic in effect, to furnish "seed money" for what will hopefully become self-sustaining socioeconomic processes rather than a long-term dole. The simple facts of world economic life are adequate prima facie evidence that, even with a maximum effort on the part of the donors, international alms would suffice for only a few fleeting years to support all countries who are acquiring more inhabitants than they are able to provide for. There is little doubt, however, that for a few small, poorly equipped areas—among them, Malta, Okinawa and other Pacific islands, the Gaza Strip, the Netherlands Windward Islands, and French Guiana—present and future survival is contingent upon the uninterrupted flow of outright subsidies. It is also clear that foreign subsidy, though often in disguised form, is a large component in the economic life of many other dependent territories and nominally independent nations; and it is possible that their ranks may swell rather than dwindle during the next few decades.

(g) The fallacy that through the age-old more or less "normal" institution of warfare, a reasonable balance between people and resources can be restored.

This doctrine, one that only rarely erupts into print, but unquestionably lurks in the minds of many individuals, is shaky on some fundamental points. First, there is little evidence that, in the past, warfare has been a **major** long-range determinant of population size among human communities, except among those small, relatively primitive tribal societies for whom a rather ritualized form of battle has been the major outdoor recreation. Secondly, the extension of European economic and political control over nearly the whole of the non-European world during the past few centuries has resulted (despite some notable lapses) in the gradual imposition of a **Pax Europaea** on those areas. Furthermore, the structure of the modern world has become such, specially during the past 20 years, that general agreement seems to have been reached, however tacitly, that military conflicts within and among the underdeveloped nations will be suppressed or contained, the alternative being devastation and bloodletting on an unimaginable planetary scale. In short, as a demographic constraint, mid-20th Century warfare appears to be a cure much worse than the disease.

The fallacy posed above is quite patently a variant of another subterranean notion, seldom uttered aloud in politer academic circles, that perhaps, after all, it is best to be "hard-boiled" and realistic about the situation and let the imbalance between people and resources take care of itself by doing nothing to avoid a rebounding of mortality to pre-modern levels in the underdeveloped areas, or by even actually encouraging the restoration of the old demographic regime. When it is objectively reviewed, however, this policy fails to make any sense on social, economic, or political grounds, quite aside from moral considerations.

(h)   The fallacious hope that the traditional, approximate balance between births and deaths can be maintained in the last few areas beyond the reach of the modernization process, or that somehow the developing countries can reverse course and return to the simple, equilibrial demographic ways of the past.

This nostalgic aspiration has no basis in fact. Again what we have is hardly a coherent, articulate doctrine but rather a set of emotions that do not altogether reach the surface of conscious deliberation. But this is an attitude that may well have affected the treatment of relatively primitive folk within certain advanced nations as well as the handling of relatively retarded communities within the developing lands. Unless another small, remote tribe or two still remains to be found in New Guinea, northern Australia, or some obscure recess of the Amazon and Orinoco basins, all of contemporary humanity has been launched upon the modernization process, with all that that implies in a demographic sense, as well as in other ways. Furthermore, there is a great mass of evidence proving beyond any reasonable doubt that this is an irreversible process. Thus there is no way of erasing the impact of the advanced nations upon the underdeveloped, to make people forget what they have learned and shun the Great World, or to declare a moratorium on change. The question is not whether the peoples of the developing lands must move forward, but rather how, at what rate, and toward what specific destinations.

7.   The unproved assumption that rapid population growth per se will damage man's habitat.

This widespread idea, which is, of course, of peculiar interest to geographers, rests precariously on two technical questions: the definition of the quality of our physical environment; and the measurement of changes therein. There appears to have been confusion of three distinct items among those who have expressed concern over the human impact upon the face of the earth— the present or potential economic productivity of the affected areas; their aesthetic attractiveness; and the preservation of the ecological integrity of "wild" areas. It must be admitted immediately that no one has yet devised ways of measuring these conditions, much less any techniques for describing their dynamics. But, even assuming that we could, it is most doubtful whether there is, in general, any direct correlation between population density or rate of increase in a specific place on the one hand and its economic worth or visual beauty on the other. Per-unit area output of agricultural and other economic goods may, in fact, increase as fast or faster than population numbers (at least to that point of total, hopeless congestion that has never yet been achieved over any appreciable land surface). Indeed the argument is credible that augmented population density is a major genetic factor in bringing about major increments in soil productivity or in the discovery, creation, or more efficient exploitation of various "natural" resources. Furthermore, archaeological evidence indicates that, among other areas, portions of Mexico, Ceylon, and Iraq maintained for long periods of the past populations greater than those now resident there and without any apparent adverse effects upon the food-producing qualities of the land.

The aesthetic quality of an area is, of course, a highly subjective matter. Nevertheless, a consensus might be reached for the view that some of the loveliest landscapes in the world are to be seen in some of the most crowded, e.g. Japan, the Low Countries, or Highland Guatemala, and that further humanization of many areas, as growth proceeds, may enhance rather than detract from their aesthetic appeal. It is equally apparent that any number of very distressing, contrary examples could be cited to show that population growth has meant both environmental and aesthetic degradation. The point to be made here is that the kinds of changes induced in the appearance and economic utility of an area undergoing brisk demographic growth is most decidedly a function of the nature, structure, and operations of the specific culture or community, not of such growth per se, and that universal postulations are probably not feasible. Thus there exists a wide spectrum of situations, from the thin, nearly static or transient population that commits the most horrendous vandalism upon its surroundings to the very dense, rapidly multiplying groups that husband their physical resources with jealous devotion and constantly add to the value and beauty of their land.

There is no logical riposte to the adherents of the wilderness mystique who are so profoundly distressed by the damage being wrought by man's activities to the delicate ecological fabric of relatively empty areas. There is little doubt that the further spatial extension or intensification of the human presence will further violate much that is priceless ethically or in any ultimate economic reckoning. As it happens, however, the virginity of even the wildest tracts has already been compromised; and there, as in the more obviously humanized areas, it is urgent that some modus vivendi be contrived that metes out the maximum benefits possible to all species of living things. But this is a concern peripheral to the agenda of the population geographer and the demographer.

8. The unproved assumption that demographic salvation is possible through modern contraceptive technology and exhortation.

If one accepts the thesis that a sharp reduction in fertility is a necessary condition for solving the population/resource pressures of underdeveloped lands, then the means for effecting such a reduction become an issue of transcendent importance. Historically, the only proved method for inducing a lasting and significant lowering of the birth rate has been to raise quite substantially a popula-

tion's levels of living—and aspiration for further gains. Unfortunately, this process is difficult to initiate, requires the generation and input of considerable capital, and consumes much valuable time. This time lag is a significant one, for not only does it take a number of years to push a population upwards to a higher socioeconomic stage but there is also a further, roughly equivalent period before the new fertility pattern reflects this achievement.

It is understandable, then, that ways are being sought whereby fertility reduction can be realized without waiting out the difficult passage through the "Demographic Transition." Two obvious techniques are not normally feasible either politically or financially—the physical separation of the sexes of prolonged periods (including the enforced postponement of marriage), or massive programs of subsidies designed to limit the number of children or to encourage voluntary sterilization. Nor are any other coercive measures likely to be considered seriously in the near future.

Currently much stress is being laid on the mass distribution of new contraceptive devices and information in the underdeveloped countries. The theory behind such programs is that a number of developing countries have now reached the point where parents realize it is to their economic and social advantage to limit family size even before the inception of significant socioeconomic advances and that they need only some cheap, simple, safe, effective, and psychologically acceptable techniques and perhaps a little official encouragement and propaganda to become successful contraceptors. The two items which seem best to meet the stringent requirements for widespread acceptability among underdeveloped populations are the oral contraceptive pill and the intra-uterine device, or coil (IUD's); and field trials for both have been initiated on a rather ambitious scale.

It is still somewhat too early to have collected and analyzed enough data from Korea, Taiwan, India, Pakistan, and elsewhere to determine whether these programs have had any significant results within the test groups, whether the new fertility pattern, if any, is likely to be a lasting one, or whether the method in question can be extended to the total population of reproductive age. A further complication is the fact that some of these experimental efforts are being carried on in areas, such as Taiwan, where significant socioeconomic development may have already initiated some spontaneous declines in fertility. Organized family limitation programs may, in such cases, simply accelerate an ongoing process, as appears to have happened in Japan during the 1940's and 1950's. Demographic history tells us that possession of advanced contraceptive technology is an incidental matter, while the truly crucial question is whether the potential contraceptors genuinely wish to achieve the small-family pattern. Quite probably the ease with which each community accepts a new, lower fertility pattern will depend upon the fundamental character of its culture and other spatially variable factors. When the need for fewer children is felt, even old, rather primitive contraceptive methods will suffice. But, insofar as the present and impending population/resource impasse is a unique episode in human history, past precedents are not necessarily binding. It is not unthinkable that major, rapid declines in the birth rate can be engineered on a national scale in advance of any important socioeconomic breakthrough, however implausible this may seem in the light of earlier experience. We do not know; we must await the evidence. But, in the interim, it would be imprudent not to examine other alternatives.

9. The unproved assumption that major socioeconomic advance can somehow be achieved in every underdeveloped country that wishes to do so.

If a nation elects to strive for a more comfortable balance between population and resources—and also to achieve other social and economic ends generally deemed desirable—by initiating major socioeconomic development, there is no assurance that it will succeed. Some nations undoubtedly can and will reach their declared goal; but historical precedents are too few in number and too distinct in character from the territories in question to offer any grounds for unqualified optimism. The various European and Neo-European nations and Japan were (with a few exceptions in Southern Europe) launched upon their developmental careers in the 19th Century or earlier. In any event, their start was made under conditions radically different from those confronting our contemporary underdeveloped countries. Economic development preceded or ran parallel with demographic expansion. Population growth was not racing ahead of economic and social capabilities so as to absorb most of the short supply of capital and physical resources.

A critical survey of the assets and liabilities for economic development of the various underdeveloped countries would indicate that the former are greatly outweighed by the latter. In addition to the severe braking effect of disproportionately rapid population growth, it is obvious that most of these territories are seriously deficient in some of the more elementary physical resources. That this is not an insuperable obstacle is shown by the attainments of such areas as Iceland, New England, Israel, Switzerland, Japan, or Finland, all of whom are at best marginal with respect to natural endowments—or perhaps best of all by the near-miracle of Hong Kong.

What is discouraging is the fact that the combination of advantages necessary to surmount physical handicaps may be lacking. Thus there may be an acute shortage of venture capital, domestic or foreign, available for developing critical components in the economy of the national infrastructure; and, in fact, much in the way of locally generated investment funds may have been exported to safer or more lucrative havens. The exploitation and export of abundant local mineral and agricultural resources can produce funds that may or may not be channeled into local growth-producing enterprises; but future problems in procuring materials needed for an advanced society may also be created thereby.

Many, perhaps most, underdeveloped countries are plagued by chronic political instability, or even military disorder, that makes it difficult to execute even the best-laid development schemes. Paradoxically, the small size of the population and market of many rapidly growing underdeveloped countries makes the formulation of valid economic plans a trying task. One's imagination strains at the prospect of any development plans that are both efficacious and primarily reliant on local resources in such "ministates" as the Maldives, Tonga, Basutoland, Bhutan, Singapore, Mauritius, Jordan, or some, such as Panama, Jordan, Malawi, or Ruanda, that are a bit ampler.

Along with the annoyances of deficiencies of physical resources, investment capital, effective government, and markets of non-economic size, there are at least two other handicaps that may prove even more frustrating: the dearth of skilled or experienced personnel, native or alien, capable of designing and managing the developmental process; and our quite limited knowledge of how best to draw up intelligent, realistic, and effective developmental blueprints to fit the peculiar needs of each individual country.

It is not even certain whether, under the best of conditions, a more or less sovereign nation can escalate itself upward to genuinely advanced socioeconomic status, and to the demographic concomitants thereof. In this connection, it will be interesting to learn whether such states as Kuwait and Bahrein, with their windfall economies—or Libya, Iraq, and Venezuela—can force-feed themselves and buy their way quickly into advanced status. The answer should be available in a few years. One final uncertainty looming over every country (except China) that aspires to better its socioeconomic standing is the attitude of the two superpowers who monopolize so much of the world's economic and military power. Without their moral, technical, and financial

support—or at least acquiescence—it would be foolish to count upon much progress.

10. The unproved assumption that the demographic consequences of major socioeconomic progress in the developing countries will replicate those experienced in the advanced nations.

Once again, we should be restrained by lack of solid historical precedent from declaring that economic development is not only a possible but is a necessary and sufficient means for achieving an efficient demographic budget, i.e. a pattern of low fertility closely approximating a low mortality rate. The assumption that the attainment of advanced socioeconomic status is **always** followed, after an interval of some years or decades, by a major reduction in fertility has not yet been fully tested in enough different countries with different historic and cultural settings. To date, the Demographic Transition and the modernization process have indeed always accompanied each other; but in every instance, development was well under way by the end of the 19th Century (as was the case in Japan, incidentally), or the country in question is European or Sino-Japanese in culture, and, without exception, the country did not start out after it had begun to suffer the symptoms of underdevelopment. Is there not some possibility that the causal connection between socioeconomic development and fertility may be culture-specific? And may it not be possible that a nation beginning its development program in an underdeveloped condition may follow a rather separate demographic course from that previously observed? In any case, is it safe to extrapolate a universal principle to cover all countries from the experience of a limited number of rather special countries?

The answers to these questions may be forthcoming in the next few years. In addition to the oil-rich states of the Middle East, there are several situations in Latin America where sustained or increasing prosperity should test the hypothesis that family limitation is a necessary sequel to socioeconomic development. These would include portions of Mexico and Venezuela, Puerto Rico, Curaçao, and possibly Jamaica, but would exclude Cuba, Argentina, Uruguay, and Southern Brazil, areas that enjoyed major influxes of European migrants during the past several decades. It may be noteworthy that substantial rises in standardized birth rates have occurred in most Latin American countries, starting in 1920 or later, even where there has been no appreciable socioeconomic progress. It must be admitted, however, that some of our difficulty in knowing just what to expect can be attributed to the fact that the earlier stages of the Demographic Transition were rarely well documented in the currently advanced nations. Thus we cannot be certain whether or not the dynamics of vital rates in the developing lands are paralleling those of earlier travelers through the Demographic Transition.

11. The unproved assumption that developing lands that succeed in attaining advanced socioeconomic status quo and then duplicate the demographic pattern of currently advanced nations will thereby have permanently solved their population/resource problems.

Entry into the charmed circle of advanced nations by no means guarantees any final, absolute resolution of imbalances between people and resources. It may simply change the terms of the problem. The advanced nations comprise a highly unstable system. Population growth does continue at a fairly brisk rate (as compared to the pre-modern period) in nearly all such countries; and economic product and per-capita wants and consumption are climbing an upward slope that has no visible crest. The problems being engendered by large, growing, affluent masses of people caught in the grip of an accelerating technology that seems to have no essential rationale except its own perpetuation and expansion are likely to be much more intense, perverse, and resistant to simple answers than those of the underdeveloped lands. But proper exploration of this point takes us into territory well beyond the range of this essay.

I hope it is evident from the foregoing discussion that we do not yet have enough facts, historical models, or general theory concerning the demography and population geography of the underdeveloped lands to describe, evaluate, and interpret their population/resource problems at all adequately, to predict the future course of these problems, or to prescribe infallible solutions. It should also be plain that it is urgent that much work and thinking be done and the proper research questions asked before much more time has elapsed. For the first time in human history, we are forced to take a hard look at the conditions of humanity in general and the forces that control our lives. And as the era of spontaneous change and piecemeal decisions draws to a close, we are being compelled not only to grasp what has been happening but also somehow to take our futures into our own hands. It is difficult; it is painful; it is necessary; and it is a tremendous challenge to the scholar.

For the geographer, the questions are particularly intriguing. Barring some catastrophe, the underdeveloped world will have at least twice its present population by the end of the century. And it is difficult to conceive how near-stability of numbers can be managed before these countries have three or four times the population now inhabiting them. What will be the geography of these crowding lands, with their burgeoning cities, their ever more mobile citizens, their intensifying ecological stresses, and tremendous, if still unforeseen, new social tensions? Some of the answers may be reportable soon in places such as Haiti, Egypt, El Salvador, Java, Mauritius, and South Korea, possibly even in the 1970's. In any case, we must begin to learn how to study this new geography of mounting population pressures, clearly, analytically, and without the incubus of myth or obsolete dogma. Then perhaps we can help in the effort to realize the full potential of our species and our planet, sanely, richly, and for many millenia to come.

Selection Thirty-five

SOME EFFECTS OF POPULATION GROWTH ON LATIN AMERICA'S ECONOMY

Alfonso Gonzaléz

The stability of Latin America rests essentially on the solution of two interrelated problems—population growth and economic development. A further corollary, and an extremely significant one, will be the social distribution of the benefits accruing from economic betterment. Latin America is both the fastest growing world region in population and also the most advanced (in terms of the death rate, literacy, and per capita income) of the underdeveloped regions of the world. It is also the only region of the underdeveloped world that had evolved from political colonial status prior to World War II. This region, therefore, has had the longest history of endeavoring to solve directly many of the problems that plague the 70 per cent of mankind that lives in the underdeveloped countries. Since mortality is lower in Latin America than in the other underdeveloped regions, undoubtedly due to the earlier and more widespread application of modern medical technology, the rate of natural increase is higher in this region than elsewhere since birth rates vary less than death rates among underdeveloped regions. Latin America serves as a harbinger of conditions that will soon prevail in the other underdeveloped regions as the latter's mortality rates continue to decline. The pressure of population on resources will increase in all the underdeveloped regions because even in Latin America mortality continues to decline resulting in an ever-widening gap between births and deaths in the absence of significant fertility control.[1]

Population Growth

In mid-1965 the population estimate of Latin America was 248 million with a forecast for

1970 ranging from a low of 278 to a high (based on continuing demographic trends) of 284 million.[2] By 1980 the estimates range from 352 to 387 million and by the end of the century the population of Latin America may be between 514 and 756 million. The range of population estimates varies with the assumptions regarding the timing of declines in fertility because a continued trend in the decline of mortality is highly likely. The fundamental reason for this rapid increase in population is the same factor that has accounted for the rapid increase in the world's population since the advent of the industrial revolution, *viz.*, control of mortality. In the 1945–50 period the crude death rate (number of deaths per 1000 population) for Latin America was 17–19 and by 1955–60 it had declined to 13–15 and about 1962–63 the average of 17 Latin American countries was 10–11.[3] This represents an overall decline of approximately 40 per cent in the post-World War II period. Since the crude birth rate (number of births per 1000 population) has remained consistently high (41–43) the rate of population growth has increased from 2.5 per cent annually in the late 1940's to about 3 per cent in the 1960's (Table 35.1). At present growth rates the population of Latin America will double in less than a quarter century. The fastest growing world subregion is undoubtedly mainland Middle America (with the Levant probably second) where every country in the 1958–64 period increased at least 3 per cent annually with a maximum (and the world leader) of 4.3 per cent in Costa Rica.

Improved health conditions have increased life expectancy over much of tropical Latin America to about 58 years and present-day trends, if projected to the end of the century, would increase this to 73 years (or approximately present-day levels in the advanced regions of the world). The Latin American

Reprinted from *Journal of Inter-American Studies,* **9,** 1967, 22–42, by permission of The University of Miami Press.

TABLE 35.1 Latin America: population characteristics[1]

	POP 1964 (M)	ANNUAL INC 1958–64 (%)	BIRTH RATE (CIS-1960)	DEATH RATE (CIS-1960)	INF MORT[2] RATE (CIS-1960)	EST POP 1980 (M)
Mexico	39.6	3.1	45.0	10.4	67.7	70.6
Guatemala	4.2	3.2	47.7	17.3	92.8	6.9
El Salvador	2.8	3.6	48.6	10.8	65.5	4.6
Honduras	2.1	3.0	45–50	15–20	47.0	3.7
Nicaragua	1.6	3.5	45–52	12–17	53.9	2.8
Costa Rica	1.4	4.3	49.9	8.5	77.6	2.4
Panama	1.2	3.3	40.1	8.0[2]	42.9	2.0
Cuba	7.3	2.0	30–34	9–13	41.8	10.0
Dominican Republic	3.5	3.6	48–54	16–20	79.5	6.2
Haiti	4.5	2.2	45–55[2]	21.6[2]	171.6	6.9
Venezuela	8.4	3.4	45–50	10–15	47.9	14.9
Colombia	15.4	2.2	43–46	14–17	88.2	27.7
Ecuador	4.8	3.2	45–50	15–20	95.6	8.0
Peru	11.9	3.0	42–48	13–18	94.8	17.5
Bolivia	3.7	1.5	41–45	20–25	86.0[a]	6.0
Paraguay	1.9	2.4	45–50	12–16	98.0[b]	3.0
Chile	8.4	2.4	34.2	11.8	111.0	12.4
Argentina	21.7	1.6	21.8	7.9	60.7	29.0
Uruguay	2.6	1.42[c]	21–25	7–9	47.4	3.1
Brazil	79.8	3.0	43–47	11–16	170[d]	123.7
LATIN AMERICA	226.8	2.9[3]	41–43[2]	13–14[2]		361.4

[1] *World Population Data Sheet.* Population Reference Bureau. December 1964.
[2] *Demographic Yearbook*, 1964 and 1963.
[3] *Statistical Bulletin for Latin America.* United Nations. Vol. II, No. 2 (August 1965). Table 1.

[a] 1959.
[b] 1945–49.
[d] 1958–62.
[c] 1940–50.

infant mortality rate (number of deaths of infants less than one year of age per 1000 live births), which along with life expectancy at birth comprise the best indexes of health conditions, has improved from about 103 in the late 1940's to about 75 in the early 1960's.[4] The latter figure is still about three times greater than that prevailing in the United States and other advanced countries.

The differences in natality between Latin America and the other underdeveloped regions are rather insignificant, especially if the low fertility countries of Latin America (*viz.,* Argentina and Uruguay) are discounted. However, the mortality rate of Latin America overall is from one-third to perhaps one-half less than in the Afro-Asian regions. This differential accounts for Latin America's greater rate of population growth. The Afro-Asian underdeveloped regions are increasing at about 2 per cent annually or slightly less, but Latin America is increasing at about 3 per cent. Current Afro-Asian mortality rates prevailed in Latin America during the 1940's. Mortality in Latin America began to decline slowly about 1920, with the post-World War I health programs, but declined precipitously with World War II programs and the decrease was especially marked during the 1950's. The decline in mortality was most significant among the younger age groups due to the application of programs combating infectious diseases and malnutrition (especially among children).

The factors lying behind the high fertility of Latin America are readily apparent: (a) the large family is an ingrained trait of the national ethos, (b) women in reproductive ages represent a relatively high proportion of the total population, (c) women enter consensual union at an early age, (d) a large percentage of women are married (either legally or by common-law) (Latin America has the highest illegitimacy rate in the world), and (e) (most importantly) the general absence of family planning—even among the urban and better educated sectors of the population.

The rate of population growth in the near future will be at least as great as at present because of the presumed continued decline in mortality over practically all of Latin America. Fertility, on the other hand, is only under effective control in Argentina and Uruguay, with incipient decline discernible in Chile and Cuba.

Demographic Consequences

There are a number of demographic consequences of considerable importance to economic development resulting from past and present population characteristics. These features are also to be found in the other underdeveloped world regions. One of these consequences is the youthful age composition of the population resulting from high natality. Slightly more than two-fifths of the population is younger than 15 years of age but due to relatively high mortality only about 3 per cent of the population is older than 65. The net result is that only about 55 per cent of the population of Latin America is in the economically productive ages, i.e., 15–64, in contrast to about 60–65 per cent in the developed countries. Only in Argentina and Uruguay, where birth rates have been less than 30 since the 1940's, are about two-thirds of the population in the productive ages. In Cuba and Chile, where fertility is intermediate between the typical high levels prevailing in Latin America and the low levels of Argentina and Uruguay, slightly less than three-fifths of the population is in the productive ages. In the remaining countries

the proportion is 55 per cent or less. The result is that in most Latin American countries only about one-third of the population is economically active whereas in the developed countries of the world the proportion is 40–45 per cent. Thereby, the dependency ratio (number of persons dependent upon each thousand of the economically productive age population) is higher in Latin America (and underdeveloped countries generally) than it is in the developed regions. Even more critical is that the dependency ratio in Latin America will actually increase from a 1960 level of 815 (compared with about 500–650 in developed countries) to 890–940 by 1975.[5]

A further demographic handicap that Latin America is facing, and it will become increasingly even more severe in the near future, is that increasingly larger groups of males will enter the labor force and that employment opportunities must be provided. In the period 1965–70 the proportion of males in the Latin American population will increase by 15–20 per cent since more than three times as many males will be entering the labor force as leaving it. At present more than 1.6 million males are entering the labor force every year and unless the economy can absorb them they constitute a potential political instability.

The youthful structure of the population virtually ensures a continued high rate of population increase in the near future. By 1975 there will be 50–60 per cent more women in the child-bearing ages than in 1960 so that unless social patterns change significantly by that time the absolute population growth (as well as the rate of growth) will be prodigious.

Population Pressure on Resources

The pressure of a rapidly expanding population is being exerted with increasing effect on the resource base of Latin America. This pressure of absolute numerical increase is being compounded by the revolution in rising expectations that is sweeping Latin America.

TABLE 35.2 Population and economic indexes: 1963[1] (1958 = 100)

	LATIN AMERICA	UNDERDEVELOPED REGIONS	DEVELOPED REGIONS	WORLD
Population	114	110	106	109
Agriculture[2]	116	117[a]	110[a]	111
Industry	128	149	136	137
Manufacturing	129	141	137	138
Mining	124	172	112	127
Energy: Production	133	151	120	126
Consumption	134	147	124	127
Foreign Trade	111	122	148	142

[1]*Statistical Yearbook: 1964*, United Nations, Table 12 and computations from Tables 3, 160, 130.
[2]*The World Agricultural Situation: Review of 1965 and Outlook for 1966*, Foreign Agricultural Economic Report No. 28, U.S. Dept. of Agriculture, Table 1.
[a]Approximate (computed); "underdeveloped regions" excludes Communist Asia.

The demand for a better livelihood now is augmenting the rising demand due to demographic increase and the combination of these two elements is severely straining the limited resources, in view of the technological level applied, of an already politically unstable region.

The rate of economic expansion in Latin America overall varies significantly according to sectors and Latin America does not compare favorably with the rate of economic development in the underdeveloped world generally (Table 35.2). The one major category in which Latin America clearly excels is in the rate of population growth and this, obviously, has a detrimental effect in terms of production increments on a per capita basis.

AGRICULTURE

Population pressure on available resources in Latin America is most critically apparent in agriculture. Although the density of population based on cultivated land for Latin America is comparable to that for the world (332 inhabitants per square kilometer of cultivated land in 1962 compared with the world average of 340), this relatively low figure for Latin America is due essentially to low densities prevailing in the three leading agricultural countries of the region (Brazil, Mexico, and Argentina). The median density for Latin America (479–500) is between one

third and one-half greater than the world average and this density is exceeded by few of the major agricultural countries of the world (*viz.*, Japan, United Kingdom, West Germany, United Arab Republic, China, Indonesia, East Germany, and the Philippines).[6]

The actual pressure of population on the cultivated land in Latin America becomes even clearer if consideration is given to the yields obtained from the land under cultivation. Although the yields obtained in Latin America are fairly high by the standards of the underdeveloped world (only the Orient, of the latter, exceeds Latin America in yields), Latin American yields are below the world average and are only about 50–60 per cent of those obtained in the more advanced world regions. The net result is that the number of inhabitants per unit of arable land (and giving weight to yields) in Latin America is about comparable to that of the Middle East and these two regions are exceeded only by the Orient among the world's regions.

The cropland-yield densities (Table 35.3) prevailing in virtually all the Latin American countries (the notable exceptions are Argentina and Brazil) are considerably above the average. In four Latin American countries (Haiti, Bolivia, Nicaragua, and Peru) the cropland-yield density exceeds that of the most dense of the major agricultural countries of the world (Sudan: 791). An additional eight Latin American countries have a den-

TABLE 35.3 World regions: comparative population and agriculture data (1962)[1]

	POPULATION (M)	ARABLE LAND (M HA)	ARABLE LAND DENSITY[2]	CEREAL YIELDS (100 KG/HA)[3]	ARABLE YIELD DENSITY[4]
Latin America	224.1	103	218	12.67	251
Middle East	190.5	113	169	9.74	253
Orient	1,645.5	383	429	13.82	451
Africa (Sub-Saharan)	178.1	207	86	7.93	158
Europe	432.5	153	283	20.84	198
USSR	221.5	230	96	10.99	127
Anglo-America	205.3	227	90	24.43	54
Oceania	16.5	34	49	12.25	58
WORLD	3,114.0	1,449	215	14.60	215

Based on data from *FAO Production Yearbook: 1963*.
[1] Number of inhabitants per square kilometer of arable land.
[2] Average for 1961–63, except for U.S.S.R. and Orient which are for 1961–62.
[3] Figure for "Arable Land Density" is divided by ratio of the region's cereal yields to the world cereal yields.
[4]

sity exceeding that of the tenth leading major world country (Pakistan: 521). It therefore seems clear that at present population pressure on agricultural productivity in Latin America already is formidable.

Agricultural development is being given considerable attention widely in Latin America and one very fundamental reason why this must be so is in order to cope with the rapidly expanding population. In addition, the rising expectations of greater food consumption and the necessities for greater export surplus in order to secure foreign exchange to further economic development also give rise to serious pressures on agriculture for increased productivity. Broadly speaking, increased productivity is being achieved in Latin America by increasing both cultivated land and yields, with the former more significant.

The area devoted to the major crops in Latin America increased overall between the 1948–52 period and 1962–63 by one-third (32.3 per cent, which was somewhat less than the overall population increment (38.3 per cent) for the same period.[7] The improvement in agricultural yields overall in Latin America was relatively small during the 1950's. The yield for maize only increased by about one-eighth between the periods 1948–52 and

1960–62 with only a slightly greater relative increase for wheat, the second crop in cultivated area in Latin America. In contrast, in the same period the yields for both crops in the United States increased by one-half and in Europe maize yields increased by more than two-thirds and wheat by one-third. Generally, the greatest improvements in agricultural yields in the post-World War II period have occurred in the more advanced regions of the world. The net result is that Latin America's maize yields have declined relatively from 67 per cent of the world's average in the 1948–52 period to 58 per cent in 1960–62.

The endeavor to increase yields can be measured by the notable increase in commercial fertilizer consumption in Latin America. The use of nitrate, phosphate, and potash fertilizers more than doubled during the 1950's in Latin America. The production, however, of commercial fertilizer in Latin America remains insignificant (by world standards) and occurs only in Chile, Peru, Mexico, and Brazil. The use of commercial fertilizers is still abysmally low in Latin America compared with the more advanced regions, especially since the increase in fertilizer consumption in the latter regions is almost as great as in Latin America. So that

TABLE 35.4 Latin America: economic characteristics

	% OF ECON. ACT. POP. IN AGRIC. (c1950–60)	CROPLAND-YIELD DENSITY[2]	CALORIES PER CAPITA[3] (1959–61)	INCOME PER CAPITA[4] (1961, $)	GDP GROWTH RATE[5] (c1960–63)	AGRIC. PROD. 1964[3] 1958 = 100 TOTAL	PER CAPITA	MFG. PROD[6] 1963–64 1958 = 100
Mexico	54	428	2,580	415	4.9	183	131	162
Guatemala	68	629	1,970	258	4.8	196	142	123
El Salvador	60	614	2,000	268		203	150	152
Honduras	66	448	2,330	252	5.4	162	117	
Nicaragua	68	868	2,190	288	10.8	226	166	134
Costa Rica	55	583	2,520	362	8.1	119	78	
Panama	46	753	2,370	371		144	104	
Cuba	42	445	2,730	516	9.07	86	68	
Dominican Republic	56	582	2,020	313		144	99	
Haiti	83	2,684	1,780	149		104	83	
Venezuela	32	768	2,330	645	4.0	176	117	175
Colombia	54	630	2,280	373	5.0	135	99	141
Ecuador	53	626	2,100	223	3.7	195	138	
Peru	46[8]	827	2,060	269	6.7	136	105	154
Bolivia	72	992	2,010	122		160	125	
Paraguay	54	564	2,400	193	3.6	117	92	92[a]
Chile	28	488	2,610	453	5.8	122	95	146
Argentina	19	179	3,220	799	−0.1	122	101	107
Uruguay		430	3,030	561		110	92	98
Brazil	58	303	2,710	375	4.7	131	94	147
LATIN AMERICA	47[4]	382	2,570	421	3.6[7]	133	98	129

[1]*FAO Production Yearbook, 1963*, Table 5a.
[2]Number of inhabitants per square kilometer of cropland divided by the ratio of cereal yields obtained to the average world cereal yields. Cropland computed from the summation of crop data available in *FAO Production Yearbook, 1963*.
[3]*The 1965 Western Hemisphere Agricultural Situation*, ERS-Foreign 113, U.S. Dept. of Agriculture, Tables 5, 1, 2.
[4]*The Economic Development of Latin America in the Post-War Period*, United Nations, 1964. Tables 51, 26.
[5]*Yearbook of National Accounts Statistics: 1964*. United Nations, Part D, Table 4B.
[6]*Statistical Bulletin for Latin American*, Vol. II, No. 2, Table 19.
[7]*Economic Survey of Latin America: 1963*, Economic Commission for Latin America (UN), Tables 257, 6.
[8]Approximate; based on *Statistical Bulletin for Latin America*, Vol. II, No. 1, Table 3.
[a] 1961.

West Germany, with only about one-twelfth the cultivated area of Latin America, uses about one and one-half the nitrates, more than double the phosphates, and about five times the potash that Latin America does. The same holds true for the mechanization of agriculture. The number of tractors in Latin America nearly tripled during the 1950's (a slower rate than Europe) yet Canada with only about a quarter of Latin America's cultivated area has appreciably more tractors.

The combined increase in cultivated area and improvement in yields has resulted in a notable increase in crop production during the 1950's in Latin America. Between the 1948–52 and 1960–62 periods maize production overall increased by three-fifths and comparable or greater relative increments in production occurred for bananas, coffee, cotton, rice, the oilseeds, and the palms. With regard to livestock numbers in Latin America, only swine have increased faster than the human population and meat production overall has fallen drastically behind in per capita output.

The net result is that overall net agricultural production between the early 1950's and the 1960's increased in Latin America by one-third.[8] This exceeds the increment for Anglo-America, both Western and Eastern Europe, and the Middle East. In this period there were nine Latin American countries in which the overall increment was one-half or greater. This prodigious increase would represent an average annual increment of 3.7 per cent or greater in agricultural production (the average for the 20 republics was 2.6 per cent).[9] Of the major Latin American countries Mexico exhibited the greatest average annual increment (6.4 per cent) and would rank among the world's leaders in the rate of agricultural expansion. In comparison, the average annual increment in the United States during the war periods when governmental policies encouraged augmented production was less than 3 per cent.[10] In only one country (Cuba) did agricultural production actually decline during the period and

Haiti and Uruguay increased production by only 5 per cent overall.

Despite the overall rapid expansion of agricultural production during the 1950's and early 1960's the agricultural sector has only been able to maintain parity with population growth during the period. Therefore, in 1964 food production per capita in Latin America overall was little different from that of the 1952–54 period.[11] No underdeveloped region is performing so poorly in agricultural output with reference to population growth as is Latin America. The fundamental reason is that population growth is more rapid in Latin America than elsewhere so that agricultural output improvements are instantaneously eroded away by further population increases.

Several Latin American countries have sustained a significant reduction in per capita food production during this period and the situation is most acute in Cuba, Costa Rica, El Salvador, Haiti, and Paraguay, and only somewhat better in Chile, Peru, and Uruguay. The greatest relative improvements (despite large population increments) have occurred in Mexico, Ecuador, Venezuela, and Bolivia.

The pressure of population can be seen in the more rapid increments accruing to crop and livestock production in Latin America destined for domestic consumption rather than for the export market.[12] This has necessitated a curtailment of the expansion of the export trade and constitutes a serious problem for Latin America's further economic development.[13] This lagging sector restricts the accumulation of necessary foreign exchange and presents serious balance-of-payments problems to a number of countries (especially Argentina, Colombia, and Uruguay).

In comparing the periods 1956–58 and 1959–61, eleven Latin American nations had a reduced caloric content in food availability per capita and one evidenced no change. Seven of the above countries (Haiti, Guatemala, El Salvador, Dominican Republic, Nicaragua, Colombia, and Panama) were below the level regarded by the U.S. Department of Agriculture as calorie-deficient (*i.e.*, 2400 calories daily).[14] In addition to these seven there were an additional five countries that had less than 2400 calories per capita in the 1959–61 period (Table 35.4). Undoubtedly, Cuba must now be added to the food-deficit countries of Latin America. Only in Uruguay and Argentina is the food consumption level comparable to that of the more advanced regions of the world. Overall for Latin America the daily caloric consumption is probably slightly in excess of 2500 calories which would represent a deficiency of about 500–600 calories daily per capita compared to Anglo-America or Western Europe. With the existing sociopolitical instability of the region it is questionable how long Latin America will be able to endure such food consumption levels (especially in view of the rate of population growth) without serious political upheavals.

INDUSTRY

The pressure of population growth on industrial output (mining, manufacturing, and utilities) is both less critical and less urgent in Latin America. This sector is growing appreciably faster than the population and, since large segments of the peoples of Latin America are in basically subsistence or local economies, the necessities of food are of more overriding immediate importance than the access to manufactured goods. However, the industrial sector must maintain a very high rate of expansion in order to ensure employment for the rapidly increasing population. Traditionally, Latin America (like other underdeveloped regions) has been basically agricultural, with about three-fifths of the economically active population in the pre-World War II period engaged in agriculture. However, the proportion had declined to 56 per cent overall for Latin America by 1945 and 1955 agriculture was exceeded by the non-agricultural sectors.[15] In 1960 the non-agricultural sectors accounted for 53 per cent of the economically active population. Since World War II the agricultural labor force has

only been increasing at one-half the overall rate for the total economically active population. With the agricultural sector, therefore, declining relatively and with the labor force increasing annually by nearly two million (about one-fifth being females) in the early 1960's, the burden of employment falls increasingly on the industrial sectors of the economy, especially manufacturing. It is questionable how long the Latin American economies can sustain a relatively high proportion engaged in the services with a relatively small industrial base.

As is the case with the economically active population, so the sector origins of the gross domestic product (GDP) reflect a decreasing share being contributed by agriculture and the opposite trend for manufacturing and (to a much smaller degree) mining. In fact, the latter two activities (along with perhaps services) are the only sectors that have rather steadily increased significantly their share of the GDP in Latin America overall from 1950 to 1963.[16] In Latin America overall the manufacturing sector exceeded the agricultural beginning in the late 1950's. Manufacturing already contributes a greater share of the GDP than agriculture in Chile, Argentina, Venezuela, Cuba, and Mexico (and almost surely Uruguay). In both Brazil and Peru manufacturing had almost reached parity with agriculture by 1963.

The industrial sector has been expanding faster in Latin America than the agricultural. Whereas the agricultural sector of the GDP increased overall in Latin America by slightly more than 3 per cent annually during the 1950's and 1960–63, the manufacturing sector expanded by 6.4 per cent annually during the 1950's and 3.8 per cent in the early 1960's—even slightly higher rates prevailed for mining. Of the 13 Latin American countries for which data are available, all countries had a more rapid rate of industrial expansion than agricultural growth during both the 1950's and early 1960's except Paraguay in the 1950's and Panama, Ecuador, Guatemala, and Venezuela for the early 1960's, with Peru exhibiting equal growth rates in the latter period.[17] Due to the appreciably greater growth rate, the industrial sector in Latin America has been in a much more favorable circumstance with regard to population than is true of agriculture. During the 1950's only Paraguay (of the 13 countries for which data was available) did not attain at least parity between industrial expansion and population growth and in the 1960–63 period only Argentina failed to expand industrially at a rate comparable to demographic increase.

SOCIAL SERVICES

Improvement in social services has been an important cornerstone of the Alliance for Progress and a change in U.S. policy about 1958 has resulted in considerably expanding social services in Latin America. The betterment of social services can help ameliorate existing conditions should some sector of the economy falter in its developmental plans.

The pressure of population growth, however, aggravates existing pressures on the already meager social services in Latin America. Notable material progress has been made in recent years in education, housing, and public health. Education now accounts for 18 per cent of national budgets overall and public health between 10–15 per cent. Also many new housing units have been constructed in Latin America due to public, private, and Alliance efforts. The infant mortality rate (probably the best gauge for determining existing medical and health conditions) may have declined by one-quarter between the late 1940's and early 1960's but still remains three or perhaps four times greater than that prevailing in the advanced countries of the world. It may take another decade and a half (or more) for most Latin American countries to attain the level prevailing now in Puerto Rico (40–45 infant deaths per 1000 live births), which is quite comparable to the non-white population of the United States. Few Latin American countries are in that category now (Table 35.1) but in the 1930's Puerto Rico's infant mortality rate (132 in 1932) was typical of Latin America. Improvements in sanitation and potable water supplies, the anti-malarial campaigns, health clinics, and other public health measures are undoubtedly having their effect on reducing mortality and, thereby, increasing population totals. But nutritional problems are of a different nature because a fundamental improvement in agriculture is necessary, despite the Food for Peace programs. The latter must increase considerably in the future to keep pace with population growth (not to mention improvement in the per capita food consumption), but U.S. domestic policy and foreign assistance have notably decreased the available surplus food stocks in the United States.

Considerable expansion of the educational facilities in Latin America has also occurred in recent years. In a recent OAS survey of 15 Latin American countries the elementary school enrollment increased from 18.5 million in 1960 to 22.7 million in 1964.[18] However, the elementary school age population of those 15 republics in that four-year period increased by approximately 4 million so that most of the expansion represents population increments. In 1964 about 42 per cent of elementary school children in Latin America were not attending classes. The deficit in higher education is also critical. Latin America has a population one-fifth larger than that of the United States but has less than a fourth of the students attending universities and advanced technical teaching centers.

A substantial housing deficit also exists in Latin America—probably about 15.5 million units and the housing shortage has been increasing since 1950 although during the early 1960's the rate of deterioration was slowed.[19] The annual rate of new housing construction (for the few countries for which data are available) represents only about one-half of 1 per cent of existing housing units and far below the 2–3 per cent construction rate that characterizes the advanced countries (the latter also have far slower rates of population growth). The net result is that the combining of poor existing housing conditions with the rapidly expanding population (especially in urban centers) creates a virtually insurmountable gap between the needs of attaining adequate housing facilities and actual accomplishments. Approximately 3.3 million units must be constructed annually during the balance of this decade and probably only a small fraction of this is actually being constructed (there is insufficient data on building activity).

Alternative Policies and Outlook

During 1964 and 1965 the Alliance for Progress recorded more significant material advances than in the earlier years of its operations. In both those years the Alliance objective of an annual increment of per capita product of 2.5 per cent was achieved for Latin America overall despite an annual population growth of 2.9 per cent.[20] Two major Latin American countries, Argentina and Brazil, that have had recent difficulties maintaining an adequate growth rate improved very significantly in 1965. Most of the remaining major countries of Latin America (Mexico, Peru, Venezuela, and Chile) are expanding economically at a satisfactory rate according to Alliance standards. Apparently the only countries encountering serious problems in the Alliance (resulting from both internal and external causes) in 1965 were Colombia, Costa Rica, Ecuador, Paraguay, and Uruguay. Under the stimulus of the Alliance, central planning agencies have now been established in all Latin American countries with the Inter-American Committee on the Alliance (CIAP) as a multilateral supervisory organization. Industrial growth overall appears to continue at a very satisfactory rate of expansion with Mexico achieving a 12.9 per cent increment in 1965, one of the highest rates in the world. Agriculture, however, continues as a major problem area despite a significant production increase in 1965 over the relatively poor harvest of 1964. Despite nearly a 12 per cent increase in agricultural output since the Alliance began in 1961, 11 Latin American countries had lower per capita food production in 1965 than a decade earlier.

The major endeavor of Latin American countries is to improve the livelihood of their inhabitants and with this objective in mind the various governments, with varying degrees of U.S. and international assistance, are attempting to utilize domestic resources more fully to further socioeconomic development. Two general approaches or programs are available to Latin America (and to the other underdeveloped regions as well) in their process of development: (1) increased productivity (including the application of improved technology)—the objective is to expand and improve the economic base in order to increase the volume of output of goods and services; and (2) population control—the objective is to restrict population so that per capita output will rise more rapidly and increasing productivity will not be nullified by population increases. Up to the present, Latin America has relied almost exclusively on increasing productivity and the application of improved technology as the solution to the problem of living conditions, although it would appear from recent developments that the role of population control may take on added importance.

INCREASED PRODUCTIVITY

Latin America continues to rely on the expansion of the economic base and the application of improved and more advanced methods in order to augment per capita output and, thereby, to raise the levels of living. Agriculture remains a serious impediment to rapid economic development despite significant increments in production. Much of the increase in agricultural output has been from the increase in cultivated area rather than from higher yields. In the case of maize, by far Latin America's leading crop (accounting for almost one-third of the total cultivated area), about nine-tenths of the augmented production between the 1948–52 and 1960–62 periods is attributable to the increased cultivated area. How long Latin America will be able to expand output in this fashion is questionable but increasing rural pressure on the land will force ever more farmers onto marginal and submarginal lands or into the already overcongested urban centers. Between 1950 and 1960 the urban population of Latin America increased by 5.3 per cent annually and represents one of the most rapidly urbanizing areas on earth. In 1965 the urban population of Latin America probably exceeded the rural for the first time.

Food output is currently about keeping pace with population growth and there may be increasing demands in the near future for higher levels of consumption from the 2500 calories daily per capita presently available. The crux of the problem remains: to increase land and labor productivity, and this will require considerable outlays of capital and rural credit facilities for improved seed, fertilizers, pesticides, irrigation projects, and the like, along with more widespread training of farmers in the more advanced techniques. The incentives under present conditions are inadequate to effectuate large-scale improvements due to fluctuating world commodity prices, heavy indirect taxation of agriculture, direct and indirect governmental price controls, and, the most serious of all, the land tenure system. As of about 1950, only 1.5 per cent of Latin American farms accounted for nearly two-thirds (64.9 per cent) of the total farmland while nearly three-quarters (72.6 per cent) of the farms contained only 3.7 per cent of all farmland.[21] The agrarian problem in Latin America involves both attendant problems of latifundia and minifundia. The overall changes of the land tenure system since 1950 are insignificant because, despite recent or planned legislation in twelve Latin American countries, little land has actually been redistributed.

Rural conditions contribute in a major way to the mass migrations into Latin American cities, especially the larger centers. This reduces the agricultural labor supply (in a region where mechanization is not widespread), places greater strain on the remaining farmers to supply the rapidly increasing urban population, and creates serious employment problems in the most politically explosive environment, the cities.

Agricultural output is also closely tied to another major problem sector of the Latin American economy—foreign trade. Overall foreign trade has not expanded as fast as population growth and Latin America's share of world trade has been gradually declining. The export market must expand rapidly in order to sustain a rising import demand of capital equipment so necessary for any further development. Production of agricultural commodities must thereby increase sufficiently to satisfy both the growing domestic market and the necessities of exportation.

Industrial growth appears to present less of a pressing problem although there is doubt whether this sector can expand fast enough to provide employment opportunities for the very rapidly expanding urban populace. Inadequate supplies of capital, skilled labor, raw materials, and restricted local markets will also present problems. However, governmental emphasis in development in Latin America is most frequently oriented toward industrialization and four-fifths of all U.S. direct investments are in the industrial sector (notably mining). Expansion of industrial output will also place increasing pressure on raw material production and also restrict the export trade further.

Two basic requirements necessary for the rapid increase in productivity are capital and education, and the latter is dependent (in large part) on the former. There are various sources of capital available for Latin America and all are used to varying degrees: (a) domestic savings, (b) foreign trade, (c) foreign investments, and (d) foreign assistance.

Domestic savings have traditionally been the major source of investment funds in Latin America but this source has been expanding inadequately. The annual per capita income in Latin America in 1961 was only $421 and income distribution is markedly uneven. For those countries where data are available, the top 5 per cent of the population in income account for at least one-quarter to nearly two-fifths of the total national income (in contrast to about one-fifth in the United

States where income distribution is hardly ideal). The rate of fixed capital formation in most Latin American countries is 13–18 per cent and this probably is as high as can be expected considering the existing levels of living and the socioeconomic structure. The encouragement of domestic savings is seriously hampered by the fact that on a regional basis Latin America has the highest rate of inflation on earth. Although very modest tax reforms have been passed in several Latin American countries resulting in the improvement of tax collections, there still is a considerable flight of local capital to the United States and Europe. As a result, in 1964 Latin American investments in the United States alone amounted to $5.5 billion and have been increasing at a faster rate than U.S. investments in Latin America.[22]

As indicated previously, the export market has not been expanding at a very satisfactory rate to warrant encouragement for expanded sources of capital from this source in the near future.

Since Castro's accession to power, foreign investment (probably four-fifths is that of the United States) in Latin America has been disappointing and in some years U.S. direct investments have withdrawn more funds from Latin America (*e.g.*, net outflow of $32 million in 1962) than have been invested. However, U.S. investments began a very modest improvement in 1963. Latin America since the 1950's has become an increasingly less significant region for U.S. direct investments accounting for only one-fifth of the world total in 1964 (in contrast to more than one-third in 1957).

Since 1959 the annual flow of U.S. direct investments into Latin America has averaged less than one-third the Alliance objective and in 1964 it had only reached about one-half the annual target of $300 million. Consequently, U.S. assistance has beome that much more important to Latin America. Economic assistance to Latin America has increased appreciably both absolutely and relatively since 1960 and amounted to more than $600 million (more than one-quarter of the world total) in 1964. This aid is concen-

trated in Brazil (more than one-quarter of Latin America's total) with significant proportions to Chile, Colombia, and Bolivia. However, net U.S. assistance to Latin America has been declining steadily since 1961 and more than one-tenth of this net aid is military.

Fundamental changes in long-range productivity and lessening of sociopolitical pressures due to existing conditions could be effectuated by basic structural reforms, *viz.*, agrarian reform, effective progressive tax structure, social welfare programs for redistribution of wealth, and drastic curtailment of military expenditures (one-tenth to more than one-quarter of the national budgets of practically all Latin American countries). Some of these measures were the founding principles of the Alliance when originally conceived in 1961 but in recent years they have been relegated to a very minor role indeed.

The net overall result is that in endeavoring to follow a course of relying almost entirely upon increased productivity for the solution to its serious problem of raising levels of living and absorbing a rapidly expanding population, Latin America is beset with difficulties of the greatest magnitude. All of the pressures described above are manifested in an increasing sociopolitical instability that has already brought about serious repercussions for individual Latin American countries, the United States, and the OAS.

POPULATION CONTROL

The other major alternative that has virtually been unutilized in Latin America is the control of fertility (except for Argentina and Uruguay, with Chile and Cuba demonstrating a transitional stage). With the population now increasing at 2.9 per cent annually, and the prospect that the rate will increase still further with the additional reductions of mortality which appear inevitable, the pressure on available resources (despite notable economic development) is considerable and will undoubtedly increase. Barring some "miraculous" birth control device, it does not seem feasible that Latin America would be able to reduce its fertility significantly before the 1980's or 1990's and by 1980 (assuming declining fertility—which at present does not appear likely) the population of Latin America will be more than 40 per cent greater than in 1965. The Puerto Rican example, which may not be valid for Latin America generally, demonstrates that the birth rate could be reduced by one-quarter from a 1945–49 level of about 40 (equaled or exceeded currently by all Latin American countries save four) to 30 by 1963–64.

Several countries of the Orient, faced with basically the same problem and the limited alternatives, have recently begun active operating programs in the field of family planning. Because of the Latin American ethos, including religious considerations, this alternative has not yet had widespread discussion in the region, let alone support. As of 1964 family planning clinics were operating in only eight Latin American countries, but by 1965 fourteen countries had some family planning services. However, President Fernando Belaúnde Terry of Peru may have been the first Latin American chief executive to recognize publicly the formidable problem that population growth poses when he established a center for demographic study in December of 1964. The Agency for International Development (AID) has recently expanded its operations and assistance in the field of population planning although it still cannot make unsolicited recommendations and proposals. Also, numerous private organizations have been active in this field in Latin America.

Governments have endeavored to avoid this approach so far, and although the attitude of the Roman Catholic Church on mechanical and chemical methods of birth control is well known, it still must definitively state its position on oral contraceptives. There is no question that Latin American fertility will be reduced regardless of the attitude of the Church (although it certainly could facilitate matters), for the historical example of European Catholic countries, the U.S. Catholic population, and Argentina and Uruguay is clear. The reason why the problem in the underdeveloped world is so critical is because population pressures on resources are already great and there is now no world region willing to accept large-scale immigration. Undoubtedly, improved education and changes wrought by the industrialization and commercialization of the economies will provide social changes that will make birth control widely accepted (even for the men).

At the heart of the struggle between population growth and economic development are basically two conflicting schools of thought: the technologists who believe that improving efficiency and technology will supply sufficient goods and services for the population (notwithstanding rapid demographic growth); and the neo-Malthusians who envision the population exceeding the available resources (despite technological innovations) with the only solution remaining that of fertility control. Latin America, of course, must decide for itself as to which approach is right or, to be safe, it can use both approaches simultaneously, but Latin America's capital and energies are (like those of all regions) limited and some decisions and some sacrifices must be made and soon.

Notes

[1]The discussion on population in this paper is based on the assumption that there will be no nuclear war, general political disintegration, or spectacular fertility control technique.

[2]Population Reference Bureau, *Population Bulletin*, Vol. XXI, No. 4, October 1965.

[3]*Economic Bulletin for Latin America*, United Nations, Vol. VIII, No. 1 (October 1962). Statistical Bulletin.

Demographic Yearbook; 1963, United Nations, Table 19.

[4]Based on the average of 16 countries for both periods from the *Demographic Yearbook: 1963*, Table 22.

[5]Irene B. Taeuber, "Population Growth in Latin America: Paradox of Development," *Population Bulletin*, Vol. XVIII, No. 6 (October 1962).

[6]Major agricultural countries are here defined as those having more than 5 million hectares of arable land according to the *Production Yearbook: 1963*, Food and Agriculture Organization of the United

Nations, Table 1. The countries of sub-Saharan Africa (except South Africa) are excluded because of the incompleteness of data regarding cultivated land.

[7]Cultivated area is based on summation of area cultivated for all crops given in the *FAO Production Yearbook: 1963*. Some significant crops are excluded from the totals (because areas are not given), viz., the deciduous mid-latitude fruits, citrus, the palms, and some tropical fruits. The population estimates are also those provided by the same FAO source (Table 3).

[8]*The 1965 World Agricultural Situation*, Foreign Agriculture Economic Report No. 22, U. S. Department of Agriculture.

The 1965 Western Hemisphere Agricultural Situation.

[9]The overall figure of 2.6 per cent annual increment for Latin America is undoubtedly too low because 1964 was a poor crop year (especially in South America) so that if either 1963 or the preliminary figures for 1965 (*The World Agricultural Situation: Review of 1965 and Outlook for 1966*, Table 1) is used instead of 1964 then the overall rate of

agricultural production increased from 1952–54 to the 1960's by about 3.1 per cent annually.

[10]*Foreign Agriculture*, Foreign Agricultural Service, U. S. Dept. of Agriculture, III, No. 50 (December 13, 1965), 4.

[11]However, if either 1963 or the preliminary 1965 production figures are used, per capita output would have been 3 per cent greater than in the early 1950's (an insignificant increase).

[12]*Economic Survey of Latin America: 1963*, Chapter III.

[13]"Latin America at Mid-Decade," *Latin American Business Highlights*. XV, No. 3 (Third Quarter, 1965), 8–9.

[14]*The 1965 Western Hemisphere Agricultural Situation*, pp. 3, 57. A daily calorie consumption of only 2400 calories would appear insufficient in view of the 3000 calories or more consumed in Anglo-America, Western Europe, European Oceania, and even in Argentina and Uruguay.

[15]*The Economic Development o Latin America in the Post-War Period*, Table 23.

[16]*Economic Survey of Latin America: 1963*, Table 17.

[17]*Yearbook of National Accounts Statistics: 1964*, Part D, Table 4B.

[18]*Alliance for Progress Weekly Newsletter*, Pan American Union, January 31, 1966. The five Latin American nations not included in the study were Mexico, Cuba, the Dominican Republic, El Salvador, and Uruguay.

[19]*Economic Survey of Latin America: 1963*, Chapter VII.

Alliance for Progress Weekly Newsletter, November 15 and December 6, 1965.

[20]*Alliance for Progress Weekly Newsletter*, August 16, 1965 and January 24, 1966.

[21]Thomas F. Carroll, "The Land Reform Issue in Latin America," *Latin American Issues: Essays and Comments*, edited by Albert O. Hirschman (New York: 20th Century Fund, 1961).

[22]Samuel Pizer and Frederick Cutler, "Foreign Investments 1964–65," *Survey of Current Business*, U. S. Dept. of Commerce, XLV, No. 9 (September 1965).

A SELECTED SUPPLEMENTARY BIBLIOGRAPHY FOR PART 8

Ackerman, E. A., *Japan's Natural Resources and Their Relation to Japan's Economic Future*. Chicago: The University of Chicago Press, 1953.

Burton, I., and Kates, R. W. (eds.), *Readings in Resource Management and Conservation*. Chicago: The University of Chicago Press, 1965.

Clark, C., *Population Growth and Land Use*. New York: St. Martin's Press, 1967, especially pp. 123–157.

Coale, A. J., and Hoover, E. M., *Population Growth and Economic Development in Low-Income Countries*. Princeton: Princeton University Press, 1958.

Cook, R. C., "Population and Food Supply," S. Mudd, H. Boyko, and others (eds.), *The Population Crisis and the Use of World Resources*. Bloomington: University of Indiana Press, 1964, pp. 451–477.

De Castro, J., *Geography of Hunger*. Boston: Little, Brown, 1952.

Fonaroff, L. S., "Was Huntington Right about Nutrition?" *Annals of the Association of American Geographers*, Vol. 55, 1965, pp. 465–476.

Ginsburg, N., "Natural Resources and Economic Development," *Annals of the Association of American Geographers*, Vol. 47, 1957, pp. 196–212.

Horst, O., "The Specter of Death in a Guatemalan

Highland Community," *Geographical Review*, Vol. 57, 1967, pp. 151–167.

Hunter, J. M., "Population Pressure in a Part of the West African Savanna: A Study of Nangodi, Northeast Ghana," *Annals of the Association of American Geographers*, Vol. 57, 1967, pp. 101–114.

Kennedy, T. F., "Land, Food, and Population in the Kingdom of Tonga," *Economic Geography*, Vol. 37, 1961, pp. 61–71.

Kovalev, S. A., "The Manpower Resources of the U.S.S.R. and Their Utilization," *Geografiya v Shkole*, No. 1, 1965, pp. 5–11.

Kuznets, S., "Long Swings in the Growth of Population and in Related Economic Variables," *Proceedings of the American Philosophical Society*, Vol. 102, 1958, pp. 25–52.

Simoons, F. J., *Eat Not This Flesh: Food Avoidances in the Old World*. Madison; University of Wisconsin Press, 1961.

Taeuber, C., "Population and Food Supply," *Annals of the American Academy of Political and Social Science*, Vol. 369, 1967, pp. 73–83.

Vaughan, T. D., and Dwyer, D. J., "Some Aspects of Postwar Population Growth in Hong Kong," *Economic Geography*, Vol. 42, 1966, pp. 37–51.

A SELECTED BIBLIOGRAPHY OF BASIC POPULATION WORKS, PERIODICALS, BIBLIOGRAPHIES, AND DATA SOURCES

BASIC POPULATION WORKS:

Beaujeu-Garnier, J., *Geography of Population*. New York: St. Martin's Press, 1966.

Bogue, D. J., *Principles of Demography*. New York: J. Wiley and Sons, Inc., 1969.

Carr-Saunders, A. M., *World Population*. Oxford: Clarendon Press, 1936.

Clark, C., *Population Growth and Land Use*. New York: St. Martin's Press, 1967.

Clarke, J. L., *Population Geography*. Oxford: Pergamon Press, 1965.

Cox, P. R., *Demography*. Cambridge, Eng.: Institute of Actuaries and the Faculty of Actuaries, University Press, 1959.

Freedman, R. (ed.), *Population: The Vital Revolution*. Chicago: Aldine Publishing Co., 1965.

Halbwachs, M., *Population and Society*. Glencoe, Ill.: The Free Press, 1960.

Hauser, P. M., *Population Perspectives*. New Brunswick, N.J.: Rutgers University Press, 1961.

Hauser, P. M., (ed.). *Population Dilemma*. Englewood Cliffs, N.J.: Prentice-Hall, Inc., 1963.

Hauser, P. M., and Duncan, O. D. (eds.), *The Study of Population*. Chicago: The University of Chicago Press, 1959.

Mudd, S., Boyko, H., and others (eds.), *The Population Crisis and the Use of the World's Resources*. Bloomington: University of Indiana Press, 1964.

Petersen, W., *Population*. New York: Macmillan Co., 1961.

Sauvy, A., *Fertility and Survival. Population Problems from Malthus to Mao Tse-Tung*. New York: Criterion Books, 1961.

Smith, T. L., *Fundamentals of Population Study*. Chicago: J. B. Lippincott, 1960.

Spengler, J. J., and Duncan, O. D. (eds.), *Demographic Analysis: Selected Readings*. Glencoe, Ill.: The Free Press, 1956.

Spengler, J. J., and Duncan, O. D., *Population Theory and Policy*. Glencoe, Ill.: The Free Press, 1956.

Stockwell, E. G., *Population and People*. Chicago: Quadrangle Books, 1968.

Thomlinson, R., *Population Dynamics: Causes and Consequences of World Demographic Change*. New York: Random House, 1965.

Thompson, W. S., and Lewis, D. T., *Population Problems*. New York: McGraw-Hill Book Company 1965.

Wrong, D. H., *Population*. New York: Random House, 1956.

Zelinsky, W., *Prologue to Population Geography*. Englewood Cliffs, N.J.: Prentice-Hall, Inc., 1966.

PERIODICALS:*

Demography, Population Association of America (annual). Chicago, 1964 to date.

International Migration, The Intergovernmental Committee for European Migration (quarterly). Geneva, Switzerland, 1963 to date.

Milbank Memorial Fund Quarterly, Milbank Memorial Fund (quarterly). New York, 1923 to date.

Population, l'Institut National d'études demographiques (three times yearly). Paris, 1946 to date.

Population Bulletin, Population Reference Bureau (bi-monthly). Washington, D.C., 1945 to date.

Population Bulletin, United Nations (irregularly). New York, 1951 to date.

Population Index, Population Association of America (quarterly). Princeton, N.J., 1935 to date.

Population Review, Indian Institute for Population Studies (bi-annual). Gandhinagar, Madras, 1957 to date.

Population Studies, Population Investigation Committee (quarterly). Cambridge, 1947 to date.

The International Migration Review, Center for Migration Studies (triannual). New York and Rome, 1964 to date (formerly the International Migration Digest).

BIBLIOGRAPHIES:

Church, M., Huke, R. E., and Zelinsky, W. (eds.)' *A Basic Geographical Library: A Selected and Annotated Book List for American Colleges*. Washington, D.C.: Association of American Geographers, Commission on College Geography, Publication No. 2, 1966.

Current Geographical Publications, Additions to the Research Catalogue of the American Geographical Society (ten times yearly). New York, 1938 to date.

Eldridge, H. T., *The Materials of Demography: A Selected and Annotated Bibliography*. New York: International Union for the Scientific Study of Population and the Population Association of America, Columbia University Press, 1959.

International Bibliography of Social and Cultural Anthropology. Population and Settlement Section

*This list is representative of periodicals devoted exclusively to demography and population study. A perusal of the sources of articles reprinted in this book, as well as those listed in the bibliographies at the end of each section, offers some indication of the number and diversity of periodicals in which literature on population appears.

and Internal and External Migration Section (annual). London, 1955 to date.

International Population Census Bibliography, No. 1, Latin America and the Caribbean. Austin: Bureau of Business Research, University of Texas, 1965.

Population, op. cit., contains a large bibliography in each issue.

Population Index, op. cit., is the single best source of current literature on population.

Referativniy Zhurnal, Akademiya Nauk U.S.S.R., Institut Nauchoi Informatsii (monthly). Moscow, 1954 to date. See particularly section 07E, Geography of the U.S.S.R., index $\frac{71338}{71339}$.

Sociological Abstracts (eight times yearly). New York, 1956 to date.

United Nations, Department of Economic and Social Affairs, Population Division, *The Determinants and Consequences of Population Trends, Population Studies,* No. 17. New York: Columbia University Press, 1954, pp. 320–369.

Wilbur, G., and Rogers, T., *Internal Migration in the United States 1958–1964: A List of References,* Sociology and Rural Life Series, No. 15. State College: Mississippi State University, Agricultural Experiment Station, 1965.

Zelinsky, W., *A Bibliographic Guide to Population Geography,* Research Paper No. 80. Chicago: University of Chicago, Department of Geography, 1962.

DATA SOURCES:

Pan-American Union. Interamerican Statistical Institute, *Boletin Estadistico.* Resumé of Latin American Census Results.

United Nations, *Demographic Yearbook,* 1948 to date. Each issue presents general data but also specific information on a selected subject.

United Nations, *Population and Vital Statistics Report* (quarterly). Latest censuses and estimates of total population, births, and deaths.

United Nations, *Statistical Yearbook,* 1949 to date. Includes economic and social topics, as well as demographic information.

U.S. Bureau of the Census. *County and City Data Book,* 1962. Washington, D.C., 1962.

U.S. Bureau of the Census. *Current Population Reports.* Series P-20 Population Characteristics, P-23 Technical Studies, P-25 Population Estimates, P-27 Farm Population, P-90 International Population Statistics Report. Washington, D.C.

U.S. Bureau of the Census. *Historical Statistics of the United States Colonial Times to 1957; Continuation to 1962 and Revisions.* Washington, D.C., 1965.

U.S. Department of Agriculture, Economic Research Service. *Net Migration of the Population, 1950–1960 by Age, Sex, and Color,* Research Foundation, Oklahoma State University cooperating. Washington, D.C.: U.S. Government Printing Office, 1965.

This is a continuing series of volumes containing migration estimates by age, sex, and color for regions, metropolitan areas, and counties of the U.S.

INDEX